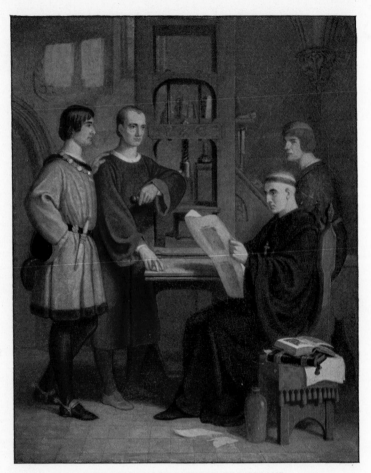

THE FIRST BOOK PRINTED IN ENGLAND

The Dictes and Sayings of the Philosophers, a collection of moral utterances, was translated by Anthony Woodville, Earl Rivers, from the French of Jean de Teonville. The English nobleman had secured the manuscript while on a pilgrimage to the shrine of St. James in Spain. In this picture the Irish artist John Doyle shows William Caxton submitting the proofs to the learned scrutiny of the Abbot of Westminster. Earl Rivers stands at Caxton's side; and in the background, setting type, is Wynkyn de Worde, Caxton's assistant and eventual successor. (From a painting in the collection of George A. Plimpton)

ENGLISH LITERATURE

A SURVEY AND A COMMENTARY

BY

BROTHER LEO

OF THE BROTHERS OF THE CHRISTIAN SCHOOLS, SAINT
MARY'S COLLEGE, CALIFORNIA

GINN AND COMPANY

BOSTON · NEW YORK · CHICAGO · LONDON
ATLANTA · DALLAS · COLUMBUS · SAN FRANCISCO

PR 85
L45
co 3

𝕿𝖍𝖊 𝕬𝖙𝖍𝖊𝖓𝖆𝖚𝖒 𝕻𝖗𝖊𝖘𝖘

GINN AND COMPANY · PRO-
PRIETORS · BOSTON · U.S.A.

TO THE TEACHER

The practical worth of a textbook depends on the extent to which the teacher enters into the spirit and intentions of the author and appreciates the point of view from which the book is written. It is not essential that the teacher be in complete accord with the author's convictions and methods, but it is desirable that the teacher should at least have an understanding of what the author is trying to do. The following paragraphs briefly indicate the principles in the light of which this book has been written and the objectives at which the author has aimed.

The Teacher's Preferences and Initiative. The teacher is the decisive factor in the teaching process. He is the artist; the textbook is his principal tool. And so this volume has been fashioned as an instrument which the teacher may employ with freedom and confidence. Every real teacher is necessarily something of an enthusiast, and enthusiasm presupposes preferences. The author, himself a teacher, has preferences of his own; but he has tried to state both his likes and his dislikes in much the same manner, and certainly in quite the same spirit, in which he might express them in intelligent conversation, not always expecting, and perhaps not invariably desiring, that his peers should see eye to eye with him. The teacher who uses this book will be in sufficient accord with the teacher who has written it if he reduce to practice the maxim of "Augustinus": "In essential things unity, in nonessential things liberty, in all things charity."

The Textbook. The word *tool* connotes some sort of mechanism, and in that respect is misleading when applied to a textbook of literature. The textbook is a tool indeed, but one less mechanistic than vital, and there is no reason in the world why it should not possess a personality and convey to the teacher an impression of real, even if sometimes irritating, fellowship. Teachers of all subjects would be appreciably happier and textbooks would become brighter and keener and more adaptable if the truth were grasped that the textbook, though a tool, is also an associate teacher, that it ordinarily is the matured expression of a man of knowledge and experience, that it embodies the findings of research in the study and of experiments in the classroom, that behind it the teacher may sense a fellow feeling and an understanding sympathy, deep and virile, however vague and inarticulate. Certainly in the teaching of literature there is need that every factor — student, teacher, textbook — be touched with human interest and animated with human emotion.

The Student's Needs and Interests. This book is neither an encyclopedia of English Literature nor a handbook for the guidance of men and women of mature mind and wide reading. Still less is it intended to be an embodiment of seasoned scholarship and erudite criticism. It is rather a guide to students whose taste is largely unformed, whose information is scrappy and chaotic, whose realization of the delights of good reading is relatively weak and limited. They need to know what to read and how to read it, what to look for in books, how to react intellectually and emotionally to what they read; they need to establish a sense of proportion in literature and in life; they need to assimilate ideas as they assimilate food and to exercise their minds as they exercise their muscles. No textbook can do all this for them; but a textbook written with a consciousness of the student's needs will, in the hands of a teacher discerning and responsive, do much to arouse and retain the student's interest in our cultural heritage, to sharpen his insight, enrich his fancy, and deepen and heighten his awareness of being alive.

From the pedagogical point of view, as Dr. Condé B. Pallen

maintains, the proper method of teaching English Literature would be to begin with the twentieth century and work back to *Beowulf*. Some day that may become the recognized procedure; it would at least retain some notion of chronology and would meet the strongest objections urged against the exclusive "type" study of literature. But for the present, counter arguments — including the attitude of teachers who have always begun at the beginning and are not unwisely suspicious of novelties — prohibit so radical a departure from established usage. What the teacher can do, what this book has tried to do, is to tell the story of English Literature with the interests of the students actively in mind. That, however, does not mean that we give them only what they like, but that we induce them to like what we give them. We can lead them to see that Chaucer is as interesting as Robert W. Service, that Fleet Street has richer traditions than Main Street, that Shakespeare is in essentials more "up to date" than yesterday's newspaper. This consideration has to a great extent determined the emphasis and proportion observed in this volume.

Without Crutches. The teacher will observe that this textbook is not embellished with review questions, discussion topics, chronological charts, and similar aids to study. The omission is deliberate. Such devices are important, to some extent even necessary, in classroom procedure; but their efficacy is negligible when they are prepared according to a standardized norm by someone unfamiliar with the personality and scholarly equipment of the teacher and the specific needs and training of the class. Different classes thrive on different review questions; just what questions, local teachers and inspectors are best competent to determine. As for discussion topics, it is evident that in considering Stevenson, for instance, students in California, where Stevenson once lived, possess information and interests far from identical with those of students in Boston or Cincinnati. Chronological charts are distinctly valuable, but only when they are made on the spot by the students, by the teacher, or by students and teacher in collaboration. In a textbook all such adventitious aids the capable teacher does not need; to the novice they are liable to prove a delusion and a snare.

Books and Books about Books. It is assumed that the student read, and read copiously, of the best that has been written, that the textbook is truly an introduction to the master works of English Literature. "What will knowledge profit thee," Thomas à Kempis pertinently inquires, "without the grace of God?" Similarly we might ask the student of literature, "Of what advantage is it that you know how many wives Milton had and how long Gray took to write the *Elegy*, if you have never thrilled to the organ tones of *Paradise Lost* and have secured no pensive pleasure from repeating

" The breezy call of incense-breathing Morn"?

Gone, happily forever, are the days when the ideal of literature study was to know everything about a writer except what he wrote. The reading of comment and criticism is, of course, to be encouraged, and the minutiæ of intensive scholarship are important and salutary; but an ounce of real literature is of more worth than ten pounds of even the best criticism, though we must not forget that criticism is sometimes real literature too. While it may be that a chosen few of our pupils are destined to walk the ascetic path of erudition, most of them will secure ample fruition from our efforts if they acquire the precious habit of reading and loving books worthy to be read and loved.

Bibliographies. The lists of books given in this volume have been prepared in consonance with the convictions just expressed. It were an easy matter to print bibliographies fearfully and wonderfully made, impressive it might be by reason of their length and valuable perhaps to the mature and intensive student; but such lists would be an encumbrance here. Present-day school libraries are never without works of reference, and such works this book is not designed to displace. In the teaching of literature encyclopedias are tools, too, and encyclopedias are lavish of library suggestions. The reading lists in this book represent a process of selection and contain recent books and studies not generally included in standard works of reference.

The Eclectic Method. The general plan of the book is indicated in the Contents. In most of its larger units it is based upon a chronological pattern; though when both common sense and pedagogical efficiency urge that certain writers be considered in groups, it ignores the vistas of the years. The treatment of individual authors may annoy meticulously methodical teachers accustomed to an unvarying classification of literary data under such captions as life, works, characteristics. The method here followed is eclectic and elastic. The aim is to secure the most effective approach to the literary significance of each author. Sometimes his life affords the open sesame, sometimes a book of his or a sentence from a book, sometimes a dominant idea or ideal, sometimes a comparison with another writer, sometimes a stimulating comment on his work and influence. Contact must be established between the facts of literature and the mind of the learner, and that method is the best method — however lacking in stringent formalism — which most promptly and vividly presents the likeliest point of contact. After all, literature is a liberal art, and the study of it may not unreasonably be invested with variety. A rigidly "scientific" treatment of literature is almost certain to inhibit sound appreciation and to quench the breath and finer spirit of the written word.

The Construction of Place. Residents of Twickenham have often seen a group of Oxford students row down the Thames, disembark at Pope's villa, and spend an afternoon in the famous grotto reading aloud from poems written there by the master of the rimed couplet. An admirable way of making literature real! Unfortunately, an actual literary pilgrimage through England is not practical, but in several portions of this volume the pupils are afforded an opportunity of vicariously visiting localities identified with books and writers, and of learning the truth of William Winter's eulogy of travel:

There is no pursuit more fascinating or in a high intellectual sense more remunerative; since it serves to define and regulate knowledge, to correct misapprehension of fact, to broaden the mental vision, to ripen and refine the judgment and the taste, and to fill the memory with ennobling recollections.

Incidentally, traveling, even by proxy, lends a freshened significance to geography and history.

The Catholic Note. Since this book is primarily intended for the use of Catholic students in Catholic schools, the relations existing between literature and the Faith are given due recognition. Catholicism is not a sect, and it is more than a form of religion; it is a philosophy of life, and as such it directly affected many English writers prior to the sixteenth century, and since then has indirectly affected many more — in most cases men who, like Tennyson, for example, were not Catholics and who were perhaps unconscious of the Catholic strain in their thoughts and writings.

On the other hand, it is important to remember that since the Reformation English Literature as a whole — and for that matter the literature of Europe generally — has been non-Catholic and sometimes even anti-Catholic. The phenomenon is interesting, and students in Catholic schools might profitably seek to discover its causes. Catholics who have contributed to English Literature are, it is hoped, adequately treated in these pages; but there has been no attempt to commemorate men and women who, however strong in the Faith and assiduous in writing devotional, controversial, and theological works, nevertheless did not produce literature. Ever so many English Catholic bishops, for instance, have written zealous and informing pastorals which are as far from being literary products as are the sermons evolved in colonial days by pious and dreary Puritan divines in New England. It takes more than zeal and loftiness of purpose to make a man of letters.

The Vital Element. In literature it is eminently true that "the proper study of mankind is man." Here, verily, heart speaketh unto heart. And while the student of literature may legitimately be solicitous about many things, human life is the one thing necessary. Edward Dowden, in concluding his essay on "The Interpretation of Literature," wrote:

> Of all our study the last end and aim should be to ascertain how a great writer or artist has served the life of man; to ascertain this, to bring home to ourselves as large a portion as may be of the gain wherewith he has enriched human life, and to render access to that store of wisdom, passion, and power easier and surer to others. If our study does not directly or indirectly enrich the life of man, it is but a drawing of vanity with cart-ropes, a weariness to the flesh, or at best a busy idleness.

No matter how industriously it busies itself with verse forms and figures of speech, with names and dates and circumstances, with schools and movements and circles, with dissections of poetry and post-mortem inquests on prose, the teaching of literature is futile and misleading unless it induce in the student the Hamlet mood of exalted wonder: "What a piece of work is man!" The great book exists that we may have life and have it more abundantly. "Know thyself" might well be set as the motto for true literary study; know thyself and thy fellow man; know life, and live more deeply, more richly, more wisely, more completely. This is essential humanism, and the spirit of humanism is the soul of literature in all ages and climes.

The Cultural Ideal. The spirit in which literature is most successfully created and appreciated has been happily indicated by an English poet, William Blake: "Nothing is pleasing to God except the glad invention of beautiful and exalted things." This book has been prepared in the belief that students, particularly in our time and in our social environment, have imminent need to learn and to realize that an essential quality of literature is that in some manner it presents a vision of beauty, that it creates an emotional expansion and exaltation, that it fosters a liking for thoughts and things that are fine and noble, uplifting and sublime. All art is based on selection, and selection implies discrimination and rejection. The literary art, using as its material the facts of human life, necessarily discriminates, selects, and rejects. That triune process exemplifies what is familiarly known as good taste, and the formation and exercise of good taste is among the most desirable results of literary study.

Esteem of Artistry and the Artist. True culture involves a sense of proportion, and there will remain something fundamentally wrong with our educational systems so long as our graduates, accepting their standards of excellence and achievement from the mass of men who despise the finer things of life, continue to regard the accumulator of millions as more admirable than the impecunious poet and the man who makes an empire as of more importance than the man who makes a sonnet. John Drinkwater says something much to the point in his critical study of William Morris:

We decorate and honor our soldiers whose business, be it to destroy or to be destroyed, is, in any case, connected with destruction; those of our lawyers who are chiefly concerned with restraint and punishment; our politicians who spend their time protecting us from assaults of neighbors and communities as commercially rapacious as ourselves, or, in their more enlightened moments, in adjusting wrongs that are the dregs in the cup of civilization. The functions of these men may be necessities of society, but they nevertheless apply to the small negative aspect of our state and not the great normal life. It is that which is, rightly, the concern of our creative artists; but our creative artists are not decorated and honored . . . we acclaim the negative and neglect the positive manifestations of man.

Such lopsided and misproportioned veneration of the negative and the material has no rightful place in any school, but least of all in the school which owes its existence and inspiration to ideals positive and spiritual. Our Catholic schools exist in order that their pupils may realize that not by bread alone doth man live, that true success consists in being something rather than in getting something, that the divine philosophy of seeking first the kingdom of God has been prolific of heroes of culture as well as heroes of holiness. If it is the function of the Church to canonize saints, it is the function of the school to canonize artists.

The World View of Literature. The modern conception of literature is neither narrowly nationalistic nor aggressively partisan. The comparative study of literary origins and influences has made it clear that truly vital books are interracial and international in both their sources and their range of appeal. "Hence," as Moulton wrote in his stimulating book, *The Modern Study of Literature*, "the unity of literature becomes the first postulate for sound literary study." Literature, rightly considered, is as catholic, as comprehensive, and as international as the Church of Christ.

And so in this book English Literature is not regarded as a mere adjunct of English history. The effort is made to rid the student's mind of provincial prejudices and preconceptions and to establish the reality and continuity of the European Tradition in literature. That is the point of view of the Catholic Church; it is the point of view of Dante, Milton, Goethe, and Sainte-Beuve; it is the point of view in complete harmony with the time-spirit of our own generation, for never since the Middle Ages has there been an epoch when, as a consequence of the World War, of facility of transportation and communication, of political and commercial relations, of scientific and artistic community of interests, our common humanity has been so emphasized and self-centered nationalism viewed with such disfavor. A textbook of English Literature regarding the subject as something purely or even mainly national would today be interesting chiefly as a divertingly flagrant anachronism.

Against what it calls narrow-mindedness the modern world, including the world of youth, lifts its voice and its eyebrows in commendable disdain. To be provincial is considered a misfortune. Yet sometimes a student, until he learns better, — and even now and then a teacher who has never learned and probably never will, — reveals the most humiliating of all forms of narrow-mindedness : provincialism in time and provincialism in place. He resents an adequate treatment of the Cavalier Poets, for instance, because the Cavalier Poets sang their songs nearly three centuries ago ; he is bored by a consideration of the Irish or the Italian contribution to English Literature because his ancestry happens to be neither Irish nor Italian. To such readers this book can hardly appeal ; but such readers are hardly on the side of the angels.

Acknowledgment for the courtesy of permitting the use of copyrighted material is due the following:

Mitchell Kennerley, New York, for an excerpt from John Drinkwater's *William Morris: a Critical Study*.

Houghton Mifflin Company, Boston, for a passage from C. A. Dinsmore's *Life of Dante*.

Henry Holt and Company, New York, for five paragraphs from Hilaire Belloc's *French Revolution*.

The Macmillan Company, New York, for a portion of the poem "A Memory," by George Russell. Copyright, 1904.

Dr. H. H. Furness, Jr., and J. B. Lippincott Company, Philadelphia, for a quotation from the late Horace Howard Furness's edition of *Much Ado About Nothing* in the Variorum Shakespeare.

Oxford University Press for Austin Dobson's poem "When Burbage Played."

Sir William Watson for his sonnet on Aubrey de Vere.

A paragraph from Augustine Birrell's *More Obiter Dicta* and Alice Meynell's poem "The Shepherdess" are reproduced by arrangement with Charles Scribner's Sons, New York.

CONTENTS

ENGLISH LITERATURE

A SURVEY AND A COMMENTARY

CHAPTER I

THE STUDY OF LITERATURE

WHAT LITERATURE IS

Our Way with Words. We all of us, old and young, use words which we should find hard to define. We are reasonably sure that we know what *into*, *very*, and *use* mean; they are words we have heard and employed since we were small children, and yet we experience difficulty in formulating their precise meaning. Such familiar words are like our own noses, so obvious that we do not see them. Then there are other words which we likewise find hard to define, but for a different reason — words such as *galvanize, socialism, scientific*. As small children we did not have those words in our vocabulary; and though they are in our vocabulary now, though we have heard them used by other persons and perhaps have used them ourselves, we should probably be a little puzzled to define them accurately. The reason is that those three words are used by different people to represent somewhat different ideas. *Socialism*, for instance, means to one man state ownership of mines and railways, to another man it means a political party, and to a third man it means a conception of history which does not take God into account.

That Which is Written. The word *literature* is one of those words which mean different things to different persons. Often it is used loosely to describe anything written or printed. Now, while in all times (except in primitive ages when there were no books and no written language) literature is indeed something written, a little thought will show us that not everything that is written or printed is literature.

A telephone directory, for example, is a printed book; yet it is not likely that many persons would maintain that a telephone directory is literature: it is merely a list of numbers and names and addresses. A dictionary is also a printed book; and though it contains more words than can be found in

AN EARLY SPECIMEN OF PRINTING

A Latin Indult of Pope Nicholas V, printed at Mainz, Germany, in 1455. (By courtesy of the British Museum)

Shakespeare's plays or Browning's poems, the dictionary is no more literature than a pile of bricks is a house. Again, a magazine advertisement for tooth paste is something printed, and it is more than a list of words; yet it is not literature, either.

Let us suppose that a realtor has taken us out in his car and shown us some property he would like to sell. When we are leaving him he says, "I will send you some of our literature." The folder he sends us is something printed, and we

The Evening Poſt.

Numb. 1967.

From Tueſday March 6. to Thurſday March 8. 1722.

London March, 8.

November 13, 1721.

HIS Houſe, (according to Order) proceeded to take into Conſideration his Majeſties moſt gracious Speech from the Throne. And the ſame being read :

A Motion was made, that this Houſe will on Friday next take into Conſideration, the Cauſes of Contracting ſo large a Navy Debt, and the beſt Methods of preventing the Contracting the like Debt for the future.

And a Queſtion being Stated thereupon.

It was propoſed to leave out theſe Words viz. (And the beſt Methods of preventing the Contracting the like Debts for the future).

Then the Queſtion was put, whether the ſaid Words ſhall ſtand in part of the Queſtion.

It was Reſolv'd in the Negative.

Content 22. Not content 64.

Diſſentient.

1. Becauſe the principal end of all Parliamentary Inquiries into Miſmanagements, being to prevent the like for the future, we thought it more agreeable to the Candour and Honour of the Houſe to expreſs it plainly in the Queſtion it ſelf, than to leave it to be imply'd only, and the rather, becauſe it ſeems to us the Words left out clearly imported, that nothing Perſonal was in view, but the Publick good only, which we thought would rather have given Satisfaction to the mind of every Noble Lord than the Contrary.

2. When the Words now order'd to be left out were for the Reaſons given ſo properly and naturally, as we conceive made a part of the Queſtion, we could not but apprehend that the laying them aſide on a Debate, might create a Suſpicion tho' unjuſt, that this Houſe did not intend to prevent, if poſſible, the Contracting a large and inconvenient Navy Debt for the future.

3. His Majeſty having in his Speech from the Throne, obſerv'd the ill Conſequences that ariſe from ſuch a large Debt remaining unprovided for, we thought it very proper if not neceſſary in the Reſolution taken to enter into the Conſideration of that Debt, to expreſs a deſire of preventing the like inconvenient Debt being Contracted for the future ; and that the doing ſo did not pre judge the cauſes of Contracting the preſent great Navy Debt for however Neceſſarily or Juſtifiably an Inconvenient thing may have once happen'd, yet we think it ought if it can to be prevented from happening ſo again.

4. His Majeſty having likewiſe obſerv'd in his Speech from the Throne, that it is part of the National Debt, is of all others the moſt Heavy and Burthenſome, and having ſet forth the Miſchiefs ariſing from the ſhi ... diſcount on the Navy and Victualling Bills, we thoug ... ſelves ſufficiently Warranted, to expreſs a deſire t ... r of the beſt

Methods of preventing the like moſt Heavy and Burthenſome Debt, whatever the cauſes of Contracting the preſent Debt, ſhall on inquiry appear to be, and this the rather becauſe the like Navy Debt can bring no manner of Benefit, either to the Publick or to any private Perſon, but to ſuch as by forceloſing when it is either to be diſcharged or provided for, may make an Exceſſive advantage to themſelves, by Buying up the ſaid Bills while under a very high Diſcount. W. Ebor. Wharton. Starſdale. Saliſbury. North and Grey. Aberdeen. Strafford. Guilford. Boyle. Cowper. Bathurſt. Bingley. Trevor. Ayleſford. W. Roſſen. Briſtol. Aſhburnham.

November 15, 1721.

The Order of the Day being read for the taking into further Conſideration his Majeſty's moſt gracious Speech. After Debate the Queſtion was put, That an humble Addreſs be preſented to his Majeſty, that he will be graciouſly pleaſed to give Order, That the Inſtructions given by his Majeſty to the Lord Carteret as Miniſter or Plenipotentiary to the Crown of Sweden, or any other Northern Crown be laid before this Houſe.

It was reſolved in the Neg'tive.

Content 21, Not Content 65.

Diſſentient.

1. Becauſe we apprehend this to be the Firſt Inſtance to be found on our Journals, where Lords have moved for a Sight of Inſtructions of any kind, and have not been ſupported by the Houſe in that Motion, and tho' we wiſh it may be the laſt, yet have we juſt Reaſon to fear that ſuch a Precedent once made, will not fail of being followed in ſucceeding Time.

2. Becauſe we do not apprehend how the calling for Inſtructions after the Concluſion of the Treaty to which they relate, and the Intervention of a General Act of Pardon can be hurtful, either to the Publick, or even to the Miniſters tranſacting ſuch Treaties ; but the refuſing to call for thoſe Inſtructions, may in our Opinion, be a Matter of dangerous Conſequence, in as much as it tends to diſcourage Enquiries of this Kind for the Future, and by that Means to Imbolden and Skreen Guilty Miniſters hereafter.

3. Becauſe tho' we acknowledge the Right of Peace and War to be in the Crown, yet we muſt be of Opinion, that this Houſe hath alſo a Right to enquire into the Tranſactions of Miniſters employed under the Crown, and to Cenſure their Conduct when Juſtice requires it, which cannot well be done unleſs it be firſt known what ſort of Inſtructions they receiv'd, and how far they have, or ought to have comply'd with them, and this ſeems to us more particularly neceſſary ſince the Act of Succeſſion has declared, That this Kingdom ſhall not be engaged in a War on Account of any of the King's Foreign Dominions : All Treaties therefore with Princes in the North, ſhould above all other, be made in the plaineſt and moſt unexceptionable Terms, or in the Way of wording ſuch Treaties, ſhall Occaſion any doubt, no Method of clearing it ought to be neglected or avoided, that ſo this Houſe and the whole Kingdom may be ſatiſfied

that

ONE OF THE FIRST ENGLISH NEWSPAPERS

Though this journal of two centuries ago was smaller and less pretentious than the daily papers we know, it was perhaps not quite so far from being literature as they are

may even find it interesting to read; yet that folder, though it contains words attractively put together, is really not literature at all.

This morning's newspaper is something printed. It is not merely a list of words like the telephone directory, or a collection of words and definitions like the dictionary; it contains many things besides advertisements for tooth paste; and, unlike the real-estate folder, it has not been written to persuade us to buy something. The newspaper gives us a great deal of information and offers us a considerable variety of reading, and yet the newspaper is not literature.

A boy's school composition on "How I spent my Vacation" is something written, and it may even be printed in the school magazine. It too is more than a list or collection of words, and it differs in its plan and purpose from the advertisement, the real-estate booklet, and the newspaper. Yet the boy's composition is not literature.

Once there was a boy in New England who wrote his composition in verse and gave it the title of "Mr. Finney's Turnip." His name was Henry Wadsworth Longfellow. Many years later he wrote another piece of verse, "The Building of the Ship." Both these pieces of verse are interesting to read; but "Mr. Finney's Turnip" is not literature, whereas "The Building of the Ship" certainly is literature. It will be profitable for us to read the boy's verse and the man's verse and try to discover why one is not literature and the other is.

The Making of a Poet. When Longfellow wrote "Mr. Finney's Turnip" he had nothing important to say, and he did not know how to say it. Though the turnip may have mattered somewhat to Mr. Finney, it did not matter at all to the rest of the world. And it does not matter to us today. It is probable that if Longfellow had written about that turnip twenty years later, he would have had something important to say about it; and then Mr. Finney's turnip, like Burns's mountain daisy and Wordsworth's primrose by the river's brim, would have mattered to all of us. Twenty years later Longfellow knew much more about human life and the ways of men, and he would have been able to tell some of the things he knew; furthermore, by that time he had a mastery of words and a skill in putting them together and making them delight us with their melody and beauty. A clever saying comes to us from the Latin: "The poet is born, not made." Like most clever sayings that statement is true, but a little misleading. In reality the poet is born *and* made; that is to say, he is born with talents, but he has to grow and learn and practice his art before he can produce genuine poetry, genuine literature.

Longfellow had so grown and learned when he wrote "The Building of the Ship." A ship as a ship is not much more important than a turnip as a turnip; and the building of a ship, like the growing of a turnip, in itself does not much matter to the world at large. But Longfellow was able, in the maturity of his life and the fullness of his powers as a writer, to make the ship and the building of it a thing of tremendous interest and importance: to show us how the forests had supplied the material, how swarms of busy workers, each of them a mortal man with an immortal soul, had used brain and brawn to make the ship almost a living being; to lift up our minds and our hearts from the ship of wood to the "Ship of State" launched upon the great ocean of history and sailing forth on its glorious voyage with swelling sails and flapping ensign. He was able to thrill us, to inspire us, to enlighten us; and that is what literature always does.

How to Recognize Literature. When we analyze and reflect upon any piece of literature,— a poem like "The Building of the Ship," a novel like *Kenilworth*, a drama like *The Merchant of Venice*, an essay like "Oxford in the Vacation," — we find that it contains certain elements none of which the real-estate folder, the newspaper, and the boy's school composition possess. The principal characteristics of real literature are the following:

1. *It makes us realize some truth of human life.* Literature is really a picture of life, and from it we get a deeper knowledge and a finer appreciation of what man is and of what he has thought and desired and done. This is one difference between Dickens's novel *A Tale of Two Cities* and the boy's composition "How I spent my Vacation."

2. *It contributes to our enjoyment.* We do not secure the right attitude toward great books until we learn to delight in reading them. The pleasure they give us is a higher and rarer and keener pleasure than the pleasure we get from palatable food or well-made clothes, from an automobile ride or the use of money. It is an intellectual, a spiritual pleasure. This is how Browning's "Pied Piper of Hamelin" differs from the real-estate folder.

3. *It is independent of time.* This morning's newspaper is old and useless by noon ; but Homer's *Iliad*, though it was composed centuries before Our Lord was born, is still fresh and new and interesting. Books that are not literature — ever so many novels, for instance — may cause a great stir when they appear, and for a little while they are read and talked about ; but soon they are completely forgotten ; they live for a short time, and then they die. But books that are literature do not die : they are immortal. Most of the books discussed in the following pages were written many years ago, yet we who live in the twentieth century can read and enjoy them ; indeed, we often find that the earliest books are the best books.

4. *It is independent of place.* We in this country are not Germans or Frenchmen or Italians, not Persians or Greeks or Romans ; but if we wish to be really cultured and to secure profit and enjoyment from our reading we do not confine ourselves to books written in the English language. One reason why we study foreign languages is that we may read works of literature written in other tongues. Perhaps the four greatest figures in all literature are Homer, a Greek ; Dante, an Italian ; Shakespeare, an Englishman ; Goethe, a German. Literature

is like the Catholic Church: it is not confined to any one country. Both the Church and literature are universal. "If," says Edward Dowden, a teacher worthy of our attention, "we are faithful children of this Catholic Church of literature and art, it will not greatly matter who may be the bishop of our particular diocese — Shakespeare, Homer, Dante, Goethe,

THE ROMAN FORUM

Without literature we should have but scanty knowledge of the men and women who, more than twenty centuries ago, thronged this center of the civilized world

Cervantes, Molière; any one of them will teach us the catholic doctrine of art — '*quod semper, quod ubique, quod ab omnibus.*'"[1]

5. *It is a thing of beauty.* Literature is one of the arts, and all the arts minister to our natural craving for beautiful things. God put a love of beauty, a desire for beauty, into our hearts, and in Heaven that noble appetite will be eternally satisfied

[1] Things accepted as true "always, and everywhere, and by everybody."

in the possession and enjoyment of Him. But meanwhile, here on earth, our longing for beautiful objects is in part gratified by music and architecture, painting and literature. The enjoyment we derive from the arts is truly a foretaste of Heaven. The advertisement, considered from this point of view, is not a thing of beauty but a thing of utility. The man who writes the advertisement is like the man who whitewashes

A GROUP OF WORLD WRITERS

From the Albert Memorial, London. Greece, Rome, Italy, England, and Germany have representatives here

a fence; the man who writes a poem is like the Spanish artist Murillo, who painted "The Immaculate Conception."

6. *It reveals a mastery of expression.* Ever so many men have a deep knowledge of human life. They feel deeply, and have, as Hamlet said, "thoughts beyond the reaches of our souls"; but they are unable to convey to others what they feel and know. They have visions of beauty, but they cannot crystallize their visions in living words. Such a man Gray had in mind when he wrote

Some mute inglorious Milton here may rest.

Most of mankind are mute inglorious Miltons. But the great writers, the makers of literature, not only know but are able to tell what they know; they not only feel but are able to convey their emotion; they are able to embody their visions of beauty in language of power and sublimity. "Writing is not literature," said Stopford Brooke, "unless it gives to the reader a pleasure which arises not only from the things said, but from the way in which they are said; and that pleasure is only given when the words are carefully or curiously or beautifully put together in sentences."

Definition. What, then, is literature? It is impossible to define literature with the accuracy with which we can define biology, to put into words the meaning of a poem as we put into formulas the solution of a problem in mathematics or the results of an experiment in chemistry. Literature is not a science but an art; and the more the human element, especially on its emotional side, enters into any art, the more impossible it becomes to apply to it the methods of science. To define and analyze are scientific processes; art is concerned with expression and creation. Hence, what are called definitions of literature are really descriptions from varying points of view; each indicates some important truth about great books, but no description embodies the whole truth.

We can see, for example, that when Carlyle called literature "the thought of thinking souls," he was engrossed with only one necessary element in great books; that when Emerson called literature "the effort of man to indemnify himself for the wrongs of his condition," he told a luminous truth indeed, but certainly did not distinguish literature from religion, from sport, from business, from education.

Here are three definitions of literature:

By letters or literature is meant the expression of thought in language, where by "thought" I mean the ideas, feelings, views, reasonings, and other operations of the human mind. — CARDINAL NEWMAN

The inspiration of some phase of life, and the stamp of some form of beauty, are the characteristics of all true works of literature.

HAMILTON W. MABIE

Literature consists of all the books — and they are not so many — where moral truth and human passion are touched with a certain largeness, sanity, and attractiveness of form. — JOHN MORLEY

We can perceive that literature has a soul and a body. Its soul is human thought, human emotion, human experience; its body is language arranged in such a way as to give pleasure to the reader. It is great literature when the thought is profound, the emotion is intense, and the verbal expression of both is beautiful and impressive. The writer is, so to say, an artist who paints with the words of human speech. He depicts some phase of human life which he well and intimately knows, and does so in language that conveys to us the thoughts of his mind and the emotions of his soul; and as we read what he has written our minds are enlarged, our hearts are thrilled, and our whole being is permeated with a joy exalted and serene.

WHY WE READ LITERATURE

To Vitalize our Knowledge. While it is true that we derive knowledge from reading works of literature, that is not our essential object in reading them. Knowledge we can and do derive from books that are not literature, books on astronomy, philosophy, economics; and perhaps the knowledge that does us most good is the knowledge we do not get from any books, the knowledge that grows out of our experience of life and our observation of men and matter. "What book is there to compare with the great Book of Life," asks Jeffery Farnol in his novel *The Broad Highway*, "whose pages are forever a-turning, wherein are marvels and wonders undreamed; things to weep over, and some few to laugh at, if one has but eyes in one's head to see withal?" But we read literature to make what we know become alive and useful; we read great books less for *knowledge* than for *realization*.

To know is one thing; to realize is another. Realization implies vitalized knowledge. I may know, for instance, that

Assisi is a town somewhere in Italy and that St. Francis lived there and founded the Friars Minor; I may know several of the events in the saint's life and have read a number of the interesting legends about the first Franciscans; I may be able to cite the dates of St. Francis's birth and death and canonization and to tell you how many Franciscans there now are throughout the world. All that is knowledge.

Then let us suppose that one day I find myself in Umbria and climb the hill whereon Assisi stands; I walk the same narrow streets through which the saint used to trip singing in the days of his youth, I kneel at his tomb in the great church raised in his honor, and gaze upon the story of his life as depicted by the artist Giotto; then I walk down the olive-clad hill and across the sunset fields to visit the noble basilica which incloses the tiny seven-hundred-year-old chapel of the Portiuncula. Let us suppose, finally, that in the moonlight I sit and ponder upon the spirit of love and simplicity and holy gladness which the Little Poor Man, as he called himself, kindled so long ago in that very place and which still burns mightily throughout the world; and that, thinking thus, I resolve to make the Franciscan spirit a part of my own life and to shed love and joy about me everywhere — then I shall not merely know, but realize, the significance of Assisi and its saint; my knowledge will be alive, vital.

In other words, knowledge confined to the intellect is dead, but it comes to life when it is realized; that is, when it arouses an emotional response and stirs the will to action. An idea in our heads is simply knowledge; but when it gets into our hearts and our hands, it is vitalized knowledge. And only vitalized knowledge profits us, gives us real delight, contributes to culture and urbanity. This same thought has been expressed in a different way by the English novelist Arnold Bennett in his little book on *Literary Taste and How to Form It*:

I am extremely anxious to avoid rhetorical exaggerations. I do not think I am guilty of one in asserting that he who has not been "presented to the freedom" of literature has not wakened up out of his pre-natal sleep. He is merely not born. He can't see; he can't hear; he can't feel, in any full sense. He can only eat his dinner. What more than anything else annoys people who know the true function of literature, and have profited thereby, is the spectacle of so many thousands of individuals going around under the delusion that they are alive, when, as a fact, they are no nearer being alive than a bear in winter.

Therefore we read great books the better to realize life, to vitalize our knowledge of life. We may know something of the strength of the love a father has for his son, but we realize its power when we read in Homer the touching story of old King Priam abjectly creeping into the tent of Achilles to beg for the mangled body of Hector. We may know that it is right to live a stainless life, but that knowledge becomes alive to us when in the lines of Tennyson we hear the chaste Sir Galahad sing,

"My good blade carves the casques of men,
My tough lance thrusteth sure,
My strength is as the strength of ten,
Because my heart is pure."

We may have accepted as true the belief that the man who desires an evil thing is punished by getting what he wants; but the awful truth of that law of morality breaks upon our souls with dazzling conviction when we follow, step by step, the absorbing drama of *Macbeth* and discover that to him who would wade through blood to a kingly throne, life is "full of sound and fury, signifying nothing." We may have heard about Westminster Abbey and even paced its aisles all bordered with monuments to the illustrious dead; but it becomes to us a living volume of history when we catch the mood of Francis Beaumont's little poem "The Tombs in Westminster Abbey" and muse in the Poets' Corner with Washington Irving in the *Sketch Book*. Though we may never gaze upon their coral-circled shores, the islands of the South Seas forever live to us when we behold them through the discerning eyes of

Charles Warren Stoddard and Frederick J. O'Brien. Far removed as we may be in life and thought from Switzerland and Poland, in the novels of Sienkiewicz we learn to appreciate the warlike spirit of the Polish heroes and in Schiller's drama of *William Tell* to realize the splendor of the Swiss struggles for freedom. Thanks to the word magic of James Stephens we can walk with Mary Makebelieve up Grafton Street in

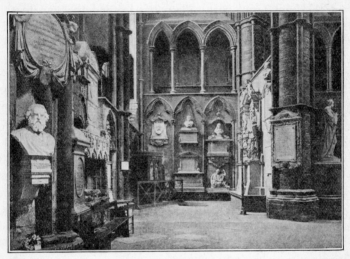

A FAMOUS LITERARY SHRINE

The Poets' Corner in Westminster Abbey is crowded with tombs and memorials of great writers

Dublin town, admire the big policeman at the corner, and delight in watching the jolly ducks cavorting in St. Stephen's Green. Shelley and Keats will attune our ears to the song of the skylark and the nightingale, and Whittier and Wordsworth will open our eyes to God's infinite artistry in the snow-clad hills and the fragrant summer fields. Books, as Dryden has well said, are spectacles wherewith to read nature.

To Live more Deeply and Richly. Because man has both a body and a soul he has both a physical life and a spiritual life. This does not mean that at one time he lives only in his body and at another time he lives only in his soul: his life is a union of both the physical and the spiritual, and he is constantly exercising both his bodily functions and his mental faculties. And he is happiest when his physical needs and cravings are controlled and directed by his reason, when there is harmony and coöperation between the material part of him and the immaterial part. Plato has likened the soul to the driver of a chariot who must maintain the mastery over his horses, and the horses to our bodily inclinations and powers. Our bodies are as essential for our life on earth as the horses are for the success of their driver's journey; but if we let our bodily life take up most of our time and attention, we are like the driver of a chariot who lets his horses run away with him. To save us from such a catastrophe Our Lord urges us to give less heed to the body and more heed to the soul. "Be not solicitous therefore, saying: What shall we eat, or what shall we drink, or wherewith shall we be clothed? . . . Seek ye therefore first the kingdom of God, and his justice." The Kingdom of God is a spiritual thing; food, drink, and clothing are material things. If we follow Our Lord's counsel and live mainly in our minds, we shall understand what it is to live deeply, richly, and happily.

We have at our disposal many ways of living the spiritual life. The practice of our religion is one, the enjoyment of good music is another, the appreciation of fine pictures and statues is a third. And among these means of thus living deeply, richly, and happily literature takes high rank. James Huneker, an American art and music critic, once wrote:

Now, while I realize that life is too vast to be compressed into any single formula, whether religious, philosophical, or artistic, universal wisdom has been distilled into certain books. All Christianity is in *The Imitation of Christ*, and the quintessence of secular wisdom may be found in Montaigne. No better gymnastic for the spirit is there than Plato, and woe to him that reads not the Bible — not alone for the style or the "quotations," but for the sake of his miserable soul.

The soul, the mind, needs food and exercise just as the body does; but the food of the mind is not bread, and its exercise is not games. It feeds on visions of truth and beauty as supplied by the master word artists in literature; its exercise is to wrestle with ideas enshrined in noble books, even as Jacob wrestled all the night with the angel; and its reward is, like Jacob's, to receive a joyful blessing at the dawn.

Sometimes a man's physical vitality runs low, and then the doctors send him away to the mountains or the seaside. There the man soaks himself in sunshine and fills his lungs with pure air and climbs over boulders or plunges through breakers day after day; and gradually he comes to feel that he is really alive and that life is truly worth living. Similarly, when we immerse ourselves in the sea of literature and bask through lengthening hours in the invigorating sunlight of truth; when we sit with Spenser or Keats, Manzoni or Verga, upon some summit of the spirit and catch the beauty of the lowlands touched with the sunset glow; when, in other words, we give the best and get the best from books — at such moments we are vividly aware of being spiritually alive and strong, supple and vigorous.

A man physically ill has no appetite for beefsteak and onions and no thrill at the prospect of taking part in a football game or a Marathon race. He is below par in his body. And the man who finds in literature only what Montaigne called a "languid pleasure" is below par in his mind: either he has not the brains or he has not trained and used them. It is not uncommon to find a person physically fit but mentally very ill indeed.

Often a reader does not get much benefit from reading a masterpiece of literature simply because he does not give himself to the work with vim, vigor, and enthusiasm. He must take an active, not a passive, attitude toward the great writer and the great book. He must read creatively; right reading is a form of living. Emerson goes to the heart of the difficulty:

One must be an inventor to read well. As the proverb says, "He that would bring home the wealth of the Indies must carry out the wealth of the Indies." There is then creative reading as well as creative writing. When the mind is braced by labor and invention, the page of whatever book we read becomes luminous with manifold allusion. Every sentence is doubly significant, and the sense of our author is as broad as the world.

To Acquire Culture and Urbanity. We say that a person is cultured when he is responsive to the appeal of the finer things in life. He enjoys good music; he relishes refined and intelligent conversation; he delights in studying masterpieces of painting and sculpture; he secures genuine satisfaction from visiting a noble cathedral, where he is susceptible alike to the architectural beauty of the building and the impressiveness of the sacred liturgy. The cultured man, furthermore, knows and loves good books. He has "a taste for reading" — rather, we might say, a passion for reading; and that is something which, as Gibbon said, he would not exchange for all the wealth of the Indies. And because through religion and art, music and literature, the man of culture comes into vital contact with ideas of truth, beauty, and goodness; because the emotions aroused in him by those refining influences are noble and elevated, — it follows that his habits of thinking and feeling are formed under the influence of the best and finest ideals. Such a man has the dignity and the simplicity, the ease and the self-control, the poise and the independence, the strength and the gentility, which are the external indications of inner culture.

The word *urbanity* comes from the Latin *urbs*, "city." In ancient days cities had walls around them, and people were definitely in the city or out of it. For the most part the people of refinement and education dwelt inside the city walls — though every city had many rude and ignorant inhabitants too — and set the standard of good taste in speech, dress, and manners. It was to the cities that foreign visitors came: legates from popes and envoys from kings, world-renowned painters and writers and musicians, philosophers and scientists and educators, all of them with fresh ideas and novel points of view. The presence within the cities of so many cultured persons naturally reacted upon the lives and customs of the inhabitants, so that they found themselves in sharp contrast with the rustic population living outside the walls. The city folks, because of their educational and cultural

THE MANUSCRIPT BOOK

By John W. Alexander, in the Library of Congress, Washington. A reminder that before printing was invented literature was preserved through the industry of monks who transcribed masterpieces of poetry and prose. (From a Copley Print. Copyright, 1899, by Curtis & Cameron, Publishers, Boston)

advantages, were recognized as *urbane*, and their knowledge and refinement, their openness of mind and ease of manner, were all summed up in the word *urbanity*.

In our day, and especially in America, that old distinction between the dwellers in town and in country no longer exists. For our cities have no walls, and railways and motor cars, the telephone and the radio, express and postal service, have made it impossible for us to be cut off from any influences affecting our fellow men. But there is still a very real danger that we may be rustic and suburban in mind. The country worker, on whom the Roman patrician looked down, was awkward and ignorant because he had not met the best people, had not engaged in cultured conversation, had not come into intimate contact with stimulating ideas. Many a worthy American citizen with good clothes, two automobiles, several servants, and a well-nourished bank account is lacking in the essentials of urbanity because he has not "met the best people" in literature. Such a man Sinclair Lewis commemorated in his novel *Babbitt*. The Babbitts lack urbanity because they do not know the best and finest things that have been thought in the world, because they have not read the great books which every cultured man reads, because it hurts their heads to talk seriously about anything except business and baseball, because they get no enjoyment from poetry, from classical music and drama, from masterpieces of prose and of painting.

In the old days one trait of the city dweller was that he could recognize important people at sight. And so in our day one trait of the man who has been accorded the freedom of the city of literature is that he can recognize literary allusions at sight. Charles Mills Gayley, in his vigorous and invigorating little book *Idols of Education*, laments that a good many college freshmen are sadly deficient in the ability to recognize the old familiar faces:

How many know the difference between Sennacherib and a floating rib, the Maid of Orleans and the Maid of Athens, the Witch of Endor and the Widow of Nain, Dionysius and Dionysus, the jewels of Cornelia and the diamond necklace, the Lion of Judah and the Lion of the North? Or, if some have some vague impression of some of these things, for how many do they possess an historical or literary flavor? If a speaker refer to Apollyon or the Houyhnhnms, to the Delectable Mountains, or Mount Hymettus, or to the Horn of Roncesvalles; if he quote a line of Horace, a French *bon mot* or a German commonplace; if he refer to the Seven against Thebes, the Electra, the Bucolics, the Télémaque, the Sorrows of Werther, to Giotto's O or Botticelli's Spring, to Gargantua or Pompilia, how many eyes light with recognition?

To a reader lacking in urbanity — that is, to a reader who wastes his time on trivial books and does not seek acquaintance with the wisest minds and choicest spirits of all countries and times — that list of names is only a list of names. To a reader who knows the Bible and Bunyan, Greek tragedy and French epic, Swift and Scott, Byron and Browning, that list of names is like the map of a country which he has traversed and dwelt in and loved.

To Learn the Art of Expression. In Robert Browning's poem "Master Hugues of Saxe-Gotha" the old organist,

HOW LITERATURE WAS LEARNED IN POMPEII

Only fragments of this luxurious dwelling have survived the scars of time and the lava of Vesuvius, but the living words recited by the Roman poet still endure.
(From a painting by E. Forti)

wrestling with the composer's "mountainous fugues," fancies he sees Master Hugues, the dead composer, regarding him from among the organ pipes, his "brow ruled like a score," and the apparition assures him that though he has mastered the technique he has missed the soul of that piece of music: "Good, the mere notes!"

We are all organists of some kind in this life of ours, and we play for the glory of God, for the profit and delight of our fellow men, and for our own improvement and enjoyment.

The music we make is human speech, and whether we write it or utter it we are engaged in the art of expression.

There are many things to be learned about effective writing and speaking, and the best way to learn them is to read and study, to analyze and imitate, specimens of good English. As art students spend long hours copying great paintings, so

A PRIMITIVE PRINTING SHOP

The art of printing has made it possible for all classes of people to read the world's great books

should students of literature play the sedulous ape, as Stevenson said, and imitate reliable models of language. In this we are like the old organist in Browning's poem; and sometimes perhaps, if we look up quickly from our work, we may catch a fleeting glimpse of Addison or Swift, Thackeray or Newman, Shaw or Chesterton, smiling down at us a little derisively; but we need not be discountenanced, for those worthies were once young and striving too.

Surely this is a matter not difficult to understand. A boy who wants to play baseball and play it very well does several sensible things. First of all, and all the time, he is most enthusiastic about the subject. Secondly, he practices at every opportunity. Thirdly, by preference, he plays, not with smaller boys who do not know the game but with larger boys who play better than he. Fourthly, he seizes every opportunity to see baseball played by professionals. And, lastly, he is grateful when persons who know tell him of his defects as a baseball player, and he takes the suggestions to heart and tries to improve himself.

Not all of us are obliged to play baseball; but all of us are obliged to express ourselves in speaking and writing, and we shall have better results and more enjoyment if we learn how to express ourselves well. Let us be truly enthusiastic about good speaking and good writing; let us practice, carefully and earnestly, all the time; let us prefer conversation with those who know more than we do, and let us read, not flimsy and superficial books, but the works of men who thought deeply and who therefore make us think deeply too; let us go out of our way to hear a good speaker or to read and study a genuine literary masterpiece; and when, in books or out of books, we get a helpful hint let us be grateful and gracious.

Some exceptions occur to us at once; but, all in all, our English Literature has been written by men who were scholars as well as writers, who were familiar figures in libraries, who knew and loved the best books of all ages and times. They learned how to express themselves in writing by attentively and enthusiastically studying the master works of universal literature. Talents vary, circumstances change, and opportunities differ; but what they did, we also can do.

CHAPTER II

AN AIRPLANE SURVEY

WORLD LITERATURE

Race and Literature. By "English Literature" we mean books written in the English language. We do not mean merely books written about England, or in England, or by Englishmen. England is neither the subject matter nor the inspiration of George Eliot's *Romola*, Carlyle's *French Revolution*, or Shelley's "Stanzas Written in Dejection near Naples." Byron wrote "The Prisoner of Chillon" in Switzerland, Stevenson wrote *Travels with a Donkey* in France, Browning wrote *The Ring and the Book* in Italy. Henry Clarence Kendall the Australian, Benjamin Disraeli the Jew, James Clarence Mangan the Irishman, Carl Sandburg the American, Robert Burns the Scotsman, Joseph Conrad the Pole, and Stephen Leacock the Canadian have all contributed to English Literature. As Greek Literature is not confined to Greece, so English Literature is not confined to England; English Literature includes more than the literature of England, even as French Literature includes more than the literature of France. Though the United States is no part of the British Empire, American Literature, because it is written in the English language, is a part of English Literature.

In this book, however, we are to confine our attention almost entirely to the English Literature which has been produced in England. To include the literature produced in Australia, in Canada, in the United States, would make the book too bulky and the course too crowded. But it is important for us to bear in mind that English Literature is something bigger and broader, something more far-reaching and more inclusive, than the English nation or the English race.

History and Literature. It is well, too, to bear in mind that English Literature is not merely an outgrowth of English history. Though events in the career of the British nation are reflected in English poetry and prose, the subject matter of much English Literature — some of its masterpieces, in fact, like Shakespeare's *Hamlet* and Browning's *The Ring and the Book* — has no relation to English history at all. "Looking at English Literature in the large," says Charles Leonard Moore, "one would say that its body has been nourished by a most minute half-pennyworth of native bread and a most unconscionable quantity of imported sack."[1] Some English writers have expressed English social ideals and, like the young Kipling, have commemorated British imperial policies; but other English writers (Ruskin, for example) have been fundamentally "agin the government" and have vigorously attacked the English conception of civilization. Byron and Keats were not the only English poets who transcended England in their interests and who died far from her shores. And some eminent English authors, judged by their writings, were singularly indifferent to the national aspirations and accomplishments of their own day. Shakespeare in his Historical Plays created a brilliant pageant of earlier English history, but "of the Englishmen of his own time he hardly tells us directly anything except that they dress outrageously, outdrink the Dutch, and are stupidly given to staring at strange monsters."[2]

Nationalism and Literature. Centuries ago even learned men, like St. Thomas Aquinas and Dante, accepted the Ptolemaic explanation of the universe and believed that the earth was the center round which the stars and planets revolved. That was the geocentric theory. We know better now; but it is still possible to find books which assume that

[1] *The Dial*, March 2, 1916.
[2] Tucker Brooke, *Shakespeare of Stratford*, pp. 136, 137.

English Literature is the center of the literary universe. We might call that the Anglocentric theory of literature, and there are several things wrong with it, the most important being that it is not true.

Copernicus and Galileo and other students of science who disputed the geocentric theory met with considerable opposition, to say nothing of inconvenience, because so many earnest

"WHAT NEWS ON THE RIALTO?"

Because of the broad sympathies and artistic power of Shakespeare, the Rialto Bridge in Venice is known far beyond the borders of Italy

scholars could not get away from the notion that the earth was the center of the universe. Similarly, at the present day, when leading thinkers and scholars recognize the universal character of literature, some people cannot get away from the notion that the particular country in which they happened to be born is the spot about which all the constellations of arts and letters revolve. And always, too, there are a few men without a country who are convinced that nothing has happened anywhere in literature since the Greek dramatists flourished in the days of Pericles, and Virgil and Horace won undying fame and the patronage of Augustus. It is the fashion now to condemn what is awkwardly called narrow-mindedness. Stressing the note of nationalism in literature is the most lamentable and certainly the most fatal manifestation of that mental affliction.

Humanity and Literature. As scientific men three hundred years ago learned to take a bigger and broader view of the heavenly bodies, so the student of books and writers may wisely learn to take a bigger and broader view of literature. English Literature is literature in English; and that implies that there has been, that there is, and that in all probability there will be literature in other languages. And as Shylock in *The Merchant of Venice* pleaded for the recognition of the common humanity of all men, irrespective of race or creed, so a textbook calls attention to the universal elements and interracial influences in great books, whether those books are written in Greek or in Persian, in English or in Chinese. Let a man envision life aglow with beauty, and what he writes is literature, even though he does not know how to write it in Arabic, in Choctaw, or in French.

In yet another respect it is important to distinguish between nationality and literature. We sometimes hear early English dramas called "the plays of our forefathers," and even ourselves referred to as the offspring of "Anglo-Saxon civilization." Now while that sort of thing may pass muster in poetry (Virgil did something of the like in inventing a venerable ancestry for the Roman people), it is distinctly misleading in history. One half of the citizens of the United States have not a drop of English blood in their veins, and a large proportion of the other half — not excepting a generous sprinkling of the countless thousands whose ancestors came over in the *Mayflower* — spring from a racial admixture as varied as that possessed by Sinclair Lewis's Martin Arrowsmith:

Martin was . . . a Typical Pure-bred Anglo-Saxon American, which means that he was a union of German, French, Scotch, Irish, perhaps a little Spanish, conceivably a little of the strains lumped together as "Jewish," and a great deal of English, which is itself a combination of Primitive Britain, Celt, Phœnician, Roman, German, Dane, and Swede.[1]

The fact that we speak the English language does not make us English. And although we Americans are indebted to England for important elements in our civic and social life, we are likewise indebted to Italy, Germany, France, and Spain, to Egypt and Israel, to Greece and Rome, and to non-national influences such as Catholicism. Our civilization, in short, is a product of no particular nation : we are the children of all Europe, and our lives and institutions are to a considerable degree determined by the traditions of European culture.

Our Literary Ancestors. To choose the nation from which we are physically descended is beyond our power : no man can select his own father and mother. But in the things of the mind it is to a large extent possible to choose our forefathers. Our thoughts and our sentiments are influenced by the books we read, by the music we hear, by the pictures we see, by the religion we profess, and these things are truly the forefathers of our minds. An American university president whose bodily ancestors were Italian once said something worth remembering :

I don't know very much about my ancestors in the flesh. It is possible that some of them were hardy Sicilian pirates who went through life with colored handkerchiefs around their heads and daggers between their teeth. But I do know a good deal about my real ancestors, the ancestors of my mind and spirit. Plato and Aristotle, Cicero and Horace, Dante and Calderón, Shakespeare and Goethe — these and men like these are my true forefathers because they have influenced my thoughts and aspirations and have helped me more than all others to shape my philosophy of life.

Thus it is that while our physical ancestors may have been Germans or Englishmen, Irishmen or Danes, Italians or Russians, or a fusion of several racial strains, our spiritual ances-

[1] *Arrowsmith*, chap. i.

tors — and spiritual ancestors are the ancestors who matter most — are the great philosophers and poets and artists and heroes and saints of all nations and times who have influenced our ways of thinking, feeling, and acting. Though in political allegiance we are of one nation, in education and culture we are of international descent. Our intellectual heritage, the great thoughts of thinking souls, comes to us from no one place in Europe and from no one race of men. We can truly say with the Latin dramatist Terence, "Nothing that is human can be foreign to me."

In this book we are to consider one portion of our literary heritage. English Literature has a noble history and comes down to us with a splendid array of thinkers and poets, storytellers and artificers in speech. Many of them have made valuable contributions to life and thought; most of them found their own inspiration in the literature of other times and races, and that accumulated wisdom they now pass on to us. When we read the masterpieces of English Literature we come into contact with what Arnold called the best that has been known and thought in the world.

THE RIVER OF LITERATURE

We shall better appreciate the significance of what is called English Literature if we reflect upon these words of an American scholar, John Macy:

Literature is a succession of books from books. Artistic expression springs from life ultimately but not immediately. It may be likened to a river which is swollen throughout its course by new tributaries and by the seepages of its banks; it reflects the life through which it flows, taking color from the shores; the shores modify it, but its power and volume descend from distant headwaters and affluents far up stream.[1]

Up the Mississippi. It is possible for a man in an airplane to get an excellent idea of the Mississippi River by taking off

[1] *The Spirit of American Literature*, chap. i.

from New Orleans, flying over the delta where the great stream pours into the Gulf of Mexico, and then following its meanderings northward, past Tennessee and Kentucky and Illinois on his right, past Arkansas and Missouri on his left, noting the important cities on either bank, observing the Arkansas and the Ohio and the Missouri and other tributary rivers, and at length locating the source of the great waterway in Minnesota. There are many things he will not find out about the Mississippi River. He will hardly have time to count all the steamers churning up and down the stream, much less to evaluate their cargoes or exchange greetings with their crews and passengers; he cannot go in swimming or estimate the depth of the river at various points; he will get only a bird's-eye view of the numerous factories and warehouses along the banks; and he will learn next to nothing of the social and commercial life of Vicksburg and Memphis, St. Louis and St. Paul. But when he shuts off his engine and comes to earth in the vicinity of Grand Rapids, Minnesota, he will have some idea of the length of the river, of its varying breadth here and at Baton Rouge, of the location and relative size of its islands, of the places where it derives increased volume from its tributaries, of the character of the country bordering its banks. He will realize, and this is knowledge of inestimable value, that the Mississippi River observable from New Madrid, Missouri, is not the whole Mississippi River.

In like manner it is possible for the student to get an airplane view of the river of literature. He can start with Conrad Aiken or John Masefield or Susan Ertz or any other writer standing where the great stream of literature flows into the gulf of present-day life, and then follow the windings of its waters between the banks of history and back through the years until he reaches a land of low visibility in the misty dawn of European civilization. On either hand he will discover nations, — England, Italy, France, Germany, Spain, and, much farther upstream, Rome and Greece, — each pouring into the river of great books contributions of varying volume and significance. He will observe here and there what look like cities, clusters of eminent and influential writers constituting definite periods in literary annals. He will notice, too, that some of the tributary streams have their source not in countries adjacent to the river, but in the distant snow-capped mountains on the dim horizon of time — thoughts and emotions which flow into universal literature from the very beginnings of human life; and, if the air is clear and his eyes are keen, the aëronaut may even trace some of the tributaries back to that Garden of Eden where they had their source close to the Tree of Knowledge and the Tree of Life. If as he flits through the air he looks upward as well as downward, he will appreciate the truth that the noble river has received much of its waters from the very heavens themselves.

Many things the student will not find out as he thus soars over the world of books. No one book will he be able to study in detail; no one author will he come to know intimately. A vast number of minor tributaries he will scarcely see at all. He will not be in a position to estimate the depth of the river of literature nor to count the thousands of human beings who have slaked their thirst at its waters, have drawn power from its flowing, have sailed for business and pleasure on its surface, have caught the sweet music of its lapping waves, and have feasted their eyes on its beauties at sunset and at dawn. But certain things about literature he will definitely realize when his thrilling journey is ended. He will know that this river is very long and that its breadth and swiftness vary. He will know that here it surges briskly between tall cliffs of thought, that there it foams and flurries among the half-submerged rocks of dissension and controversy, that yonder it glides smoothly and sweetly between level plains where birds sing and flowers bloom and children's laughter fills the air. And he will grasp the important fact that we who stand beside the river in America in the twentieth century do not see it all.

In short, before he proceeds to explore any section of the river of literature in detail, he will have a general idea of what the river is.

Up the River of Books. Let us now, with this analogy of the river vividly in mind, take an airplane view of literature. Here, in England and Ireland, Canada and the United States, are a host of writers: Chesterton and Shaw, Winifred Letts and Sean O'Casey, Paul Elmer More and W. B. Maxwell, Katharine Tynan Hinkson and Isabel Clarke, Galsworthy and Sara Teasdale, Gertrude Atherton and Winston Churchill, and ever so many more. All these writers greater and less, poets and novelists, essayists and dramatists, have made contributions to literature. Some of their inspiration and some of the elements in their methods they have drawn from the life of today; but if there lay the sole source of their power they would be not littérateurs but journalists. Journalism it is which is exclusively concerned with contemporary happenings; literature looks before and after — and above. And just as contemporary life itself draws much of its knowledge and many of its customs from earlier ages, so contemporary literature derives most of its force and inspiration and beauty from books written in past centuries. It is hardly an exaggeration to say that if the living writers just mentioned had not read much and thought deeply in the literature of the past they would not be writing books at all; and if we who read them read no books of earlier epochs we cannot properly judge and cannot vitally enjoy the books of our own day and generation.

The writers of today are influenced by the writers of yesterday. The contemporary novel would be something very different from what it is if Stevenson and Walter Scott, Turgenev and Dostoevski, had not written novels in the nineteenth century. And the nineteenth-century novelists were in turn influenced by yet earlier story-tellers — Richardson and Fielding and Daniel Defoe, who themselves, consciously or unconsciously, were affected by Cervantes, the author of the great Spanish novel *Don Quixote*, and by tellers of tales in Italy and France. And what is true of the novel, the most ephemeral of the forms which literature assumes, is true in even greater measure of the drama, the poem, and the essay. In what they write, and in the way they write, the literary men of the hour are the heirs of the ages.

The Victorians. Looking backward along the course of literature in English we see within the last hundred years certain outstanding figures and certain especially significant movements. John Ruskin tried to open the eyes of his fellow men to the finer things of life, and he went to the old books and paintings and churches of Europe for much of his material and illustrations. Carlyle, developing his theory of great men as the motive forces of civilization, chose his heroes in Germany, in England, in Scotland, in Switzerland, in Italy, in Turkey, in Scandinavia. Tennyson not only probed the thought of his own day and in imagination constructed the life and ideals of years to come, but found his themes in many climes and times. Browning was a traveler in body and in spirit; his poems are a mosaic of unfamiliar names and times and events. The Oxford Movement, which so notably affected life and literature, is most adequately represented by Cardinal Newman, who gained his knowledge from deep study of the past, and who perfected his clear and beautiful style by imitating Cicero and other ancient writers.

Romanticism and Classicism. Next we find the Romantic Movement in England, Germany, and France. In English Literature the principal writers identified with it are Byron, Scott, and Wordsworth. It was many-sided, as we shall see elsewhere in this book, and its power came from many sources; but, among other things, it was a revolt against the artificiality in literature and the conventionality in life which characterized the Classicism of the eighteenth century. Most prominent in that Classicism of the Augustan Age, as the period is called, were Addison and Johnson in prose and

Alexander Pope in verse. The leading ideas of the English Classicists came from French critics and philosophers and from the Latin writers in the days of the Emperor Augustus.

Pope claimed to have learned how to write by reading John Dryden, the leading figure in the epoch immediately preceding his own; and Dryden, poet, dramatist, critic, and translator, busied himself with Early English Literature, with writers of France and Spain and Italy, with the Greek and Roman classics. His best-known poem, written in honor of St. Cecilia, the patroness of music, brings us back to the conquest of Persia by Alexander the Great.

Puritan and Cavalier. And now comes the mighty Milton, a blind man with an inner vision, who embodied in his *Paradise Lost* the fruits of intense living and seasoned scholarship, of a life spent first in rustic England and foreign travel, then in the turmoil of civil war and Puritan politics, and ending in obscurity and what the world called disgrace; of a scholarship which fed upon the great epic poems of Virgil and Homer, upon innumerable works of philosophy and theology, upon the Bible, which to him, as to us, was the written word of God.

The power of literature, as we have seen, does not issue from history, but the river of books sometimes reflects momentous events that take place along its banks and receives torrents that flow down neighboring hillsides; and here and there along its course are rocky islands which divide its flow. A series of momentous events in English history were the conflict between the Cavaliers and the Puritans, the execution of King Charles I, the establishment of the Commonwealth, and the Restoration of the Stuarts in the person of Charles II. While Milton is identified with one phase of that troubled epoch, another reaction is observed in Robert Herrick, the unspiritual clergyman who composed fanciful lyrics in his sheltered retreat, paid literary tribute to imaginary ladies, and sang of life and destiny in a thin but sweet voice and in the spirit of an ancient pagan returned to earth. The opposition to Puritanism found expression in Samuel Butler's metrical satire *Hudibras*; and the courtly and laughter-loving Cavaliers have secured immortality in the poems of Sir John Suckling and Richard Lovelace. They were to a great extent the literary heirs of the poets who in the troubled and prosaic days of Queen Elizabeth formed "a nest of singing birds."

STRATFORD-UPON-AVON

Here Shakespeare was born, and here he lies beneath the pavement of Holy Trinity Church

The Elizabethans. Shakespeare could, on occasion, be a singing bird too, as the delightful lyrics strewn through his plays bear ample witness; and so could his friend Ben Jonson, one of whose little songs still rings sweetly in our ears, "Drink to me Only with thine Eyes." And as we of today often turn to Shakespeare for memorably worded comments on life (he and Pope are the most popularly quoted writers in the English language), so we turn to Francis Bacon for shrewd and pithy embodiments of practical philosophy and worldly wisdom.

Bacon wrote other things, but he lives in literature by reason of his *Essays*. Ben Jonson wrote essays, too; and both Bacon and Jonson here followed after the French thinker Montaigne, the Roman philosopher Seneca, the Greek slave Epictetus, and the Wisdom Books of the Bible.

Shakespeare and Jonson were primarily dramatists, and they leaned heavily on dramatists who had gone before them. Jonson took pains to point out how faithfully he was following in the footsteps of ancient writers and hearkening to the counsel of learned authorities. Shakespeare, as Jonson complained, had small Latin and less Greek, but for all that he was widely read in dramatic and narrative literature. His plots are not original; he took them from chronicles, from popular stories, from earlier plays. Of his supremely great tragedies, one is set in legendary Britain, one in Scotland, one in Denmark, and one in Italy.

Shakespeare began his career as a dramatist by revising and adapting old tragedies and by coming into contact with the work of Marlowe and other writers for the theater. And the men from whom Shakespeare learned his trade might have traced their descent as dramatists from the plays of college and of court and from the devotional dramas in which the medieval guilds, in England and on the Continent, celebrated the great feasts of the Christian year. Those pious dramas themselves derived directly from the liturgy of the Catholic Church.

Shakespeare, Ben Jonson, Bacon, and Edmund Spenser represent the Elizabethan Age. Spenser has been called the poets' poet because his poems have stimulated the brain and fired the imagination of John Keats and many another singer. His *Faerie Queene*, he himself assures us, was planned to show the workings of the Christian virtues in the times in which he lived. That object necessarily required a moral and a patriotic element; but it is remarkable that the excellence of the poem is due almost entirely to the brilliancy of its conceptions, the quaintness of its language, and its attempt to reconstruct the medieval metrical romance of chivalry. The Spenserian stanza is a modification of an Italian verse-form and has been imitated by later poets.

Ballads and Romances. Spenser's poems introduce to us the spirit of poetry in masquerade costume; the English and Scottish Ballads of the era preceding disclose the spirit of poetry in scant and primitive garb. They recount homely tales of love and war, border raids and fairy charms, tragedies by flood and field, and sad stories of the death of kings. The same relish for dangers and warfare, for courage and nobility, we find on a higher plane and against a broader background in the prose romance of Sir Thomas Malory, the *Morte d'Arthur*. This was one of the many versions of the tales of King Arthur and the Knights of the Round Table which, both before and since the publication of Malory's work in 1485, have appeared and reappeared in European Literature from Iceland to Italy.

The Morning Star of Song — Chaucer. Stories of the most widely different kinds make up most of *The Canterbury Tales* of Chaucer, though the charm of that unfinished masterpiece lies mainly in the shrewd and kindly humor of their telling and in the clever and appealing portraiture of the tellers. For several reasons the name of Geoffrey Chaucer deserves to be remembered by the student, but chiefly because with him English Literature really begins. This is so, first, because Chaucer is the first really great writer in English; secondly, because he is the first writer in English to exert any notable influence on subsequent English Literature; and thirdly, because like a man rowing from a narrow inlet into a broad and far-extending river, he swung English poetry into the current of European literary tradition.

Literature before Chaucer. Before Chaucer there had been literature in England, but to a great extent it was provincial and isolated from the literature of Europe even as England itself, for long a group of divided principalities and a prey to invading sea rovers, was (except for its religious affiliation with Rome) isolated from the Continent. Looking back upon it we find groups of writers on religion, philosophy, history, and science, most of them, like Roger Bacon and St. Bede the Venerable, members of religious orders, and one of them, Alfred the Great, a king and national hero; and we find early Christian poetry as in the Cædmonian poems, and early pagan poetry as in *Beowulf*. But that pre-Chaucerian literature in English stands apart from the European Literature which we can trace in an unbroken line from England and France in the twentieth century to Rome and Greece in the first and fifth centuries before the birth of Christ. It is like a small stream starting among low-lying hills and fed partly by the mighty river; but after a time its supply from the river is diverted, and the little stream dries up because it has no further source of power. *Beowulf*, for instance, has exerted no influence on subsequent literature and is farther removed from our thought and spirit than the Greek *Iliad* and the Spanish songs of the Cid.

The World Stream. Chaucer affords a splendid illustration of the non-national nature of literature. He floats placidly on the surface of the river, enjoying the sights and sounds and odors of the fragrant English fields through which he passes and observing with humor and insight the knights and monks and farmers and nuns and housewives and students he meets along the way; but he is borne on waters that come from other lands and by a force that has its origin in far-distant mountains. That force is the European Tradition in literature. It came to Chaucer through several French romances, through Dante and Petrarca and Boccaccio; and behind those French and Italian writers were the classics of Rome and Greece.

THE EUROPEAN TRADITION

We have now made a rapid exploration of the stream of literature in English. Before we bring our airplane to earth let us make a hasty survey of the great river of European Literature of which our English Literature is a part and from which it derives its force and volume. We shall first consider the literary forces in modern Europe which have especially influenced writers in English; secondly, we shall note the diffused but very real effects of the Catholic tradition in literature; and, thirdly, we shall glance at the part played in the development of English Literature by the leading authors of Greece and

GOETHE

Rome. From all this we shall acquire a bird's-eye knowledge of what we have called the European Tradition in literature.

Germany. The German contribution to European culture has not been predominantly literary; it can be traced more adequately in music, science, and philosophy. The majority of English writers have not been directly affected by German Literature at all. Yet certain outstanding works of German Literature are part of our intellectual inheritance. The gaily lithographed books of fairy tales which we read when we were little children were translations and adaptations of the folklore garnered by the Grimm brothers or by the Danish writer Hans Christian Andersen. Freytag and Lessing have affected our notions of dramatic literature, and German scholars such as Ulrici and Gervinus have helped us to understand our own Shakespeare, precisely as English scholars such as Moore and Toynbee and American scholars such as Lowell and Grandgent

THE SCHLOSS, OR CASTLE, HEIDELBERG

have helped the Italians to appreciate Dante. Schiller is accepted as a world poet by English readers. Goethe, the great name of German Literature, has for long been a name to conjure with in England and the United States. Bayard Taylor translated his *Faust*, and others of his books have been introduced to English readers by Carlyle, Coleridge, and Scott. German influences can be traced in Browning, George Eliot, and Matthew Arnold. It may not be without point to recall that in our own day a popular German influence, both before and since the World War, has been exerted by the German play *Old Heidelberg*, in its musical form known as *The Student Prince*.

Spain. We cannot realize the extent of the Spanish influence on European Literature until we remember that for centuries Spain was the dominant nation in Christendom, that her soldiers and statesmen in the Old World and her colonizers and missionaries in the New were impressive figures even in the eyes of her enemies. The relations between Spain and England, inimical as well as friendly (for they were alternately one and the other), brought the masterpieces of Spanish Literature to the notice of the admiring islanders. Until the defeat of the Armada the educated Englishman looked up to Spain and recognized, even while he patriotically regretted, the superiority of Spanish writers. The popularity of Spanish Literature among reading Englishmen in the days of the Tudors is astonishing; and the Spanish dramatists, notably Calderón and Lope de Vega, vitally affected the Elizabethan stage. The writings of St. Teresa, the leading woman in world literature, influenced Crashaw and other English religious poets. Cervantes, the father of the novel in European Literature, achieved a world masterpiece in *Don Quixote* and strongly influenced the art of fiction in England, from Defoe's *Robinson Crusoe* and Fielding's *Joseph Andrews* to Donn Byrne's *Blind Raftery* and John Masefield's *Odtaa*. Much of the Spanish influence on English Literature came through Ireland.

France. It would be possible to cover several pages of this book with nothing more than the names and writings of French authors who have shed their influence on English Literature. France has conquered and invaded England, England has conquered and invaded France; and between wars, as good warriors will, Frenchmen and Englishmen have found the temperamental English Channel no barrier to social intercourse. The bookstore in an American town will not fail to offer for sale a translation of the latest novel by André Maurois or Paul Bourget, and the bookstalls at Waterloo Station in London display

French books as old as the *Song of Roland* and as new as Louis Bertrand's *St. Augustin*. Boileau and other seventeenth-century critics were the inspirers of Dryden and Johnson. It was in a Frenchman, Chateaubriand, that Romanticism found its most complete embodiment, and in another Frenchman, Voltaire, that Classicism found its most literary expression. Both men lived for a time in England: one eulogized Milton and the other depreciated Shakespeare, and both affected English Literature. Some of the French novelists are as familiar to English readers as Dickens and Henry James, and some of the French critics are more familiar than Saintsbury and Paul Elmer More. French essayists, especially Montaigne, have served as models for English stylists, and vast quantities of French poetry have been taken over bodily by English verse writers. The spiritual letters of St. Francis de Sales have shaped the traits of English devotional literature, and the Protestant *Pilgrim's Progress* has its Catholic forefather in a French monk's allegory, *The Pilgrimage of Man*. In addition, very much of the ancient literature which came into English came through French channels.

Italy. As the direct inheritor of the European Tradition from the great writers of imperial Rome, Italy, more than any other nation, influenced the development of literature in English. Repeatedly in the course of our study of individual English writers we shall observe their indebtedness to Italian methods and Italian thought. There were times, as in the sixteenth century, when in England "the love of all things Italian became a veritable passion: Italian art, music, manners, language, and finally letters, became the first necessities of gentle life, and poetry awakened from her long sleep to breathe forth Italian melody through the lips of Wyatt and Surrey."[1] At once a link with the vanished Roman Empire and the living heart of the Catholic world, Italy appealed to thoughtful minds and fired creative imaginations. Padua, Salerno, and

[1] Maud F. Jerrold, *Francesco Petrarca, Poet and Humanist*, p. 298.

BOSSUET

The "Eagle of Meaux" holds an honored place in French Literature. He was
a distinguished pulpit orator and a zealous bishop in the days of King Louis XIV

Bologna were world-famed university foundations in days when learning in England was sparse and uncertain; Rome and Florence were centers of literature, art, and culture when English poets were, so to say, learning their trade, when English prose had not yet reached maturity, when English art and artists were as yet undreamed of. For centuries, even to our own day, the ambition of every man who thirsts for the finer things in life has been to visit Italy and draw inspiration from her churches, her monuments, her libraries, and her art galleries. Practically every one of the great English authors made the grand tour, either actually like Chaucer and Milton or in imagination like Shakespeare. The three supreme makers of Italian literature, Dante, Petrarca, and Boccaccio, not to speak of innumerable minor writers, have profoundly affected English poetry and prose. John Addington Symonds has well remarked:

As poets in the truest sense of the word, we English live and breathe through sympathy with the Italians. The magnetic touch which is required to inflame the imagination of the North is derived from Italy. The nightingales of English song who make our oak and beech copses resonant in spring with purest melody are migratory birds who have charged their souls in the South with the spirit of beauty, and who return to warble native wood-notes in a tongue which is their own.[1]

Other Countries. Every other country of Europe has in some degree affected English Literature, from little Holland to titanic Russia. For riming verse English and all modern poetry is indebted to the ancient bards of Ireland. From Holland came that wonderful *Imitation of Christ*, by the monk Thomas à Kempis, a book popular in every language and eulogized by such a diversity of English writers as Johnson, George Eliot, and Hugh Walpole. Another instance of the Dutch influence is furnished in the resemblances existing between Milton's *Paradise Lost* and the *Lucifer* of Joost van den Vondel, a convert to the Catholic faith and the leading poet

[1] *Sketches and Studies in Southern Europe*, Vol. I, pp. 112, 113.

DANTE'S TOMB, RAVENNA

of the Netherlands. As for Russia, the influence of Tolstoy on much recent English Literature is obvious, and our novelists and short-story writers have learned much from the Russian masters of fiction. A persistently popular poem is Edward Fitzgerald's *Rubáiyát of Omar Khayyám*, a free translation from a Persian poet. The *Rubáiyát* is not the only instance of the influence of Persia on English Literature. Dryden, as has been said, "brought Persia upon the stage"; the Irish poets Moore and Mangan turned to Persia, the one for his *Lalla Rookh*, the other for his *Karaman*; and we must not forget William Collins's *Persian Eclogues* and Matthew Arnold's "Sohrab and Rustum" and "The Sick King in Bokhara." Portugal, too, has brought its contribution to English letters, mostly through Spanish channels, as in the romance of *Amadis de Gaul*. From Switzerland we have the legends of William Tell, the naturalism of Rousseau, the inspiration of some of Ruskin's finest prose and of some of the noblest poetry of Byron, Shelley, and Coleridge. The Polish novels of Henryk Sienkiewicz, admirably translated into English by Jeremiah Curtin, have had some effect on twentieth-century romancers and on the historical dramas of John Drinkwater; and from the Scandinavian countries have come the influence of the ancient sagas and of the dramatic technique of Ibsen.

THE CATHOLIC INFLUENCE

The Catholic Spirit. It is difficult for us who live in twentieth-century America to realize how intimately religion entered into the lives of the peoples of Europe in the ten centuries preceding the Protestant Reformation. Among us religion assumes literally hundreds of forms, and many of our fellow citizens profess no religious belief at all. In the days of Dante in Florence or in the days of Chaucer in England all the people, with the notable exception of the Jews, professed the Catholic faith. Though then as now differences of opinion existed concerning some matters of morals and belief, there existed a real Church unity. It was not necessary to prohibit religious teaching in the schools or religious discussion in the clubs, for everybody was agreed upon the fundamentals of religion and assisted at the same Sacrifice of the Mass and partook of the same Sacraments and professed spiritual allegiance to the same Vicar of Christ. Religion was recognized as the most important thing in the world; it inspired architects and painters and poets. That is why such small towns as Orvieto in Italy and Chartres in France and Wells in England had their vast and magnificent cathedrals, why nearly all the masterpieces of painting which we can still see in European art galleries were holy pictures, why the early English plays and the

THE "GOLDEN CATHEDRAL" OF ORVIETO

The façade of this church is covered with mosaics of a religious character, their dominant theme being the Fifth Glorious Mystery of the Rosary. Nearer the ground the entire Bible is illustrated in bas-relief

dramas of Calderón were mostly on religious topics, why Dante made his immortal poem a vision of Hell, Purgatory, and Heaven, why Chaucer wrote his "A B C," a prayer to Our Lady, and based his principal poem on a religious pilgrimage to the shrine of a saint.

In those days as in ours there were people who did not lead devout lives, others who were mainly interested in arguing about religion, and still others who were not conspicuously interested in religion at all. But to them all Catholicism was a real thing. Even when they did not talk about it, people took religion for granted, just as we take electricity for granted; and in ever so many ways the spirit of Catholicism entered into and profoundly affected their lives. It was like the air they breathed and the food they ate. And because it influenced their lives, it likewise influenced the expression of their lives in literature. Even when poems and stories were not on distinctively religious themes, they reflected in some measure the religious ideals of the times in which they were written. We can see this very clearly when we examine Chaucer's *Canterbury Tales*.

But the spirit of Catholicism in great measure continued to exert an influence even on later literature when England was no longer a Catholic country. People may change their minds quickly about a form of belief, but they cannot so quickly change their habits of acting and feeling; without being aware of it they retain much of the spirit of the belief they have abandoned. Nearly all Protestants, for example, refused to honor the Blessed Virgin; yet Scott writes a prayer to her in *The Lady of the Lake*, Poe makes her the subject of a truly beautiful poem, Wordsworth pays a tribute to her Immaculate Conception. Ruskin rambles about the Catholic cities of Europe and sneers at monks and rants at sundry Catholic devotions; but when the same Ruskin seeks to understand the idea behind the Cathedral of Lucca or to recount the story of the building of St. Mark's in Venice, he has to see through Catholic eyes and thrill with Catholic fervor. Carlyle can speak commiseratingly of "the poor old Pope" tottering on the Throne of the Fisherman, and fancy he sees the end of that unbroken spiritual rule; but when Carlyle proceeds to explain the significance of Dante he forgets his anti-Catholic spirit and, through the Scotch mist, listens entranced to that "voice of ten silent centuries."

Church Hymns. The Catholic spirit in the Middle Ages found prominent expression in Latin hymns, most of which we now find in the Roman Missal and in the Divine Office of the priest's Breviary, or Book of Hours. The twelfth and thirteenth centuries were the golden age of these poetic compositions, which are true literature by reason of their human

ST. THOMAS AQUINAS

The Dominican philosopher wrote the "Tantum Ergo" we sing at Benediction. This painting, the work of the Blessed Angelico, is preserved in the monastery of San Marco, Florence

interest, their exalted thought, their deep emotion, and their rare beauty of form and expression. Representative Church hymns are the "Vexilla Regis" and the "Lauda Sion." The "Dies Iræ," read in our Masses for the Dead, is one of the supreme poems of the world; its author was an early Franciscan, Thomas of Celano. Scarcely less celebrated is Jacopone da Todi's exquisite "Stabat Mater," numberless times translated into English and set to music by a multitude of composers. The Church hymns were written sometimes by popes and prelates, sometimes by humble men whose very names we do not know. It would be difficult to find a happier instance of the universality of literature. Among their authors were Frenchmen like Adam of St. Victor and Peter Abelard, Irishmen like Sedulius, Englishmen like St. Bede the Venerable, and Italians like John of Capua.

The Legends of the Saints. The veneration paid by Catholics to men and women of exceptional holiness of life brought into being a rich literature based on the lives of the saints. In consequence we find, spreading out into story and poetry in all the languages of Europe, legends such as those contained in *The Little Flowers of St. Francis*, the story of St. Elizabeth and the roses, the account of St. Gregory the Great and the English boys in Rome. Many of these legends filtered into English Literature, and we find them in Shakespeare, in Southey, in De Quincey, in Keats, and in other writers. They have inspired poets and dramatists as well as artists and musicians.

The Cycles of Romance. From the saints the story-telling spread to other heroes, to great warriors, great patriots, great lovers, and so there grew up legends, mostly in verse-form, dealing with such figures as Charlemagne, Tancred, and Tristram of Lyonesse. The most noted of all these cycles, and the one which has left the deepest impress on English Literature, is made up of various stories concerned with King Arthur and the Knights of the Round Table. Originating in Britain, the King Arthur romances were spread on the Continent by Irish bards and were brought back to England by the Welsh Geoffrey of Monmouth in his *History of the Kings of Britain*. The King Arthur stories, as Dr. Lennox of the Catholic University has well said, have "formed the blood and bone and sinew" of much subsequent English Literature from Layamon's *Brut* in the thirteenth century down to Tennyson's *Idylls of the King* in the nineteenth. In our own day they have inspired poets like John Masefield and E. A. Robinson. The Arthurian legends have assumed such varied forms as Swin-

ward es nach im ber schlappfen vñ mit seinē knyen
das kinde in seinen hindern lindlich stossen/vnd da
mit also hinweg treybend/Das vil zart kind ward
rewsamlich nach seiner lieben mütter vmbsehen vnd
gütlich nach ir senftzgent gemachsam wainend/vñ
gar süßlich den namen seyner lieben mütter antüffen/
vnd sprechen/mütterlin mütterlin/Des erschrack hört
der blütuerkauffer/vnd zucket bald auß seiner täschē
einen silbren pfennig; vnd gab den dem vnschuldigē
Kind vnd beschwayget es mit semften worten.

℄ Nach dem aber vnd er den weg nahend haym mit
dem vnschuldigen kind komen was/vnd sich allent
halben ob in nyemandt mit dem kind sahe vmsahe/
Da sach er einen letzer zů der lincken seyten arbetend
Er erschrack seruast vñ stůnd mit dem villieben kind
vntz sich der letzer mit seinē gesicht abkerte/Er hůb
sich schnell auf sein füß vnd eylte mit dem kind tzů
dem hawß des iuden Samuels/vnd schlappfte das
mit im hin ein in das hawß.
℄ Der Samuel als er das schön kind amblickte/als
ein tiger tier/begerte er des blütes des vnschuldigen

FROM THE LIFE OF A SAINT

Printed at Augsburg about 1480. The story of the boy martyr, St. Simeon,
of Trent in Italy, who was kidnaped and killed by wicked men in 1475

burne's poem *Tristram of Lyonesse*, Wagner's music dramas, and G. F. Watts's painting of Sir Galahad. The Romantic Movement in English Literature was largely the not unsuccessful effort of such writers as Percy, Chatterton, Scott, and Coleridge to fan to a flame the embers of medieval romance smoldering beneath the ashes of Puritanism and Classicism.

THE INFLUENCE OF ROME

Christian Rome. The strong Roman influence on English Literature can be traced in part to Christian writers of the first few centuries who, though chiefly solicitous about teaching faith and safeguarding morals and defending Catholicism against the pagan world, nevertheless managed to write in such a way as to produce real literature and to affect writers of later eras. Prudentius was the poet par excellence of this school; by chanting the beauties and splendors of Catholic faith and worship he secured in verse in the fourth century the effect which Chateaubriand secured in prose in the nineteenth century. Lactantius, a philosopher and man of letters, has been styled the Christian Cicero. St. Jerome translated the Holy Scriptures into what is known as the Latin Vulgate, the version from which the Bible used by Catholic English readers today is a direct translation; and he wrote a vast number of commentaries, treatises, sermons, and letters characterized by a fiery and imaginative style. St. Ambrose, the great Archbishop of Milan, carried the patrician tradition of ancient Rome into Christian life and literature.

But greatest of all stands St. Augustine, teacher and orator, philosopher and historian, who knew life from many angles and came into sympathetic contact with all sorts and conditions of men. His *City of God* was the first philosophy of history; his immortal *Confessions* gave the first prominent example of a form of literature which has since developed such diverse books as the autobiography of St. Teresa in Spanish, the *Journal* of Amiel and the *Confessions* of Rousseau in French, the *Biographia Literaria* of Coleridge and the *Apologia* of Newman in English. St. Augustine carried the influence of Plato into Christian literature even as in the thirteenth century that other great Christian philosopher, St. Thomas

ST. JEROME AND THE LION

The beautiful legend relates that the learned saint interrupted his studies to draw a thorn from the lion's paw. (From a painting by G. Van Eyck)

Aquinas, following the lead of Albert the Great, correlated the teachings of Aristotle with the doctrine of the Catholic Church.

The transition from pagan to Christian Rome is most completely effected in *The Consolations of Philosophy*, by Boethius, "the last of the Romans," a scholar and statesman who suffered the death penalty under Theodoric in 525. While in prison in Pavia he drew peace and comfort from thoughts about the inconstancy of fortune and the permanence of truth. His reflections he cast into a dialogue, interspersed with poems, between himself and the Lady Philosophy. Then he went to his unjust doom. But his little book lived on, and today finds an assured place in the literature of the world. Sometimes readers have doubted that Boethius was a Christian at all, so thoroughly is his book saturated with the highest teachings of pagan philosophy; on the other hand, Boethius has been enrolled among the holy martyrs of the Church and, under the name of St. Severinus, is commemorated on October twenty-third. King Alfred and Chaucer translated *The Consolations* into English; with that book the Blessed Thomas More, a man in life and in death much resembling Boethius, whiled away his imprisonment in the Tower of London and faced execution on Tower Hill.

Ancient Rome. It would be difficult to overestimate the importance of the Roman classical writers as formative factors in the European Tradition of literature, including literature in English. Until very recently a familiarity with the masterpieces of Latin Literature was regarded as an unfailing mark of real education, and for centuries the Latin language was the means of communication between scholars in different countries, as it continues to be the official language of the Universal Church. Even today the man with no pretension to classical scholarship speaks Latin without knowing it. If we scan a column in this morning's newspaper we shall find a large number of words of Latin origin; and if we analyze the ideas contained in a modern English book on history or science, literature or philosophy, we shall discover that its author has been thinking thoughts once expressed, and probably expressed better, by Cicero and Virgil, Horace and Tacitus. We are the children of Rome in a deeper and more fundamental sense than we are the children of our parents.

Latin Literature is a swift stream, deep and broad, bearing on its surface the intellectual wealth of modern nations and

ST. AUGUSTINE

From a painting by Murillo

¶ Cy commence le second liure

¶ De la maniere qui est a adiouster a sa
necessite des disputacions.   i.

Se le sens humain qui pour cau
se de lumanite qui est fraisle et
malade par coustume nosoit
cõtredire a sa clere raison de verite mais
sousmeist a sa brape doctrine de sa foy cre
stienne sa langueur comme a brape me=
decine iusques adce que par seide diuine
esse fut garie par dousce impetracion de
soy il ne seroit ia mestier de song sermõ
a ceulx q sentent droitement de sa foy ca=

tholique et qui par paroses ne sceuent de
clairer ce qui sentent a conuaincre chascu
ne erreur de baine oppinion. Mais pour
ce q cest sa plus grant masadie et sa plus
obscure de sentendement des folz et nõ sa
chans en ce que apres ce que sen seut a ren
due brape rapson telle comme esse se peut
dõner de homme a hõme par seurs mou=
uemens des raisonnables ou par ceulx
sont si aueuglez quilz ne boyent pas ses
choses qui se demonstrent appertenēt ou
par mauuaise obstinacion par laquesse
ilz ne peuēt souffrir ne acorder les choses
                                          ei.

A PAGE FROM *THE CITY OF GOD*

This French edition was printed at Abbeyville in 1486. (By courtesy
of the British Museum)

fertilizing every land through which it flows. Through it the European Tradition spread west and north and shaped and sustained the splendid literature which we possess in the English tongue. And as Dante took the Roman poet Virgil for his guide through Hell and Purgatory, the vast majority of

IN THE HOUSE OF MÆCENAS

Mæcenas was a wealthy Roman who befriended writers and encouraged the arts. He is shown with Virgil and Horace

writers in English have turned to Latin authors for inspiration and to Latin Literature for models of construction. Bacon, Milton, Dryden, Johnson, Pope, Addison, Burke, Gray, Coleridge, Landor, Byron, Tennyson, Newman, Arnold, were all university men, and the backbone of English university training has ever been Greek and Latin literature. English preparatory schools, almost without exception, have emphasized Latin; so even those writers who did not go on to the universities secured at least a formative knowledge of ancient books and authors. Merely to list the Latin writers whose influence is discernible in English Literature would require more space than we can afford. Let us, however, indicate the Latin writers who most notably affected our English writers.

Quintilian, who lived under the Emperor Trajan, was the leading Latin rhetorician; he laid down the rules of good

VIRGIL

writing and formed in his readers sound taste in language and construction. Juvenal was the most prominent Roman satirist; he painted brilliant pictures of the times in which he lived and criticized life and manners. Ovid in his *Metamorphoses* preserved many of the tales of ancient mythology which reappear time and again in English Literature, and in his *Art of Love* conveyed bits of worldly wisdom utilized by writers in every language of Europe. Horace, one of the great Augustans, was a poet, a thinker, a satirist, and a man of the world, loving alike the tumult of the city and the quiet delights of his Sabine farm and, in his *Odes* and *Epistles*, commenting pleasantly and shrewdly on the ways of mankind. Virgil, the supreme name in Latin Literature, was in the Middle Ages an object of almost superstitious veneration, and through the centuries his tomb at Naples has been a literary shrine. In his *Georgics* Virgil sang of country scenes and gave vivid and pleasant descriptions of the farmer's life; and in his *Æneid*, an epic poem written in imitation of Homer, he recounted the legendary origin of the Roman people. He has been called the Pagan Prophet of Christ, because in one of his *Eclogues* he wrote a passage which seemed to foretell the birth of Our Lord. An English poet, Tennyson, penned Virgil's highest eulogy:

Wielder of the stateliest measure ever moulded by the lips of man.

If Virgil is supreme in Latin verse, Cicero is the master of Latin prose. He played many parts in the course of his varied and eventful life; he was a statesman and an exile, a lawyer and a philosopher, an orator and a poet, a teacher and a moralist. But his most enduring claim to recognition is the mature and polished language with which he wrote his delightful letters, his essays sparkling and profound, and his exquisitely designed and powerful orations. Even across the gulf of twenty centuries it is possible to visit the ruins of his villa above Frascati, where he took his ease and looked down upon Rome

CICERO

across the plains, and there to come into contact with the spirit of him who was the most perfectly balanced man of letters the world has ever known. "Cicero," declared Quintilian, "is less the name of a man than of eloquence itself." The highest compliment that can be paid to any writer in any tongue is to say that his style is Ciceronian.

Cicero lived in the days of Julius Cæsar; and Cæsar, though preëminently a soldier and statesman, was a writer as well.

The American high-school boy wrestling with Cæsar's *Commentaries* may well exclaim with Shakespeare's Brutus, "O Julius Cæsar, thou art mighty yet!" Cæsar was the first of the Roman historians in point of time, and wrote of his "conquests, glories, triumphs, spoils" with soldierlike brevity and journalistic precision. Other Latin writers on history who contributed to the European Tradition were Cornelius Nepos, whose *Chronica* is a little history of the world; Sallust, who commented on historic events with the keenness of Chesterfield and the practical wisdom of Benjamin Franklin; Livy, who, though as misleading as Froude or Macaulay in his handling of facts, wrote with dignity and charm; and Tacitus, the noblest Roman of them all, "the first of historians," says Gibbon, "who applied the science of philosophy to the study of facts."

Philosophy — thinking about the why of life and the how of living — was a matter of much concern to the Romans. Besides Cicero, who was great in this field as in every other, there were Pliny the Elder and Pliny the Younger; Lucretius, a poet-philosopher, a thoughtful expounder of the doctrine of Epicurus; Seneca, the teacher of the Emperor Nero, who applied the principles of Greek philosophy to his own time and race, and who, though a pagan, anticipated more than one Christian idea. Seneca was a playwright too, and his tragedies exerted an influence on Shakespeare and especially on Marlowe. Roman dramatists of an earlier period were Plautus and Terence, names to be reckoned with in the history of dramatic literature. They affected the art of Molière, and the plot of Shakespeare's *Comedy of Errors* is taken from one of Plautus's plays turning on mistaken identity.

Julius Cæsar is reported to have exclaimed to Varro, a writer on many subjects: "You have taught us all things human and divine!" With less exaggeration we might apply Cæsar's words to all Roman Literature, pagan and Christian. Certainly, though the world has learned much and done much since Horace strolled in the Forum greeting friends and reluctantly shaking hands with bores; though a new and brilliant light has broken on the human mind since Seneca sought to justify the cruelties of Nero; though such profound and enduring literary creations as Dante's *Divine Comedy* and Shakespeare's *Hamlet* and Cervantes's *Don Quixote* and Corneille's *Polyeucte* and Goethe's *Faust* were far in the future when Cicero discussed life and letters with congenial friends on the heights of Tusculum, it is nevertheless true that much of the experience of mankind and a large proportion of wisdom both human and divine are embodied in the Latin tongue, the language of the grandest earthly empire and of the strongest spiritual force that universal history can furnish. From Rome comes a goodly measure of our intellectual heritage.

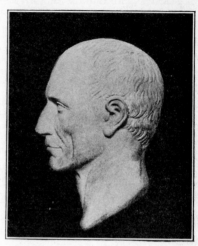

JULIUS CÆSAR

THE INFLUENCE OF GREECE

Rome has been the teacher of the modern world, but Rome was not less truly the pupil of Greece. The Roman legions in scarlet and gold carried the imperial eagles in resistless conquest to the uttermost boundaries of the known world; but long before the political empire, weakened and decayed, succumbed to the attacks of barbarians from north and west, the conqueror was conquered — not by the force of arms but by the power of thought. From a tiny tongue of land thrust south into the Mediterranean, and from a handful of island colonies too insignificant to figure on a map of the world, came an army against which no legionaries could prevail — an army of teachers and scholars, of philosophers and poets, of carvers of statues and makers of plays; and to that peaceful invasion of ideas Rome accorded the freedom of the city and the world. The grandeur that was Rome capitulated before the glory that was Greece.

The Greek influence reached English Literature through three channels. First, some English writers (Browning and Shelley, for instance) read the Greek poets and studied the Greek philosophers at first hand; the Greek language was long an essential part of English university education. Secondly, Greek thought came into English Literature by way of the Latin, for most of the great Roman writers, whether Christian or pagan, echoed and imitated the authors of Greece. And, thirdly, the Grecian influence was brought to England as a result of that important movement in life and thought known as the Renaissance, or New Birth, of learning. The Renaissance began in Italy and spread to France. Italian and French writers, enthusiastically reading Greek Literature and philosophy, absorbed the ideas and the spirit of the ancient culture and gave to intellectual Greece a new life. Their books, brought into England and read by English writers, conveyed the Greek influence into our literature.

Christian Greece. Although the Christian writers of Greece did not so profoundly affect English Literature as did the Christian writers of Rome, their influence was and continues to be real and important. Chief among them is St. John Chrysostom; that is, St. John of the Golden Mouth, so called because of his extraordinary gifts as an orator. So impressive was he as a preacher that his congregation would frequently break forth into spontaneous applause. Those of his sermons which have been preserved are vigorous and eloquent and surprisingly modern, and they have done much to fashion pulpit oratory in all the countries of modern Europe. Then there is

St. Basil the Great, like St. Chrysostom a Catholic bishop and an able orator. He was a thinker, too, and in his serious treatises harmonized the philosophy of Plato with Christian teaching.

It was necessary in the fourth century (for that was when all these Greek Christian writers flourished) to defend the doctrines of the Church against the attacks of dying paganism and to show that Catholicism could utilize the best products of ancient thought. To this important work another great churchman, St. Athanasius of Alexandria, brought the qualities which we should find of service in the modern world. He was alert and fiery, a man of action as well as of thought, a vigorous orator (public speaking was preëminently a Greek accomplishment), and one of the first historians of the Church. Another and even more noted Greek writer on history was Eusebius. These and other Greek Fathers of the Church have left their mark on religious writings in English both Protestant and Catholic. An immediate result of the reading of the Greek Fathers was the Oxford Movement in the nineteenth century.

Ancient Greece. "Plutarch's *Lives* there was in which I read abundantly, and I still think that time spent to great advantage," wrote Benjamin Franklin in his *Autobiography*; and the American statesman and thinker but voiced the experience of countless men in various countries and climes. "Of all the Grecian authors," declares an eminent French critic and teacher, Émile Faguet, Plutarch "has perhaps been the most read, the most quoted, the best loved, and the most carefully edited."[1] Yes, and the most frequently translated and the most persistently borrowed from. Writing of distinguished Greeks and Romans, this last of the Greek historians, whatever may be his shortcomings as an accurate chronicler, achieved the literary touch that makes his portraits live. English Literature is heavily in his debt. And we are under obligations too to other Greek writers on history: to Polybius, no word artist

[1] *Initiation into Literature*, p. 36.

but an industrious compiler of facts; to Xenophon, general and philosopher, immortalizing himself in his account of the Retreat of the Ten Thousand; to Thucydides, one of the glories of the age of Pericles and one of the master historians of the world, as scholarly in his handling of material as John Richard Green and as dramatic and forceful as Hilaire Belloc;

MARCUS AURELIUS

to Herodotus, happily styled the Father of History, delightfully innocent of modern "scientific" methods and unconcernedly mingling fact and fable, the first in the long line of literary historians, the men who write charmingly even if (as was charged against Macaulay) they would tell a lie to round a period.

The greatest contribution made by Greece to the European Tradition was in the realm of philosophy. It might be said that though not every Greek philosopher was a writer, every Greek writer was a philosopher. The commingling of Greek thought with Roman action was symbolized in the person of the Roman Emperor Marcus Aurelius, whose *Meditations*, or *Golden Book*, as it was named in a famous translation, ranks high in the wisdom literature of Western civilization. Aurelius belonged to the Stoics, one of the great schools of Greek philosophy; and in the occasional spare moments of his busy life, often at the end of a hard day's march at the head of his troops, the imperial thinker would find satisfaction and repose in jotting down random reflections on life and duty, on his projects and motives, on the means he employed to control his passions and regulate his conduct. At the other end of the social scale was the freed slave Epictetus, who, in his *Discourses,* inculcated the eminently Christian truth that the soul is of vastly more importance than are material things. Some of his comments have a direct application to twentieth-century conditions. For instance:

ARISTOTLE

> As, if you were to breed lions, you would not be solicitous about the magnificence of their dens, but the qualities of the animals themselves; so, if you undertake to preside over your fellow citizens, be not so solicitous about the magnificence of the buildings, as careful of the fortitude of those who inhabit them.

The Greek philosophers who most vitally influenced subsequent writers and whose ideas are part and parcel of our very lives were Plato and his brilliant disciple Aristotle. Aristotle did not himself write literature. We possess only notes and fragments of his discourses, but his teachings have been fountain heads of philosophy and theology, of dramatic construction and literary criticism. The German critic Lessing claimed that Aristotle's teachings are as infallible as the elements of

Euclid. Catholics are especially indebted to the great Stagirite (he was born in Stageira, a town in Macedonia, in 384 B.C.) because his system of thought forms the pattern or framework of the Church's doctrine; the Catholic child studying the little catechism is learning to think according to the plan of Aristotle and sometimes in his very words.

PLATO

After a drawing by Raphael

Unlike his most famous pupil, Plato was a literary man. Though in his wonderful *Republic* he would banish poets from his ideal commonwealth, he was truly a poet himself — a thinker of searching thoughts and a dreamer of glorious dreams. His most typical work is to be found in his *Dialogues*, in which with delicacy and power he depicts the Athenian life of his day, records and preserves the teachings of his master Socrates, and gives an impressive picture of the trial and death of that noble philosopher. Since the thirteenth century, when St. Thomas Aquinas correlated Catholic teaching with the system of Aristotle, Plato's influence on Catholicism has lessened; but before that time many of his ideas had been adapted to the Church's theology, and several eminent Catholic writers, notably St. Augustine, were Platonists. Plato's influence on English and other modern literatures has been enormous. We might almost say that it is impossible for a man to be a poet without being a Platonist as well.

Another phase of Greek thought was represented by Lucian of Samosata, a native of Syria, who lived in the second century of the Christian Era. Were Lucian living today he would be writing clever special articles for the papers and giving pungently humorous talks over the radio. In certain respects he resembles Juvenal in Rome, Voltaire in France, and Swift in England; certainly he is prominent among world satirists, men who lash the follies of the age with the whip of ridicule. Like most satirists, Lucian sometimes shot the arrows of his wit at worthy men and sacred institutions; but his *Dialogues of the Dead*, his social satires, and his ironic suggestions on how to write history have affected writers far removed from him in time and place and intellectual outlook. Indebted to Lucian are More, Marlowe, Ben Jonson, Shakespeare, Beaumont, Prior, Dryden, Barham, Browning, Pater, Lang, and other English writers.

Six hundred years earlier lived a man of whose personality we know next to nothing, but whose writings have become part of the favorite reading of children throughout the Western World. This was Æsop, whose *Fables* have been adopted into later literature, notably into French verse by La Fontaine. When as little children we laughed over the stories of the fox and the grapes, the dog and the shadow, the boy who raised the cry of "Wolf, wolf!" and the old crow that fancied she had a good singing voice, we were enjoying the wit and wisdom of a deformed Greek slave who told those tales five hundred years before the Christian Era.

Much of the Greek spirit flowed into European Literature through the dramatic form, for the Greeks have given us some of the most thoughtful and well-constructed plays we know. The very word *tragedy* comes to us from the Greek language; it is derived from *tragos*, meaning "goat," and gained its application to the drama through the fact that early Greek actors wore goatskins. The prominent names in Greek Tragedy are Æschylus, Sophocles, and Euripides. They took old and well-known stories of gods and heroes and made of them vivid and soul-searching dramas of great beauty and rich educational value. Going to the theater in the Athens of Pericles was almost like going to church; people attended plays not mainly for amusement but for instruction and inspiration. In comedy the Greeks gave us Menander, and especially Aristophanes, who kept soldiers and politicians, rulers and philosophers, from taking themselves too seriously. To this day actors are often called Thespians, after Thespis, the earliest of the Greek players.

In poetry, too, the Greeks exerted a vast influence on their own and later literature. Nearest to us in point of time stands Theocritus, a poet who in his idyls drew delightful pictures of life in town and country and beside the flashing sea; he is of the brotherhood of Longfellow and Stoddard, of Goldsmith and Gray, and of Milton and Shakespeare in their milder moods. Of the poems of Pindar the Theban only fragments have come down to us, but even those shreds of his lyric fancy have served to animate and inspire numerous English singers from Cowley to Francis Thompson. From the odes of Anacreon many of our poets, like Robert Herrick and Thomas Moore, caught the secret of grace and daintiness in word melody.

Most famous of all the Greek poets and, with the exception of Hesiod, the earliest is Homer. His life is lost among the clouds of primitive history. Stories tell that he was blind and poor; but he saw visions splendid, and in mind was rich beyond computation. Some modern scholars maintain that no such person existed, and in the Homeric Question have invented a subject of discussion upon which the learned can display their erudition and exercise their wits. But the Homeric poems have survived; and whether they are the work of one man, or the product of several poets, or merely a collection of songs first sung by countless unknown bards, they stand

¶ The fyrst fable maketh mencyon of the foxe and of the rapsyns

He is not wyse/ that desyreth to haue a thynge whiche he may not haue/ As reherith this fable Of a foxe/ whiche loked and beheld the rapsyns that grewe vpon an hyghe vyne /the whiche rapsyns he moche desyred for to ete them ¶ And whanne he sawe that none he myght gete/ he torned his sorowe in to Joye/and sayd these rapsyns ben sowre/and yf I had some I wold not ete them/ And therfore this fable sheweth that he is wyse / whiche fayneth not to desyre that thynge the whiche he may not haue/

¶ The second fable is of the auncyent wesel and of the rat/

Witte is better than force or strengthe / As reherith to vs this fable of an old wesel / the whiche myght no more take no rats/wherfor she was of hir sore hongry

i iij

THE FOX AND THE GRAPES

A page from an edition of Æsop's *Fables* printed by Caxton in 1484. (By courtesy of the British Museum)

as fine examples of the poetic art and as undying inspirers of world poesy. Homer is the father of epic poetry; that is,

HOMER

the poetry which, like the painting on a huge canvas, commemorates events of vast scope and universal interest. The *Iliad* is the great epic of war, the *Odyssey* the great epic of travel and adventure. Both waft us back to an epoch before the dawn of written history and keep fresh and fair to all succeeding ages the personality of the frail and beautiful Helen, the long conflict between the Trojans and the Greeks, and the personalities of heroes and of gods. Homer has been the model of all succeeding epic poets, of Virgil and Dante, of Tasso and Milton. Perhaps the most exquisite instance of his tremendous influence on English Literature is Keats's glowing sonnet "On First Looking into Chapman's Homer."

SUMMARY

We have now completed our rapid airplane exploration of the river of English Literature. Beginning with outstanding writers of our own day, we have traced the stream of the European Tradition to its sources. We have glanced at its principal tributaries and have seen how it has been here shadowed by impending cliffs, here diverted by islands and promontories, here fed and freshened by rain clouds floating from distant mountains. We have gone back to Tennyson, to Wordsworth, to Dryden, to Milton, to Shakespeare, to Chaucer. We have noted the contributions made to English Literature by Italy and France, Spain and Germany, and the other countries of modern Europe. We have seen the waters troubled by events like the Puritan rebellion and swollen by movements like the Renaissance. We have glimpsed something of the pervading influence of Catholicism. We have flown over Rome and Greece and recognized the truth of Sir Gilbert Murray's statement that "*Paradise Lost* and *Prometheus Unbound* are . . . the children of Virgil and Homer, of Æschylus and Plato."[1] Thus far ours has been but a bird's-eye view, but we have tried to see literature steadily and see it whole.

And now, in the succeeding chapters, we shall study the stream more in detail as it flows through fair English meadows. We shall pause now and again to breathe the scented air and glory in the prospect of the distant hills. We shall swim and row and sail, and perchance picnic on delectable islands. We shall pluck the yellow primrose from the river's brim and make to ourselves bright garlands of the golden gorse. We shall float softly in the moonlight and, if we are wise in our generation, we shall lift our hearts in happiness and our voices in song. And sometimes, as we idly trail our fingers in the cool water, we shall think long, long thoughts and say: "These glistening drops have journeyed far. They come from lands I have never seen, from ages I have never known. They can tell me much, if I but try to hear them, of life and men. For this river, winding through history far back into the beginnings of things, has been brightened by human laughter and salted with human tears, and its music it has caught from human loves and human strivings, human sorrows and human hopes."

[1] *The Religion of a Man of Letters*, p. 40.

CHAPTER III

THE HAMMER AND THE CROSS

EARLY ENGLISH LITERATURE

The Beginnings. English Literature before the time of Chaucer might be considered as a prologue to a play. The prologue precedes the play, but it has no vital connection with the action of it, and if there were no prologue at all, the drama would still be complete. A convenient example of the relation of prologue and play is Shakespeare's *Taming of the Shrew*. The induction, or prologue, tells the story of the tinker who, abducted in his sleep by a frolicsome nobleman, wakes up to find himself clad in gorgeous raiment, refreshed with delicious food, and surrounded with all manner of luxury. The drama which follows the prologue unfolds a story and presents characters not in the least associated with Christopher Sly and his adventures in high society: it is the tale of a girl with a sharp tongue and an ungovernable temper reduced to sweetness and docility by a domineering bridegroom. In practice it often happens that when *The Taming of the Shrew* is staged, the curtain rises on a street in Padua, the scene of the first act, and the induction is not shown at all. In that case the audience gets no impression of anything lacking, for the prologue is not necessary to the drama.

Such is the relation of what we call Old English Literature, dating from the fifth century to the Norman Conquest, to the literature which, beginning with Chaucer, extends in an unbroken line down to our own day. The pre-Chaucerian literature was but the prelude, or induction, to the literature which caught up and continued and even notably enriched the litera-

A SPECIMEN OF OLD ENGLISH

This passage from an eleventh-century manuscript of the *Chronicle* records the defeat of the Danes by King Alfred in the Valley of the White Horse

ture of the European Tradition. Some of the literature in that prologue is interesting and beautiful and even intrinsically important, but it produced no effect on the great literature that followed. Shakespeare knew nothing of *Beowulf* and would have written his masterpieces just as they are if that poem of terror and adventure had never existed; the sonnets of Keats and Wordsworth would be precisely as we find them if there had not been a single English poem written before *The Canterbury Tales*. "The Seafarer" and "Deor's Lament" are as far removed from our lives and our interests and have had as little effect on our great books as the folklore of Polynesia or the Nō plays of Japan.

Language and Literature. Early English Literature was written in the English language, but not the English language which we speak and read and write. To read *Beowulf* or Cædmon in the original it is necessary for us to learn what amounts to another tongue. The Old English language is as different from our speech as German is, and more difficult than German in its grammar. As in German, we recognize many words in Old English, though from our point of view they seem to be badly spelled, like *heard*, "hard"; *neah*, "near"; *strengu*, "strength"; *sunu*, "son"; most of the connectives in our modern speech, the little words which act like cement in holding the structure of language together, are substantially the same as those used by the earlier writers; and we have retained the Old English way of putting words in order — nouns before the verbs they govern, adjectives usually before and not after nouns, and modifiers close to the words to which they relate. But there are ever so many words in Old English which we should not recognize at all: *bearu*, "grove"; *wlencu*, "pride"; *tela*, "properly"; *wreon*, "to cover"; *deman*, "to judge." Nouns and verbs and adjectives were inflected in Old English somewhat as they are inflected in Latin. And there are ever so many words in our vocabulary which — since they have come into the language later from Greek and

Latin and from modern European languages — we should not discover in Old English at all. The man who does not know Old English has to read Cædmon in a translation, just as he has to read Homer in a translation if he does not know Greek.

Here is a specimen of none too difficult Old English in the West Saxon dialect (for dialects, or varying forms of the language, were used in different parts of England). The matter of it is familiar to us, for it is the opening of the Gospel according to St. John, the last Gospel always read in the Mass when the book is not removed after the priest's blessing. It will be interesting to compare it with the modern English version, which we probably know by heart:

1. On frymðe wæs Word, and ðæt Word wæs mid Gode, and God wæs ðæt Word.
2. Ðæt wæs on fruman mid Gode.
3. Ealle ðing wæron geworhte ðurh hyne; and nān ðing næs geworht būtan him.
4. Ðæt wæs līf ðe on him geworht wæs; and ðæt līf wæs manna lēoht.
5. And ðæt lēoht lȳht on ðȳstrum; and ðȳstro ðæt ne genāmon.

1. In the beginning was the Word, and the Word was with God, and the Word was God.
2. The same was in the beginning with God.
3. All things were made by him: and without him was made nothing that was made.
4. In him was life, and the life was the light of men.
5. And the light shineth in darkness, and the darkness did not comprehend it.

To trace the changes that have taken place in the English language during twelve centuries is a fascinating occupation, but one which in a study of literature does not immediately concern us. We can observe, however, the marks of some changes in our modern spelling. The best usage of today requires that we spell *knife, knight, through, thoroughly*. Yet in our pronunciation the *k* is silent in the first two words, and the others are pronounced *thru* and *thoroly*. Why? Because our manner of pronouncing has softened in the course of centuries. In the days of Cædmon men said something like *kah-nife* and *kah-ni-ght*, and gave a throaty sound to the *ugh* in *through* and *thoroughly*.

So although the language has changed, — so much, indeed, that, as we have seen, to read English as it used to be requires considerable study, — it is nevertheless in its essentials the same language. Most inaccurate is the statement so often heard: "English is derived from Latin." Many words have come into English from Latin, though they have changed their forms and in some instances their meanings; but the structure of English, its pattern, its organization, — its skeleton, so to speak, — is preserved, with only incidental variations, from the Old English speech. Distinctively Latin grammar is not English grammar. All languages have certain properties in common, and the grammars of all languages have a common core of principles, which principles we best learn from the study of a highly developed and unchanging language like Latin or Greek; but of neither of those ancient tongues is English in any proper sense the offspring. Old English is the father of modern English speech, Norman French is its mother; and Latin and Greek are benevolent uncles, Dutch is a first cousin, German is a second cousin once removed, Spanish and Italian are relatives outside the fourth degree of blood kinship, and Persian and Russian and Chinese are neighbors who at times have come bearing gifts.

To avoid the possibility of having confused notions on the subject, it is well for us to understand clearly that literature is one thing and that language is another. Language is the medium through which literature expresses itself, but to maintain that language and literature always have the same origin is as ridiculous as to assume that we are all Missourians because the street cars we ride in were made in St. Louis. Our literature descends to us from Continental sources, it is part of the great stream of the European Tradition, though some of it reflects English life and embodies English ideals; but our language is a development of the Old English speech, though it has been enormously enriched by accretions from other tongues.

Pagan and Christian Literature. In considering the outlines of Early English Literature we can conveniently divide the topic into two sections: the Pagan and the Christian. The

STONEHENGE

In the south of England stand these impressive remains of a race whose history is lost in the mists of time

men who first spoke in the English tongue and reduced to runes and alliterative verse the emotions aroused in them by contemplation of the sea and of the stars, were not sharers in the religious life of cultured Europe: they were alien alike to the paganism of Cicero and Horace and Marcus Aurelius and to the Christianity of St. Basil and Lactantius and St. Augustine. Some of them, a minority, belonged to the Celtic race and worshiped Celtic gods; about a thousand years before the birth of Our Lord they had crossed the seas from France and from Spain and settled in what today are Ireland and Great Britain. The Scotch and the Welsh and the Irish of our own time — that is, those of them who represent no racial admixtures — are the descendants of those distant invaders, whose strain likewise exists in that extremely composite racial product, the modern Englishman. The Celts conquered the earlier inhabitants of the land, about whom we know little, but some of whose traces, like the ring of rocks at Stonehenge in England, still remain. Then in the sixth and seventh centuries of our era, and periodically in later times, came raiders and colonizers from the north of Europe, Jutes and Saxons and Angles, all members of the Teutonic race from which likewise the modern Germans are sprung, and these brought with them their racial traditions and the worship of their gods. These Teutonic tribes in their turn overcame the Celtic inhabitants, many of whom were killed, others withdrew to Scotland, Wales, and Ireland, and yet others mingled with their conquerors. And the gods of the Teutons became the gods of England.

The chief of those gods — like Zeus in Greece and Jupiter in Rome — was Thor. When thunder rolled and lightning flashed, it meant that Thor was swinging his mighty hammer and the sparks were flying from his anvil. And so the first English Literature might not inappropriately be called the Literature of the Hammer. Then Christian missionaries came to England — some from Ireland, some from the Continent — and after a time converted the inhabitants. And so the second division of Early English Literature was the Literature of the Cross.[1] Whenever religious ideas are vigorous they profoundly affect literature ; and as the English people of long ago took their religion, whether pagan or Christian, very seriously, literature reflects much of the intensity of their religious emotion.

[1] W. B. Wright, in his essay on Shakespeare's *Hamlet* in the *Atlantic Monthly* for May, 1902, gives a stimulating interpretation of the play as a conflict between the religious ideals symbolized by the Hammer and the Cross.

PAGAN LITERATURE

Beowulf. It is remarkable that the first notable piece of English Literature is not English at all, except for the fact that the tenth-century manuscript containing the poem (now in the British Museum) is written in the West Saxon dialect. That poem is the epic of *Beowulf*. The scene of the action is Denmark, and the characters are men of the race from which the invaders were descended. It is like one of the stories of Henryk Sienkiewicz translated into English by an American citizen whose ancestors came from Poland.

Beowulf is less important as literature than as a landmark in the history of literature. The poem is clearly several centuries older than the manuscript of it; it may have appeared in earlier manuscripts now lost, or it may have been preserved orally for hundreds of years. Poetry, we must remember, existed before the art of writing, and the literature which we now keep in books men used to keep in their heads. Scholars have disputed much regarding the date at which *Beowulf* was composed, but the best authorities place it somewhere in the sixth century. There are good reasons for believing that, like other national epics, *Beowulf* is a collection of several songs composed at several times. As to the author or authors of the poem we have not the faintest idea. The people who in primitive days listened to the gleeman reciting verse cared no more about finding out who composed the piece than our motion-picture audiences care about finding out who wrote the scenarios. And *Beowulf* is primitive. Indeed — and this is its greatest distinction — it is, at a conservative estimate, five hundred years older than any considerable bit of poetry in French or Spanish, German or Italian.

The story of *Beowulf* is available in excellent summaries in manuals of literature and in several readable translations into modern English. Beowulf is the hero, a very wonderful person who is not at all backward about boasting of his exploits. He comes to King Hrothgar at Heorot and in single combat and unarmed overcomes the monster Grendel, who for twelve years has been nightly visiting the mead hall and devouring alive thirty of Hrothgar's warriors. Then Beowulf undertakes to put Grendel's witch mother out of the way. He plunges into a dark pool, and after an incredibly long swim and all manner of strange encounters he finds the witch in a submarine cave, fights with her furiously, and at length kills her with a magic sword hanging conveniently near by. Then he comes up for air and the praise of Hrothgar and, bearing numerous presents, departs into his own country.

Many years go by, rapidly as they often do in stories and plays; and now we find Beowulf an old man and a king, with but one thing to annoy him. It seems that a dragon, impolitely addicted to spitting fire, has been roaming the land and destroying residences, not excepting the king's. Beowulf grows angry and decides that something should be done about it. So, with a band of followers, he advances upon the dragon's lair. Leaving his men outside, he goes in, and he and the dragon fight furiously. Beowulf, aided by his faithful Wiglaf, succeeds in slaying the dragon, but the old king has received a mortal wound. He bids Wiglaf bring out from the cave a vast hoard of treasure which the dragon had guarded for three hundred years, makes arrangements for his funeral, and expires. He is buried in barbaric splendor and mourned by his subjects.

So much for the story of *Beowulf*. Let us now examine some of its literary characteristics, nearly all of which we find in other examples of primitive poetry. There is, for one thing, a complete absence of the conventional love story: Beowulf does not seek the hand of a beautiful princess in marriage and live happily with her ever after; in fact, there are no beautiful princesses visible in the poem. Hrothgar's queen pours out the mead at the feast and gives the conquering hero a necklace, but she evidences neither beauty nor brains and occupies no prominent place in the narrative. Neither is humor discern-

A PAGE FROM THE MANUSCRIPT OF *BEOWULF*

Courtesy of the British Museum

ible; rather, over all the poem there hangs a thick mist of melancholy, of melancholy that is wrought of mystery and terror. The characters, including Beowulf himself, are sketched only in the faintest outline; no attempt is made to portray them to the life. Striking events are described better than natural objects, and all the descriptions are brief though not infrequently vivid. That vividness is largely secured by the copious employment of those vigorous epithets in which Old English is so rich: *ice-bright, wave-paths, battle-sweat, ring-breaker*.[1] Here an atmosphere of desolation is well suggested:

> Harp-joy is vanished,
> The rapture of glee-wood; no excellent falcon
> Swoops through the building, no swift-footed charger
> Grindeth the gravel.

The narrative of *Beowulf* is in places rapid and the dialogue dramatic, but there are dreary stretches of clotted history and desert wastes of moralizing; also numerous repetitions and considerable confusion and inconsistency — these due, most probably, to diversity of authorship or the carelessness of copyists. The Cotton Manuscript of the poem, so called because it was among the documents collected by Sir Robert Cotton, was written after the Cross had conquered the Hammer, and the copyist or compiler (very likely a monk) here and there inserted the name of God and tried, though far from convincingly, to give the work a Christian tone. "Wielder of Glory" surely suggests less the God of the Christian Gospel than Thor, the Thunderer of pagan mythology. Religion of no sort furnishes motives for action in the poem, but the background is obviously pagan.

In reading *Beowulf*, says a distinguished English critic, Sir Edmund Gosse, "we seem to be looking down into a translucent pool of ocean, fringed and shaded by seaweeds, in whose

---

[1] Meaning a generous king. Wealthy men often wore spirals of soft gold on their arms and would break off pieces to bestow as presents.

depths monstrous fishes are slowly swimming, and fierce crustaceans are energizing, and noiselessly engaging in combat." [1] That impression applies especially to the first part of the poem, for Beowulf's fight with Grendel's mother really is a submarine conflict; but even in the second part we seem to observe events through a mist which shuts out sound and gives a suggestion of vagueness of contour and deliberation of movement to the man and the monster engaged in the death struggle.

Beowulf appealed somewhat differently to Longfellow. "It is," he wrote, "like a piece of ancient armor; rusty and battered, and yet strong. From within comes a voice sepulchral, as if the ancient armor spoke, telling a simple, straightforward narrative; with here and there the boastful speech of a rough old Dane, reminding one of those made by the heroes of Homer." [2] Thus wrote Longfellow the teacher and critic; and thirty years later Longfellow the poet utilized the same idea in "The Skeleton in Armor."

Minor Pagan Poetry. Needless to state, most of the poetry of the pre-Christian period has completely disappeared. Much of it was never committed to writing at all, and the converts to the religion of the Cross would likely enough exercise their zeal in destroying evidences of their former faith. But some fragments of an older devotional literature remain, most of it in the form of metrical charms to ward off the evil arrows shot from the sky by witches or valkyries, or to repeat while rubbing an aching joint or a rheumatic limb. There were also poetical prayers to Woden and other gods, used in connection with religious ceremonies that accompanied the gathering of medicinal herbs and the turning of the first furrow in the spring.

"Widsith" is the remnant of a poem which antedates *Beowulf*, and which is of more interest to the student of history than to the student of literature. The word *Widsith* means a man who has done much traveling, and the poem recounts the journeys and adventures of a wandering gleeman, or minstrel

---

[1] *More Books on the Table,* p. 163.   [2] *Poets and Poetry of Europe,* p. 4.

Attila, the "Scourge of God," whom St. Leo the Great met near Mantua on his way to attack Rome in 452, is mentioned in this poem. "Deor's Lament" has not the epic character of *Beowulf* and "Widsith": it is an elegy voicing grief because of misfortunes which have befallen the singer. "The Seafarer," another elegy, strikes a note which seems true to human nature at all times. The poet admits that he has suffered much while sailing the ocean and yet he would not exchange the perils of the sea for the comfort of the landsman. So did Ulysses feel when in his old age he gathered together his faithful followers and sailed into the sunset.[1] The finest of these minor poems is "The Wanderer." It tells of a loyal warrior who has lost his chief. In desolation he sails the ocean, and in his dreams he lives again the days gone by, fighting and feasting with his lord and his brave comrades. Then he awakes, and sorrow fills his heart at sight of the falling snow and the gray, cheerless waves.

CHRISTIAN LITERATURE

The Standard of the Cross. Christianity came into England from Rome and from Ireland. The Cross followed the Imperial Eagles; missionary efforts were begun not long after the Roman occupation of the island, but achieved little or nothing. The first permanent movement to spread the Christian faith in England was the result of the zeal of Irish missionaries who, leaving their native houses of learning, traveled all over Europe and even into Asia. The Irish apostles preached the faith in Scotland and in the north and west of what is now England. St. Gregory the Great, having seen some handsome English youths in Rome, greatly desired to preach the Gospel in their land; and when he became pope he sent St. Augustine (not to

---

[1] Tennyson has admirably handled this event in his poem "Ulysses." The speech which he puts into the mouth of the hero ranks among the masterpieces of English eloquence.

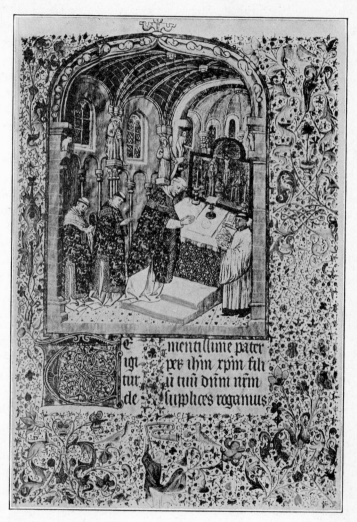

PAGE FROM AN ILLUMINATED MANUSCRIPT

be confused with the St. Augustine who wrote *The City of God*)
to evangelize England. Accordingly the faith was implanted
in the south of the island. Thus, as a result of the labors of
priests and monks — some from Ireland, some from Rome —
Christianity gradually spread throughout England, and the
Cross of Christ replaced the Hammer of thundering Thor.

ST. GREGORY SEES THE ENGLISH SLAVE BOYS

The change was not abrupt and violent. "The church was
built where the pagan temple had been, and the people walked
to the shrine of Christ by the same well-worn path by which
they had sought the sacred enclosure of the god. Where
the consecrated tree had stood was now the Holy Rood. The
groves, devoted to the Nature-god, became the groves of the
convent."[1] We continue to speak of the Christmas season as
Yuletide, and our word *Easter* comes from *Eastre*, the name of
a pagan goddess whose feast was replaced by that of the Resur-
rection of Our Lord.

[1] Stopford Brooke, *Early English Literature*, p. 195.

The change in religion produced a change in literature. Delight in conflict, voiced in *Beowulf* and "The Fight at Finnsburh," took on a Biblical background; Teutonic melancholy dissolved into the wistfulness of the Celt, the self-consciousness of the conquering Roman, and the gentleness of the Christian spirit. Poetry acquired "a lofty religious tone which reveals itself in outbursts of praise to God, in the glorification of apostles and saints, and of martyrdom, in a vivid personal feeling of sorrow for sin, in a frequently expressed desire for eternal happiness higher than the mead-hall or spear-play can give."[1]

The Cædmonian Poems. Cædmon is the first English poet whose name has come down to us; and though it is certain that not all the poems attributed to him are his personal work, they are products of his example and influence. He has been called the Anglo-Saxon Milton, rather inaccurately, for it is far from certain that he was descended from either the Angles or the Saxons,[2] and he resembles Milton only in the selection of some of his themes. The beautiful story of his divine call to be a poet, itself a little masterpiece of English Literature, has been told by another monk, St. Bede the Venerable, in his *Ecclesiastical History*.

It would not be very misleading to speak of Cædmon as the first cowboy poet. No noble lord was he, no dignified bishop, but a humble cowherd; and it was in a rude stable, as he lay on the straw warmed by the breath of oxen, that there came to him the double vocation to the religious life and to the writing of poetry. One night people made merry at a feast, and the harp passed from hand to hand. But the cowherd did not sing — perhaps because he had no skill; perhaps, as Brother

---

[1] E. W. Edmunds, *An Historical Summary of English Literature*, p. 10.

[2] Cædmon's very name seems to imply that he was of Celtic descent. . . . At all events, the section of the country where he dwelt and the monastery to which he belonged owed their Christianity to Irish monks; and it was Irish or Irish-trained clerics who read him those portions of the Bible which he versified. — P. J. LENNOX, *The Catholic University Bulletin*, May, 1913

Azarias has brilliantly suggested,[1] because he would not sing the old pagan songs. Instead, Cædmon slipped from the gay hall and sought shelter in the stable. And in his sleep there came to him a mysterious visitant who said, "Cædmon, sing." Cædmon answered, "I cannot sing." "You must sing," insisted the stranger. Cædmon was impressed and asked, "What must I sing?" And the stranger answered, "Sing of the Creation." And then ideas of a sudden filled the mind of the cowherd, and words of strength and beauty flowed from his lips, and he composed a noble poem of the creation of the world.

In the morning Cædmon went to the neighboring monastery of Whitby and obtained an interview with the abbess, St. Hilda, a remarkable woman, who ruled over a double monastery (one of monks and the other of nuns), and who, so many centuries before woman suffrage had been recognized in England, had been summoned to Parliament because of her piety and her widsom. St. Hilda received Cædmon into her establishment as a monk; and henceforth, says Bede, the erstwhile cowboy was "marked in a special manner by the grace of God, for he was wont to make songs of piety and religion, so that whatever was expounded to him out of Scripture, he turned erelong into English verse expressive of much sweetness and penitence."

The story of Cædmon lives for us anew when we make a literary pilgrimage to Whitby, on its cliff beside the North Sea. We traverse some ten miles of the Whitby moor, where scraggy, half-wild sheep perpetually roam and feed upon the scant vegetation; and we recall that in his depiction of the desert through which the Israelites wandered it was this very piece of English waste land Cædmon had in mind. Beyond are upland meadows fertile still, remnants of the historic five farms adjoining the cloister — remnants because since Cædmon's day the sea has bitten deep into the coast line. On either side of the river Esk sprawls the modern town of Whitby,

[1] *The Development of Old English Thought*, p. 100.

all the year an abode of fishermen and in summer a vacation place for invalids and children. Not a vestige can we find of the monastery where St. Hilda's Benedictine monks and nuns labored and studied and sang the praises of the Lord; but the ruins of a later abbey church still stand at the summit of the east cliff; and below we can hear the beating of the waves against the rocks. Even today Whitby is a place apart:

WHITBY ABBEY

seventy miles lie between it and the walled city of York. In the seventh century it was almost in another world. No more fitting spot could a poet find to meditate upon the truths of faith and of life and thus, perched between the blue sky and the churning ocean, to reproduce the story of the fall of man and the triumph of the Cross. Here is the birthplace of the Cædmonian poems.

The Cædmonian poems consist of metrical paraphrases of portions of the Old Testament, chiefly of the books of Genesis, Exodus, and Daniel; and of the "Christ and Satan" group, pertaining to the fallen angels, Our Lord's descent into Limbo, and His temptation by the devil. There is, finally, a brief poem known as "Cædmon's Hymn":

> Praise we the Lord
> Of the Heavenly Kingdom,
> God's power and wisdom,
> The works of His hand;
> As the Father of Glory,
> Eternal Lord,
> Wrought the beginning
> Of all His wonders!
> Holy Creator!
> Warden of men!
> First, for a roof,
> O'er the children of earth,
> He stablished the heavens,
> And founded the world,
> And spread the dry land
> For the living to dwell in.
> Lord Everlasting!
> Almighty God! [1]

Numerous passages of the Cædmonian poems possess a strong dramatic quality. Here, for instance, is a prose translation from the "Genesis," based upon the Satanic pronouncement "I will not serve."

Why should I slave? I need not serve a master. My hands are strong to work full many a wonder. Power enough have I to rear a goodlier throne, a higher in the heavens. Why should I fawn for His favor, or yield Him such submission? I may be God, as well as He! Brave comrades stand about me; stout-hearted heroes who will not fail me in the fray. These valiant souls have chosen me their lord. . . . It seemeth no wise right to me that I should cringe a whit to God for any good. I will not serve Him longer.

[1] The manuscript of the Cædmonian poems is now preserved in the Bodleian library at Oxford. It was discovered in the seventeenth century by James Ussher, the scholarly Protestant Archbishop of Dublin, and was given to Francis Dujon, known in literature as Junius. (Dujon is not to be confused with the writer of the *Letters of Junius*.) Hence the manuscript is known as the Junius Cædmon.

And a vivid realism animates many another passage, notably Cædmon's account in the "Exodus" of the drowning of the Egyptians in the Red Sea:

> The host was overwhelmed. The seas flowed forth; an uproar rose to heaven, a moan of mighty legions. There rose a great cry of the doomed, and over them the air grew dark. Blood dyed the deep. The walls of water were shattered; the greatest of sea-deaths lashed the heavens. ...A madness of fear was upon them; death wounds bled. The high walls, fashioned by the hand of God, fell in upon the marching army. ...Never came any survivor of all that countless host back to his home again to tell of his journey or to relate to the wives of heroes in the cities the grievous tidings; but a mighty sea-death came upon them all and swallowed their legions, and slew their heralds, and humbled their boasting. For they had striven against God!

Cynewulf. Practically nothing is known about Cynewulf. It is likely that he was a priest, possibly a bishop, and he lived in the eighth century. The poems attributed to him reveal several authors who are conveniently comprised in the School of Cynewulf. The principal poems associated with Cynewulf are these:

"Christ," dealing with the Advent and the Birth of Our Lord, His Ascension, and His second coming at the Last Judgment.

"Elene," the finest piece of literature in the Cynewulf group. It recounts the story of the finding of the true cross by St. Helen, the mother of the Emperor Constantine, and dwells upon some of the historical consequences of the discovery. It has the vigor of *Beowulf*, a delicacy and charm which suggests the Celtic influence, and a strong infusion of the Christian philosophy of life.

"Juliana," an instance of the contribution made by the legends of the saints to literature. St. Juliana suffered martyrdom under the Emperor Maximian, and her life and sufferings and ultimate triumph constitute the subject matter of this poem.

"The Dream of the Rood," an example of vision-poetry, wherein the poet tells of a Cross which appeared to him in his sleep and brought him comfort and happiness.

St. Bede the Venerable (673-735). When we mention a date in modern history — 1066, for example, or 1928 — we

DEATH OF ST. BEDE THE VENERABLE

His last hours were spent in completing his translation of the Gospel according to St. John. When Wilbert, the boy to whom he was dictating, announced that the work was finished, the Saint significantly commented: "Thou hast spoken truth; it is indeed finished." Then singing "Glory be to the Father and to the Son and to the Holy Ghost," he peacefully breathed his last breath

count from the Birth of Christ. The man to introduce this custom into Europe was a monk of Jarrow, a holy man, an ardent scholar, and a writer of no little skill, St. Bede the Venerable, the "first father of our English learning." From personal observation he knew little of the wide world. Many monks of long ago — St. Thomas Aquinas, for instance —

traveled much and far; but Bede lived practically his whole life (for he entered when a little boy) in the monastery, where he prayed and studied and wrote. Yet his fame as a scholar spread abroad, and even before his death his name was held in reverence.

St. Bede did not write in English, and for that reason his immediate importance in the history of English Literature is not great. But he was great in his influence; for to him we owe substantially all we know about Cædmon, and his most famous work is still a source book for students of history. That work is his Latin *Ecclesiastical History of the English People*, in which he covers his subject from the Roman invasion under Julius Cæsar to the events of four years before his own death. He was an excellent historian, surprisingly modern in his methods, careful to distinguish between fact and hearsay, and untiring in his quest for documents upon which to base his statements. Other branches of learning occupied him in books on grammar, on natural science, on theology, on Holy Scripture, and on the lives of the saints. His last work was a translation of the Gospel of St. John. That finished, he sweetly and cheerfully passed through the gates of death, for, said he, "My soul much desires to behold my King Christ in His beauty."

Alfred the Great. Famed in history and legend, "England's Darling," as Alfred has been called, is an important figure in the story of European civilization. He unified England, withstood the invading Danes, reformed the laws, by example and precept supported the Church, and encouraged education and culture by establishing schools and bringing teachers from the Continent. He translated, in person or through secretaries, several famous Latin books, including *The Pastoral Care* of St. Gregory the Great, Orosius's *History of the World*, Boethius's *Consolations of Philosophy*, and Bede's *Ecclesiastical History*. Alfred did more than translate: he added comments and explanations and often enlarged upon the thought of the originals. He was the inventor of the now familiar device of supplying chapter headings and prefixing a table of contents. If Cædmon is the Father of English poetry, Alfred is the Father of English prose; indeed, he might well be considered the Father of English Literature in general, since more than any other man he labored to bring English learning into the current of the European Tradition. His translations are all from Continental sources, with the one exception of Bede's *Ecclesiastical History*, and that was written in Latin. Two English poets laureate — Henry James Pye and Alfred Austin — have written poems on Alfred the Great, and at least two plays of which he is the hero are in existence, one by Sheridan Knowles, the other by the American Jesuit Father Henry Van Rensselaer; but he is best known in subsequent literature by the century-old legend of the old woman and the cakes and by Chesterton's stirring "Ballad of the White Horse."

ALFRED THE GREAT

Other Christian Prose Writers. King Alfred's interest in learning prompted him to collect, organize, and complete existing historical records, a work which continued long after his death and resulted in *The Old English Chronicle*. The chroniclers were chiefly monks in four different monasteries, and they produced a summary of historical events which is more continuous and scholarly than any similar chronicle of Continental Europe.

As *The Old English Chronicle* preserves something of the learning of the monks, so numerous fragments of sermons and devotional treatises preserve the fruits of their piety and zeal. The most famous collection of such discourses is the *Blickling Homilies*, so called because the manuscript containing them is kept at Blickling Hall in Norfolk. They date from the tenth century, and in the development of English prose stand midway between the writings of Alfred the Great and the writings of Ælfric. There are nineteen sermons in the collection, some of them not complete. In places they are beautiful and poetical as well as devout; in one of them, which recounts the Mystery of the Annunciation, the Angel Gabriel says to the Blessed Virgin, "The redness of the rose glitters in thee, and the whiteness of the lily shines."

Ælfric (955?–1023?). A monk and a master of novices, a teacher and a scholar, Ælfric enjoys the further distinction of being the most prolific as well as the most finished and literary of all the Old English writers of prose. He had read abundantly in the Christian writers of Rome and deliberately tried to imitate the graces of style he recognized in St. Gregory the Great and St. Jerome. Ælfric wrote both in Latin and in English. His works include a vast number of sermons, lives of the saints, explanations of Christian Doctrine, a textbook of Latin grammar, familiar dialogues, and letters. As it flowed from his pen the Old English language lost much of its roughness and became a thing of charm and variety. Ælfric was the first writer in English to indulge in what is called poetic prose, a style of writing in which the prose has something of the music and cadence of verse. We can observe this sort of writing in the essays of De Quincey and in Francis Thompson's essay on Shelley.

Other prose writers need not long detain us. Two centuries before Ælfric there was a monk of Malmesbury (afterwards an abbot and a bishop) who wrote in both Latin and English and who was a scholar, a linguist, a musician, and a poet. This was St. Aldhelm[1] (656?–709), known by the beautiful title of the Knight of Virginity because he wrote so much in prose and in verse about the virtue of purity. He was a hymn-writer, too, and composed popular chants to replace the old pagan songs which the common people continued to sing long after the introduction of Christianity. Alcuin (735–804), though not prominent in English Literature, is worthy of attention on account of his vast scholarship and his work as teacher at the court of Charlemagne. The earliest of all these prose writers was St. Gildas the Wise, who lived in the sixth century and wrote sadly of sad times.

---

[1] The word *Aldhelm* signifies "old hat." It is possible that one of the saint's ancestors received this nickname because of his addiction to unfashionable head-gear. Many of our modern family names were originally nicknames suggested by peculiarities of body and of dress.

CHAPTER IV

MONK AND MINSTREL

MIDDLE ENGLISH LITERATURE

In our review of Old English Literature we saw that men dedicated to God in the religious life or in the secular clergy were among the principal writers in English from Cædmon and Gildas the Wise down to the Norman Conquest. Though less pronounced, there is likewise in the record of our earliest literature the note of the minstrel, scop, or gleeman, the maker and singer of popular songs, the teller of ancient tales, the uncrowned laureate of bloody strife and domestic happiness and love's young dream and other aspects of human life on which monks and priests are not authorities and about which they could hardly be expected to sing with the enthusiasm born of personal experience. Now these two classes of writers, the monk and the minstrel, continued to make literature in the era known as the Middle English Period.

Middle English Literature begins with the Norman Conquest of England and extends to and includes the age of the first supreme English poet, Geoffrey Chaucer. In the present chapter we shall see the monk and the minstrel — even though they frequently regarded each other with distrust and disapproval — contributing to the literature of the learned and to the literature of the simple and unlettered. Both the monk and the minstrel followed in the wake of the Norman fleet that brought William the Conqueror to the shores of England, and both carried with them stories and songs and learning from the Continent, and so united the literature of England with the literature of the European Tradition.

The details of the Norman Conquest — one of the most important and dramatic episodes in English history — are set forth in many books, and in them we can read of the death of Edward the Confessor, of the rival claimants to the English throne, of the landing of the Normans at Pevensey, and of the death of Harold and the triumph of William at the Battle of Hastings, or Senlac, on the southern coast. These are all matters of considerable importance to the student of literature; but of even more importance are the effects of the Conquest on education, on language, and on literature.

Effects of the Norman Conquest. One notable result of the Conquest was the gradual migration of distinguished Continental scholars to England and the development of the universities of Oxford and Cambridge. The incoming teachers were nearly all members of religious orders. In the thirteenth century — the century which contributed so much to education, to art, to literature, and to philosophy throughout Europe — the Franciscans and Dominicans gave a strong impetus to education and culture not only in the universities but in the old and the more recent monasteries. The result was a large number of writers on history, on philosophy, on science — men of piety and learning whose writings, however, need not detain us here because for the most part they are in the Latin tongue, which was and for centuries continued to be the language of scholarship.

Chief among the clerical writers were two archbishops of Canterbury, both Italians by birth, Lanfranc and St. Anselm, writers on philosophy and theology; William of Malmesbury and Giraldus Cambrensis, historians who treated events in English history as parts of the history of Western Europe and who wrote with considerable charm and polish; John of Salisbury, secretary to St. Thomas of Canterbury and afterwards Bishop of Chartres in France, who displayed his unusual learning in numerous treatises on grammar, on logic, on philosophy, and on the principles of government; Roger Bacon, an Oxford Franciscan, whose name figures in the history of scientific thought; and Richard of Bury, Bishop of Durham, a friend of the Italian poet Petrarca, whom he met at Avignon in 1330, and a delightful lover of books. His *Philobiblon* is one of the most fascinating books about books ever written.

The Norman Conquest wrought a number of important changes in the English language. These came about gradually as the result of the slow fusion of the native English tongue with the French speech of the court and the nobility. It was in the years following the Conquest that English became what it is today, a comparatively grammarless tongue; the old inflections were dropped, and the preposition *of* came into use to denote possession. Though a great many French and Latin words had come into the English language before the Conquest, the native vocabulary was now further enriched with synonyms, or words of almost the same meaning, coming from the French.[1] The conversation between Gurth and Wamba in the second chapter of Scott's *Ivanhoe* affords an admirable illustration of how foreign words found their way into English speech. The manner of writing poetry was also affected. Old English verse depended mainly on alliteration and on accent or stress; French verse had rime and a regular number of accented syllables. In Middle English verse rime is adopted, alliteration is partly abandoned, and the accents are determined by the number of syllables.

THE CYCLES OF ROMANCE

The Middle English Period of English Literature is chiefly interesting for the adoption into English of the Medieval Romances; that is, of stories (usually in verse) of saints, heroes, and lovers. To the development of the Romances

[1] Strictly speaking, we have no synonyms, since each word has its own connotation and atmosphere. There is point in the small boy's definition of a synonym: "The word you use when you don't know how to spell the other."

both monks and minstrels contributed. The subject matter of the Romances came from history and legends of many countries and times — of Thebes, of Troy, of Greece, of Rome, of France, of Ireland, of England; from events as widely separated as the wars of Alexander the Great, the exploits of Charlemagne, and the adventures of the Crusaders. The Romances were of vast length, their plots were loose and rambling, and their language was colorful and picturesque. The earliest of them date from the tenth century; the fourteenth was their age of highest splendor. In form and in theme the Romances had a tremendous influence on subsequent English Literature. They inspired some of the most representative work of Spenser, Scott, Byron, Moore, Southey, Tennyson, Arnold, Morris, Swinburne, Longfellow, and Lowell. In our own day we can trace their effects upon the poems of John Masefield and Alfred Noyes.

King Arthur and his Knights. Most famous among the Romances and most intimately connected with English Literature were the legends of King Arthur and the Knights of the Round Table. In two Latin chronicles, dating from the ninth and eleventh centuries, Arthur is mentioned as a brave leader of the Britons. In the *Mabinogion*, a thirteenth-century collection of Welsh stories, Arthur appears as a friend of the fairies and an adept in the art of magic; but long before the thirteenth century the legends of King Arthur had been sung in Britain and had been spread on the Continent of Europe by monks and minstrels, first in Brittany, then throughout France. A good tale never loses anything in the telling, so in the course of years the stories took on fresh details and absorbed stories from distant lands.

As we read the story of King Arthur and his Knights in Tennyson's *Idylls of the King* we find in their most finished form various strands of legends which had appeared in earlier versions in both prose and verse; the nineteenth-century poet profited by the work of numberless monks and minstrels.

77

FROM A MEDIEVAL ROMANCE

Printed at Nuremberg, Germany, in 1517. (Courtesy of the British Museum)

Merlin the Magician is a character in the Arthurian Romance whose repute as an enchanter goes back to the very dawn of written speech. He appeared in a poem by Robert de Borron in the twelfth century, in a lengthy romance in prose, and then a hundred and fifty years later in an English poem (its author unknown) called *Arthur and Merlin*. The tale of Tristram and Iseult, which ranks among the supreme love stories of the world, is Celtic in origin; a suburb of Dublin, Chapelizod, or Iseult's Chapel, is still named after the heroine. It was put into French verse by Chrétien de Troyes (1150?–1190), into German by Gottfried von Strassburg about the year 1200, and a century later into English, probably by Thomas of Erceldoune. Finest of all the Arthurian stories in Middle English is *Sir Gawain and the Green Knight*, the work of an unknown author who reveals a noble mind and a devout soul, rare artistry in descriptions, and a wholesome delight in the mere fact of being alive.

The Arthurian story of the Holy Grail goes back to the very days of Our Lord. The Grail was the chalice used by Jesus at the Last Supper when He changed the bread and wine into His Body and Blood. After the tragedy of Calvary, says the legend, the chalice was hidden by Joseph of Arimathea at Glastonbury in the southwest of England, and none might find it save a knight absolutely pure of heart. Sir Percival, who figures as the successful seeker in so many versions of the Holy Grail legend, was originally a Welsh hero. In some of the later accounts he is replaced by Sir Galahad, the son of Sir Lancelot. The story of Sir Lancelot and Queen Guinevere was combined with the story of the Holy Grail in a medieval French prose romance called *Lancelot of the Lake*, which was based on a Latin version probably written by Walter Map, a twelfth-century Welsh priest, who wrote "for the love of his lord, King Henry." We know how prominently the Grail legend figures in *Parsifal*, the German music-drama by Wagner; but as early as the year 1200 the story was told by a German

A SCENE FROM THE ARTHURIAN STORIES

Drawn by the French artist Paul Gustave Doré

poet, Wolfram von Eschenbach. The Holy Grail appears likewise in the literature of Norway, Portugal, and Italy.

The Arthurian Romance is a remarkable instance of the universality of literature: its roots spring from many soils, and its flowers bloom in many lands. "In the productions of the early romance writers it may be seen how the Western world was moving away from the separate national traditions, and beginning the course of modern civilization with a large stock of ideas, subjects, and forms of expression common to all nations."[1] In other words, the Romances of the Round Table were a means of forming and perpetuating the European literary tradition.

Geoffrey of Monmouth (1100?–1154). Then came a book which had a wonderful effect on the history of Arthurian Romance. It was a dignified work in Latin and was intended by its author as a serious and scholarly contribution to history. That book was the *History of the Kings of Britain*, by Geoffrey of Monmouth. Geoffrey had drunk deep of the lore of the monks and the lays of the minstrels, for he had been a man of the world for many years before he became a priest and a bishop. He gathered together all the stories of King Arthur he could lay his hands on and presented them as authentic exploits performed by a national hero. Even from the first he was not taken seriously as a historian; but in the history of literature, however much he might be surprised to know of it, he ranks as a person of more importance — as the source and inspiration of one of the world's greatest cycles of poems. Not all the stories that came to be associated with the Arthurian Romance were known to Geoffrey: he has not a word to say about Tristram or Lancelot, the Round Table or the Holy Grail. But he brought back from Brittany the Arthurian legends to the place of their origin, and he fired the imagination of countless poets. Without Geoffrey of Monmouth there would have been no Sir Thomas Malory; and without Malory,

[1] W. P. Ker, *Epic and Romance*, p. 350.

there would have been no *Idylls of the King* and no versions of the Tristram story by Arnold, Swinburne, and Masefield.

Wace and Layamon. What a monk began, a minstrel developed. Attached to the court of King Henry II was a *trouvère*[1] named Robert Wace, who found in the *History of the Kings of Britain* likely material for his songs. So he translated Geoffrey's Latin prose into French verse, added something about the Round Table and the death of King Arthur, and called the poem *Brut*.[2] This was about the year 1155. Fifty years later an English parish priest named Layamon translated Wace's French verse into English verse and called his riming chronicle *Brut* also. Layamon's version is not a literal translation by any means and contains numerous details not found in the *Brut* of Wace. The priest added to the minstrel's account of the Knights of the Round Table, wrote with considerably more enthusiasm about strife and peril, and brought in the fairy element and sundry tales of magic which he had doubtless heard from the lips of peasants along the borders of Wales. Layamon's *Brut* illustrates the changes which were slowly coming into the language. It contains relatively few French words and clings to the Old English alliterative verse; but some rimes are introduced, and the nouns are losing their earlier inflections. The *Brut* is at once a landmark in the development of the English language and an important link in the progress of the Arthurian Romance.

Sir Thomas Malory (1400?–1471?). The next phase of the development of Arthurian Romance brings us to the second half of the fifteenth century when Caxton published the *Morte d'Arthur* of Sir Thomas Malory. About Malory the man we know next to nothing. He was recognized as "a gentleman of an ancient house, and a soldier," and he was probably a native

---

[1] One of the names by which poets or minstrels were known in France.

[2] *Brut* comes from *Brutus*, the name of a legendary king of Troy. The full title of Wace's poem is *Brut d'Angleterre*, that is, The Brutus of England, meaning that King Arthur was as great a hero in England as Brutus was in Troy.

of Warwickshire, the county in which Shakespeare was born. He seems to have been a member of Parliament too, and may have fought in the Wars of the Roses in defense of the House of Lancaster. His prose version of the King Arthur cycle was completed in 1470. For his sources he turned chiefly to French

A KNIGHT KEEPING HIS VIGIL

The candidate for knighthood consecrated his sword and his service to God and spent the night in prayer before the altar

originals, and some of the finest of the tales, such as *Sir Gawain and the Green Knight*, he completely ignored. Malory is worthy of attention for two things: he wrote in a style vivid, pictorial, artistic, which beautifully suggests the atmosphere and spirit of the "days of old when knights were bold"; and, despite looseness of plot and inconsistency of episodes, he succeeded in giving the entire narrative unity by making King Arthur the dominant and heroic figure. The *Morte d'Arthur* makes splendid reading today; indeed, there are many lovers of Arthurian Romance who prefer Malory's prose to Tennyson's verse.

MIDDLE ENGLISH POETRY

Literature in the Middle English Period was largely concerned with religious issues; it is difficult for us to realize how deeply Catholicism entered into the lives of people in all stations of life. Even tiny English hamlets had magnificent parish churches, and everywhere throughout the land were convents and monasteries. Phases of that prevailingly religious epoch have been presented in our own time in two novels worthy of more than passing notice: *Richard Raynal, Solitary*, by R. H. Benson, and *The Anchorhold*, by Enid Dinnis. Especially was the fourteenth century, as Sister Madeleva has well said, "religious in its traditions, subject-matter, and purpose. The drama was almost entirely so; prose divided itself between secular and religious interests, chronicles, translations and paraphrases of the Bible, catechisms, sermons, treatises, and proverbs; narrative poetry was as devoted to saints' legends and Mary stories as to romance and fabliaux; and the secular lyric was inconspicuous beside the religious lyric of the period." [1]

Laurence Minot (1300?-1352?). The secular lyric is best represented by Laurence Minot, certainly not a great poet, but a ready and popular singer whose originality, as Ten Brink says, "consists in the blending of the technique of the gleemen's song with that of the clerical lyric." [2] He was a court minstrel, a forerunner of the poets laureate of a later day, and he celebrated in verse the victories of King Edward III. In form he marks the transition from the Old English alliterative verse to the use of rime; in spirit he sounds a strong nationalistic note and embodies the unfeeling and blustering character which war (and that was a warlike era) invariably develops.

Religious Poems. But, as we have seen, the poetry of the age was prevailingly religious. An example of the attempt to

---

[1] *The Pearl: A Study in Spiritual Dryness*, p. 38.
[2] *History of English Literature*, p. 322.

utilize the poetic form for purposes of religious instruction is the *Ormulum*, by Orm, a Lincolnshire monk. He translated and expanded thirty of the Sunday gospels. The result is not remarkable for its poetic value, but it is interesting as an early instance of unrimed iambic verse. Typical, too, is the *Pricke of Conscience* by Richard Rolle (1290?–1349), the Hermit of Hampole, a poem written in both English and Latin. It is a series of meditations on the great truths of faith — Heaven, Purgatory, and Hell, death and judgment, and the fleeting character of earthly life. Rolle was saintly and learned, and his personality and his writings had a wide influence. He lived in Yorkshire, as did the unknown author of *Cursor Mundi*, or *Way of the World*, a metrical history written from a deeply religious point of view and with considerable literary skill and warm human feeling.

But best of all is *The Pearl*, evidently the work of a religious who records a rich spiritual experience under the allegory of a man who has lost a pearl of great price. Some scholars have found in *The Pearl* the lament of a father over the death of his daughter; but beautiful as that interpretation is, there can be little doubt that the poet is easing his heart because he is suffering from dryness in prayer, because the sweetness and consolation which he once found in the practice of his religion have passed away. That is a spiritual condition frequently met with in the lives of the saints and in the experience of religious persons, but never has it been given a more touchingly beautiful expression. It is an interesting coincidence that *The Pearl* was found in the same manuscript with *Sir Gawain and the Green Knight* and two religious poems, "Cleanness" and "Patience." Conceivably they were all written by the same gifted man, whose songs come to our ears like the melodies of some sweet-throated thrush unseen and unidentified.

William Langland (1332?–1400?). The religious poetry of the fourteenth century assumed another form in *Piers Plowman*, a series of "visions" generally attributed to William

RICHARD ROLLE'S PSALTER

The Psalms in Latin and English, with an English commentary by Richard Rolle.
(By courtesy of the British Museum)

Langland, or Langley, who exhibits the singing gift of the minstrel, the devotional fervor of the monk, and the "nose for news" of the modern journalist. Of the personality of Langland very little is known. He seems to have been a cleric and a man who had seen and suffered much, who in his verses exposed the hardships of the common people and the abuses that existed among some of the monks and the higher clergy. That Langland was a loyal and devout Catholic cannot be doubted; and because he was loyal and devout he could write with bitter indignation of the lives of religious men who disgraced their noble calling. He was an English Dante without Dante's genius and learning and culture.

Piers Plowman is written in the old alliterative verse. It is often rough and uncouth in expression but is not lacking in passages of real eloquence. As the poem stands, it gives evidence of more than one author. The conjecture is that Langland died before the work was finished, and a certain John Butt completed the task. Then the entire poem was revised by two editors, one of them outspoken and violent, the other gentle and diplomatic. *Piers Plowman* is today of less interest to the student of literature than to the student of history; like Chaucer's *Canterbury Tales*, though with less charm and with absolutely no humor, it reflects the popular life of the times.

OMIT **A Typical Poem.** The one piece of literature which most adequately conveys the essential spirit of the Middle English Period is *The Owl and the Nightingale*, generally attributed, though on slight grounds, to Nicholas of Guildford. In this clever and spirited collection of verses monk and minstrel engage in friendly though animated debate on the merits of their respective attitudes toward life. The owl is the spokesman of the monk and upholds the worth and dignity of the ascetic standard of conduct; the nightingale symbolizes the minstrel and pleads for the recognition of beauty and of song. The birds of controversy are evenly matched, and together present an impartial statement of the theory of beauty and the theory of goodness. "The characters and arguments of the disputing birds are well distinguished, and the slight dramatic touches with which the narrative is enlivened are in excellent taste." [1] The author reveals humor, a knowledge of life, considerable power of imagination, and a measure of skill in description. He uses only a few French words, but shows the influence of French verse structure.

OMIT MIDDLE ENGLISH PROSE

Religious Prose. *The Ancren Riwle.* We can easily understand that priests and monks, many of them profound scholars as well as pious men, wrote extensively on religious subjects. From the literary point of view the most interesting piece of Middle English religious prose is a rule or code of directions for nuns who lived a solitary life, *The Ancren Riwle*, sometimes ascribed to Richard Poor, Bishop of Salisbury in the thirteenth century. The author shows himself familiar with the science of the saints and with the standard authorities on the religious life; but what makes *The Ancren Riwle* literature is the rich human sympathy and the keen understanding of life which its lines reveal. The three ladies for whose guidance the rule was written are given minute directions regarding their dress and their daily habits; it is even suggested that they keep a cat for their recreation. They are reminded that the thing of chief importance in their way of life is to preserve interior union with God.

The inward rule is always alike. The outward is various, because everyone ought so to observe the outward rule as that the body may therewith best serve the inward. All may and ought to observe one rule concerning purity of heart, that is, a clean unstained conscience, without any reproach of sin that is not remedied by confession. . . . This rule is framed not by man's contrivance, but by the command of God. . . . But

[1] W. J. Courthope, *A History of English Poetry*, Vol. I, p. 135.

the external rule, which I call the handmaid, is of man's contrivance; nor is it instituted for anything else but to serve the internal law. . . . Wherefore, this rule may be changed and varied according to everyone's state and circumstances. For some are strong, some are weak, and may very well be excused, and please God with less; some are learned, and some are not, and must work the more, and say their prayers at the stated hours in a different manner; some are old and ill-favored, of whom there is less to fear; some are young and lively, and have need to be more on their guard. . . . The confessor may modify the outward rule as prudence may direct, and as he sees that the inward rule may thus be best kept.

In this passage the author of *The Ancren Riwle*, enlarging on Our Lord's saying that "the letter killeth, but the spirit giveth life," modifies the general law according to particular circumstances, even as in our own day the Church grants dispensations in matters such as fasting and abstinence. It is common sense applied to the religious life. And in another place the writer establishes a beautiful comparison between nuns and birds:

True anchoresses are compared to birds; for they leave the earth; that is, the love of all earthly things; and through yearning of heart after heavenly things, fly upward toward heaven. And, although they fly high, with high and holy life, yet they hold the head low, through meek humility, as a bird flying boweth down its head, and accounteth all her good deeds and good works nothing worth. . . . Fly high, and yet hold the head always low. . . . True anchoresses are indeed birds of heaven, that fly aloft, and sit on the green boughs singing merrily . . . that is, in such meditation they rest in peace and have gladness of heart as those who sing.

At the end of the treatise the author strikes a delicious personal note: "As often as ye read any thing in this book, greet our Lady with an Ave Mary for him that made this rule, and for him who wrote it, and took pains about it. Moderate enough I am, who ask so little."

Secular Prose. *The Travels of Sir John Mandeville.* As the religious prose of the Middle English Period is represented by

The Ancren Riwle, so the secular prose of the same epoch finds its most famous example in *The Travels of Sir John Mandeville,* a work written originally in French in 1371. Who wrote it we do not know; but we do know that Sir John Mandeville, for centuries accepted as a historical person, was no more a real human being than the Lemuel Gulliver of Swift's satire or the

MONASTIC SCHOLARS

The scriptorium, or library, of English monasteries was a center of culture in an age when literature was largely neglected outside the cloister

Andrew Gump of American caricature. The imaginary Sir John, an English knight, recounts his adventures on the way to Jerusalem and in lands beyond; he describes visits to the court of the Great Cham and to the land of Prester John; he narrates startling adventures in India and the islands of the seas. From his diverting pages we learn how diamonds grow, what dreadful monsters dwell in secluded valleys, how certain mountains draw to themselves men and beasts by magnetic power, that a great river flows with precious stones instead of water, where a family of extraordinary ants live on hills of gold dust; and we can discover all we need to know about the Garden of Eden and the Fountain of Youth. The book is a medley of the real and the fanciful, of sober truth and wild-eyed fiction, written with vigor, with simplicity, and with a fine command of language. No wonder it was translated into a dozen European tongues. The English version is recognized as the best piece of English prose before Malory's *Morte d'Arthur*.

SUMMARY

We have now completed our survey of Old English and Middle English Literature. We have distinguished between Pagan and Christian Early English poetry and have seen how the latter derived from the Catholic European Tradition. Indeed, the development of English Literature in both poetry and prose, in both its mood of prayerful thought and its mood of human passion and swelling song, consists almost entirely in an imitation of the literature of the Continent. Both monk and minstrel looked for inspiration across the English Channel. The relationship was thickened as a result of the Norman Conquest, with an influx of scholars and singers and the spread of the Cycles of Romance. The time was at hand for the advent of a great poet who by the force of his genius and the charm of his songs should make a contribution to world literature and let the full force of the great stream of literary culture gladden English meadows. And so we pass to a consideration of Chaucer.

CHAPTER V

THE AGE OF CHAUCER

FASHIONS IN LITERATURE

The Hero Theory. Thomas Carlyle, in his *Heroes and Hero Worship*, developed a theory of history which seeks to explain events by means of great men or heroes. The men make the events. Carlyle believed that the great man is not merely one man in the crowd whose head happens to be a little higher than other men's heads, but a sort of superman, a being of deeper insight and finer skill than his fellows, and that he directs and even determines the course of history. Carlyle writes:

For, as I take it, Universal History, the history of what man has accomplished in this world, is at bottom the History of the Great Men who have worked here. They were the leaders of men, these great ones; the modellers, patterns, and in a wide sense creators, of whatever the general mass of men contrived to do or to attain . . . the soul of the whole world's history, it may justly be considered, were the history of these.

We are not here concerned with Carlyle's hero theory in the field of history. Perhaps he carried it to extremes and ignored the existence of other factors — for instance, Roman Imperialism, religion and feudalism, climate and geographical position, trade routes and industrial conditions — which have affected the rise and fall of nations. But it is true that the great-man theory has a degree of application to the history of literature. The great writer, far more than the great statesman or the great general, formulates men's thoughts and molds men's language and colors men's intellectual backgrounds. The more we think about it the more clearly we see that Virgil and Horace did more than Augustus to impress

Roman civilization on the world. Italy had many rulers and countless fighting men in the Middle Ages, but not one of those heroes of the sword and the council chamber exerted so strong and deep an influence as Dante, the hero of the pen; many of them we should not even remember if he had not immortalized them in his poem. Dante definitely made the Tuscan dialect the literary language of his country; and by writing his masterpiece in the language of the people instead of in Latin, the language of scholars, he set the fashion for writers in his own and in other lands and became in a way the father of all modern literature. Besides, Dante took as the basis of his writings the Christian philosophy of life. When Carlyle says that "a man's religion is the chief fact with regard to him," he is only uttering a truth to which Dante had given the supreme literary expression in his *Divine Comedy* and which became henceforth a foundation stone of the European Tradition in literature.

And what Dante did in Italy other great writers achieved in France and Spain, Germany and England. We can readily understand how they did so if we grasp this idea that there are fashions in literature even as there are fashions in clothes. Twenty years ago the American college boy who came to class wearing golf knickers was looked upon as a freak. Then the correct thing was corduroy trousers. What has brought about the change? Clearly, golf knickers were first worn by some prominent and influential student, a man who enjoyed the respect and esteem of his fellows, whose brain or brawn was such that his companions admired him. Now admiration leads to imitation; so when he began wearing golf knickers instead of corduroys, in a few weeks everybody was doing it. Let any man very much in the public eye — a popular moving-picture actor or the Prince of Wales, for example — wear a green tie instead of a white one with conventional evening dress, and it is almost a certainty that green ties will become the vogue.

Conditions are the same in literary production, with this important difference, however : that fashions in literature go deeper than fashions in clothes and are therefore harder to establish and harder to change. It is easier to change a necktie than to change an idea. Now the great writers in literature have, so to say, made certain ideas and certain ways of writing fashionable. Some Italian and French critics at one time made it a law of dramatic writing that the unities should be observed : that a play must have one plot, must have no change of scene, and must have all its events take place within the space of one day. Here and there dramatists rebelled against that fashion in the drama, but they were not influential enough to change it. Then along came Shakespeare in England and, more than two centuries later, Victor Hugo in France and ignored the unities altogether. They were big men, and their example was followed, with the result that today no dramatist, big or little, feels it necessary to think about those once sacred unities at all. It does not seem at all odd to us to see the first act of a play set in ancient Egypt, the second in medieval France, and the third in modern Chicago. Our notions of what is fitting on the stage have been formed by writers of great plays. And so it is that Carlyle's hero conception of history is justified in literature.

CHAUCER

The First Modern Poet. Earlier literature in English is an interesting prelude, but it is with Chaucer that, properly speaking, the history of English Literature begins. *Beowulf* and Cædmon, the *Ormulum* and Minot, are to us like the ancient pottery and the wax figures swathed in outmoded garments which we gaze upon in a museum : they smell of the ages ; they do not seem alive. But when we come to Chaucer, when we catch the shrewd and mellow humor of his character portraits and follow the lilting melody of his verses, we know that we are communing with a man of flesh and blood, a real man, a man who, despite his quaintness of costume and his unfamiliar manner of speech, in essentials belongs in the twentieth century as much as in the fourteenth. We do not take long to get acquainted. Some of the stories he has to tell us we already know; we do not have to consult an encyclopedia to appreciate his little jokes. We can feel with him, not merely for him, when he suggests a thought of suffering and sadness. We can heartily agree with ever so many things he says, and when we disagree it is in much the same manner that we disagree with Kipling or Galsworthy. A truly great poet, he is not of an age, but for all time. Most of his thoughts are our thoughts, only we have not thought them out so thoroughly; and his view of life is largely our view, only we have not lived so magnificently as he, "a man," says Dryden, "of a most wonderful comprehensive nature." "With him," Matthew Arnold declared, "is born our real poetry." He is the "father of English poetry,"[1] the "prince of English poets."[2] Of English Literature Wordsworth hailed him as the "great Precursor, genuine morning Star."

> Old Chaucer, like the morning star,
> To us discovers day from far;
> His light those mists and clouds dissolved,
> Which our dark nation long involved,

sang Sir John Denham, the Irish Englishman. And in similar vein young Joseph Addison pays tribute:

> Long had our dull forefathers slept supine,
> Nor felt the raptures of the tuneful Nine;
> Till Chaucer first, a merry bard, arose,
> And many a story told in rhyme and prose.

And Southey summarizes the general opinion of Chaucer when he says, "The line of English poets begins with him, as that of English kings with William the Conqueror."

[1] Dryden.   [2] Thomas Fuller.

CHAUCER READING TO EDWARD III

From a painting by Ford Madox Brown

In other words, as William the Conqueror brought England into the European tradition of history, so "Dan" Chaucer[1] brought English poetry into the European Tradition of literature. "He stood at the great divide and waved the final farewell of English Literature to the rune and saga of Celt and Saxon retreating into the North."[2]

CHAUCER

A tradition maintains that this portrait was painted under the direction of Thomas Occleve. (From an original painting in the collection of George A. Plimpton)

The Man. What manner of man was this English poet who occupies so important a place in the history of our literature? What are the significant events in his life? What did he write, and why do his readers, including other poets, wax so enthusiastic about it? And how may we learn to read Chaucer for our learning and delight?

The best description we possess of Geoffrey Chaucer (1340?–1400) is furnished by himself in little hints and random comments and joking reflections scattered through his writings. Putting all such material together we can construct a composite portrait of the man. Physically he was of goodly girth, and on

---

[1] Geoffrey Chaucer has been called "Dan" Chaucer by Tennyson and others. The word *Dan* was originally *Dom*, which was and is the title of Benedictine monks; as, Dom Gasquet, Dom Vonier. It is applied familiarly and humorously to Chaucer as it is to the mythical son of Venus in "Dan" Cupid. Similarly, we speak sometimes of old "Father" Time.

[2] Thomas Walsh, *New York Times*, February 9, 1913.

his face there gleamed a roguish look. He enjoyed company, but was soft-spoken and retiring. In particular, he enjoyed the companionship of books. So fond was he of reading that nothing could draw him from his study save the coming of spring; for though he loved books much, he loved nature more. The pleasure he secured from books he held to be the greatest earthly joy, and he never grew weary of

> olde appreved stories,
> Of holynesse, of regnes, of victories,
> Of love, of hate, of other sondry thynges.
> .   .   .   .
> And as for me, though that I can but lyte,
> On bokes for to rede I me delyte,
> And to hem yeve I feyth and ful credence,
> And in myn herte have hem in reverence
> So hertely, that ther is game noon
> That fro my bokes maketh me to goon,
> But hit be seldom on the holyday,
> Save, certeynly, whan that the month of May
> Is comen, and that I here the foules singe,
> And that the floures ginnen for to springe, —
> Farwel my book, and my devocioun!

Chaucer was a religious man too, though there was nothing long-faced about his piety. And he was so good a Catholic that he could on occasion poke sly fun at monks who were lovers of good cheer and at clerics who took themselves too seriously. His authentic portrait shows him with inkhorn and rosary, with a rounded face and a merry twinkle in his eyes. When Chaucer lived there England was still "Merrie" England.

Chaucer's father was a prosperous vintner in London, and the boy had opportunity to loiter along the bank of the Thames and watch the ships and the sailors from many lands. But he went to school too, and later probably to one of the universities, for he knew his Latin classics well, Ovid especially, and he had more than a passing intimacy with philosophy and science. He was early a member of the household of Lionel, Duke of

Clarence, and so came to understand court life. Then he was a soldier in the English army in France, was taken prisoner and ransomed, and later received a pension for his services and continued to be in attendance at court. In due course he married, and, it would seem, with not much happiness; most men of genius (Socrates and Shakespeare are notable instances) appear to have been unfortunate in their choice of wives. Chaucer was a diplomat also, going on an embassy to Italy and visiting Genoa and Florence; and several other times he went abroad. He was Comptroller of Customs for the port of London, though how successful he was in that office it is impossible to say. For a long time he enjoyed worldly prosperity; but afterwards, when his patron, John of Gaunt, fell into disgrace, Chaucer was deprived of position and pension, his wife died, and he tasted the hardships of poverty until King Henry IV took the throne from Richard II, when Chaucer again enjoyed royal favor for about a year before his death. His life was long, filled with variety, and rich in contacts with men in every grade of society. It was a fine training for a poet.

Chaucer's Poems. Though Chaucer is in some respects the most English of English poets, his writings are all strongly influenced by foreign literature. Wars and politics he left severely alone: we look in vain in his writings for any account of his experiences as a soldier or any comments on the troubled times in which he lived. But he gives us many beautiful descriptions of the English countryside and the coming of the English spring with its sweet scents and riot of coloring and the little birds that "maken melodye"; and he has drawn to the life a wide variety of English men and women. His reading and his several journeys to France and Italy, as well as his presence at court, where French fashions were still in vogue, brought him into contact with foreign thought and foreign points of view; hence we find that nearly all his poems are reproductions of material that already existed in other literatures.

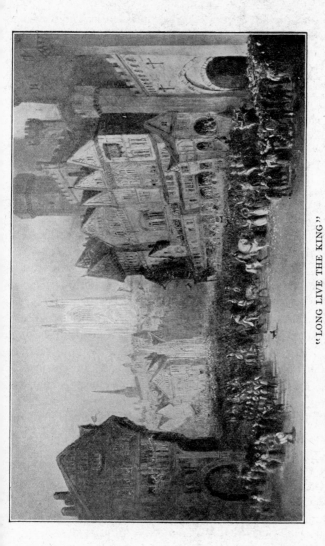

"LONG LIVE THE KING"

Chaucer witnessed the entrance into London of the unfortunate Richard II, soon to be deposed, in company with Bolingbroke, who became King Henry IV. (The painting is reproduced with the permission of the Corporation of Liverpool)

Chaucer's earliest writing can be discerned in *The Romance of the Rose*, a translation of a French allegory of the same name though the English version was in part made by other writers. The French influence is equally strong in *The Book of the Duchess*, which Chaucer wrote in 1369 in memory of the recently deceased Lady Blanche, the wife of his friend and patron, John of Gaunt. From this early period dates the most religious poem of Chaucer, known as the "A B C." It is a beautiful prayer to the Blessed Virgin, and derives its name from the fact that the stanzas follow the order of the alphabet, the first beginning with A, the second with B, the third with C, and so on.

Several of Chaucer's poems are chiefly Italian in their source and inspiration. The best of these, and one which from the modern point of view is more appealing than *The Canterbury Tales*, is *Troilus and Criseyde*, a love story of the Trojan war freely translated from the *Filostrato* of the Italian writer and scholar Giovanni Boccaccio.[1] Shakespeare took the same story for the subject of one of his plays. Chaucer in this case improved upon his model. He equals Boccaccio's skill in narrative and excels the Italian in character-drawing. *The Parliament of Fowls* is an example of what is called "occasional" poetry, that is, of verses written to commemorate some particular event. The particular event here was the marriage of King Richard II with Princess Anne of Bohemia in 1382, and Chaucer, following both French and Italian models, tells of the wooing of an eagle by three royal birds in presence of Dame Nature and the feathered folk assembled to keep St. Valentine's Day. Chaucer manifestly enjoyed writing this poem; it is fresh and vivid and seasoned with humor and satire.

[1] The evil that men do lives after them, and Boccaccio is mainly remembered in our day as the writer of some immodest stories. He has, however, a higher claim to immortality. From the point of view of style, he is one of the three supreme writers of Italian. He was a very learned man, and the first lecturer on Dante. And during his mature life he was deeply religious and had to be warned by his confessor not to carry exercises of mortification to excess.

It is mainly about himself that Chaucer writes in *The House of Fame*, a poem that reveals the English poet's indebtedness to Dante. Like every man who lives widely and thinks deeply, Chaucer was convinced that reputation is but an empty bubble and earthly fame only vanity of vanities. But that is no reason why the poet should not continue to write. No, Chaucer says in substance, it is nevertheless needful that I study humanity and faithfully paint mankind as I see it ; and what people shall think of me is no great matter :

> Suffyceth me, as I were deed,
> That no wyght have my name in honde.
> I woot my-self best how I stonde.
> For what I drye or what I thinke, —
> I wol my-selven al hit drynke,
> Certeyn, for the more part,
> As forferth as I can myn art.

The poet finds himself carried through the air by an eagle to the House of Fame, and, like Dante in *Paradise* looking down upon "the little threshing-floor" of the earth, from that exalted station he is able to see human affairs in their true perspective. The poem is unfinished.

The Latin influence predominates in Chaucer's *Legend of Good Women*, a work which prompted Tennyson to write one of his earlier and not unpleasing poems. In *Troilus and Criseyde* Chaucer was rather hard on the devout female sex : the story turns upon the unfaithfulness of a sweetheart, and Chaucer does not spare the fair and fickle lady. In *The Legend of Good Women* he makes ample amends by recounting nine stories (he planned for twenty, but did not complete the design) of women noted for constancy and fidelity. Some of his heroines were not in other respects ornaments of their sex, but even the glamorous Cleopatra and the languishing Dido served to point his moral and adorn his tale. The best thing in this poem is its prologue, a delightful description of Chaucer's dream. The stories are based on Virgil and Ovid.

The Canterbury Tales. To mention Chaucer is to think at once of *The Canterbury Tales*, another unfinished collection of stories in verse, on which the immortality of the poet rests. They represent his richest experience of life and his keenest skill in analyzing characters, and they are like nothing else in English Literature for their depictions of human customs and natural scenery. They remind us of an excellent picture in an even more excellent frame. The picture is the varied stories told by Chaucer's pilgrims — some noble, some vulgar, some dainty and delicate, some brusque and vigorous — and the frame is Chaucer's description of the pilgrims themselves and of the circumstances which bring them together. The frame is richly and convincingly English; the picture is almost entirely drawn from foreign literature, ancient and modern.

To understand the setting of this great poem we must recall something of the religious background of England in the fourteenth century. As we have seen, Catholicism was an essential part of the nation's life, and religious interests affected everybody deeply. In their religion people not only had a source of consolation in trouble and of strength at need and a means of giving expression to their deepest desires and their fondest hopes; they had also a living link which united them with departed saints and heroes of their own race and with noble men and women of other countries and times. They knew, as we know, that the great commandment of the law is to love God and to love one's neighbor, but they had a more broad-minded understanding of the word *neighbor* than is possessed by the modern world. To a man in Chaucer's day his neighbor meant not only the man in the next house or the next village, nor even only the man in Paris or Madrid or Rome; it meant likewise the man who had passed through the gates of death and who lived temporarily in Purgatory or eternally in Heaven. And hence the devotion to the Holy Souls, and hence the veneration of the Saints. People understood that love is stronger than death. They ceased to understand it only when the Reformers came and told them that there is no such state as Purgatory and that to continue to love their neighbor after death is to be guilty of superstition.

But Catholicism was still the religion of the people of England in Chaucer's day, and it was not yet considered a crime to pray for the dead or to invoke the intercession of the blessed.

CANTERBURY CATHEDRAL

So men and women, besides praying to God, prayed to the saints and cherished their relics and adorned their shrines. And to the shrines of certain saints they often went in pilgrimage to do reverence to the places where great Englishmen had lived and to ask the blessing of God and of His holy ones upon their works and their lives. One such shrine, the most famous in all England, was in the city of Canterbury near the south coast, where St. Thomas Becket had been archbishop and where, in one of the chapels of the magnificent cathedral, he had been murdered at the instigation of King Henry II. If we were in Canterbury this very day we could see a little square hole in the floor where a bit of the pavement, stained with the martyr's blood, had been cut out and carried to Rome. And we could see where the great shrine of the saint once stood, and the marble steps worn hollow by the passing of numberless pilgrims through the centuries. In the sixteenth century, King Henry VIII, after he had renounced his allegiance to the pope, broke up that shrine and robbed it of the priceless ornaments of gold and silver and jewels with which it was adorned.

It is a pilgrimage to the shrine of St. Thomas Becket which Chaucer describes in *The Canterbury Tales*.[1] A company of pilgrims gather in the Tabard Inn near London Bridge to set out through Dartford and Rochester to the ancient walled city of Canterbury. And they agree to tell one another stories on the way. Chaucer recounts some twenty-four of the stories so narrated, all of them but two in verse. The stories are as varied as the tellers; but the finest story of all, though it is much more than a story, is the "Prologue," wherein the poet introduces the pilgrims and in a few clever touches makes them live for all time. A Crusader is there, a man who had seen service overseas and who had tilted in tournaments and bled upon fields of battle, "a verray parfit gentil knight"; a Lawyer, with the professional manner of the man of law, "discret he was and of gret reverence"; a Friar, fat and worldly, as some friars through too much prosperity had in fact become, who, "in stede of weping and preyeres," encouraged men to "yeve silver to the povre freres"; a "Clerk of Oxenford," a dreamer and student who spent what little money he had on books,

---

[1] It has been suggested by a recent writer that Chaucer's sense of religious propriety prevented him from finishing *The Canterbury Tales*. "To him and the men of his time there was something awful and impressive about the shrine of St. Thomas; he could not treat it in a jesting way, and he must have felt that it would be incongruous suddenly to adopt a profoundly devotional tone; it would have suited ill with the bulk of his work; it would have suited ill with the temper of mind in which he wrote the series." — FRANCIS WATT, *Canterbury Pilgrims and their Ways*, p. 81

FROM WILLIAM BLAKE'S "CANTERBURY PILGRIMS"

Among the characters shown in the engraving are the Host, the Pardoner, the Monk, the Friar, the Prioress, and the Knight versed in "Aristotle and his philosophye"; a country squire, or "Frankeleyn," with red face and white beard, in whose house it snowed of "mete and drinke"; a Prioress, or superior of a convent of nuns, Madame Eglantine by name, dainty and ladylike and devout; the Wife of Bath, a coarse, vulgar woman of the middle class; a sailor from Dartmouth with a mighty thirst and a ready hand on his dagger; the knight's gaily attired son; a saintly parish priest; a scoundrelly hypocrite of a "Pardoner"; a merchant with a forked beard; a Doctor who maintained that "gold in phisik is a cordial"; and many more. Here are rich and poor, saints and sinners, the learned and the ignorant, the wise and the otherwise, all united in a profession of faith. Most of them take their religion seriously; few of them take it sadly. Their general attitude resembles that of the Italian peasant woman who, rebuked by a prim American tourist for laughing in church, quietly put the question "But should not a child be at home in her Father's house?"

The stories told by the pilgrims vary in literary excellence and human appeal from the Oxford scholar's simple and pathetic tale of the patient Griselda — culled from Chaucer's reading of Petrarca — to the holy priest's very holy but deadly dull prose sermon on the seven deadly sins. Several of them are fables from the French or tales told in the French manner. The Second Nun appropriately recounts the legend of St. Cecilia; the worldly Monk unfolds several anecdotes of misfortune; and the Wife of Bath, not at all a fairylike individual, tells a fairy tale. The Doctor repeats the story of the Roman girl Virginia, and the Lawyer the Catholic legend of Constance. Chaucer himself, when called on by the host to contribute to the entertainment, begins in verse with a burlesque on the Romances, a form of literature he disliked, and finishes in prose with a story celebrating the virtues of a loyal wife.

Chaucer's Minor Works. Besides two stories in *The Canterbury Tales*, Chaucer wrote two works in prose, neither of great importance. The first was a translation of Boethius's ever-popular meditation, *The Consolations of Philosophy*; the other, a simple treatise on the Astrolabe,[1] written for the enlightenment of Lewis, his "litel sone." In verse he wrote several shorter pieces, including the "Balade de Bon Conseyl" and "Lak of Stedfastnesse"; but the one poem of Chaucer's which even a hard-headed business man would admit to be worth the writing was a "Complaint to his Empty Purse." It was this poem, whimsically setting forth the poet's inability to keep his purse properly filled, that induced the new king, Henry IV, to restore and increase Chaucer's pension. An interesting trifle is the bit of verse addressed to Adam, his copyist, complaining good-naturedly of the secretarial shortcomings of a man otherwise unknown to fame. Thus, by being careless in his work, Adam has secured immortality! Many poems were once attributed to Chaucer which recent scholarship has pronounced spurious.

How to Read Chaucer. It will be seen, even from the few quotations in this chapter, that Chaucer's writing looks like English very badly spelled. So, for that matter, does Shakespeare's in the First Folio. So far as Chaucer is concerned we may profitably ignore his spelling. Indeed, though the advice may seem ridiculous at first, the best plan is to read him not with the eye but with the ear: his poetry does not sound as unfamiliar as it looks. Some words which we pronounce in one syllable Chaucer pronounced in two, like *swete*, "sweet"; and his manner of accenting syllables does not always conform to ours. But read properly, his lines make music. Then there are some words of French origin which have not continued in use and a fair number of Middle English words no longer employed. The notes in any good edition of the poems will solve such difficulties. There is, too, the alternative of reading Chaucer in modern prose or verse; but real lovers of

---

[1] An instrument which, in Chaucer's time, served somewhat the same purpose as the modern sextant.

Chaucer scorn such a procedure. Concerning such "translations" Walter Savage Landor wrote:

> Pardon me if I say I would rather see Chaucer quite alone, in the dew of his sunny morning, than with twenty clever gentlefolks about him, arranging his shoestrings and buttoning his doublet. I like even his language. I will have no hand in breaking his dun but rich-painted glass, to put in (if clearer) much thinner panes.

A little time and effort spent in learning how to read Chaucer will result in a power that satisfies and in the enjoyment of real literature at first hand. Here, as Dryden said, "is God's plenty."

THE SCHOOL OF CHAUCER

The word *school* is used in several widely different senses. Thus we speak of a parochial school, of the Lake School in English poetry, and of a school of fishes; and when we speak of poets and fishes belonging to a school we do not mean that they say "Good morning, teacher" and study their lessons and run out to play when the bell rings for recess. A school of poetry no more means an institution of formal instruction than the Apostolic College or the College of Cardinals means a group of buildings, diffident professors, self-possessed students, an alumni organization, and a football team. A school in literature means simply the influence which writers and books exert on other writers and books. So when we speak of the School of Chaucer we do not imply that Chaucer was a schoolmaster and Lydgate and Occleve sat at his feet and learned wisdom, but we merely indicate the fact that some of his contemporaries and successors paid him the tribute of their imitation. In other words, Chaucer, even without knowing that he did so, established a fashion in literature, and other writers tried to do in their small way what he had done in his great way.

John Gower (1330?–1408). The "moral Gower," as Chaucer called him, was a courtier, a lawyer, and a man of considerable wealth who "wrote in three languages with equal facility and equal mediocrity."[1] In French he wrote *Speculum Meditantis*, that is, a "mirror" of meditation on sin and human life; in Latin, *Vox Clamantis*, or "Voice of One Crying," a poem dealing with the rebellion of Wat Tyler and other disturbing events in the reign of King Richard II; and in English *Confessio Amantis*, or "The Lover's Confession," wherein a young man seeks advice of Genius, a priest of Venus, and the confessor discourses on the seven capital sins and relates some hundred stories as illustrations. Several of the stories are interesting, but rather lengthy for confessional material. As a young man Gower had written some French poems which discerning critics esteem more highly than his three longer works.

James Russell Lowell voiced the opinion of many readers who have begun but have not finished Gower's poems: "Gower has positively raised tediousness to the precision of a science, he has made dulness an heirloom for the student of our literary history."[2] But Gower suffers most because he is inevitably compared with his great contemporary, Chaucer: so doth the greater glory dim the less. Gower was no master mind, but neither was he a driveling idiot; he had considerable learning, much industry, and a real gift for writing verse. His tomb in Southwark Cathedral in London — where Dyer, Fletcher, Massinger, and Shakespeare's brother Edmund were also buried — serves to recall that Gower was a liberal contributor to the fund for repairing that church, a fact which inspired a roguish wit to compose an epitaph which does *not* appear on the poet's tomb:

> This church was rebuilt by John Gower, the rhymer,
> Who in Richard's gay court was a fortunate climber;
> Should any one start, 'tis but right he should know it,
> Our wight was a lawyer as well as a poet.

[1] George Moore, Preface to *The Coming of Gabrielle*.
[2] Essay on Chaucer, in *Literary Essays*, Vol. III, p. 329.

Lydgate and Occleve. An admirer and conscious imitator of Chaucer, John Lydgate (1370?–1450?), a Benedictine monk, completed the Knight's story in *The Canterbury Tales* by writing *The Story of Thebes*, and in *The Fall of Princes* he dilated on the misfortunes of illustrious men recounted by Chaucer's Monk. This lengthy series of sad tales, told in nine books of seven-line stanzas, is about the best thing that Lydgate did. Besides Chaucer he had Boccaccio as his model. Another very long poem of his is the *Troy Book*, an adaptation of Guido delle Colonne's thirteenth-century Latin *History of Troy*. In quantity (two hundred and fifty works bear his name) Lydgate is impressive; in quality he is ordinary and commonplace. Thomas Occleve (1370?–1450?), if his own account may be believed, led a wild life as a young man and confessed his failings and professed his repentance in "La Male Regle"; and in his *Regiment of Princes* he gave abundant good advice to the Prince of Wales, the Prince Hal of Shakespeare, who seems to have needed it and heeded it. The *Regiment*, or rules for right living, was based on a Latin work by Egidic de Colonna, a disciple of St. Thomas Aquinas. As a moralist Occleve commands respect, but as a poet he does not rank high.

Scottish Writers. The School of Chaucer flourished in Scotland, where King James I (1394–1437) imitated the Chaucerian versification and borrowed numerous Chaucerian phrases in his *Kingis Quair*, or King's Book, an allegory based upon his wooing and winning of Lady Jane Beaufort. He was happier as a poet than as a king. Robert Henryson (1425?–1500?), a Glasgow University man, continued the story of Chaucer's Trojan heroine in *The Testament of Cresseid* and imitated the Chaucerian stanza form in *Orpheus and Eurydice*. He is less of a poet and more of a journalist than his master, though his poetic gifts are more evident in "Robene and Makyne," the first English pastoral poem, and in his brisk and clever *Fables* from Æsop.

William Dunbar (1460?–1525?) was a priest-poet, sometimes called the Chaucer of Scotland; his is the leading name in Scottish Literature until the advent of Robert Burns. Refinement is not one of his conspicuous virtues, but he reveals power and skill and mother wit in his satirical allegory, *The Dance of the Seven Deadly Sins*. The priestly side of him comes to the fore in *The Golden Targe*, a poem based on the eternal human conflict between love and reason; and the poet prevails in *The Thistle and the Rose*, celebrating the marriage of James IV of Scotland with Princess Margaret of England. Dunbar's constant desire, never gratified, was to become the pastor of "a wee country kirk covered with heather." He had been a Franciscan novice in youth; but, as it seems, having abandoned voluntary poverty, he was destined to taste involuntary poverty for the rest of his life. Another priest, and a learned man, who eventually became Bishop of Dunkeld, was Gawin Douglas (1474–1522). He imitated Chaucer in two allegories, *The Palace of Honour* and *King Hart*, bearing upon the pursuit of pleasure and ultimate repentance; and he translated Virgil's *Æneid* and did it more than passing well, even though he speaks of "the nuns of Bacchus" and has the Sibyl advise Æneas to recite the Rosary. Douglas was a Renaissance Humanist born out of due season.

Hawes and Skelton. University honors are here evenly divided, for Stephen Hawes (1483?–1523?) was an Oxford man, and John Skelton (1460?–1529) a Cambridge scholar. Though their names are conveniently bracketed, Hawes and Skelton were as different as two poets could be. Hawes is a link in English Literature between Chaucer and Spenser; he favored the allegory of an elder day and delighted in presenting the Trivium and Quadrivium[1] of the medieval universities in the guise of fair ladies who might have stepped out of some old

---

[1] The Trivium consisted of grammar, logic, and rhetoric; the Quadrivium of arithmetic, music, geometry, and astronomy. These were the "three" and "four" groups of liberal studies.

metrical romance. Skelton, though on occasion he could imitate Chaucer too, was much more himself when writing coarse
and biting satires on men and institutions. And, rather oddly,
Hawes, who had the poet's soul, was less successful in the
mechanics of verse-making than Skelton, who was a sharp and
destructive critic. It has been said that Hawes "was held by
the ears when he was dipped in Helicon." [1] Hawes is best remembered for his *Pastime of Pleasure*, the story, involved in
form and moral in purpose, of the "Great Love and the Beautiful Maiden"; Skelton, for his fierce satire on the clergy, *Colin
Clout*, and his ungracious attack on Cardinal Wolsey, who had
once befriended him.

THE BALLADS

The fifteenth century was the golden age of popular songs or
ballads, many of which came from earlier ages. The ballads
sprang not from the monastery, the court, or the university,
but from the fireside, the battlefield, and the glen. They were
simple lays of simple folk, passed on in speech from generation
to generation, and they dwelt, often with real poetic beauty,
on simple themes. Many of them were written down much
later and collected by men like Bishop Percy,[2] who published

[1] Henry Morley.

[2] Percy was not yet a bishop, and in his editing of the ballads showed more
enthusiasm than scholarship; but, as events proved, in his case enthusiasm
was of more importance than scholarship. His collection of the old songs fired
poetic imaginations and profoundly affected subsequent English Literature.
Wordsworth hardly exaggerated when he wrote, "I do not think that there is
an able writer in verse of the present day who would not be proud to acknowledge his obligations to the *Reliques*" (Essay supplementary to the Preface of
the *Lyrical Ballads*). There had been collectors and admirers of the ballads
before Percy, notably John Selden and that versatile Samuel Pepys, John
Dryden and Joseph Addison, and especially Allan Ramsay. Walter Scott's
Minstrelsy of the Scottish Border has historical as well as personal importance.
The most complete and scholarly collection is *The English and Scottish Popular
Ballads*, the work of two American university men, Francis J. Child and George
L. Kittredge.

his *Reliques of Ancient English Poetry* in 1765. We now have a number of printed collections of the ballads and several books explaining their literary characteristics.

The Ballad Form. A ballad consists of any number of stanzas, and the stanzas usually take this form:

> The king sits in Dumferline town,
>   Drinking the blood-red wine;
> "Oh where will I get a good sailor
>   To sail this ship of mine?"

There are four lines, of which the second and fourth rime; the first and third lines have four accents and the second and fourth lines three. This is the typical ballad stanza, though in instances there are departures from it in placing the accents and in the number of syllables. That the ballads were transmitted orally and not by writing is shown in the existence of verses which are irregular to the eye but not to the ear, and by the use of the chorus, or refrain, a sort of first-aid device for the comfort of memory-fagged minstrels. The refrain further served to enable the listeners to join in the singing and so enjoy the occasion all the more. It is human nature to esteem more highly a game or an entertainment or other enterprise in which we individually take part.

Ballad Subjects. What were the themes of the ballad singers? Love, of course, in which the minstrel always finds material ready to hand and his audience a stimulus to long thoughts of the future and the past; and as hatred is the reverse side of the shield of love, so the ballads dealt too with family quarrels and tribal feuds. Representative ballads of this class are "Earl Crawford," "Fair Annie," and "Willie's Lady." And the singers sang of other kinds of fighting, fighting done for love of country and of glory, and so it is that some of the ballads are battle songs running red with blood. Such are "Flodden Field," "The Battle of Otterburn," and "The Hunting of the Cheviot," also known as "Chevy Chase."

Then, as children of all ages like to shudder and thrill over stories of ghosts and fairies and witches and mysterious happenings, the simple audiences that listened to the wandering bard enjoyed such ballads as "Lady Margaret," "Allison Gross," and "Sweet William's Ghost." There were ballads too, though not many, of sailors and the sea, the best known of which is "Sir Patrick Spens." Finally, the ballads commemorated the stirring lives and noble deeds of outlaws and robbers, intent on that "something good in the worst of us," which genuine optimists like St. Francis de Sales and the old ballad singers knew how to bring out. A whole cycle of such songs revolve round the personality of Robin Hood, the Locksley of Scott's *Ivanhoe*, who, tradition says, lived in Sherwood Forest with his merry men in suits of Lincoln green and robbed the wealthy and bestowed alms on the poor.

Influence of the Ballads. Now and then in the following pages we shall have occasion to note the influence of the ballads on writers in the nineteenth and twentieth centuries. In form and in spirit that influence was considerable. The ballad stanza was adopted by many poets, and writers weary of the complexity and artificiality of modern life have sought freedom by recapturing the primitive mood and the simple outlook of the early bards. Examples of the influence of the old ballads on more recent poetry may be found in Aytoun's *Lays of the Scottish Cavaliers*, Coleridge's "Rime of the Ancient Mariner," Keats's "La Belle Dame sans Merci," Rossetti's "King's Tragedy," Browning's "Hervé Riel," Tennyson's "Revenge," Longfellow's "Wreck of the Hesperus," Wilde's "Ballad of Reading Gaol," and Chesterton's "Ballad of the White Horse." [1]

[1] It may not be out of the way to guard against the possible confusion of the English ballad with the French *ballade*, a very different poetic form, consisting of three eight-line stanzas and an *envoi*, or conclusion, of four lines. The *ballade* was favored by that diverting scholar, thief, and poet, François Villon, and has been widely imitated in English Literature from the days of John Gower down to our own times.

CHAPTER VI

THE REVIVAL OF LEARNING

THE RENAISSANCE

Human thought has its tides which ebb and flow as the tides of the sea. A glance back along the history of European Literature reveals now a period of advancement, of development, of abounding energy, and now a period of reaction, of timidity, of what is sometimes called literary decadence. One of the most interesting of the periods of advancement, an era when the tide of life swept riotously across the sands of time, occurred in the fifteenth century in Italy and is known as the Renaissance, or New Birth. It is also known as the Revival of Learning, for that was the form which the Renaissance mainly assumed: men developed a new interest in literature, especially in the literature of Greece, and since one effect of the study of great books is to give the mind added clearness of vision the scholars of the Renaissance began to look upon human life and human institutions with renewed interest and discernment. Their enthusiasm spread, and presently arose artists who greatly desired to create beautiful things; much of their work we can still see in the architecture and the sculpture and especially in the great paintings of the period. Michelangelo and Raphael and Leonardo da Vinci are products of the Renaissance; so is the world-renowned Vatican Library, founded by Pope Nicholas V and enlarged and enriched by his successors, especially by Pope Leo X, who might be called the Pope of the Renaissance. The center of the movement, however, was not Rome but Florence, where, under the rule of the Medici family, architects builded and poets sang and painters flung master-

THE POPE OF THE RENAISSANCE

Giovanni dei Medici, afterwards Pope Leo X, occupies a prominent place in the
Revival of Learning. This portrait by Raphael is in the Pitti Palace, Florence

pieces on palace walls and deep-browed scholars delved into the literature of the past.

The Renaissance may be traced to many causes, including the encouragement given to learning by some of the popes and by influential families like the Medici of Florence. The fall of the Eastern Empire before the Turks in 1453 drove many

SAVONAROLA DECLINING HONORS

This painting by Bargellini is in the Gallery of Modern Art, Rome

learned men into Italy, carrying with them priceless manuscripts and works of art. The refugees were received with honor and became teachers and inspirers of Western Europe. It so happened that just then Italy was enjoying comparative prosperity and peace, and so men found time to give themselves to study and to writing. The leading scholars and writers were called Humanists, and the new interest in literature was known as Humanism.

Like every other great movement in human thought, the Renaissance had some unfortunate consequences. Its devotion to pagan literature brought about in some quarters a return to pagan standards of living and an admiration of pagan ideals, and that was not good for the cause of the Catholic religion and even paved the way for the revolt against the authority of the Church known as the Reformation. It was against these evil effects of the Renaissance that Savonarola and St. Philip Neri so vigorously protested and that eventually the Council of Trent was compelled to legislate. But though the Renaissance did not lead men to God along the path of holiness, it opened men's eyes to that beauty in life and art which is a reflection of the Eternal Beauty and urged them on in the pursuit of that wisdom which is the echo of the Eternal Truth.

The Revival of Learning spread from Italy into other countries of Europe, particularly into Germany and Holland and somewhat later into England. While Italy was making rapid strides in literature and art, England, torn by the civil Wars of the Roses (a series of conflicts not nearly so picturesque as their name would imply), was lagging behind in culture and scholarship. But when Henry VII — the Earl of Richmond in Shakespeare's *King Richard III* — came to the throne peace was established, a fresh interest was taken in the things of the mind, and there set in a flood tide of learning and literature which reached the high-water mark in the days of Shakespeare and Bacon. Even in the dark days of the civil wars the devout King Henry VI had founded colleges at Eton and Cambridge and in other ways labored for the spread of learning, and his uncle the Duke of Gloucester, "the good Duke Humphrey" of popular tradition, had collected books and tried to foster scholarship; and later the influence of the Italian Humanists profoundly affected the English universities. Englishmen went to Italy to study, Italian scholars came to England to teach, and English writers busied themselves in translating the ancient classics and in imitating the modern Italian writers. Cultural influences flowed in likewise from France; from Spain

MICHELANGELO WORKING ON HIS STATUE OF MOSES

It is said that when the task was finished the sculptor struck the marble with his chisel, crying "Speak!" Originally intended for the tomb of Pope Julius II, the statue now stands in the Church of St. Peter in Chains, Rome

came the Renaissance educator Luis Vives to live in London and lecture at Oxford; and Erasmus, the eminent Dutch scholar and a leading Humanist, studied at Oxford and taught at Cambridge and, through his friendship with the Blessed Thomas More and other learned Englishmen, brought England into vital touch with the Revival of Learning. And thus it was that England, though a full century behind the rest of Europe in the procession of scholarship, at length shared in the intellectual fruits of the Renaissance and began to contribute heavily to the literature of the world.

HOLBEIN'S PORTRAIT OF ERASMUS

William Caxton (1422?-1491). One of the leading factors in the spread of the Revival of Learning and a thing which, as has been happily said, gave wings to literature was the invention of printing from movable type. In the days when books could be multiplied only by the tedious labor of copyists, libraries were necessarily small and opportunities for learning limited; but when it became possible to duplicate books by the thousand, more men acquired the reading habit and could devote themselves to study with less difficulty and expense. And so it is that in the history of English Literature it is fitting to commemorate William Caxton. A great author he certainly was not; a Renaissance Humanist he certainly was not; he was eminent not in what he did but in what he made it possible for other men to do. Caxton was a printer and publisher and a lover of good books; and his importance lies in the fact that by means of the books which he printed and published European Literature flowed freely into England, and English writers found a medium of expression.

A native of Kent, young Caxton was apprenticed to a London merchant, and in 1441 crossed over to Bruges, the city of the celebrated belfry, and successfully established him-
self in business. But he was
not content to spend his
life measuring cloth and
counting money. His spare
time he devoted to reading
and then to translating.
One of his translations, that
of Raoul Lefèvre's *Collection of the Histories of Troy*,
was the first book printed
in English — at Bruges in
1474. He now took up
printing on his own account
and published a translation
of a moral and political al-

WILLIAM CAXTON

legory, *The Game and Play of Chess*. He returned to England and set up a printing establishment in Westminster in
1476; and there, for the rest of his life, he gave himself to
the congenial task of translating, editing, and publishing
books. From his press in 1477 came the first book ever
printed in England, Earl Rivers's *Dictes and Sayings of the
Philosophers*. It was followed by numerous other publications, including Malory's *Morte d'Arthur*, Chaucer's *Canterbury Tales*, Gower's *Confessio Amantis*, and a translation of
the allegory *The Pilgrimage of Man*, which is the source of
Bunyan's *Pilgrim's Progress*. In fourteen years he printed

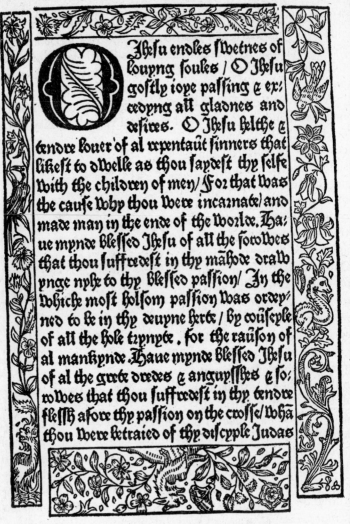

Ihesu endles swetnes of louyng soules / O Ihesu gostly ioye passing & excedyng all gladnes and desires. O Ihesu helthe & tendre louer of al repentaut sinners that likest to dwelle as thou saydest thy selfe with the children of men / For that was the cause why thou were incarnate / and made man in the ende of the worlde. Haue mynde blessed Ihesu of all the sorowes that thou suffredest in thy manhode drawynge nyhe to thy blessed passion / In the whiche most holsom passion was ordeyned to be in thy deuyne herte / by couseyle of all the hole trynyte. for the rauson of al mankynde. Haue mynde blessed Ihesu of al the grete dredes & anguysshes & sorowes that thou suffredest in thy tendre flessh afore thy passion on the crosse / whan thou were betraied of thy discyple Judas

A SPECIMEN OF CAXTON'S PRINTING

A page from the *Fifteen Oes and other Prayers*, printed in 1491. (By courtesy of the British Museum)

Thus ende I this book whyche I haue translated after myn Auctor as nyghe as god hath gyuen me connyng to whom be gyuen the laude and preysyng / And for as moche as in the wrytyng of the same my penne is worn/myn hande wery and not stedfast myn eyen dimmed with ouermoche lokyng on the whit paper / and my corage not so prone and redy to laboure as hit hath ben / and that age crepeth on me daytly and febleth all the bodye/and also be cause I haue promysed to dyuerce gentilmen and to my frendes to adresse to hem as hastely as I myght this sayd book / Therfore I haue practysed and lerned at my grete charge and dispense to ordeyne this said book in prynte after the maner and forme as ye may here see / and is not wreton with penne and ynke as other bokes ben / to thende that euery man may haue them attones / ffor all the bokes of this storye na= med the recule of the historyes of troyes thus enpryntid as ye here see were begonne in oon day / and also fynys= shid in oon day / whiche book I haue presented to my sayd redoubtid lady as afore is sayd. And she hath wel acceptid hit / and largely rewarded me/ wherfore I beseche almyghty god to rewarde her euerlastyng blisse after this lyf. Prayng her said grace and all them that shall rede this book not to desdaigne the symple and rude werke. nether to replye agaynst the sayeng of the ma= tres towchyd in this book / thauwh hyt accorde not vn= to the translacon of other whiche haue wreton hit / ffor dyuerce men haue made dyuerce bookes / whiche in all poyntes acorde not as Dictes. Dares. and Homerus ffor dictes and homerus as grekes sayn and wryten fauo=

THE FIRST BOOK PRINTED IN ENGLISH

A page from the *Recuyell of the Historyes of Troye*, or *Collection of the Histories of Troy*. (By courtesy of the British Museum) upwards of one hundred books, most of them big ones. By making and keeping rules for the guidance of his compositors he did much to establish standards in English grammar and spelling. A good book handsomely printed is doubly a work of art, and the production and multiplication of such books was the life work of such men as Aldus Manutius in Venice, the four Estiennes in Paris, and Caxton in London.

A PRINTING SHOP FOUR HUNDRED YEARS AGO

Caxton found numerous imitators. By the beginning of the sixteenth century there were more than one thousand printers in England and some thirty thousand editions of books. "Assuming," says Dr. Preserved Smith, "that the editions were small, averaging 300 copies, there would have been in England by 1500 about 9,000,000 books. . . . In a few years, the price of books sank to one-eighth of what it had been before. 'The gentle reader' had started on his career."[1]

[1] *The Age of the Reformation*, p. 9.

The Blessed Thomas More (1478–1535). The Church in raising Sir Thomas More to her altars conferred the knighthood of Christ upon the most prominent of all the English Humanists. Indeed, the sage of Chelsea was a many-sided man. More was "a martyr and a saint — canonized not only by his Church, but by all who love a white-souled courage."[1] More was a model family man and a successful statesman, a lover of books and a social celebrity, a grave scholar and a maker of jests, a lawyer and a friend to truth, a favorite of his king and a defender of the faith.

We are here concerned with More's place in the history of English Literature. He has been accorded very high rank. Samuel Johnson, in the "History of the English Language" prefixed to his celebrated Dictionary, devotes nearly one third of his space to a consideration of More, whose "works were considered as models of pure and elegant style." Professor Fletcher points out that as a stylist More was far in advance of his generation : "For nearly a hundred years afterwards we do not meet with such a vigorous, perspicacious, and above all such an evidently thoughtful style."[2] " Elizabethan prose is tawdry and mannered compared with his," a distinguished Glasgow University man[3] insists; "at his death Chaucer's thread is dropped, which none picked up till Clarendon and Dryden. With his colloquial, well-bred, unaffected ease he is the ancestor of Swift." Sir James Mackintosh styles him the father of English prose in recognition of the style, at once dignified and sprightly, of More's English writings.

These fall into two divisions: his *History of King Richard III* and his controversial works. The former as history is misleading, but as literature it has been proclaimed by Hallam "the first example of good English language." It inspired one of the most popular of Shakespeare's plays and thus settled for

---

[1] Bliss Perry, *The Praise of Folly and Other Papers*, p. 2.
[2] *The Development of English Prose*, p. 7.
[3] J. S. Phillimore, *Dublin Review*, July, 1913.

all time the picture of Richard III as a vile and cold-blooded villain, deformed alike in body and in mind. As a matter of fact, Richard was not so bad as More and Holinshed and Shakespeare have painted him. More was misled in his estimate of the monarch through his early association with Cardinal Morton, a friend of Henry VII, Richard's conqueror and successor. The best of More's controversial writings is *The Apology of Sir Thomas More*, a piece of real literature and the eloquent outpouring of a noble soul. In other tracts he disputes with Tyndale and other opponents of the Catholic position and reveals himself as a vigorous fighter and a master of argumentation.

But an odd thing about the Blessed Thomas More is this: the master work of this thoroughly English Englishman is a contribution to world literature written in the Latin tongue and published in Louvain in 1516, and not translated into English until Ralph Robinson brought out an edition of it in 1551. This is the famous *Utopia*, which has put the adjective *utopian* into every European language, a book which describes an imaginary commonwealth with such an air of reality that some zealous souls contemplated sending missionaries to the land of Utopia, deeming it a pity that such naturally good people as the Utopians should be denied the light and consolation of the Catholic faith. The *Utopia* of More belongs to a class of writings fathered by Plato in the *Republic*; other notable books of the kind are Bacon's *New Atlantis*, Campanella's *City of the Sun*, Hobbes's *Leviathan*, Swift's *Gulliver's Travels*, and Lytton's *Coming Race*. The list of such books in European Literature is a lengthy one. In excellence and variety and literary art More's is second only to Plato's, and in originality and wit and delicate irony it surpasses the *Republic*. And — this is surely a crucial test of genuine literature — More is surprisingly modern. "He sketched an ideal, or rather perhaps a fanciful social system, with something of the ingenuity of Mr. H. G. Wells, but essentially with much more than the flippancy attributed to Mr. Bernard Shaw." [1] It is a little amazing for a modern reader to find in the *Utopia* sane and satirical discussions of such topics as eugenics, the humane treatment of criminals, religious toleration, hospital equipment, secret diplomacy, and the concentration of wealth.

MORE'S DAUGHTER, MARGARET ROPER, VISITS HER FATHER IN THE TOWER

This painting by Herbert is reproduced by courtesy of the Grosvenor Museum, Chester, England

More also wrote considerable Latin verse, but the *Utopia* was the first notable contribution made by an Englishman to the literature of the European Tradition.

The Blessed Thomas More was born in Cheapside, London, and as a boy lived in the household of Cardinal Morton. At Oxford, whither he went in 1492 (a date not difficult to remember), he studied Greek and came under the influence of the Renaissance spirit. Then he studied law, and became suc-

[1] G. K. Chesterton, *A Short History of England*, p. 157.

cessively undersheriff of London, a member of Parliament, Treasurer of the Exchequer, and, in 1529, Lord Chancellor of England. He was a close friend of King Henry VIII until he refused to sanction that monarch's separation from the Roman communion. He was twice married, and lived happily at Chelsea on the Thames, now in the heart of London, where he entertained many of his Humanist friends, especially Erasmus, who wrote of him as follows:

More hath built near London upon the Thames side a commodious house, neither mean nor subject to envy, yet magnificent enough; there he converseth with his family, his wife, his son, and daughter-in-law, his three daughters and their husbands, with eleven grandchildren. There is not any man so loving to his children as he; and he loveth his old wife as well as if she were a young maid; and such is the excellency of his temper that whatsoever happeneth that could not be helped, he loveth it as if nothing could happen more happily.

From this happy and successful life More went as prisoner to the grim Tower of London in 1534, and the next year mounted the scaffold on Tower Hill. Like Sir Walter Raleigh, who was destined to meet the same fate some years later, More jested even in the face of death. "Help me up," he said smilingly to his guards at the foot of the rickety steps. "Coming down I shall have to shift for myself." He embraced the headsman; and then, before the fatal stroke fell, he pulled his long white beard from out the path of the ax. "This," he murmured, "hath done no treason." Truly, as Chesterton has said, More "was above all things a Humanist, and a very human one."

The Revival of Learning Impeded. Since More was the leading representative of the Revival of Learning in England, — one of the few Englishmen, in fact, who could meet the Humanists of Italy on terms of equality, — it is evident that his execution for high treason, while conceivably beneficial to the policies of King Henry VIII, was not beneficial to literature. And the Englishman who had done most to introduce into English Literature the refined and civilizing influence of Italian poetry was also executed for high treason in the reign of the same monarch. That man was Henry Howard, Earl of Surrey. Bishop Fisher, the Humanist chancellor of the University of Cambridge, met the same fate. It is a fact worthy of remark that King Henry VIII, a ruler celebrated or notorious for many things, — for writing a book against Luther, for the number of his wives, for his political insight, for his spiritual scruples, for his adipose tissue, — should be remembered likewise for having chopped off the heads of More, Fisher, and Surrey, three of the most enlightened and accomplished scholars in the kingdom.

Considered in itself, the thing may be only a matter of one king and three heads; but the tragedy of More, Fisher, and Surrey is a symptom of a social disease which ravaged England for half a century and more, and which ever since has returned periodically like the pestilence or the influenza. That disease was a rebellion against authority in religion. With delicious irony it is called the Reformation; and from rebellion against authority in religion it spread to rebellion against authority in other departments of life. When the English nation broke away from the Catholic Church, it cut itself off likewise from the European Tradition in literature and from the fullness of the spirit of the Renaissance. "Had not Europe shared one mind and heart, until both mind and heart began to break into fragments a little before Shakespeare's birth?"[1]

In literature, as in religion, it was impossible to make the separation complete, for the literature of Europe, like the religion of Rome, was something too vast and too influential and too pervasive to be altogether abandoned and ignored; but a manifest result of the Reformation in England was the impeding of the cultural influences which had begun to flow into English Literature from the Catholic countries of Europe. Had there been no interruption in the course of the Revival of

[1] W. B. Yeats, *Autobiographies*, p. 237.

Learning, had there been no profitless blasts of religious controversy and no chopping off of learned heads, England would have secured her due share in the fruits of the Renaissance and English Literature would have developed more rapidly and harmoniously. Great as English Literature is, it would be greater still had there been no such king as Henry VIII and no such incident as the Protestant rebellion.

The Coming of the Sonnet. Fortunately for English Literature the poetic form known as the sonnet had been introduced before the Reformers had established their embargo upon ideas brought from afar. It is a species of poetry that has flourished mightily in English soil, the key whereby some of the greatest English poets, including Shakespeare, Milton, Wordsworth, and Keats, have unlocked their hearts. Theodore Watts-Dunton, himself a poet and the friend of a greater poet, Swinburne, has happily described the sonnet :

> A sonnet is a wave of melody :
> From heaving waters of the impassioned soul
> A billow of tidal music one and whole
> Flows, in the "octave"; then, returning free,
> Its ebbing surges in the "sestet" roll
> Back to the depths of Life's tumultuous sea.

The sonnet originated in Italy, and the first poet of importance to employ it was a monk, Fra Guittone of Arezzo, who died toward the end of the thirteenth century. It was perfected by numerous Italian poets, especially by Dante, by his friend Guido Cavalcante, and by Petrarca. To Sir Thomas Wyatt (1503-1542) is due the honor of bringing the sonnet into English Literature. With Wyatt is rightly associated the name of Henry Howard, Earl of Surrey (1518-1547), his friend and disciple. The English sonnets of Wyatt and Surrey were first published, ten years after Surrey's execution, in Richard Tottel's *Miscellany*, the first collection of printed English poems. Both men were enthusiastic admirers of Petrarca, and their sonnets (in some instances translations from the great

Italian poet) brought the Petrarchan spirit into English Literature and opened a golden door to English poets.

Sir Thomas Wyatt was a native of Kent and a graduate of Cambridge, a courtier and an ambassador, who visited Italy in 1527 and ten years later was England's representative in Spain. He was imprisoned in the Tower of London in 1540, was tried for high treason, and narrowly escaped the fate of the Earl of Surrey. His acquittal gave him a two years' lease on life; he died of fever on his way to meet the Spanish ambassador. As a poet Wyatt was inferior to his friend Surrey, but to him belongs the fame of the pioneer. His poems reveal him as a man of character, even of piety, as an untiring experimenter in verse-forms, as a remarkable combination of the original thinker and the careful imitator of Italian models. It is just to place him among the makers of English Literature.

Wyatt was primarily a thinker and a courtier; the Earl of Surrey was mainly a poet and a soldier. His grandfather had fought and won at Flodden Field, and the young Howard carried on the family tradition by fighting against the Scots and the French. His father, the Duke of Norfolk, fell under the suspicion of Henry VIII, and Surrey was involved in the alleged conspiracy. The outcome was the execution of the brave and cultured poet on Tower Hill in 1547. As a master of the sonnet Surrey gleaned where Wyatt reaped. Less powerful than the older man and less original in thought, Surrey is the finer stylist and the more authentic poet. To his work at its best — much of it is not his best — Mrs. Browning, herself a poet of feeling and insight, paid ungrudging tribute: "His poetry makes the ear lean to it, it is so sweet and low." [1]

As Petrarca sang the praises of his Laura, so Surrey, adapting the sonnet form to English song, extolled the virtues of the "Fair Geraldine, bright object of his vow." Besides his sonnets, Surrey is to be remembered as the first English poet to employ that blank verse which eventually, in the hands of

[1] *The Book of the Poets*, p. 129.

Shakespeare and Milton, was to be accepted as the most characteristic of all English poetic forms. Surrey's blank verse, with much of the roughness and uncertainty of pioneer work, can be seen in his translation of the second and fourth books of Virgil's *Æneid*. Surrey was only twenty-nine years old when he went to his death. It is not improbable that his best work was still to be written and that the headsman of Henry VIII lopped off a blossoming branch from the tree of English poetry. Alexander Pope, in "Windsor Forest," supplies Surrey's epitaph :

> Matchless his pen, victorious was his lance,
> Bold in the lists, graceful in the dance.

Sir Philip Sidney (1554–1586). Changes which took place on the throne of England during the sixteenth century produced no corresponding changes in the development of literature. The obstruction of the Renaissance movement under Henry VIII continued under Edward VI, under Mary, and under Elizabeth, Edward's reign being too brief and Mary's being too troubled for the introduction of any fresh foreign influences. Under all the Tudors, but especially under Elizabeth, the effort was in the direction of intensive nationalism in politics, and that spirit could hardly be expected to foster the world view in literature. But the Humanistic tendency, though impeded, was not wholly crushed, and it asserted itself in the leading writers of the Elizabethan Age. Some of its most interesting characteristics may be traced in that gallant soldier and scholar and courtier, "the last knight of English chivalry," Sir Philip Sidney.

Sidney was not a great writer, but his influence on other writers was considerable, and his personality embodied some of the salient traits of the Renaissance spirit. In the course of his short life he enjoyed varied contacts. A Protestant and an Oxford man, he visited Paris, Vienna, Venice, Heidelberg, and Antwerp, and everywhere made the acquaintance of learned men and absorbed cultural ideas. European scholars dedicated their books to him; Poland even sought him for her king. As a courtier he did much to form the fashion (borrowed from Italy) of attaching as much prestige to verse-making as to riding or fencing; and the writing of poetry became one of the accomplishments of a gentleman. Sidney fell, mortally wounded, on the field of Zutphen. His last recorded act was to decline a drink of water and send it to a common soldier who lay near.

Sidney is remembered for three literary works: *A Defense of Poesie*, written about 1580 and published after his death as *An Apologie for Poetrie*; the *Arcadia*, written to amuse Sidney's sister Mary, the Countess of Pembroke; and *Astrophel and Stella*, a sequence of sonnets. The first is all in prose, the second is partly in prose and partly in verse, and the third is all in verse. The *Apologie*, written to offset *The School of Abuse*, by Stephen Gosson, is a defense of poetry and the drama; it shows a wide acquaintance with ancient and modern literature and abounds in kindly humor and the tolerance bred of culture and refinement. It still makes pleasant reading, even though the style, like most Elizabethan prose, is rambling and involved. The *Arcadia* is a lengthy and rather dull romance of pastoral life, inter-

SIR PHILIP SIDNEY

From an original painting in the collection of George A. Plimpton

spersed with little poems, chiefly notable because it reveals a strong Spanish and Italian influence. In *Astrophel and Stella* — the Star-lover and the Star — Sidney recounts with poetic license the story of his love for Lady Penelope Devereux. Its models are the sonnets of Surrey commemorating his devotion to Geraldine and the sonnets of Petrarca enshrining his affection for Laura. Sidney's sonnets are very uneven, some beautiful and poetical, others almost mechanical imitations. Something of his noble character and of his ability as a poet may be gleaned from the last sonnet he wrote:

> Leave me, O Love, which reachest but to dust!
> And thou, my mind, aspire to higher things!
> Grow rich in that which never taketh rust;
> Whatever fades, but fading pleasure brings.
> Draw in thy beames, and humble all thy might
> To that sweet yoke where lasting freedomes be;
> Which breakes the clowdes, and opens forth the light
> That doth both shine, and give us sight to see.
> O take fast hold! Let that light be thy guide
> In this small course which birth drawes out to death:
> And think how evill becometh him to slide,
> Who seeketh heav'n, and comes of heav'nly breath.
> Then farewell, world! Thy uttermost I see!
> Eternall Love, maintaine Thy life in me!

SPENSER

Charles Lamb, who had a knack of saying memorable things, called Edmund Spenser (1552–1599) the poets' poet, and it would seem to be true that only poets can rightly appreciate the author of *The Faerie Queene* and that many poets have been aroused and awakened by such appreciation. Milton esteemed him, and Dryden, and Cowley; Prior and James Thomson frankly imitated him; to Wordsworth he was an inspiration; and to Keats his fine phrase "sea-shouldering whales" flung open the magic casement of poetic imagination. Yet Spenser's formative influence has been sharply limited to literature in

English: in the gallery of world poets he simply does not belong. Other English writers have been known and esteemed abroad. Shakespeare is a household word in every land; Milton is more highly regarded on the Continent than he is at home; Byron during most of his life was less a national than a European figure; Whitman and Poe and even Joaquin Miller were accepted in Europe before their worth was recognized in their native America; and Sidney, as we have just seen, was highly esteemed from Italy to Holland. But Spenser's influence, great though it has been on English Literature, has never reached beyond the chalk cliffs of Dover.

EDMUND SPENSER

From an original painting in the collection of George A. Plimpton

Perhaps one reason for this singular limitation of a poet admittedly above the average in ability is that Spenser suffered from the obstruction to the Renaissance spirit in Tudor England. Some of the writers of his time, like Sidney and Shakespeare, carried on the Renaissance tradition in spite of the narrow nationalism of the hour. Spenser, a child of the Renaissance if there ever was one, devoted himself to the furtherance of the national ideals: he desired to be the English Virgil, chanting the glories of his race; he sought the favor of Queen Elizabeth by incorporating that very remarkable lady in his most pretentious poetic offering. Like Sidney he was a Protestant, but unlike Sidney he allowed his work to be sullied by expressions of religious prejudice and sectarian strife. "Sage and serious" Milton called him, and so he was; but in constructing his masterpiece upon a national conception rather than upon the broad basis of humanity Spenser was more serious than sage.

Edmund Spenser was a poet and a great poet, but he sought likewise to be a prophet like Isaias and Jeremias of old. He was a fairly well-read man, and he knew that Virgil in Rome and Dante in Italy had both of them united the poet's charm with the prophet's authority. The *Æneid* and the *Divine Comedy* voice patriotic ideals. But he overlooked the vital fact that to those two superb thinkers and singers Rome and Italy represented the idea of a world empire. Rome was to Virgil not merely mistress of the world but, in very truth, the center of world civilization. To Dante the individual city states like Venice and Siena and his own Florence did not particularly matter: the nationalism which he so passionately championed was the continuation and perpetuation of the Roman Empire with the pope supreme in spiritual affairs and one universal monarch supreme in temporal affairs. There was nothing narrow or local about the nationalism of Virgil and Dante, but it was a sheer impossibility for Spenser to share their comprehensive vision. He knew that England was but a small and remote section of the civilized world. He knew that the heritage of culture and art had flowed into England from nations still vast and powerful. He knew that it was only in his own day that England had even so much as disputed the supremacy of the world with a great nation like Spain. He knew that his own education had come to him chiefly from the reading of Latin and Italian and French books. He knew that England could never be to him what Rome was to Virgil, what Italy was to Dante. He knew that since the Reformation the spiritual unity of the world no longer existed. He could dream, indeed, of a world-conquering England, but his common sense made it clear to him that such a dream had scant possibility of fulfillment. If some recent students of the poet have interpreted him aright[1] he lived to taste the bitterness of disenchantment. He saw his dreams of patriotic glory grow vague and dim. And, apart from the personal disasters which overtook him, Spenser died a broken-hearted and disappointed man.

Edmund Spenser, a Londoner by birth, received his early training under the famous educator Mulcaster at the Merchant Taylors' School, and in 1576 he took the degree of Master of Arts at Cambridge. In four years he had set out on that political career in Ireland which culminated eighteen years later in the burning of his castle at Kilcolman near Doneraile by the people he had insulted and exploited. Spenser was one of those land-hungry Englishmen who, ever since the conquest of Ireland under Henry II, have sought to secure something for nothing by oppressing and maligning the peasantry and currying favor with English sovereigns. From his point of view the Irish were rebels, and in his prose dialogue, *View of the Present State of Ireland*, he advocated rigorous measures against them. He fled with his family when his home was destroyed, first to Cork and then to London, where he died early in 1599.

Before taking up his residence in Ireland, Spenser, fresh from the university, was a member of a London literary club called the Areopagus, and came to know Sir Philip Sidney, Gabriel Harvey, and other men interested in poetry. It was in this environment that his first poems were written. Then in Ireland he became intimate with Sir Walter Raleigh, to whom he dedicated *The Faerie Queene*. They were both among the English "adventurers" who secured pickings from the confiscated estates of the Earl of Desmond.

Spenser's Minor Poems. *The Shepherd's Calendar*, published in 1579 and dedicated to Sidney, consists of a series of twelve poems, one for every month, which in form imitate the eclogues, or pastoral poetry, of Theocritus and Virgil. The

[1] H. E. Cory, for instance, in his *Edmund Spenser: A Critical Study*.

characters are the poet's friends and prominent persons of the day; "Eliza" is Queen Elizabeth, "Hobbinol" is Gabriel Harvey, and "Colin Clout" is Spenser himself. The language is deliberately old-fashioned and modeled upon the diction of Chaucer. These eclogues are artificial and affected but are not without beauty and insight, and they reflect some of the controversies which were then stirring men's minds.

The "Epithalamion" and the "Prothalamion" are wedding odes. The names will be more intelligible to us if we remember that they are taken directly from the Greek, the word *thalamos* meaning a "bridal chamber." Both are truly beautiful poems. The "Epithalamion," which was written first, celebrates Spenser's marriage in 1594 with Elizabeth Boyle, a relative of the first Earl of Cork. This work alone would be sufficient to establish Spenser's right to the title of poets' poet; it shows him a master of melody and word magic. With the "Epithalamion" was published the *Amoretti*, or love songs, a sonnet sequence which may have been merely a literary exercise but which more probably is a collection of poems written in honor of the lady whom he married. The "Prothalamion" commemorates the marriage of two daughters of a nobleman, and a considerable portion of it offers subtle flattery to the Earl of Essex, at whose house the ceremony took place and to whom Spenser looked for political preferment. The poem is delicate and graceful and makes lingering music with its recurring refrain,

Sweete Themmes! runne softly, till I end my Song.

Under the title of *Complaints* (1591) Spenser grouped a number of poems, including "The Ruins of Time," "The Tears of the Muses," "Mother Hubbard's Tale," and some translations from Petrarca. The most significant of these is "The Tears of the Muses," in which the poet laments the decayed condition of learning in Elizabethan England; it is the voice of a man of the Renaissance regretting the check which the Revival of Learning had encountered.

"Colin Clout's Come Home Again" may possibly suggest a display of humor, but that impression is misleading. There was no humor in Spenser: he and Milton are standing proof that humor is not essential to great poetry. This poem is a pensive and in places a brilliant and impressive account of his return to England in 1591 and of his reflections on that occasion. Here, as so often elsewhere, Spenser shows himself a lord of language.

In 1596 Spenser brought out Four Hymns, a little volume but a great book, and the greatness of it is largely due to the completeness with which it dips into the European Tradition in literature. In this group of poems Spenser has for the subject of his poetic reflection the same general truth of life embodied a few years earlier by the Venetian artist Titian in his wonderful picture called "Sacred and Profane Love," now in the Borghese Gallery in Rome. The first two hymns are devoted to Love and Beauty, the third and fourth to Heavenly Love and Heavenly Beauty; all four present in noble and picturesque language the immortal theory of love first set forth by Plato and then incorporated into Catholic teaching by the Neoplatonists. Spenser states with fresh imagery the sublime truths that "of the soul the body form doth take," that true beauty comes from the thinking of beautiful thoughts, and that from the contemplation of beautiful objects we rise to a perception of the Eternal Beauty of God. Here again is an utterance of the Renaissance spirit giving a reason for the faith that is in it.

The Faerie Queene. As it stands, The Faerie Queene, the poem upon which Spenser looked with most partial eye, is a lengthy piece of work; but, as the poet explains in his letter to Sir Walter Raleigh, the plan called for eighteen books in addition to the completed six. The Faerie Queene, like The Canterbury Tales, was never finished. The project was almost too vast for mortal man to realize. "Spenser was undertaking the equivalent of a dozen novels in addition to reducing all his material to an elaborate and artificial metrical form." [1] That form is the Spenserian stanza, properly so called, for Spenser not only used it first but wrote more Spenserian stanzas than all other poets combined. As we read the poem today we notice that the language is archaic, and the men who read it in Spenser's day observed the same thing; as in some of his other poems, the poet designedly affected an old-fashioned style in grammar, spelling, and vocabulary.

King Arthur was to be the central figure of the poem, and each of the first twelve books was to be devoted to one of the twelve moral virtues listed by Aristotle, each virtue to be personified in a knight. This plan is followed in the six books we possess:

Book I. Holiness, represented by the Red Cross Knight
Book II. Temperance, represented by Sir Guyon
Book III. Chastity, represented by Britomart
Book IV. Friendship, represented by Cambel and Triamond
Book V. Justice, represented by Sir Artegall
Book VI. Courtesy, represented by Sir Calidore

The poem is, therefore, moral and didactic in purpose. It is cast in the form of an allegory, and the allegory is complicated and inconsistent. Besides the conflict between virtues and vices, it involves religious controversy (with a strong Protestant bias, naturally), reflections on recent historical events, such as the defeat of the Armada and the Irish situation, and the statement of political issues. "Duessa" is Queen Mary, "Calidore" is Sir Philip Sidney, "Arthur" is the Earl of Leicester (it was Spenser's hope that that nobleman would marry Queen Elizabeth and so further the progress of English nationalism), and the Fairy Queen, "Gloriana," is Elizabeth herself. There is nothing in history, as Dean Church has remarked, which can be compared to the "gross, shameless, lying flattery" that Spenser proffered to his sovereign. "He

[1] J. M. Manly, *English Prose and Poetry*, p. 781.

deck'd Eliza's head," sang Prior, "with Gloriana's beams." The story goes that Elizabeth was not indifferent to such lavish praise and intended to reward the poet handsomely; but when Lord Burghley remonstrated with "What! All this for a song?" Elizabeth contented herself with bestowing upon Spenser an annual pension of fifty pounds.

The Faerie Queene, despite its word music and its gorgeous display of poetic fancy, is more admired and talked about than studied and read. Its allegory is too elaborate and wearisome; its presentments of history and controversy are so much dead wood; its incense smoke of flattery, however it may have pleased the avid nostrils of Queen Elizabeth, can only incite the modern reader to languor or move him to profane mirth. We might almost say that for the student to be compelled to read the six books through would partake of the nature of cruel and unusual punishment, forbidden by the Constitution of the United States. But, on the other hand, not to know something of the poem, not to have dipped into it at random and to have enjoyed brief sessions with its imagery and fine poetic sweep, is to have missed one of the rarest delights which English Literature affords. This, at all events, can be said of Spenser, and it is high praise: he was an exceptionally clean-minded man. In an age almost unparalleled for coarseness of speech and looseness of morals he preserved purity of soul and wrote no line that would sully the most delicate imagination. In this he was unlike his contemporary, Shakespeare, whom we have to expurgate for class use; he was unlike his great predecessor, Chaucer, and his great successor, Dryden, both of whom felt obliged to retract and regret the unworthy things they had written.

The Faerie Queene is a poem at once finished and incomplete, gloriously alive and irrevocably dead. The poet did not live to realize his design, but he did succeed in creating for us a large number of impressive pictures and of composing a veritable symphony of sweet sounds. Controversy, politics, and flagrant flattery are not the stuff of which great literature is made, and in so far as these constituents enter into Spenser's master work, the poem is lifeless and inert. But Spenser evoked a vision of living beauty when he looked into his own heart and wrote and when he sat at the feet of other writers, many of them nameless, who had contributed to world literature. He learned much from his predecessors: from the Medieval Romances, from Malory, from Tasso and Ariosto and Dante; from the French *Romance of the Rose*, from Langland and Chaucer, and from the Greek philosophers and the Latin poets. His weakness is due to his absorption in the insular idea of nationalism and his concern with narrow religious and political issues; his strength lies in his possession of a high poetic gift, in his moral purpose and the grandeur of his design, and in the richness of the heritage he derived through the Revival of Learning from the European Tradition in literature.

ELIZABETHAN POETRY

The literary flowering of the Renaissance in the sixteenth century was very pronounced on the Continent. Ariosto, the author of *Orlando Furioso*, died in 1533, and the *Jerusalem Delivered* of Torquato Tasso, another eminent Italian poet, appeared in 1581. A group of French poets, fittingly called the Pléiade, or cluster of bright stars, were seeking to improve verse-writing under the inspiration of classical models. In Spain, though Calderón was not born until 1600, the world writer, Cervantes, was a contemporary of Spenser and Shakespeare, and Lope de Vega had begun to pour out his eighteen hundred plays. This was an age, too, of progress in other fields, for here was the time when Tycho Brahe, Kepler, and Galileo made their contributions to science. The Revival of Learning, in short, was bearing fruit in many departments of life and in many countries of Europe, though its course was impeded in Germany and in England by the Reformation.

"The smoke of theological strife, which darkened so many years of the Tudor period, blinded the eyes of the masses to the high artistic merits of England's old masters of letters,"[1] not to speak of masters of letters in Catholic lands. In scholarship and in prose-writing England still lagged behind Italy, France, and Spain.

But poets are like birds and will pour forth their songs even in wintry weather. And there were not lacking numerous verbal songsters in the England of Tudor times. Some of them were unusually sweet singers, and their melodies still endure. Yet the enthusiasm manifested by writers on English Literature when they come to consider the poetry of the Elizabethan Age is frequently untouched by a sense of proportion. If England was "a nest of singing birds," it was not the only spot alive with melody. As far back as the thirteenth century Italy had been filled with the poetry of innumerable writers who practiced "the sweet new style," and the French poets of Provence had fashioned their lays. In the sixteenth century neither movement was wholly spent, and new incentives to verse-making had come as one of the results of the Revival of Learning. Not even the Tudor policy of national isolation could prevent the echoes of Continental poetry from gladdening and stimulating English singers, nor could the fierce and cruel religious persecutions under Henry, Edward, Mary, and Elizabeth entirely check the ardors of poetic English hearts. While theologians raged and politicians devised vain things, the English poets, looking upon life and seeing that it was good, lifted their hearts and their voices in song. To have many poets at one time was a commonplace in Italy and France; but it was a new experience in England, and students who never look beyond England in their investigation of literature sometimes assume that it was a new experience in the world.

A Mirror for Magistrates. "Old habits," says Thomas à Kempis, "are with difficulty relinquished," and the truth holds

[1] S. H. Gurteen, *The Arthurian Epic*, pp. 6, 7.

in literature as in life. Thus it was that a series of poems written in Tudor times harks back to earlier models and continues the spirit of Lydgate's *Fall of Princes* and Boccaccio's *Fall of Illustrious Men*. This collection of poems is known as *A Mirror for Magistrates*, and constituted a gallery of men in high places who had suffered tribulation. "Here, as in a looking-glass, you shall see, if any vice be in you, how the like hath been punished in others heretofore." Its authorship has been erroneously attributed to Thomas Sackville, afterwards Lord Buckhurst, who was only a boy of eighteen when the first edition of the *Mirror* appeared; he contributed the "Induction" and the "Complaint" of Buckingham to the third edition. The originator of the series was probably George Ferrers, a lawyer and master of the revels at the court of Henry VIII, who began the series, assisted by William Baldwin, in the reign of Queen Mary. Several other writers, including Thomas Phaer, assisted in bringing the work to completion, and Richard Niccols edited it in its final form. As might be guessed from the diversity of authorship, the work is very uneven, and as might be inferred from the subject matter, it is uniformly gloomy in tone; but some portions rise to the level of genuine literature, notably the "Induction," which shows the influence of Virgil and Dante and reveals considerable skill in allegory.

Lyrics. Some of the best Elizabethan poetry consisted of songs scattered through the dramas written by Peele, Greene, Lodge, Lyly, Dekker, Ben Jonson, Beaumont and Fletcher, and especially Shakespeare. In general, they are distinguished for their fanciful figures of speech and for the smoothness of their versification. There were also several sonnet sequences, like Spenser's *Amoretti* and Sidney's *Astrophel and Stella*. Of these the most famous is that of Shakespeare, which has occasioned much controversy regarding the purpose and meaning of the sonnets. In addition, this period produced a number of Miscellanies, or collections of lyric poems, dealing with various

POLY-OLBION
IOHN MORRIS.

GREAT BRITAIN

By
Michaell Drayton
Esqr

London printed for M. Lownes. I. Browne. Iohn Busbie, I. Helme J. Busbie

TITLE-PAGE OF DRAYTON'S *POLYOLBION*

subjects, such as religion, love, and the coming of spring — topics which have inspired poets in every country and in every age. Of these *Tottel's Miscellany* (1557) is historically the most important, but some excellent specimens of lyric verse are contained in George Gascoigne's *A Hundred Sundry Flowers* (1572); in *A Gorgeous Gallery of Gallant Inventions* (1578) and *A Handful of Pleasant Delights* (1584); in *The Passionate Pilgrim* (1599), containing, besides several anonymous lyrics, five of Shakespeare's sonnets and Marlowe's exquisite "Come Live with me and be my Love"; in *England's Helicon* (1600), with poems by Sidney, Spenser, Lodge, Peele, and Barnfield; and in Davison's *Poetical Rhapsody* (1602).

Seven Minor Poets. *Michael Drayton (1563–1631).* Michael Drayton has been likened by Hazlitt to a soil which produces an abundant harvest but very few flowers. Several of his poems commemorate events in English history, and his *Polyolbion* is a sort of real-estate circular in verse — "a chorographical description of all the tracts, rivers, mountains, forests, and other parts of this renowned Isle of Great Britain, with intermixture of the most remarkable stones, antiquities, wonders"; but of all Drayton's patriotic writings the only one which really lives is the "Battle of Agincourt," a vigorous and stirring ballad. "Nymphidia," a fairy poem which Drayton wrote when he was over sixty years of age, was for long thought to be the source of Shakespeare's *Midsummer Night's Dream*. The fact is just the other way around, Drayton having obviously helped himself freely from Shakespeare's fairy lore. Like Shakespeare, Drayton was a native of Warwickshire.

Samuel Daniel (1562–1619). Samuel Daniel is also remembered mainly because of a Shakespearean association. Shakespeare's sonnets differ slightly in form from the Petrarchan model, consisting of three quatrains, or stanzas of four lines, to which a couplet is attached, and not of the combination of eight lines and six lines favored by most sonneteers. The Shakespearean sonnet is sometimes called the English sonnet, and its father and inventor was "the well-languaged Daniel," whose influence on Shakespeare is manifest. Daniel's sonnet sequence, *Delia* (1592), contains several poems that for "sweetness of rhythm, delicate imagery, and purity of language nearly surpass Shakespeare's efforts."[1] Daniel wrote much besides, including an epic on the Wars of the Roses; the best that can be said of his work was said by Pope: he is unpoetical, but "has good sense often."

Thomas Campion (*1567?–1619*). Thomas Campion, born either in London or in Dublin of an English family long settled in Ireland, illustrates the not unusual combination of doctor and poet; and he was a very good poet. A student of music, too, he delighted to make

GEORGE CHAPMAN

experiments in unusual kinds of verse, and engaged in a controversy with Daniel on the merits of rime. Campion argued against the use of rime, but happily did not practice what he preached. Whatever his religious convictions may have been — we know that he detested the Puritans, that he had many Catholic friends, and that he was possibly related to Father

[1] S. L. Lee, *Dictionary of National Biography.*

Edmund Campion — his devotional poems rank among the finest hymns in the English language and unite a true lyric gift with genuine spiritual exaltation. One of his most delightful love poems, "Cherry-Ripe," may be compared with Robert Herrick's tiny lyric with the same title.

George Chapman (*1559?–1634*). To mention George Chapman is to think at once of Homer and of John Keats, for it was Chapman's version of the *Iliad* that inspired that sublime sonnet "On First Looking into Chapman's Homer." That Chapman gave a faithful literal rendering of Homer nobody would maintain, and exact scholars have delighted to point out the weaknesses of his translation; but he did succeed in reproducing much of the Homeric spirit and of conveying to his readers (and Chapman continues to have readers) a sense of expansion and exultation. The painter Barry is reported to have remarked, "When I went out into the street after reading Chapman's *Iliad* every man I met seemed to be ten feet high." Barry said in prose what Keats said in poetry; both bestowed high praise on Chapman's achievement, for it is an infallible sign that a piece of writing is great literature if it gives us an impression of growth and enlargement. Chapman, an heir of the Renaissance spirit, wrote poems and plays, none of which has attained the celebrity of his translations from the Greek. He was well thought of both as man and as littérateur. Ben Jonson, never too lavish in compliments, maintained that, except himself, Fletcher and Chapman were the only two authors then living who knew how to write a masque. Praise from Sir Hubert is praise indeed.

Robert Southwell (*1561?–1595*). Even more enthusiastic praise Jonson bestowed upon another poet of the day. William Drummond of Hawthornden in Scotland, a poet himself and a recorder of conversations with rare Ben, summarizes Jonson's opinion of Robert Southwell as follows: "That Southwell was hanged; yet so he [Jonson] had written that piece of his, the 'Burning Babe,' he would be content to destroy many of his."

Jonson seems to have been correct both in his statement of fact and in his literary estimate. Southwell was hanged, drawn, and quartered at Tyburn — the Hyde Park Corner of modern London — because he was a Catholic priest; and his poem, "The Burning Babe," is a finer thing than any piece of verse that Jonson wrote. And close to it in excellence is another of Southwell's poems, "A Child of my Choice," less emotional and more restrained. Both poems suggest Southwell's real distinction in English Literature: he was the first poet to sing with real power of a child, and the Child of his choice was the Divine Child. "The Burning Babe" is like an Infant Jesus brought to life by some Italian Renaissance painter on a refectory wall. Southwell had been in Italy and doubtless had seen such pictures. And later, as he lay in the Tower of

ROBERT SOUTHWELL

London, between periods of excruciating torment on the rack he wrought those consoling visions into melodious verses.

Other poems Southwell wrote in prison, — the selfsame Tower of London where Raleigh was to write his *History of the World*, — but none of them attains the level of "The Burning Babe." Some, like the familiar one beginning

Shun delays, they breed remorse,

are good advice in rime. Others, undeniably genuine poetry, remind us of that style of architecture which is called the baroque: they are overdecorated with metaphors and "conceits," as artificial bits of verbal cleverness were called. "St. Peter's Complaint" illustrates this aspect of Southwell's poetry and reflects a fashion of verse-writing already in vogue in England, though best exemplified by the Italian poet Marino.

Robert Southwell came of a Catholic family which had enjoyed the friendship of King Henry VIII and even had profited by that monarch's looting of the monasteries. He became a Jesuit, studied in France and in Italy, and then, despite the severe Elizabethan laws against priests, returned to England to minister to the persecuted Catholics. For a time he was chaplain to the Countess of Arundel. He was arrested in 1592, cast into prison, tortured some thirteen times, and finally executed on the charge of "constructive treason." His poetry was but a side issue in his short and busy life.

Henry Constable (*1562–1613*). Henry Constable was a Cambridge man, a convert to Catholicism, and an ardent imitator of French and Italian writers. Like Southwell he spent several years abroad, and on his return served a term in the Tower. He is among the most capable Elizabethan practitioners of the sonnet form. He wrote love poems and religious poems, and especially in the latter he is distinguished for depth of feeling and coherence of thought. He has grace and picturesqueness, a manifest but not excessive liking for "conceits," and an exceptional structural skill; he generally manages to invest his concluding lines with emotional emphasis. *Diana*, a sequence of love sonnets, was published in 1592. His religious poems, though remaining in manuscript, were widely read, and some of them were, until recently, ascribed to Donne and other poets. Constable's essential qualities are all evident in this sonnet to Our Blessed Lady:

> In that, O Queen of Queens, thy birth was free
> From guilt, which others do of grace bereave,
> When in their mothers' womb they life, receive,
> God as His sole-borne daughter lovèd thee.

To match thee like thy birth's nobility,
He thee His Spirit for thy spouse did leave,
Of whom thou didst His only Son conceive,
And so was link'd to all the Trinity.

Cease then, O Queens who earthly crowns do wear,
To glory in the pomp of worldly things;
If men such high respect unto you bear
Which daughters, wives, and mothers are of Kings,
What honor should unto that Queen be done
Who had your God for Father, Spouse, and Son?

John Donne (*1573–1631*). One of the last offshoots of the
Renaissance in England is the poetry of John Donne; and
Donne himself is a remarkable specimen of the contrasts and
inconsistencies which characterized the Revival of Learning
in some of its manifestations. Descended on his mother's side
from Sir Thomas More, Donne was brought up a Catholic,
but a heritage that fell to him in his early manhood was the
occasion of his renouncing his faith: Catholics were heavily
fined and taxed. He joined an expedition to Spain and Portugal and saw something of the world; then, well on in life, he
became a minister and eventually Dean of St. Paul's Cathedral
in London, where he enjoyed the reputation of a learned and
effective preacher. The visitor in London can still see the
dean's ghastly marble effigy in St. Paul's; he is represented
in his grave-clothes and winding-sheet — a costume of his own
choosing.

Donne's poems fall into two classes: those of a worldly and
even licentious character, and those on religious themes. The
former were the products of his irregular life as young Jack
Donne, and their circulation in manuscript (for they were not
printed until after his death) caused the Dean of St. Paul's
some embarrassment. His more sedate poetry is much concerned with the themes of repentance, death, and judgment.
In manner Donne's poems, both secular and religious, are
elaborate experiments in meter and mosaics of "conceits"

and forced and tortuous language. Donne was, indeed, a juggler of words and seems to have been less intent on expressing emotion than on writing something different from existing poetry. He is a poet of the head rather than of the heart, "a queer and surprising but not a great mind."[1] His "verses gnarl'd and knotted," as Walter Savage Landor styled them, have but a limited appeal. There can be no halfway estimate of Donne: either we like him very much or we dislike him intensely.

ELIZABETHAN PROSE

With the exception of Francis Bacon, the later Renaissance in England produced no really great scholar. Ben Jonson was esteemed a marvel of learning, but his erudition was light and scrappy in comparison with that of the Continental scholars of his own and the preceding era. And the art of writing prose lagged behind in England. Sir Philip Sidney's sentences are long, rambling, and uncertain and reveal a mind striving ineffectually to master the art of clear and logical expression. As prose writers Lodge, Greene, and Nash are noted more for vigor than for grace and give the impression of having carved out the language with a chipped chisel and a wabbly mallet. It is much the same with Sir Walter Raleigh. The great age of prose was still in the future. Five prose writers of this epoch demand more than passing attention.

Roger Ascham (1515-1568). Secluded among books at Cambridge University for some forty years, and subsequently tutor to the Princess Elizabeth (afterwards Queen Elizabeth) and Latin secretary for Queen Mary, Ascham contrived to write in plain and strong and fairly flexible English two works that have importance in the history of English Literature. They are *Toxophilus*, or Lover of the Bow, a dissertation on archery; and *The Schoolmaster*, published after the author's

[1] *The Times Literary Supplement* (London), March 11, 1926.

death. Both deal with education and show Ascham to have been a sane and practical teacher. Like real educators in every country and every age, Ascham believed that teaching is not merely pounding facts into youthful memories and that the secret of true education is kindness and sympathetic understanding. "Love is fitter than fear," he wisely says, "gentleness better than beating, to bring up a child rightly in learning." And his estimate of the average parent's interest in education may not be entirely without application to twentieth-century America:

It is pity that commonly more care is had, yea, and that among very wise men, to find out rather a cunning man for their horse, than a cunning man for their children. For to the one they will gladly give a stipend of 200 crowns by year, and loth to offer to the other 200 shillings. God that sitteth in heaven laugheth their choice to scorn, and rewardeth their liberality as it should; for He suffereth them to have a tame and well-ordered horse, but wild and unfortunate children.

Ascham was well read in the ancient classics and had absorbed much of the learning of the Renaissance; yet, unlike Bacon and so many other men of his day, he realized the importance of the English language. In his dedication of *Toxophilus* to Henry VIII he thus professes his creed: "Although to have written this book either in Latin or Greek ... had been more easier[1] and fit for my trade in study, yet ... I have written this English matter in the English tongue for Englishmen."

John Lyly (1553-1606). *Euphues, or the Anatomy of Wit* and *Euphues and his England* are two books which, though rarely read nowadays, still live by reason of the fact that they gave a noun and an adjective to the language. When a man speaks

---

[1] Observe the double comparative, like the double superlative in Shakespeare's famous "most unkindest cut of all." That usage has since gone out of fashion. It was acceptable enough when Ascham and Shakespeare wrote, but is no longer "good grammar," because educated speakers and writers do not employ it today.

or writes in an obscure, ornamental, and affected style, using strained resemblances and forcing words out of their normal meaning, we say that his style is euphuistic or that he is given to the use of euphuisms.[1] The words come from the title and leading character in the two *Euphues* books by John Lyly.

The euphuistic style in literature is not confined to English Guevara in Spanish and Marini in Italian were in some respects Lyly's models; indeed, within proper limits euphuism in small doses is as diverting as fancy-dress costume, but neither is adapted for everyday use. Lyly set a fashion in English writing, and his most distinguished imitator was Shakespeare, who employed numerous euphuisms in some of his earlier plays, though he outgrew the practice and even ridiculed it later on.

Lyly was an Oxford graduate and a scholar of some repute; he preferred the life of a man of fashion and became a hanger-on at the royal court. Perhaps his strongest claim to our remembrance is that he was the first author in universal literature who wrote a book designed for the amusement of ladies. That was his admitted object. He would, he said, rather have his work lie "shut in a lady's casket than open in a scholar's study." The two books of *Euphues* consist of long-drawn-out moralizings and sentimental discourses strung along a line of slight narrative. Euphues is described as a "young gallant of more wit than wealth and yet of more wit than wisdom," and the story of his conversations is thus commended to feminine readers:

---

[1] It may not be amiss to remember the difference between *euphuism*, meaning a verbal conceit or affectation, and *euphemism*, meaning a softened or round-about way of saying things. The two words are often confused. Euphuism sometimes called preciosity, from the word used to designate the same tendency in French Literature. An example of euphuism: "Sweet air! Go, tenderness of years; take this key, give enlargement to the swain, bring him festinately hither" (Shakespeare's *Love's Labour's Lost*, III, i). An example of euphemism: "Oswald is purposely inaccurate in his statements," meaning that Oswald tells lies.

It resteth, ladies, that you take the pains to read it, but at such times as you spend in playing with your little dogs, and yet I will not pinch [1] you of that pastime, for I am content that your dogs lie in your laps, so Euphues may be in your hands, that when you shall be weary of the one, you may be ready to sport with the other.

Lyly was thus the father of what might be appropriately called lapdog literature.

Robert Burton (1577-1640). Burton is a good example of a man of one book. He studied at Oxford and lived there most of his life, apart from the world and its ways, nosing into all manner of curious literature. In 1621 appeared the first edition (there were several more during the author's lifetime) of *The Anatomy of Melancholy*, over the pen name of Democritus Junior, and so Burton established himself among the composers of books quaint and charming, eccentric and scholarly, humorous and wise. The very title is misleading. Burton employs the word *anatomy* as Lyly had used it, to mean examination or analysis; and despite the portentous suggestiveness of "Melancholy," the book is really cheerful if sometimes a bit cynical. Its subject matter is not melancholy at all; in modern language it might be called Facts and Fancies of Psychology. "It is a museum which we enter in a mood of idle curiosity and leave thinking less about the multitude of strange things collected there than of the man who gathered them together." [2] Among those strange things are innumerable quotations from learned Renaissance writers of Latin, most of whose names are so unfamiliar that some readers have suspected Burton of inventing them; an array of formidable marginal notes and comments often more absorbing than the text itself; and a style, not merely bristling with Latin quo-

---

[1] *Pinch*, as in recent American slang, here means to steal or deprive of. Some not altogether reputable language of our own day is older than we think. When, for example, a man loses his position he is vulgarly said to be *fired*; and in sonnet cxliv Shakespeare uses the same term: "Till my bad angel fire my good one out." Some slang is really so old that it is new.

[2] J. M. Murry, *Countries of the Mind*, p. 63.

tations, but actually part Latin — a sentence sometimes beginning in English, continuing in Latin, and then coming to a close in English. Burton was called a "devourer of books," and he here unloaded much of his curious learning. The *Anatomy* has been warmly admired by discerning readers. Dr. Johnson claimed that it took him out of bed two hours before he wanted to get up, but that savors of exaggeration. Nothing could make Johnson get up before he wanted to, and Burton's *Anatomy*, though a striking book, is not at all like an alarm clock.

THE BEGINNINGS OF LITERARY CRITICISM

Whereas on the Continent the Renaissance produced numerous men who passed judgment on books, estimated literary values, compared different texts of masterpieces, and sought to teach appreciation of literature, critics in England were few in number and uncertain in their methods. Criticism implies scholarship and familiarity with the best that has been known and thought in the world, as Matthew Arnold has well said; and in the sixteenth and early seventeenth century English scholarship had not attained its highest level.

Gascoigne and Gosson. The first of the Elizabethan critics in the order of time was Thomas Gascoigne (1525?–1577), whose *Certain Notes of Instruction* is an essay on verse-writing. He pointed out that English meter depends on accents rather than on quantity and the number of syllables. This is the chief distinction between English and Latin versification, and Gascoigne was the first man to recognize it in theory, though, of course, all English verse writers had recognized it in practice. Stephen Gosson (1555–1624), a very rigid and strait-laced gentleman, attacked the drama and poetry as immoral agencies in his *School of Abuse* and drew a sharp reply from Thomas Lodge and a more urbane remonstrance from Sir Philip Sidney in *A Defense of Poesie*.

Ben Jonson. Most prominent among the critics of this period was Ben Jonson, who, though best known as a writer of plays, was keenly interested in literary theories and much given to evaluating the work of his contemporaries. Like Bernard Shaw in our own day, Jonson wrote prefaces to his plays, and these prefaces were practically critical essays. His *Underwoods*, though poetical in form, are critical in matter; they are somewhat like Pope's metrical *Essay on Criticism*. Though not a great scholar according to the Continental standard, Jonson was more widely read in ancient literature than most men of his day, and formed his critical standards on the theories of Aristotle, Horace, and Longinus, and on the practice of the Greek and Latin dramatists. His chief contributions to literary criticism may be read with interest and profit in *Timber, or Discoveries made upon Men and Matter*, a collection of random notes on books and life. Jonson had a considerable following among the literary men of his day, — "the Tribe of Ben," as they liked to call themselves, — and his influence did much to form taste and determine literary style. He was the first of the long line of literary dictators in England.

Jonson's leading critical theories may be briefly summarized. He bowed, first of all, to the authority of the ancients and disapproved of novelties. He recognized the power and beauty of Shakespeare's plays, but none the less he lamented Shakespeare's lack of classical learning. The moral element, he maintained, is necessary in a poet, and he agreed with Longinus that a good writer must be a good man. As for the critic, Jonson held that he must be sincere and fearless, and that if he undertakes to criticize poetry he must be a poet himself. This brings us to a very interesting problem. If the critic of poetry must be a poet, must the critic of music be a musician and the dramatic critic a playwright and an actor? Best of all are Jonson's suggestions regarding the art of writing English: "For a man to write well, there are required three necessaries

— to read the best authors, observe the best speakers, and much exercise of his own style." Rugged and burly man that he was, Jonson despised euphuism and set the example of plain, straightforward prose.

BACON

A Thinking Machine. Euphuism, however, found its strongest opponent in a most remarkable man, who, while primarily a politician, occupies a prominent place in the history of English prose. Francis Bacon (1561-1626), Baron Verulam and Viscount St. Albans, is the author of those famous *Essays*, which stand as models of keen thought and simple style. Lyly and his followers favored a manner of writing all spangled and decorated, bejeweled and befringed; Bacon set down his ideas with directness and simplicity, discarded ornaments and conceits, and made his style a flawless windowpane through which his readers might observe the workings of his mind. Bacon had no sentiment, no emotion, no poetic fancy. There is in him no touch of Ben Jonson's sturdy indignation, no suggestion of Shakespeare's imaginative sweep. He was a thinking machine, well oiled and noiseless; and his *Essays* represent the mathematics of thought and speech.

Pellets of Wisdom. The *Essays* of Bacon rank high among the wisdom books of English Literature and, indeed, the literature of the world. Their author was a truly learned man, who, as he himself said, took all learning for his province, and who studied men in public and private life as thoroughly as he studied books; and in these short, pithy comments on Truth, on Death, on Superstition, on Travel, on Friendship, on Gardens, on Studies, on Riches, he set down the cream of his reflections and the distillation of his worldly wisdom. They were written now and then in the intervals of an exceptionally busy life. Ten of them appeared in 1597, thirty-nine in 1612, and fifty-eight in 1625, a year before his death. They were influenced by the French essays of Montaigne — there has been at least one ardent Baconian who tried to prove that Bacon really wrote Montaigne's essays as well as Shakespeare's plays! — and by the wisdom books of the Bible and the ancients; but Bacon is truly an original writer and thoroughly assimilated the learning he had derived from his predecessors.

Almost every sentence in the *Essays* is a fit subject for wholesome meditation and reflection, a bit of concentrated mental food to be "chewed and digested" and turned over in the mind. His phrases are like bouillon cubes (only richer in nutritive values), which are not to be swallowed whole, but require to be dissolved and watered and seasoned according to taste. Bacon puts much in little, and his readers must say in their own thoughts ever so many things which he does not say. A lengthy magazine article could be written on every one of the following remarks culled at random from the essays:

Men fear death, as children fear to go in the dark.

Friendship . . . redoubleth joys, and cutteth griefs in half.

That is the best part of beauty, which a picture cannot express.

A man that hath no virtue in himself ever envieth virtue in others.

Let states that aim at greatness take heed how their nobility and gentlemen do multiply too fast.[1]

He that travelleth in a country before he hath some entrance into the language, goeth to school, and not to travel.

Read not to contradict and confute; nor to believe and take for granted; nor to find talk and discourse; but to weigh and consider.

They that deny a God destroy man's nobility; for certainly man is of kin to the beasts by his body; and if he be not kin to God by his spirit, he is a base and ignoble creature.

A Latinist. Though Bacon wrote other books in English, — *The Advancement of Learning*, a *History of Henry VII*, *The New Atlantis* (an unfinished account of an imaginary

---

[1] Observe how the same thought was expressed by Goldsmith:

Ill fares the land, to hastening ills a prey,
Where wealth accumulates and men decay.

island inhabited by a superior race like the Utopians of More), — he wrote what he considered his most important work, *Novum Organum*, in Latin; and he even translated his *Advancement of Learning* into Latin and made additions to it in that tongue. He held the view that nothing written in English could last long or affect the thought of the world; that

BACON

"these modern languages will at one time or the other play the bankrupt with books." Bacon is a great English writer in spite of himself. Students of science and philosophy may delve into his *Novum Organum* and *De Augmentis Scientiarum*; but by the student of literature and by the man who likes good reading, Bacon is remembered for his *Essays*, of which their author thought so little that he did not bother to turn them into Latin. In this respect he resembles Petrarca, who

wrote much and learnedly in Latin, but in his sonnets to Laura unburdened his heart in Italian; those Italian poems have given Petrarca his surest immortality.

"**Wisest, brightest, meanest.**" As a man Bacon was less admirable than as a writer. Pope, who had a way of saying rather unkind things, characterized Bacon as "wisest, brightest, meanest of mankind," and the "meanest" part of it is not without point. Bacon was ambitious for place, power, and wealth, and in order to keep in the good graces of Queen Elizabeth he turned against his friend and benefactor, the Earl of

Essex. He rose, though slowly, and became Lord Chancellor of England in 1618. But three years later he was impeached for taking bribes, forced to confess his guilt, and deprived of his offices and honors. Among the exhibits in the Record Office in London is a letter written by Bacon to King James I begging "for a cell to retire unto." He was asking not for a place in a prison or a monastery, but for the position of provost of Eton College. His request was ignored, so he retired to his estate at Gorhambury and buried himself in study. While traveling through Highgate on a winter day he wished to find out (what we with our refrigerators know so well) if cold would delay decomposition. He bought and plucked a fowl and stuffed it with snow. The experiment was a costly one, for he contracted pneumonia and died. The incident is in a way symbolic of Bacon as a scientist: he was rich and ingenious in theories, but in practice and experiment uncertain and unfortunate.

SUMMARY

Beginning in Italy the Renaissance, or Revival of Learning, spread eventually into England and affected the most representative poets and practically all the prose writers of the sixteenth and the early seventeenth century. The Renaissance spirit manifested itself in translations from the Greek, the Latin, the Italian, the Spanish, and the French, and in imitations of literary forms evolved on the Continent. Although the Protestant Reformation was an outgrowth of the Renaissance, it is clear that the Reformation did not affect literature favorably. Some of its consequences in England, all of which had a bearing on literature, were the suppression and despoiling of eight hundred monasteries and the destruction of their libraries; the depopulation of the Oxford colleges; religious controversies, which are rarely favorable to literary production; the persecution and in some cases the execution of learned men; the isolation of England from the thought and progress of Continental Europe; and a partial check in the transmission of the European Tradition in literature.

It is the fashion for writers on this period to emphasize such national events as the organization of the Church of England, the defeat of the Spanish Armada, the buccaneering exploits of Sir Francis Drake, and the development of exploration and discovery in the New World. These things are deeply significant in English history, but they have had little effect on English Literature. Spenser is a great poet not because of his patriotic spirit, but in spite of it. The merchant adventurers and their invasion of marts of trade overseas have been celebrated in poetry not by Shakespeare or Spenser, but in our own day by Alfred Noyes. Drayton's best poem commemorates not the defeat of the Armada, but a victory over the French in the days of King Henry V. As we shall see in the next chapter, when Shakespeare looked to England for material for some of his plays he ignored the present and derived inspiration from the past. And practically all the writers of the period caught their enthusiasm from the Renaissance spirit, the spirit of the ancient world reasserting itself in the European Tradition.

CHAPTER VII

THE AGE OF SHAKESPEARE

The most complete expression of the Renaissance spirit in English Literature and the richest transmission of the European Tradition in letters we find in the stage plays of the late sixteenth and early seventeenth centuries. It is here that Shakespeare looms above his contemporaries as Mont Blanc, viewed from the lake front at Geneva, dwarfs surrounding peaks. His is the great name in the drama, the great name in English Literature, one of the three or four great names in the literature of the world. And his greatness is adequately manifested not in the narrative poems which he wrote in his youth, nor even in the sonnets which contain some marvelous lines and provoke not less marvelous controversy, but in less than thirty of the dramas he composed for the rude and disreputable London stage and for the fashionable circle of the royal court. To study Shakespeare and to study his times it is needful to know something of the dramatic form which he utilized.

THE DRAMA

The Spoken Word. Just as a lyric poem is written to be recited or sung, so a drama is written to be acted on a stage before an audience. A lyric usually exists before it is recited or sung, and nowadays most poems are not interpreted vocally at all, but are read in silence as novels or histories are read; but to secure the full enjoyment of Jonson's "Drink to me Only with thine Eyes," Oliver Wendell Holmes's "Last Leaf," or William Allingham's "Fairies" we must hear it read aloud. One reason why poetry is not so highly esteemed and intimately loved as it might be is that in our day the art of reading aloud is almost a lost art; and the lyric poem needs to be interpreted by means of the musical human voice. And so the drama, to yield its best results, needs to be acted. To be sure, *Hamlet* or *She Stoops to Conquer* is a genuine play when we read it out of a book as we read a novel; but it usually means more to us when as members of an audience in a theater we see it acted by competent artists or when we ourselves enact a rôle in a wisely directed performance. When it is not possible for us to see or to take part in a play but we must content ourselves with reading it, we do well to stage the drama in our imagination, to make believe we see the characters moving about and speaking their lines aloud. And the next best thing to seeing a play performed or to acting in it ourselves is to read it aloud, assuming now one rôle and now another and entering into the spirit of all the parts.

Not all dramas are literature, but nearly all dramas were written to be acted. There is a literary form known as the closet drama, a poem written in dialogue form but intended to be read in the closet or study. Strictly speaking, the closet drama is not drama at all, even as an essay written in verse is not, strictly speaking, poetry. The great dramatists did not write closet dramas. Sophocles and Calderón and Shakespeare and Molière wrote with the intention of having their works interpreted by actors on the stage; and most of the great dramatists, like Molière and Shakespeare, were themselves actors and producers and understood theatrical conditions. It is important that we should remember these facts and regard the drama (when it happens to be literature) as literature designed for presentation on a stage, just as we should bear in mind when reading a great oration that it is literature intended to be spoken directly to an audience.

The Art of Make-Believe. The dramatic instinct is a profound human trait. Even as at times we all feel like singing and dancing, so at times we all feel like acting. Children in most of their games manifest the dramatic instinct; they make believe they are soldiers or mothers or wild animals. And children of a larger growth like to make believe too, as we can clearly understand when we reflect upon the popularity of lodge initiations and masquerade balls. The dramatic instinct has been utilized to symbolize some of the deepest truths of life and to express man's noblest emotions. Thus we find in the Holy Sacrifice of the Mass a pronounced dramatic element; it is a sacred drama which enacts the story of our Redemption. Indeed, at all times in the world's history, religion has utilized the dramatic instinct. In ancient Greece the drama had its origin in ceremonies connected with the worship of the god Dionysus. It was much the same with the Jews. When we read that David the King, to the great annoyance of his wife, danced before the Ark of the Covenant, we are simply learning that the holy monarch gave vent to his religious fervor in a dramatic form.[1] It is a deep truth that in both pagan and Christian times the drama was born at the foot of the altar.

Epochs of the Drama. Four times has the literature of Europe witnessed a pronounced flowering of the drama: first, in Greece, before the Christian Era, in the age of Pericles; secondly, in the late sixteenth and early seventeenth centuries in Spain; thirdly, in England during the same epoch; and lastly, in France in the second half of the seventeenth century, the golden age of French Literature. And the splendor of the drama in Spain, England, and France, coming in those three countries almost at the same time and having several important characteristics in common, was to a great extent a far-

---

[1] The dance continues to be associated with religious liturgy. Twice a year, on the feasts of Corpus Christi and the Immaculate Conception of Our Lady, ten boys attired as pages in the court of King Philip III perform a traditional dance before the high altar in the Cathedral of Seville. They click castanets and are accompanied by a full orchestra in the sanctuary. A readable description of this Spanish religious dance is given by J. B. Trend in *Alfonso the Sage*, pp. 179–190.

flung reflection of the much earlier dramatic activity in Greece. The Renaissance had, as it were, rediscovered Greece, and to the influence of the Renaissance spirit must the masterpieces of Spanish, English, and French dramatic literature be largely attributed. Several of the great French plays are on the same themes chosen by the Greek dramatists, sometimes preserving even the same titles. Of the English dramatists the majority were university-trained scholars who had read Sophocles and Euripides in the original Greek; the greatest of them, Shakespeare, though not a scholar, absorbed the Greek influence and the Renaissance spirit at second hand through the reading of English works based on the ancients.

The Catholic Influence. Stronger than the influence of Greece and Rome was the spirit of Catholicism as manifested in the ceremonies of the Church, especially the ritual of the Mass. The proof of this is that in its beginnings the modern drama was essentially religious in nature and purpose. And, though this may seem strange to us who live in times when priests do not often go near the theater at all and when the theatrical profession is not held in special honor, the first actors were churchmen; and devout persons like St. Gregory Nazianzen and the German nun St. Hroswitha were dramatists. After a time (for we can see how the custom of priests taking part in dramas might lead to abuses) the Church forbade the clergy to act, but she did not, wise Mother that she is, attempt to suppress the dramatic instinct. All over Europe there were religious plays, plays based on the life of Our Lord and on episodes in the Bible; and such plays continue to be acted. Instances are the passion plays produced periodically by the peasants of the Tyrol and by the people of the little village of Oberammergau in Bavaria. In Spain several of the leading dramatists, like Calderón and Lope de Vega, were priests, and many of their dramas are based on religious themes. Some of Calderón's best work is found in his *Autos Sacramentales*, a cycle of plays devoted to the Real Presence of Our Lord in the Blessed Sacrament. History and religion are impressively blended in a French dramatic pageant commemorating the lifting of the siege of Orléans by St. Joan of Arc in 1429; this long play (it has over two hundred scenes and nearly one hundred and fifty speaking parts) in structure anticipates the English chronicle plays of the next century.

THE DRAMA BEFORE SHAKESPEARE

English Religious Plays. Dramas growing out of the ceremonies of the Catholic religion existed as early as the tenth century in England, but they reached their full growth and achieved great popularity during the fourteenth and fifteenth centuries. They were of three sorts. The *mysteries* dealt with events recounted in the Bible, especially with the life of Our Lord; the *miracle plays* gave dramatic expression to the legends of the saints; the *moralities* had for characters abstract ideas and virtues and vices, such as Sin, Death, Good Deeds, Pride, Confession.[1] One of the moralities which is fairly well known even today and is occasionally presented on the modern stage is *Everyman*, a translation of a fifteenth-century Dutch play attributed to Peter Dorland, who, says Ernest Rhys, "must have been a man of profound imagination, and of the tenderest human soul conceivable."[2] *Everyman* will repay careful study as an example of the morality play, and it offers excellent material for student actors. Less known is a morality of the fourteenth century recently discovered in Dublin, written into the blank spaces of an old book of housekeeping accounts of Christ Church Cathedral. The leading character is the King of Life, who is served and flat-

---

[1] The words *mystery*, *miracle*, and *morality* were not, of course, employed by the people with the precision here suggested. Religious dramas of all sorts were frequently called simply *moral plays*. The three words represent a classification made by recent students of the drama. Similarly, dialogues or bits of music between plays were called *interludes* long before the sixteenth century.

[2] Everyman edition of *Everyman*, Introduction, p. xviii.

tered by two attendant knights, Health and Strength, and is entertained by a jester, Mirth. He is proud and careless and scoffs at the power of God and Death. The Queen and the Bishop warn him, but in vain. The conclusion of the play has not been found, but even from the fragment in our possession we can recognize the work as one of unusual force and dramatic intensity. It was acted in Dublin, probably in College Green, six hundred years ago. Another noteworthy morality is *Magnificence*, by John Skelton.

The religious plays were presented on feast days by the members of the various guilds of workingmen. At first the stage was some open space, usually the square in front of the parish church; but eventually the actors came to recite their lines on the top of a huge wagon, somewhat like a furniture van, drawn from place to place by horses. The plays were grouped into cycles named after the cities where they were acted: thus we have the Wakefield Plays,[1] the Chester Plays, the York Plays, and the Coventry Plays. Coventry is not far from Stratford-upon-Avon, and it is credible that the boy Shakespeare had his imagination fired by witnessing some of the pageants. Performances were held at Coventry as late as 1580.

The Interludes. Though the mysteries and moralities were religious in tone and subject, they were not necessarily solemn and sad; for England was Merry England, and the writers of the religious dramas managed to create a good deal of genuine comedy and even of broad farce. Almost always they poked fun at the Devil, and King Herod was a stock comic character. The religious element was less pronounced in a new form of the drama which appeared early in the sixteenth century. This was the interlude, meaning literally "between plays," because at first it was a short piece sandwiched between longer dramas. One of the earliest interludes is Skelton's *The Nigra-*

[1] More generally known as the Towneley Plays "because the manuscript of the plays was for a long time in the hands of a family of that name." — H. C. Schweikert, *Early English Plays*, p. 26

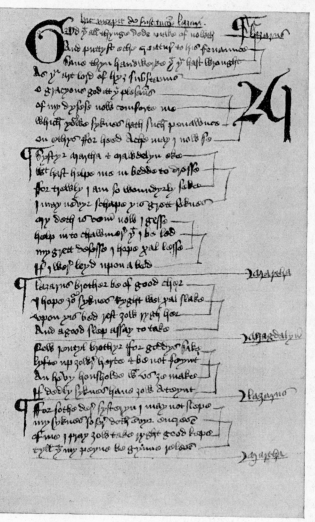

FROM A FIFTEENTH-CENTURY MYSTERY

Courtesy of the British Museum

mansir (1504). The man most closely identified with the interludes was John Heywood (1497?–1580?), a friend of the Blessed Thomas More and well known as an actor and singer at the court of Henry VIII. He remained a Catholic at the time of the Reformation and was still at the court during the reign of Queen Mary, but when Elizabeth came to the throne he crossed over to Belgium and lived at Mechlin. His best-known interlude is *The Four P's*, wherein a Palmer, a Pardoner, a 'Pothecary, and a Pedlar engage in a brisk and humorous contest to discover which of them can tell the biggest lie, the Palmer winning with the statement that in all his travels he had never seen "any woman out of patience."

Comedies. The interludes grew into full-length plays under the hand of university men who knew their Plautus and Terence and imitated the devices of the classical writers. The first English comedy is *Ralph Roister Doister*, which appeared in the middle of the sixteenth century. Its author, Nicholas Udall (1506–1556), was a teacher, first at Eton and later at Westminster. A free adaptation of the *Miles Gloriosus* of Plautus, the play abounds in humor of a somewhat boisterous sort and has a well-constructed plot and a number of distinctly amusing situations. Rougher and coarser and less artistic is *Gammer Gurton's Needle*, generally attributed to John Still but probably the work of William Stevenson, a scholar-dramatist of Cambridge. George Gascoigne, who tried his hand at every sort of writing, brought out an adaptation from the Italian of Ariosto, *The Supposes*, first acted in 1566. The Continental influence on English comedy was carried on in plays written and acted at the universities and by men about the court, particularly by John Lyly, who wrote a number of scholarly dramas in which the dialogue is better than the plot and characterization. All these writers, though they did not know it, were preparing the way for the great Shakespearean comedies; Shakespeare learned from most of them, and bettered the instruction.

Chronicle Plays. Shakespeare was even more indebted to a long line of writers of historical plays, dramas which were for the most part poor things but which gave him much of his material and supplied him with fundamental ideas. In them he discovered the germs of *King Lear* and his ten plays dealing with English kings. His three parts of *King Henry VI* are mainly revised versions of existing chronicle plays, and his *King John* follows a chronicle play by an unknown writer, *The Troublesome Reign of King John*, which in turn borrowed from a drama by John Bale (1495–1563), a voluminous producer of miracle plays, mysteries, interludes, and tragedies. In *Richard III* Shakespeare drew upon the Blessed Thomas More's historical treatise and the chronicle of Holinshed; in the three plays concerned with *King Henry V* he depended both on Holinshed and a popular chronicle play called *The Famous Victories of Henry V*.

Tragedies. The first English tragedy is *Gorboduc*, by Thomas Norton, a London lawyer and politician, and by that Thomas Sackville, afterwards Lord Buckhurst, who had a hand in the writing of *A Mirror for Magistrates*. It follows classical models in its observance of the unities of time, place, and action,[1] and in its avoidance of scenes of violence and bloodshed. Later English tragic writers, though they showed a strong classical influence, were less particular about avoiding scenes of violence, and eventually there developed on the English stage a school of play-writing which specialized in the "tragedy of blood." Such a drama is *The Spanish Tragedy* of Thomas Kyd (1558–1595),

---

[1] The unities were rules for the writing of tragedy which were evolved by certain Italian critics in the sixteenth century; they were called classical because they were supposed to be based on the teachings of Aristotle and on the practice of the Greek writers of tragedy. They found their strongest advocates in France in the seventeenth century. The unity of action insisted on but one plot in a drama; the unity of place forbade any change of scene; the unity of time required that all the events in a play must take place on one day. In France the unities were held to be essential until about a hundred years ago, when Victor Hugo demonstrated what Marlowe and Shakespeare had demonstrated two hundred years earlier in England, that great dramatists rather than learned critics determine what is or is not proper to the dramatic form.

a writer who also wrote a play, now lost, on the story which Shakespeare was to make immortal in *Hamlet*. Robert Greene (1560?–1592) and George Peele (1558–1598) were university men who engaged in varied literary work, including the writing of tragedy. Their dramatic writings had considerable influence on Shakespeare and served to convey to him, who was not a classical scholar, some of the classical heritage in literature. Greene seems to have held Shakespeare in contempt, and one of the last things he wrote contains a disparaging comment on "the only Shake-scene in a country."

Christopher Marlowe (1564–1593). In the historic city of Canterbury, a place rich in literary associations of Chaucer and Dickens, the visitor finds in a public park a monument commemorating the dramatist Christopher Marlowe, the son of a Canterbury shoemaker, who attended (we fear irregularly) the King's School near the famous cathedral where St. Thomas Becket met his death. On the four faces of the pedestal are carved the names of Marlowe's principal plays : *Tamburlaine, Doctor Faustus, Edward II*, and *The Jew of Malta*. Above the titles are niches for appropriate statues, but only one is filled ; and the incompleteness of the memorial symbolizes the character of Marlowe's writings, a promise of unrealized greatness. Marlowe studied at Cambridge and then went to London, "a boy in years, a man in genius, a god in ambition." Like Greene, he led a wild, turbulent life, mingled in shady politics and in the spy system of the Privy Council, and while still in the twenties was stabbed to death in a quarrel at Deptford, a village east of London. Marlowe was an undisciplined genius. Next to Shakespeare he was the greatest dramatist of the times, and, like Shakespeare, he was a poet of delicacy and power. What he might have achieved had he lived longer and more wisely is one of the fascinating "ifs" of literary history ; but now, in the words he wrote upon the sad ending of Faustus,

> Cut is the branch that might have grown full straight,
> And burned is Apollo's laurel bough.

Tamburlaine the Great, in two parts, Marlowe's first tragedy, is disfigured by crudity and carelessness, by rant and bombast, but it possesses force and dramatic intensity. Its hero is Tamerlane, the barbarian conqueror of India and Asia in the fourteenth century, whom Marlowe reveals as a man of ruthless ambition and an insatiable thirst for power. In *Faustus* he took the old German legend which in the nineteenth century was to furnish the material for Goethe's *Faust*, the supreme masterpiece of German Literature, and made of it an impressive dramatic picture of the unhallowed thirst for knowledge. It has numerous shortcomings and it is vulgar and irreverent, but it is easily the best of Marlowe's dramas. *Edward II* suggests comparison with Shakespeare's *Richard II* : both plays deal with a weak character in an exalted station. In point of self-control and artistic reserve in language *Edward II* is very different from the unrestrained impetuosity of *Tamburlaine*, but it is lacking in dramatic force. The scene of the unhappy monarch's death is repulsive in its accumulation of horrors. Barabas, the leading character in Marlowe's *Jew of Malta*, has often been compared with Shakespeare's Shylock in *The Merchant of Venice*. Marlowe's creation is less human than Shakespeare's, though both illustrate the inordinate thirst for wealth. *The Jew of Malta* is a well-constructed drama, but the story seems to run away from the author, and the play degenerates into unreal and ghastly melodrama in the scene in which Barabas fiendishly destroys his enemies.

With all his faults Marlowe had vitality and vigor, and his influence on the English drama and especially on Shakespeare can hardly be overestimated. "He cast in clay what Shakespeare recast in marble," declared John Churton Collins, a learned and thoughtful nineteenth-century critic; "it is more than probable that without the tragedies of Marlowe we should never have had, in the form at least in which they now stand, the tragedies of Shakespeare."[1] He did much to develop

[1] *Essays and Studies*, pp. 149–150.

blank verse, the form of dramatic poetry which in the hands of Shakespeare and Milton has become the most representative and powerful medium of poetical expression in English. "He gave English tragedy sublimity, intensity, breadth, and order; he freed blank verse from rigidity and mechanical correctness, and gave it the freedom, harmony, variety of cadence, and compelling music which imposed itself upon all later English tragedy."[1] Most important of all, and despite such limitations as his blindness to the importance of religion and his inability to portray the character and personality of woman, Marlowe never lost sight of literature as a picture and interpretation of life. His three leading plays deal with three consuming human passions: the lust of power, the lust of knowledge, and the lust of wealth.

SHAKESPEARE

Shakespeare is recognized as the world's supreme dramatic writer. He created a large number of men and women who live in memory: Falstaff and Desdemona, Cassius and Lady Macbeth, are more truly alive than most men and women we meet in the street. He either invented or popularized a vast number of phrases that have become part of our daily and familiar speech; expressions such as birds of a feather, dead as a doornail, bag and baggage, fast and loose, dancing attendance, wild-goose chase, to the manner born, the course of true love, getting even, give and take, more sinned against than sinning, and more honored in the breach than in the observance are bits of glittering mosaic chipped from Shakespeare's plays. He evolved numerous passages of sustained and incomparable beauty and sublimity. He said some profound things about human nature and said them better than anybody else. He knew how to construct plays that have in many cases survived the changes in dramatic fashions and the development of dramatic art. He is at once a classic and a "best seller."

[1] Hamilton W. Mabie, *William Shakespeare, Poet, Dramatist, and Man*, p. 23.

What Shakespeare was not. So prominent is Shakespeare's place in the history of literature and so compelling and captivating the force of his genius that there is danger of getting false impressions of the man and his art. Shakespeare was not deliberately and consciously a man of letters, writing with the purpose of contributing to world literature and enjoying the thought that his works were destined for immortality. Save in his youth, when he wrote some narrative poems and sonnets, Shakespeare does not seem to have concerned himself with fame as a writer. He was an actor, a reviser of old plays, a manager, and incidentally a playwright; he gave slight attention to what became of his plays once they were acted, and if it were not for the care and loyalty of two of his fellow actors, John

TITLE-PAGE OF THE FIRST FOLIO

The 1623 edition of Shakespeare contained several plays not previously published and which, but for the devotion of Heminge and Condell, would probably have been lost to the world

Heminge and Henry Condell, who brought out the celebrated First Folio of 1623, we probably should never have possessed his greatest dramas. William and Isaac Jaggard and Edward Blount deserve remembrance as the publishers of the Folio.

Shakespeare was not a flawless writer. He set little store by mere grammatical correctness, partly because his education was meager, partly because he generally wrote in great haste, partly because he shared the practical man's indifference to the niceties of expression. He wrote speeches to be heard, not poems to be read; if a passage gave promise of sounding well on the stage, he was indifferent as to whether it might read well in the closet. At times he imitated Lyly's euphuism and Marlowe's bombast and Kyd's lack of artistic restraint. We are told that Patrick Henry, our Revolutionary orator, sometimes started a sentence and trusted to the Lord to see him through; numerous passages in Shakespeare show that he was equally daring if not equally devout.

Shakespeare was not an inventor of original plots. Nowadays we regard plagiarism, or literary theft, as something dishonorable; Shakespeare, in common with other writers of his day, had no such scruples. Nearly all his plays can be traced to older plays, to books of history, to stories translated into English from Latin and Italian. His *Julius Cæsar*, for example, contains long passages almost literally copied out of Sir Thomas North's translation of Plutarch's *Lives*. The plot of every one of his great plays was borrowed from some preceding writer.

Shakespeare was not a philosopher. Some poets, such as Lucretius and Dante, were deep thinkers who put into their poems profound reflections on human life and destiny. That is something which Shakespeare did not and could not do. His plays do, indeed, show a penetrating knowledge of human life, but it is the sort of knowledge to be gained by observation rather than by philosophic analysis and classification. Shakespeare, in short, was no more original in his thinking than he was in his plot construction. Though in Hamlet he presents a man "sicklied o'er with the pale cast of thought," and though the Prince, like Romeo and Brutus, is much given to philosophic reflection, analysis will show that there is nothing either very profound or very original in the substance of such well-known passages as those beginning with "What a piece of work is man," and "To be or not to be, that is the question." To praise Shakespeare for philosophical insight is like praising Thomas A. Edison for theological acumen.

Shakespeare was not a moral preacher. Unlike Sophocles and Calderón, he did not write his plays to instruct and enlighten and edify mankind; unlike Spenser and Bacon, he had no intention of purifying men's hearts and training their intellects. The crowds who came to the Bankside theaters were not seeking sermons, even sermons artfully disguised: they wanted to be thrilled and amused, and Shakespeare gave them what they wanted. Some of the lines at which they laughed would make a modern audience blush, though it must be added that in this respect Shakespeare was less an offender than the majority of his fellow dramatists. Shakespeare had no "message" to deliver, no gospel of "uplift" to preach. He was simply a member of a disreputable profession who worked hard and wrote plays because he had to, made a snug sum of money out of his labors, and left the stage and London when he had secured all the money he wanted.

Why Shakespeare is Supreme. All this being so, we might well wonder how it came to pass that Shakespeare, who did not bother much about the art of writing, is hailed as a master of English style; that Shakespeare, who never invented a plot, is the most distinguished playwright the world has known; that Shakespeare, who was not a philosophic thinker, is incessantly quoted and referred to by philosophers and psychologists and theologians; that Shakespeare, who had no high ambition to improve men's morals, is so constantly on the lips of preachers and teachers and other men who work for the betterment of humanity. What is the key to the riddle?

The answer is not difficult to find. Shakespeare builded better than he knew. Like men in every department of life whom we call great, this actor-manager-dramatist unconsciously achieved infinitely more than his actual performance seemed to warrant. Like young Saul who went forth to look for his father's asses and found a royal crown, like little James Watt who sat idly watching his mother's teakettle and invented the steam engine, like Columbus who sailed westward to find a trade route and discovered a world, Shakespeare wrote for the rough London theater and made his audience all succeeding ages. And this he did because, whether he was aware of it or not, he possessed in a high degree the art of expression; he knew how to write.

The mystery of William Shakespeare, in so far as it is a mystery at all, is the mystery of genius. He had scant education, few opportunities for travel, little time for reading, limited association with learned men [1]; but God had dowered him with a keen mind, a power of accurate observation, an uncanny knowledge of the human soul, a pictorial imagination, and an unparalleled mastery of words. Like the young Murillo, who learned how to paint while mixing pigments, Shakespeare acquired the art of supreme literature while reshaping and editing dull and humdrum stories to suit the requirements of the stage. That is the way of genius. And that is why an uncouth Scottish peasant became the poet Robert Burns and why an unschooled backwoods lawyer achieved the power and perfection of Lincoln's Gettysburg Address.

Like all geniuses, Shakespeare was prolific, and while writing the plays that poured from his tireless pen he learned craftsmanship and patience, artistic sense and discipline. Though as he wrote them his dramas were not divided into five acts, he developed a feeling of dramatic symmetry and

[1] Yet we must not underestimate the extent of Shakespeare's cultural opportunities. The Stratford school was better staffed than the average country school; and Shakespeare's London association with the Earl of Southampton brought him into contact with Continental scholars, including John Florio, the translator of Montaigne, and gave him access to one of the richest private libraries in England.

proportion in the unfolding of his plots. His growth in the art of writing blank verse we can trace from the rigid and monotonous regularity reminiscent of *Gorboduc* to the ease and variety and dexterity he exhibits in *Coriolanus* and *The Tempest*.[1] His characters changed from vague types like Launce in *The Two Gentlemen of Verona* and the Queen in *King Richard II* to clearly defined individuals like Launcelot Gobbo and Lady Macbeth. And from the farce and superficiality of the early comedies and the blood and thunder of the first tragedies, Shakespeare's interpretation of life deepened into the mellow humor of *As You Like It* and *The Tempest*, and the steady, searching, soul-revealing vision of *Othello* and *King Lear*. Shakespeare's mature plays moved Goethe to say that he felt he was reading in the book of life with the wind of fate tossing the pages to and fro. The difference between Shakespeare's early and later works is the difference between an amateur photographer's snapshot and Leonardo da Vinci's "Mona Lisa" in the Louvre. His gifts of genius were stupendous; but those gifts had to be developed through work and experience, through increased knowledge of human life and persevering efforts at self-expression.

---

[1] Excellence in blank verse, like excellence in most things, consists not in slavish submission to rules but in mastery of the principles which the rules embody. The basic rule of the blank verse is that there be five iambic feet, thus:

If mú | sic bé | the foód | of lóve, | play ón.

Shakespeare came to vary it by often adding an unaccented syllable at the end, or by occasionally substituting a trochaic foot, as in

Find tongúes | in trées, | *boóks in* | the rún- | ning broóks,

or a dactyl (one long and two short syllables, like the joints of a finger), as in

Lís ten ing | their feár, | I coúld | not sáy | Amén,

and by employing run-on lines — that is, verses the proper reading of which demands that no pause be made at the end:

In my good brother's fault: I know not why
I love this youth.

Furthermore, in the beginning of his career he used frequent rimes; as he progressed he avoided them.

Self-expression in the dramatic writer is evidenced by his ability to get into his characters and think their thoughts, feel their emotions, and see all things from their several points of view. This Keats did not try to do, for Keats is essentially a lyric poet. This Byron tried to do, but failed, for Byron could never succeed in sinking his own personality in his creations. But Shakespeare's self-expression was the art of concealing self. Notwithstanding all he wrote, we know very little about him. In Keats's sonnets we find the real Keats; in *Manfred* and *Childe Harold* we find the real Byron; but in *Macbeth* we find the sinful Thane of Cawdor and his resolute lady, in *Hamlet* we find the imaginative Prince of Denmark and his weak mother and his sensual uncle, in *Othello* we find the wily Iago and the baffled Moor and the innocent Desdemona and the simple Cassio and the silly Roderigo. In each of them and in all of them Shakespeare lives and moves; but in the truth and splendor of the creations we catch no hint of the personality of the creator.

Theories of Authorship. Shakespeare's complete artistic self-effacement is one of the reasons why in recent years his authorship of the dramas associated with his name has come to be disputed by some men who like to defend an improbable cause and who deny the validity of literary traditions.[1] The principal names put forward as candidates for the Shakespearean authorship are Marlowe, Sir Walter Raleigh, several noblemen (for example, the Earl of Southampton and the Earl of Rutland), a group of dramatists including Marston,

[1] To the United States belongs the questionable distinction of starting the war on Shakespeare. The first gun — a mere toy pistol — was casually fired by J. C. Hart in *The Romance of Yachting* in 1848; the battle was definitely on eight years later when Delia Bacon, ultimately consigned to a lunatic asylum, posited the Baconian thesis in *Putnam's Monthly* (January, 1856). Shortly afterwards the first shot was fired on English soil by W. E. Smith in his book *Bacon and Shakespeare*. Then in 1888 came a blast of artillery from Minnesota when Ignatius Donnelly published *The Great Cryptogram*. In the twentieth century the question has evolved into a spectacular guerrilla warfare with much sniping and few casualties.

Drayton, and Dekker, and Anthony Bacon and his more famous brother, Francis. The champions of Francis Bacon claim to have discovered in the plays cryptograms or secret hints indicating that the authentic author was not Shakespeare, and they have made ado over the admittedly careless and inconsistent draftsmanship in portraits of "the Stratfordian," as they call him. It is all very good fun, but it is not scholarship; the same sort of evidence might be used to deny the historic reality of Pontius Pilate, Napoleon Bonaparte, and Amy Lowell. Against all and sundry claims to other than Shakespearean authorship of the plays stand certain indisputable facts:

1. In his own day and for three centuries afterwards Shakespeare was accepted as the author of his plays, and numerous contemporary writers acclaimed his genius.

2. The main events in Shakespeare's life are known, and there is nothing in them to show either that he did not exist or that he could not have written the plays attributed to him.

3. An examination of the Shakespearean plays proves that the man who wrote them was closely identified with the theater. Shakespeare was, as Greene contemptuously called him, a "Johannes factotum," or Jack-of-all-trades, of the stage. The Bacons were not, the Earls of Rutland and Derby and Southampton were not; with the possible exception of Thomas Heywood, no Elizabethan dramatist was so essentially a theatrical man as Shakespeare was.

4. A comparison of the Shakespearean plays with the known writings of the others shows fundamental differences of style, of vocabulary, of power of expression, of range of interest, and of outlook on life. For instance, it is simply incredible that the same man could have written Bacon's essay on Love and Shakespeare's *Romeo and Juliet*.

The Man Shakespeare. Stratford-upon-Avon is a little town in Warwickshire, and there William Shakespeare was born on April 23, 1564. He received the rudiments of education in the Guild Grammar School (which still stands), a school maintained by the workingmen's association known as the Guild of the Holy Cross. The school was suppressed under Henry VIII; but, like many other such foundations throughout England, was reopened in the reign of Edward VI when the citizens protested. At the age of eighteen Shakespeare married

ANNE HATHAWAY'S COTTAGE

On holidays, when numerous visitors to Stratford-upon-Avon cross the fields to Shottery, the children of the neighborhood distribute flowers from the Hathaway garden

Anne Hathaway, a woman eight years his senior, who lived across the fields in Shottery. Some four years later, leaving his wife in Warwickshire, Shakespeare went up to London and joined a company of players. He was never distinguished as an actor; tradition has it that three parts which he assumed in his own plays were Friar Laurence in *Romeo and Juliet*, Adam in *As You Like It*, and the Ghost in *Hamlet*. His first work was revising and adapting old plays, and from that he passed to the making of new plays from stories and histories.

A few years ago an American university professor found documents in the Public Record Office in London which indicate where Shakespeare lived during a part of his long sojourn in the capital; his residence was in the house of a Huguenot named Mountjoy a little off busy Cheapside. After a time Shakespeare became director of plays and part owner of a theater. He waxed well-to-do, and about 1603 retired to his native town, where he bought a fine piece of property, New Place, and there he lived until his death on April 23, 1616. He is buried in Holy Trinity Church, Stratford.

Such is the bare outline of Shakespeare's life. If the recorded facts seem scanty, we must remember that in his day there were no newspapers to exploit theatrical personages, that he belonged to a profession not in good repute, and that externally he did nothing spectacular or notorious. Even in our times, when publicity has become an art, great artists, writers, and thinkers rarely get into the headlines. If there is anything to wonder at, it is not that we know so little about him, but that we know so much. As the late H. H. Furness has said:

It is merely our ignorance which creates the mystery. To Shakespeare's friends and daily companions there was nothing mysterious in his life; on the contrary, it possibly appeared to them as unusually dull and commonplace. It certainly had no incidents so far out of the common that they thought it worth while to record them. Shakespeare never killed a man as Jonson did; his voice was never heard, like Marlowe's, in tavern brawls; nor was he ever, like Marston and Chapman, threatened with the penalty of having his ears lopped and his nose split; but his life was so gentle and so clear in the sight of man and of Heaven that no record of it has come down to us; for which failure I am fervently grateful, and as fervently hope that no future year will ever reveal even the faintest peep through the divinity which doth hedge this king.[1]

Shakespeare was not what would be called today an up-to-date person. There is nothing in his life and nothing in his plays which would indicate that he took much interest in the

[1] Preface to the Variorum Edition of *Much Ado About Nothing*.

thrilling events of his time.[1] Unlike Marlowe, he played no party politics; unlike Jonson, he served no prison term for writing indiscreetly; unlike Spenser, he possessed no enthusiasm for English Protestantism and English national expansion. At the death of Queen Elizabeth he was publicly reproached by Henry Chettle for not paying poetical tribute to her memory and achievements. We look in vain among his plays for a glowing description of the defeat of the Spanish Armada or a rapturous picture of the merchant adventurers sailing out from Plymouth Sound. The themes he chose for his dramas were England of an elder day and stories in the European Tradition of literature. He was a small-town man, and as soon as he made his competence he was glad to escape from the bustle and intrigues of London. He was a keen observer and liked to study faces and characters, but (and this his plays amply attest) he was a hard worker and an omnivorous reader. He little dreamed that whole libraries would be written about his ideas and his craftsmanship and that the stage plays he hastily put together would be translated into all languages and studied by boys and girls in school.

Gossip, crystallized in the statement of Archdeacon Davies that "he died a Papist," has long been busy with the subject of Shakespeare's religious beliefs, and more than one industrious scholar has claimed that the great dramatist was a child of Mother Church. The possibility is unquestionable. He lived in times when Catholics were persecuted and when they did not unnecessarily call attention to their religious beliefs. His friend and patron was the Catholic Earl of Southampton. In his plays he treats monks and ecclesiastics with respect, in marked contrast with other dramatists of the time; and in at

[1] Charles Mills Gayley, kindly and capable scholar, was induced during the World War to write an interesting little book, *Shakespeare and the Founders of Liberty in America*, in which the effort is made to establish that Shakespeare was on terms of intimacy with the early colonizers in the New World; but it proves little beyond the fact that scholarship and enthusiasm can make a readable book out of nothing.

least one instance, that of *King John*, he toned down the anti-Catholic virulence of his sources. He shows too a surprisingly correct knowledge of Catholic beliefs and of Catholic customs, as when in *Romeo and Juliet* he speaks of evening Mass, for in Verona the practice of offering the Holy Sacrifice in the evening lingered long after his day. But, on the other hand, there is nothing in his plays that shows him to have been a man conversant with the spiritual life or animated by supernatural motives. His is a humanistic spirit, and his thoughts, even when garbed in the singing robes of poetic eloquence, are of the earth, earthy. He was alien to the religious exaltation of Calderón and Dante. He was no more a saint than he was a philosopher or a savant. Religious persons and events he could depict with fidelity and sympathy, but only as a modern newspaper reporter might record the sermon of a holy bishop or describe the Eucharistic Congress. In the passages in his plays — and they are numerous — which commemorate spiritual experience and embody religious ideals, Shakespeare tells what he sees and recounts what he imagines; he does not utter, from the heart to the heart, that which he feels and knows.

The Shakespearean Stage. We make a grave mistake if we fancy that the theater in Shakespeare's day was a substantial and well-equipped building like the Haymarket in London, the Opera in Paris, or the Century in New York. And we err still more grievously if we liken the Elizabethan actor to one of our modern gentlemen players who lives in a luxurious hotel, owns an expensive car, dresses in the height of fashion, and is an honored guest at college commencements and exclusive clubs. A London preacher in 1577 exaggerated as sometimes preachers do, but he voiced the view of many honest citizens when he called the playhouses "schools of vice, dens of thieves, and theaters of all lewdness." As late as the time of Molière the actor was under the ban of the Church, and it is only in our own day that he has ceased to be under the ban of society. As for actresses, they were simply nonexistent in Shakespeare's day. No woman who valued her reputation would appear even in the audience, and for any woman to show herself on the stage was simply unthinkable. Years after Shakespeare's death, when some imported actresses tried to play on the London stage, they were driven off with boos and catcalls and partly eaten apples. On Shakespeare's stage Juliet and Rosalind and Lady Macbeth were impersonated by boys, which in part explains the dramatist's fondness for having so many of his heroines masquerade in men's clothes.

Sometimes plays were given in a royal palace, as at Whitehall or at Hampton Court, Cardinal Wolsey's princely dwelling on the Thames about twenty miles from London; and sometimes there was a performance on the estate of a nobleman or in the lawyers' quarters in the Temple or Gray's Inn. In such cases the setting was often elaborate and the costumes were rich and splendid. But even when royalty smiled upon the player, it was much in the way modern wealth and fashion countenance the sleight-of-hand performer or the Egyptian dancer. The fact that Shakespeare's *Love's Labour's Lost* was acted before Queen Elizabeth at Whitehall, or the legend that she requested Shakespeare to write another play about Sir John Falstaff, does not warrant the assumption, sometimes indulged in by fanciful commentators, that the actor-dramatist hobnobbed with royalty. Many a lady in our day sends a request to a café musician to play a favorite melody who would not dream of saluting him on the street or inviting him into her home.

All the theatrical companies (they were never numerous) played part of the year "on the road"; one reason was that the bad weather affected the attendance of Londoners, the other that the authorities closed the theaters in time of plague — and it was often time of plague. No theater was permitted within the city limits, so the managers had to erect their ram-

Changling   Simpleton

French Dancing M.ͬ

S.ͬ I   Falstafe   Hostes   Clause

AN ELIZABETHAN STAGE

shackle buildings in Shoreditch and Finsbury Fields. Ther
was little pretense of scenery: that the imagination of th
spectators had to supply. Often there was a curtain to b
dropped before a small inner stage; but most of the actio
took place on a long, narrow platform that stretched out amon
the groundlings, as the occupants of the pit were called. Th

THE GLOBE THEATER

From an old print

groundlings stood in the mud or the dust and were unprotecte
from the weather. They were rude and outspoken and sorel
tried the temper of actors and the patience of managers. I
some of the theaters men of fashion occupied stools on th
stage and were not averse to exercising what wits they ha
at the expense of the struggling Thespians. All performance
were held during the daylight hours.

Shakespeare was associated with several such theaters, th
most famous of which was the Globe, located on the Banksid
in Surrey, across the Thames from the city. During a pe

ormance of *King Henry VIII* in 1613 the Globe was burned down as a result of fireworks set off on the stage; and one aftermath of the destruction of "that virtuous fabric" is recorded by Sir Henry Wotton in the following affecting terms: "One man had his breeches set on fire, that would perhaps have broiled him, if he had not by the benefit of a provident wit put it out with bottle ale." It is something of a coincidence that on the site of the Globe there stands today one of London's leading breweries.

Shakespeare's Plays. Of the thirty-seven dramas ordinarily attributed to Shakespeare, there are several with which he had very little to do. In *Pericles*, for example, Shakespeare's style is visible only in a few scenes. The same is largely true of the three plays of *King Henry VI*, which come very early in Shakespeare's dramatic career, and also of *King Henry VIII*, which is certainly the last of his plays in order of time. On the other hand, there are two dramas not included in the Shakespeare canon in which it is probable he had a hand: *King Edward III*, a Marlowesque tragedy with several passages possessing the authentic Shakespearean ring; and *The Two Noble Kinsmen*, a version of the story of Palamon and Arcite out of Chaucer and probably, like *King Henry VIII*, the joint work of Shakespeare and John Fletcher. *The Taming of the Shrew* is a revision of a play of the same name by an unknown author.

We shall now briefly consider the principal plays of Shakespeare. It is possible to approach the study of them in various ways: to follow them in the order in which Shakespeare wrote them; to begin with *Julius Cæsar*, because it is the easiest to read; to trace certain characters or ideas from play to play, finding, for example, Romeo, Brutus, and Hamlet to be embodiments of the meditative temperament. But we shall confine ourselves to a fivefold classification: the Comedies, the Histories, the Classical Plays, the Tragedies, and the Romances.

The Comedies. Though *Love's Labour's Lost* makes hard reading at first, irritates by reason of its reflection of Lyly's euphuism, and is at best a thing of froth and frivolity, it demands attention because it is the first play that is really Shakespeare's work and the only one with a plot not borrowed from existing plays or stories.

MAXINE ELLIOTT AS PORTIA; NAT GOODWIN AS SHYLOCK

Farce rather than comedy, because broader in its fun and improbable in its situations, *The Comedy of Errors* is an early example of that hearty humor, relieved by an occasional hint of tragedy, which we have come to recognize as essentially Shakespearean. The plot comes from Plautus, but the young Shakespeare already reveals himself a master of flowing language and a student of characterization.

The Two Gentlemen of Verona, derived from stories by the Spaniard Montemayor and the Italian Cinthio, is chiefly of interest as a preliminary study for some of the characters more carefully and sympathetically drawn in *The Merchant of Venice*, one of the most popular of the plays on the stage. It is evident that the character of Shylock took the principal rôle in spite of the author's intention. The Jew was to serve as a complication and to supply a suggestion of tragedy; but so forceful

You stand within his danger, doe you not.

An. I, so he sayes.

Por. Doe you confesse the bond?

An. I doe.

Por. Then must the Iew be mercifull.

Shy. On what compulsion must I, tell me that.

Por. The qualitie of mercie is not straind,
it droppeth as the gentle raine from heauen
vpon the place beneath: it is twise blest,
it blesseth him that giues, and him that takes,
tis mightiest in the mightiest, it becomes
the throned Monarch better then his crowne.
His scepter showes the force of temporall power,
the attribut to awe and maiestie,
vvherein doth sit the dread and feare of Kings:
but mercie is aboue this sceptred sway,
it is enthroned in the harts of Kings,
it is an attribut to God himselfe;
and earthly power doth then show likest gods
vvhen mercie seasons iustice: therefore Iew,
though iustice be thy plea, consider this,
that in the course of iustice, none of vs
should see saluation: vve doe pray for mercy,
and that same prayer, doth teach vs all to render
the deedes of mercie. I haue spoke thus much
to mittigate the iustice of thy plea,
vvhich if thou follow, this strict Court of Venice
must needes giue sentence gainst the Merchant there.

Shy. My deeds vpon my head, I craue the law,
the penalty and forfaite of my bond.

is his portrayal that he throws the play out of balance, and after the gripping trial scene the clever comedy of the last act seems incongruous. For years Shylock was interpreted in the spirit of broad farce. Charles Macklin was the first actor to play the Jew as a tragic human figure. The plot, grossly improbable in both the casket strand and the pound-of-flesh story Shakespeare took from Italian sources. In this play we have some of the most beautiful of Shakespeare's dramatic poetry.

SIR HENRY IRVING AS SHYLOCK

The basis of *As You Like It* was a romance by the versatile Thomas Lodge (1558?–1625) which Shakespeare enriched with graceful lyric passages and the introduction of several original characters, especially the melancholy Jaques and Touchstone sprightliest of all Shakespeare's fools. Here he made free use of contrast as a dramatic motive, and in Rosalind gave us one of the most fascinating of his heroines. The atmosphere of the play is delightful, with its suggestion of woodland life its pervasive humor, and its delicate seasoning of irony. Nearer perfection as a comedy is *Twelfth Night*, which, however improbable the plot derived from Bandello, achieves distinction through its characters: Viola and Olivia, the sparkling maid Maria, the gruff and Puritan-hating Sir Toby Belch, the incomparable ass Sir Andrew Aguecheek, and especially the

THE HALL OF THE MIDDLE TEMPLE, LONDON

Here *Twelfth Night* was performed for the first time early in 1602. (From a photograph taken expressly for this book with the kind permission of the Honorable Society of the Middle Temple)

pompous and self-important Malvolio. The songs in *As You Like It* and *Twelfth Night* represent the perfection of Shakespeare's lyric art.

A note of seriousness, almost of pessimism, creeps into *Much Ado About Nothing*. The story of Hero and Claudio comes from a French source, Belleforest's *Histoires tragiques*; but Shakespeare deepens the characterization and gives the center of the stage to the big-hearted and fun-loving Beatrice and the whimsical, woman-hating Benedick, the prototype of the confirmed bachelor who ultimately succumbs to feminine charm. Dogberry, the booby constable, is another original creation. The shadows deepen in *Measure for Measure* and *All's Well that Ends Well*, both dramas which in spirit and outlook on life are not comedies at all. They are distinctly unpleasant plays and indicate that Shakespeare wrote them in a mood of sadness and cynicism; most of their characters are frail and mean and cowardly, though Isabella in *Measure for Measure* takes her rightful place in the Shakespearean gallery of noble women. *All's Well that Ends Well* was inspired by a translation from Boccaccio, and *Measure for Measure* by Whetstone's *Promos and Cassandra* and his translation of the *Heptameron* of Margaret of Navarre. Some commentators profess to discover hints of Shakespeare's own personality in the Duke in *Measure for Measure*.

VIOLA ALLEN AS VIOLA

The Histories. The Histories are dramatic renderings of episodes in earlier English history, based on the chronicles of Holinshed, Hall, and other writers, and on plays concerned with national events. *King Richard III*, strongly suggestive of Marlowe in its mingling of grim tragedy and bombast, is the finest melodrama ever written. It is a play of thrills and horrors, ever a favorite with actors because of the opportunities for theatrical display inherent in the leading rôle; the other parts do not matter. The stage version which is usually given is an adaptation of Shakespeare's play by Colley Cibber, an eighteenth-century actor and playwright.

RICHARD MANSFIELD AS RICHARD III

A finer play is *King Richard II*, with numerous passages of sustained poetry, with an atmosphere of haunting melancholy and doom, and with at least one masterly scene perfectly conceived and dramatically realized — the deposition scene in Westminster Hall, where Richard reluctantly resigns the throne of England in favor of his cousin Bolingbroke. Some of the most impressive instances of Shakespeare's phenomenal skill in character creation are found in *King John*: the boy Arthur; Hubert, the diamond in the rough; the sturdy, outspoken Faulconbridge; John himself, a royal braggart and weakling; Cardinal Pandulph, the pope's legate; and especially the Lady

Constance, a part so exacting and difficult in its portrayal of maternal grief that more than one accomplished actress has declined to undertake its interpretation.

Three of the Histories might be called the Prince Hal Trilogy, since they are concerned with the life and development of the son of Henry IV, who succeeded his father on the throne and waged triumphant warfare against the French. They are the two parts of *King Henry IV*, and *King Henry V*. In the First Part of *King Henry IV* Shakespeare institutes a double contrast between court life and tavern life and between two young men and rivals in arms, Prince Hal and Hotspur. The Prince is represented as a wild youth who leaves the royal palace and consorts with disreputable characters, but when there arises need of his services he dons his armor and distinguishes himself in battle. His upward development is traced in the Second Part and in *King Henry V*, where he is a wise ruler, a devout sovereign, a skilled general, and an appealing wooer. He is the only male character in all Shakespeare's plays who is really a heroic hero. And in these three plays and in that rough, hilarious comedy *The Merry Wives of Windsor* we encounter Shakespeare's supreme comic creation in the person of Sir John Falstaff, a wit, a braggart, a glutton, a liar, a thoroughly unprincipled old rascal who nevertheless wins our sympathy. His downward development, in contrast with the upward development of Prince Hal, is indicated with tact and discernment.

The Classical Plays. The Classical Plays are so called not because they imitate the work of Greek and Roman playwrights but because their themes are drawn from classical sources and their scenes laid in ancient times. The best known of them is *Julius Cæsar*, immortal by reason of the surpassing oration of Marc Antony over the corpse of Cæsar, the quarrel scene between Brutus and Cassius, and the firm delineation of the idealistic character of Brutus, the reader and thinker who fails when he comes into the arena of practical life. The facile and pleasure-loving Antony, the man to whom success came easily and who therefore missed the discipline of struggle, Shakespeare follows to Egypt in *Antony and Cleopatra* and reveals the gradual deterioration of a character not strong enough to resist the force of passion and the lure of an enervating environment. Sardou and several other dramatists have turned to the same theme; but Shakespeare excels them all in his reproduction of the gorgeous East, his analysis of the siren Cleopatra's charms, his depiction of the man who for a woman threw a world away. *Coriolanus*, difficult to read though sustained and concentrated in construction, is the story of a man ruined by his pride of birth and breeding. The mother and wife of Coriolanus rank high among Shakespeare's feminine creations. In *Troilus and Cressida* Shakespeare wrote in a vein of bitter satire of the Homeric heroes of the Trojan War and evolved a strong though unpleasing illustration of Hamlet's familiar saying "Frailty, thy name is woman." The last of the Classical Plays, *Timon of Athens*, approximates to the theme which Shakespeare later on so magnificently developed in *King Lear*; it is uneven in workmanship and obviously is one of the dramas in which Shakespeare collaborated with somebody else.

The Tragedies. The five great tragedies of Shakespeare — a performance unparalleled in the history of world literature — depict with consummate artistry and marvelous knowledge of the human heart the ravages of five consuming passions each of which assails man at a definite period of his life. Were all his other plays lost, these five tragedies would suffice to keep Shakespeare the undisputed master dramatist of all countries and all times. Taken together they reveal the perfection of his literary power, his keen sense of dramatic values, and especially his comprehension of human emotion as an influence that makes or mars the life of every man. They can be read repeatedly and witnessed a score of times on the stage, and never can their action grow stale or their inspiration be exhausted. To know these five plays is truly and essentially to know everything it is possible to know about human life.

The first of them, *Romeo and Juliet,* is the tragedy of youth and love. "Violent delights have violent ends"; and in the story that so picturesquely unfolds itself "in fair Verona, where we lay our scene" we recapture the wonder and the wild desire

THE GHOST APPEARS AT ELSINORE

What if it tempt you toward the flood, my lord,
Or to the dreadful summit of the cliff
That beetles o'er his base into the sea,
And there assume some other horrible form,
Which might deprive your sovereignty of reason
And draw you into madness?

of ardent, inexperienced youth and realize anew the tragedy that issues from the planting of the rose of love in a world finite and material and overgrown with the thorns and brambles of vulgarity and caste and hereditary hatred. The play literally sings itself into our souls, so potent is the dramatist's command of word melody. Shakespeare bettered his source (Arthur

Brooke's translation of Bandello's story) with his glowing fancy and with his dramatic relief supplied in the dashing, laughing, unsentimental Mercutio. All the world pays tribute to *Romeo and Juliet* as the greatest love play ever written. In present-day Verona — though Shakespeare's characters had, in fact, no historical existence — strangers from all lands visit the house of the Capulets, and the alleged tomb of Juliet

OPHELIA

From a painting by Millais

overflows with visiting cards left there by admirers of Shakespeare who have caught the glamour and the pathos of his ill-starred lovers twain.

As Romeo typifies the emotion of love, so Hamlet typifies the emotion of self-esteem; that is to say, Romeo's love flows out from him, whereas Hamlet's love is forced back upon himself by a number of interior conditions and external circumstances. He is what today would be called egocentric, the first man to see that *Hamlet* is nothing with Hamlet left out. Like his creator, and despite a popular opinion to the contrary,

Hamlet is no philosopher, but he is an adept at poetic introspection, at envisaging himself in a variety of situations possible or fantastic. The fact that there were two editions of the
play besides the version given in the Folio of 1623 has brought
confusion and inconsistency into modern texts and has made
possible the most di-
verse interpretations of
Hamlet's character and
motives. This is the
play upon which Shake-
speare seems to have
worked most diligently
and revised most
thoroughly from an
older play and from
Belleforest's *Histoires
tragiques*. It is also the
most popular of his
plays with learned and
unlearned alike. Ham-
let is an exceptionally
appealing figure; sev-
eral of the other char-
acters, such as Polonius,
are admirably drawn;
and the drama is gener-

EDWIN BOOTH AS HAMLET

ously sprinkled with commonplace thoughts expressed in novel
and picturesque language. The passion for introspection which
is so potently illustrated in the person of Hamlet, a man in
the thirties, is the emotional trait of most thoughtful men in
the same period of life. Readers and spectators consciously
or unconsciously identify themselves with the gentle and self-
regarding Prince.

As Hamlet is the man of thought, so Othello is the man of action; and Shakespeare presents him in those critical years of

middle life when impulses long suppressed seem to make a last fight against ideas and habits fostered by education and civilization. A strong disciplinarian, and therefore self-controlled, the Moor suddenly loses both discretion and self-command and involves his lovely wife Desdemona in his tragic doom. Hamlet thinks too much, Othello thinks too little, and so for opposite reasons they meet a similar fate. As the instrument of

THE WEIRD SISTERS

destruction Shakespeare introduces Iago, his super-villain, the very incarnation of the spirit of evil. *Othello* has the swiftness and tragic sweep of the strongest of the ancient Greek plays, with a rich humanism and a flood of pictorial language which Sophocles never equaled.

Inordinate ambition, the typical passion of later middle age, is the subject of Shakespeare's *Macbeth*. The Thane of Cawdor, aided and encouraged by his devoted and unscrupulous wife, wades through blood to gain the throne of Scotland, and all too late learns the significant truth that the evil desire is punished through its own attainment. Like most of Shakespeare's heroes, Macbeth is an unconscious poet, and some of his utterances are among the most glowing passages in universal literature. Out of Holinshed's matter-of-fact history Shakespeare created a drama of lurid force and heartrending horror and a graphic picture of the problem of evil. "Fair is foul, and foul is fair."

EDWIN FORREST AS LEAR

And, finally, in *King Lear* we have a powerful and soul-wracking exposition of the tragedy of old age: its childishness, its waywardness, its petulance, its pathos, its unknowing injustice, and its inherent nobility. Dr. Johnson, with a flash of that insight more than once revealed in his comments on Shakespeare, maintained that Polonius in *Hamlet*, once a shrewd and capable man of affairs, became a doddering old fool because he failed to change with changing times and relied too much on his past successes. That analysis applies even more accurately to King Lear, whose indiscretions bear such bitter fruit. He is truly a "man more sinned against than sinning," and yet those who most flagrantly sin against him are his children, the children of his blood and of his conduct. Against the grim and storm-tossed background of castle and desert heath move some of Shakespeare's most unforgettable creations: the loyal Kent, the loving fool, the villainous Edmund, the devoted Edgar, the unnatural Goneril, the tender Cordelia. The play moves us as a masterly rendition of some superb piece of music or a devastating storm viewed from a mountain peak.

The Romances. Four plays, often classed as Comedies, are so fanciful in subject matter and treatment that they may be conveniently considered apart. *A Midsummer Night's Dream*, compounded of elements from Chaucer, from Plutarch, and from Ovid, is at once a delightful fairy tale, a charming love story, and a humorous rendition of human weakness and absurdity. Bottom, the self-important weaver magically changed into an ass and loved by the enchanted queen of the fairies, is not only an immortal comic creation but an enduring type of human experience. Of sterner stuff is *Cymbeline*, the highly improbable plot of which Shakespeare borrowed from Holinshed and Boccaccio, and out of unlikely material evolved Imogen, one of his most appealing heroines. To Robert Greene's *Pandosto* Shakespeare was indebted for the plot of *A Winter's Tale*, a sage poetical romance in which the roguish thief Autolycus shares dramatic honors with the sweet and dainty girl Perdita and with Hermione, the patient and virtuous wife. But finest of the Romances, and one of the best of

SIR HENRY IRVING AS LEAR

all the plays, is *The Tempest*, in which some students have discovered a hint of Shakespeare's own individuality and an expression of his personal theory of life. Perhaps they are wrong; but nevertheless it is fitting to associate the playwright who went down to Stratford again with the magician Prospero who breaks his magic staff and relinquishes his power over the creatures of air and sea. It is in this play that Shakespeare anticipated the scientific theory of evolution by introducing the monster Caliban, the "missing link," part human and part brute.

HELENA MODJESKA AS IMOGEN

Summary. Two factors mainly contributed to the marvelous literary riches of the drama of Shakespeare: his own abounding genius and the spirit of the European Tradition in literature. He took his material and caught his inspiration from the past: from Greece and Rome, from Italy, France, and Spain, from early Britain and more recent England, and — whatever was his own religious belief or absence of belief — from Catholicism. Thomas Carlyle, certainly no partial witness, wrote in his *French Revolution*, "Catholicism, with and against feudalism, but not against nature and her bounty, gave us English a Shakespeare and era of Shakespeare, and so produced a blossom of Catholicism." Like Michelangelo and the cathedral builders, like the composer Palestrina and the painter Velasquez, Shakespeare achieved high art, which is a vision of life in terms of beauty. Chatham said that he learned history from Shakespeare, and many readers have professed to find in Shakespeare great truths of philosophy and a new perception of moral values; but the one thing that all of us must discover in the great plays is the living face of beauty, an earthly reflection of the Heavenly Beauty which is God. "Beauty needs no arguments, for it is itself the strongest argument in the world; and the work of art is a burning-glass which so concentrates the rays of beauty as to set the soul aflame." [1]

And so today the little village of Stratford-upon-Avon, with its memories and its relics and its associations, is a world shrine of literature whither pilgrims go — men and women whose souls have been kindled and purified by the art and imagination of a man born there nearly four hundred years ago.

DRAMATISTS AFTER SHAKESPEARE

Ben Jonson (1573–1637). The life of Jonson possesses variety and interest, but it has little to do with Jonson as a dramatist. He was a big, corpulent man, swollen of features and ungainly of gait, who paid poetic tribute to "my mountain belly and my rocky face," and who could on occasion drink deep and bear a part among the Elizabethan roisterers. He served a prison term too, and was in peril of execution, whereupon he became a Catholic; but, the danger past, Jonson conveniently shifted out of his new-found faith. His stepfather, Thomas Fowler — sometimes contemptuously referred to as a bricklayer, but really a contractor and surveyor and "Controllor of the Queen's Majesty's Works" — gave young Jonson a good education at Westminster School; and whether or not Jonson appreciated his stepfather, he certainly appreciated

[1] W. Macneile Dixon, *Tragedy*, p. 142.

his teacher, William Camden, to whom he dedicated his first and greatest play:

> Camden! most reverend head, to whom I owe
> All that I am in arts, all that I know.

Much that he knew, however, Jonson had picked up in the army in Flanders and in London taverns; but Camden's in-

BEN JONSON

fluence never deserted him, and through all his varied activities he preserved an interest in books and learning. Like his later namesake, Dr. Samuel Johnson, he had a Scottish biographer. Jonson's Boswell was William Drummond, who has recorded, with what accuracy it is difficult to determine, some of the conversations he had with Jonson at Hawthornden, near Edinburgh. Jonson's tomb in the Poets' Corner of Westminster Abbey bears the laconic epitaph "O rare Ben Jonson!"

As a dramatist Jonson is to be remembered for two things: he frankly imitated the technique of Greek and Latin dramatists and he emphasized the portrayal of human nature in eccentric moods or "humours." In his plays he made a display of his classical learning, his "learned sock," as Milton termed it; and he reveled in satire, coarse wit, and vigorous dialogue. Several of his fifty dramas are attacks on contemporary writers for the stage, for Jonson was prominent in the "War of the Theaters" which was waged late in the sixteenth century, and echoes of which we find in Shakespeare's *Hamlet.* "Our English Horace," as Henry Chettle called Jonson, produced comedies, tragedies, and masques. Of the comedies the best is *Every Man in his Humour*, abounding in cleverness though marred by "licentious jests"; *Volpone* is a study of a melancholy man-hating man; *Epicene* gives an almost farcical account of the doings of a "silent woman"; *The Alchemist* turns on the passion for money; *Bartholomew Fair*, of all Jonson's plays the most popular with the groundlings, is strong and vulgar. In tragedy Jonson is most distinguished for his *Sejanus* and *Catiline*, very classical and dignified but, in comparison with Shakespeare's classical dramas, lifeless and formal. None of Jonson's

JOHN FLETCHER

From an original painting in the collection of
George A. Plimpton

masques is equal to Milton's *Comus*, but there is real beauty in *Oberon* and *The Masque of Queens*. In general Jonson's plays are more scholarly than vital; they are not, and they never were, favorites with theatergoers. As William Collins put it, "Nature in him was almost lost in art."[1]

Beaumont and Fletcher. Francis Beaumont (1584–1616) and John Fletcher (1579–1625) formed a literary partnership

[1] *Epistle to Sir Thomas Hanmer.*

and produced in collaboration over fifty dramas. Both were university men, Beaumont hailing from Oxford, Fletcher from Cambridge. Beaumont was the more serious-minded of the two and seems to have been something of a critic as well as a dramatist. Ben Jonson, Dryden tells us, "submitted all his writings to his censure, and, 'tis thought, used his judgment in correcting, if not in contriving, all his plots."[1] Fletcher, who collaborated also with Massinger and Shakespeare, wrote easily and lightly (and sometimes very dirtily) but lacked Beaumont's feeling for tragedy. The best-remembered of the plays by Beaumont and Fletcher are *Philaster*, a romance weak in characterization, improbable in plot, but rich in dramatic poetry; and *The Knight of the Burning Pestle*, a sprightly "take-off" on the Romances, its mood recalling the comic spirit of *Don Quixote*.

Philip Massinger (1583-1640). Though Massinger was not untouched by the licentiousness of the English stage, he revealed in his plays moral earnestness and religious convictions. He was an Oxford man and a convert to the Catholic Church who settled in London and engaged in dramatic work, sometimes with others, sometimes on his own account. He seems to have taken the theatrical profession seriously, and in one of his dramas, *The Roman Actor*, made a fine defense of the stage. *The Duke of Milan* clearly owes some of its inspiration to Shakespeare's *Othello*, though Massinger was no slavish borrower; the drama is well constructed and has passages of genuine eloquence. Massinger's masterpiece is *A New Way to Pay Old Debts*, a gripping picture of St. John's "lust of the eyes" in the person of the heartless miser, Sir Giles Overreach. There is nothing of the blood and thunder element in Massinger's plays: they are noted for their restraint, their fine workmanship, and their balanced style.

John Webster (1580?-1625?). It is difficult to conceive a greater contrast than that between the dramatic works of

[1] "Essay of Dramatic Poesy."

Massinger and of Webster. With Webster we sup full with horrors: he is the most powerful representative of the "tragedy of blood." *The Duchess of Malfi* and *The White Devil* are grim and horrible but great — some say, next to Shakespeare's, the greatest tragedies in English Literature. But their greatness is literary rather than dramatic; they are too chaotic in form as well as too "unpleasant" in matter for stage presentation. Webster had a knack of writing sententiously, putting much in little, as in the oft-quoted lines

> We cease to grieve, cease to be fortune's slaves,
> Nay, cease to die, by dying.

But his limitations are evident. He has no sense of either comedy or romance; he sees but one side of life, the tragic side, and that chiefly in its accumulation of terrors. In contrast with Shakespeare, he lacks balance, sanity, perspective. Vittoria in *The White Devil* reminds us of Lady Macbeth, but she utterly lacks the revealing human touches which soften and even ennoble Shakespeare's undying creation.

Other Dramatists. Writing plays in partnership with somebody else was a favorite occupation of Thomas Dekker (1570?–1641?), whose name occurs in conjunction with those of Marston, Webster, Massinger, Ford, and other dramatists. He and Marston were ridiculed by Jonson in *Cynthia's Revels* and *The Poetaster*. Dekker made a real contribution to English comedy in *The Shoemaker's Holiday*, a comedy of life in London. Thomas Heywood (1575?–1650) — "I hold he loves me best who calls me Tom" — was another prolific collaborator: he claimed to have had a hand in the making of over two hundred plays. Charles Lamb called him a prose Shakespeare and was justified in the compliment, for Heywood at his best, though not a master dramatist, is a capable and even brilliant writer. His best-remembered play is *A Woman Killed with Kindness*. Yet another man of many partnerships was Thomas Middleton (1570–1627), a writer of abounding energy whom at least one competent critic, Dr. Charles H. McCarthy, regards as in some respects second only to Shakespeare.[1] But his work is seriously marred by coarse comedy and depraved views of life. Representative dramas of Middleton are *The Changeling*, *Woman Beware Woman*, and *A Mad World, My Masters*. John Ford (1586–1640?), unlike most of the dramatists of this period, had tenderness and gentility and was likewise a successful lyric poet; but, like Massinger and Fletcher, he was

JAMES SHIRLEY

often theatrical rather than dramatic, that is, he constructed scenes and created characters which are startling but improbable and unreal. His principal plays are *The Lover's Melancholy*, *The Broken Heart*, and *Love's Sacrifice*.

James Shirley (1596–1666). Shirley was the "last of the Romans"; he carried the Elizabethan dramatic tradition through the troubled years of Charles I and fought at Marston Moor in the Royalist army. He studied at both Oxford and Cambridge, became a Catholic, and for a while taught school at St. Albans. He went to Ireland with Lord Strafford and founded in Dublin the first Irish theater, for which he wrote several plays, notably *St. Patrick for Ireland*, the first of many dramatizations of the story of the Irish national saint.[2] In London he was a favorite both at the court and the popular

---

[1] "Methods in the Study of English Literature," in the *Catholic School Journal*, October, 1926.

[2] For an account of this play see John Eglington's *Anglo-Irish Essays*, pp. 57 ff.

theaters and won distinction in every kind of dramatic composition. Among his plays are the comedies *The Witty Fair One* and *Hyde Park*; *The Traitor*, a well-constructed tragedy; and *The Triumph of Peace*, a court masque. Shirley was a notable poet too, and some of the lyrics scattered through the plays are tuneful and eloquent. One such occurs in his masque *The Contention of Ajax and Ulysses*:

> The glories of our blood and state
>   Are shadows, not substantial things;
> There is no armour against fate;
>   Death lays his icy hands on kings:
>   Sceptre and crown
>   Must tumble down,
> And in the dust be equal made
> With the poor crooked scythe and spade.
>
>   ·   ·   ·   ·   ·   ·   ·
>
> The garlands wither on your brow,
>   Then boast no more your mighty deeds;
> Upon Death's purple altar now
>   See, where the victor-victim bleeds:
>   Your heads must come
>   To the cold tomb;
> Only the actions of the just
> Smell sweet, and blossom in their dust.

CHAPTER VIII

THE AGE OF MILTON

James Shirley, with his capable work in drama and in lyric poetry, serves to bridge the slight gap between the age of Shakespeare and the age of Milton and, in particular, to introduce us into the company of that "mob of gentlemen who wrote with ease," as Pope described the Cavalier Poets. Shirley was a fighter as well as a writer, and most of his fellow Cavalier Poets were writers as well as fighters. They all had this in common, that though they sympathized with the cause of King Charles and detested Cromwell and the Puritans, they derived their literary inspiration not from the stirring episodes of the Civil Wars and the Puritan Commonwealth, but from such universal themes as love and nature and the delights of solitary musing.

The execution of Charles I and the establishment of the Commonwealth profoundly affected the course of English history, and the noises of the conflict of arms and of ideas inevitably echoed in the literature of the period; but the surprising thing is that the echoes were not more dominant and prolonged. The leading writers on both sides — when they were producing literature and not journalism or controversy — wrote little of war and politics. Puritanism produced a literary star of the first magnitude in Milton and a solitary satellite in Marvell; the Royalist cause evolved a numerous group of minor poets, several of them immortalized by reason of single songs. And besides the two Puritan writers and the host of Cavalier Poets there was a third group, a little band of men, like Crashaw and Herbert, who ignored the strife of the hour and took refuge in thoughts of God and the things of the soul. The literature of this period therefore falls into three divisions: the poems of the Cavaliers, the contribution of John Milton, and the lyrics of the Religious Poets.

THE CAVALIER POETS

Robert Herrick (1591-1674). Unregarded for two centuries after his death, the poems of Robert Herrick are now securely established in the canon of English Literature, and the pagan parson who in his youth chummed with Ben Jonson and in his old age lived obscurely on the edge of Dartmoor has become the object of a literary cult. Such a caprice of fame seems appropriate in the case of this man, whose life was a tissue of contrasts and contradictions and whose verses are sometimes exquisitely sweet and graceful and occasionally crude and vulgar.

Herrick was born in Cheapside, London. As a young man he joined the "Tribe of Ben" and participated (if his own account can be believed) in more than one feast of reason and flow of bowl. The ode in which he pays his compliments to Jonson is as eloquent in spirit as it is curious in form:

> Ah, Ben!
> Say how or when
> Shall we, thy guests,
> Meet at those lyric feasts
> Made at the Sun,
> The Dog, the Triple Tun,[1]
> Where we such clusters had
> As made us nobly wild, not mad,
> And yet each verse of thine
> Outdid the meat, outdid the frolic wine?

This enthusiastic disciple of rare Ben went to Cambridge and took his degree when he was thirty years old. When he was nearly forty he became a clergyman and was given charge

---

[1] The names of London taverns.

of the parish of Dean Prior in Devonshire. He was Royalist in sympathy; so when the Cromwellians came into power he was deprived of his living, but returned to it in 1662 by favor of Charles II. He tells us that he was glad to get back to London and glad to get back to Devonshire, a complaisance which proceeded less from Christian resignation than from an accommodating human spirit. He was sometimes in debt, and now and then he drank more than was good for him; but on the whole his long life seems to have been uneventful and happy. He never married; and there is no reason to believe that his numerous love poems were more than addresses to imaginary ladies — Julia, Anthea, Electra, Dianeme, and the rest. He was neither a saint nor a hero, but a peaceful, moderately self-indulgent follower of the paganism of Catullus, Horace, and Martial, whose writings most of his poems resemble.

The subject matter of his poems Herrick charmingly indicates in the "Argument" prefixed to the *Hesperides*, a collection of over eleven hundred of his secular verses:

> I sing of brooks, of blossoms, birds and bowers,
> Of April, May, of June, and July-flowers;
> I sing of May-poles, hock-carts,[1] wassails, wakes,
> Of bridegrooms, brides, and of their bridal-cakes;
> I write of Youth, of Love, and have access
> By these, to sing of cleanly wantonness;
> I sing of dews, of rains, and piece by piece,
> Of balm, of oil, of spice, and amber-greece;
> I sing of times trans-shifting; and I write
> How roses first came red, and lilies white.
> I write of groves, of twilights, and I sing
> The court of Mab, and of the Fairie King.
> I write of Hell; I sing, and ever shall,
> Of Heaven, and hope to have it after all.

He did, indeed, devote some of his poems to sacred things, in the collection called *Noble Numbers*; but somehow Herrick was never either very convincing or very poetical when he was

[1] The hock-cart was the wagon that brought home the last load after harvest.

pious. There is, however, a quaint and simple charm about his "Grace for a Child":

> Here a little child I stand,
> Heaving up my either hand;
> Cold as paddocks [1] though they be,
> Here I lift them up to Thee,
> For a benison to fall
> On our meat and on us all.   Amen.

Every modern collection of English poetry contains the best and most delicate of Herrick's lyrics. Through most of what he wrote runs a strain of sadness at the prospect of death; indeed, Herrick might be called the Poet of Fleeting Life. His familiar verses beginning "Gather ye rosebuds while ye may" voice a thought on the brevity of life expressed by Spenser, by Tasso, by the Latin poet Ausonius, and in Holy Scripture, a thought that is beautifully framed in a familiar German song.[2] He was impressed by the fact that all things decay with time, that youth passes and beauty fades and violets wither and die; and in rare moments he abandoned his care-free paganism and dwelt in devout meditation:

> If after rude and boist'rous seas,
> My wearied pinnace here finds ease;
> If so it be I've gained the shore,
> With safety of a faithful oar;
> If having run my barque on ground,
> Ye see the aged vessel crown'd;
> What's to be done, but on the sands
> Ye dance and sing, and now clap hands?
> The first act's doubtful, but we say,
> It is the last commends the play.

[1] Paddocks are toads or frogs.

[2] Freuet euch des Lebens
    Weil noch das Lämpchen glüh't;
  Pflücket die Rose
    Ehe sie verblüh't!

  Delight in life while its lamp yet glows,
  And ere its fading pluck the rose.

Sir William Davenant (1606–1668). Typical of the career of many of the Cavalier Poets is the life of Davenant, who was knighted by Charles I, fought on the Royalist side, three times suffered imprisonment in the Tower of London, shared the exile of Queen Henrietta Maria in France, and basked in the favor of Charles II after the Restoration. His father kept an inn at Oxford where Shakespeare sometimes stayed on his journeys between Stratford and London; several bits of gossip connect Shakespeare with Davenant, one maintaining that the great dramatist was William's godfather. When the Royalist cause was lost Davenant set sail for America but was captured by a ship of the Commonwealth. While in France he became a Catholic, a fact which doubtless affected his life but which exerted little influence on the tone of his later writings. It must be said, however, that his poems and plays are more decent than most of the literature of the Restoration era — an epoch rebounding from Puritan repression and enamored of strange gods.

SIR WILLIAM DAVENANT

Davenant's dramas are of no importance, though it is interesting to observe that his *Siege of Rhodes* (1656) is the first English opera. His long poem, *Gondibert*, was well thought of in his day, but modern readers find it dull and dreary. His lyrics are tuneful and often spangled with real poetic gems. Here is the first half of his "Soldier Going to the Field," which may profitably be compared with poems on the same theme by other Cavalier Poets:

Preserve thy sighs, unthrifty girl,
    To purify the air;
Thy tears, to thread instead of pearl
    On bracelets of thy hair.

The trumpet makes the echo hoarse
    And wakes the louder drum;
Expense of grief makes no remorse
    When sorrow should be dumb.

For I must go where lazy Peace
    Will hide her drowsy head,
And, for the sport of kings, increase
    The number of the dead.

Sir John Suckling (1609-1642). As a poet Suckling is remembered for a few dainty, care-free songs, notably the one beginning

Why so pale and wan, fond lover?
    Prithee why so pale?

That little masterpiece occurs in *Aglaura*, one of four poor plays from Suckling's careless pen. His life was a queer combination of opéra bouffe and grim tragedy. He was a soldier and a spendthrift, a courtier and a prisoner. At his own expense he raised a company of cavalry to fight for the king, and they set forth for the fray attired in "white doublets, scarlet breeches and scarlet coats, hats and feathers." But they looked better than they fought, for at the first smell of powder they one and all ran away; upon which feat of valor Suckling remarked, "Posterity must tell this miracle, that there went an army from the south, of which there was not one man lost nor any man taken prisoner." Troubles gathered about Suckling in subsequent years, and he took his own life in Paris.

Richard Lovelace (1618-1658). Some of the world's finest literature has been written in prison, and so it is not surprising to discover that the poems for which Lovelace is best remembered were composed to beguile the tedium of his captivity as a prisoner of the Commonwealth. "To Althea from Prison," with its familiar lines

> Stone walls do not a prison make,
> Nor iron bars a cage,[1]

and "To Lucasta, on Going to the Wars," with its beautiful statement of the triumph of loyalty over love,

> I could not love thee, dear, so much,
> Loved I not honor more,

are deservedly universal favorites and have made Lovelace the most popular of all the Cavalier Poets. Yet neither of those two songs is characteristic of his poetry as a whole. Generally Lovelace was neither so simple in thought nor so clear and straightforward in expression. He was a bit of a euphuist and imitated the strained expressions of Donne. Though he can hardly be classed among the religious poets, Lovelace often resembles Crashaw and Habington in his fanciful imagery, and he anticipated some of the traits of Cowley and the "metaphysical" poets.

Like so many of his fellow Cavaliers, Lovelace knew much of the ups and downs of fortune. As a student at Oxford he was accounted "the most beautiful and amiable person that eye ever beheld," a fact which, more than academic worth, secured him academic honors; for he was so gentlemanly and devoted in entertaining feminine visitors in 1636 that he received the

---

[1] It is interesting to note that very similar sentiments were expressed by a French poet, Pellisson, who, from his cell in the Bastille, wrote as follows:

> Doubles grilles à gros cloux,
> Triples portes, forts verroux,
>   Aux âmes vraiment méchantes
> Vous représentez l'infer;
>   Mais aux âmes innocentes
> Vous n'êtes que du bois, des pierres, du fer.

But there is no suggestion of plagiarism on the part of Lovelace. Pellisson wrote in 1661, three years after the English poet's death.

degree of Master of Arts "at the earnest request of a great lady in attendance on the Queen." As representative of the people of Kent he delivered a petition in the House of Commons for the restoration of the king, with the result that he

was cast into prison. Both his sword and his wealth he devoted to the Royalist cause. There spread a rumor of his death, and on his return to London from the wars he found, like Enoch Arden, that his "Lucasta" (Lucy Sacheverel) had married another man. Then came another term in prison, and the gallant Cavalier died in poverty in Gunpowder Alley.

Sir John Denham (1615–1669). Close to Chaucer in Westminster Abbey lies a Cavalier Poet who in his day wrote a number of popular things, includ-

SIR JOHN DENHAM

ing a now forgotten play, *The Sophy*, in which, said Waller, he "broke out, like the Irish Rebellion," but who is now remembered because he is the author of a few lines beautiful and meditative as the river they commemorate:

> O could I flow like thee, and make thy stream
> My great example, as it is my theme!
> Though deep, yet clear, though gentle, yet not dull,
> Strong without rage, without o'erflowing full.

His theme is the river Thames, seen as it flows so placidly through the meadows near Runnymede; and the brief description occurs in a lengthy poem called *Cooper's Hill*, the first sustained piece of descriptive and reflective verse in English Literature. It is a work which suggests a calm-eyed, contemplative spirit meditating on nature and human life. That, however, is what, most emphatically, Denham was not. English by ancestry, Irish by birth, gypsy by temperament, Denham, from his student days at Oxford to his quarrelsome career in London, was a stormy petrel in exceptionally stormy waters. He was an inveterate gambler and inveterate loser, and those of his possessions which did not slip from him at the gaming table were confiscated by the Puritans. An obscure poet, George Wither, was a captain in the Parliamentary army and was captured by the Royalists. Denham begged the king to pardon the Puritan poet because, said he, "while that man lives I shall not be the worst poet in England."

Abraham Cowley (1618–1667). John Dryden[1] was the first literary critic to apply the name of metaphysical poets to Donne and his imitators, and Cowley is the most prominent example of the metaphysical tendency in poetry. The word does not mean what it seems to mean. It has nothing to do with philosophy in this connection, but connotes a style of verse-making characterized by metrical cleverness, learned allusions, strained and unusual metaphors, and a play of fancy often bordering on absurdity and extravagance. Today Cowley is little read, but during his lifetime and for many years after his death he was much admired and was regarded as something of a literary dictator. His influence on the development of English poetry was considerable. He introduced the Pindaric ode and thus set the fashion for several succeeding poets, including Dryden, Gray, and Thompson.

---

[1] In the preface to his *Juvenal*, in 1693, when he wrote that Donne "affects the metaphysics, not only in his satires, but in his amorous verses." Dr. Johnson popularized this unique use of the word *metaphysics* in his *Life of Cowley*.

Though in the eyes of mature critics Cowley could hardly be designated "a mighty genius," there is point and judgment in this estimate of him from the pen of young Joseph Addison:

> Great Cowley then, a mighty genius, wrote,
> O'er-run with wit, and lavish of his thought:
> His turns too closely on the reader press;
> He more had pleased us, had he pleased us less.
> One glittering thought no sooner strikes our eyes
> With silent wonder, but new wonders rise;
> .   .   .   .
> Thy fault is only wit in its excess.

Cowley was a Londoner, born in Chancery Lane. He attended Cambridge, was expelled by the Puritans for his Royalist devotion, and with Denham and others joined Queen Henrietta Maria in France. Returning to England in 1654, he studied medicine at Oxford. He lived at Chertsey on the Thames. He loved rural life. "God the first garden made," he wrote, "and the first city, Cain." He lies in the Poets' Corner in Westminster Abbey.

As a prose writer Cowley was master of a graceful and pleasing style, as revealed in his slender sheaf of essays, one of them entitled "On Myself"; and he tried his hand at dramatic writing as well. But his historical importance rests upon his collection of love poems, unimpassioned but clever, *The Mistress*; on his unfinished epic, *Davideis*, a pale imitation of Milton, but dignified and stately; and most of all on his *Odes*, in which he exercised himself in metrical experiments and indulged his fondness for elaborate conceits and artificial imagery. In one of his poems he calls attention to the similarity of the human brain to the kernel of a walnut.

Thomas Carew (1598?–1639). Dainty, graceful, polished, and written slowly and with fastidious care, the lyrics of Thomas Carew still please, even though they do not and never did appeal to the deeper emotions and the nobler sentiments. They are far removed alike from the dashing carelessness of

Suckling and the vital richness of Herrick, but they hang in the
Cavalier gallery like little paintings neither striking in coloring nor bold in composition but still attractive because of their
delicacy and subdued tones. Bits of Carew's verses have a way
of haunting the memory:

> Beauty, youth, and endless spring
> Dwell upon thy rosy wing.
>
> Amongst the myrtles as I walked,
> Love and my sighs thus intertalked;
> "Tell me, said I, in deep distress,
> Where may I find my shepherdess?"
>
> Give me more love, or more disdain:
>   The torrid, or the frozen zone
> Bring equal ease unto my pain;
>   The temperate affords me none:
> Either extreme, of love or hate,
> Is sweeter than a calm estate.

His "Approach to Spring," on a topic irresistible to all poets
and poetasters and near poets, invests the familiar subject
with fresh and fragrant charm. Carew's lines are finer than
his life, if half the stories told of him be true; but all lovers of
true poetry will rejoice with Clarendon that Carew died "with
the greatest manifestation of Christianity that his best friends
could desire."

Edmund Waller (1606–1687). Waller was a Cavalier poet,
but with reservations. He adhered to the Royalist cause until
it became a lost cause, when he prudently wrote some graceful
complimentary verses to Cromwell and secured safety and
the post of provost of Eton College. As a poet he was much
thought of in his day; but time has a way of reversing the
judgments of an age, and now Waller lives chiefly in two or
three delightful lyrics like "On a Girdle" and "Go, Lovely
Rose." Waller resembles Carew. Both lacked strong convictions and deep emotion, and both were assiduous in the
pursuit of grace and perfection of form.

Samuel Butler (1612–1680).   Although to classify Butler with the Cavalier Poets is like putting Saul among the prophets, *Hudibras*, the one work associated with his name, is the most notable example of poetry reflecting the spirit of the times.   Most of the poet followers of King Charles, including those who outlived the Puritan régime, fought and spoke in defense of their sovereign, but wrote of love and loyalty and the promise of the spring; and nearly all of them were university men and members of the nobility. Butler, on the contrary, achieved his fame with a vigorous satire on Puritanism with all its works and pomps; and he came of an obscure Worcestershire family and had little formal education. He was a clerk or secretary in the household of Sir Samuel Luke, a

SAMUEL BUTLER

From an original painting in the collection of George A. Plimpton

colonel in Cromwell's army; and when Charles II came to the throne Butler won great popularity by his metrical caricature of his former master, for that is what *Hudibras* is. The leading character, Hudibras, is a Presbyterian Don Quixote, and Ralpho, an Independent, is his booby squire. The poem, a bit lengthy for sustained reading, is in octosyllabic verses. It is not great poetry — indeed, for the most part, it is frankly doggerel; but it is a very good burlesque, and even some of the remote descendants of the Puritans wince a little at its shafts of irony.

Hudibras hits, and hits hard, at long-faced religionists of all countries and all times. The Pharisees, we must remember, were Jewish Puritans, and the Jansenists were French Puritans; and even in the land of the free and the home of the brave we have a few earnest persons who seek to merit Heaven by making earth a Hell. Many a quip of Butler's is susceptible of a present-day application:

> He could distinguish and divide
> A hair 'twixt south and south-west side;
> On either which he would dispute,
> Confute, change hands, and still confute.
>
> For all a rhetorician's rules
> Teach nothing but to name his tools.
>
> He could raise scruples dark and nice,
> And after solve 'em in a trice;
> As if divinity had catch'd
> The itch, on purpose to be scratch'd.
>
> Compound for sins they are inclin'd to,
> By damning those they have no mind to.
>
> His wit was sent him, for a token,
> But in the carriage crack'd and broken.
>
> For saints themselves will sometimes be,
> Of gifts that cost them nothing, free.
>
> For disputants, like rams and bulls,
> Do fight with arms that spring from skulls.
>
> To cheat with holiness and zeal,
> All parties and the common-weal.

Needless to say, Charles II and his court were enthusiastic about this coarse and pungent satire; but that put no money in Butler's purse, and he died in poverty. He lies today beneath the green sod of the churchyard of old St. Paul's in

Covent Garden. In 1721 a monument to Butler was erected in Westminster Abbey, where he is commemorated as "the curious inventor of a kind of satire among us, by which he plucked the mask from pious hypocrisy and plentifully exposed the villainy of rebels"; and that Westminster memorial moved Samuel Wesley to write what is perhaps the bitterest epigram in the English language:

> While Butler, needy wretch, was yet alive,
> No generous patron would a dinner give;
> See him, when starved to death and turned to dust,
> Presented with a monumental bust.
> The poet's fate is here in emblem shown:
> *He asked for bread, and he received a stone.*

Andrew Marvell (1621-1678).

> But at my back I always hear
> Time's wingèd chariot hurrying near;
> And yonder all before us lie
> Deserts of vast eternity.

The man who wrote that was an authentic poet; and the poet who could envisage eternity as an expanse of "deserts" might well be regarded as a Puritan laureate, even though no such office existed in the Lord Protector's court. In Marvell the man and the poet were miles asunder. The man was, with his friend Milton, made Latin secretary to Cromwell and accommodated himself to the Restoration, though writing vigorously against its abuses; the poet idled in the garden of fair imaginings and wrote such delicious pieces as "A Drop of Dew," "The Picture of Little T. C. in a Prospect of Flowers," and "To his Coy Mistress," one of the truly memorable love poems in English Literature. There is a hint of a stronger and more thoughtful Herrick in Marvell's "Thoughts in a Garden":

> How vainly men themselves amaze,
> To win the palm, the oak, or bays,
> And their incessant labors see
> Crowned from some single herb or tree

> Whose short and narrow-vergèd shade
> Does prudently their toils upbraid,
> While all the flowers and trees do close
> To weave the garlands of repose!

Marvell's poems were collected by his widow in 1681, but their printing caused little stir, and, like Herrick, Marvell had to wait centuries for adequate recognition. It was a poet of a later day, William Wordsworth, who in a sonnet of 1802 paid tribute to Marvell; and a quaint lover of poetry, Charles Lamb, who rendered becoming homage in prose. Finally in 1921 his native city of Hull proudly celebrated the three-hundredth anniversary of his birth. "It has occurred to me," remarked the worshipful Lord Mayor on that occasion, "that Andrew Marvell was the greatest advance advertisement agent Hull ever had." Thus does fame play queer pranks on her favored children!

MILTON

Next to Shakespeare, John Milton (1608–1674) was the weightiest contributor to the goodly treasure of English Literature, and Milton's name, like Shakespeare's, is familiar to cultured readers in every land. The man, indeed, is frequently more intimately known than his writings; and even though *Paradise Lost* is listed among the books people mean to read some day but never do, a present picture in the popular imagination everywhere is that of the prematurely aged Puritan poet seated at his organ, his sightless eyes closed but his soul flooded with supernal visions. The world cherishes the memory of two blind bards, Homer and Milton. Homer is legendary, Milton is real; but the songs of both make immortal music.

Man and Poet. The contrast between Milton the man and Milton the poet was drawn with unconscious humor by the schoolboy who wrote that "Milton married three times and wrote *Paradise Lost*," a statement correct in its facts but unwarranted in its implications. Milton was a scholar and a

Puritan saint; a good man and learned, but in many ways disagreeable. An unsympathetic husband, a harsh father, a scurrilous controversialist, he reveals numerous irritating personal traits. Though richly read in the books of the European literary tradition and an heir of the culture of the Renaissance, he maintained and championed ideas and theories uncongenial to the mass of men in his day and not less uncongenial now. His religious opinions, for example, were far removed from ours. He denied the divinity of Jesus Christ. He was opposed to forms of prayer and was blind to the dramatic beauty and spiritual suggestion of church liturgy. He advocated divorce and half tolerated polygamy. He believed that the soul cannot live apart from the body. All such views he held with firmness and promulgated with

JOHN MILTON

Milton's grandfather was a stanch Catholic, and the poet's brother Christopher became an enthusiastic convert; but, despite a persistent and ill-founded legend that he entered the Roman communion in his declining days, Milton was and continued to be violently anti-Catholic in his controversial writings. (From an original painting in the collection of George A. Plimpton)

vigor, so that theologians have always found in his writings ample grounds for disagreement and condemnation. He was a bigot and something of a fanatic, and neither bigots nor fanatics are persons we can easily admire and like.

But that is not the whole story, and others of his characteristics must win our sympathy and esteem. He was a zealous and intelligent student, and as a boy devoted so many hours daily and nightly to his books that eventually he injured his eyesight. In an age when virtue was often openly scoffed at, Milton revered personal purity and guarded himself against temptation. If a vindictive and implacable enemy, he was a loyal and devoted friend. Though his conception of duty was harsh and narrow, he had the courage of his convictions and lived his life with high seriousness; and though his notion of religion seems to us strained and severe, he unfailingly recognized man's obligation to God.

And Milton the poet was one of the world's supreme makers of visions of beauty. Some of his sonnets are the finest in the English language, and when he wrote in Latin he succeeded, as few modern poets have done, in making his verses not mere literary exercises but the expression of genuine emotion. In lighter vein he evoked the powers of a delicate fancy, and in his more serious works he displayed a massive imagination and a splendid command of words. More truly even than Wordsworth, he was to poetry a dedicated spirit : in the days of his youth he determined to write such verses as the world would not willingly let die. He drew lavishly on the best that had been written before him, and his influence on subsequent writers, both at home and abroad, has been far-reaching and impressive.

Milton and Dante. In several important respects the Puritan Milton closely resembles the Catholic Dante. Though their theological positions were far apart, both were essentially religious men, both were very great writers, both were prevailingly intense and serious, and both could on occasion be gentle and winning. Both gave spiritual masterpieces to the world, and both — because the bulk of mankind are incapable of appreciating the highest art — are more talked about than read. And the thirteenth-century poet of Italy and the seventeenth-century poet of England led lives that are similar in their general outlines.

The career of each was divided into three distinct periods of nearly equal length. Each enjoyed a studious and leisurely youth, rich in opportunities for gathering poetic material and for refining his genius, each early won generous fame for lyrics and sonnets of unusual beauty, each at about the same age dedicated himself to a lifelong task by which he hoped to gain terrestrial immortality. . . . Then for each there followed approximately two decades of severest discipline. The contemplative singers, dreaming of immortality, were snatched from their gentle, iridescent worlds of ideals and cast violently upon the rocks of actual evil conditions. Each was made fit to write a world poem by experiencing the world's fiercest passions and its elemental struggles. . . . In despondency, disillusionment, and faith the one proposed to justify the ways of God to men, the other to reveal to men the true path to God. Milton was engaged for some six years on his *Paradise Lost*, beginning in 1658 and finishing in 1665. Dante was absorbed in the *Divina Commedia* for an equal period.[1]

In yet another respect Dante and Milton are akin: both demand much from their readers in scholarship and application. It would hardly be accurate to say of Milton, as certainly it can be truly said of Dante, that to know his works intimately is to secure a liberal education; but there can be no doubt that the intensive reading of Milton broadens and deepens the intellect and exalts and purifies the imagination. And as many of the most enthusiastic students of Dante are men who do not share his intense Catholicism, the reader of Milton, however averse to Arianism and Puritanism, will secure both learning and inspiration from contact with the Englishman's vigorous and well-disciplined mind. For Milton is truly a classic, and the student of literature who does not know intimately and love ardently at least one true classic — Homer or Virgil, Dante or Goethe, Shakespeare or Milton — will never win to the finer and deeper fruitage of literary culture.

The Springtime of Life. John Milton was a Londoner, born in Bread Street, Cheapside. His father, originally a Catholic,

[1] C. A. Dinsmore, *Life of Dante*, pp. 110–113.

had adopted the Protestant faith; Milton's younger brother
Christopher returned to the Church and was a judge of some
prominence in the reign of James II. Milton's father gave
his son ample opportunities for study, and John, after attending St. Paul's School in London, entered Christ's College, Cambridge. He was not popular with his fellow students,
who nicknamed him "the Lady of Christ's," partly because
of his refinement of manners and his almost feminine appearance but also because young Milton had higher standards of
morality and of conduct than were possessed by the general
run of undergraduates. His university career was not a source
of happiness. His relations with his instructors and with
the college administration were not congenial (exceptionally
brilliant students are often difficult subjects), and he was
"rusticated," or suspended, in 1632. He had entered the university with the intention of becoming a clergyman, but his
views of religion were changing, and he discovered for himself
another vocation. He felt that God wanted him to be a poet,
and he took the call seriously. So for the next six years he
lived a quiet, studious life on his father's estate at Horton.

Horton is a tiny village in the Thames valley but a few
miles from Eton and Windsor. Even today, despite a mill or
two and some ugly modern houses, it is a picturesque spot.
Green pastures flank it, through the heart of it runs the little
river Colne, and on minute islands in the stream cattle lie
ruminating in the softened sunlight. It was an ideal retreat
for a young poet intent on perfecting himself in his art, and
here Milton wrote some of his most graceful and delightful
verses. He had begun his poetic endeavors at Cambridge, but
it was at Horton that Milton the poet grew to man's estate.

Early Poems. Milton's "Hymn on the Morning of Christ's
Nativity" is an ode, stately and pictorial, with here and there
a touch that suggests one of Botticelli's sacred paintings. Like
everything that Milton wrote, it reveals wide reading and original reflection. Some of its language is strained and affected,

indicating the influence of Donne and suggesting something of the imagery of Crashaw without Crashaw's burning fervor.

"L'Allegro" and "Il Penseroso" present the poet in a cheerful mood and in a thoughtful mood.[1] As "L'Allegro" shows, Milton took his cheerfulness very soberly indeed, and there is a gravity of tone even in his mention of

> Jest, and youthful Jollity,
> Quips and cranks and wanton wiles,
> Nods and becks and wreathèd smiles,
>
> . . . .
>
> Sport that wrinkled Care derides,
> And Laughter holding both his sides.

The poet is more himself in "Il Penseroso" with his invocation

> Hail, divinest Melancholy!
> Whose saintly visage is too bright
> To hit the sense of human sight.

But both pieces are true poems in their play of fancy, their refined imaginings, their unhackneyed language, and their high measure of metrical perfection. The student who learns to know and appreciate these two poems will never make the mistake of accepting vulgarity for art or doggerel for poetry.

The purity of young Milton's mind and his esteem for the virtue of chastity are expressed in the masque of *Comus*, for which Henry Lawes wrote the musical score. Its dramatic quality is weak, for Milton was too lyric and personal to write effective drama; but when rightly staged and sympathetically interpreted *Comus* has still the power to hold an audience by reason of its splendid poetry and its moral earnestness. "Love Virtue, she alone is free" is the summary of its teaching — a teaching conveyed through the story of a maiden lost in the

---

[1] L'Allegro may be translated the Cheerful Man, and Il Penseroso the Pensive Man. At this period of his life Milton was not a thorough Italian student. There is no such word in Italian as *penseroso*. The correct form is *pensieroso*, which means not *thoughtful*, but *solicitous, anxious, full of care*. Later on Milton came to read Italian fluently and to write it rather well.

forest, enchanted by Comus and his crew, and delivered on account of her holiness of life. Even in his youth Milton was, like Shakespeare, a copious borrower from other men's writings, and it is possible to trace in *Comus* ideas and turns of language taken from Fletcher's *Faithful Shepherdess*, Peele's *Old Wives' Tale*, and Ben Jonson's masques. But Milton took nothing that he did not improve.

A shepherd in one of the eclogues of Virgil and in an idyl of Theocritus is named Lycidas, and this name, bestowed upon Edward King, a fellow student at Cambridge, gives the title to the last of the Horton poems. Milton and King were not intimate friends, but King's untimely death moved the poet to contribute an elegy to a memorial volume planned by King's admirers. Elegiac poetry is not uncommon in English Literature, but Milton's "Lycidas" and Cowley's elegy on Crashaw are the first notable instances of it; Shelley's "Adonais," Arnold's "Thyrsis," Tennyson's *In Memoriam*, and Swinburne's "Ave atque Vale" are all lineal descendants of "Lycidas." The poem is in strict accord with the pattern of the Greek pastoral, and, as in Dante, there is a blending of characters from mythology, like Æolus; from Christian history, like St. Peter; and from fancy, like Camus, the god of the river Cam, which flows through Cambridge. What perhaps most appeals to the modern reader in "Lycidas" is the speech of St. Peter, "the pilot of the Galilean lake," who bewails the unworthiness of the clergy, a theme which Dante in his day more than once utilized. In this passage occurs the beautiful line

> The hungry sheep look up and are not fed.

The Strife of Noonday. After a visit to Italy in 1638 Milton entered upon a semipublic career coextensive with the Cromwellian régime in England. He married, and not happily. For a time he engaged in teaching, but chiefly he devoted his pen to the cause of the Commonwealth and entered into numerous literary quarrels with contenders at home and abroad. He sought to justify the execution of King Charles I and was made a Latin secretary under Cromwell. At the age of forty-five he completely lost his sight, but his fierce activity ended only with the Restoration, when some of his books were burned by the common hangman, and he was obliged to go into retirement.

This storm-and-stress period of Milton's literary life must sadden even his most devoted admirers. He was a cutting and vindictive adversary and in controversy recognized neither common decency nor "the rules of the game." His fall, declares Pattison, was worse than Bacon's, a descent "to that despicable region of vulgar scurrility and libel, which is below the level of average gentility and education."[1] He wrote on divorce; on the execution of the king, which he venomously defended; on church government, in treating which he revealed what was least worthy in his character. Two living documents, neither lengthy, emerge from the welter of his prose writings, his *Tractate on Education* and *Areopagitica*, a plea for the liberty of the press. The *Tractate* holds an assured place in the universal library of education. In many of the practices it sponsors it is repellent and antiquated, but its basic principles — the fruits of classical training and the Renaissance — are enduring and often couched in language worthy of the subject. The Areopagus was the civic tribunal in ancient Athens (it was before that learned assembly that St. Paul preached his wonderful sermon on the Unknown God), and the word *Areopagitica* means matters deserving the attention of Parliament, the English Areopagus. In *Areopagitica* occur several instances of Milton's misreading of history, of his blind religious prejudices, of his weakness for imputing evil; but here, too, occurs that splendid definition "A good book is the precious life-blood of a master spirit, embalmed and treasured up on purpose to a life beyond life." Milton's pleading for unlicensed printing is eloquent and impressive;

[1] *Milton*, in the English Men of Letters Series, p. 113.

but eloquent and impressive too is the fact that not so long afterwards he himself occupied the post of licenser or censor of publications under the Commonwealth.

Of Milton's prose writings generally Professor Saintsbury has said, "Cut the abuse out, and there is not much left of them."[1] Now and then they contain flights of impassioned diction and some well-constructed sentences; but in writing prose Milton was using an instrument not yet brought to its perfection of keenness and pliability, and he often, indeed usually, wrote English that is lacking in construction, order, and finished ease. It is a mistake to hail him as one of the masters of English prose, though, on the other hand, it is possible to pick from his pages several gems of well-fashioned eloquence. He is one of the few poets in the world's literature who could not write distinguished prose.

The Sunset Glow. Cromwell died, the son of Charles I came back from France and mounted the English throne, some of the leaders of the Commonwealth fled to the Continent, and others, charged with treason, went to their death. The erstwhile Latin secretary, poor and blind, relapsed into obscurity. Milton had married for the third time in 1663, and now with his wife and daughters he lived sometimes in London, sometimes in a country cottage at Chalfont St. Giles in Buckinghamshire. In the eyes of the world his life seemed a failure. He was poor, he was in disgrace, he was blind and in failing health. He was the lone survivor of a lost cause. Gone from his life was the sunshine of his happy Horton days; no longer blew about his head the winds of controversy. A stroller in Bunhill Row at evening time, seeing the blind poet sitting silent on his doorstep and smoking his solitary pipe, might sigh or sneer according to the direction of his sympathies, but in either case conclude that here was a man whose life of promise had gone up in smoke; that the Great Plague and the Great Fire, which in quick succession had devastated London,

[1] Chapter on Milton in the *Cambridge History of English Literature*.

were amply reproduced in the career of John Milton. For his spirit had been blackened by the plague of politics and his heart seared by the fire of bitter disappointment.

And yet out of this season of obscurity and poverty and crushing failure blossomed the supreme work of the poet's genius. It was now that he composed *Paradise Lost*. Michael

MILTON'S COTTAGE, CHALFONT ST. GILES

Here the poet began what he considered his master work, *Paradise Regained*

Munkácsy's well-known painting represents Milton seated in an armchair, the light of inspiration on his brow, dictating his master poem to his devoted daughters. It is a pretty picture but misleading as to facts. Milton's daughters did not take down his poem in dictation, for the simple reason that they had never learned to write; Milton had some very rigid views regarding the education of woman. *Paradise Lost* and the other works of his later period Milton dictated to a few faithful friends who often visited him to console him and to assist him in his labors. Then came death in November, 1674, and the body of John Milton was deposited in the Church of St. Giles, Cripplegate, in the tomb where his father already lay. The spot is marked to this day by a slab of stone in front of the chancel screen; but it is almost a certainty that the tomb was broken open in 1790 and the poet's bones dispersed. His true monument is his cenotaph of song.

Paradise Lost. Three of the world's literary masterpieces are each the work of a lifetime. The young Dante, filled with grief at the death of Beatrice, determined to raise to her memory a literary monument, to write a poem such as had been written of no woman; and a few years before his death he completed his *Commedia*. The story of the man who sold his soul to the devil first impressed Goethe when he was a little boy watching a puppet show; he wrote the first line of his *Faust* when he was twenty-three years of age and the last when he was eighty-one — a lesson, as Brother Azarias remarks, that who runs may read. Milton while still at Horton determined to write a supreme poem and considered several subjects for his potential masterpiece. As early as 1642 he had chosen the fall of man for his theme and had drafted a number of outlines of the story in the form of a Greek tragedy. Through the tumultuous years of the Commonwealth the design was postponed but not abandoned, and the strife and excitement of that epoch in Milton's life, the affliction of his blindness, and the suffering and privation of his declining days, all were distilled into *Paradise Lost*. It is truly, in his own words, "the precious life-blood of a master spirit."

Lamartine described *Paradise Lost* as "the dream of a Puritan fallen asleep over his Bible." It is that, and much more. It is a conscious attempt to "justify the ways of God to men." It is an exalted poetic delineation

> Of man's first disobedience, and the fruit
> Of that forbidden tree, whose mortal taste
> Brought death into the world, and all our woe,
> With loss of Eden. . . .

Abdiel that ſight endur'd not, where he ſtood
Among the mightieſt, bent on higheſt deeds,
And thus his own undaunted heart explores.

O Heav'n! that ſuch reſemblance of the Higheſt
Should yet remain, where faith and realtie
Remain not; wherfore ſhould not ſtrength & might
There fail where Vertue fails, or weakeſt prove
Where boldeſt; though to ſight unconquerable?
His puiſſance, truſting in th' Almightie's aide,
I mean to try, whoſe Reaſon I have tri'd   120
Unſound and falſe; nor is it aught but juſt,
That he who in debate of Truth hath won,
Should win in Arms, in both diſputes alike
Victor; though brutiſh that conteſt and foule,
When Reaſon hath to deal with force, yet ſo
Moſt reaſon is that Reaſon overcome.

So pondering, and from his armed Peers
Forth ſtepping oppoſite, half way he met
His daring foe, at this prevention more
Incens't, and thus ſecurely him deſi'd.   130

Proud, art thou met? thy hope was to have
The highth of thy aſpiring unoppos'd,   (reacht
The Throne of God unguarded, and his ſide
Abandond at the terror of thy Power
Or potent tongue; fool, not to think how vain
Againſt th' Omnipotent to riſe in Arms;
Who out of ſmalleſt things could without end
Have rais'd inceſſant Armies to defeat
Thy folly; or with ſolitarie hand
Reaching beyond all limit, at one blow   140
Unaided could have finiſht thee, and whelmd
Thy Legions under darkneſs; but thou ſeeſt

All

A PAGE FROM THE FIRST EDITION OF *PARADISE LOST* (1667)

It is one of the world's supreme epics of art,[1] impregnated with classical and Renaissance learning and in a broad way imitating the form of ancient epic poetry and reproducing the atmosphere of the Greek drama. It is a work of art based upon a truth of human history and human nature recognized everywhere and in every age; for the fall of man from a state of happiness and virtue is a tradition among early peoples in every part of the world, and even should a modern man, as some do, deny the fact of original sin, he cannot deny its effects — a clouded understanding, a weakened will, and a strong inclination to evil. It is a symphony of word music, dignified and exalted, suggesting the horn effects in Wagner and the choral strains in Handel's *Messiah*. It is a vision of beauty conceived in the grand style, brought forth in reverence, and adorned with jewels of English diction that far outshine "the wealth of Ormus and of Ind."

Objections of varying force have been urged against *Paradise Lost*. (1) Milton was very much of an individual poet, and he put into the poem so much of his own thought and emotion that in some respects it is more lyric than dramatic, more subjective than objective in its interest. But then the mind and the experience of Milton — experience of books and of life — are well worth our while. (2) In the astronomical system utilized in *Paradise Lost* the earth is stationary, with the sun and the planets circling around it,[2] and this is not good science. True. But we do not as a rule turn to poetry for our scientific

---

[1] It is well to distinguish between the epic of art and the epic of life. The latter is usually of unknown authorship and the expression in poetry of the life of a people in an early stage of civilization; the former is the work of a scholarly poet writing in a period of mature civilization and utilizing the experience of earlier writers. The *Iliad*, *Beowulf*, and the *Song of Roland* are epics of life; the *Æneid*, *Jerusalem Delivered*, and *Hiawatha* are epics of art.

[2] The Ptolemaic system, so called after Ptolemy, an Egyptian astronomer who lived in the second century. His theory of the earth as the center of the universe was supplanted by the heliocentric theory of Copernicus, a Polish priest.

knowledge, and Milton's adherence to the older planetary theory does not destroy the beauty of his poem; this is no more vital an objection against Milton than it is against Dante, who also follows the Ptolemaic system in his *Commedia*. (3) Milton confuses our notions of the material and the spiritual when, for instance, he pictures the rebel angels using the mountains of the earth for projectiles. But must we be so precise and literal-minded in reading poetry? Milton wants to convey an impression of tremendous conflict, a war with big issues involved, and he has his warriors fling at their adversaries the biggest things they find lying around; he has them do, so to speak, what men would do if men were rebel angels. (4) In comparison with the crispness of outline and the picturesqueness of detail in Dante, Milton is vague and shadowy and lacking in color. This limitation — though young Macaulay esteemed it a merit when he wrote his essay on Milton — is, of course, traceable to the fact that the poet had been blind for years and had acquired the habit of imagining things with less and less dependence on form and coloring. (5) But the most persistent objection brought against Milton is that he makes a hero of Lucifer, the prince of the rebel angels. The charge is fundamentally unjust. True, Milton has done an exceptionally fine piece of character-drawing in his portraiture of the devil, and enters into his point of view somewhat as Shakespeare gets inside his villains like Iago and Edmund; but Milton shows a downward development in the devil from the proud and brilliant Lucifer of the first books of *Paradise Lost* to the mean and scheming Satan of the temptation in Eden. The fault, if fault there be, is not with Milton but with Milton's modern readers. On this point, writes a recent commentator,

Milton could hardly have guessed the extraordinary future of his creation; for the rebel, as a human type entitled to respect and often to sympathy, was not recognized in Europe till the period of the French Revolution. Cromwell and the Puritans might be rebels, but only in the eyes of the Royalists: in their own eyes they were liberators. The term "rebel" was in itself a term of reproach and was to remain such till the days of Byron. Milton, therefore, would be not a little perplexed at our strange modern sympathy with Satan, which to him would be almost incomprehensible.[1]

Even if the student does not attempt to read the entire poem, he will secure a satisfying impression of its excellence, first, by reading a summary or outline of it and then by dipping into it and enjoying representative passages. What might be called the "high places" of the poem are the invocation to the heavenly Muse and the picture of the fallen angels in the burning lake (Book I); the council of the devils (Book II); the description of the Garden of Eden (Book IV); Raphael's account of the battle between the hosts of Lucifer and Michael (Book VI); the story of the temptation of Eve and the fall of man (Book IX); and Adam and Eve expelled from Paradise (Book XII).

Other Poems. Milton continued the story of the human race in the four books of *Paradise Regained*, a poem which he regarded as superior to *Paradise Lost* and for which his story of the fall of man was designed as a prelude. Most readers judge Milton entirely by *Paradise Lost*, just as with greater injustice they estimate Dante's work by the *Inferno*; but some critics (including Coleridge and Wordsworth) consider *Paradise Regained* the best of all Milton's writings. This poem treats at considerable length of the temptation of Our Lord by Satan; in Books III and IV some truly glorious passages occur, and in Book II he puts a touching speech into the mouth of the Blessed Virgin.

Closely approximating to the form of a Greek drama with its few characters, its chorus, its lengthy speeches, and its off-stage action, *Samson Agonistes* is the work into which the poet put most of his own mood and personality. The blind Samson

[1] R. E. Neil Dodge, "Theology in *Paradise Lost*." Cited by C. H. Grandgent in *Old and New*, p. 5.

held captive by the Philistines and compelled to hearken to their revelry in the temple of their idol is a prototype of Milton during the Restoration. The drama is interesting as the last flare-up of Milton's genius. The preface on tragedy is a good statement of the author's theory.

Aside from his lengthier works in poetry and prose, Milton kept a poetic record of his reactions to life and circumstances in thirty-odd sonnets (a few of them in Italian), which he wrote from time to time, from his young manhood to his old age. Perhaps the best of them are "On his Having Arrived at the Age of Twenty-three" — despite the fact that he speaks of God as a Task-Master — and "On his Blindness," with its pathetic reflection leading to the line that has become an English proverb,

> They also serve who only stand and wait.

Milton's Creditors and Debtors. In a general way Milton was deeply indebted to the literature of Greece and Rome and to the leading Italian writers, including Dante, Tasso, and Petrarca. His writings are an unceasing reminder that literature is a derivation of books from books. In form he had no hankering after novelties, and in his sonnets he was faithful to the Petrarchan model; in *Samson Agonistes*, to the so-called classical unities of time, place, and action; and in *Paradise Lost*, to the canons of epic poetry formulated by Italian critics. More than all else, he drew heavily on the Bible for both diction and inspiration. And he learned much from several of his predecessors, especially Shakespeare and Spenser. It is not unworthy of remark that one reason why he achieved greatness was that he sedulously read and imitated truly great models of literary expression.

For many of the ideas and for some of the specific speeches in *Paradise Lost* Milton was indebted to preceding writers on the subject of the fall of man. Francis Dujon was one of his friends, and through him Milton certainly came to know

Cædmon and to secure from the early poet at least one hint
for his characterization of Satan; both Cædmon and Milton
make the devil desirous to seduce Eve in revenge for his expulsion from Heaven. It is likely too that he drew on the
Adamo of the Italian Andreini, published in 1613, and on the
Adamus Exul of Grotius, which appeared about the same time;
but his amplest borrowing was from the Dutch drama *Lucifer*,
brought out in 1654, the work of Joost van den Vondel, the
leading poet of Holland and a convert to the Catholic faith.
Milton knew Dutch (was taught it by Roger Williams, the
founder of Rhode Island), and investigators have found numerous points of resemblance between *Lucifer* and *Paradise Lost*.

Milton's influence on other writers has been conspicuous.
His masterpiece has taken its place in the European Tradition
and is better known on the Continent than it is in the English-
speaking countries. One of his great foreign admirers was
Chateaubriand, who translated *Paradise Lost* into French, and
in his *Genius of Christianity* used Milton to prove that a religious subject makes the best possible theme for a poetic masterpiece. Of the English poets Pope, James Thomson, Gray,
Wordsworth, Shelley, and Keats were especially indebted to
Milton. Thanks to Shakespeare and Milton blank verse is
recognized as the standard form of exalted poetry in English.
De Quincey exaggerated the popular appeal of Milton when
he wrote that "Milton is justly presumed to be as familiar to
the ear as nature to the eye"[1]; but though Milton's longer
works are not widely read, several of his sonnets and his Horton poems are familiar to school children in England and
America, and many of his characteristic expressions have been
woven into the fabric of everyday speech. And the man himself, triumphing over his afflictions, steadfast in the pursuit of
his ideals, faithful to the last to his vocation as a poet, is an
impressive figure in the eyes of succeeding generations.

[1] *Reminiscences of the English Lake Poets*, p. 6 (Everyman edition).

THE RELIGIOUS POETS

Richard Crashaw (1613?-1650). The remarkable poetic contribution of Richard Crashaw is Catholic and catholic; that is, while on the one hand it is strongly and vitally inspired by the principles and devotions of the Catholic religion, it is on the other broadly and richly influenced by the ancient classics, by the literature of Spain and Italy, and by the theories of the English metaphysical poets, among whom Crashaw is conspicuous. His work is a happy illustration of both the literary possibilities of the Catholic faith and of the extranational character of literature. His most recent commentator, the Italian Mario Praz, maintains that Crashaw has given to Spanish mysticism its most perfect poetic expression. Crashaw as man and as poet was the subject of one of the most successful poems by his friend Cowley, where he is addressed:

> Poet and saint, to thee alone are given
> The two most sacred names of Earth and Heaven.

Crashaw was a minister's son. His father was a vigorous Puritan preacher in London, a man of narrow views and intemperate zeal whose pet abomination was the Church of Rome. Young Crashaw went to Cambridge, and there, while devoting himself to literature and languages (especially to Spanish), fell under the spell of the beauty and sanctity of the writings of St. Teresa and the other Spanish mystics. In them he discovered a depth and a charm which in the rigid Puritanism of his clerical father he had never discerned; religion now disclosed itself to him as a thing of beauty, as an artistic inspiration. The result was his conversion to Catholicism. "In Crashaw's poetry," writes Professor Grierson, "as in the later poetry of the great Dutch poet Vondel, a note is heard which is struck for the first time in the seventeenth century, the accent of the convert to Romanism, the joy of the troubled soul who has found rest and a full expansion of heart in the rediscovery of a faith and ritual and order which give entire satisfaction to the imagination and affections."[1]

In 1644 Crashaw left the university and, being a Royalist in sympathies, crossed over to Paris and joined the group of Englishmen in the train of Queen Henrietta Maria, the widow

THE SHRINE OF OUR LADY OF LORETO

The Church of the Holy House was completed in the sixteenth century. The campanile contains a bell weighing eleven tons donated by Pope Leo X

of Charles I. Then he went to Rome, became a priest, and was assigned to a chaplaincy at Loreto. In a few months he contracted a fever and died in the shadow of the Holy House, and there he lies buried. Cowley beautifully sang his elegy:

> How well, blest swan, did Fate contrive thy death,
> And made thee render up thy tuneful breath
> In thy great mistress's arms! Thou most divine
> And richest offering of Loretto's shrine!
> Where, like some holy sacrifice to expire,
> A fever burns thee, and Love lights the fire.

[1] *The Background of English Literature*, p. 153.

Besides being a poet and a mystic, Crashaw was a musician and an artist; like Blake, he sometimes illustrated his poems with a delicate and sensitive pencil. His poetical works include *Epigrammata Sacra* (in Latin and English), *Steps to the Temple*, and *Delights of the Muses*, the last being a collection of secular lyrics. He made free translations of the "Dies Iræ" and other Latin hymns. His essential worth is best revealed in his religious poems, especially in his tribute to St. Teresa, the "Hymn to St. Teresa" and "The Flaming Heart." The student will find interest in comparing Crashaw's "On the Holy Nativity of Our Lord God" with Southwell's "Burning Babe" and Milton's "On the Morning of Christ's Nativity." He resembles Southwell in his ardent devotion and his fondness for verbal conceits, and he is like to Milton in his powers of visualization and his suggestive word pictures, but unlike him in his passionate intensity of religious emotion. Crashaw has been styled the Catholic Shelley, and his poetic quality in many respects resembles that of the Romantic lyricist, though there is, of course, a vast difference in the philosophy of life held by the seventeenth-century Catholic and the nineteenth-century atheist.

What Swinburne called the "dazzling intricacy" of Crashaw's style sometimes runs to excess, and, like all the metaphysical poets, Crashaw occasionally marred his work by far-fetched comparisons and an extravagance of fancy. But his best verse is flowing and radiant and marked in a high degree by originality. Significant as expressing Crashaw's conception of the universality of Catholicism and of literature are the following lines on St. Teresa:

> Souls are not Spaniards, too: one friendly flood
> Of baptism blends them all into a blood.
> Christ's faith makes but one body of all souls,
> And Love's that body's soul; no law controls
> Our free traffic for Heaven; we may maintain
> Peace, sure, with piety, though it comes from Spain.

> What soul soe'er, in any language, can
> Speak Heaven like hers, is my soul's countryman.
> O 'tis not Spanish, but 'tis Heaven she speaks!

Many of Crashaw's poetical epigrams are gems of condensed beauty. The most popular of them, on the miracle wrought by Our Lord at the wedding feast in Cana, has been happily translated by Dryden,

> The conscious water saw its God and blushed.

Another is on the Pharisee and the Publican:

> Two went to pray! O, rather say,
> One went to brag, the other to pray.
> One stands up close, and treads on high,
> Where the other dares not send his eye.
> One nearer to God's altar trod:
> The other to the altar's God.

George Herbert (1593–1633). One day a clerical gentleman, dressed in his best, was on his way to a music social when in a muddy lane he met "a poorish man with a poorer horse," and the horse had fallen down in the mire. The clergyman assisted the "poorish man" to unload the horse and get him up and then to load him again; and in so doing he soiled his nice black clothes. When he reached the house and the musicians the clergyman apologized for his appearance and explained the circumstances, whereupon somebody remarked that he had "disparaged himself by so dirty an employment." But the clergyman replied that the thought of what he had done would be music to him at midnight, and added: "If I be bound to pray for all that be in distress, I am sure that I am bound, so far as it is in my power, to practice what I pray for. And though I do not wish for the like occasion every day, yet let me tell you I would not willingly pass one day of my life without comforting a sad soul or showing mercy; and I praise God for this occasion. And now let's tune our instruments."

The clergyman was George Herbert, like Crashaw a Cam-

bridge man and a poet; and the story, which Izaak Walton
tells so quaintly in his life of Herbert, would seem to show that
the rector of Bemerton could live religion and poetry as well
as preach the one and write the other. He was a friend of
Donne's, and his poems were influenced by the dean's literary
peculiarities. He lived a peaceful and holy life, and the spirit
of his life animates the poems which he wrote in Greek, in
Latin, and in English. His English poems were published
under the title *The Temple* in the year after their author's
death. Herbert lacks Crashaw's intensity of spirit and vivacity of imagination, but he shares his devotional spirit. He is
seen at his best in "Virtue" ("Sweet day, so cool, so calm, so
bright") and in "Love," which begins:

> Love bade me welcome; yet my soul drew back,
>   Guilty of dust and sin.
> But quick-eyed Love, observing me grow slack
>   From my first entrance in,
> Drew nearer to me, sweetly questioning,
>   If I lacked anything.

Henry Vaughan (1622-1695). A young Oxford man in
London, supposed to be studying law but actually consorting
with the survivors of the "Tribe of Ben" and inditing cheerful
little songs on youth and love and good cheer, Vaughan was
brought to serious views of life, as he tells us, "by the sudden
eruption of our late civil wars." Joining the army of King
Charles, in 1645 he saw some slight service near the old walled
city of Chester; but the Cavaliers were worsted, and Vaughan
was no fighter and retired to his family home in South Wales.
There he read some of Herbert's writings, and their beauty so
moved him that henceforth he gave his thoughts and his pen
to religion. The Silurist, as Vaughan was called because of his
birth in Wales, busied himself in translating the *Moralia* of
Plutarch and that book which is always appearing in the history of European Literature, *The Consolations of Philosophy*,

by Boethius. He practiced medicine, though where he secured
his training is a matter of conjecture. He was given chiefly to
early rising, to the contemplation of nature, and to writing
poems, many of them excellent, on pious themes. Three collections of his "sacred" poetry came out within ten years:
Silex Scintillans, *The Mount of Olives*, and *Flowers of Solitude*.
"The Retreat," one of his most appealing poems, was a strong
influence on Wordsworth's "Intimations of Immortality";
and there is something of the majesty and splendor of Francis
Thompson in these lines from Vaughan's poem "The World":

> I saw Eternity the other night,
> Like a great ring of pure and endless light,
> All calm, as it was bright;
> And round beneath it Time in hours, days, years,
> Driven by the spheres
> Like a vast shadow moved; in which the world
> And all her train were hurled.

William Habington (1605–1654). Vaughan sang, among
other things, his cordial appreciation of his faithful wife, and a
few other poets before and since have derived inspiration from
the married state; but it is an interesting fact that two Catholic singers, Habington in the seventeenth century and Coventry Patmore in the nineteenth, made the love they had for
their wives the burden of their song. Habington's *Castara* and
Patmore's *The Angel in the House* are both glorifications of
conjugal love blessed and sweetened by the spirit of religion.
Both series of poems are literary embodiments of a scene so
often observed in church, husband and wife kneeling shoulder
to shoulder at the communion rail.

William Habington was born in an old Catholic family of
Worcestershire. A persistent tradition states that it was the
poet's mother who wrote the letter to Lord Mounteagle which
disclosed the Gunpowder Plot. Debarred on account of his
faith from attending an English university, the boy made his
studies in France at the celebrated College of St. Omer. On

his return to England he fell in love with Lucy Herbert, a nobleman's daughter, whom he eventually married and with whom he lived happily. He did a little historical writing and produced a play with some success; but his place on the roll of English poets was won by *Castara*, the collection of poems about his wife, which he wrote before and after his marriage.

Castara is a love story in three parts, mostly in verse but with a number of interludes in prose. The first part is taken up with the young lover's hopes and fears, his ardors and his dreams, with dainty word pictures of the wished-for lady and regrets that his fortune and station in life are obstacles to their immediate union. The second part voices the sentiments of the husband who has not ceased to be a lover, who daily finds in his Castara more and more to admire and esteem; and, indeed, and apart from the not altogether impartial judgment of her husband, we know that Lucy was a woman of singular charm and good sense, a perfect wife and mother. In the third part of the poem Habington's love has deepened and widened, and the lyrics are here of a strongly religious taste; the love of husband for wife has become for him a symbol of the love of the soul for God.

Quarles and Traherne. Two other Royalist poets who wrote mainly on religious themes were Francis Quarles (1592–1644) and Thomas Traherne (1636?–1674). Quarles lacked the ecstatic glow of Crashaw and the occasional sublimity of Vaughan, but he possessed much of Habington's quaintness of fancy and the ease and agreeableness of Waller and Marvell. He enjoyed considerable popularity during his lifetime. His poetical work falls into two divisions: poems on Biblical subjects, for the most part paraphrases of the sacred text; and *Emblems Divine and Moral*, a series of devotional verses written to accompany Biblical illustrations. Traherne's poems were unheard of until 1896, and when discovered by Bertram Dobell they were first attributed to Vaughan — a natural mistake, for the two poets resemble each other in their simple childlike devotion and in their habit of rising from the contemplation of nature up to nature's God. Traherne's leading characteristic is joyousness. "He holds out eager hands, like a child, to the glories of the visible world, but, unlike many children, he never tires of his toys."[1]

Sir Edward Sherburne (1618-1702). The last of the Cavaliers, a loyal Catholic, a sweet singer of love both human and divine, Sherburne was likewise a scholar and a collector of books. Though he fought for Charles I and held offices under that monarch, he suffered the confiscation of his estates because of his religious convictions and was deprived of his library, "which was great and choice, and accounted one of the most considerable belonging to any gentleman in or near London." Some slight reparation was made him after the Restoration. Sherburne's secular poems are good, but his religious poems are better. In the former he resembles Carew in the latter he resembles Herbert. Typical of his style and imagery is this poem:

> Love I'd of Heaven have bought when He, (this who
> Would think?) both purchase was and seller too.
> I offered gold, but gold He did not prize;
> I offered gems, but gems He did despise;
> I offered all; all He refused yet: "Why,
> If all won't take, take what is left," said I.
> At this He smiled, and said, "In vain divine
> Love's price thou beatest; give nothing and she's thine."

[1] Miss G. E. Hodgson, *English Mystics*, p. 260.

CHAPTER IX

THE AGE OF DRYDEN

PROSE WRITERS

Sir Thomas Browne (1605-1682). Even as there is a fascination in antique furniture, so there is a charm and restfulness in leaving our own giddy-paced times and communing with writers whose point of view is different and whose style is quaint and obsolescent. Like the desire to visit the old home town, the longing for a book of an elder day comes to most of us at times, and then two authors we remember are Browne and Fuller. One was a doctor, the other a minister; both were great readers and writers, each with an individuality of his own. And to both has come a quiet, grateful celebrity; they are not known to the general run of readers, but by a discriminating few they are treasured and esteemed.

Religio Medici (the Religion of a Doctor) is the book principally associated with the name of Sir Thomas Browne. It is not a formal treatise or an example of exact scientific thinking, much less an ordered contribution to theology; and the literal-minded scientist or theologian can have a very enjoyable time exposing Browne's ignorance and inconsistency and perhaps his religious and scientific heresies. But the book, like his *Urn Burial* and *The Garden of Cyrus*, is filled with things quaint and queer, "rarities, and that of the best collections," as Evelyn said of the contents of Browne's house and garden. And the pensive Cavalier physician wrote a sort of prose poetry (or should we say poetic prose?) that with its cadences lulls the mind and blunts the edge of ill-tempered criticism.

Browne was born in London, went to Oxford, and studied

medicine abroad. He settled in the country at Norwich in 1637, and there spent the rest of his life in fellowship with the rare plants in his garden and the old books on his shelves. He resembles Burton in his digressive style and his curious assortment of scholarship; and, like Herrick, his pensive brooding frequently turned on death and decay and the inevitable passing of earthly things and conditions:

> There is no antidote against the opium of time, which temporarily considereth all things; our fathers find their graves in our short memories, and sadly tell us how we may be buried in our survivors. Grave-stones tell truth scarce forty years. Generations pass while some trees stand, and old families last not three oaks.

Sir Thomas Browne is a true physician of the mind whenever we need a literary sedative.

Thomas Fuller (1608–1661). Fuller was a Cavalier parson who lost his Savoy living because of his devotion to the Royalist cause. His writings were numerous, many of them on religion and others on history; but he is remembered and loved because he was a genial soul and gentle and because he had a humorous outlook and a lively style. The very titles of some of his volumes — *Good Thoughts in Bad Times*, *Good Thoughts in Worse Times*, *Mixed Contemplations in Better Times* — indicate something of his vivacity and wit as a writer of the king's English. His most famous work is *The Worthies of England*, familiarly known as Fuller's *Worthies*, a delightful assemblage of biography and gossip concerning men more or less (often less) prominent.

Fuller shares Browne's delicious old-fashioned air, but his style has less gravity and more spice. We can still enter into the dry humor of his description of the devout soldier shooting " out his prayer to God and his pistol at the enemy." We can appreciate his delineation of negroes as "images of God cut by Him in ebony, not ivory." We may even chuckle at that passage in *The Holy State* wherein he represents the Elizabethan pirate Drake "persuaded by the minister of his ship" that he might lawfully prey upon Spanish commerce: "The case was clear in sea-divinity; and few are such infidels, as not to believe doctrines which make for their own profit." And we must realize that we have risen to the higher reaches of literature when we encounter such a thought as the following: "Who hath sailed about the world of his own heart, sounded each creek, surveyed each corner, but that there still remains much *terra incognita* to himself?"

Izaak Walton (1593–1683). Knowledge, vision, and personality go into the making of every real book, and the greatest of these is personality. Our American Bishop Spalding once wrote that he who has the literary personality can make anything interesting, even dusty roads; and it may well be that the prelate, who probably was not fond of going forth to fish, had old Izaak Walton in mind. Here is a kindly and devout and unobtrusive man who likes fishing and writes a book about it; and through succeeding years readers (most of whom either do not care a straw about the sport of angling or else have forgotten more about it than Walton ever knew) fondle the pages of his *Complete Angler* because they are captivated by his gentle personality and his quaint comments on the weather and the scenery, on labor and on life. Experts have picked flaws in some of his theories of angling, but all who read him recognize that the man was bigger than the fisherman. Surely it is novel and refreshing to find a man who smiles serenely and goes a fishing when everybody else is busy deposing and restoring kings.

Though Walton lived to be ninety (his life stretching from the time of Shakespeare to the time of Pope), and though he knew much of sorrow (for he lived in troublous times), he remained ever a boy at heart. He even had a boy's bad habits, for he scratched his initials and the date of his visit on one of the tablets in Westminster Abbey. He made a modest fortune in his linen shop in London and then retired to the country and busied himself with fishing and with writing the lives of

Donne and Herbert and other men whom he esteemed. His last years were spent in Winchester, and there he is buried in the cathedral; and every knowing visitor to the historic structure, pausing before his tomb, enters into the spirit of Louise Imogen Guiney's tribute to his memory:

> While thought of thee to men is yet
> A sylvan playfellow,
> Ne'er by thy marble they forget
> In pious cheer to go.
> As air falls, the prayer falls
> O'er kindly Winchester:
> O hush thee, O hush thee! heart innocent and dear.

Walton's *Complete Angler* appeared in 1653, and it is illuminating to consider that during the next quarter of a century — years filled with war's alarms and religious controversy and political contentions — the book passed through five editions. It remains one of the most unassuming and delightful books in English Literature. The author's amiable disposition and shrewd humor and kindly strain of leisurely meditation, as well as his picturesque and idiomatic language, have appealed to readers in all generations who are wise enough now and then to retreat from the bustle and struggle of life and pensively dangle their baited hooks in the flowing stream of time.

Of biographies of prominent men it has been said that often they lend a new terror to death. That charge cannot be laid against Walton's lives of Donne, Wotton, Hooker, and Sanderson. He was one of the first biographers to introduce copious extracts from letters, and he succeeded in making his portraits lifelike and convincing.

John Bunyan (1628–1688). Before the Reformation even unlettered people were able through the practice of the Catholic religion to gratify their desire for beautiful things. They heard the sonorous Latin chant; they followed the dramatic liturgy of the Mass; they gazed upon statues and paintings; they derived a high and symbolic pleasure from the odor of incense, the vestments of the priests, the blaze of candles on the altar; and from all the associations of religion they secured some measure of æsthetic delight. The Reformers changed all that. The language of the street and the shops took the place of the language of the Church, the Mass was proscribed, paintings and statues were defaced and broken to bits, and all the appurtenances of the Catholic ritual were condemned as being idolatrous and superstitious. Beauty was exiled from the house of the Lord. Without knowing it, people hungered for something to feed their imaginations, to lift up their hearts to the contemplation of the Eternal Beauty as well as the Eternal Good. From that hunger and to appease that deeply human need came a religious allegory, *The Pilgrim's Progress*, by John Bunyan.

JOHN BUNYAN
By courtesy of the British Museum

The Pilgrim's Progress has been and still is a widely read book, and ever so many commentators on English Literature have given it extravagant and indiscriminate praise; but in the fragrant smoke of their eulogies, the enthusiasts have lost sight of the fact that the Bedford preacher debased the high simplicity of the Bible to the plane of the vulgar and the ordinary. Why eulogize Bunyan for writing down to the dull-minded and illiterate? What would be thought of the man who would attempt to impart the spirit of Shakespeare or Milton in a style homely and commonplace? It is freely admitted that Bunyan did considerable service to the cause of evangelical religion, that his book is a sermon suited to the limited comprehension and the narrow emotions of ignorant men; but that does not make *The Pilgrim's Progress* a master work of literature. Nearly all great literature appeals to men who possess or are striving to secure at least the rudiments of intellectual culture; the truly great book is almost invariably "over our heads," and one of the joys of good reading is increasing our mental stature in order to understand it. *The Pilgrim's Progress*, for better or for worse, is over nobody's head. "Bunyan's prose is so simple and straightforward that children to-day can understand and enjoy it," as Professor Manly [1] correctly says; but does that fact make it literature? Bunyan was a profoundly ignorant man. He read his Bible without understanding much of what he read, and because he picked up much of the Biblical vocabulary some of his admirers conclude that he also caught the sublime simplicity of the Biblical style.

From the literary point of view the two outstanding merits of *The Pilgrim's Progress* are the vocabulary and the story, and for both of these Bunyan was indebted to the European Tradition in literature. The vocabulary is Biblical, and the Bible is one of the foundation stones of European letters. The allegorical narrative is derived from a beautiful French poem by William de Guileville, a Cistercian monk of the fourteenth century. It was called *The Pilgrimage of Man*, and had been translated into English verse by Lydgate under the title of *Pilgrimage of the World*, in 1426. Another version of it, *The Pilgrimage of the Soul*, was printed by Caxton in 1483. There were other translations in both prose and verse of the French monk's poem, "and these translations continued in popular favor and influenced our literature down to the time of the

[1] *English Prose and Poetry*, p. 807.

Great Rebellion. . . . It is impossible to read *The Pilgrim's Progress* in the light of these translations without arriving at a moral certainty that Bunyan's inimitable allegory was suggested by De Guileville's romance, and was largely indebted to it and to the Romances of Chivalry for much that has contributed to the popularity of his work." [1]

Here is a synopsis of *The Pilgrimage of Man*, which the student may compare with the adventures of Christian and Hopeful in Bunyan's story. The Pilgrim has a vision of the Heavenly Jerusalem and sets forth to reach it, passing the angels who guard the road. A beautiful lady, Grace of God, brings him into her house, where he is baptized and confirmed, receives Holy Communion, and is given a staff, the girdle of Justice, and the book of Faith. Resuming his journey, he faces many dangers symbolical of the passions, but Reason and Grace of God assist him. Tribulation besets him, and he is led from the path by Fortune. He finds shelter in a monastery and is helped by Discipline, Abstinence, Poverty, Chastity, and Obedience. The monastery is poorly guarded, and enemies enter. The Pilgrim escapes and continues his journey until Infirmity takes hold of him, and finally Death strikes him down. And then we discover that it all has been a dream, and the clock strikes and the cock crows.

Bunyan wrote many devotional works besides *The Pilgrim's Progress*. In *Grace Abounding* he recounts the irregularities of his early life, one of which was the reading of stories of chivalry. He suffered much on account of his religious convictions, and in his closing years was a popular preacher. Above his grave in Bunhill Fields, London,— hard by the spot where Milton spent his last years,— is an imposing monument showing Bunyan reclining, a closed book in his hand; and on the sides of the tomb are two reliefs suggesting his principal work, a pilgrim with a staff and bundle and a pilgrim bearing a cross.

[1] S. Humphreys Gurteen, *The Arthurian Epic*, pp. 26, 27.

The Diarists. In recent years interest has focused on two unusual books: the Diaries written by John Evelyn (1620–1706) and Samuel Pepys (1633–1703). A Royalist country gentleman, Evelyn fled to France in 1643, returning four years later to live a quiet life in disturbed and disturbing times. But his eyes were open and his ear was close to the ground,

SAMUEL PEPYS

By courtesy of the British Museum

and the observations on men and events which he recorded day by day for nearly seventy years constitute valuable and interesting comments on the public life of the period. The world knew Pepys as Secretary to the Generals of the Fleet and the capable organizer of the British Navy, as a patron of music and the drama and a collector of books, as something of a social celebrity and a man about town, a person eminently respectable and respected. His *Diary* — begun when he was twenty-six years of age and continued during ten years — reveals him as he knew himself, a man with moral weaknesses and occasional moods of devotion, a bit of a grafter but prevailingly honest, good-hearted and generous, yet sometimes envious and greedy — what Kipling would call, and what nearly every man is, a "general averagee." Pepys had no notion that his *Diary* would ever be published; he intended it for no eye but his own, and he even wrote it in a system of shorthand which was unriddled only a hundred years ago. A good deal of the present-day interest in this unusual work is a manifestation of our human delight in gossip and petty scandals; Pepys was no master of style and even no faithful observer of the rules of grammar, and from one point of view the literary value of his *Diary* is slender indeed. But if Terence was right, if nothing human can be foreign to us, then Pepys has contributed, though in no exalted degree, to our knowledge of life. For the man was able to see himself, he was frank and impartial in recognizing his shortcomings, and he had an artlessly alluring way of setting down what he saw.

THE DRAMA

The Restoration Era. The Puritans were strongly opposed to the theater, which they regarded (not altogether without justification) as a school of abuse, as Gosson had called it, so that during the period of the Commonwealth the playhouses were closed and performances forbidden. But when Charles II came to the throne there was a renewed flourishing of dramatic activity. Nearly all the plays of the Restoration period are grievously disfigured by coarseness and indecency — a reflection of the loose morals of the royal court and a reaction against the rigidity of the Puritan régime. The seventeenth century was the golden age of the drama in France, and French influences affected the English stage. Several of Molière's plays were translated and presented in London, but no English Molière appeared, nor any English dramatist with the nobility of Corneille or the artistry of Racine. It was at this time that women first appeared on the English stage; one actress, Nell Gwyn of Drury Lane, won notoriety in history and in historical fiction.

Representative Dramatists. Besides John Dryden, whose dramatic works will be considered later in this chapter, the Restoration period produced a group of dramatists whose offerings, for the most part licentious and cynical, have little permanent worth. The prevailing type of play was the comedy of manners, best represented by *The Double Dealer* and *The Way of the World*, by William Congreve (1670–1729), who came nearest — though that was not very near — to Molière's brilliancy and skill in character-drawing. William Wycherley (1640?–1716) was educated in France and wrote *The Country Wife* and other dramas under the influence of the French spirit. The plays of Sir John Vanbrugh (1664–1726) were so indecent that they disgusted even Voltaire. George Farquhar (1678–1707), born in Londonderry, Ireland, and for a time a student at Trinity College, Dublin, was a bad actor and nearly killed a man in a stage duel in one of Dryden's plays; but when he came to London he managed to write three or four comedies, notably *The Recruiting Officer*, which were gay and original and less objectionable morally than the comedies of his contemporaries. The leading exponent of the serious, or "heroic," drama was Thomas Otway (1651–1685), who translated some of Racine's dramas and whose *Venice Preserved*, though marred by strains of coarse humor, is a well-planned and powerful tragedy. Colley Cibber (1671–1757) wrote a number of weak dramas and is chiefly memorable for his adaptations of Shakespeare (one of which, *King Richard III*, still holds the boards) and for his reminiscences of the theatrical history of the early eighteenth century. Cibber is the connecting link between the drama of the Restoration and the period of Goldsmith.

LITERARY CRITICISM

The latter half of the seventeenth century saw a renewed interest in the theory of literature and the most marked effort since the Renaissance to apply the literary canons of the ancients to English poetry. In this movement, as we shall see, Dryden was the leading figure; but other men, most of them well read and studious, were concerning themselves with literary criticism and, in imitation of Horace and Boileau, writing their precepts and opinions in verse — doing in a small way what Pope, with his metrical *Essay on Criticism,* was to do in a more memorable way early in the next century. Sir William Soames in 1683 brought out a verse translation of Boileau's *Poetic Art,* all in all a good piece of work performed under the eye and in places with the collaboration of Dryden; about the same time appeared an *Essay on Poetry* by John Sheffield, Earl of Mulgrave (1648–1721), and in the last year of the century a verse treatise on *Unnatural Flights in Poetry,* by Lord Lansdowne. Davenant's preface to *Gondibert* and Hobbes's comments on it are significant of the interest taken in the theory of poetry.

Criticism in the form of attack and denunciation is represented by Jeremy Collier (1650–1726), a Protestant minister, who denounced the evil tendencies of the drama in his *Short View of the Immorality and Profaneness of the English Stage.* Collier united with his stern clerical outlook a power of logical argument and a vigorous wit, and drew unconvincing replies from Vanbrugh and Congreve.

Thomas Rymer (1641–1713).   The most prominent of the destructive critics was Rymer, who is now recognized as about the poorest commentator on literature that ever lived, though by most of his contemporaries he was esteemed the best. Pope called Rymer "a learned and a strict critic"; and so he was, though strictness is not an exalted critical virtue, and learning, though indispensable, is no substitute for the ability to recognize real literature. On every one of his decisions this learned judge has been reversed. He was very difficult to please. He held that the *Divine Comedy* is "of a sad and woeful contrivance," and that "Dante has a strain too profound, Petrarch too vast, and Boccaccio too trivial and familiar, to deserve the name of heroic poets." He made a savage attack on Shakespeare as a literary artist, holding *Othello* in especial scorn. Rymer was a Yorkshire man educated at Cambridge, and a lawyer. His opinions are disclosed in *Tragedies of the Last Age* and *A Short View of Tragedy.*

Wentworth Dillon (1633?–1685). Wentworth Dillon, Earl of Roscommon, was born in Ireland. His father "had been reclaimed from the superstitions of the Romish Church." His uncle, the Earl of Strafford, sent him to Yorkshire for his education; thence he went to Normandy and to Italy and carried on his studies. Wealth and prominence came to him on his return to England after the Restoration, and he received honorary degrees from both Oxford and Cambridge. He was an enthusiastic student of literature, founded an organization on the plan of the French Academy "to refine and fix the standard of our language," and enjoyed considerable repute as a poet. Pope's tribute to his cleanness is often quoted:

> In all Charles' days
> Roscommon only boasts unspotted bays.

In Dillon's view "want of decency is want of sense," an opinion later expressed in *An Essay on Criticism* in almost identical words. He made blank-verse translations from Virgil and Horace. Dillon's outstanding contribution to literary criticism was his *Essay on Translated Verse* in heroic couplets, preceded by a fine tribute to Dryden. He is further memorable as being, with the exception of Dryden, the first critic to praise *Paradise Lost*, which was not otherwise acclaimed until Addison wrote of it in the *Spectator*.

DRYDEN

The outstanding figure in every department of literature during the second half of the seventeenth century is John Dryden (1631–1700), whose work "overtops the expanse of contemporary English Literature like the temple shining from the Sunian height over the sea."[1] He was not a mere dabbler in the art of writing, but adopted it as his life work and profession. He practiced it in its several phases and studied it

[1] A. W. Ward, *Cambridge History of English Literature*, Vol. VIII, p. 64.

from every angle, and he stands between Jonson and Johnson in the succession of literary dictators. As an authority on books and writing he was acknowledged during his lifetime even by his enemies, and we of a later generation recognize his supremacy as a prose writer, as a critic, and as a satiric poet. He wrote metrical chronicles and odes and developed the rimed couplet; he was a prominent dramatist and a popular pamphleteer; he made translations from the Greek, the Latin, the French, and Middle English; he transmuted religious controversy into literature; and he wrote prefatory essays that are recognized not only as important contributions to literary criticism but as the beginnings of modern English prose.

JOHN DRYDEN

From an original painting in the collection of George A. Plimpton

The Life of Dryden. John Dryden was born at Aldwinkle near Oundle in Northamptonshire on August 9, 1631. He came of Puritan stock, though Puritanism never made a deep impression on his mind. He received his schooling at Westminster and at Trinity College, Cambridge. On leaving the university he returned to London and engaged in literary labors for the remainder of his life. He was a keen student of literature and of criticism, being especially interested in French plays and essays. His marriage in 1663 with Lady Elizabeth Howard appears to have contributed but little to his happiness. In 1670 he was made royal historiographer and succeeded

Davenant as poet laureate. He entered the Catholic Church in 1686, and in consequence, when William and Mary came to the throne, was deprived of the laureateship and his other official posts. We get a vivid picture of him in his last years, seated in an armchair in front of Will's coffeehouse in Covent Garden, surrounded by a group of admirers and discoursing of politics and literature. He died on May 1, 1700, and was buried in Westminster Abbey.

The externals of Dryden's life are uneventful and anything but spectacular. His satires and criticisms made him numerous enemies, but he was slow to convert a literary quarrel into personal animosity; he was not thin-skinned, and many of the attacks made upon him he passed over in contemptuous silence. Dryden was a hard-working professional man of letters, eminently kind and helpful to the younger tribe of writers and appreciative of the best work of his fellows. His friend Congreve wrote:

He was of a nature exceedingly humane and compassionate, easily forgiving injuries, and capable of a prompt and sincere reconciliation with them who had offended him. . . . His friendship, where he professed it, went much beyond his professions. . . . To the best of my knowledge and observation he was of all men that ever I knew one of the most modest.

Though some of his writings, especially his comedies, are disfigured by the indecency which characterized so much of the literature of the period, Dryden was personally a man beyond reproach. Accusations have been repeatedly made against his personal character, but not one of them has ever been proved. In his mature years he publicly expressed regret for the licentious element in his earlier writings. Dryden was like a newspaper man of the present day employed on a sensational journal, who writes luridly of crime and debauchery and yet lives a decent personal life and has high principles of faith and honor.

Dryden's Conversion. Dryden's changes of religious belief motivated at least two of his poems, one of them the longest e wrote; and as he has been put down as a timeserver and opportunist, a man who changed his religion to curry favor with the reigning sovereigns, it is important to understand the facts in his conversion. The Puritanism in which he was brought up was uncongenial to his nature, and he shifted out of it as soon as he had freedom of choice. For a time he was indifferent to religion (the life of a dramatist in the days of Charles II was hardly conducive to the practice of piety), and although nominally a communicant of the Church of England he was really something of a skeptic. But reading and thinking and deepened experience of life brought about a change of views. Dryden was a logical thinker, and having seen, from his study of literature, the need of standards and principles and some sort of authority in matters of art, he was led to recognize the necessity of organization and government in matters of religion and life.

The outcome was his poem, *Religio Laici* (the Religion of a Layman), in which he manifests a freshened interest in religious problems and makes a spirited defense of the Church of England. The next step was natural and inevitable. Like Newman and like Chesterton, he perceived that the fullness of spiritual authority, the perfection of religious organization, and an unbroken connection with apostolic times existed only in the Catholic Church. The fact that James II, who succeeded his brother, Charles II, was a Catholic was a circumstance which had no perceptible bearing on Dryden's conversion. Already, before he entered the Church, he had been confirmed in his offices of poet laureate and historiographer royal. He gained absolutely nothing in a material way from his conversion, and he exposed himself to gossip and calumny. Finally, when James was deposed and the Protestant William of Orange was made king, Dryden persevered in the profession of his Catholic faith, though he lost his offices and his pension and had the humiliation of seeing his old enemy Shadwell supplant him as poet laureate.

The Dramatist. Dryden wrote, in all, nearly thirty plays, most of them of slight worth, but the best of them such as to make him the leading dramatist of the time. *The Indian Emperor* and *The Conquest of Granada* were his ablest contributions to the heroic play, a type of drama characterized by an oratorical style, high-flown language, and impossible situations. These faults Dryden overcame in his second dramatic period, owing to his study of Shakespeare and the French dramatists; his *All for Love* is a free adaptation of Shakespeare's *Antony and Cleopatra.* Though he engaged in it rather extensively all his life, Dryden never really cared for dramatic writing, and in 1693 he abandoned the stage in disgust. He was most successful in the writing of dialogue, and the practice forced upon him by his dramatic activity undoubtedly did much to develop the clear and flexible prose style which gives him his high rank as a writer.

The Poet. Dryden was a verse writer first and last, and his earliest efforts were poems on current events. His "Heroic Stanzas on the Death of Cromwell," lacking the vigor and abounding vitality which characterize most of Dryden's poetry, was followed by *Astræa Redux*, celebrating the coronation of Charles II. *Annus Mirabilis* commemorated the unusual things that took place during the "wonder year" of 1666, chiefly the war with the Dutch and the Great Fire of London. In these early poems Dryden shows that he was finding himself as a writer; but he developed his powers slowly, and here, as in his first plays, was prone to indulge in rhetorical flights and what in our day is disparaged as "fine writing."

Dryden reached his full stature as a poet in his satires, the first of which was *Absalom and Achitophel* (1681).[1] This is

---

[1] The second part of *Absalom and Achitophel*, which appeared in the following year, is mainly the work of Nahum Tate (1652–1715), who engaged in a variety of literary work, including a translation of the Psalms in collaboration with Nicholas Brady.

one of the comparatively few works of English Literature inspired by political events. There was a plot to have the Duke
of Monmouth succeed to the English throne, and Dryden
ridicules the leading figures in the conspiracy under the names
of characters involved in the Biblical revolt of Absalom against
his father David. Monmouth is Absalom, of course; the Earl
of Shaftesbury is Achitophel, the rascally counselor; the Duke
of Buckingham is Zimri; Titus Oates is Corah; and Shadwell
the poet is Og. The late Professor Walter Raleigh has called
Absalom and Achitophel "the deadliest document in English
Literature, splendid in power, unrelenting in purpose."[1] It
was followed by *The Medal*, a "satire against sedition," occasioned by a movement to strike a medal because of the
acquittal of the Earl of Shaftesbury. Like most sequels, it is
less effective than the first heir of the satirist's invention. But
Dryden struck his old stride in *Mac Flecknoe*, an excoriation
of Shadwell, whom Dryden elects to the throne of the dunces,
then assumed to be occupied by Richard Flecknoe, a writer of
greater ambition than ability.

Dryden's satires hold their assured place in English Literature not because they are grossly abusive, for such they are
not, but because they are remarkable for adroit characterization, for real power of denunciation, for their tone of urbanity
and amused self-possession, and for the point and cleverness
of their style. Though, as Saintsbury says, "there are passages
of Dryden's satires in which every couplet has not only the
force but the actual sound of a slap in the face,"[2] the poet
always gives the impression that he is not hitting nearly so
hard as he might, that he is exercising self-control in dealing
with the villainies and absurdities of human nature. And
most of what he wrote is of universal application. As applicable to the fanatics of our own day as to the supporters of

---

[1] In his collection of essays entitled *Some Authors*.
[2] *Life of Dryden*, in the English Men of Letters Series, p. 76.

the Duke of Monmouth are these verses from *Absalom and Achitophel*:

> A numerous host of dreaming saints succeed
> Of the true old enthusiastic breed:
> 'Gainst form and order they their power employ,
> Nothing to build and all things to destroy.
> But far more numerous was the herd of such
> Who think too little and who talk too much.

Dryden's two religious poems, *Religio Laici* and *The Hind and the Panther*, consist almost entirely of argument and yet retain their poetic status. Many sides of religion are easily susceptible of poetic treatment, assuming that there is a poet to do the writing, but controversy is rarely fit literary material. The preface to *Religio Laici* is an interesting expression of Dryden's religious opinions at the time the poem was written. He confesses that he is "naturally inclined to skepticisms in philosophy," but points out that religion is something beyond the reaches of mere philosophy; "that we have not lifted up ourselves to God by the weak pinions of our reason, but He has been pleased to descend to us." In the course of the poem Dryden answers current objections against religion, expresses his fear of the Church of Rome and of the Jesuits, and establishes the important point that the Bible is not the sole rule of faith and that obviously tradition is a factor in belief. The Church of England, he maintains, is the safest form of religion because it avoids the extremes of Catholicism on one side and of the evangelical sects on the other. His plea is eloquent, and the poem contains many passages of sustained beauty.

Five years later came *The Hind and the Panther*, Dryden's defense of the Catholic faith, to which he now professed allegiance. Here the religious discussion is carried on by various animals, each of which represents a form of religion. The Catholic Church is the "milk-white Hind, immortal and unchanged"; the Episcopalian is the "spotted Panther"; the Quaker is the "quaking Hare"; the Freethinker is the "buffoon Ape"; the Presbyterian is the "insatiate Wolf"; the Unitarian is "Reynard the Fox"; the Anabaptist is the "bristled baptist Boar." The discussion between the Hind and the Panther,

> . . . sure the noblest next the Hind,
> And fairest creature of the spotted kind,

is carried on with courtesy and dignity. Dryden's reasons for entering the Catholic Church are set forth with clearness and convincing sincerity. He had found the necessity for an infallible teaching authority:

> What weight of ancient witness can prevail,
> If private reason hold the public scale?
> But, gracious God, how well dost thou provide
> For erring judgments an unerring guide!
> Thy throne is darkness in the abyss of light,
> A blaze of glory that forbids the sight.
> O teach me to believe thee thus concealed,
> And search no farther than thyself revealed;
> But her alone for my director take,
> Whom thou hast promised never to forsake!
> .   .   .   .
> Why choose we then like bilanders to creep
> Along the coast, and land in view to keep,
> When safely we may launch into the deep?
> In the same vessel which our Saviour bore,
> Himself the pilot, let us leave the shore,
> And with a better guide a better world explore.

Dryden successfully experimented with other forms of verse. He wrote numerous complimentary poems to his fellow literary craftsmen, and he added to his fame (and incidentally put money in his purse) by writing prologues and epilogues for new plays. He also composed several odes and handled the complex meter with skill. Of these the best known are the two odes in honor of St. Cecilia, especially "Alexander's Feast," of which Dryden said, "Nobody has written a nobler ode, and nobody ever will" — rather a strong saying from modest John, but a verdict not foreign to the truth. His elegy "To the Memory of Mrs. Anne Killigrew" is one of the finest poems Dryden ever wrote, voicing his admiration for a pure and beautiful soul and his disgust with the low moral standards then prevailing on the English stage. Dr. Johnson was not far wrong when he applied a venerable dictum and said that Dryden found English poetry of brick and left it of marble.

Translations. Dryden produced, especially during his last years, when the deprivation of his offices and pensions made it necessary for him to engage in remunerative writing, a large group of translations of classics in the European Tradition. His leaning was toward the great Latins, and so he concentrated on spirited English versions of Juvenal, Ovid, Horace, and particularly of Virgil. In his work, as he explained in his prefaces, he aimed at being readable rather than scholarly; his object was to popularize classical literature with readers unable to read Latin. His *Fables* contain stories from Chaucer and Boccaccio retold with force and vivacity but without a minute fidelity to the originals. Dryden was the first writer to modernize Chaucer, and he defended the procedure on the ground of practical expediency:

If the first end of a writer be to be understood, then, as his language grows obsolete, his thoughts must grow obscure. When an ancient word, for its sound and significancy, deserves to be revived, I have that reasonable veneration for antiquity to restore it. All beyond that is superstition. Words are not like landmarks, so sacred as never to be removed.

Prose Works. The critical essays which Dryden prefixed to his plays, poems, and translations constitute a valuable collection of remarks on the theory of literature and have been recognized as "the first pieces of good modern English prose." [1] Sir Walter Scott even went so far as to say that "the prose of Dryden may rank with the best in the language. . . . It is dignified where dignity is becoming, and is lively without the

[1] Matthew Arnold, in his edition of Dryden's *Essay of Dramatic Poesy* (Oxford, 1889).

The Fifth Paſtoral.

OR,

DAPHNIS.

The Argument.

Mopſus *and* Menalcas, *two very expert Shepherds at a Song, begin one by conſent to the Memory of* Daphnis ; *who is ſuppoſ'd by the beſt Criticks to repreſent* Julius Cæſar. Mopſus *laments his Death,* Menalcas *proclaims his Divinity. The whole Eclogue conſiſting of an Elegie and an Apotheoſis.*

MENALCAS.

SInce on the Downs our Flocks together feed,
And ſince my Voice can match your tuneful Reed,
Why ſit we not beneath the grateful Shade,
Which Hazles, intermix'd with Elms, have made?

5   *MOPSUS.*

Whether you pleaſe that Silvan Scene to take,
Where whiſtling Winds uncertain Shadows make:
Or will you to the cooler Cave ſucceed,
Whoſe Mouth the curling Vines have overſpread?

     MENALCAS.

10   Your Merit and your Years command the Choice:
Amyntas only rivals you in Voice.

     MOPSUS.

What will not that preſuming Shepherd dare,
Who thinks his Voice with *Phœbus* may compare?

     MENALCAS.

Begin you firſt; if either *Alcon's* Praiſe,
Or dying *Phillis* have inſpir'd your Lays:

                 If

FROM DRYDEN'S *TRANSLATION OF VIRGIL*

This edition, which was published by Jacob Tonson in 1697, is the first example of modern bookmaking. Compare it with the *Paradise Lost* shown on page 261

accumulation of strained and absurd allusions and metaphors, which were unfortunately mistaken for wit by many of the author's contemporaries." [1] Energy and clearness, together with modernity in paragraph formation and sentence structure, are characteristics of Dryden's prose style. "If any journalist or reviewer were to write his to-morrow's leader or his next week's article in a style absolutely modelled on Dryden, no one would notice anything strange in it, except perhaps that the English was a good deal better than usual." [2] In short, Dryden's essays constitute one of the English prose classics.

In his essays Dryden discussed a variety of literary issues, many of them still of vital interest. Some of his topics are the use of rime in dramatic writing; imagination in literature, a theme which Addison later amplified; the principles of plot construction; the characteristics of opera, a form recently introduced into English by Davenant; the relative excellence of ancient and modern writers, a question subsequently taken up by Swift in *The Battle of the Books*; the limits of poetic license; ideals and standards of criticism.

Dryden was the first English critic to introduce the inductive method into dramatic criticism. Though he had a deep reverence for the rules of writing set down by Aristotle and other ancient dictators, he did not hold that the standards of literature "were fixed long ago by certain inspired writers whose authority it is no longer lawful to question." [3] On the contrary, he conceded the possibility of development in the literary art and was prompt to recognize the merits of a drama written in violation of long-established rules. Good sense, he urged, rather than tradition should be the basis of our literary judgments.

[1] Scott's *Life of Dryden*, Sect. viii, p. 436.

[2] Saintsbury, Preface to Scott's *Life of Dryden*.

[3] This extraordinary belief in the papal infallibility of the ancients was expressed in an article on Southey in the *Edinburgh Review*, October, 1802. The Italian Scaliger had previously said that "Aristotle is our emperor, the perpetual dictator of all the fine arts."

In Dryden's day as in ours literary criticism was popularly assumed to be a species of faultfinding, and that view Dryden vigorously assailed:

We are fallen into an age of illiterate, censorious, and detracting people, who, thus qualified, set up for critics. . . . In the first place, I must take leave to tell them, that they wholly mistake the nature of criticism who think its business is principally to find fault. Criticism, as it was first instituted by Aristotle, was meant a standard of judging well; the chiefest part of which is, to observe those excellencies which should delight a reasonable reader. . . . 'Tis malicious and unmanly to snarl at the little lapses of a pen, from which Virgil himself stands not exempted.

Unlike Bacon and so many others who looked down upon the English language, Dryden, though his admiration of the classics was profound, realized the possibilities of modern tongues and urged the careful, systematic study of the language of Shakespeare and Milton. He did not think that the best way to learn to write living English is to write lifeless Latin, that if a man secures proficiency in the classics a knowledge of English will come unsought like a blessing from Heaven. "There are many," he says, "who understand Greek and Latin, and yet are ignorant of their mother tongue." And then he proceeds to indicate what he considers the essential factors in a good English course: "A liberal education, long reading and digesting of those few good authors we have amongst us, the knowledge of men and manners, the freedom of habitudes and conversation with the best company of both sexes." And he adds that the student of Latin and Greek cannot write good English until after "wearing off the rust which he contracted while he was laying in a stock of learning."

Dr. Johnson, in his *Lives of the Poets*, pays a graceful but not fulsome compliment to Dryden's essays: "The criticism of a poet, not a dull collection of theorems, nor a rude detection of faults, which perhaps the censor was not able to have committed; but a gay and vigorous dissertation, where delight is mingled with instruction."

Dryden as a dramatist was no Shakespeare, as a poet was no Milton, as a prose writer was no Newman; but he was the outstanding literary figure of his day, the first really professional man of letters, and he won distinction and supremacy in every sort of writing he attempted. Satiric poetry is certainly not the most exalted literary form; but in both ancient and modern literature it has its assured place, and Dryden ranks high among the satirists of all time. As a writer of odes he challenges consideration with Collins, Shelley, and Francis Thompson. His prose style, though unadorned and business-like in its texture, is limpid, graceful, and clear, and it set the example for Addison and other writers. Dryden the critic had a background of wide reading, a first-hand knowledge of the literary art in its several branches, a well-balanced judgment, and an openness of mind that made him one of our most dependable if not one of our most brilliant commentators on books and writing.

To ignore John Dryden is to conceive of English Literature as an arch without a keystone. He is the connecting link between the past and the present in the history of poetry and prose.

CHAPTER X

THE CLASSICAL INFLUENCE

WHAT CLASSICISM IS

If a man wants to build a house he can go about it in one of two ways: he can lay down some bricks for foundations and then set up on the bricks wooden beams of various lengths and nail across the beams what odds and ends of planks he finds lying about. He can saw off here and patch there, now making jagged holes for windows, again hacking and fitting until he has constructed a pair of serviceable stairs, and so on until the house is finished. Houses have been built in that way, and they may be comfortable enough to live in, but they are usually queer things to look at.

In civilized countries houses are generally not built in that fashion. The man who builds the house is something of an expert: that is to say, he knows how other houses are built; he has studied problems of construction; he has actually built houses himself. The first thing he does is to make a plan; and the better builder he is, the more is his plan ample and detailed. He draws upon his knowledge of houses he has seen and he tries to embody their most attractive features. Then he goes on to the actual building of the house; and in laying his foundation and erecting his superstructure, in shaping his windows and slanting his roof, he follows the plan he has made. When the house is finished, it probably will not be the least bit freakish or spectacular or unusual, and in its general outlines will be pretty much like other houses; but it will be comfortable to live in, and may even be a thing of beauty as houses go.

Now just as there are two possible ways of building a house, so there are two possible ways of writing a play or a poem. Some writers and groups of writers try to get away from the methods of earlier writers ; for one reason or another they want to be different. Such writers — and painters and sculptors and musicians too — are known by various names. They are called primitives, eccentrics, individualists, impressionists, radicals, Romanticists. And other writers and groups of writers study the masterpieces of the past, seek to imitate the best models, and do their writing according to a prepared plan and in obedience to certain rules derived from masterpieces of literature. Writers who proceed in this way are called Classicists, and their way of writing and the spirit in which they write is known as Classicism.

The word *classics* is in a narrow sense taken to mean the literary masterpieces written in Latin and Greek ; but in its broader meaning the word includes the greatest works of literature in every language and the most highly esteemed pictures and statues and musical compositions. No piece of literature was a classic at the time it was written. Before they were recognized as classical writers, Virgil and Dante and Shakespeare had to stand the test of time ; their writings had to become mellowed and seasoned, like fine wine or the wood which goes into an airplane. A classic author is a sort of literary saint, canonized by the admiration of educated readers through succeeding generations. A saint is a man who has practiced virtue in a heroic degree, a man who has been a very good Christian ; and years after he is dead we speak of him as St. Louis or St. Charles. A classic author is a man who has practiced literature unusually well, who has been a very good writer. A classic painter is a man who has practiced art in a high degree, who has been a very good painter ; and he is, so to say, canonized when, years after he is dead, we speak of him as an old master.

The best explanation of a classic of literature is given by

the French critic Charles Sainte-Beuve, in his essay "What is a Classic?"[1] The classical writer, he tells us, is "an author who has enriched the human mind, increased its treasure, and caused it to advance a step; who discovered some moral and not equivocal truth, or revealed some eternal passion in that heart where all seemed known and discovered; who has expressed his thought, observation, or invention, in no matter what form, only provided it be broad and great, refined and sensible, sane and beautiful in itself."

Such, then, is a classic; and what in English Literature we call Classicism or the Classical Influence is the effort of certain writers and groups of writers to imitate the spirit and skill of master authors in other countries and other times, especially the poets and prose writers of Greece and Rome. Ben Jonson, for instance, wrote his plays in imitation of ancient dramatists and explained in his prefaces just how closely he had followed good models. Dryden, as we have seen, did much the same thing, his essays being largely a showing of the plans or patterns he employed in constructing his dramas. And in the eighteenth century, which we are now about to consider, the representative English writers sought to emulate the style and the spirit of earlier masters of literature. This period is often called the Augustan Age, because there was so much admiration and imitation of the great Roman writers who flourished in the reign of the Emperor Augustus.

POPE

Alexander Pope (1688–1744) is the leading exponent of English Classicism in the eighteenth century. And we might learn much about Pope and about Classicism could we visit his villa at Twickenham on the Thames, where he lived with his books for more than a quarter of a century, and explore

[1] This essay may be found in the Harvard Classics, C. W. Eliot's "five-foot shelf."

what remains of his famous grotto. Pope's grotto is a remarkable symbol of eighteenth-century Classicism.

Pope's Grotto. Pope's property, sloping gently down to
the bank of the river, was bisected by the public road leading
from Richmond to Teddington. To avoid the inconvenience
of having to cross the highway every time he went from his
house to his sunny lawn, Pope constructed a tunnel under the
road. That tunnel he called his grotto, and he adorned it in an
eminently characteristic way. There were tiny caverns within
caverns, "marbles, spars, gems, ores, and minerals" fastened
into the walls and roof, bits of mirror set everywhere to reflect
light from outside, and all arranged in conventional designs.
Pope delighted to describe it:

> . . . where Thames' translucent wave
> Shines a broad mirror through the shadowy cave;
> Where lingering drops from mineral roofs distill,
> And pointed crystals break the sparkling rill,
> Unpolished gems no ray on pride bestow,
> And latent metals innocently glow.

The grotto was at once practical and artificial, and was
stippled with odds and ends picked up in a variety of places.
And Pope's poetry, so characteristic of English Classicism, was
very like Pope's grotto. Indeed, the verses wherein he describes his grotto are illustrative of the Classical conception
of poetry, which maintained that "the business of the poet was
not to represent nature, but to decorate her and then work
himself up into as much rapture as gentility would allow over
the decorations."[1] Then, too, the present condition of the
grotto resembles the fate of the poetry. Most students of
English Literature have never visited Twickenham, but in
many a dwelling in England and elsewhere are pebbles and
bits of glass pilfered from that tunnel beneath the Teddington
road; most readers have never read Pope's writings through,

[1] Theodore Watts-Dunton, "The Renaissance of Wonder," Chambers's
Cyclopædia of Literature, Vol. III.

but every person who speaks English at all consciously or unconsciously uses fragmentary quotations from Pope's poetry. Some of his verses have become familiar proverbs. Next to the Bible and Shakespeare, Pope is the most frequently quoted of all English writers.

Pope the Man. The sage of Twickenham afforded a remarkable example of a sound mind in an unsound body.[1] His

POPE'S TWICKENHAM

life, as he said, was one long disease. He was a little man with a large head. Physically frail and deformed, he was mentally keen and alert; he read much, wrote extensively, and was skilled in the art of conversation. In character he was a curious compound. He was vain and sensitive, spiteful and quarrelsome, often coarse in his language, and sometimes inconstant in his friendships. Yet he was a devoted son to his aged mother, frequently kind and generous to the needy, and sincere and earnest in his efforts to improve conditions in literature and life.

[1] "*Mens curva in corpore curvo*," as the unkind Atterbury put it.

Pope was born in London of a Catholic family. Debarred because of his faith from attendance at the universities, he studied under tutors and made rapid progress. In his youth he lived near Windsor and later at Chiswick, but always he was much about town and early enjoyed the reputation of a man of intellect. He made money by his writings and was

ALEXANDER POPE
From a painting in the collection of
George A. Plimpton

recognized as the leading poet of his day. After the death of his father in 1717 he removed to Twicken-ham, only a dozen miles away from London; there he died, and there he was buried in Twickenham church. No act of his life became him like the ending of it : he insisted on getting out of bed and receiving the last sacraments on his knees.

Translations and Imitations. The work which brought Pope both fame and fortune was his trans-lation of the *Iliad* of Ho-mer, which he completed in 1715 after five years of intensive application. He was no Greek scholar, and his translation is really an adaptation of existing Latin and English versions. Richard Bentley's comment on it still stands : "A fine poem, Mr. Pope, but you must not call it Homer." For all that, Pope's *Iliad* is a vigorous and readable work and, despite the disdain of Greek scholars, remains the most popular English translation of the Greek epic. He gave the weight of his name to a translation of Homer's *Odyssey*, which appeared in 1726, but he had comparatively little to do with it ; William Broome

nd Elijah Fenton were the men chiefly responsible for the
version, which falls far below the level of the *Iliad*. Pope
urned to Chaucer in 1715 and produced a free modern version
f *The House of Fame*; but more typical and intrinsically
nore important are his six *Imitations of Horace*, the fruits
f his last years of thought and study. The poems are uneven, but they contain some of the finest and keenest things
Pope ever wrote. They are preceded by the "Epistle to Dr.
Arbuthnot," of which an American critic, literally quoting
Johnson, has said: "If it is not poetry, I do not know where
poetry is to be found."[1]

It was in imitation of Horace that Pope when only twenty-
three years old wrote in rimed couplets his *Essay on Criticism*,
a work which might be regarded with Boileau's *Poetic Art* as
he Apostles' Creed of Classicism. "Follow nature, of course,"
says Pope in substance, "but do so according to the fashion
set by Aristotle, Homer, and Virgil." This work is filled with
clever comments and memorable lines; and his advice is good,
though, like most advice, it must be watered according to
taste. A warning to students who dismiss a book as overestimated because they see little or nothing in it is contained
n his lines regarding the literary artifices of great writers.
Long before, Horace had said that sometimes Homer nods;
Pope suggests that the failure is not always on the author's
side:

> Those oft are stratagems which errors seem,
> Nor is it Homer nods, but we that dream.

Pastorals and Elegies. Like most poets, Pope early manifested an itch for verse-making:

> As yet a child, nor yet a fool to fame,
> I lisp'd in numbers, for the numbers came.

His *Pastorals*, published when their author was only twenty
years old, have the defects of youth and are sometimes dis-

[1] Paul Elmer More, *Shelburne Essays* (Tenth Series), p. 140.

missed as mere schoolboy exercises; but that is unjust, for Pope was old for his age and no ordinary schoolboy. Not to know his "Windsor Forest" is to miss some very good descriptive passages and to overlook the soothing fact that the Classical Pope had a heart as well as a head — and a liver. Much the same thing might be said of his elegies, especially of "Eloisa to Abelard" and "On an Unfortunate Lady." Here Pope tried (not with complete success) to be a poet of the heart rather than of the head; in both cases he succeeded in writing a number of noble and rhetorical passages and in demonstrating that his forte was not lyric poetry. He was a poet, certainly; but not that kind of poet.

Satires. As a young man Pope joined the group of admirers round the armchair of Dryden in Will's coffeehouse and determined to learn the art of satire which the elder poet had so brilliantly exercised. That he learned his lesson he presently showed in *The Rape of the Lock*, a mock-heroic poem unique in English Literature. It so happened that a young nobleman in a moment of giddiness snipped a lock of hair from a young lady's head. That was before bobbing had become the vogue, and the young lady resented the robbery. So did her family and her friends, and the result was a tempest in the teapot of fashionable society. Here was Pope's opportunity, and so in *The Rape of the Lock* he pretends to treat the affair as a matter of grave importance:

> What dire offence from amorous causes springs,
> What mighty contests rise from trivial things.

The poem reaches its height of absurdity in the account of what happened after the fell deed had been done:

> Then flashed the living lightning from her eyes,
> And screams of horror rend th' affrighted skies.
> Not louder shrieks to pitying Heaven are cast,
> When husbands, or when lap-dogs breathe their last;
> Or when rich China vessels, fallen from high,
> In glittering dust and painted fragments lie!

It is not correct, as sometimes is done, to speak of *The Rape of the Lock* as a burlesque. The art of burlesque consists in ridiculing great things by making them little; the art of the mock heroic consists in ridiculing little things by making them great.[1] Butler's *Hudibras* is a burlesque, and burlesque is the spirit of much written by Mark Twain and Anatole France. But in Pope's masterpiece satire achieves its effects in precisely the other way. The whole point of the poem is that it is a pompous treatment of an insignificant theme — much ado about nothing.

A literary drink prepared with insufficient honey and an excess of gall is the *Dunciad*, or Epic of Dunces, three books of which appeared in 1728 and the fourth book in 1742. This eminently characteristic production was inspired by Dryden's *Mac Flecknoe* and was occasioned by Pope's quarrels with Lewis Theobald and Colley Cibber. Pope had brought out an edition of Shakespeare, and Theobald, who was a Shakespearean commentator of considerable scholarship, called attention to some of Pope's slips in textual criticism. Pope retorted with the *Dunciad*, wherein he enthrones Theobald as king of the dunces and satirizes some of the men and movements in the literature of the day. In the fourth book Cibber replaces Theobald as ruler of the realm of dullness; Cibber had poked fun at a play in which "the wicked wasp of Twickenham" had a hand. In places the poem is coarse and bitter and some of its judgments are unfair, but none the less it is a great satire. Pope was sincere in his castigation of literary abuses and in his contempt for inefficiency and low standards. The *Dunciad* has many fine lines such as "Damn with faint praise, assent with civil leer," of which Chesterton has well said: "A great poet would not have written such a line, perhaps. But a minor poet could not."[2]

---

[1] This distinction is well drawn by A. F. B. Clark in his *Boileau and the French Classical Critics in England*.

[2] *Five Types*: "Pope and the Art of Satire."

The Rape of the Lock and the *Dunciad* establish Pope as the second greatest satirist in English Literature. "If Dryden was the Mars of English satire, Pope was the Venus ... quite as conspicuous for malice as for elegance."[1] It is in his satires that Pope is a complete embodiment of the Classical spirit, with his imitation of accepted models, his devotion to definite standards of literature, and his display of intellectual cleverness. He spiced his lines with frequent antitheses and showed a surprising mastery of the art of riming.[2] The concluding passage of the *Dunciad* rises to heights of genuine eloquence. It describes the universal reign of dullness and in many ways is applicable to our own day and generation.

Moral Essays. Pope planned but never completed a vast poem on the conduct of life, one of the parts being his *Essay on Man*, written in rimed couplets. Pope rushed in where angels fear to tread. His avowed intention was to give a reason for the faith that was in him, to justify Christianity and expose the errors of unbelief. But philosophy and theology were not fields where he could feel at ease, and his work left him exposed to the attacks of philosophers of varying schools and theologians of diverse creeds. Many of his arguments he derived from Bolingbroke and Shaftesbury, but that was only petty larceny. The poem — for it is a poem — abounds in vivid phrasing and contains several passages of beauty and dignity; and, like the grotto at Twickenham, the *Essay on Man* has been rifled by souvenir hunters. Here occurs the familiar saying "Whatever is, is right." Here Pope gives graphic expression to the thought so beautifully worded

[1] Francis Thompson, *A Renegade Poet.*

[2] He has been accused of writing imperfect rimes like *join* and *line, obey* and *tea.* But his modern critics forget that English pronunciation in the eighteenth century in numerous respects approximated to what is called the Irish brogue. Pope and his contemporaries pronounced *join* "jine" and *tea* "tay." In an elder day Shakespeare pronounced *soul* "sowl," as in a familiar passage in the Trial Scene in *The Merchant of Venice.*

by Bulwer-Lytton, "The veil which covers the face of futurity was woven by the hand of mercy," in the sprightly couplet

> The lamb thy riot dooms to bleed to-day,
> Had he thy reason, would he skip and play?

Here are the lines

> Lo, the poor Indian! whose untutored mind
> Sees God in clouds, or hears Him in the wind,"

which have given rise to the journalistic custom of speaking of a redskin as "Lo." Some of the other "moral" verses which Pope intended for his projected masterpiece contain specimens of his finest style and his most earnest thought.

Pope's Place in Literature. Much of the adverse criticism vented upon Pope takes the form of complaint that he did not write the kind of poetry that found favor in the nineteenth century. He is often labeled artificial. But artificiality in literature is like superstition in religion : it is something which we personally do not practice or approve of. Nobody considered Pope artificial until a new style, Romanticism, came in and the leading eighteenth-century Classicist was discredited. It is hardly fair to condemn Raphael because he did not paint like Sargent, or to call Verdi artificial because his compositions differ from the more recently accepted style of Wagner or Puccini. The sane question to ask about any writer or painter or musician is simply this : What did he try to do, and how did he succeed in doing it?

Pope did not try to write certain kinds of poetry at all. But the kind of poetry he did try to write — the critical, the didactic, the satiric — he wrote exceptionally well. He was recognized as the leading poet of his day; and though his fame has since fluctuated, nobody can deny his wit, his brilliancy, his mastery of the rimed couplet. It is idle to fight over the question Is Pope a poet? "The *Essay on Man* is as surely designed to stir the feelings as Shelley's lyrics are. If its aim *were* to give instruction, that aim could be attained much better in prose."[1] Pope, in short, did something which in our day is well-nigh impossible, for literary satire is practically a lost art, like the illumination of manuscripts or the making of stained glass. There is much justification for Chesterton's dictum: "Pope was really a great poet; he was the last great poet of civilization."[2] Certainly he was the last great poet of the Classical tradition.

ADDISON AND STEELE

Literature in Journalism. As we have seen elsewhere in this book, the journalist and the poet, the newspaper man and the littérateur, are no more to be confused because they both use written speech than are the dentist and the bricklayer because they both use cement. It might be said, indeed, that literature and journalism are as different as day and night; and, like day and night, literature and journalism have twilight zones wherein we find pieces of writing which partake of the character of both. Now and then in our daily newspaper we come across an editorial utterance or a humorous or pathetic description of some current event which possesses the essential characteristics of true literature; and from time to time a recognized man of letters — a poet or an essayist or a writer of fiction — may publish his distinctive literary work in the columns of a newspaper. Such are instances of literature existing in journalism, and it was a condition of publication that enjoyed considerable vogue during the eighteenth century in London.

Newspapers as we know them did not then exist. The first English daily paper, *The Daily Courant*, which started in 1702, was smaller and decidedly less newsy than the *Express* of London or the *Tribune* of Chicago. And most of the periodicals

[1] C. T. Winchester, *Principles of Literary Criticism*, p. 233.
[2] *Five Types*: "Pope and the Art of Satire."

of the eighteenth century appeared only once or twice or thrice a week. They were a combination, in primitive form, of our newspapers and our magazines. Daniel Defoe had a good deal to do with several of them; but from the point of view of literature the most important were the *Tatler*, the *Spectator*, and other publications edited by Sir Richard Steele. None of Steele's papers existed for a long time, but they contained some of the most representative literature of the day, the informal essays of the editor and of his friend Joseph Addison.

SIR RICHARD STEELE

Sir Richard Steele (1672–1729). Irish by birth, Steele was a big boy playing on the green hard by St. Patrick's Gate in Dublin when Jonathan Swift was a little boy rolling his hoop in Hoey's Court. Then Steele went to London and studied at the Charterhouse School and at Oxford. In both places his chum and confidant was Addison, with whom he was destined to form a famous literary partnership. Some interesting pictures of the two, as boys and as men, are given by Thackeray in *Henry Esmond*.

Steele led a careless and highly varied life. He was a soldier and a member of Parliament, a playwright and a journalist; and always he was in good humor and in debt. He died in Wales in 1729. His plays have today only a historic interest; but they did something to purge the English stage of the licentiousness of the Restoration era and to establish that curious line of Irish dramatists — Goldsmith, Sheridan, Synge,

Shaw — who have so notably affected the London theater. He established five periodicals, one after another, and to them contributed essays characterized by kindliness of outlook, pervasive humor, and a vigorous and unaffected style. It is eternally to his credit that in an age of cynicism and vulgarity he invariably showed respect for womanhood.

Joseph Addison (1672-1719). Both as man and as writer in marked contrast with Steele, Addison was methodical and industrious, and eventually became Secretary of State. Though politics occupied much of his attention, he was always devoted to literature. He wrote a number of poems, one of which, "The Campaign," commemorating the English victory at Blenheim, brought him celebrity and political preferment; he produced an unsuccessful opera *Rosamond*, and *Cato*, a cold and stately tragedy on classical lines; but his signal claim to recognition is based on the essays he wrote to oblige his friend, the editor of the *Spectator*. "I fared," said Steele, "like a distressed prince who calls in a powerful neighbor to his aid. I was undone by my auxiliary. . . . The paper was advanced indeed. It was raised to a greater thing than I intended it."

Always a reading man and something of a philosopher, with a keen eye on the fads and foibles of the day and the follies and inconsistencies of human nature, Addison was admirably fitted to write essays of more than passing worth. Best known of them all today are the papers dealing with the life and character of the imaginary Sir Roger de Coverley and his associates and friends. "The Vision of Mirza" is a specimen of Addison's philosophical allegories, and his lighter vein, wherein he mingled humor and satire, is revealed in his literary analyses of a beau's head and a coquette's heart. Others of his essays were deliberate attempts to inculcate respect for Christian principles and to elevate the moral standard of the times. Repeatedly he busied himself with popular literary criticism, writing a series of papers on Milton and discussing problems of style, the pleasures of the imagination, and the characteristics of comedy and tragedy. He made no important contribution to criticism, but he was a good literary middleman and popularized the teachings of great European critics.

After all, what Addison wrote is of less importance than the manner in which he wrote it. He is one of the great English stylists. He steered a straight course between aloof, impersonal dignity and flippant, eccentric intimacy. Not every reader admires Addison. One of the curiosities of literature is the opinion which Jane Austen entertained of the *Spectator*: "A voluminous publication, hardly any part of which would not, either by its matter or manner, disgust a young person of taste."[1] But the consensus of opinion more nearly coincides with the well-known eulogy penned by Johnson: "Whoever wishes to attain an English style, familiar, but not coarse, and elegant, but not ostentatious, must give his days and his nights to the volumes of Addison." Fashions in writing have changed since the early eighteenth century, and the modern world favors a more hurried and flurried manner than Addison's; but we praise the virtues which we cannot claim, and in describing a writer as "Addisonian" we convey a high compliment.

SWIFT

A Lover of Liberty. The second half of the eighteenth century witnessed two remarkable risings of subject nations: the American Revolution of 1776 and the French Revolution of 1792. It is not generally known that the basic principle upon which both assertions of the rights of the people were founded was phrased as early as 1722 by Dean Swift in one of the pamphlets, called *The Drapier's Letters*, which he wrote in defense of the oppressed Irish people. In the Fourth Letter occur these momentous words, which singularly forecast the spirit of our own Declaration of Independence:

[1] Cited by Sir Walter Raleigh in *The English Novel*, chap. ix.

For in reason, all government without the consent of the governed is the very definition of slavery. . . . The remedy is wholly in your own hands, and therefore I have digressed a little in order to refresh and continue that spirit so seasonably raised amongst you, and to let you see that by the laws of God, of nature, of nations, and of your own country, you are and ought to be as free a people as your brethren in England.

The Drapier's Letters were occasioned by an attempt to foist a copper coinage on Ireland, one of many projects to exploit the people of that suffering land. Thanks to Swift's energetic denunciation the plan came to naught. The English authorities issued a proclamation against the anonymous pamphlets, and offered a reward of three hundred pounds for the apprehension and conviction of the writer. The authorship of *The Drapier's Letters* was no secret in Dublin, but no informer dared to claim the reward. Swift was idolized by the Irish people, and in Dublin his memory is still held in affection. The municipal officials granted him the freedom of the city in 1729, "moved by a just sense of the past services he has rendered to his country," and the patriotic leader Grattan invoked his spirit in defense of Irish nationalism.

The Man. Swift's activity on behalf of the Irish people is largely responsible for the dislike of him entertained by many Englishmen of the day and for the prejudiced views of his personality recorded by subsequent English writers. He has been pictured as a vulgarian, a scoffer, a hater of mankind. His vulgarity was a fault of the age in which he lived, his cynicism (often exaggerated) was likewise characteristic of his day and generation, and his hatred was fed by his first-hand knowledge of the misery of the Irish people and of the tyranny and despotism of the English rule in Ireland.

Jonathan Swift (1667–1745) was born of English parents in Dublin and was educated in Trinity College of that city. He was a great reader but an indifferent student, and received his degree "by special favor." The implied humiliation spurred him to unwonted industry, and for seven years following his graduation he devoted eight hours daily to concentrated study. He went to England, became secretary to Sir William Temple at Moor Park, and there met Esther Johnson, the little girl with whom, up to her death in 1728, he preserved a tender and beautiful friendship. Those who wish to discover the real

LITTLE ESTHER AND HER TEACHER

Esther Johnson, the "Stella" of the *Journal*, was Swift's appreciative pupil at Moor Park, and in succeeding years was his confidante and friend

Swift might look into the *Journal to Stella*, written to her during his life in London. Composed in "little language," or baby talk, these letters to Esther Johnson reveal Swift as kindly, whimsical, humorous, and affectionate, as a man very different from the savage ogre of popular misconception.

Swift was ordained in the Church of England in 1694, left Moor Park four years later, and engaged in varied literary and journalistic work in London. His pen was devoted largely to political issues and had considerable influence in putting the Tory party in power. He was recognized as one of the leading literary men of the age and enjoyed the friendship of Pope and other members of the Scriblerus Club. Swift was ambitious for place and power, but he was never willing to pay for preferment by sacrificing his own convictions and fawning upon the mighty ones of earth. He was made Dean of St. Patrick's Cathedral in Dublin in 1714, and the remainder of his life was spent in the city of his birth. Though by no means a spiritual man (he had entered the clergy through ambition rather than devotion) Swift discharged his duties conscientiously and proved himself a capable administrator and a good financier. His mind failed him toward the end of his life. He lies

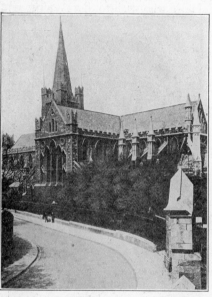

ST. PATRICK'S CATHEDRAL, DUBLIN

Founded in the twelfth century, this finely proportioned Gothic edifice has had a varied history. It has been used for a school, a prison, a court of law, a military barracks, and even for a stable. Since the Reformation it has been the principal Protestant church in Ireland

today beneath the pavement of St. Patrick's Cathedral; and beside him lies Esther Johnson, who was here laid to rest one stormy day in 1728.

A recent scholar, after devoting many years to a study of Swift's works and character, has given us the following estimate of the man:

Swift's was an eminently majestic spirit, moved by the tenderest of human sympathies, and capable of ennobling love — a creature born to rule and to command, but with all the noble qualities which go to make a ruler loved. . . . Above all things Swift loved liberty, integrity, sincerity, and justice. . . . If a patriot be a man who nobly teaches a people to become aware of its highest functions as a nation, then was Swift a great patriot and he better deserves that title than many who have been accorded it.[1]

The Satirist. Swift is best known today through *Gulliver's Travels*, which shares popularity with Defoe's *Robinson Crusoe* as a gift book for children — an odd destiny for the most grim and biting satirical prose work in the English language. The volume was written (1726) as part of an extensive work projected by the Scriblerus Club, and Swift's avowed purpose was to "vex the world," convinced as he was that there are times when the world needs to be vexed. It is a satire on human life in general and on English court life in particular. Many of its allusions to persons and events are missed by the modern reader (unless he reads the illuminating notes in W. C. Taylor's edition), but no adult reader can fail to feel the force and sting of its comments on human weakness and absurdity. Gulliver's adventures among the Lilliputians and Brobdingnagians are narrated with consistency and humor. Here, as it were, Swift looks at man through a telescope, holding to his eye first the large end and then the small. The shadows deepen in his depiction of life among the Houyhnhnms, a race of intelligent horses; and there is no "sweetness and light" — that famous phrase is of Swift's invention — in his dismal picture of the Yahoos. *Gulliver's Travels* is one of the most original books in English Literature and has supplied all modern languages with words and all modern literatures with ideas.

While still at Moor Park and shortly after his ordination, Swift wrote his *Tale of a Tub*, a religious satire composed in a

[1] Temple Scott, *The Prose Works of Jonathan Swift, D.D.*, Introduction to Vol. VI.

thoroughly irreligious spirit. It purports to be an attack upon Catholics and Lutherans, and so it is; but it is likewise an effective blast of raillery against the pretensions of the Church of England. The book is brilliant, witty, irreverent, but it is not bitter and venomous. Some of the ablest of Swift's satires deal with Irish subjects. Thus, his *Modest Proposal* is a biting arraignment of English cruelty and incompetence. The proposal is the ironical suggestion that since the Irish people unfortunately have children, and since parents are often the victims of extreme poverty, the paternal English government might arrange to have the children killed like cattle and sold as food in the English market. The satire was lost on some literal-minded readers, who declared that Swift must have been an inhuman monster to think of such a thing!

The Classicist. Swift was always interested in language problems and in theories of literature. His *Proposal for Correcting, Improving, and Ascertaining the English Tongue* urges the formation of a body of learned men similar to the French Academy, having for object the "fixing and ascertaining of our language for ever." It was characteristic of the Age of Classicism for Swift to assume that language should not change and develop, to deplore the introduction of new words and the use of slang, abbreviations, and phonetic spelling. He made a plea for the official recognition of good writers and insisted that they should be rewarded with pensions and honors. Several of his essays, such as "A Letter of Advice to a Young Poet," deal with similar themes.

The Classical tendency of Swift is most clearly manifested in his *Battle of the Books*, published when he was thirty-seven years of age. The battle is the never-ending conflict between old books and new, and Swift ranges himself on the side of the ancients. The work abounds with humor and with characteristic satire; and though the author's bias in favor of the classics is manifest and his disparagement of recent writers not always judicious, it has an abundance of sane criticism and sound sense. Applicable for all time is his fable of the Bee and the Spider, which points the contrast between the writer of thoughtful charm and the mere spinner of words.

The Stylist. Swift wrote some verse, but his claim to recognition is based upon his prose performance. He began to write when in the thirties, so that everything from his pen is seasoned and mature. His writing is prevalently in what the old-fashioned rhetoricians used to call the plain style: he is sparing of adjectives, avoids roundabout phrasing, and aims at clearness, vigor, and precision. Swift's manner of writing is *loquitive* [1]; that is, it is much like the style of ordinary good speech. Here are some examples, interesting alike for their matter and their manner:

That was excellently observed, say I, where I read a passage in an author where his opinion agrees with mine. When we differ, there I pronounce him to be mistaken.

A very little wit is valued in a woman, as we are pleased with a few words spoken plain by a parrot.

The reason why so few marriages are happy is because young ladies spend their time in making nets, not in making cages.

What they do in heaven we are ignorant of; what they do not do we are expressly told, that they neither marry nor are given in marriage.

Physicians ought not to give their judgment of religion, for the same reason that butchers are not admitted to be jurors of life and death.

As universal a practice as lying is, and as easy a one as it seems, I do not remember to have heard three good lies in all my conversation, even from those who were most celebrated in that faculty.

JOHNSON

Writer and Man. Were we to ask a tolerably well-educated man "What comes to your mind at mention of Dr. Samuel Johnson?" the reply would probably be "Johnson as a ragged student at Oxford" or "Johnson trying to teach school," "Johnson dominating conversation at the club" or "Johnson

---

[1] See Sir William Watson's little essay "Pencraft," in which he explains the characteristics of the *cantative*, the *scriptive*, and the *loquitive* styles.

walking down Fleet Street with Jamie Boswell to attend services at St. Clement Danes." But in every case it would be an impression of Johnson the man rather than of Johnson the writer. Where most writers are concerned — Shakespeare, Milton, and Dryden, for example — we think first of what they wrote; in Johnson's case, even when his *Rasselas* or his essay

© Emery Walker Limited

JAMES BOSWELL

on Cowley is on the desk before us, we are envisaging the burly, shortsighted, snuff-smeared, big-hearted, and devout-minded dictator of English Literature. "When he talked," as H. W. Mabie happily expressed it, "his words were charged with the electric current of his tremendous personality; when he wrote, the circuit was broken; at some point the current escaped into the air, and the reader never receives any emotion or impulse approaching a shock in intensity. . . . In some cases we remember the man because of the work he did; in Johnson's case we shall remember the work because of the man who did it." [1]

And how comes it that we know Johnson the man so very well and very intimately? Because his personality made a strong impression on all who knew him and on all who have studied the man and his times. Sir John Hawkins, a charter member of the Club that used to meet at the Turk's Head, described him; Sir Joshua Reynolds painted his portrait;

[1] *Essays in Literary Interpretation*, p. 21.

Washington Irving almost made him the leading figure in the *Life of Goldsmith*; Macaulay hit off some of his eccentricities with journalistic vividness and lack of proportion; Carlyle introduced him into that gallery of oddly assorted celebrities called *Heroes and Hero Worship*. But we feel so close to Johnson the man chiefly because a certain young Scot, otherwise unknown to fame, wrote a big book about Johnson's life and conversation and so immortalized both his subject and himself.

The Complete Biographer. James Boswell (1740–1795) has recently been considerably written about and his letters have been published; but as a man he is important only because he was a thorough hero worshiper, and as a writer he counts only because

SAMUEL JOHNSON

of his *Life of Johnson*. No hero himself, he could appreciate noble traits in others; and he wrote down everything he observed in Johnson and everything he heard Johnson say. Boswell was not a mere shallow-minded flatterer — not, as Macaulay contemptuously called him, a Scotch bur on Johnson's coat tail: he was something of a student, he had an active, open mind, and he was a pleasant companion and a consistent friend. He was neither a knave nor a fool, for Johnson really liked and esteemed him. But he secures his place in the history of English Literature solely because he contributed to it a supreme piece of biographical writing.

Thanks to him and his immortal book, Johnson the man becomes more real and alive to us than Johnson the writer.

In Boswell's *Life of Johnson* we have a series of living, speaking pictures of the Great Cham of English Literature. We see him grimacing beneath his untidy, ill-fitting wig; we hear him snorting and growling and silencing opposition with one of those thunderous "sir's"; we listen to him defending Catholicism on the Harwich coach and discussing men and books and political issues at the Club; we observe him consuming innumerable dishes of tea and enjoying the society of his friends and familiars. And we secure a singularly adequate idea of the sort of man Johnson really was — a voracious reader, a brilliant talker, a respecter of honor and virtue. His limitations are here too. Hannah More, the story goes, besought Boswell to soften and idealize the portrait of Johnson; but Boswell indignantly replied that he would not "cut off his claws nor make a tiger a cat to please anybody." And all succeeding readers applaud that sturdy resolve.

Who Johnson Was. A hungry boy rummaging in his father's bookshop for apples found a volume of Petrarca and eventually became, as Heine called him, the John Bull of Erudition. The bookshop was in Lichfield, in the Midlands, where Johnson was born in 1709. The scholar and writer and dictator died in London in 1784. A varied and eventful life was crammed between those two eighteenth-century dates. The boy went to Oxford and attended Pembroke College there, but left before taking his degree; it was many years later that he received the title of Doctor. Then he tried teaching for a living, and from that drifted into hack work for Birmingham booksellers. His marriage in 1735 to a widow many years his senior brought him domestic happiness but necessitated his going to London to add to his income. There for years he struggled against poverty, engaged in various literary pursuits, edited the *Rambler*, and ultimately won fame and a measure of fortune.

Characteristic of Johnson's years of plenty was his association with Goldsmith, Burke, Reynolds, Garrick, and other prominent men in the famous Club which he started in 1764. It was at this period that Boswell made his acquaintance, and most of the *Life* is devoted to picturing Johnson in the height of his prestige as writer and critic. Though the long struggle for success left its scars, Johnson, however rough and uncouth externally, was a devout man, an assiduous scholar, a loyal

A MEETING OF THE CLUB AT THE TURK'S HEAD IN GERRARD STREET

friend. He was generous of help to those in need, going out of his way to be of service to aspiring writers and maintaining a number of poor people at his own expense. The memory of his wife he ever cherished. On March 28, 1753, he made this record: "I kept this day as the anniversary of my Tetty's death, with prayers and tears in the morning. In the evening I prayed for her conditionally, if it were lawful."

Jonson and Johnson. A similarity in name is not the only likeness between the author of *Timber* and the author of *Rasselas*.

Both were confirmed Londoners; both felt the town to be their element. Both were huge, unwieldy, unhealthy men. Both possessed vast memories and mighty erudition, and were of a stamp to have been eminent in many branches of human activity if circumstances had not made them authors. Both, as characters, were greater and more influential even than as men of letters. Both, as it happens, made short journeys into France and Scotland; and each found in a Scotchman his biographer.[1]

Both, too, were stanch admirers of ancient literature and held that modern writers could do nothing better than to imitate the classics. Incidentally, both had a style of penmanship neat, small, and even dainty.

On the other hand, there were notable differences between the two leonine writers. Dr. Johnson, though he was a convinced Tory, never became involved in political intrigue to the extent that Ben Jonson did. He served no prison term, and, in contrast with the riotous Ben, he lived a well-ordered and Christian life. The elder man won considerable fame with his numerous dramas; Johnson, though he tried the dramatic form, achieved no success. The critical writings of Ben Jonson are shreds and fragments scattered through the prefaces to his plays and his hasty, unfinished notes; Samuel Johnson's critical dicta are embodied in essays and presented in complete and dignified form. In their subsequent influence they differ also, for Ben Jonson exercised little authority after his own time, whereas Samuel Johnson affected not only his contemporaries but many writers even to our day.

What Johnson Wrote. In verse young Johnson wrote imitations of two of Juvenal's *Satires*: *London* and *The Vanity of Human Wishes*. His satire is less biting than either Juvenal's or Pope's, and his poems are distinguished for sound thinking and ornate expression, but he was not possessed of high poetic gifts. He tried the drama with his Classical tragedy *Irene*, but the play was not successful, though his friend Garrick did everything possible in its production. He made an attempt at the novel in *Rasselas*, a story hurriedly written to pay the expenses of his mother's funeral. *Rasselas* has little plot

[1] John A. Symonds, *Ben Jonson*, p. 156.

interest, but it makes good reading. It deals with the eternal quest of happiness, points out that nobody on earth is as happy as our capacity for happiness warrants, and reaches the conclusion that there must be a state after death in which we shall enjoy complete and noble pleasure.

Johnson's essays in the *Rambler* have never secured the prominence gained by the essays of Addison and Steele in the

THE HEART OF JOHNSON'S LONDON

Fleet Street was the center of Johnson's life and literary labors. He enjoyed its noise and activity and often strolled with one of his intimates from the foot of Ludgate Hill to the Strand. Temple Bar is shown in the background

Spectator; they are heavy and learned, but they lack the delicate touch of Addison and the care-free geniality of Steele. He brought out an edition of Shakespeare in 1765 and made numerous weighty comments in his introduction, but the work as a whole has long since been antiquated owing to the advance of Shakespearean scholarship since the eighteenth century. His *Journey to the Hebrides* is an account of a tour made in company with Boswell in 1773.

The principal works of Johnson are the *Lives of the Poets*

(1777–1781), and the *Dictionary*, which he completed in 1755 after several years of intensive labor. When we take up the *Lives of the Poets* we are struck by the fact that at least half the men Johnson wrote about are unfamiliar to modern readers; some of his dwarfs, it has been said, are giants, and

HIS LORDSHIP WAS "IN CONFERENCE"

Johnson learned while waiting in Chesterfield's antechamber that "hope deferred maketh the heart sick." (By courtesy of the National Gallery, London)

many of his giants are dwarfs. This does not necessarily reflect on Johnson's judgment, for his essays were written as an introduction to an edition of poetry, and he was not free in his choice of subjects. The essays vary in merit. In dealing with Gray, for instance, Johnson is out of sympathy with the approaching Romantic Movement; but he is at his best when writing of Dryden and Pope, of Waller, and especially of Cowley. The *Dictionary*, as dictionary, is now of little practical value; but a very enjoyable occupation is to pick from it some of Johnson's unusual definitions. The *Dictionary* occasioned one of the most remarkable pieces of writing in English Literature, the letter to the Earl of Chesterfield. When beginning the book Johnson had appealed to Chesterfield for assistance, but in vain; when the *Dictionary* was finished, Chesterfield became officiously friendly. Johnson's letter rejects the belated favor:

Seven years, my lord, have now passed, since I waited in your outward rooms, or was repulsed from your door; during which time I have been pushing on my work through difficulties, of which it is useless to complain, and have brought it at last to the verge of publication, without one act of assistance, one word of encouragement, or one smile of favor. Such treatment I did not expect, for I never had a patron before. . . . Is not a patron, my lord, one who looks with unconcern on a man struggling for life in the water, and, when he has reached ground, encumbers him with help?

How Johnson Wrote. It has been said of Carlyle that he could write in three languages: English, Scotch, and "Carlylese." Johnson, although he spoke in English, habitually wrote in "Johnsonese." Now, what is sometimes sneeringly condemned as "Johnsonese" is really literary English, what Watson calls the *scriptive* style. It is much the same way of writing favored by De Quincey, and by Francis Thompson in his essay on Shelley, with this important difference, that Johnson lacked the imaginative fire and the emotional overflow that makes ornate writing convincing. He had a fondness for mouth-filling words (one of his critics maintains that Johnson would never use a word of two syllables if he could find one of six), and he favored stately and rounded sentences. He distinguished, as so many modern writers fail to do, between the language of conversation and the language of literature. Thus, in a letter to his friend Mrs. Thrale, he wrote, "When we were taken upstairs, a dirty fellow bounced out of the bed on which one of us was to lie." That is as colloquial as one could wish. But in his *Journey to the Hebrides* he writes the same thing as follows: "Out of one of the beds on which we were to repose, started up, at our entrance, a man black as a Cyclops from the forge." Perhaps, as Macaulay said, "Johnsonese" is "a language in which nobody ever quarrels, or drives bargains, or makes love." Perhaps Johnson carried dignity and ornateness to extremes; perhaps, as Lamb remarked, even Johnson's jokes are no laughing matter. In any case a liberal reading of Johnson at his best is a literary tonic for the modern student who finds in newspapers and popular books a language that is sometimes below the level of conversation, and who is prone to turn up his nose at a paragraph from Johnson mainly because he lacks the vocabulary and the mental concentration to follow the meaning of its carefully constructed sentences.

JOHNSON'S HOUSE, GOUGH SQUARE

In this sturdy brick building, now a Johnson museum, "Ursa Major" lived from 1748 to 1758. It is one of seventeen lodgings occupied by Johnson during the forty-eight years of his London life

The Classical Dictator. To certain men of letters, because of the range of their influence over other writers and because of the reverence in which their opinions were held by their contemporaries, we give the title literary dictators. Such was Ben Jonson, such Dryden, and such Dr. Johnson. The compiler of the *Lives of the Poets* had a consuming interest in literature and in theories of writing, and he tried to encourage wholesome tendencies in the study and the production of books. Boswell's biography records many of Johnson's conversations on literary subjects and supplies us with an

AT THE CHESHIRE CHEESE

A tradition more interesting than dependable holds that this tavern in Wine Office Court was a rendezvous of Johnson and Goldsmith. It is popular with visitors by reason of its antique atmosphere and the excellence of its lark-and-beefsteak pie

unsystematized digest of his principles and theories. What Boswell does not furnish as an aid to the understanding of Johnson as a literary dictator, the Doctor himself affords us in his numerous writings. In eighteenth-century Classicism Johnson and Pope are the outstanding figures: Johnson, in prose; Pope, in verse. In the writings of both we can discern the most significant traits of Classicism.

Johnson, as we have seen, frankly imitated the Latin satirist Juvenal, and he deeply admired the classics generally. From them and from their current interpreters, Boileau and Pope, he drew the fundaments of his critical theories. That he had limitations as a critic and that he was sometimes brusque and intolerant as a dictator must not blind us to his real importance as a formulator of literary judgments. He had sterling good sense, absolute honesty, and a sturdy vigor in expressing his opinions, and not all his opinions are to be dismissed as old-fashioned and arbitrary. In our day, as in Milton's day, the problems involved in the rights of censorship and the liberty of the press clamor for solution, and no solution will be satisfactory except one consonant with the sound and liberal views here set forth by Johnson :

The danger of such unbounded liberty, and the danger of bounding it, have produced a problem in the science of government, which human understanding seems hitherto unable to solve. If nothing may be published but what civil authority shall have previously approved, power must always be the standard of truth : if every dreamer of innovations may propagate his projects, there can be no settlement; if every murmurer at government may diffuse discontent, there can be no peace; and if every sceptic in theology may teach his follies, there can be no religion. The remedy against these evils is to punish the authors; for it is yet allowed that every society may punish, though not prevent, the publication of opinions which that society shall think pernicious; but this punishment, though it may crush the author, promotes the book; and it seems not more reasonable to leave the right of printing unrestrained because writers may be afterwards censured, than it would be to sleep with doors unbolted, because by our laws we can hang a thief.

GOLDSMITH

In eighteenth-century England some political movements were especially corrupt, and party leaders found it expedient to enlist the services of capable writers in what nowadays is called propaganda. One such leader, the infamous Earl of Sandwich, found himself in need of a graceful and persuasive pen, so he sent Parson Scott, his chaplain, to induce Oliver Goldsmith to defend the administration. Goldsmith was recognized as a capable writer and known to be in financial difficulties. He was then living in wretched quarters in the Temple.[1] To the astonishment of the political emissary the writer absolutely refused to gain financial independence by devoting his pen to the cause of the party. "And so," said Parson Scott, "I left him in his garret."

The Man Goldsmith. This little-known incident reveals Oliver Goldsmith as a man of ideals and of honor: he refused to barter his birthright for a mess of pottage. Not long afterwards he gained a sum of money from his play *The Good-Natured Man* and was

TEMPLE BAR

The word *bar* means "gate," and this entrance to the old city of London got its name from its closeness to the Temple. It stood where Fleet Street merges into the Strand. Temple Bar is now but a memory; it was removed because it blocked traffic

[1] The Temple, which figures so largely in the history of English Literature, is a group of buildings between Fleet Street and the Thames, originally occupied by the military religious order of the Knights Templars. The old church still stands with its medieval ornaments and its tombs of Crusaders. The Knights Templars were suppressed by the Church in 1312. Their London property passed into the hands of two societies of lawyers and became a favorite place of residence for men of law and of letters.

able to abandon his garret and occupy the second floor of a fine house elsewhere in the Temple grounds, No. 2 Brick Court. Ever lavish of hospitality, he nightly invited in a group of friends and joined with them in singing and dancing and playing noisy games. A scholarly writer on legal subjects lived on the floor below and was driven to distraction by the din overhead. And so it was that the great authority on English law, Sir William Blackstone, had to remonstrate with the author of "The Deserted Village," though without much success. Few present-day students of law realize how much Goldsmith had to do with the style and spirit of Blackstone's *Commentaries*!

Thanks largely to Boswell, who did not like Goldsmith and disparages him in several places in his *Life of Johnson*, the popular notion of the gifted Irishman is that of an inspired simpleton who, as Garrick jocosely said, "wrote like an angel and talked like poor Poll." Let it be remarked emphatically that Goldsmith was no fool, though like many another wise man he could play the fool for the delectation of his friends. Grave defects of character undoubtedly were his. He was lazy, inconstant, diffident, and — to the great scandal of Jamie Boswell — extremely careless in handling money; but he had an alert mind, considerable education, a high sense of honor, and a generous heart. The gentleness and sweetness of his disposition, which made his friends love him deeply, and sincerely mourn his untimely death, we can discover in everything he wrote.

Born in a parsonage in County Longford, and brought up at Lissoy, Oliver Goldsmith (1728–1774) came to know at first hand the conditions of Irish rural life which subsequently formed the background of his best-known poem. His father, a poor Protestant pastor, aided by some well-to-do relatives, sent the boy to Trinity College, Dublin ; and Oliver, though an irregular student, managed to get his degree. He thought for a while of each of the learned professions, theology, law, and medicine, though he liked none of them much, and finally chose medicine as the least of three evils. Meanwhile he managed to cross the Channel and spent a year in wandering and study, visiting Flanders, France, Germany, Switzerland, and Italy, "a guinea in his pocket, one shirt to his back, and a flute in his hand," often earning his supper with a rollicking tune, and sleeping in some hospitable monastery. At the age of twenty-eight he began his London career, like Johnson finding ill-paid literary work as a bookseller's hack. But his talents ultimately won recognition, and when he died at the age of forty-six he was one of the best-known writers of English and a favorite member of Johnson's Club.

OLIVER GOLDSMITH

The Poet. Some of the observations made during his year of wandering and the reflections they occasioned are contained in "The Traveller," a poem noted for its graceful descriptions and cheerful sentiments. "The Deserted Village," still a general favorite, reflects his impressions of Irish life. Goldsmith's humorously pathetic character sketches of the village parson and the pedantic and kindly schoolmaster, his pictures of country sports, and his arraignment of the oppressive English rule in Ireland are impressive and eloquent. "Retaliation" and "The Haunch of Venison" were written for the amusement of his literary friends; the former engages in good-natured sallies at the expense of Johnson, Garrick, Reynolds, and others. Some of his best work is to be found in shorter pieces; for example, "An Elegy on the Death of a Mad Dog." Goldsmith favored the rimed couplet, which in his hands became smoother and more musical than Pope's verses, and in other respects he adhered to the traditions of the Classical school. There are numerous echoes of his reading in ancient authors, as in "The Deserted Village," where the passage beginning "As some tall cliff that lifts its awful form" is a paraphrase from the *De Consulatu Theodori* of Claudian.

The Prose Writer. During the days of his early struggles for a livelihood Goldsmith wrote a vast quantity of prose, ranging in subject from a *Short English Grammar* and histories of England, Greece, and Rome to a *History of Animated Nature* and a *Survey of Experimental Philosophy*. Much of his prose has no importance now save for its always graceful English style; but his *Citizen of the World*, a series of letters purporting to be the reflections of a Chinese philosopher on a visit to England, still lives on account of its shrewd observation and kindly satire. Goldsmith derived the idea of the *Chinese Letters* (as the book was originally called) from Horace Walpole's skit "A Letter from Xo Ho, a Chinese Philosopher at London, to his friend Lien Chi, at Pekin." Walpole in turn had taken the idea from the *Persian Letters* of the Frenchman Montesquieu.

As a prose writer Goldsmith is best known by his novel *The Vicar of Wakefield*, a well-constructed story for seventeen chapters, and after that weak and conventional. In the Vicar he idealizes his father and in Moses he caricatures himself. Washington Irving remarks:

How contradictory it seems that this, one of the most delightful pictures of home and homefelt happiness, should be drawn by a homeless man; that the most amiable picture of domestic virtue and all the endearments of the married state should be drawn by a bachelor, who had been severed from domestic life almost from boyhood; that one of the most tender, touching, and affecting appeals on behalf of female loveliness, should have been made by a man whose deficiency in all the graces of person and manner seemed to mark him out for a cynical disparager of the sex.[1]

[1] *Life of Goldsmith*, chap. xvii.

Goldsmith, in fact, was like Richard Steele: conspicuous among eighteenth-century writers for his chivalrous treatment of women.

The prose style of Goldsmith constitutes a genuine contribution to English Literature. It is more easy and flexible than Johnson's, more genial than Addison's, more correct and better balanced than Steele's, more warm and picturesque than

GOLDSMITH'S GRAVE

One of the first objects to draw the attention of the visitor in the Temple precincts is the low mound of marble which marks the resting place of "Goldy"

Swift's. A generous reading of Goldsmith's prose is the best possible antidote against the smart, uncouth, inelegant fashion favored by so many of our present-day newspaper men and writers of advertisements.

The Dramatist. It is remarkable that some of the strongest influences on the English drama have been furnished by Irishmen. Steele did much to purge the English stage of indecency, and Goldsmith did more to free it from the affectations of the sentimental comedy of sighs and tears and to introduce the comedy of wholesome laughter. *The Good-Natured Man* disconcerted the ladies who had been accustomed to come to the theater with extra large handkerchiefs in the expectation of finding the play something to weep over. *She Stoops to Conquer* has established itself as one of the classic English comedies. Dramatic fashions change rapidly, but a good play survives their mutations, and Goldsmith's really comic plot and his inimitable characterization of Tony Lumpkin will continue to appeal to readers and to spectators intent on something more than crude jokes and mechanical farce situations.

BURKE

In front of Trinity College, Dublin, facing College Green, stand statues of two of Trinity's sons: Oliver Goldsmith and Edmund Burke. Though both men were makers of literature and both had a strong attachment to the land of their birth and breeding, it would be difficult to find two Trinity graduates more dissimilar in character, mental attitude, and life work. Those statues — conveying, like all Dublin statuary, an impression of vigorous declamation — are a striking reminder that colleges cannot make men over, but merely bring out what is in them.

The Statesman. Edmund Burke (1729–1797) presents the unusual spectacle of a sincerely patriotic Irishman who achieved fame as a constructive English statesman, of a devout Protestant who fought for Catholic Emancipation and the higher education of the Irish priesthood, of a Parliamentary orator who converted political speeches into living literature. He was a truly great man. When somebody asked Johnson if Burke did not remind him of Cicero, the burly dictator replied, "No, sir; but Cicero reminds me of Burke." Sir James Mackintosh remarked that the historian Edward Gibbon might have been cut out of a corner of Burke's mind without being missed. The French orator Mirabeau paid Burke the practical compliment of borrowing freely from the Irishman's

EDMUND BURKE

From a portrait by Hoppner in Trinity College, Dublin

speeches, and Disraeli adorned in his own lively style ideas lifted from Burke's statements of political principles.

Burke was born in Dublin, the son of a Protestant father and a Catholic mother. It was the custom at that time in Ireland when parents were of different faiths to bring up the boys in the father's religion and the girls in the mother's. Burke's mother was an exceptionally cultured and devout woman and had a profound influence on his character. And the lady whom he married was also a Catholic, the daughter of Dr. Nugent, a member of Johnson's Club. Burke was a consistent friend of Catholic interests not only in Ireland but in France, and received warm expressions of esteem and gratitude from the French bishops and from the pope.

Burke's long Parliamentary career was filled with various activities, the most noted being his defense of the American colonies, his opposition to the French Revolution, — "that putrid carcass, that mother of all evil," — and his prominence in the trial of Warren Hastings. That trial, which occupied fourteen years, has been commemorated in one of Macaulay's most brilliant essays. Hastings was governor-general of India and was accused by Burke and others of cruelty and corruption. The prisoner was acquitted, but the mass of evidence gathered by Burke and so ably presented by him in Westminster Hall brought out grave irregularities in the English rule in India and affected the subsequent course of English imperialism. A true statesman, not a mere politician, Burke rose above party considerations and contributed many important ideas to the science of government. When Goldsmith in "Retaliation" jokingly remarked that Burke "to party gave up what was meant for mankind," he stated what he and every other member of the Club knew to be the exact opposite of the truth : it was not a lie, because it could deceive nobody and was not meant to be taken seriously.

The Orator and Writer. The good-natured Goldsmith was responsible for another false impression of his friend and fellow

Irishman when he called Burke the dinner bell of the House of Commons, meaning that when Burke got up to speak the benches were rapidly emptied. Burke's speeches were well worth listening to and are still well worth reading. He was a forceful and finished orator, and a writer with a fine command of words, a nervous style, and a fund of accurate information. Burke was to Matthew Arnold "our greatest English prose writer"[1] and the "greatest English statesman."[2] "Of all great English prose writers," the late Sir Walter Raleigh tells us, "Burke is most like Shakespeare. . . . He brought to the service of politics an imagination that would have given him high rank among dramatists and poets."[3] Burke invented the expression "the Fourth Estate," which he applied to journalism. Many phrases which appeared originally in his speeches and essays have become part and parcel of familiar discourse. Here are some of his maxims, ideas, and memorable epithets:

Numbers in their nature imply poverty.

The malignant credulity of mankind.

Rather well meant than well considered.

The zeal of foolish good intention.

Falsehood has a perennial spring.

A modification is the constant resource of weak, undeciding minds.

Too much logic and too little sense.

Factious fury.

The calumnies of malice and the judgments of ignorance.

To innovate is not to reform.

Government is a contrivance of human wisdom to provide for human needs.

Your representative owes you, not his industry only, but his judgment; and he betrays you instead of serving you if he sacrifices it to your opinion.

At college Burke was the leader of a student group who formed a literary society and engaged in debates. The out-

---

[1] *First Essays*, p. 63.

[2] *Irish Essays*, p. 283.

[3] *Some Authors*. Raleigh was an Oxford professor who died in 1922.

come of one such debate was his earliest published work, *A Vindication of Natural Society*, brought out when he was twenty-seven years old. About the same time appeared his *Inquiry into the Ideas of the Sublime and Beautiful*, an essay which is still widely read. It is an attempt to discover and formulate the principles of beauty and sublimity in literature and art, and in a day when English literary criticism was largely undeveloped it constituted a weighty contribution to the subject. *Thoughts on Present Discontents* is the best of his utterances on English affairs. Of his three great expressions of opinion on the American Revolution the speech "On Conciliation with America" is deservedly the most popular; it is one of the most perfect examples of oratory in modern times. In *Reflections on the Revolution in France* and *Letters on a Regicide Peace* we have the gist of Burke's eloquent arraignment of the violence and fanaticism which accompanied the deposition of Louis XVI and the establishment of democratic rule in France. His *Letter to a Noble Lord*, occasioned by the protest of the young Duke of Bedford against a pension granted to Burke at the close of his Parliamentary career, is a masterpiece of eloquence comparable to Johnson's letter to Lord Chesterfield.

OTHER WRITERS

Chesterfield. By no means a great man, but certainly a useful public official and a successful and knowing member of polite society, Philip Dormer Stanhope, Earl of Chesterfield (1694–1773), was in a minor way a patron of letters and something of a literary dictator as well as a writer of distinction. A thoroughly worldly man, with no conception of the higher values of life, Chesterfield's writings show him to have been cold, calculating, and intent on selfish ends; but at the same time they abound in good sense and in clever sayings. His *Letters to his Son* failed in their immediate object, for the young man to whom they were addressed had no desire for gentility and no ambition for power; but they have today an appreciative audience. Some of the bits of advice Chesterfield gives his unworthy offspring have value for a later generation:

A man's own good breeding is his best security against other people's ill manners.

Whoever is in a hurry shows that the thing he is about is too big for him.

If you will please people, you must please them in their own way; and, as you cannot make them what they should be, you must take them as they are.

The good name that we leave behind us at one place often gets before us to another, and is of great use.

Men who converse only with women are frivolous, effeminate puppies; and those who never converse with them are bears.

Wear your learning, like your watch, in a private pocket; and do not pull it out and strike it merely to show that you have one. If you are asked what o'clock it is, tell it; but do not proclaim it hourly and unasked, like the watchman.

Richard Bentley (1662-1742). Richard Bentley was not a popular writer, but as an educator and a classical scholar he exercised influence on the thought of his time. He was a Yorkshire man who spent most of his life at Cambridge University as student and teacher and master of Trinity College. We might assume that he lived a quiet, scholarly life, buried in books and aloof from the world and its ways; on the contrary, though his ability was undoubted and his learning immense, Bentley was aggressive and even quarrelsome and stirred many a tempest in the academic sea. He was a conspicuous figure in Cambridge, with his vigorous stride and the enormous hat which he insisted on wearing on all occasions. It was characteristic of him that he acquired the habit of smoking when he was seventy years old and indulged in it with violence up to the time of his death. His literary work included critical editions of Horace, Terence, and Milton.

Junius. During three years, beginning in January, 1769, there appeared in the *Public Advertiser* a series of letters over the pen name of Junius, dealing with government policies and public men. They were well written, though often bitter and vindictive, and they occasioned an extraordinary amount of comment and controversy. Though the *Letters of Junius* were concerned chiefly with purely political issues and contained a

JOSEPH JEFFERSON AS BOB ACRES

large journalistic element, they are assured a place in English literature on account of the vivid and brilliantly caustic quality of the style. "In the *Letters of Junius*," says Alfred Bougeault, a French critic, "invective and sarcasm rise into genius. The language is worthy of Tacitus, and English prose does not contain anything more solid, more vigorous, or more truly classic."[1]

Who was Junius? Who was this man "who dwelt apart in honorable pride and scorn, condemning from his secret judgment-seat the evils of his time; who was more powerful than cabinets and more feared than kings; who lived his silent life with the iron mask ever on his face, and died and made no sign"?[2] Dr. Johnson thought that Burke was Junius; but the author of the *Letters* was manifestly a lesser man, with a more limited range of knowledge and intellect. The Earl of Chatham has been

[1] *Histoire des littératures étrangères.*
[2] W. J. Dawson, *Makers of English Prose*, p. 20.

named as Junius, too, and so have Chesterfield, Charles Sackville, Thomas Paine, Horne Tooke, and numerous others. A good case can be made out in favor of the historian Edward Gibbon; but, though the mystery of the authorship never has been and probably never will be satisfactorily solved, the weight of evidence points to an Irishman, an official of the English government, Sir Philip Francis (1740–1818), as the writer of the *Letters of Junius*.

RICHARD BRINSLEY SHERIDAN

Sheridan. Early in 1775 a young man recently married and in need of ready money had his maiden play produced at Covent Garden Theater and thereby made a lasting contribution to English dramatic literature. For the young man was Richard Brinsley Sheridan (1751–1816), and the play was *The Rivals*. Here were introduced some immortal characters: the swaggering Irishman, Sir Lucius O'Trigger; the gruff and blustering Sir Anthony Absolute; the countrified Bob Acres; above all, the inimitable Mrs. Malaprop with her diverting variations on the King's English. Who can "illiterate" from memory her "contagious" countries, "the very pine-apple of politeness," and "as headstrong as an allegory on the banks of the Nile"? Two years later, having meanwhile produced three less important dramas, Sheridan brought out his greatest work, *The School for Scandal*, a masterpiece of social satire, a play still delightful to read and more delightful to see capably acted. In many respects

The School for Scandal challenges comparison with the great comedies of Molière, though it is thinner and more superficial than the best work of the French genius. *The Critic* (1779) is the third of Sheridan's brilliant and humorous comedies. Twenty years later he attempted a tragedy in *Pizarro*, an adaptation of the German dramatist Kotzebue's *Spaniards in Peru*; but Sheridan had no high gifts for writing tragedy, and in any case his powers had declined.

"He who has written the two best comedies of the age is surely a considerable man," Dr. Johnson declared of Sheridan. And Sheridan has further justified his claim to remembrance by the large number of quotations from his writings which we often employ without remembering where they come from. Such Sheridanisms are "defence, not defiance," "I own the soft impeachment," "no scandal about Queen Elizabeth," "easy writing's vile hard reading," and "as easy as saying Jack Robinson."

A Dubliner by birth and characteristically Irish in his virtues and defects, Sheridan was only incidentally a writer and a dramatist; he lived a varied and well-filled life and knew at first hand both affluence and poverty. He was for a time manager of the Drury Lane Theater in London, and the story persists that when that fabric was destroyed by fire and brought him serious financial losses he calmly sat in a neighboring public house with a bottle of wine beside him on the table. "A man," he whimsically remarked, "may surely be allowed to take a glass of wine by his own fireside." He enjoyed a Parliamentary career too, and distinguished himself as an orator, assisting Burke in the trial of Warren Hastings. He claimed that his philosophy of life was to work like a race horse and loaf like a lizard. Loafing proved more congenial than working, and he died in destitution. He lies among the literary immortals in Westminster Abbey.

CHAPTER XI

THE ROMANTIC MOVEMENT

WHAT ROMANTICISM IS

The word *romantic* has several meanings. In popular language it is loosely applied, often with humorous intent, to the emotion of love. Thus the young lady unduly interested in sentimental stories and the butcher boy who lingers long in conversation with a pretty housemaid are said to be romantic. More accurately, the word is used in connection with the medieval stories in verse or prose known as the Romances, or with later stories, like Sir Philip Sidney's *Arcadia*, which in some respects resemble them. As the word is employed in histories of literature and in literary criticism it connotes a tendency, a mood, or a manner of writing opposed sometimes to Classicism and sometimes to what is known as Realism. In this chapter we are considering Romanticism as a reaction against the Classicism that prevailed in eighteenth-century English Literature.

Let us go back for a moment to the illustration of building a house. We have seen that the Classical writer — that is, the writer who deliberately imitates great writers of the past — is like a man who builds a house according to a detailed plan and tries to make it resemble other houses. There are streets in London, Paris, and New York where the houses look as though they were all turned out of the same mold, where the resemblance between house and house is so complete that the numbers are about the only thing to distinguish one from another. One day a man grows weary of that monotony, and says something like this: "I am going to build a new house, and it is going to be something different. Instead of many small windows with large panes, I shall install a few large windows with small panes. Instead of a flight of long, straight stairs, I shall have a series of steps on different levels and running in various directions. Those vast living rooms in all the houses in this street are cold and depressing; I am going to have several small and cosy living rooms, each decorated in a different style. And instead of buying spick-and-span standardized furniture and chairs alike as peas in a pod, I am going to collect odds and ends from various parts of the earth — Navajo rugs and Spanish stools and Greek statues and mural decorations suggested by the Cathedral of Chartres."

Such, in a general way, is the attitude of the Romantic writer, and such is the spirit of the Romantic Movement in literature. It is a movement away from the formalism and conventionality and standardization of the Classical idea; it is an effort to secure freshness, originality, spontaneity, to get away from rules and models, to secure inspiration from life rather than from books. The Romantic writer grows weary of hearing what Virgil did and what Aristotle said should be done; he feels smothered by literary precedents and conventions. Boileau and Pope seem to him stilted and artificial and mechanical; he wants nature unadorned, and fresh air, and primitive rapture. He is like young David discarding the cumbrous armor of Saul and going forth to slay Goliath armed only with some smooth stones and a sling.

The Classical attitude and the Romantic attitude are both necessary to complete living, and manifestations of them are to be found in every department of life. St. Francis of Assisi is from this point of view an eminently Romantic figure in the history of religion, just as at their best the Pharisees represent the conservative and imitative school of religious thought. In education the present-day tendency toward uniformity in the training of teachers and toward standardization of entrance requirements and credit hours in colleges is an expression of

Classicism. On the other hand, St. de la Salle with his popular teaching and Froebel with his kindergarten were educational Romanticists. In music Bach and Handel were Classical; Weber and Wagner were Romantic. Sir Joshua Reynolds was a Classical painter; Manet and Corot were Romantic painters. We can easily observe the distinction between the Classical and the Romantic spirit in two kinds of public speakers: the one dignified and deliberate and given to stilted and carefully rehearsed gestures, and the other free, spontaneous, natural.

In literature, as in other forms of art, Romanticism comes as a protest against the formality and artificiality of extreme Classicism, and Classicism comes as a reaction against the license and freakishness of extreme Romanticism. Classical writers, like Boileau in France and Pope in England, were followed by numerous admirers and imitators who tended to make literature a thing of rhetoric instead of life and who regarded the form of literature as of greater importance than its substance. The inevitable reaction took place in the late eighteenth and early nineteenth century. In Germany, Schiller, Bürger, Novalis, and Friedrich von Schlegel were leaders in the Romantic revolt; in France, the Romantic ideal, first realized by Rousseau, was fostered by Chateaubriand, Lamartine, Madame de Staël, Alfred de Vigny, Victor Hugo, and many other writers of drama, of prose, and of verse. The German Romanticists influenced the French, and the French Romanticists influenced the Germans, and between the Romanticists in England and those on the Continent there was an interplay of ideas. And always there were a few eminent writers, like Goethe in Germany and Sainte-Beuve in France, who tried to avoid the excesses of both Classicism and Romanticism and to utilize the best in both movements. The close of the eighteenth century was a period of revolution in life generally. In France it overthrew the monarchy, in Germany it chiefly affected philosophy, and in England it disclosed itself in a literary way, especially in new conceptions of poetry.

ROMANTICISM IN THE EIGHTEENTH CENTURY

The Dean of Dabblers. As Pope's grotto at Twickenham
was the symbol and the stronghold of Classicism, so Horace
Walpole's Gothic castle at Strawberry Hill was typical of
the Romantic Movement. Strawberry Hill is on the Thames

STRAWBERRY HILL

From an old print

less than a mile from Twickenham, and here in 1747 Horace
Walpole (1717–1797) built a residence as different as could
be imagined from Pope's villa and filled it with all manner
of curious and unusual furnishings.[1] The son of Sir Robert
Walpole, the owner of the Gothic castle had attended Eton
and Cambridge, had rambled on the Continent, had entered

[1] It is interesting to observe that the estates of Pope and Walpole are today
the sites of Catholic educational institutions, Pope's villa being occupied by a
convent school conducted by the Sisters of Mercy, and Walpole's gardens by
the teachers' colleges of the Vincentian Fathers and the Brothers of the Christian Schools.

Parliament and held several offices; but most of his long life he spent among his books and statues and paintings at Strawberry Hill. He was by temperament and by choice what the Italians call a *dilettante* and what the French call an *amateur* — a man who made a profound and scholarly study of no one subject but who dabbled in a variety of intellectual interests. He was something of a social celebrity and a man of fashion;

THE CHURCHYARD AT STOKE POGES

he set up a printing press and brought out editions of various writings, including his own; and he wrote on history, on painting, on politics, on gossip, and commemorated the virtues of Pope Benedict XIV in Latin verse.

As a writer Walpole is best remembered for his voluminous correspondence. He was an untiring letter writer, and his epistles form an interesting commentary on literature, on art, and on the history of the eighteenth century. His *Historic Doubts* was the earliest attempt to whitewash the character of King Richard III as that monarch is depicted by the Blessed Thomas More and Shakespeare; and his novel *The Castle of*

Otranto, a tale of mystery and terror, was the first manifestation of the Romantic Movement in English fiction.

The Author of the "Elegy." An eyewitness[1] declares that on that memorable night when the English troops were slipping down the St. Lawrence River to scale the steep cliff at Quebec

THOMAS GRAY
From a painting in the collection of
George A. Plimpton

and defeat the French on the Plains of Abraham, their commander, General James Wolfe, "repeated nearly the whole of Gray's 'Elegy' to an officer who sat with him in the stern of the boat"; and then he, who, like his rival Montcalm, was to fall mortally wounded the next day, made this statement: "I would prefer being the author of that poem to the glory of beating the French tomorrow." The poem which Wolfe so admired was the familiar "Elegy written in a Country Churchyard," a piece of verse remarkable for its simplicity, its wistful melancholy, its delicate word-music, and its gemlike bits of natural description. To compare it with Pope's "Windsor Forest" is to realize much of the difference between Romanticism and Classicism.

The country churchyard immortalized by Gray is at Stoke Poges, some twenty miles west of London, where the poet and

[1] John Robison, afterwards a professor at Edinburgh University. The story of Wolfe and the "Elegy" may be found in Playfair's *Biographical Account of Professor Robison*, published in 1815.

his mother lie buried beside the old parish church. The churchyard is beautiful on a summer's day, but not more so than dozens of others in England; yet it is most famous of all, and is visited annually by thousands of tourists, because it had the good fortune to be commemorated in a poem that has captivated popular fancy. Gray took eight years to write the

ETON COLLEGE FROM THE THAMES

This famous school was founded by the pious King Henry VI, whose statue adorns the principal inner court. Across the river is the town of Windsor

"Elegy," and even then was diffident about having it published; but his friend Walpole induced him to give it to the printer. For this as for his other writings Gray would never accept any money, considering it beneath his dignity as a gentleman to write for pay; and his publishers were perfectly satisfied to humor his scruples.

Thomas Gray (1716–1771) was born in London, and at Eton formed a friendship with Walpole which, though strained on one occasion when they went to Italy together and disagreed as even friendly travelers sometimes will, continued until his death. He was a man of retiring habits and spent most of his life deep in his books at Cambridge, where he held a professorship, never gave a lecture, and amassed a vast store of learning. In proportion to his talents and his opportunities his literary output is slight, but everything he wrote has a high degree of excellence. Though he was familiar with the great authors of ancient and modern times, and though he lived in a prevailingly Classical period, he showed a truly Romantic interest in nature, in the early poetry of Wales, and in "the short and simple annals of the poor." He avoided both the formalism and artificiality of the Classicists and the excessive emotional display and lack of restraint that characterized much Romantic literature.

Besides the "Elegy," the poem by which he is most widely known, Gray wrote several memorable odes. Of these "The Bard" and "The Progress of Poesy" take high rank in the early Romantic Movement. Singularly impressive is his picture of the Welsh bard lifting his voice in protest against the invading English under Edward I and then plunging to his death. Another ode, "On a Distant Prospect of Eton College," captures the mood in which with the eyes of a mature man he gazes upon "ye distant spires, ye antique towers" where his schooldays were spent; and it concludes with the much-quoted and much-misapplied reflection

> . . . where ignorance is bliss,
> 'Tis folly to be wise.

In a vein of gentle humor he discourses of his favorite cat in a poem entitled "The Long Story," an ode undeserving of the oblivion which has overtaken it. Like Walpole, Gray was a graceful and urbane letter writer. "I once thought Swift's letters the best that could be written," Cowper wrote to a friend, "but I like Gray's better. His humor, or his wit, or whatever it is to be called, is never ill-natured or offensive, and yet, I think, equally poignant with the Dean's."

Nature and Indolence. A young theological student at the University of Edinburgh was given the task of translating one of the Psalms, and he electrified the class and scandalized the professor by handing in a highly ornate and figurative version. We can see the professor pursing his lips and shaking his head. "Young man, you must put a curb on your fancy," the poet

RICHMOND BRIDGE
Spanning the Thames between Surrey and Middlesex

was admonished, "if you wish to be useful in the ministry." The young man was not at all sure that he wished to be useful in anything, so he abandoned his studies in divinity and betook himself to the delights of the muses. Thus it was that James Thomson (1700–1748), a capable but admittedly easygoing son of Scotland, found his vocation.

Thomson went to London in the early 20's, a sheaf of poetry in his pocket, and after the usual lean years gained recognition and a modest fortune. He made his home in Richmond, and from Richmond Hill he could overlook a pleasant stretch of the valley of the Thames and see both Pope's Villa and, shortly before he died, Walpole's Gothic castle. He was affected by the ideals represented by both those objects, for Thomson's poetry is Classical in form and Romantic in substance. *The Seasons*, now little known, was once a widely popular poem; and *The Castle of Indolence* sparkles with beautiful lines and sings itself smoothly along. Both poems make it clear that Thomson had a discerning eye for color and a delicate ear for sound, and that at the same time he was unable or unwilling to free himself from the trammels of trite and conventional diction. "Thomson has sometimes been commended for the novelty and minuteness of his remarks upon nature," Cardinal Newman writes[1]; and he adds, "this is not the praise of a poet." Certainly not in Newman's day, when the Romantic Movement had brought forth profuse fruits, nor, indeed, in any day if the poet has merely photographed nature; but it was commendable in Thomson to regard nature with the naked eye rather than through the spectacles of his friend at Twickenham and to invest his descriptions of scenery and country life with alluring splendor. Thomson is best known now because of his patriotic poem, "Rule Britannia," which occurs in *Alfred: a Masque*, written in collaboration with a fellow Scotsman, David Mallet.

The Revival of the Past. A conspicuous trait of the new poetry was an interest in primitive life as that life was expressed in early popular ballads. Percy's *Reliques of Ancient English Poetry* (1765) and Charlotte Brooke's *Reliques of Irish Poetry* (1789) are typical of the tendency, for they fastened attention on the Ballads, literary products infinitely removed in both form and spirit from the poetry of the Classical school. Interest in the past, so prominent in Gray, received an unusual stimulus through the translations of early Gaelic verse which James Macpherson (1736–1796) claimed to have made. His work occasioned a controversy which echoes yet, however faintly, in the history of English Literature. *Fingal*, *Temora*, and other poems he professed to have translated from

[1] *Poetry, with Reference to Aristotle's Poetics.*

a third-century poet, Ossian; but his claims were disputed, and Macpherson never satisfactorily cleared his name. The Ossianic poems, which it is probable Macpherson invented rather than translated, have a weird and other-worldly beauty about them, and suggest something of a Homeric spirit amid the Highland mountains and the fog of the Hebrides. They were accepted as genuine on the Continent, and exerted considerable influence on French and German Romanticism.

If the poetic forgeries of Macpherson are only probable, those of Thomas Chatterton (1752–1770) are certain. He was a precocious lad, this "boy poet of Bristol," and used to spend many hours poring over old books and dreaming dreams of vanished days. He claimed to have discovered some poems written by a fifteenth-century monk named Thomas Rowley, verses remarkable for their truly poetic qualities but obviously the invention of a clever but unscholarly mind. The so-called Rowley poems caused considerable stir, and Chatterton came to London to enjoy his celebrity; but disheartened by poverty and neglect and disgraced by the discovery of his forgeries, the youth of eighteen swallowed poison and died. It is astonishing that such clever work could have been produced by a mere boy. He was only thirteen when he wrote the first of the alleged fifteenth-century poems. This blighted genius had a large influence on the development of the Romantic Movement. Several later poets, including Blake and Coleridge, are heavily indebted to Chatterton.

Minor Romanticists. An unhappy victim of laziness, of sadness, and at last of insanity, William Collins (1721–1759), while still an undergraduate at Oxford, wrote his *Persian Eclogues*, creations marked by dreamy fancy, rich imagery, and a splendid command of words. Like so many others Collins settled in London, and was befriended by Johnson and Thomson. His collection of odes, published in 1746, reveal him as deeply imaginative and surpassingly musical, a genuine if undisciplined poet. "The Passions, an Ode to Music" is a symphony in words, inevitably suggesting Dryden's "Alexander's Feast"; and his "Ode to Evening" is at once strong and delicate and pervaded by a pleasing melancholy. He won enduring remembrance with his short fragment, "How Sleep the Brave."

Once extremely popular but now of little more than historical importance, Edward Young (1683–1765), while rector of Welwyn, wrote *Night Thoughts*, a meditation in blank verse on life and death and the life beyond life. John Gay (1685–1732) was a burlesque writer with a real lyric gift, still potent by reason of *The Beggar's Opera*, a satire upon the courtiers of George II. When Congreve read the script he remarked that it would "either take greatly or be damned confoundedly." In both particulars he was a prophet. Gay's burlesque is even now sometimes revived, and suggests something between the brilliant comedies of Sheridan and the tuneful wit of the Gilbert and Sullivan operas. In a far different mood James Beattie (1735–1803), professor of moral philosophy at Aberdeen University, wrote *The Minstrel* in Spenserian stanzas. It is long and spineless, with some quotable passages and a mild flavoring of Romanticism. Beattie was, with reservations, a vaguely outlined forerunner of Wordsworth.

Gray and Young were widely imitated by a group of writers conveniently and not inaccurately labeled "the Graveyard School." One of these, Robert Blair (1699–1746), produced in *The Grave* a blank-verse meditation that rivals *Night Thoughts* but falls short of the exquisite "Elegy written in a Country Churchyard." William Shenstone (1714–1763), a more cheerful soul, pleasingly imitated Spenser in *The Schoolmistress*, and in his verses "Written at an Inn at Henley" voiced the sentiments of many a seasoned traveler:

> Whoe'er has travell'd life's dull round,
>   Where'er his stages may have been,
> May sigh to think he still has found
>   The warmest welcome at an inn.

As Wordsworth took occasion to point out in the appendix to his *Lyrical Ballads*, Anne Finch, Countess of Winchilsea (1661–1720), was the earliest of all the English poets of the eighteenth century to manifest essentially Romantic qualities. In her "Nocturnal Reverie" there are abundant signs of Classicism; but the spirit of her verses is vital rather than bookish, and her descriptions of nature are fresh and lifelike. Another early Romanticist was the Irish clergyman Thomas Parnell (1679–1718), a friend of Swift and Pope, the latter of whom sponsored an edition of Parnell's poems in 1723. His best work includes "The Hermit," "A Night Piece on Death," and "A Hymn of Contentment." "The Hermit" is thoroughly Classical, but in his other poems Parnell pictures scenes from nature with imaginative power and in the true Romantic spirit.

The Romantic Movement, thus far affecting verse, extended to prose in *The Natural History and Antiquities of Selborne*, by Gilbert White (1720–1793). In the form of letters to learned friends, White, a country parson, writes simply and entertainingly of the fields and the skies, the freaks of the weather, of finches and larks and daws. Like Walton's *Complete Angler*, White's book is not a scientific treatise or a naturalist's record of fact and observations; it is the comment of a kindly and learned man (White was a graduate of Oriel College, Oxford) who finds peace and comfort "exempt from public haunts."

BURNS

Scotland's Contribution. An American visitor in Edinburgh was being shown about the historic castle, a place singularly redolent of the shames and glories of past centuries. In the citadel his guide, a grim, bristling, enthusiastic Scot, pointed out the treasured regalia of the kings of the land: the crown once worn by Robert Bruce, the richly ornamented scepter of James V, the two-handed sword of state presented to James IV by Pope Julius II. Perhaps the visitor's face showed a trace of disappointment at the scantiness of the treasures, for the guide took occasion to remark in tones of mingled indignation and rapture, " 'Tis na muckle against what they have at Westminster, but a' the jewels in Europe couldna' buy what ye see before ye."

Like the kingly regalia in Edinburgh Castle, the literary treasures of Scotland may seem comparatively slight, but to the people of the land they are infinitely precious and beyond price. The Protestant Reformation, which assumed an especially rigorous form in Scotland, impeded during two centuries the growth of a learned literature in harmony with the European Tradition; but the homely poetry of the people — a development from the Old Scottish Ballads — "was cherished in defiance of the ministers. It went on, underground but vigorous."[1]

The contributions made by Scotland to English Literature have been of great value and of far-reaching influence. Several Scottish writers we have already considered in their relation to the rise of the Romantic Movement; but scores of others, singers of songs and tellers of tales, many of them nameless and forgotten, find utterance in the writings of Robert Burns and Sir Walter Scott. The romance and splendor of the Highlands were captured and enshrined in the stories told by Scott in prose and in verse, and the comedy and tragedy, the nobility and sordidness, of the Lowlands were framed and glorified in the poems of Burns. For Burns was in a very real sense the heir of Dunbar, Ramsay, Semple, Fergusson, and other earlier Scottish bards.

Life and Personality. Born in a little two-roomed cabin at Alloway in Ayrshire, Robert Burns (1759–1796) knew the meaning of hardship and poverty and grilling bodily labor. His father was a gardener and farmer in a small way — a man

---

[1] *The Times Literary Supplement* (London), January 20, 1927, in a review of Gavin Greig's *Last Leaves of Traditional Ballads and Ballad Airs.*

always struggling, and never with success, to wrest a living from the soil. The boy got a few years of schooling of sorts, and there were some good books in the humble home. Like Shakespeare and like Lincoln, young Bobbie made the most of his limited educational opportunities. Though never a learned man, he read everything he could lay his hands on, and, what is more to the purpose, he learned the lessons of the coming of

WHERE BURNS WAS BORN

spring and the passing of the birds and the doings of men. He differed from most of the peasant boys in one thing: that while they trudged the fields and followed the plow empty-minded and dull, he had an active intellect and a brilliant imagination, and his spirit was thrilled with the stories he had heard beside the peat fire and with the songs that were sung of summer evenings on the green. And the itch for writing came to him; and in his brief spells of leisure he set down his first poems, with only a vague notion of an audience but in compliance with an inner urge that gave him no rest until he had put his fancies and emotions into verse.

Troubles and difficulties (mostly of his own making) crowded upon Burns when he became a man and had gone with his brother to a farm at Mossgiel. He decided to leave Scotland and in distant Jamaica to begin life anew; but the unexpected popularity of his poems, published at Kilmarnock in 1786, induced him to change his mind. He went to Edinburgh, this crude, unfashionable plowboy, unused to city life and social manners, and he and his poems became the sensation of the day. He was petted and feasted and lionized, he made some good friends and a number of bad ones, and he "lived dangerously" while his vogue endured. He married Jean Armour in 1788 and settled on a farm at Ellisland beside the river Nith; but he was better as a poet than as a farmer, and his fortunes failed to prosper. He secured the office of exciseman at Dumfries, but the last years of his life were irregular and depressing. It is not exact to say, as sometimes has been said, that he drank himself to death, but there can be no doubt that his intemperance affected his health and hastened his end. "The great misfortune of my life," Burns wrote, "was to want an aim." He was truly a gifted man, but he was morally weak and undisciplined and failed to hold his passions in check.

Poems of the Land. Burns wrote a number of poems in standard English, but in these he is not at his best. Scotch dialect was his true medium, for writing thus he was able to get close to the life he knew and the land he loved. And so the finest of his writings are poems that convey the joys and the sorrows, the doubts and the aspirations, of the rough country boy — the poems that hold his feelings when he beheld a mountain daisy and when his plow ran through the nest of a field mouse and the "cowrin, tim'rous beastie" scuttered away. And it was in his native dialect too that he wrote those ringing verses beginning "Scots, wha hae wi' Wallace bled," and his gallant defense of the sturdy peasant in "A Man's a Man for A' That." In "The Cotter's Saturday Night" he paints a beautiful picture of the home life he knew so intimately as a boy; and in "Halloween," taking his text from Goldsmith, he presents the rural folk at their merrymaking. Less pleasing but not less authentic are the snapshots of vulgar life he offers in "The Jolly Beggars."

Humor and Satire. Burns did not go to the Greeks and the Romans for models of satirical verse; to contrast his "Address to the Deil" and his "Holy Willie's Prayer" with the representative satires of Dryden and Pope is to perceive both the catholicity of literature and the disparity between the Romantic and the Classical spirit. His caustic "Address to the Unco Guid" has in its turn become a classic, one of the strongest pleas for charity and one of the most crushing and scathing denunciations of self-esteem in all literature. Burns's humor, brightening ever so many of his poems and dominating several, is typical of his native land: broad and farcical, sometimes coarse, but always pungent and frequently veiled by an assumed seriousness.

Burns's Masterpiece. The Ayrshire plowboy wrote but one narrative in verse, but that one reveals him as a superb story-teller, unsurpassed by Chaucer or anyone else. In "Tam o' Shanter" he takes up a legend of the countryside and gives it a rendering concise and sparkling, utilizing all his poetic gifts, his humor, his satire, his zest in country sights and sounds, and his first-hand knowledge of life. Tam has been in town drinking more than was good for him. On his way home, astride his gray mare Meg, he meets a band of witches and escapes a serious mishap only because the sturdy Meg dashes with him to safety, leaving her tail behind her. Despite the difficulty the reader may find in the dialect, a difficulty by no means insuperable, the poem is well worth the trouble involved in its reading.

Songs. If we were to seek for the reason why Burns is the poet dearer than all others to his own people, why many of his lines have been converted into national proverbs, why his birthday is commemorated the world over, why his statue stands in public parks all the way from Dumfries to San Francisco, we should find the answer in the songs which he wrote, mostly for Johnson's *Scots Musical Museum*. He fitted words to old Scotch airs as Moore wrote his poems to old Irish airs, but the Scot to a greater degree than the Irishman succeeded in putting the heart of a nation into his verses: audiences everywhere in the English-speaking world respond to the melody of "The Minstrel Boy," but they stand up and sing the words of "Auld Lang Syne." Burns's songs are true lyric poems. Each is faithful to the mood of the moment, and there is a directness and simplicity about them that goes from the heart to the heart. Many of these exquisite songs he composed on the banks of the Nith, walking up and down and waving his arms; and then he would go home and write them down. Not to know "To Mary in Heaven," "Comin' thro' the Rye," and "John Anderson, My Jo" is not to know pricelessly beautiful expressions of human feeling; it is not to know Robert Burns.

An Estimate. The shortcomings of Burns as a poet are obvious; many of them spring from his limitations as a man. He is narrow in his outlook on life and narrow in his range of interests. He is one of the poets who defy translation, not only because of the dialect in which he wrote his best work but because his poems have but slight appeal to men who are unfamiliar with Scotland in life or in books, and whose literary tastes have been formed in the tradition of Continental literature. Indeed (and we have but to recall his biographers and his critics in justification of the statement), Burns is best understood and most fondly loved by the simple and unlettered; he is inscrutable to both the Oxford manner and the Cambridge mind, which is at once the best and the worst thing that can be said of him. Burns is a poet of the heart rather than of the head. It is a curious fact that though the Scotch are in mental trend philosophic and have thought heavily enough and perplexingly enough in prose, Scottish poets have indulged in little speculation on the why and wherefore of existence. Burns never analyzes and dissects and invites his soul; and though he was not unacquainted with remorse and felt the need of God (see his pathetic "Prayer in the Prospect of Death"), there is in him no gleam of real spiritual vision.

On the other hand, his poems are remarkable for their warm sympathy with man and with nature, vibrant in their insistence on human brotherhood and on the ideals of human liberty. They rank high in the universal literature that voices intense feeling and various phases of the passion of love. They spring from the soul and from the soil, and to them clings much of the beauty and something of the sordidness of their origin. There is in them evidence of true art but none of artifice,

ROBERT BURNS

and here, again, Burns stands in contrast with Tom Moore. They are homely in the best sense of the word; their imagery, their comparisons, and their diction are suggestive of the open fields and the cottage fireside, the rural village and the northern skies. We enjoy Burns in proportion as we enjoy the wholesome, elemental things of life, as we are unspoiled by artificiality and insincerity and affectation. And to read Burns in our day of overstuffed furniture and formal evening dress is a tonic as well as a joy.

THE DEVELOPMENT OF ROMANTICISM

William Cowper (1731–1800). Cowper has an assured place in the history of the Romantic Movement because of the ease and simplicity of his style of writing and the charm of his portrayal of nature and humble life. Like Burns, he had a narrow

WILLIAM COWPER

From a painting in the collection of George A. Plimpton

outlook and a limited experience of the world and its ways; unlike Burns, he possessed but a slight measure of vigor and vitality. The poetry of Burns stimulates like some rough and potent drink; the poetry of Cowper warms and cheers like a cup of tea.

Cowper was, indeed, a tea-table poet: much of his work was done under the inspiration of Mrs. Unwin and other women and in the atmosphere of the old-fashioned sitting room. *The Task*, in blank verse, was the reply to a challenge made by Lady Austen to write a poem with a sofa as its subject. That was the task, and Cowper produced a series of metrical meditations not on a sofa alone, but on a clock, a garden, and three aspects of winter. In ballad measure he wrote a humorous account of the misadventures of a London tradesman in "John Gilpin," and his considerable lyric gift is to be seen in "On the Receipt of my Mother's Picture" and other shorter poems. He also made a translation of Homer's *Iliad*, wrote personal letters characterized by unaffected and pleasing comments on men and books, and composed a collection of religious hymns, the best known of which begins

> God moves in a mysterious way
> His wonders to perform;
> He plants His footsteps in the sea
> And rides upon the storm.

The hymns are especially characteristic of Cowper, whose religious views were very strong and very melancholy; he held the belief that he was predestined for eternal damnation, and this thought induced several periods of temporary insanity and impelled him on more than one occasion to attempt suicide. His most famous hymn was written after he had determined to drown himself, had set out in a carriage for the river, had lost his way in the fog, and had found himself again at his own door. So he thanked God and kept on living.

COWPER AT HOME

From a painting in the collection of George A. Plimpton

George Crabbe (1754–1832). Crabbe was a poor boy at Aldeburgh on the coast of Suffolk whose delight was to gaze out upon the North Sea, to listen to the tales of sailors, and to inspect the curious souvenirs they had brought home from distant lands. He got a little schooling and then became an apothecary's apprentice and studied medicine. One of Crabbe's poems attracted the attention of Edmund Burke in 1781, and the statesman ever after manifested a friendly interest in the obscure poet, sometimes paying his bills, and, when Crabbe decided to become a clergyman, securing him a place as curate. Crabbe went to London, where Burke's friendship opened to him the Literary Club and the good will of Dr. Johnson, who pronounced Crabbe's *Village* "original, vigorous, and elegant." That poem was written as a direct reply to Goldsmith's "Deserted Village," Crabbe contending that the Irishman had invested his descriptions with too much glamour. Nobody would ever urge that objection against Crabbe, for in all his poems he stresses the drab and dull and sordid side of life. He is in poetry what Hogarth is in painting. His principal poems, besides *The Village*, are *The Newspaper*, *The Parish Register*, *The Borough*, and *Tales of the Hall*.

Crabbe is rightly placed among the Romanticists, inasmuch as his poems show a reaction against the Classical spirit and are distinguished for their simple style and their successful effort to avoid affectation and literary primness; his characters are not the conventional swains and shepherdesses of the Classical tradition, but plain Jesse Bourn and Colin Grey. But, from another point of view, Crabbe is one of the leading English Realists in his insistence on the seamy side of things. He has a "sad sincerity" and a strong sense of justice, considerable narrative skill, and keen powers of description. It will be interesting to compare this passage from *The Village* with a familiar portion of Goldsmith's poem:

> Fled are those times, when, in harmonious strains,
> The rustic poet praised his native plains:
>
> . . . .
>
> Rank weeds, that every art and care defy,
> Reign o'er the land and rob the blighted rye;
> There thistles stretch their prickly arms afar,
> And to the ragged infant threaten war;
> There poppies, nodding, mock the hope of toil;
> There the blue bugloss [1] paints the sterile soil;

[1] The bugloss (the first syllable pronounced to rime with *new*), the mallow, and the charlock are three species of weeds.

Hardy and high, above the slender sheaf,
The slimy mallow waves her silky leaf;
O'er the young shoot the charlock throws a shade,
And clasping tares cling round the sickly blade;
With mingled tints the rocky coasts abound,
And a sad splendour vainly shines around.

William Blake (1757–1827). Blake is at once a conspicuous rebel against the spirit of Classicism and a horrible example of Romanticism gone wild. Nowadays it is the fashion to discuss a poet's "message." Why a poet or any other artist should have a message does not seem clear; but if messages are in order, the most salutary moral to be derived from Blake's work is the danger of running to extremes. Fleeing from conventionality as from the face of a serpent, Blake arrived at literary and artistic anarchy. He was a good man; he loved his wife; he was honest and cordial and kind; he was intensely religious-minded, — all these things we are told, and all these things are true. Swinburne canonized him in a prose rhapsody in 1868, and thus founded what has since become a devotional cult. But Blake's personal virtues do not atone for his artistic vices. There have been writers who strictly observed the laws of literature and flouted the laws of morality; Blake respected the laws of morality but refused to recognize any laws of literature at all.

The result of Blake's confusion of license with liberty is that he is today glorified as a lay preacher, a Methodist saint, a prophet, an eccentric philosopher, an artist, a humanitarian, an animal worshiper — as everything, in fact, except a poet. Of course he wrote some genuine poetry; but even the best of it is marred by the inconsistency, the incoherence, the freakishness of a man who ignored tradition and common sense and the world of things as they are, and who persisted in living in and writing about a weird world of his own imagining. Blake was a brilliant man but a grievously ignorant one. He had but a chaotic education; he was not widely read; he lacked alike the benefits of foreign travel which secured the literary salvation of Shelley and the keen and canny eye for things at home which secured the literary salvation of Burns.

A Londoner by birth and by all but continuous residence, Blake learned engraving as a boy and practiced that art, and exercised himself as a painter. Only incidentally was he a writer. Many of his drawings are on literary themes: on the Bible, Virgil, Dante, Chaucer, Milton, Gray, and Thomson. He also illustrated some of his own writings. His artistry is more than original: it is eccentric almost to the point of insanity. His later writings, the "Prophetic Books," such as *The Marriage of Heaven and Hell*, partake of the character of his drawings: they contain real beauties, manifest absurdities, a queer and often baffling symbolism, and numerous evidences of lack of salutary discipline in thought, in feeling, and in style.

As a poet Blake is nearest to being readable and inspiring in his early offerings: *Poetical Sketches* (1783), *Songs of Innocence* (1789), and *Songs of Experience* (1794). The introduction to *Songs of Innocence*, beginning "Piping down the valleys wild," and that even better-known poem on the Tiger in *Songs of Experience*, reveal him at his most appealing and best. He had a delightfully childlike fancy and a freshness of expression which had not yet degenerated into the cloudy "mysticism" of his more mature years. Blake holds his place in the history of English Literature by reason of several beautiful and original lyrics and a number of keen and stimulating prose aphorisms scattered through his writings.

Robert Southey (1774-1843). Southey, man and writer, began as a radical and a Romanticist and ended as a conservative and a Classicist. He was born in Bristol and was sent to Westminster School and to Oxford by his maiden aunt, a lady with strong literary interests. Young Southey gave every promise of leading a short life and a sensational one. He was expelled from school, he was a trouble center at the university, and on one occasion he so tried his lady aunt that she thrust him out of doors on a stormy night. He studied in turn for the ministry, medicine, and law; married in due course; rambled on the Continent and in Ireland; dreamed with Coleridge of founding an ideal commonwealth in America; and finally settled down to literary work and respectability at Keswick in the Lake Region, was appointed poet laureate, and became wealthy and self-satisfied. He lost sympathy with the revolutionary friends of his youth, though he continued manfully to come to their aid when they needed ready money or a night's lodging.

If quantity were the only thing that counted in literature, Southey would be a greater writer than Shakespeare. He poured out volume upon volume in prose and in verse, and wrote uniformly well; but he lacked the gift that keeps books alive. His *Life of Nelson* is a standard school text in England, and a few of his shorter poems, such as "The Battle of Blenheim," "The Cataract of Lodore," and "The Inchcape Rock," are embalmed in school readers throughout the English-speaking world; but his *History of Brazil*, a capable yet uninteresting account of dead and buried happenings, *The Doctor*, a lengthy prose meditation influenced by Rabelais, Sterne, and Burton, and *The Curse of Kehama*, a theatrical Hindu romance in alternating rime and blank verse, are rarely read and are lightly esteemed. Because he lived in amity with Coleridge and Wordsworth in the Lake Region, Southey is sometimes united with them under the title of the "Lake Poets"; but he had little in common with that gifted twain even in his youth, and nothing at all as he grew older.

Campbell and Rogers. Campbell and Rogers are appropriately bracketed here, for in many respects they resemble each other, they were associated in readers' minds during the days of their now vanished vogue, and in at least one edition their representative poems were brought out in the same volume. Thomas Campbell (1777–1844) was born in Glasgow and made his studies at the university there, but lived most of his life at Sydenham in London, writing nearly as assiduously as Southey and enjoying himself as a popular literary man. Of all his output in verse and in prose nothing appeals to our generation save a few short poems, such as "Lochiel's Warning" and "Ye Mariners of England." His most ambitious performances were *The Pleasures of Hope*, an expression of the Romantic spirit in Classical heroic couplets, and *Gertrude of Wyoming*, a pale imitation of the metrical narratives of Scott. Samuel Rogers (1763–1855), partner in a London banking firm, devoted his ample leisure to reading, to writing, and to entertaining literary celebrities in his cheerful house overlooking the Green Park. His *Pleasures of Memory* and other mildly Romantic poems are now completely forgotten. Rogers refused the post of poet laureate, but it is interesting to recall that it was in his court dress that both Wordsworth and Tennyson made their laureate bow to Queen Victoria.

William Cobbett (1762–1835). Cobbett was a big man physically and a strong man intellectually, a fearlessly independent thinker, a vigorous and hard-hitting critic of what he deemed abuses, and an enthusiastic admirer of country life and the social ideals of medieval England. His *Peter Porcupine*, which was written after a visit to the United States, is a castigation of Americans for falling short of the ideals of their Constitution; his *History of the Protestant Reformation* is a scathing exposure of the rapacity and hypocrisy which accompanied the revolt against the authority of Rome; and his *Rural Rides* — from the literary point of view the best of his writings — is an interesting and vivacious collection of comments on social and industrial conditions. His strictures on political abuses brought upon him a fine and a term in prison. Other books of Cobbett's are unconventional treatises on French and English grammar, *An Account of the Horrors of the French Revolution*, a history of Rome, and *Advice to Young Men and Women* — this last still helpful and practical.

As a stylist Cobbett was a plain, blunt man, averse to verbal fireworks and dazzling figures of speech; he thought clearly and wrote vigorously. The following excerpt is from his advice to young men contemplating matrimony. In both style and substance it has some bearing on twentieth-century tastes and conditions:

A mark of industry is a quick step and a somewhat heavy tread, showing that the foot comes down with a hearty good will; and if the body lean a little forward, and the eyes keep steadily in the same direction, while the feet are going, so much the better, for these discover earnestness to arrive at the intended point. I do not like, and I never liked, your sauntering, soft-stepping girls, who move as if they were perfectly indifferent as to the result; and, as to the love part of the story, whoever expects ardent and lasting affection from one of these sauntering girls will, when too late, find his mistake: The character runs the same all the way through; and no man ever yet saw a sauntering girl who did not, when married, make a mawkish wife and a cold-hearted mother; cared very little for either by husband or children; and, of course, having no store of those blessings which are the natural resources to apply to in sickness and in old age.

Charles Waterton (1782–1865). A striking manifestation of the Romantic spirit, though less in what he wrote than in how he lived, was furnished by Charles Waterton, explorer and naturalist, landed gentleman and writer, athlete and saint. He came of an old Yorkshire family, was educated at Stonyhurst, traveled much, penetrated into the wilderness of British Guiana, and told of his explorations with piquancy and charm in *Wandering in South America*. He was always doing the unexpected, like trying to make a Catholic out of Thackeray and standing on the angel's head on the Castel Sant' Angelo in Rome. A warning to all acrobats, this vigorous gentleman who liked to amaze dignified friends by walking into a room on his hands and who at the age of seventy-seven could scratch the back of his head with his toe, met his death by stumbling over a bramble on his estate at Walton Hall. A friend thus describes a part of Waterton's daily regimen:

He went to bed early, and slept upon the bare floor, with a block of wood for a pillow. He rose for the day at half-past three, and spent the hour from four to five at prayer in his chapel. He then read every morning a chapter in a Spanish life of St. Francis Xavier, followed by a chapter of *Don Quixote* in the original, after which he used to stuff birds or write letters till breakfast.

Waterton's *Essays in Natural History* and his *Autobiography* are highly esteemed by readers who know something of the unique personality of the man and of his really important contributions to science.

TRAITS OF ROMANTICISM

After following the rise and development of the Romantic tendency in English Literature, and before considering the outstanding Romantic poets of the nineteenth century, it will be convenient to summarize the leading traits of the movement. Romanticism included so many elements and took such varied and even contradictory forms that a satisfactory definition of it is impossible; but it will be helpful to indicate the principal characteristics which the student may trace in the writings of individual authors. No one writer — neither Gray nor Burns, neither Blake nor Cobbett, neither Wordsworth nor Byron — embodies every one of these traits of Romanticism; but the work of every Romantic writer will show the influence of at least several of them:

1. Emotional stress rather than intellectual activity. This is why the overwhelming majority of the Romantic writers were poets, since poetry is a more facile medium of emotion than prose.

2. Interest in distant times and places, particularly times and places not included in the European Tradition of literature. Thus Gray went to Wales for his inspiration; Southey to India; Byron, to ancient Israel and modern Greece.

3. An enthusiasm for the religious ideals and social institutions of the Middle Ages. Hence the Gothic romance in fiction

the medieval interests of Chatterton and Scott, the devotion of Cobbett to remote "Merrie" England.

4. A freshened perception of natural scenery and an effort to describe and interpret nature with directness and simplicity. This is especially notable in the poetry of Thomson, Scott, and Wordsworth.

5. Religious and patriotic fervor. Blake and Shelley — though they were as different in their positions as two men could be — illustrate the religious interest. The patriotic interest was ordinarily not in the here and the now, but in other lands, such as France, Ireland, or modern Greece, and in other times.

6. Wonder, mystery, and sublimity. Macpherson's Ossian poems and Coleridge's "Rime of the Ancient Mariner" are representative of this trait.

7. Subjectivity, lyricism, the intrusion of the ego, emphasis on the personal note. Stress on the individuality of the writer was caught from Rousseau. At its best it may be seen in Wordsworth; at its worst, in Byron, with his assumption of the rôle of "blighted being."

8. A revolt against the literary canons of eighteenth-century Classicism. This made for variety and freedom on the one hand, and for chaos and absurdity on the other.

9. Experimentation with new themes and new forms of expression.

10. Interest in the problems of the working classes and appreciation of the literary possibilities of men and women in low stations in life. This democratic note was struck most emphatically by Burns, and found numerous echoes. Later on it degenerated into Realism (notably in France) and into caricature and satire.

CHAPTER XII

FIVE ROMANTIC POETS

WORDSWORTH

The Lake Region. A district something over thirty miles square in Cumberland and Westmoreland is the country of the English Lakes. Lake Windermere, the largest of the Lakes, is but ten miles long, and Rydal Water, justly famed for its picturesqueness, is less than a mile in extent. No, the Lake Region is not "mammoth"; but it has bits of forest still, and the little river Greta, and that Cataract of Lodore about which Southey wrote an ingenious poem; it has paths leading to all manner of unexpected vistas on the mountain sides and to the sight of nature in her sterner moods when mists obscure the glory of the hills. The Lake Region has attracted many literary men to dwell there for a few summers at least, and some to make it their permanent abode. It is here, at Coniston, that Ruskin is buried, preferring a grave among the Lakes to a tomb in Westminster Abbey. Here young Shelley lived for a brief while after his marriage to Harriet Westbrook; and here John Wilson, who used to write over the name of "Christopher North," had a country home for forty years. De Quincey had a cottage beside Rydal Water, and admired Wordsworth and Coleridge with the ardor of hero-worshiping youth; and, especially, here dwelt Wordsworth, Coleridge, and Southey, the members of what is sometimes called the Lake School.

But William Wordsworth (1770–1850) is the Lake Poet paramount. Here he was born at Cockermouth; here, save for a few years, he lived all his life, at Grasmere and at Rydal Mount; and here he lies buried in the peaceful Grasmere

churchyard. Here he sat under the elms on fine days convers-
ing with his sister Dorothy and his poet friends; here he paced
the gravel path composing his verses and dreaming his dreams;
here he set forth on long walks among the hills and observed
nature in her manifold aspect. He caught the spirit of the
Lake Region and, more than any other writer, found here his
inspiration. Southey commemorated India in verse and South

WORDSWORTH'S COTTAGE, RYDAL MOUNT

America in prose; Coleridge in imagination traveled far, even
to the wraith-infested ocean and the uncharted land of Xanadu; but the bulk of Wordsworth's writings and practically
all his great poems contain descriptions of the Lake Region
and the fruits of his meditations among the Cumberland hills
and dales.

A Dedicated Spirit. Having studied at the Hawkshead
Grammar School and at the University of Cambridge, Wordsworth went abroad and became an enthusiastic sympathizer
with the French Revolution. Like Southey, he was at first a
radical in politics, in religion, in art; and, like Southey, he

lived to become a sedate and mild-tempered conservative. The Reign of Terror disgusted him with the republican movement in France, and a deeper knowledge of human nature made him suspicious of novelties in religion. He married in 1802, went on occasional journeys into Scotland and to the Continent, but preferred the quiet and relative solitude of the Lakes to the annoyances of travel and the tumult of cities. Externally his life was serene and uneventful. He was appointed poet laureate seven years before his death, at a time when his best work had long since been completed and his poetic powers had waned.

© Emery Walker Limited

WILLIAM WORDSWORTH

From a painting by H. W. Pickersgill in the National Portrait Gallery, London

Like Milton, Wordsworth accepted the writing of poetry as his vocation in life; he regarded himself as a "dedicated spirit" and devoted his thought and his art to metrical meditations on nature, life, and man. There was nothing of the journalist in Wordsworth; though he took his writing with high seriousness, he was indifferent to the reception his poems received and little concerned over the adverse criticism they encountered. Unlike Burns, who wrote because poetry, so to say, was bubbling inside him, Wordsworth carefully and thoughtfully evolved a theory of his art and then wrote to exemplify his ideas of what poetry should be. His principles, embodied in the prefaces and appendixes published with several editions of his works, have been a source of enlightenment to many of his successors and form a valuable contribution to literary criticism in English.

Wordsworth had no sympathy with the notion that the poet should give the people what they want. On the contrary, he protested against the "degrading thirst for outrageous stimulation," and held that the poet's office is to distill the fine essence of his accurate observation and profound thought. Poetry was to him the "spontaneous overflow of powerful feelings . . . emotion recollected in tranquility," the "still, sad music of humanity." Its purpose was "to teach the young and gracious of every age to see, to think, and feel, and therefore to become more securely and actively virtuous." And it was derived, not as the Classicists held, from books, but directly from life and nature.

> Thus informed,
> He had small need of books; for many a tale
> Traditionary round the mountains hung,
> And many a legend, peopling the dark woods,
> Nourished imagination in her growth,
> And gave the mind that apprehensive power,
> By which she is made quick to recognize
> The moral properties and scope of things.

The Romantic element in Wordsworth took several forms, but chiefly his theory and his practice of simplicity. He maintained that the proper subject of poetry is the persons and events of normal everyday life, and that the language of poetry should be the language of conversation. He often carried his principles to extremes, as when he composed "The Idiot Boy" and in "Peter Bell" seriously attempted to evoke pathos by entering into the mental processes of a donkey; and his insistence on commonplace language justified the cutting criticism that much of what he wrote wavers "between simplicity and silliness." But his influence was considerable in combating the artificiality of extreme Classicism and in calling attention to "a primrose by the river's brim" and other humble objects as appropriate poetic themes. In substance he spoke to makers of verse as the voice spoke to St. Peter: "That which God hath cleansed, do not thou call common."

Those "Purple Patches." Wordsworth was a stimulating theorist, but a poor critic, especially of his own work. Some of his short poems and some passages in his long poems are among the finest specimens of pure poetry in English; but, most unequal of poets, he has dreary lengths of verse flat and prosy, bald and uncouth. Matthew Arnold, one of his earliest admirers, tried to show Wordsworth at his best by making a selection of the short poems and the "purple patches" in the longer ones. Every reader is wise in doing something of the sort on his own account.

To illustrate: Few things that Wordsworth wrote are more truly poetical than the first half of the poem beginning

> There was a Boy; ye knew him well, ye cliffs
> And islands of Winander!

We enter heartily into the spirit of the verse and identify ourselves with the lad who

> Blew mimic hootings to the silent owls,
> That they might answer him.

And we secure the joy and rapture and sense of infinite peace that comes from contact with high art as we read the living lines:

> Then, sometimes, in that silence, while he hung
> Listening, a gentle shock of mild surprise
> Has carried far into his heart the voice
> Of mountain-torrents; or the visible scene
> Would enter unawares into his mind
> With all its solemn imagery, its rocks,
> Its woods, and that uncertain heaven received
> Into the bosom of the steady lake.

TINTERN ABBEY

The thirteenth-century abbey church, on the right bank of the Wye, is impressive even in its ruins. Cistercian monks occupied this site from 1131 until the dissolution of the monasteries under Henry VIII. (By courtesy of Ralph Adams Cram)

Wordsworth could write that haunting, exquisite, suggestive passage; and right after that he could perpetrate this descent to the commonplace:

> This boy was taken from his mates, and died
> In childhood, ere he was full twelve years old.
> Preëminent in beauty is the vale
> Where he was born and bred: the churchyard hangs
> Upon a slope above the village school.

The poems of Wordsworth are full of such contrasts.

The Best of Wordsworth. To know Wordsworth at his highest and most inspiring, the student should read "Tintern Abbey" and other poems contained in *Lyrical Ballads*, first published in 1798; *The White Doe of Rylstone* and "Yarrow Revisited"; a generous garland of the sonnets, including "The World is too much with us"; the "Ode: Intimations of Immortality"; and then dip into *The Prelude* and savor the admirable fancies there embedded like luscious plums in a soggy pudding. In general, it may be taken as a working rule to read any poem by Wordsworth that is not lengthy, and that he wrote in his youth or his middle age.

His Influence. Wordsworth has sometimes been saluted as a profound and original philosopher. A thinker he was, but along paths remote, and, like most poets, a thinker who frequently confused thought with emotion — an eminently human but most unphilosophical habit. We have little need of his philosophy or of his general view of life; but we can derive inspiration from his appreciation of nature as the handiwork of God and a solace to struggling, suffering humanity. The spirit of Wordsworth's most representative nature poetry is close akin to the spirit (though it lacks the joy and the spiritual fervor) of St. Francis of Assisi, who felt a true brotherhood with the beasts and the birds and the flowers and all created things. There is a high nobility, a delicacy of perception, a singular beauty of expression in numerous passages in Wordsworth's poems, as his glowing white tribute to the Blessed Virgin,

> Our tainted nature's solitary boast.

And from his life, as from his writings, we can learn the importance of solitude and silence and intent communings with nature and with our own thoughts. Wisely he wrote

> Strongest minds
> Are often those of whom the noisy world
> Hears least!

The influence of Wordsworth on English poetry was immediate, and it still continues. Even poets who, like Shelley, did not subscribe to his theories of poetry or who even, like Byron, ridiculed Wordsworth, are nevertheless indebted to him for incentive and example. The Wordsworthian influence may be traced in both *Childe Harold* and *Alastor*; and Shelley learned the lesson of Wordsworth's devotion to nature so well that he carried it into veritable nature worship. Tennyson in "Dora" conformed to Wordsworth's principles of poetry by using simple, everyday language and employing commonplace types; and he caught something of Wordsworth's mania for preaching. Aubrey de Vere was consciously and deliberately a disciple of Wordsworth; and so, with reservations, was Matthew Arnold. Father Faber's "Cherwell Water Lily" was an Oxford man's reaction to the Cambridge poet's delineation of natural scenery. The increasing vogue of Wordsworth among readers of our own day is in part accounted for by the homage of imitation paid him by many of the poets of the early twentieth century. Indeed, some of them have learned their lesson only too well; Witter Bynner, for instance, out-Wordsworths Wordsworth in devotion to the simple and the commonplace when he likens the look in the beloved's eyes to "the underside of soap in a soap dish."

COLERIDGE

A Damaged Archangel. It is easy to get an impression that is ill proportioned of the man who wrote "The Rime of the Ancient Mariner," because he was a medley of diverse qualities and because his biographers, even when they meant well, managed to show him in unfavorable lights. Little Charles Lamb, who often allowed his cheery, stammering tongue to run away with him, was the first to call Coleridge a damaged archangel, and he was not far from the truth; but often a superficial study of Coleridge reveals less of the archangel and more of the damage. Was he not eccentric, and strangely indifferent to money matters and to domestic dignity? Was he not flogged when a schoolboy for reading Voltaire? Did he not irresponsibly break his college career by suddenly enlisting in the army under the preposterous name of Silas Tompkin Comberbach? Did he not try many things, from raising vegetables to preaching? Did he not dream an impossible dream — shared with young Southey — of a mad socialistic community in America? Was he not an opium addict, a lecturer who often allowed his audiences to wait for him in vain, an extremely trying friend, a philosopher without system, a writer without method, often a poet without inspiration? Truly, there is abundant evidence to support the contention that Coleridge was shiftless and inconstant and even not quite sane.

But there is another side to the story. When he wished to be, he was one of the most gracious and companionable of men. He was a voracious reader and possessed a retentive memory and a wide knowledge of books. He was a scholar, a gentleman, a poet, a philosopher, a critic, even a theologian of sorts — "the only person I ever knew," declared Hazlitt, "who answered to the idea of a man of genius." He was a talker of assiduity and charm; the testimony is practically unanimous that to listen to him was a liberal education. He towered intellectually above his fellows: as Shelley puts it, "a hooded eagle among blinking owls." With all his admitted shortcomings, he achieved, in both prose and verse, a high and unique excellence. In life and in literature he encouraged appreciation of the finest and best. And he could say of himself in his *Table Talk* : "For one mercy I owe thanks beyond all utterance — that with my gastric and bowel distempers, my head hath ever been like the head of a mountain in blue air and sunshine."

Samuel Taylor Coleridge (1772–1834) was a Devonshire man, born at Ottery St. Mary's. He was, as the saying goes, old for his age, and while still a boy he was deep in his father's books of poetry, philosophy, and theology. Most of Coleridge's eccentricities, including the opium habit, were due to his ill health; he caught rheumatic fever as a boy of seventeen by imprudently swimming a river with his clothes on, and the malady induced complications. He studied at Cambridge, but left without taking a degree, and married Sara Fricker soon after. A turning point in his life was his acquaintance with Wordsworth in 1796. They discussed theories of poetry, and Coleridge contributed "The Rime of the Ancient Mariner" to Wordsworth's *Lyrical Ballads*. The friends went together to Germany, and there Coleridge became immersed in philosophy. But his family needed support, and so he engaged in editorial work in London. His poor health and his unsystematic habits seriously interfered with his prosperity through most of the ensuing years — a record of aimless ramblings, projects taken up and abandoned, rare moments of joy and inspiration alternating with long periods of despondency and mental stagnation. From 1816 until his death eighteen years later he lived in the house of a stanch friend, Dr. James Gillman, at Highgate in London.

The real Coleridge is best revealed in two works of an autobiographical character, both published after his death, *Table Talk* and *Biographia Literaria*. From these volumes we can understand why it was that his friends were glad to have him scribble notes in the margins of books he borrowed, for often his comments were more valuable than the texts. His *Table Talk*, though less famous than Johnson's opinions as recorded by Boswell, contains matter of wider range and of a more stimulating character. The *Biographia Literaria* is not narrowly personal: it includes interesting and informing dicta on Wordsworth, Southey, and other literary friends; on "literary inertia" (a state of mind the author knew so well); on philosophers from St. Thomas to Hobbes; on how to read English and how to study German; on the principles of poetry and of criticism; on the French drama and the Latin language. The student may not find all of it easy reading, for, as Talfourd said, "the palm trees wave and the pyramids tower in the long perspective of his style"; but it is well worth wrestling with, and, like Jacob's angel, it will confer a blessing.

Coleridge's Poetry. Because of his exceptional talents and his genuine if fitful powers as a poet, Coleridge is one of the great figures in the Romantic Movement; and his Romanticism is most in evidence in his early masterpiece, "The Rime of the Ancient Mariner." Wordsworth had a slight hand in the composition of this extraordinary poem, suggesting the lines

> And listens like a three years' child:
> The Mariner hath his will.

But the credit of the poem as a whole rightly belongs to Coleridge, who was an excellent critic of his own work and revised and polished the seemingly simple lines. Though the work was a frank attempt to embody an atmosphere of mystery and terror, Coleridge was too sensitive an artist and too judicious a critic to allow every startling detail he had first written to see the light. Thus, he eliminated this stanza, in which he had rather overdone in the matter of horrific details:

> His bones were black with many a crack,
>   All black and bare, I ween;
> Jet-black and bare, save where the rust
> Of mouldy damps and charnel crust
>   They're patch'd with purple and green.

In his hands the old ballad form became the vehicle of a kind of poetry new in English Literature and destined to influence several subsequent writers, particularly among the Pre-Raphaelites.

Wonder, mystery, nature in her awe-compelling moods, vague terror, are the keynotes of "The Rime of the Ancient Mariner" and of other poems representative of Coleridge's queer but powerful genius. So "Christabel" takes as its theme the conflict between the gentle heroine and the evil enchantress. The originality of the metrical scheme and the subtle but pervasive suggestion of mystery and the supernatural are illustrated in these lines:

> The night is chill; the forest bare;
> Is it the wind that moaneth bleak?
> There is not wind enough in the air
> To move away the ringlet curl
> From the lovely lady's cheek —
> There is not wind enough to twirl
> The one red leaf, the last of its clan,
> That dances as often as dance it can,
> Hanging so light, and hanging so high,
> On the topmost twig that looks up at the sky.

It is typical of Coleridge that "Christabel," like "Kubla Khan," remains unfinished; the poet's inspiration came and went (too often went), and his works remain like exquisite fragments of unearthly sculpture.

"Kubla Khan" is a poem the inspiration of which came to Coleridge in a dream. On awakening he at once proceeded to write; but as he completed the lines

> For he on honey-dew hath fed,
> And drunk the milk of Paradise,

he was interrupted by a visitor, a "person on business from Porlock," and when he attempted to resume his work he found that his ideas and images "had passed away like the images on

the surface of a stream into which a stone had been cast."
The fragment is a wonderful fantasy; one of the supreme examples of Romantic imagery and imaginative splendor, with
its "sunless sea" and "sinuous rills" and "incense-bearing
tree," its "sunny-dome" and "caves of ice" and "ancestral
voices prophesying war." And the poem was but barely begun. Alas, that "person on business from Porlock" has much
to answer for!

Coleridge's sense of the mysterious yields to a mood of
pathetic melancholy in "Dejection: an Ode," a melancholy
occasioned by the poet's awareness of his inability to give expression to the thoughts and fancies surging in his soul. This
is an eminently human mood, for what man's grasp equals his
reach? But only here, and in Francis Thompson's "Hound of
Heaven," has it been given supremely poetic treatment. In
Coleridge's case the pathos is all the more poignant because
in his life, as in his poem, he found no hint of Thompson's
abiding consolation.

Coleridge wrote other poems, mostly short bits and promising fragments. The "Æolian Harp," written in 1795, contains
a pantheistic[1] conception of nature, which Coleridge afterwards abandoned. "Frost at Midnight" is a good example of
his second-class poetry, which is better than the first class of
most poets. His "Nightingale" and the "Hymn before Sunrise in the Vale of Chamouni" reveal his ability as a manipulator of words and a master of rhythm and his freshness of
natural description; but they fall short of the grandeur of
imagination and emotional ecstasy that animated his three
supreme poems. For the rest, his verse sinks below even his
medial level.

---

[1] Pantheism is a form of belief — or, if you like, a school of philosophy —
which identifies God with His creation. According to the pantheists men and
animals and vegetables and rocks are all God in nature and substance. Wordsworth came very near to pantheism in some of his poems, and a good many
recent singers are infected with it. Pantheism is the basis of some religious sects
just now the fashion in the United States.

Coleridge's Contribution to Literary Criticism. Some critics are not poets, and some poets are not critics. Coleridge was both. His *Lectures on Shakespeare and Milton*, the outcome of note-taking activity on the part of some auditors, contains in unsystematic form a treasure of sound and stimulating remarks on literature. Some of his views were wrong-headed from the start and others have been disproved by recent scholarly research; but in the main Coleridge ranks high among the English literary critics. He dealt with big subjects in a big way. He was the first, for instance, to classify all men as Aristotelians or Platonists, according as they are dominated by thought or by emotion. Coleridge owed much to German writers, especially to August von Schlegel, and his enthusiasm for German literature and philosophy was instrumental in preparing the way for Carlyle's not always judicious missionary labors on behalf of German art and thought.

KEATS

Youth and Genius. Often and rather absurdly, John Keats (1795–1821) has been likened to Shakespeare; absurdly, for, as Frederic Harrison has well observed, "We could no more compare Keats with Shakespeare than we could compare Mont Blanc with one of its own snowy pinnacles."[1] Yet there are three points on which the two poets resemble each other. First, each of them produced literature of a very high order. Secondly, neither of them sounded a personal note or made their writings a medium for self-revelation: what they wrote gives us few indications of what they were. This is all the more remarkable in Keats, since he was a lyric poet, not a dramatist, and the lyric poet almost necessarily writes about himself. Thirdly, both Shakespeare and Keats strikingly illustrate the miracle of genius. The Stratford rustic and the son of the London liveryman had but a meager formal education, and

[1] *Tennyson, Ruskin, Mill, and Other Literary Estimates*, p. 178.

the externals of their lives were not such as to develop distinguished gifts; yet both the Elizabethan player and the Cockney medical student achieved greatly and enjoy undying fame.

Surely it was one of nature's feats of legerdemain to compound a being so exquisitely fine amid foul air, stale straw, the reek of oil, leather, animal heat, the needs and easements of dumb beasts, while menials washed coach wheels and jested in Billingsgate. The origin of John Keats is an instance of the personal equation of genius, elusive of law. Perhaps there may be forces in earth and heaven which are not dreamed of in our philosophy.[1]

Keats is further remarkable as illustrating the truth that in literature quality counts for more than quantity. Most supreme writers have written copiously as well as excellently, but to Keats falls the distinction of being represented by but three small volumes of verse. And his best work — for, like all writers, he had to pass through a period of apprenticeship and experimentation — was done within the small space of two years. A prey to tuberculosis, he died in Rome at the age of twenty-six, an age when most writers have not yet found themselves or tested their powers.

Born in the room above his father's livery stable at Moorfields, London, John Keats received some schooling at a private institution and then took up the study of medicine; but his heart was not in the work of dissection and clinical diagnosis. He read and he dreamed: read Spenser's *Faerie Queene* and Chapman's translation of Homer, Shakespeare's plays and Dante's *Commedia* in English; dreamed a poet's dreams of truth and beauty and set them down in living words. "I feel assured I should write from the mere yearning and fondness I have for the beautiful," he wrote to Richard Woodhouse in 1818, "even if my night's labors should be burnt every morning and no eye ever shine upon them." He had friends, among them Leigh Hunt, who helped him to develop his mind

[1] A. E. Hancock, *John Keats*, p. 10.

and exercise his gifts, and two Fannys — his little sister and Miss Brawne — brought a feminine influence into his life; but as a poet he depended very little upon others and truly lived a life apart. In 1821, accompanied by a friend, the artist Joseph Severn, he went to Rome to escape the rigors of the English climate, and there, in a house beside the Spanish Steps leading up to the Church of Santa Trinità dei Monti, he breathed his last. He was a poet even to the end: "I feel the daisies growing over me." And upon his grave in the Protestant Cemetery his self-composed epitaph was inscribed, "Here lies one whose name was writ in water."

WHERE KEATS LIVED IN HAMPSTEAD, LONDON

The notion once prevailed, due mainly to Shelley's indignant lament in "Adonais" and Byron's flippant jest in *Don Juan*, that Keats was practically killed by harsh criticism of his writings in English reviews. We know now that he was not "snuff'd out by an article"; that, as Matthew Arnold said, he had "flint and iron in him." But recently there has been a tendency to run to the other extreme and to make of Keats a stocky, virile, "two-fisted" individual, a sort of pugilist poet, a Hercules with a lyre. All we need do to correct either misleading impression is to read Keats's poems and Keats's letters. We there discover him no weakling indeed, but certainly no blustering blade, no early nineteenth-century cave man. The truth is that the man was almost completely lost in the poet; that the poet was greater than the man.

Narrative Poems. Keats wrote several stories in verse. *Endymion* and *Hyperion* he took from Greek mythology — Classical material certainly, but eminently Romantic in spirit as Keats transfused the theme. He knew no Greek, and he derived the conceptions of both poems from a reading of John Lemprière's *Classical Dictionary*. *Endymion*, written in riming couplets, recounts the story of the youth who captured

PIAZZA DI SPAGNA, ROME

Keats died in the house at the reader's right beside the picturesque Spanish Steps. It is now a museum containing portraits and relics of the poet and a small library of books about him and his poems

the affection of Diana. It is the moon myth, and by Keats haltingly told; but the confused narrative is redeemed by numerous touches of verbal splendor. It shows the poet, still immature, already intent on the quest of beauty. The Endymion story had been already handled in English Literature by Drayton in "The Man in the Moon." Drayton showed far more narrative skill than Keats, but had less descriptive power and poetic glow. *Hyperion*, never completed, is a version of the Greek sun myth written in powerful blank verse which shows the influence of both Dante and Milton. Book I, with its impressive description of the fallen Titans, inevitably recalls Milton's portraiture of the fallen angels.

"The Eve of St. Agnes" has been declared "a vision of beauty, deep, rich, and glowing as one of those dyed windows in which the heart of the Middle Ages still burns."[1] This is a pretty comparison, but fundamentally misleading. For the heart of the Middle Ages, as Dante manifested and as even Carlyle perceived, is the Catholic faith; and Keats's poem conveys not the slightest inkling of the Catholic spirit: it is gorgeously but unmistakably pagan. Keats here retells an eminently Romantic tale in Spenserian stanzas replete with magnificent imagery; from the point of view of imaginative splendor it is perhaps the finest sustained example of pure poetry in the English language. Keats turned to the Middle Ages again in *Isabella; or the Pot of Basil,* a vivid illustration of the great truth that genuine art can take an essentially repulsive theme and transmute it into a thing of beauty. The story had been already told by Boccaccio. The same tale, under the title *A Sicilian Story,* was given a poetical rendering by Barry Cornwall. It is interesting to see how the three writers vary in their handling of the subject and how Keats excels the others in delicacy and color. In *Lamia* Keats took a story of enchantment which he found in Burton's *Anatomy of Melancholy* and retold it in heroic couplets with increased narrative power. It is especially beautiful, even dramatic, in its closing passages, wherein by allegory the poet proclaims poetry a surer path to the attainment of truth than philosophy.

The Odes. Many a Londoner has visited the British Museum and seen the specimens of Greek sculpture known as the Elgin Marbles[2]; but Keats beheld those symbols of a vanished

---

[1] H. W. Mabie, *Essays in Literary Interpretation,* p. 255.

[2] Thomas Bruce, Earl of Elgin, was an English diplomat who collected numerous pieces of Greek sculpture in Athens early in the nineteenth century and sold them to the British Government for half of what it cost him to transport them. Most of them are now located in the Elgin Room of the British Museum.

civilization with the discerning eye of a poet, and fancifully reconstructed the life and passion of an elder day in his "Ode on a Grecian Urn." Not that Keats describes any particular urn in the British Museum or elsewhere: he was a poet, not a journalist; but the bits of Greek sculpture which he saw fired his inventive imagination, and we have his vision of the fleeing maidens, the sacrificial procession, the youthful piper, and the little town of silent streets. Nearly as fine is his "Ode to Autumn"; and most exquisite of all is his "Ode to a Nightingale," with its seductive word music, its description of the moonlit dream forest where the flowers can be detected only by their odors, and especially its poetic rendering of the idea that death is not to be dreaded since the song of the nightingale can never die. Keats wrote several other odes, all of them distinguished, but inferior to the superb three.

Other Poems. In a truly Romantic mood, a mood of wonder and mystery and magic, Keats wrote a fairy ballad, "La Belle Dame sans Merci" (The Beautiful Lady without Mercy), based on an English translation of a fifteenth-century poem by Alain Chartier. Like many more of the poems of John Keats, this is not to be read with an eye to "the geography of the piece" or with rigidly literal appreciation; rather, it is to be read as we listen to music. In a lighter mood is "Lines on the Mermaid Tavern," conceived in a spirit of pensive playfulness and yearning for the days when Shakespeare and Ben Jonson foregathered at the feast. "Sleep and Poetry" shows the young Keats at his best; he wrote it at the age of twenty-two. His unfinished "Eve of St. Mark" has much of the lightness of touch of the "Lines on the Mermaid Tavern" and something of the Chaucerian spirit; its influence can be traced in Tennyson and Rossetti.

Finally, John Keats stands forth as one of the supreme masters of the difficult sonnet form. In structure and true poetic eloquence he did nothing more magnificent than the well-known "On First Looking into Chapman's Homer." To appreciate those fourteen lines is to get close to the secret of the poet's art; and when we have shared the fine rapture of his vision splendid, what care we for the historical inaccuracy whereby he credits the conqueror of Mexico with the discovery of the Pacific Ocean? Though false to fact he is true to truth, as we well know when at some crisis of our lives we discover a Pacific of our own. At least five other of his sonnets, including "The Grasshopper and the Cricket," "On the Sea," and that glorious one beginning

> Bright star! would I were steadfast as thou art,

are among the supreme examples of short poems to be found in English. They are like drops of dew that mirror the morning sun, tiny jewels reflecting both the ache of human hearts and the wonders of God's universe.

Why we Read Keats. We are justified in seeking a profound knowledge of human life and character in great literature, in expecting to come in contact with great and luminous thoughts, and in looking for inspiration to put verve into our lives and our tasks. Yet true literature and great literature can exist without giving us any of these things. Keats's poetry reveals little or no knowledge of human nature; certainly it contains no lightning-like flashes of discerning comment such as we find in Browning, no lifelike and original character portraits such as those painted by Shakespeare. Nor does the poetry of Keats afford us thoughts beyond the reaches of our souls. Its author was plainly a man possessed of no extraordinary intellectual powers and no vast and comprehensive grasp of ideas. Least of all does Keats's poetry belong to what is sometimes vaguely styled the literature of "uplift." Nothing that he wrote in the least resembles a sermon or a moral treatise or a patriotic appeal to make the most of life. No; we do not read John Keats for knowledge, for philosophy, for moral inspiration. We may learn from him neither the science of sanctity, the art of thinking, nor the knack of practical success.

Why, then, are we to consider Keats's poems literature, and what is to be our purpose in reading them? The answer is simple and fundamental. Keats's poems are true literature, Keats's poems are worthy of our study and our love, solely because they open our eyes and our minds, our imaginations and our hearts, to visions of immaterial beauty.

JOHN KEATS

That beauty in itself and of itself is a fitting object of our devotion, that (as Plato taught so long ago) all created beauty is a pale and ineffectual reflection of the Uncreated Beauty which is God, that a man is doing something in accord with the better part of his nature when he makes or admires any truly beautiful thing, are truths too often forgotten. Heirs as we are of the stern Hebrew spirit through the direct and indirect influence of the Bible; of the Jansenistic spirit [1] through a body of devotional literature which has rigorized our conception of religion; of the Puritan attitude through the example and the influence of a number of popular English and American writers who held the ideal of beauty in suspicion and mistrust, — we are too prone to regard the enjoyment of beautiful things as unworthy or even as sinful. And, added to that, we of the Western World, with our absorption in practical results, in our concern with how much a thing costs and what it can be used

[1] Jansenism, named after Cornelius Jansenius, a seventeenth-century bishop of Ypres, was a narrow devotional movement that flourished for a time in France. The Jansenists held to certain rigorous beliefs which were condemned by the Church; but some of their teachings and much of their rigid spirit infected many devout men and continue to exert an influence in France and elsewhere even to this day.

for and what we can get out of it, are liable to fall into the error of despising objects and ideas which serve no immediate material purpose. The result is that while we esteem efficiency and utility and virtue, we are liable to hold beauty in slight regard and even to condemn it as a delusion and a snare. Thus we narrow our outlook and enslave our lives; thus we deprive ourselves of a source of noble and refined pleasure; thus we turn away from a path glad and glorious mounting to the very throne of God.

One function of literature — by no means its least important function — is to open our eyes and our minds to a perception and enjoyment of the beautiful; and some literature, and especially some poetry, does this and nothing more. Such is the nature and such is the function of the poetry of John Keats. We do not turn to him for information, for religious exhortation, for practical advice on the conduct of life; we shall not learn from him how to become saints or thinkers, how to succeed in business, or how to study human character. But if we read his best poems with attentive minds and active imaginations and responsive hearts we shall experience a vision of splendor and a subtle and constantly increasing inner glow of delicate delight. Our memory will be stored with well-turned and gracious phrases; the picture gallery of our imagination will be enriched with images evoked by

> . . . the sad heart of Ruth, when, sick for home,
> She stood in tears amid the alien corn,

and by

> The moving waters at their priestlike task
> Of cold ablution round earth's human shores;

and our souls will be refreshed in the contemplation of things and thoughts of quiet loveliness,

> Full of sweet dreams, and health, and quiet breathing.

And so it is that this mere boy, sickly and weak and often sore at heart, will share with us his God-given perceptions of beauty. Across the years he reminds us of his limitations and of his enduring greatness:

> What though I am not wealthy in the dower
> Of spanning wisdom; though I do not know
> The shiftings of the mighty winds that blow
> Hither and thither all the changing thoughts
> Of man; though no great ministering reason sorts
> Out the dark mysteries of human souls
> To clear conceiving; yet there ever rolls
> A vast idea before me.

And that vast idea is a hint, however fragmentary and finitely defective, of what was in the Mind of God Himself when at creation's dawn He looked upon the world of His making and saw that it was good.

SHELLEY

The Making of a Poem. In the year 1818 an Englishman, twenty-six years of age, arrived in the city of Naples. Varied, troubled, and disordered had been his brief life. He had quarreled with his father, he had been expelled from Oxford, his first wife had committed suicide. He had wandered much in England, in Scotland, in Ireland, and on the Continent of Europe. And now, with his second wife and their two children, with his wife's half-sister and her child, he came to Southern Italy in quest of peace. Naples, with its magic bay and its bright air and its tempering contrast in the ever-menacing presence of Vesuvius, smoke-crowned against the bluest of blue skies, is an admirable city to be happy in; but happiness, as Shelley and other poets have discovered and have taught, is conditioned less by where we are than by what we are. What Shelley was did not make for happiness. His was a spirit restless and perturbed, darkened ever by sad memories, unlightened by fair prospects, bereft of the consolations of belief in God our Father. His troubles came with him, and

even in that singularly fair city new troubles began to brew.
And so the young man, in many ways still a child and in other
ways older than his years, decided that he had had enough of
earthly life and swallowed a potion of laudanum.

But he did not die. His wife and his friends discovered what
he had done, and they gave him antidotes and made him walk
off the effects of the drug. And then it was that, physically ill,
nerve-shattered from the effects of the poison, utterly weary
of life and yet unable to cease living, Shelley wrote a poem.
Few readers of his "Stanzas written in Dejection near Naples"
realize how much human experience, how much sorrow and sin
and anguish and despair, went into the making of those verses;
how much of the poet's weariness and sense of failure find expression in the lines:

> I could lie down like a tired child,
>   And weep away the life of care
>   Which I have borne and yet must bear,
> Till death like sleep might steal on me,
>   And I might feel in the warm air
> My cheek grow cold, and hear the sea
> Breathe o'er my dying brain its last monotony.

The "Ineffectual Angel." A memorable piece of literary
criticism is Matthew Arnold's frequently quoted comment on
Shelley: "The Shelley of actual life is a vision of beauty and
radiance, indeed, but availing nothing, effecting nothing. And
in poetry, no less than in life, he is a beautiful and ineffectual
angel, beating in the void his luminous wings in vain." In
both his life and his poetry Shelley is a mass of contradictions:
a life of generous and noble impulses and foolish and unworthy
actions; poetry of sublimity and gorgeous music marred by
numerous shortcomings and disfigured by crazy theories and
meaningless rhapsodies. Without realizing what he was doing,
Shelley drew his own portrait, as man and as poet, in "Ozy-
mandias," a graphic picture of splendid fragments and unrealized greatness.

Born at Horsham, some forty miles out of London, Percy Bysshe Shelley (1792–1822) studied at Isleworth and Eton and then went to Oxford, where a silly pamphlet he wrote in defense of atheism brought about his expulsion in 1811. He had been given no adequate religious training and possessed little practical sense, so his life became a tissue of errors and absurdities.

PERCY BYSSHE SHELLEY

From a sketch by E. E. Williams in the collection of George A. Plimpton

He was interested vaguely but intensely in human liberties and the rights of man, he wrote a tract urging the Irish people to rise in rebellion against English domination, he became involved in the domestic life and political views of William Godwin ("What a set!" cried the fastidious Arnold at thought of that group of social reformers), and in 1818 he left England never to return. His last years were spent in various places in Italy. He was drowned in a squall while sailing in a small craft in the Gulf of Spezia near Leghorn. His body was washed ashore and was cremated; his ashes were buried in the Protestant Cemetery at Rome. At his worst he was an undutiful son, an unfaithful husband, a preacher of anarchy and irreligion; at his best he was "like an angel who has lost his way back to Heaven; and in his poetry, as in the music of Mozart, we hear the wailing, the questioning, the beating of wings in the void."[1]

Shelley's Best Poems. Much that Shelley wrote has no permanent value, and several of his lengthier poems are

[1] A. Clutton-Brock, *Essays on Literature and Life*, p. 100.

redeemed only by occasional passages of iridescent beauty. Several of his shorter poems are exquisite lyrics, revealing truly poetical conceptions and characterized by rare harmony, by rich variety of meter, by arresting and unusual imagery, and by a splendid surging of undisciplined emotion. Among these the finest are "Ode to the West Wind," "To a Skylark," "The Indian Serenade," "Lines written among the Euganean Hills," "The Cloud," and "Hymn to Intellectual Beauty." The death of Keats moved Shelley to write "Adonais," a moving tribute to the author of *Endymion* and a series of imaginative reflections on death and immortality conceived in Shelley's characteristically pagan spirit.

Essentially a lyric poet, one who looked into his own heart and wrote, Shelley is rightly placed among the poets of the Romantic Movement. He emphasizes the note of revolt and is fiercely if ineffectually dissatisfied with things as they are; he avoids conventional images and traditional methods of writing; he takes as the themes of several of his longer poems — *Alastor, The Revolt of Islam, Hellas, Prometheus Unbound* — persons and places of other times, and ideas far removed from ordinary life and experience. Like the other Romantics, Shelley revealed a vivid interest in nature, though the spirit in which he interprets nature is different from that animating Wordsworth, Coleridge, and the rest. Scott contented himself with simple, lifelike pictures; Wordsworth, a parson in poetry, was intent on the moral lessons to be drawn from the contemplation of starlight and forest gloom; Coleridge was captivated by the suggestion of wonder and of mystery which he found in created things; Keats lost himself in nature and mingled his soul with the spirit of the universe; Byron turned to nature for consolation and redress and found in her wilder moods a background against which to exhibit the scars and wounds of his "blighted being." To Shelley nature was an intoxicating incentive to pour out his misty philosophy of life, a starting point for the invention of a natural world of his own imaginings. He never wrote, like Scott and Wordsworth, with "his eye on the object." He was as much out of touch with nature as he was with men; yet his best poems help us to discover in the world of creation unsuspected beauties and implications. His muse was all wings and no feet.

Shelley's Prose. Like most poets, Shelley was master of a graceful and vigorous prose style. He never had much to say, but he was adept in saying it. Sometimes where his poems (that juvenile indiscretion, *Queen Mab*, for instance) are merely torrents of wild and whirling words, his notes thereon are penetrating and rational — for Shelley. Thus it is that in his preface to *The Cenci* — a poetic drama of intrigue and blood laid in sixteenth-century Rome — Shelley pointed out, though not without misunderstanding and unconscious prejudice, certain distinctive traits of Catholicism, a faith which he had seen functioning in Italian life:

To a Protestant apprehension there will appear something unnatural in the earnest and perpetual sentiment of the relations between God and man which pervades the tragedy of the Cenci. . . . But religion in Italy is not, as in Protestant countries, a cloak to be worn on particular days; or a passport which those who do not wish to be railed at carry with them to exhibit; or a gloomy passion for penetrating the impenetrable mysteries of our being, which terrifies its possessor at the darkness of the abyss to the brink of which it has conducted him. Religion co-exists, as it were, in the mind of an Italian Catholic with a faith in that of which all men have the most certain knowledge. It is interwoven in the whole fabric of life. It is adoration, faith, submission, penitence, blind admiration, not a rule for normal conduct. . . . Religion pervades intensely the whole frame of society, and is, according to the temper of the mind which it inhabits, a passion, a persuasion, an excuse, a refuge.

Shelley's most important prose contribution is his *Defence of Poetry*, written in 1821, in answer to an attack made by Thomas Love Peacock on poetry in general and the Romantic poets in particular. Here, as was the case with Sir Philip Sidney and his *Apologie for Poetrie*, we have a poet entering the lists on behalf of his craft. Several of Shelley's observations deserve to be recalled because of the soundness of their thought and the beauty of their expression:

A poet is a nightingale, who sits in darkness and seeks to cheer its own solitude with sweet sounds; his auditors are as men entranced by the melody of an unseen musician, who feel that they are moved and softened, yet know not whence or why.

Poetry is a sword of lightning, ever unsheathed, which consumes the scabbard that would contain it.

... how the gentleness and elevation of mind connected with these sacred emotions can render men more amiable, more generous and wise, and lift them out of the dull vapors of the little world of self.

Poetry is the record of the best and happiest moments of the best and happiest minds. ... Poetry thus makes immortal all that is best and most beautiful in the world. ... It creates anew the universe. ... It justifies the bold and true words of Tasso — *Non merita nome di creatore, se non Iddio ed il Poeta.*[1]

A poet, as he is the author to others of the highest wisdom, pleasure, virtue, and glory, so he ought personally to be the happiest, the best, the wisest, and the most illustrious of men.

A Poet's Heart. When Shelley's body, in accordance with a government ordinance, was burned on the Italian shore in 1822, the heart, as his friend Trelawny records, remained entire and unaffected by the fierce flames. That was an impressive symbol of Shelley's poetry. Much that he wrote now shares the oblivion of his ashes; but his finest poems, his matchless songs of lyric loveliness, remain, like the heart of him — "tameless, and swift, and proud" — untouched alike by the waters of forgetfulness and the flames of censure. Unwittingly he composed his own epitaph:

> He liv'd, he died, he sung, in solitude.
>
> . . . .
>
> The fire of those soft orbs has ceased to burn,
> And Silence, too enamour'd of that voice,
> Locks its mute music in her rugged cell.

[1] No one deserves the name of creator save God and the poet.

BYRON

A Living Paradox. In 1924, the centenary of Lord Byron's death, a proposal to place a tablet to the poet's memory in Westminster Abbey was frowned upon by Dean Ryle: "A man who outraged the laws of our Divine Lord and whose treatment of women violated the Christian principles of purity and honor, should not be commemorated in Westminster Abbey." We may dissent from the dean's conclusion, but we cannot deny his statement of facts. Byron was neither a good man nor a good Christian, and yet he attracted and continues to hold the interest and even the sympathy of Europe. He was neither a scholar nor a poet of supreme achievement, and yet he wrote many a line that has become an English proverb and composed a number of poems that will live as long as any poems endure. The man and his work bristle with incongruities. Byron rather than Coleridge lived up to the characterization of "damaged archangel."

Biographers and critics never tire of pointing out the strange contrasts that appear in his life and writings. Even physically he was a creature of extremes: "He had a head," says Macaulay, "that statuaries loved to copy, and a foot the deformity of which the beggars in the streets mimicked."[1] And the contrast extended to his life and character: "He had a conscience which never modified his conduct, a refinement which could not mitigate his coarseness, a kindness which was obscured at the smallest firing of his pride or his desire, and, oddest of all, a sense of humor which never assisted him to observe proportion."[2] He was, in the words of a recent biographer, John Drinkwater, "a rake, a rebel, an iconoclast, something of a mountebank, a cynic of deadly aim, an unashamed egotist,"[3] and at the same time he was tender and manly and generous; a friend to men like Moore and Shelley;

[1] Review of Moore's *Life of Byron*, in the *Edinburgh Review*, June, 1831.
[2] J. C. Squire, *Books Reviewed*, p. 132.   [3] *The Pilgrim of Eternity*, p. 46.

a benefactor to men like Leigh Hunt; and at the last something of a hero of romance, giving his very life in the cause of a nation other than his own.

And Byron the poet was not less inconsistent than Byron the man. He could assail certain writers of his day with insult and satire, unfairness and indecent spleen, and he could recapture something of the nobility of Biblical literature in his *Hebrew Melodies* and create in his apostrophe to the ocean a piece of meditative verse almost sublime; he could write passages that no man dare read aloud, and he could create visions of poetic beauty which are part of the literary inheritance of every English-speaking child; he could wade through dirt and depravity and coarseness and vulgarity in *Don Juan*, and in *Childe Harold's Pilgrimage* he could thrill ecstatically

LORD BYRON

From a painting in the collection of George A. Plimpton

to the glory and sacredness of Rome, the city of the soul; he could sponsor lines that in their clumsiness and disregard of elementary grammar would disgrace a schoolboy in the sixth grade, and he could fashion sentences so well wrought and flawless as to reveal unsuspected possibilities of English diction. No poet has ever sunk lower than Byron, and few poets have excelled him in power and impressive grandeur.

A Tale of Mud and Stars. George Noel Gordon, Lord Byron (1788–1824), was born in England, spent his childhood in Scotland, studied at Harrow and Cambridge, lived much in

Switzerland and Italy, and died in Greece. He was sprung from a wild and willful family, and all his life showed the traits of a spoiled and undisciplined child.

> And thus, untaught in youth my heart to tame,
> My springs of life were poisoned.

While still a young man he became a social lion and a literary celebrity, married indiscreetly, and shortly found himself ostracized by the fashionable people who but recently had fawned upon him. He fled from England, never to return, and lived abroad, sometimes wasting himself in unworthy excesses, sometimes for weeks at a stretch concentrating on writing and study. Geneva knew him, and Venice and Ravenna and Pisa. And then, in 1823, he joined the Greeks in their war for independence, caught a fever the following year, and died in the swamps of Missolonghi at the age of thirty-six. His body was brought back to the England he despised and now rests in his ancestral home at Newstead Abbey beneath a monument donated by the King of Greece. His life was a tissue of shreds and patches — sordid shreds and brilliant patches; and his poetry partook of the qualities of his life. Incidentally, despite the vast amount of his published work, Byron professed never to take himself seriously as a poet; yet his poetry is his sole claim to remembrance.

The Satires. Some juvenile and very ordinary verses which while still a boy Byron published under the title *Hours of Idleness* elicited a severe criticism from the *Edinburgh Review*; and the young poet, stung to fury, dashed off his satire *English Bards and Scotch Reviewers*, wherein he discharged his spleen upon the just and the unjust. The work was powerful but utterly unrestrained, ill-tempered, and inconsiderate and Byron afterwards regretted what he called "this miserable record of misplaced anger and indiscriminate acrimony."

[1] Byron wrote his condemnation of *English Bards and Scotch Reviewers* in a copy of the poem now the property of Thomas J. Wise of London.

His satirical masterpiece is *The Vision of Judgment*, wherein he pokes bitter fun at Southey, who, in a poem of the same name, had made a hero out of King George III of England. Byron has that monarch standing outside the gates of Heaven while St. Michael and Lucifer discuss his character; there seems no chance for George III to gain admission, until Southey threatens to read his own poems aloud, and that prospect so terrifies St. Peter and the angelic host that the

NEWSTEAD ABBEY

The ancestral home of the Byrons had been one of the numerous monastic foundations suppressed under Henry VIII

king slips into Heaven unobserved. Another satire is *Beppo*, a tale with a Venetian background. It is brilliant and capable, though marred by flippancy and an unwholesome moral tone. Most representative of Byron is his lengthy satire, *Don Juan*, a poem that exhibits its author at his worst and best. Some of it is indecent and vulgar, and in places it is flat and banal; but other portions reveal a sparkling wit and contain passages of sustained beauty animated by a not ignoble spirit. If poetry is essentially self-expression, then Byron was never more a poet than here. Like Byron's life, *Don Juan* is a tale of mud and stars.

One of the results of *Don Juan* was a crop of imitations of it by English rimesters, some of them worthy of more than passing notice. Thus Winthrop Praed, in the same stanza form (the *ottava rima*, which Byron had borrowed from the Italian), bitterly but not unjustly indicated the essential weakness of the poem and its author:

> But I have moved too long in cold society,
> 　Where it's the fashion not to care a rush;
> Where girls are always thinking of propriety,
> 　And men are laughed at if they chance to blush;
> And thus I've caught the sickness of sobriety,
> 　Forbidden sighs to sound, and tears to gush;
> Become a great philosopher, and curled
> Around my heart the poisons of the world.
>
> ＼　.　.　.　.　.　.　.　.　.
>
> To me all light is darkness; — love is lust,
> 　Painting soiled canvas, poetry spoiled paper;
> The fairest loveliness a pinch of dust,
> 　The proudest majesty a breath of vapor;
> I have no sympathy, no tear, no trust,
> 　No morning musing and no midnight taper
> For daring manhood or for dreaming youth,
> Or maiden purity, or matron truth.

Childe Harold's Pilgrimage. Byron toured Europe and the East shortly after leaving college, and the outcome was Cantos I and II of *Childe Harold's Pilgrimage*, the publication of which in 1812 brought such sudden popularity that Byron said he woke up one morning to find himself famous. The third and fourth cantos were written later. *Childe Harold* has less cynicism and vulgarity than *Don Juan*, though in it Byron insists on maintaining the rôle of a "blighted being" which he found pleasure in affecting. Here are numerous bits of brilliant and artistic description and several splendid meditations on life and history. Some of the best-known selections from Byron — for instance, the Apostrophe to the Ocean, the Eve of Waterloo, the Dying Gladiator, and the wonderful description of the Roman Colosseum by moonlight — are to be found in *Childe Harold's Pilgrimage*. This can be said of it: it is a poem which grows upon the reader, a poem to which we can turn more than once for enlightenment and pleasure; and it serves to make real and lifelike the great cities and natural beauties of Continental Europe and to reconstruct some of the most thrilling episodes in Western history.

Dramas and Tales. Byron was too theatrical to be dramatic. That is to say, though he had no connection with the actual theater as Shakespeare and Sheridan had, he was by nature an actor, and even something of a bad actor. His stage was the world; and he delighted in playing a part — the part of a handsome and noble soul, very melancholy and very proud, more sinned against than sinning, and hating and despising his fellow men. This attitude is shown most clearly in *Manfred*, though it runs through *Cain* and Byron's other dramas. Byron may have been, as Sir Sidney Colvin styles him, "the greatest attitudinist in literature as in life,"[1] but he was too egositic, too self-absorbed, too subjective ever to adopt the impersonal outlook which really dramatic writing demands. There is substantially but one character in all Byron's dramas, and that character is Byron as Byron thought he was or pretended to be.

Several tales in verse are rather better than his dramas, though the Byronic figure of the melancholy and disillusioned nobleman is always present. Among these are *The Giaour*, *The Bride of Abydos*, *The Corsair*, *Lara*, and *The Siege of Corinth*. Of them all the most distinguished are *Mazeppa* and "The Prisoner of Chillon." The Chillon poem is still widely read and deserves its immortality, though it is utterly unreliable in its historical details. The prisoner, Francis Bonnivard, was not by any means the tragic figure envisaged by Byron; he was imprisoned for political and not religious

[1] Preface to *The Letters of John Keats*, p. xv.

reasons, his captivity was not of the heart-rending nature described in the poem, and, in fact, he suffered far more in Calvinist Geneva after his release than he did during his forced stay within the picturesque castle on the shore of Lake Leman. Byron wrote the poem in three days when he and Shelley, making a round of the lake in a small boat, were

THE CASTLE OF CHILLON

On the Lake of Geneva, near the town of Villeneuve

held up by a protracted spell of bad weather at Ouchy, the port of Lausanne. He immortalized Chillon and Bonnivard.

Various Poems. Though often classed among the satires and not devoid of the satirical element, Byron's *Hints from Horace* is really a liberal translation of the Augustan poet's *Ars Poetica*. Certainly it is not without interest that the Romantic poet should enjoy putting the precepts and suggestions of the Classical Roman into acceptable English verse. *Hints from Horace* is unfortunately neglected in too many studies of the poet; it constitutes, says Lane Cooper of Cornell,

"one of the permanent gifts of Byron to English Literature." [1]
But Byron continues to be best remembered by some of his
shorter poems: his "Ode on Venice," "Darkness," his "Sonnet on Chillon," "Maid of Athens," and several of the *Hebrew
Melodies*, especially "She Walks in Beauty," "Vision of Bel-
shazzar," and that miniature masterpiece, "The Destruction
of Sennacherib" with its embodiment of the Hebraic spirit:

> And the widows of Ashur are loud in their wail,
> And the idols are broke in the temple of Baal;
> And the might of the Gentile, unsmote by the sword,
> Hath melted like snow in the glance of the Lord!

Byron the Romanticist. The father of French Romanticism
was that eccentric creature Jean Jacques Rousseau, and the
bulwark of French Classicism — in literature, though in nothing else — was the blasphemous Voltaire. Both of them,
though each repelled and disgusted Byron the man, profoundly
affected Byron the poet. "By a sort of miracle," says a Swiss
professor, "Byron unites in his spirit the two opposing types
of Voltaire and Rousseau." [2] Certainly he had Rousseau's
overweening egotism and much of Rousseau's freshened interest in nature; and, like Rousseau, though in different ways,
he was a revolutionary and a scorner of conventions. His
bitterness and cynicism, his tendency to scoff at beliefs which
other men held sacred, he learned (if, indeed, he needed tui-
tion) from Voltaire. What he did not learn from Voltaire,
or from anybody else, was Classical precision in the art of
writing. As has been well said, "If we admit Byron to the
company of great English poets, we have to accept him as the
most slovenly of them all." [3] But that conspicuous failing was
due less to Romantic contempt of Classical ideals of diction

---

[1] *The Dial*, January 16, 1913.
[2] L. F. Choisy, "Byron aux bords du Leman," in *Bibliothèque universelle*
(Lausanne), June, 1924.
[3] John Drinkwater, *The Pilgrim of Eternity*, p. 164.

than to innate carelessness, perverse haste, and a thoroughly undisciplined spirit. Utterly alien to him were the "labor of the file," the "art that conceals art," Michelangelo's "purgation of superfluities," Carlyle's "eternal patience." He had but a slight sense of order, a slender conception of proportion, and no appreciation of that intellectual and emotional poise which is an infallible sign of the Classical spirit. He was a poet born, not a poet made. Byron's supreme gift was a torrential energy, but an energy unharnessed and uncontrolled. He was completely Romantic, however, in his abandonment to emotional moods, in his rapturous devotion to the isles of Greece, and in his melancholy musings over Rome, the mother of dead empires. Patriotism for him meant the love of any country — except England.

CHAPTER XIII

THE NOVEL

THE BEGINNINGS

Romanticism and Realism. The Romantic Movement, although manifesting itself chiefly in poetry, likewise exerted a strong influence on English prose; and that influence was most notable in fiction. As Romanticism was in conflict with the Classical idea in poetry, so in prose Romanticism was in opposition to still another attitude toward literature and life — an attitude conveniently called Realism. And as Romanticism was a revolt against the excesses of Classicism, so Realism was in turn a protest against the excesses of Romanticism. The English novel, especially in the nineteenth century, affords numerous examples of both Romanticism and Realism.

What is Realism? The word connotes many things and, like the word *Romanticism*, has been very loosely used; but it stands for something manifest and definite in both books and life. Two men, for instance, go out together for a day in the country, and when they return home they tell their families about their outing. The first man says: "It was a wonderful experience to step blithely along the winding road, where every turn and every rise revealed a new aspect of nature. There was tonic in the invigorating western breeze. We ate our luncheon on a mossy carpet beside the running stream and listened to the orchestra of birds and insects. And in the afternoon we breasted the challenging slopes of Mount Agnon and stood enthralled at the maneuvers of the cavalry of the clouds." And the second man says: "Next time I'm going to take that trip in a car. The road was hot and dusty and seemed to have no end, and savage dogs barked at us at every turn. The wind was strong enough to blow us away, I thought; it did blow my hat away. Luncheon was fine: those pickles and sandwiches were just the thing for the occasion, and the thermos bottle kept the coffee piping hot. But the bank of the creek was damp, and I know I've caught cold; and the birds kept squawking, and ants got into the mince pie. And I'm tired to death from dragging myself up to the top of that scraggy old Mount Agnon, where there was not a thing to see but the clouds." The first man is a Romanticist; the second man is a Realist.

Now, as our two men can adopt two distinct attitudes toward an outing, two novelists — Dickens and Thackeray, for example — can adopt differing points of view in their portrayal of life. The Romantic novelist sees life in softened outlines, perhaps even through rose-colored eyeglasses; his book is like a stage in a theater on the evening of a distinguished performance. The Realistic novelist sees life at close range and often picks out the less pleasant parts of it to look at; his book resembles a stage without lights and with cluttered scenery at ten o'clock in the morning. The characters in the Romantic novel tend to be prevailingly noble and beautiful; the Realistic novelist feels like telling them to go and wash the grease paint off their faces and engage henceforth in some useful form of industry. Realism is so called because it professes to show life just as it is; but the devotee of Romanticism might retort that it is the concern of art to ennoble and beautify life as it is, that the stage of human life has no meaning until the scene is set and the lights are on and the orchestra discourses sweet music. Both attitudes have produced great literature. Some world novelists are Romanticists, some are Realists, and still others manage to combine the two views of life.

What is a Novel? It is easy to find and to formulate numerous definitions of the novel. The most liberal and elastic is that given by Professor Phelps of Yale: "A good story well told." But that would seem to include other forms of literature — the short story, for example, and the tale in verse — which, properly speaking, are not novels. More exact and satisfying is the definition by Robert Herrick, a man who has written novels and taught literature: "A prose narration of events involving the interests of possible, conceivable human beings in a possible, conceivable world." Some of us might prefer the definition given by Anthony Hope Hawkins, the author of *The Prisoner of Zenda*: "A fictitious narrative comprising a number of interrelated situations, by means of which human life, manners, and feelings are exhibited."

In general it can be said that the novel possesses the following traits:

1. It is a relatively lengthy story told in prose.

2. The story is composed of plot, or "interrelated situations."

3. It is fictitious, not rigidly and literally factual or historical.

4. The characters in the novel are "possible" and "conceivable," not freaks or monstrosities.

5. The background, or setting, of the story is broadly true to life, though not necessarily "founded on fact."

6. Though the novel may instruct and edify, its essential purpose is to give refined pleasure.

Origins of the Novel. The germ of the modern novel is to be found in popular tales in prose or verse, which among all peoples have been means of entertainment. The Romances of Chivalry had some of the traits of the novel, though many of their characters were unreal and their plots generally lacked sustained structure. Saintsbury traces some of the elements of the novel to the *Colloquies* of Erasmus.[1] Cervantes's masterpiece, *Don Quixote*, is the first novel in the history of literature; it is more than a short story and more than a collection of stories. In English the nearest approaches to the novel in Elizabethan times were Lyly's *Euphues*,

[1] *The Earlier Renaissance*, pp. 82, 83.

Sidney's *Arcadia*, Nash's *Unfortunate Traveller, or the Life of Jack Wilton*, and Thomas Deloney's coarsely realistic stories, *Jack of Newbury, The Gentle Craft*, and *Thomas of Reading*. Deloney, whose writings were overlooked until 1912, was a weaver of Norwich with scant education and little

knowledge of the wide world but with the story-teller's native gifts and a shrewd eye for the absurdities and follies of tradesmen. His stories are interesting as curiosities and as milestones in the history of fiction, but intrinsically they lack artistry and broad human appeal.

Daniel Defoe (1661?–1731). The first English novel, and some would say the best, is the never-failing favorite of boys of all ages: *The Life and Strange Surprizing Adventures of Robinson Crusoe, of York, Mariner*, published in 1719. Few books are so widely known. It has been translated into a dozen languages, including Hebrew and Persian, and the shipwrecked mariner and his man Friday are familiar figures in every land.

Robinson Crusoe owes much of its appeal to its union of Romantic material and Realistic method. The voyage and the shipwreck, life on the desert island, the discovery of the footprint on the sand, encounters with savages and perilous adventures on sea and shore form a theme essentially Romantic;

but Defoe handles it with the simplicity, the directness, the wealth of detail, which he might employ in describing a crossing of the Thames or a stroll down Fleet Street. He makes his Robinson Crusoe a real person — real in his stupidity, his fears, and his depression not less than in his decency, his resourcefulness, and his not too heroic valor. Here, assuredly, is a "good story well told."

Defoe was nearly sixty years old when he turned to fiction. Before that he had been almost everything: a student for the ministry, a biographer, a versifier, a historian, a political pamphleteer, a journalist, and incidentally he had served a term in prison and had been pelted in the pillory. After *Robinson Crusoe* he wrote several other fictitious narratives, the best of which is *Captain Singleton*, a story of wanderings in darkest Africa. Despite his fame as a novelist he

DANIEL DEFOE

From an original painting in the collection of George A. Plimpton

was, more than anything else, a newspaperman born two centuries too soon. His *Journal of the Plague Year* was long thought to be an authentic history of the Great Plague; it is really a piece of clever realistic fiction. His pamphlet *The Shortest Way with Dissenters* is a masterpiece of irony worthy of comparison with Swift's *Modest Proposal*.

Daniel Defoe, as writer and as man, was not wholly admirable. Some of his less-known novels are disfigured by coarseness, and in none of his writings does he manifest a lofty soul or create a truly noble and heroic character. He was a shifty politician and something of a timeserver; he was no stickler for truth and no conspicuous example of virtuous living. But he has won to true immortality because of *Robinson Crusoe*. He here created a world classic. Over his grave in Bunhill Fields in London there stands an obelisk erected in 1870 by the boys and girls of England, and on a bench near it children sit and pay their silent tribute to the man who wrote a book that never grows old.[1]

Samuel Richardson (1689-1761). Thackeray, in his masterly historical novel, *Henry Esmond*, gives us glimpses of an elderly gentleman surrounded by a group of feminine admirers and frankly basking in their adulation. That elderly gentleman is Richardson, who wrote stories which men have never liked but which (in his own day at least) women found consoling and exquisite. Richardson, like John Lyly of *Euphues* fame, is a ladies' man in literature. He is sentimental and prolix (his masterpiece, *Clarissa, or the History of a Young Lady*, was published in seven volumes), and he delights in exhibiting the charm and virtue of women in all stations of life against the contrasting background of masculine coarseness and selfishness. He is the father of the Romantic novel in English, and his work was highly esteemed by Romanticists at home and abroad, especially by Rousseau, by Diderot, and by Goethe. Today he is not much read. Taste, including feminine taste, has changed; his sugary sentimentalism is wearying to our abrupt generation, and the very length of his novels is forbidding.

Richardson was a printer and stationer in London who was obliging enough to write letters for people (especially for

[1] In justice to Defoe's memory it should be stated that charges of plagiarism sometimes made against him must be dismissed as "not proven." A Dutch analogue of *Robinson Crusoe* was published in 1708, but it is probable that Defoe never saw the book and could not have read it if he had seen it. As a piece of literature the Dutch narrative is far inferior to the English novel. Defoe's inspiration sprang from the sensational shipwreck of Alexander Selkirk, a Scot whose adventures had all London agog.

women) less skillful than he in the epistolary art. It was possible to learn a good deal about human nature by writing letters for milady and milady's maid, for the butcher's wife and the alderman's daughter, and Richardson stored away his impressions and mused on the ways of the human heart. He decided to prepare a book of model letters, but the plan changed into a novel in letter form. The result was *Pamela*, his first story, published when its author was more than fifty years old. It was an eighteenth-century variant on the theme that Heaven will protect the innocent working girl. Pamela Andrews is a servant whose beauty and virtue so impress her dissolute master that she reforms that dubious worthy and eventually marries him. Pope said of *Pamela* that it would do more good than twenty sermons, but the sermons that Pope was familiar with must

SAMUEL RICHARDSON

From an original painting in the collection of George A. Plimpton

have been low-grade clerical ore. There is plenty of dirt in the story, and the much-heralded virtue is mere worldly prudence. Better in every way is *Clarissa*, a series of letters dealing with middle-class life. Here Richardson shows that he really knew human nature, though never on its higher levels; there are interminable lengths of tragedy and pathos, leading to a conclusion in which the fascinating villain is killed in a duel. His third novel, *Sir Charles Grandison*, a story of life among the nobility, presents the kind of hero which appealed to the feminine heart as the perfect gentleman, but which masculine readers — not wholly disinterested judges, possibly — even then condemned as the perfect prig.

Henry Fielding (1707–1754). Disgusted with Richardson's sirupy sentimentalism, a dramatist and journalist published a parody, *Shamela*, in 1741, and followed it with *The History of the Adventures of Joseph Andrews*, Pamela's brother. Thus Fielding, one of the leading English novelists, made his début as

TOBIAS SMOLLETT

a story-teller. In *Jonathan Wild* he described the life and adventures of a thief; and in his best work, *Tom Jones*, he produced a story that is powerful and well constructed, strong in its characterization, keen in its satire, and rich in its humor, but soiled and streaked by the vulgarity and loose ideas of morality which were typical of both Fielding and his age. Late in 1751 appeared his last novel, *Amelia*, in every respect inferior to its predecessors.

Born at Glastonbury, Henry Fielding studied at Eton and at the University of Leyden, came to London at the age of twenty-three, and wrote for the stage. His plays were technically efficient, but for the most part grossly indecent and are deservedly forgotten. Then he turned to journalism, was a lawyer and a commentator on English law, a justice of the peace and a social reformer, and an active and progressive politician. He died in Portugal at the age of forty-seven. A recent biographer, Wilbur Cross of Yale, has demonstrated that as a man Fielding was by no means as black as he was painted by Scott, Thackeray, Stephen, Henley, Gosse, and

Saintsbury; but no apologist can ignore the fact that Fielding's truly important work in the development of the English novel was largely vitiated by his low ideals of conduct and his offensive emphasis on the seamy side of life.

Tobias Smollett (1721-1771). Following the lead of Nash's *Jack Wilton* and Fielding's *Jonathan Wild*, Smollett, a Scotsman who had failed as a dramatist and barely managed to get on as a surgeon, wrote several stories in which the leading character is a rogue and a rascal. This type of fiction is called the *picaresque* novel, from *picaro*, "rogue." It originated in Spain, the first example being *The Life of Lazarillo de Tormes*. Smollett's best-known rogue stories are *Roderick Random* and *Peregrine Pickle*, both loosely constructed and depending for their interest on the realism of the male characters and the variety of the incidents.

LAURENCE STERNE

From an original painting in the collection of George A. Plimpton

Humphrey Clinker is a series of letters describing a journey to Scotland. Thackeray was in an unusually genial mood when he wrote that *Humphrey Clinker* "is, I do think, the most laughable story that has ever been written since the goodly art of novel-writing began." The humor of Smollett has been vastly overrated, and his rogue romances are liberally marred with the indecency and lack of delicacy which must be accepted as characteristic of eighteenth-century English fiction. Smollett traveled considerably, and it is diverting to hear him, who, in his books, was no stickler for the proprieties, complaining that in Michelangelo's "Pietà" in St. Peter's in Rome he found "something indelicate, not to say indecent." He was an admirable judge of indecency.

Laurence Sterne (1713–1768). Cloying sentimentalism, leering obscenity, irresistible humor, and convincing pathos are all singularly blended in the two episodic novels written by Sterne: *Tristram Shandy* and *A Sentimental Journey through*

THE PARSONAGE AT COXWOLD, YORKSHIRE

Where Sterne gave intermittent attention to the spiritual needs of his flock

France and Italy. Irish by birth, Sterne entered the ministry and lived for twenty years in a Yorkshire rectory, neglecting his parishioners and devoting himself to reading and to less worthy pleasures. A thoroughly disagreeable man and a thoroughly unprincipled writer, he nevertheless had the art of putting words pleasantly together, and so his two books will be quoted for their frequent felicitous phrasing and for their moving and sometimes powerful characterization. For good and for ill he is in a small way in English Literature what Rabelais is in a large way in French Literature. The description of the death of Le Fèvre in *Tristram Shandy* is a little

masterpiece of tragedy, richly human in substance and original
in style; the chapter "The Sword" is one of the earliest instances in English of the almost perfect short story; and the
portrayal of such characters as Parson Yorick, Corporal Trim,
and especially Uncle Toby shows what Sterne could do when
at his best. Unfortunately, both morally and artistically, he
was rarely at his best.

THE "REIGN OF TERROR"

Forerunners in Romanticism. We shall now trace the two
main channels which prose fiction followed during the nineteenth century, considering, first, the writers of Romantic
novels and then the novelists whose method was Realistic.
The outstanding figure in the history of the Romantic novel in
English is Sir Walter Scott; but Scott was preceded and followed by writers whose contributions to Romanticism, though
less than his, cannot rightly be ignored. One of these was the
Strawberry Hill dabbler, Horace Walpole, whose *Castle of
Otranto* (1764) constituted the first English novel wherein mysterious midnight noises, subterranean passages, a murderous
sable helmet, a magic sword borne by a hundred men, and
other accessories of the romance of terror were utilized in a
yarn far removed from actual life and experience but thoroughly consistent in itself.

William Beckford (1759-1844). Another eighteenth-century
Romanticist was William Beckford, a man who spent his life
in travel and literary dabbling and, during twenty years,
dwelt in the south of England at Fonthill Abbey, where he
constructed a "fairy palace" as odd as Walpole's Gothic castle
on the Thames. Like Walpole he busied himself in collecting
engravings, pictures, rare books, and artistic curios, and like
Walpole he wrote one Romantic novel, *Vathek*, an Arabian
tale. The history of this novel is as unusual as the story itself.
Beckford turned it out during his stay in Lausanne, Switzer-

land, in an uninterrupted session of three days and two nights, when he was a mere youth of twenty-two. It was written in French and published at Lausanne and Paris, but an English version, the work of Samuel Henley, appeared in 1784. It is a grotesque but powerful story of Oriental luxury, romance, enchantment, and terror, recounting the amazing adventures of the wicked Caliph Vathek. It progresses steadily to a conclusion at once ghastly and gorgeous in an underground palace, the Hall of Eblis, where men and women who have selfishly pursued pleasure and wealth prowl about forever, their hearts burning with an unconsuming flame. *Vathek* equals the *Arabian Nights* in splendor and outdoes that collection of stories in mystery and horror.

Mrs. Radcliffe (1764-1823). Most representative of the Gothic romance, however, were the several novels written by Ann Radcliffe during a brief but intensive period of production. Her vogue did not last long; but at its height her books were widely read in England, were translated into foreign languages, and were declared by some supposedly competent critics to be second only to the plays of Shakespeare. Even after her popularity had abated, her influence on English fiction was considerable. She became the nucleus of a legend, the rumor gaining ground that meditating upon her own stories had driven her insane. Among Mrs. Radcliffe's tales are *The Romance of the Forest, The Italian, or the Confessional of the Black Penitents*, and especially *The Mysteries of Udolpho*, the novel most characteristic of her imaginative resources. A French girl finds herself imprisoned in a grim castle in the Apennines where the Lord of Udolpho conducts plots against the Italian government and pillages towns on the mountain slopes. Her days and nights are filled with terrors. The wind wails, hidden doors creak, mysterious rappings resound; she looks from her window and sees a shrouded figure flit across the courtyard and observes the lances of the sentries tipped with death-foretelling flame; strains of vaguely familiar music rise from the dungeons, and swords clash in passageways hidden in the thick walls. The seemingly supernatural happenings are all rationally explained before the story reaches its conclusion, but no explanation prevents the reader from forgetting his own life and circumstances and experiencing a copious plenty of shocks and thrills.

"Monk" Lewis (1775–1818). Such shocks and thrills so wrought upon the nerves and the imagination of one Matthew Gregory Lewis, then just twenty years of age, that he determined to write a mystery story of his own. The result was *Ambrosio, or the Monk*, a tissue of horrors, absurdities, and manifestations of bigotry and ignorance, all so repulsive and indecent that the author prudently eliminated many particulars in his second edition. The story then entered upon a long career of popularity — a popularity due in part to the now widely awakened appetite for thrills, but also in part to the credulity of a large portion of the English reading public where the Catholic Church and her institutions are aspersed. The story is laid in Spain, and offers a panorama of crowded churches, hypocritical confessors, monstrous lady abbesses, convent torture chambers, and all the other theatrical properties dear to the souls of the ignorant blinded by religious prejudice. "Monk" Lewis, as the author came to be called, did nothing else notable in a literary way, though he exercised himself in verse-making and play-writing. He was a little pop-eyed man, by Byron and Scott frankly considered a bore, who appropriately died of yellow fever on a voyage home from Jamaica. *The Monk*, though in substance a travesty and in style an affliction of spirit, has this importance in the History of English Literature: first, it is one of the most conspicuous examples of that strain of anti-Catholic prejudice which runs through many books written since the sixteenth century; secondly, it served to create and to foster those queer ideas of religious and the religious life which find embodiment even in the pages of numerous later stories.

SCOTT

The Lame Boy and the Ballads. In Princes Street in Edinburgh, one of the half-dozen most picturesque cities in the world, the visitor is attracted to a tall Gothic monument which is as much an object of interest as Holyrood Palace or the grim castle perched upon its beetling rock. That

THE SCOTT MONUMENT, EDINBURGH

monument, rising like a cathedral spire amid the traffic of the city, is a memorial to a little lame boy named Walter Scott who was born here, and here went to school and college; who spent most of his life beside the Tweed but a little distance south who now reposes beneath the pavement of St. Mary's aisle in the ruined Abbey of Dryburgh. The lad was delicate and spent much of his time in the country at Sandy Knowe: in rugged weather beside the roaring fire; on pleasant days out on the hillside watching the grazing sheep and the blooming heather and the magic of the sky. And his mind was ever busy and his imagination aflame; for his grandmother and the shepherds and the servants all told him stories of the olden days — of border raids and the clash of factions in Edinburgh town, of the glory of the Highland lakes and mountains, of the fascination of Bonnie Prince Charlie and the beauty of Mary Queen of Scots, of the fairies that danced in hidden glens,

DRYBURGH ABBEY

Founded in the twelfth century, Dryburgh is beautifully situated on a sweeping curve of the Tweed. It was one of many houses of prayer and good works converted into pathetic ruins as a result of the Reformation

and of the mighty warriors who centuries agone crossed the seas to fight in the Crusades. Many such stories the lame boy heard, often sung to simple tunes, and he developed a love of romance and chivalry and delighted in the ballads of an otherwise forgotten past. That was the richest part of the education of Sir Walter Scott (1771–1832).

When he grew older he busied himself collecting many such traditionary songs, and his first literary production was *The Minstrelsy of the Scottish Border* (1802), containing some of the old Scottish Ballads and some original poetry in imitation of them. He learned German, and translated some of the ballads of Goethe, Bürger, and Herder; all his life he was indifferent to the German scientists and philosophers, but responsive to the strains of the German poets. Through much reading and the use of his imagination he reconstructed the Middle Ages and lived in fancy as a minstrel in medieval castles, where knights strode about in flashing armor and time-stained banners rustled on the walls. Thus he became imbued with the spirit of Romanticism and made that spirit the living soul of everything he wrote.

Romances in Verse. Scott was a story-teller both born and made. Even as a boy he delighted his school companions by narrating the tales he had learned at Sandy Knowe, and almost without exception his voluminous writings assumed the story form. During some ten years, beginning when he was thirty-four years old (he had meanwhile studied law and married), Scott wrote a series of tales in verse, among them *The Lay of the Last Minstrel*, *Marmion*, *The Lady of the Lake*, *Rokeby*, and *The Lord of the Isles*. Of these the best are *Marmion*, with its pictures of Tudor days, its description of life in abbeys and castles, and its graphic reproduction of the tragedy of Flodden Field; and *The Lady of the Lake*, its scene set on Ellen's Isle in Loch Katrine, with its fine characterization, its splendid natural descriptions, and its dramatic episodes, such as the hunt, the gathering of the clans, and the wanderings of the disguised king and his hand-to-hand conflict with the chieftain Roderick Dhu. But all Scott's verse romances make delightful reading. The boy or the girl who overlooks them misses one of the greatest pleasures of youth.

Abbotsford. Scott might have continued writing narrative poetry indefinitely but for one thing. Young Lord Byron had begun his long series of metrical tales, and Scott was able to perceive that the younger man had, as he generously conceded, "overshot me with my own bow." Scott's poems had brought him both fame and fortune, but he gracefully decided to abandon the field. He had purchased an estate at Abbotsford, and there he furnished a large mansion and lived the life of a country gentleman, spending his mornings at his desk, his afternoons out of doors, and his evenings in extending hospitality to his numerous friends. Abbotsford is within convenient walking distance of Melrose Abbey, and the visitor finds it in much the same condition as when Scott there lived and wrote.

ABBOTSFORD

His library is intact; and one can see his desk, his pictures, his guns and fishing rods, and his curios and relics drawn from many lands, among them the crucifix which Mary Queen of Scots carried in her hands when she went to her execution.

Scott was a rapid writer and turned out a tremendous quantity of work. At Abbotsford he wrote the last of his verse romances and most of the novels by which he is best known, as well as several productions now ignored. He wrote lives of Swift and Dryden and edited their writings, and brought out a life of Napoleon in nine volumes. He was offered the post of poet laureate in 1813, but refused the honor. Kindly, hearty, industrious; a charming host and a loyal friend; a gentleman with ample means and no desire for empty display,—Scott at Abbotsford enjoyed his books and his dinners, his dogs and his trees, the greetings of farmers on the highroad and the companionship of men of letters before the blazing fire in the hall. That happy existence was destined not to last, but while it lasted Scott knew the acme of human happiness.

As far back as 1802 Scott had entered into partnership in a publishing firm with his old school friend James Ballantyne, and Ballantyne and his brother built up a promising business. Much of Scott's wealth came from this source. Then, in the winter of 1825–1826, a financial crisis arose and the firm failed. Though not bound by the letter of the law to discharge the obligations of the firm, Scott decided that honesty obliged him to repay his creditors, and so he set to work to pay off the debt of 120,000 pounds by the labors of his pen. He cut down his lavish expenditures at Abbotsford, he sold many of his possessions, and he wrote feverishly for many hours a day. He succeeded in his task, but at the cost of his health and his life. Paralysis attacked him, and, a weary, prematurely old man, he visited Italy in the forlorn hope of recovering his health and strength; but it was too late.

The last words Scott ever wrote were written in Rome. Scrawled in the journal of his trip, this entry appears for April 16, 1832: "We slept reasonably, but on the next morning —," and there the journal stopped forever. Scott was hurried back to his beloved Abbotsford, and in September he died. "It was a beautiful day," says his biographer and son-in-law, John Lockhart, "so warm that every window was wide open — and so perfectly still that the sound, of all others most delicious to his ear, the gentle ripple of the Tweed over its pebbles, was distinctly audible as we knelt around the bed, and his eldest son kissed and closed his eyes."

The Waverley Novels. As early as 1805 Scott had begun a prose narrative of life in Scotland in the eighteenth century, but grew disgusted with his work and tossed it aside. Nine years later he took up the discarded manuscript, finished it in three weeks, and published it without disclosing his name as author. The year was 1814 and the book was *Waverley*, the first of the long line of Romantic fiction called the Waverley Novels. For a time Scott concealed his identity as their author; but the secret leaked out, and the reading world discovered that the "Great Unknown" was the master of Abbotsford. In this remarkable collection there are twenty-nine stories, most of them considerably more lengthy than the average novel of our own day, and they present a pageant of life and circumstance almost as varied and colorful as in the plays of Shakespeare. The last of the Waverleys and not the least of them, *Castle Dangerous*, appeared in 1831, the year before the author's death.

SCOTT'S GRAVE, DRYBURGH ABBEY

In a group of stories so diverse and numerous it is inevitable that we should find some better than others, though critics are by no means in accord in attempting to arrange the Waverley Novels in the order of their excellence. For richness of historical setting the palm is justly awarded to *Ivanhoe*, with its reproduction of a medieval tournament, its atmosphere of chivalry and adventure, and its portraiture of gallant King Richard the Lion-hearted and his mean and calculating brother, John Lackland. From the point of view of logical structure (never a conspicuous literary virtue with Scott) the best examples are *The Bride of Lammermoor* and *Quentin Durward*. The former furnished the theme for Gaetano Donizetti's opera *Lucia di Lammermoor*; the latter has contributed to a number of plays and stories dealing with the times and

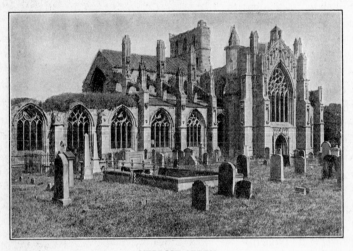

MELROSE ABBEY

The monastic buildings of St. Mary's Abbey, Melrose, were burned by the soldiers of Henry VIII in 1544, and twenty-five years later a mob mutilated most of the artistic stone carvings and statues. Fragments of exquisite stonework, pilfered from the ruins, may still be seen in houses in the neighborhood and in Scott's Abbotsford

personality of King Louis XI of France. Best of the Waverleys in original and convincing characterization, as also in the qualities of humor and pathos, are some of the stories with their scene laid in Scotland: *The Antiquary, Guy Mannering, A Legend of Montrose, Old Mortality*, and *Waverley* itself. Opinions are sharply divided regarding the merits of *St. Ronan's Well*, an attempt by Scott to adopt the Realistic method of Jane Austen's novels of manners.

The subtitle of *Waverley* is *'Tis Sixty Years Since*, and that was the nearest in point of time that Scott came to his own day and generation. Twelve of the novels are set in the eighteenth century, six in the seventeenth, three in the sixteenth, three in the fifteenth, one (*Castle Dangerous*) in the fourteenth, and in the other novels Scott goes back as far as the eleventh century for his background. As for location, the majority of the Waverley Novels unfold their action in Scotland, and Scottish characters appear in several of the stories taking place in other lands; five of them, notably *Ivanhoe* and *Kenilworth*, are English in their locale, two are Continental, and three are Oriental. Several of the Scottish stories present a little difficulty to the American reader because of Scott's use of dialect conversations; but the obstacle is not insurmountable. Scott's dialect is more intelligible than much of the jargon appearing in the alleged comic sections of American newspapers.

Scott proceeded on the assumption that the essential concern of a novelist is to tell a story. He did not try to preach sermons or to reform the world, to engage in psychological study or psychic research, to solve social and moral problems or to exploit filth and depravity in the name of art; he proffers no disquisitions on philosophy, religion, or socialism; his characterization is not "scientific," for which may the Lord make us truly thankful! He gives us real stories, — stories with movement and episode and intrinsic interest, — and he presents real human beings without attempting to analyze their motives, expose their "complexes," and dissect their souls. To read him and enjoy him we need but an open mind, a clean heart, and a willingness to be entertained.

" The Wizard of the North." We have several weighty reasons for acclaiming Sir Walter Scott one of the supreme masters of English fiction. He was able to tell a story, and usually to tell it more than passing well. Generally he is slow in starting, as in *Waverley* and *Ivanhoe*; but once well begun, his novels move steadily if not briskly, revealing a number of "high places" rather than a single climax, and culminate in a conclusion warranted by the preceding action. He had a keen dramatic instinct and knew how to organize his action and his characters in such a way as to secure intensity and suspense. Several of his novels have been successfully converted into stage plays, and nearly all of them are potential dramas. Again, he created a large number of memorable characters. Some enthusiast has gone through the Waverleys and discovered that Scott gave us two thousand eight hundred and thirty-six characters in all, "including thirty-seven horses and thirty-three dogs." Ignoring the live stock and the human beings who do not particularly impress our imagination, we find that Scott has contributed to world literature a generous plenty of enduring characters: men like

SIR WALTER SCOTT

From an original painting in the collection of George A. Plimpton

Leicester, Graham of Claverhouse, Captain Dalgetty, Gurth and Wamba, the Templar, Jonathan Oldbuck, Edie Ochiltree, and Dandy Dinmont; women like Rebecca, Di Vernon, Jeanie Deans, Meg Merrilies, and Amy Robsart. Finally, Scott knew how to write. He had a fine command of words, considerable variety of style, and the gift of arousing a sympathetic mood in his readers. He was a rapid writer, flowing but by no means careless, and many of his paragraphs seem too verbose and lengthy for our syncopated times; but that fault, if fault it be, he shares with most writers of a century ago.

Many of Scott's novels are set in Catholic times, and in his treatment of Catholic themes and persons their author is open to moderate censure. His monks, for instance, are always unworthy monks. They approximate to two types: the thin, scheming, villainous, stiletto-up-the-sleeve sort of monk, like the Black Priest of St. Paul's; and the fat, greasy, indolent, gluttonous, luxury-loving monk, like the diverting but not entirely edifying Friar Tuck. There have been religious gentlemen of both types, — we know that from good Catholics like Dante and Chaucer, — but there have been devout and worthy clerics too, and in common fairness Scott should have given us both sides of the story. He was in this, as in most matters concerned with Catholicism, a victim of an unconscious prejudice fashioned by the early Reformers and fostered by life in a non-Catholic community.

That unconscious prejudice, so manifest not only in the Waverley Novels but throughout the bulk of English Literature produced since the sixteenth century, blinded Scott's eyes to many of the finer and more characteristic traits of Catholic and medieval life.

Scott apprehended the Middle Ages on their spectacular, and more particularly, their military side. . . . The motley mediæval world swarms in his pages, from the king on his throne down to the jester in his cap and bells. But it was the outside of it that he saw; the noise, bustle, color, stirring action that delighted him. Into its spiritualities he did not penetrate far. . . . It was the literature of the knight, not of the monk that appealed to him. . . . He could not draw a saint.[1]

This limitation has been noted more than once. It has been well indicated by the late Richard Holt Hutton: "I do not think there is a single study in all his romances of what may be called a pre-eminently spiritual character."[2] True; but to how many otherwise great writers, in English Literature and other literatures, may the same stricture apply!

[1] H. A. Beers, *History of English Romanticism in the Nineteenth Century*, pp. 39, 40.   [2] *Sir Walter Scott*, p. 126.

Whatever charges may be laid against his work, Scott remains as a man noble and inspiring, as a writer great and enduring. "Scott is still read," wrote Brother Azarias, "and will continue to be read, as long as men will appreciate the spontaneous outpourings of a genius who writes with all the ease and joyousness with which the blackbird sings. There is about his books the freshness of the morning dew."[1] That freshness, that never-staling novelty, is a mark of all great literature. Homer has it; and Horace and Manzoni and Chaucer and Dickens. It is the freshness which comes of abounding life.

THE SCHOOL OF SCOTT

Novels of History and Adventure. If we are to measure the greatness of a writer by the extent of his influence on writers of his own and of following times, then Sir Walter Scott must take high rank in English letters. In his verse romances he opened a path which Byron and others followed, and in his prose tales he established the historical novel as an assured literary species. Abroad he enjoyed great popularity and was recognized as the founder of Romantic prose fiction. Several French novelists, especially Hugo and Dumas, frankly set about emulating his example, and his novels less directly inspired the development of history and adventure fiction in Germany and Italy. At home Scott established the novel as a reputable literary form. Before he began to pour out his Waverleys the novel was an object of suspicion and the novelist was regarded as a person not quite respectable. There were exceptions, of course; but, in general, novel-reading was assumed to be something of a vice. That attitude toward fiction has long since disappeared, and chiefly through the sterling goodness of Scott's personal character, the literary excellence of his novels, and the wholesomeness and sanity

[1] *Books and Reading*, p. 50.

of his moral outlook. We shall now consider the most prominent of the nineteenth-century novelists who followed Scott
in the Romantic tradition.

Readers who respond to simple poetry of the heart, and
students who have investigated certain circumstances in the
career of Cardinal Newman, will alike recall the name of
Charles Kingsley (1819–1875), preacher, social worker, controversialist, poet, university professor, novelist, and all-round
advocate of muscular Christianity. Among his novels are
Alton Locke, Hypatia, Westward Ho, and *Hereward the Wake,*
some of them dealing with existing social conditions, but
most of them narratives of earlier times. He wrote with breezi-
ness and vigor; but much of his work, especially *Hypatia* and
Westward Ho, is defaced with virulent anti-Catholic bigotry.
More capable as a novelist was his younger brother Henry
Kingsley (1830–1876), who, failing to make his fortune in
Australian gold fields, wrote *Geoffrey Hamlyn,* a novel based
on his travel experiences, and achieved fame as a writer.
Ravenshoe, a story in which a Catholic priest figures as the
scheming villain, is accounted his best work.

William Harrison Ainsworth (1805–1882) was a prolific
writer of historical fiction and a best seller of fifty years ago.
His representative works are *Guy Fawkes* and *The Tower of
London.* Ainsworth was conspicuously free from the religious
bigotry which marred the work of many of Scott's followers,
something that cannot be said of Charles Reade (1814–1884),
whose fifteenth-century tale *The Cloister and the Hearth,* in
some respects a powerful book, fairly bristles with anti-
Catholic prejudice. Most of Reade's novels are exposures of
social abuses of his own day : thus *It is Never too Late to Mend*
attacks the English prison system, and *Hard Cash* deals with
the inhuman treatment meted out to inmates of private asy-
lums for the insane.

Boys of all ages have a weakness for *Peter Simple, Mr. Mid-
shipman Easy,* and other sea-swashing tales by Frederick

Marryat (1792–1848), who caught the tradition of novels of adventure from Smollett and Scott and handed it on to Stevenson and Conrad. His books are vivid transcripts of his experiences and observations in the British navy, written with artlessness and abounding spirit. Upward of a hundred novels, besides historical studies, poems, and plays, are credited to George P. R. James (1801–1860), whose literary ambitions were encouraged by Sir Walter Scott. He was in the diplomatic service, holding posts at Boston, at Norfolk, Virginia, and at Venice, where he died. He is known as "Solitary Horseman James" because of his fondness for introducing his novels with the appearance of a man on horseback. Most of his novels are of the historical type, and include *Richelieu, Darnley, The Black Prince, Attila*, and *Ticonderoga*. A thorough Romantic, though most delightfully original, was the Reverend Charles Lutwidge Dodgson, whom the world dimly knew as a professor of mathematics at Oxford, but whom lovers of glorified nonsense — which is really the most uncommon of common sense — esteem and love as that Lewis Carroll (1832–1898) who wrote *Alice in Wonderland* and *Through the Looking-Glass*. His Mad Hatter, his tearful Walrus, his March Hare are as truly characters in English Literature as are Shakespeare's Othello, Addison's Roger de Coverley, and Kipling's Gunga Din.

"Let me have men about me that are fat," said Julius Cæsar anxious to avoid the snares of conspirators and the machinations of traitors; and practically all writers of fiction agree that their bad men must possess, like Cassius, a lean and hungry look. Wilkie Collins (1824–1889) enjoys the distinction of having demonstrated in *The Woman in White* that a villain may have a double chin and a mountainous expanse of waistcoat. His Count Fosco in that sensational story of mystery and adventure is as wicked as he is obese, and he is quite the amplest figure in English fiction. Fosco is a fat man whom nobody can consistently love. Collins, a friend and disciple of

Dickens, had numerous limitations as a novelist, but he possessed the essential art of knowing how to construct a story. He wrote several novels, but his best are *The Woman in White* and *The Moonstone*.

Joseph Henry Shorthouse (1834–1903), a Birmingham business man, when over fifty years old wrote *John Inglesant,* a remarkable historical novel set in the reign of Charles I. It possesses imaginative sweep and unusually profound transcripts of religious experience. *John Inglesant* exerted a strong influence on Monsignor Benson and on other writers of religious and historical fiction. In more recent times the Romantic idea in fiction was preserved and exemplified by H. Rider Haggard (1856–1925), who wrote his first story, *King Solomon's Mines*, in the course of his daily train journeys between Norwich and London. The book was the result of a bet that he could produce a better story than Stevenson's *Treasure Island,* which had just appeared. Haggard was a favorite writer in the 90's, *Allan Quartermain* and *She* running into many editions. His stories are imaginative to the point of extravagance, and embody several of the traits of Byron, Scott, Disraeli, Bulwer-Lytton, and Stevenson. Romantic fiction could hardly go much farther.

The Brontë Sisters. Chateaubriand, dwelling with his mother and his sister and his stern and melancholy father in a bleak Brittany castle, never had a real boyhood. His youthful energies spent themselves in somber musings and heroic dreams, and his eventual literary work became impregnated with the Romantic spirit. Three girls, living with their father, an Irish clergyman, at Haworth in the midst of the desolate Yorkshire moors, never had a girlhood; and, like the French writer, Charlotte, Emily, and Anne Brontë lived in their imaginations and stamped the stories they wrote with the impress of Romantic fancies. Using the pen names of Currer Bell, Ellis Bell, and Acton Bell, they set down the products of their scant knowledge of life and of their weird, distorted, and sometimes truly beautiful imaginings. The front windows of the parsonage opened on the churchyard, the back windows on the dim and purple moor; and that outlook and the dull gray of the village houses are of the soul of the Brontë books.

Anne Brontë (1820–1849) was the gentlest spirit of the three, and in her poems — some of them delicate reproductions of soul experience — and in her novels, *Agnes Grey* and *The Tenant of Wildfell Hall*, she gave in conventional form her girlish versions of love's young dream. Emily Brontë (1818–1848) wrote poems too, and they are original and powerful, though uneven and unbalanced. Her one novel, *Wuthering Heights*, a tale of the Yorkshire moors, is crude and ill-constructed, grim and repulsive, even melodramatic and unreal; but despite its faults it is a triumph of Romantic fiction, the sort of thing which Coleridge did in verse and Edgar Allan Poe in prose. *Wuthering Heights* is a book that is alive, and critics are coming to see in it the greatest novel produced by the Brontë sisters.

Charlotte Brontë (1816–1855) had a slightly more extensive experience of life than her sisters enjoyed, and her literary output is considerably larger in quantity. She was the little mother of the Yorkshire household, and spent two years at a private school in Brussels. Much of her own life and character went into *Jane Eyre*, the novel which brought her recognition and which still holds its place with readers. In this strong and capable novel there is evidence of the influence of Mrs. Radcliffe and the Gothic romance, and Rochester, the bold, bad hero-villain, has a good deal of the "blighted being" pose and of the cruel fascination of the Byronic heroes. The book shows skill in dialogue and the ability to put startling emotions into simple language; some of its descriptive passages, as in the thirteenth chapter, are exceptionally suggestive. But the most distinctive thing about *Jane Eyre* is the heroine — a governess, neither pretty nor accomplished, but a well of powerful feeling. Charlotte Brontë here struck a new note in English fiction: "She chose the ugliest women in the ugliest of the centuries, and revealed within them all the hells and heavens of Dante."[1]

Charlotte Brontë is remembered likewise for *Shirley* and *Villette*, two novels in which she succeeded in transferring into fiction men and women she had met in actual life. In both these books she is largely Realistic in manner, as, indeed, she tried to be; she had a warm admiration for the work of Thackeray and won his praise and recognition. Yet she never entirely lost her Romantic outlook. All her heroines are eminently Romantic combinations of ice and fire, of poise and passion; her conscious Realism is rarely convincing.

Bulwer-Lytton (1803–1873). A veteran cartoonist on the staff of *Vanity Fair* thus describes Edward Bulwer:

> Lord Lytton had a remarkably narrow face with a high forehead; his nose was piercingly aquiline, and seemed to swoop down between his closely-set blue eyes, which changed in expression as his interest waxed and waned.... Carefully curled hair crowned his forehead, and his bushy eyebrows, beard, and mustache gave a curious expression to his face, which was rather pale, except in the evening, when he slightly "touched up," as the dandies of his day were in the habit of doing.[2]

It is a picture not merely of the man but of the writer. His books partake of the characteristics of his face and appearance. They are sensational and artificial, often keen, but narrow in their interpretation of life; and they are dandified to a degree and frequently suggest the rouge pot and the fashionable tailor.

Bulwer-Lytton was a voluminous writer, his published works running to seventy-five volumes. He brought out a collection of poems at the age of fifteen, he wrote historical and political essays, he translated the odes of Horace. But he is best remembered by two plays — *Richelieu* and *The Lady of Lyons* — and by numerous and rapidly written novels. *Richelieu* still

---

[1] G. K. Chesterton, *Varied Types*, p. 5.
[2] Leslie Ward, *Forty Years of "Spy."*

holds the boards, being included in the repertoire of every Shakespearean actor; it is a theatrical but impressive drama, with the great French cardinal as its protagonist. In *Richelieu* occur several phrases which have become familiar sayings, such as "The pen is mightier than the sword" and "In the lexicon of youth . . . there is no such word as *fail*."

Of the novels of Bulwer-Lytton some are philosophical, like *The Caxtons* and *My Novel*; some are novels of manners, like *Pelham* and *Ernest Maltravers*; but most of them are embodiments of the Romantic spirit in tales based on history, on criminal cases, and on mystery. *Eugene Aram* and *Paul Clifford* are melodramatic romances of crime; *Zanoni* and *The Pilgrims of the Rhine* are revivals of the Gothic romance of Mrs. Radcliffe and her followers; and his historical novels, like *Rienzi, The Last of the Barons*, and especially *The Last Days of Pompeii*, are a mixture of guidebook information and mechanical melodrama. Some of his stories have an unwholesome moral tone, and practically all of them illustrate the artistic faults of Romanticism degenerating into sensationalism.

Benjamin Disraeli (1804-1881). In many respects there is a kinship between Bulwer-Lytton and Disraeli as men and as writers. Both were dandies and poseurs, both were active in practical politics, both were men of brilliant though superficial mind, and both wrote in a style characterized by exaggeration of sentiment and excessive devotion to theatrical effect. But while Bulwer-Lytton was mainly a writer and only incidentally a politician and man of affairs, Disraeli was essentially a statesman and parliamentarian who wrote novels as an outlet for an extraordinary intellectual activity.

Disraeli, the Jew who by cleverness, by shrewdness, and by force of character rose to be Prime Minister of England, is a figure that looms large in the history of the Victorian era. To his adroit policy England is indebted for the possession of India and for the development of her imperial ambitions. He began as a radical and ended as a conservative, and all through his political career he was opposed to Gladstone, who began as a conservative and ended as a radical champion of Irish home rule.

When Disraeli was a law student aged twenty-two he took the reading public by storm with his first novel, *Vivian Grey*, a clever social satire abounding with telling thrusts at men in public life; and throughout his subsequent stormy career he continued to turn out stories based upon his experiences and observations. Disraeli is the leading exponent in English Literature of the novel dealing with political life, and his stories are interesting commentaries on the times in which he lived. In them, slightly disguised, appear many of the men who for good or for ill were identified with the events of Queen Victoria's long reign. *Coningsby* was origi-

BENJAMIN DISRAELI

nally planned as a tract to uphold the Tory party: it is less a novel than a disquisition on political affairs. *Sybil* is concerned with industrial conditions in England between the years 1837 and 1842. *Tancred*, Disraeli's masterpiece, is an attempt to reconcile Judaism and Christianity, and was written after a tour through Palestine and North Africa. In *Lothair* Disraeli turned his attention to the Catholic revival in England, and several prominent churchmen, such as Cardinal Manning and Monsignor Capel, were the models for the leading characters. Disraeli's last novel is *Endymion*, a story largely autobiographical and containing portraits of Cardinal Wiseman, of Bismarck, of Napoleon III, and of Dickens as "Mr. Gushy" and Thackeray as "Mr. St. Barbe."

Disraeli the man was fond of perfume, of jewelry, and of eccentric attire; Disraeli the novelist was given to exaggeration, verbal display, and a theatrical outlook on life. Writing mostly of the upper classes and of developments in existing politics, he constructed narratives eminently Romantic in spirit and tinged with melodrama and superficial cleverness. Life itself was pretty much of a play to Disraeli, and he accepted novel-writing as his minor rôle. Nobody reads him for the sake of his plots or because of his characterization, but his books appeal as specimens of clever writing and as commentaries on nineteenth-century politics. *Tancred* and *Lothair* are like Madame Tussaud's Waxworks, wherein we may gaze upon the decorated and highly colored effigies of men who once figured prominently in public life.

Richard Doddridge Blackmore (1825–1900). Adjoining Strawberry Hill on the Thames is the town of Teddington, and here Blackmore spent most of his life raising fruit and vegetables and writing stories. He had tried many things and had failed. His health could not stand the strain of law practice, the public made no response to his efforts at writing poetry, and of his several novels but one attained real popularity; but that one novel is sufficient to make its author famous. *Lorna Doone* was written when Blackmore was forty-six years old, and much to his surprise (for he had grown accustomed to failure) the book slowly but surely attained a wide and constantly increasing vogue. Blackmore went on raising peaches and greens for the London market; but his gallant hero John Ridd and the sweet heroine Lorna made his name a household word on both sides of the Atlantic and brought so many literary pilgrims to his vegetable patch as seriously to interfere with market-gardening, which he regarded as his main occupation in life. Blackmore insisted that *The Maid of Sker*, which nobody reads, was his master-piece; but he is destined to go down in the history of English fiction as a man of one book, and that book is *Lorna Doone*.

Blackmore's story has all the elements that make a tale immortal. It is a love story clean and fresh and fragrant; it is filled with fighting and adventure and moments of breath-taking suspense; it has a whole family of villains, an outlaw band, ranging from the sinister Sir Ensor to the fierce and powerful Carver Doone; it has delightful pictures of home life and captivating accounts of John Ridd's adventures in the London world — the manner of his introduction to Shake-speare's plays is one of the most humorous and unique episodes in all English fiction; it has delineations of rural conditions in Devonshire and Somerset as delicious (as an Exmoor man would say) as the local clotted cream; it has several char-acters that live in memory; and it reproduces in vivid tints a definite period of English history. In short, *Lorna Doone* challenges comparison with Scott's novels in exemplifying the finest and most enduring traits of English Romanticism in fiction.

Borrow and Besant. Two differing phases of Romanticism are illustrated in the novels of George Borrow (1803–1881) and Sir Walter Besant (1836–1901). A twin passion for ram-bling and for languages justified Borrow in describing himself at the age of twenty as

> A lad who twenty tongues can talk,
> And sixty miles a day can walk.

His walks took him all over England and Wales and later, as agent of a Protestant Bible society, into Russia, Portugal, and Spain. The outcome was several books, some of them frankly novels in form but all of them largely fiction in substance. He had an amusing mistrust of Catholicism, and "his methods of controversy were as absurd as they were often unmannerly."[1]

[1] *The Times Literary Supplement* (London), August 28, 1924.

The Romany Rye and *Lavengro* are novels pertaining to gypsy life, a subject on which Borrow posed as an authority; it is now demonstrated that his gypsies are as unreal as his "Papists." As a writer Borrow is unique and highly autobiographical. He has a considerable following of devout "Borrovians." Besant wrote *Ready-Money Mortiboy* and other novels in collaboration with James Rice, and yet others unaided. The best of these, a fine specimen of a Romantic story based on London life, is *All Sorts and Conditions of Men*. Besant made a plea in this book for the introduction of culture and beauty into the lives of London's degraded poor, and the result was the erection of the People's Palace in the Mile End Road.

Robert Louis Stevenson (1850-1894). In the last quarter of the nineteenth century, when Romanticism seemed to have finished its course and when Realistic novels in English and translations of French novels dealing with the squalid and disgusting side of human existence attained unmerited celebrity, a gaunt, sickly Scotsman wrote a boys' story that reopened men's eyes to the glamour of youth, to the stirring of adventure, to the lure of buried treasure, to the fascination of sailing uncharted seas. From one point of view *Treasure Island* was only a glorified dime novel, but from another angle it was the revival of the Romantic Movement in the closing years of the last century. Long John Silver, the sea cook, with his suave speech and his cold-blooded plans, his facile crutch and his masterful ways, forthwith took his rightful place in the gallery of immortal villains.

Robert Louis Stevenson, born in the royal city of Edinburgh, early was forced from the rigorous northern climate in search of health and sunshine. The quest led him to France and Switzerland, to the Adirondacks, across the American continent to San Francisco, and to Samoa in the South Seas, where he died. And all the places he visited furnished him materials and incentives for the writing which he carried on persistently throughout his relatively short life. His childhood in Scotland he commemorated in *A Child's Garden of Verses*; his South Sea experiences he translated into the *Vailima Letters*; his wanderings in France he recorded in *Travels with a Donkey*; his sojourn in Hawaii he signalized with his eloquent letter defending the character of Father Damien; his transcontinental journey he recounted in *Across the Plains*; his stay in California he enshrined in the prose of his *Silverado Squatters* and the verse of his little-known poem "Beside the Gates of Gold."

© Emery Walker Limited

ROBERT LOUIS STEVENSON

From a painting by Sir W. B. Richmond in the National Portrait Gallery, London

As a poet in his *Underwoods* and as an essayist in his *Virginibus Puerisque* and *Familiar Studies of Men and Books*, Stevenson secured distinction; but it is as a novelist that he won his title of "Tusitala," or story-teller. His Romantic tendency first appeared in *New Arabian Nights*, a collection of unusual stories concerned with the imaginary adventures of Prince Florizel in modern life. After *Treasure Island* came *Kidnapped*, a well-wrought historical tale of thrilling adventure and glad emprise, and his tragic and sensational story of dual personality in *The Strange Case of Dr. Jekyll and Mr. Hyde*. His most powerful work is *The Master of Ballantrae*, a grim story of a family feud set in the atmosphere of a bleak Scotch estate, remarkable for its portraiture of two brothers animated by a hatred of each other. Other of his Romantic tales are *The Black Arrow, David Balfour*, and *The Wrecker*.

Literary estimates of Stevenson are often confused with adulation of the man as he was or as he is thought to have been. "There is little doubt," writes Miss Agnes Repplier, "that the somewhat indiscriminate admiration lavished upon Mr. Stevenson himself was due less to his literary than to his personal qualities. People loved him, not because he was an admirable writer, but because he was a cheerful consumptive."[1] But Stevenson was an admirable writer, in the sense that he possessed an artistic mastery of a seemingly artless style together with great inventive power — a very rare combination of excellences. He concerned himself little with anything except the novelist's essential business : to plan a story and to tell it well. Perhaps his chief limitation — a limitation that another vigorous story-writer, Jack London, shared — was his inability to create feminine characters. Women do not figure prominently in his novels. According to Andrew Lang one of the virtues of *Treasure Island* is that "there are no interfering petticoats in the story."[2]

THE REALISTS

Fanny Burney (1752–1840). Side by side with the development of the Gothic romance, so conspicuously sired by Horace Walpole and so solicitously nursed by Mrs. Radcliffe, there arose a school of fiction which avoided sensationalism, declined to impart thrills, and centered its attention on familiar everyday life. The earliest example of this kind of novel is *Evelina*, written by Miss Frances Burney in 1778. In the form of letters the story recounts the experiences of a young lady reared in seclusion and then flung into social life in London. The book met with an unexpected success, was for years a topic of discussion, and won the hearty commendation of Dr. Johnson and Edmund Burke. Because of its emphasis on

[1] "The Gayety of Life," in *Compromises*, p. 30.
[2] "The Works of Mr. Stevenson," in *Essays in Little*, p. 30.

domestic and social life, its attempt to paint men and women as they really were, and its shafts of humorous satire aimed at the innate follies of human beings and the conventionalities of fashionable society, *Evelina* set the example for novels depicting ordinary men and women in ordinary surroundings. Miss Burney wrote other stories, *Cecilia, Camilla,* and *The Wanderer,*

MARIA EDGEWORTH

a life of her father, and a highly entertaining diary, but she never reached the heights of her first story and developed something of a "Johnsonese" quality of style. She married a French refugee from the Revolution and became Madame d'Arblay in 1793.

Maria Edgeworth (1767–1849). Though born in England, Maria Edgeworth spent most of her life in Ireland, keeping the accounts and managing the family on her father's estate in County Longford. She acquired a knowledge of Irish life among both the peasantry and the landed gentry and presented realistic studies of it in *Castle Rackrent, The Absentee, Ormond,* and *Garry Owen.* Several of her earlier works were merely moral preachments in story form, written for the edification of her younger brothers and sisters; but Maria Edgeworth wrote at least two or three of the finest Irish novels in existence. She is free from both the Romantic excesses of writers like Lever and Lover and the offensively extreme Realism of certain Irish novelists of our own day. Scott praised her work highly and found in it a stimulus for his novels dealing with the Scottish peasantry.

John Galt (1779–1839). Scotland, which produced in Scott the prince of Romantic fiction, has given us in John Galt a writer of Realistic novels noted for their accurate observation, their bitter irony, their dry humor, and their effective characterization. Born in Ayrshire, Galt came to London as a young man and engaged in commercial life, traveled on the Continent to report on trade conditions, and engaged in colonization efforts in Canada. Galt in Ontario is named after him, and to him the city of Guelph owes its origin. After three years he returned to England and devoted the rest of his life to writing, but the best of his work had been done many years before. Galt's most representative novels are *The Ayrshire Legatees*, *The Entail*, and *The Last of the Lairds*, all dealing with the details of Scotch village life. He shows a hardheaded, tight-fisted, unimaginative people intent on driving bargains and making money — the antithesis of the Scottish character as depicted by Scott. *Lawrie Todd* is a story based upon his experiences in Canada. Galt is one of the claimants for the honor of having written "The Canadian Boat Song."

Jane Austen (1775–1817). A calm-eyed, clear-headed, singularly observant young lady sitting beside the tea table in an English rectory read specimens of the Gothic romance, was amused and a little irritated at the extravagances of that fictional "reign of terror," and registered her reaction in a novel of her own, *Northanger Abbey*, in which she poked sly fun at the mystery and pomposity of the Radcliffe school. That story, not published until after Jane Austen's death, is a key to the literary ideals of its author and to the spirit of her other and better-known novels.

Few lives have been less eventful and more circumscribed than Jane Austen's. A clergyman's daughter, she dwelt mostly at Steventon in Hampshire and at neighboring Chawton, spent eight years in historic Bath, and died at Winchester in 1817 at the age of forty-two. Never did she travel two hundred miles from home. And home was no exciting place.

Steventon lies in a shallow valley cupped by low-lying hills; it has one of those churches dating from the Middle Ages so frequently found in English towns, and a churchyard with a solitary yew tree drooping above the graves — another Stoke Poges waiting to be immortalized by another Gray. Here, in the elm-shaded parsonage at the end of a row of drab cottages, the rector's daughter played decorous games with her brothers and her sisters, entertained the blacksmith's wife, noted the anomaly of a corpulent widow in a tearful mood, and listened to the baker's grandmother unfold the tale of her backache and her "putrid sore throat." Here, in the "general sitting-room," she observed her father's clerical visitors and listened to their conversation, and revenged herself for that boredom by telling the unvarnished truth about them in her novels. At first she wrote to amuse herself and the family circle, but presently she found a wider audience.

The list of Jane Austen's novels is not extensive. Besides *Northanger Abbey* and *Persuasion* (both published posthumously), it includes *Sense and Sensibility*, *Pride and Prejudice*, *Mansfield Park*, and *Emma*. Some of her unfinished stories have recently been published. Structurally considered, the best of her novels is *Emma*; but the perennial favorite is *Pride and Prejudice*, with its taking portraiture of the keen and sprightly heroine, Elizabeth Bennet, her cynical and disillusioned father, the stiff-jointed Colonel Brandon, and that dawdling and timeserving clerical booby Mr. Collins. Nothing in English Literature compares with the subtle absurdity of that silly gentleman's proposal of marriage.

Some readers there are who do not care for Jane Austen's novels at all. They find them tame, commonplace, uneventful, narrow in outlook, and lacking in incident, and greatly wish, with Edward Fitzgerald of *The Rubáiyát*, that one of Fielding's heroes would dash in on the gentry and swear a round oath or two. But that is only complaining because the novelist did not do what she had no intention of doing. As Scott, who admired her greatly, observed, hers was not the design of writing in the "big bow-wow" style. She was content to follow the advice of Horace and the procedure of Molière and note and reproduce the manners of her age. It is true that she "has little idealism, little romance, tenderness, poetry, or religion"[1]; but she was a keen observer, a consistent if not brilliant writer, an exponent of what Meredith called the comic spirit. If worth is conditioned by the degree in which we succeed in doing what we want to do, then Jane Austen's high reputation is justified.

Thomas Love Peacock (1785-1866). A Realist who was the possessor of considerable gifts but whose novels have never attained popularity was Thomas Love Peacock, the friend and executor of Shelley and one of the most original and eccentric men of letters in the early nineteenth century. He was a real poet, and yet affected to despise poetry and even wrote an essay to show that poetry is a survival of barbarism. His novels are distinguished for a form of Realism that stresses comedy and even approximates to farce, and for a social satire that is withering and yet not unkindly. His characters are not individuals but stock types, such as were used in the miracle plays and moralities of the fifteenth century. His plots are slight and his style undistinguished; yet his stories have distinction because of the author's unusual view of life and the energy with which he conveys his ideas. Representative novels by Peacock are *Headlong Hall*, *Nightmare Abbey*, *Crotchet Castle*, and *Gryll Grange*.

Anthony Trollope (1815-1882). The man who wrote *Barchester Towers* was a less competent artist than Jane Austen and an immeasurably less caustic critic of upper middle-class society than Thackeray; hence from the strictly literary point of view, Trollope does not loom large on the horizon of English fiction. But there is more to be considered than the strictly literary point of view. Literature, among other things, holds the mirror up to social life; and it is a remarkable fact that it is the books of the lesser writers rather than the books of the

[1] William and R. A. Austen-Leigh, *Jane Austen: her Life and Letters*, p. 274.

geniuses which most adequately reflect a definite period or so-cial condition. This seems to be true in all literatures. How little, after all, of the real life of the French people do we find in the writings of the galaxy of brilliant dramatists and poets of the seventeenth century, and how slightly do Bacon and Shakespeare and Jonson reproduce the manners of their age! But if we wish to hear literature performing its function as what Madame de Staël called the voice of society, we must turn to writers who had no soaring imagination, no revealing insight into the human heart, perhaps even no exceptional gifts of construction and of style.

Such is the importance of Anthony Trollope, whose own life would be more promising material for a realistic novel than the plot of any of the fifty tales he wrote. Trollope's *Autobiography*, says Bernard Shaw, is "one of the honestest books ever written, because Trollope had the good sense to omit everything that he knew he could not be honest about." His father was a lawyer who turned farmer and made a failure of it and spent a good portion of his life dodging his creditors; his mother was an energetic woman who, not succeeding in her hare-brained scheme of establishing a store in our Middle West, wrote a book on American life which became a best seller. Anthony was an awkward, untidy schoolboy, a trouble-making and unreliable young man, and for many years a post-office employee. When he approached middle age he settled down in his character and his habits, lived strictly according to a schedule, and devoted several hours of each day to systematic writing. He made a business of grinding out novels, and in his case it was a business that paid.

Trollope is to be seen at his best in the several novels of the Barsetshire series, especially *Barchester Towers*, *The Warden*, and *The Last Chronicle of Barset*. In taking up one of his novels we can be sure that we are not going to be thrilled and surprised, also that we are not going to be disgusted and dis-appointed. For Trollope is one of the most even of writers, never achieving a masterly scene or description, yet never plodding through pages of verbal undergrowth. His characters — not one of which stands out like Mr. Collins or Becky Sharp or Sam Weller or Maggie Tulliver — are faithful portraits of the kind of people who lived in Victorian England, and his descriptions are lifelike reproductions of cathedral towns and sheltered villages. "My mechanical stuff" he called his fiction; and his stories are just that — mechanical, with both the merits and the defects of machine-made products.

George Eliot (1819–1880). Some critics maintain that the greatest woman novelist in English is Mary Ann Evans, who wrote over the pen name of George Eliot; others are prone to point out that her vogue has rapidly declined, that much of her work is today utterly unreadable, that she was a near-poet and a near-philosopher and a near-social-reformer rather than a novelist. The truth, as is usually the case, lies between the two extremes. Some of George Eliot's novels are chunky and misshapen, clogged with what we consider outworn notions of philosophy and disfigured with wrong-headed views of religion and of life: "wearisome, stodgy, careful, lifelike, untransfigured books, the books that are so long and lifelike that when you have finished reading one of them you almost feel that you have spent twenty years with these deplorable people."[1] On the other hand, George Eliot came very near the highest achievements of English fiction in at least three of her stories, and in *Silas Marner* she produced a classic well-nigh flawless. Many passages in her books are splendidly conceived and glowingly written, such as her immortal tribute to *The Imitation of Christ*; and she created a large number of impressive characters — Tom and Maggie Tulliver, Mrs. Poyser, Felix Holt, Tito Melema, Dinah Morris.

---

[1] Arthur Machen, *Dr. Stiggins* (Introduction), p. 10. This censure, it must be remembered, is the reaction of a twentieth-century Romanticist to the work of a nineteenth-century Realist. To be "lifelike" when writing of dull people is, in Machen's view, to be guilty of the unforgivable sin.

George Eliot's life began in Shakespeare's Warwickshire and closed in Carlyle's Chelsea. Eight years of it were spent in the town of Coventry with her father. Educationally she was self-made, learning languages and studying philosophy. She was strongly influenced by German rationalism and abandoned her belief in Christianity. Going to London in 1849, she contributed to learned reviews and became a prominent figure in literary and philosophical circles. As editor of the *Westminster Review* she was associated with Spencer, Huxley, and other apostles of "advanced" thought, and outraged the proprieties by living with George Henry Lewes. A few months before her death she married John Walter Cross, a London banker. Besides her novels, she made

SAVONAROLA

In *Romola* George Eliot gives a sympathetic if somewhat spectacular portrait of the famous Dominican

translations of Strauss and Spinoza and wrote *The Spanish Gypsy* (a drama) and other poems, mostly verse sermons.

George Eliot began her fiction-writing with *Scenes of Clerical Life*, stories distinguished for clever characterization and insight into human nature. Then came what is commonly considered her masterpiece, *Adam Bede*, a story that does not start until it is almost half finished, but then moves briskly and absorbingly to its tragic conclusion. In *The Mill on the Floss*, on the contrary, she did her best work in the first half of the book, the childhood of her heroine being especially well depicted. *Silas Marner* came next and, from the purely literary point of view, is the finest thing she ever did; it contains less of her queer philosophy and more of her artistry than any other of her books. A distinguished historical novel is *Romola*, a study of the downward development of a gifted man in the

THE LEARNED LADY OF FLORENCE

Romola and her father in their scholarly retreat, with the fascinating and unprincipled Tito entering the room

person of Tito, containing colorful if not always accurate pictures of Florence in the days of Savonarola. Less successful, perhaps because more a novel of purpose and of preaching, was *Felix Holt. Middlemarch* is a story that leaves some readers cold but that greatly impresses others. "I said to myself," Canon Barry tells us, "this is how Shakespeare would have written, if he wrote in our century."[1] In *Daniel Deronda* she made a fine defense of the Jews, and that, wrote Maurice Francis Egan, "was

the most Christian thing she ever did."[2] Her literary Realism is indeed sweetened with moral idealism: she is never cynical, never coldly ironical, never consciously superior.

Thomas Hardy (1840–1928). Prominent among the English Realists is Thomas Hardy, a novelist of power and high technical skill, whose story-telling period ended with *Jude the Obscure* in 1895. From that time he devoted himself to poetry,

[1] *Memories and Opinions*, p. 142. [2] *Lectures on Literature*, I, chap. i.

producing, among other things, a dramatic trilogy on Napoleon in nineteen acts and one hundred and thirty scenes. He is a pagan and a pessimist, intent on depicting the folly and the misery of mankind and the cruelty and blind impassiveness of nature. He opened upon a less fearsome note with *Under the Greenwood Tree*; but speedily his work began to vibrate to the tragic aspects of life in *Far from the Madding Crowd*, *The Return of the Native*, and *The Mayor of Casterbridge*. His most popular book, *Tess of the D'Urbervilles*, occasioned no small stir on its appearance in 1891 on account of its frank presentation of the seamy side of life and human character; but it is unjust to assume that the author's motives were unworthy or that his methods were designedly sensational. Hardy never wrote down to his audience, never sought notoriety and self-advertisement. We may consider his view of life inadequate, his criticism of life fundamentally unjust, but we cannot withhold from him the tribute due a conscientious literary artist.

In a little red-brick house veiled in vines and ivy on the outskirts of the town of Dorchester lived the man who has written some of the most beautiful and direful stories in English fiction. They are beautiful because for the most part they are well planned and almost faultlessly written, because their characters become real men and women to the reader, because often their descriptions of nature rise to true poetic levels. And they are direful because almost uniformly they deal with the grim and depressing side of life, because they are animated by the spirit of brooding, hopeless tragedy, because in the dull stretches of that "Wessex" sky there shines no star of energizing faith. Some superficial writers have professed to find paganism a thing of joy; Hardy is too profound and too logical to accept that view. Once we take God and His Providence out of the world, if we think at all we must agree with Hardy that "the cruelty of fate becomes apparent" and that life is empty and meaningless.

For weal or for woe Thomas Hardy is a thoroughly consistent pagan. Like a good many other men of the modern world, he had no belief in religion or in Christ; but unlike most followers of unfaith he carried his philosophy to its practical conclusions. What Frederic Harrison has written of Hardy's poems applies equally well to Hardy's novels:

> Nature is a graveyard; man is a hopeless mystery; love works out tragedies; Death ends all — but it leaves ghastly wraiths on earth. . . . There is no affectation in them [Hardy's lyrics]. They are his own inmost thoughts — his philosophy of life. This monotony of gloom, with all its poetry, is not human, not social, not true. . . . It is not so much — *Mors janua Vitæ*, as it is rather — *Vita janua Mortis*. And the Portal opens to the Netherworld, not to any world above.[1]

Other Realists. Mrs. Elizabeth Cleghorn Gaskell (1810–1865), the biographer of Charlotte Brontë, wrote over forty novels, including *Mary Barton*, an exposure of the English factory system, and *Cranford*, a quietly delightful delineation of English village life. Though a strong Romantic note pervades *Erewhon*, that story of an imaginary people — a nineteenth-century *Gulliver's Travels* — is a caustic satire on modern life. Its author was Samuel Butler (1835–1902), a minister's son who departed radically from the faith of his father and voiced his revolt in *The Way of All Flesh*, a novel characterized by cleverness and a realism sometimes vulgar and offensive. A man of queer views and wide learning, Butler wrote on many subjects. One of his opinions, expressed in *The Authoress of the Odyssey*, was that Homer was a woman. George Gissing (1857–1903) was a gloomy and poverty-tortured man who put some of his experiences of London life into *The New Grub Street*, *The Old Woman*, and other well-written and pessimistic novels. A real artist, Gissing lacked the human touch and a popular appeal. He is best remembered not by his stories, but by a collection of meditations on books and life entitled *The Private Papers of Henry Ryecroft*.

[1] *Novissima Verba*, pp. 29–33. The Latin quotations mean "Death is the gateway to life" and "Life is the gateway to death."

DICKENS AND THACKERAY

A Study in Opposites. The two leading English novelists of
the nineteenth century are often spoken of together, not because they resemble each other but because, both as men and
as writers, they are in marked and often aggressive contrast.

DICKENS'S HOME ON GADSHILL

"Divers birds sing here all day, and the nightingales all night. . . . My room is
up among the branches of the trees, and the birds and the butterflies fly in and
out, and the green branches shoot in at the open windows, and the lights and
shadows of the clouds come and go with the rest of the company"

They both wrote stories; but, how different their stories, in
matter, in manner, and in mood! Thackeray looked out at life
from the window of his aristocratic club in Pall Mall and recalled his mature impressions of journeys abroad; Dickens,
after intimate contact as a journalist with the poorer streets
and winding alleys of London, mused and wrote in the quiet
of his airy study at Gadshill near Rochester. Thackeray was

a thoroughgoing Realist and, some would say, a censorious cynic, crisply exposing the vanity of social ambition and the sordidness of human motives; Dickens was an out-and-out Romanticist and a good deal of a sentimentalist as well, drawing his characters from the masses and enfolding them in a glamorous veil of exaggeration, literally weeping as he wrote his pathetic scenes, and investing his books with the spirit of "uplift" and optimism. Both novelists have their enthusiastic admirers; but it is rare to find a devotee of Thackeray who does not disparage Dickens, or a Dickensian who does not find Thackeray dry and uncongenial.

© Emery Walker Limited

WILLIAM MAKEPEACE THACKERAY

From a painting by S. Laurence in the National Portrait Gallery, London

As Men. The contrast includes their personal lives and their characters. William Makepeace Thackeray (1811–1863), born in Calcutta, India, came of a well-to-do family and enjoyed a Cambridge education, inherited a moderate fortune, and as a young man toyed luxuriously with art and literature. Charles Dickens (1812–1870) was born in Portsmouth, England, knew poverty and want and hard labor, and as a mere child of ten was forced to drudge in a shoe-blacking warehouse for six shillings a week; his education, such as it was, he got in the streets of Chatham and London. Thackeray lived much of his life on the Continent, knowing Paris and Rome; Dickens, though he made brief trips to Italy and to the United States, lived almost entirely in England. Thackeray was careless in money

matters, let his fortune slip through his fingers, and had little
personal ambition; Dickens was a good business man, made
himself wealthy through the labors of his pen, and strove
energetically for fame and success. It was an odd turn of circumstances that once brought Thackeray, then working as an
illustrator, to submit certain drawings to Dickens and to have
them declined with thanks. Dickens gained literary celebrity
while still a young man, but Thackeray was much slower in
developing his powers. Eventually they became friends but
never intimates; they were thoroughly uncongenial in character and were incapable of appreciating the excellence of each
other's writings.

Their Novels. Almost without exception Dickens's stories
are softened and heightened transcripts of life among the lowly
and the poor. The principal of them are *Pickwick Papers*, a
series of loosely constructed episodes characterized by farcical
humor; *Oliver Twist*, a tale of poverty, of crime, of social injustice; *Nicholas Nickleby*, a variegated narrative including
a vigorous attack on educational abuses of the day; *The Old
Curiosity Shop*, a study of life in London remarkable for its
extremes both of humor and of pathos; *Barnaby Rudge*, a historical novel turning on the Gordon Riots; *Martin Chuzzlewit*,
containing bitterly distorted pictures of conditions in the United
States; *Dombey and Son*, *Great Expectations*, and *Our Mutual
Friend*, all three typically Dickensian in their alternation of
scenes grave and gay and their loose but well-constructed plots;
David Copperfield, to some extent an account of Dickens's own
life and experience; *A Tale of Two Cities*, a splendid story of
the French Revolution which competes with *David Copperfield*
for the distinction of being its author's masterpiece; and an
unfinished story, *The Mystery of Edwin Drood*, its scene laid
in "Cloisterham," that is, in Rochester, the city which Dickens
knew well as a boy living in adjoining Chatham and close to
which he lived at Gadshill during the last fourteen years of his
life. Here is a baker's dozen of novels, each an outstanding

book, each representative of Dickens on at least his moderate level of achievement, all still potent and still widely read.

The list of Thackeray's representative novels is not so lengthy. We remember him because of *Vanity Fair, Pendennis, Henry Esmond, The Newcomes,* and *The Virginians*; and it is only through a wish to err on the side of leniency that we include *The Virginians*, a not wholly satisfying sequel to *Henry Esmond*, its scene laid in Colonial America and George Washington one of its characters. But the other four are veritable masterpieces. *Vanity Fair* (the title comes from Bunyan's *Pilgrim's Progress*) is a huge canvas whereon is painted a pageant of human life and human strivings and human hopes, rich in memorable scenes, such as a description of the Battle of Waterloo from the Brussels aspect of it, and filled with shrewd comments and dicta embodying worldly wisdom. Thackeray gave it the subtitle of *A Novel without a Hero*. *Pendennis* is the story of a young man who makes a fool of himself in several eminently human ways and manages to learn a little in the process; there are pictures of university life, of social life,

GATEWAY TO THE HIGH STREET, ROCHESTER

Dickens commemorated Rochester in his first book and in his last. The genial ghosts of Mr. Pickwick and his companions still haunt the stairways of the old Bull Inn, and the streets and the cathedral are shadowed by the mystery of Edwin Drood

of life among London journalists, and many other views of English conditions. In *Henry Esmond* Thackeray goes back to the eighteenth century and creates an exalted example of the historical novel, bringing numerous persons famous and infamous into the story and writing it in a style reminiscent of Joseph Addison's. *The Newcomes* is a little world in itself filled with a diversity of men and women and giving a lifelike picture of upper-class London.

Dickens and Thackeray did a vast amount of other writing, most of which has little value today. Dickens edited *Household Words* and afterwards *All the Year Round*; he revealed himself as a good deal of a bigot in *Pictures from Italy* and *American Notes*, and wrote *A Child's History of England*, a very poor work relieved only by his description of the Battle of Hastings and his delineation of Henry VIII. Thackeray wrote numerous essays and sketches for *Fraser's Magazine*, the *Cornhill Magazine*, and *Punch*. Some of his work was so offensive to the Catholic sensibilities of Richard Doyle that that capable artist resigned from *Punch* in protest. Thackeray's *Yellowplush Papers*, *Roundabout Papers*, and *The Book of Snobs* contain some excellent pieces, but for the most part they are dull and mediocre. His lectures on the *English Humorists of the Eighteenth Century* and the *Four Georges* are animated and vigorous in style, but often unreliable in content. Thus, "Thackeray's lecture on Swift, which is full of animosity and misconception, is a well-written revelation of Thackeray."[1] The best of his minor writings are *Catherine*, a caricature of Bulwer-Lytton's crime stories; *Codlingsby*, a burlesque on Disraeli; and *Rebecca and Rowena*, a humorous continuation of Scott's *Ivanhoe*.

Their Creations. Dickens is unsurpassed in English fiction as a creator of characters that live in the reader's memory and that become more real even than many persons we meet in daily life. Dora is the original brainless beauty of that ilk;

[1] John Macy, "The Critical Game," *Literary Review*, January 7, 1922.

Pecksniff and Uriah Heep are eternal types of hypocrites; Sam Weller and Dick Swiveller and Mark Tapley are familiar examples of likable and eccentric young manhood; Alfred Jingle is the gabbler paramount; Daniel Quilp is the personification of meanness and cruelty; Mr. Squeers is the ideal portrait of the ignorant schoolmaster; Mrs. Nickleby is the representative of

ROCHESTER CASTLE ON THE MEDWAY

This Norman stronghold, its walls twelve feet thick, was built by William de Corbeuil, Archbishop of Canterbury, in the second quarter of the twelfth century. Today it stands in the midst of a park and is occupied by a garrison of pigeons

the pretty, fluttering, ineffectual woman; Bill Sykes is the heavy villain of fiction and of life. The list could be almost indefinitely extended, for few, indeed, are the men, women, and children in Dickens's novels who are not drawn in a distinct and lifelike way.

Not many of Thackeray's characters are so vivid and arresting, but several of his creations are superb portraits. The contrast he establishes in *Vanity Fair* between Amelia Sedley, the good woman without much intelligence, and Becky Sharp, the unscrupulous woman with plenty of brains, is a high artistic achievement; and he has a number of outstanding portraits, such as Colonel Newcome, Major Pendennis, Rawdon Crawley, the Old Pretender, Laura, and Beatrix, which constitute an important contribution to literature. Unlike Dickens, Thackeray does not exaggerate human traits to secure his effects. His men and women are not larger than life; but Dickens emphasizes and expands and overdraws, as in the case of Little Nell and Nancy Sykes and old Chuzzlewit and Mr. Dick. Thackeray's art resembles that of the portrait painter; Dickens's, that of the cartoonist.

Their Style and Spirit. As a writer of English Thackeray far excels Dickens; he has a delicacy, a suggestiveness, a species of aristocratic fastidiousness in the use of words which is utterly alien to the style of his great contemporary. Much of his writing represents what Michelangelo called "the purgation of superfluities": he secures his effects by chiseling away superfluous verbiage. Dickens, on the contrary, gives the impression of writing with a paintbrush in either hand: he adds stroke upon stroke, and achieves his aim by putting the paint on thick. In short, Thackeray demands more of his readers, and Dickens demands less.

© Emery Walker Limited

CHARLES DICKENS

From a painting by Ary Scheffer in the National Portrait Gallery, London

Two opposing charges are made against our two eminent novelists. Dickens is often called mawkish, theatrical, sentimental; Thackeray is condemned as soulless, cold, and cynical. These are simply two ways of saying that Dickens had too little control over his feelings and that Thackeray had too much; that Dickens wrote from his heart, and Thackeray from his head. If modern readers find Dickens's comedy too broad and Dickens's pathos too tearful, it is partly because they are slaves to the present-day fashion of not making much display of emotion in ordinary life. He seems to them unrestrained because they have schooled themselves in emotional repression. And if they complain about Thackeray's alleged cynicism, it is because they have not learned to think, to analyze, to reflect. Nowadays we are too prone to accept a person or an idea that appeals to us as in all respects perfect, to assume that criticism of an individual or an institution is proof of the critic's disloyalty. Thackeray, says Lionel Johnson, was "too clear-sighted to accept delusions, too reverent to despair, too kindly to be always glad."[1] After all, the least we can expect of a Realist is that he be real. And so it is that Andrew Lang can thus address Thackeray:

> Your pathos was never cheap, your laughter never forced; your sigh was never the pulpit trick of the preacher. Your funny people — your Costigans and Fokers — were not mere characters of trick and catch-word, were not empty comic masks. Behind each the human heart was beating; and ever and again we were allowed to see the features of the man.[2]

THE END OF THE CENTURY

Romantic Novelists. The closing years of the nineteenth century found Realism still dominant in English fiction and a new school of Romanticists, mostly inspired by Stevenson, producing popular books. In 1894 appeared *Trilby*, a story of studio life in Paris, by George Du Maurier (1834–1896). The

---

[1] *Post Liminium*, p. 236.　　[2] *Letters to Dead Authors*, p. 3.

author, an artist on *Punch*, won instant celebrity; and the book, with its rich characterization and its creation of the sinister hypnotist Svengali, has taken an assured place among the lesser English novels. Du Maurier's earlier novel, *Peter Ibbetson*, is in some respects a finer work. A second Mrs. Radcliffe of sorts was Marie Corelli (1864-1924), a decidedly lurid lady who wrote on a great many lurid subjects. Her name was originally Minnie Mackay; she was of Scottish and Italian ancestry and was educated in a French convent. She is best known for *Barabbas*, a melodramatic novel of the first Holy Week, *Wormwood*, a ghastly study of the effects of the drug habit; and *Temporal Power*, a frenzied appeal to the popes to leave Rome and become bishops of the world.

Another cosmopolitan was Henry Harland (1861-1905), born in Russia, educated at Harvard, and broadened by much European travel. Some of his earlier stories he published over the pen name of "Sidney Luska." He achieved sudden fame in 1900 with *The Cardinal's Snuffbox*, a delicate and original story of Italian life. He became a Catholic, and in his succeeding stories, like *The Lady Paramount* and *My Friend Prospero*, he achieved religious novels at once artistic and original but frothy and superficial. Sir Anthony Hope Hawkins (1863-   ), an Oxford man and a lawyer, has written numerous stories, including *Quisanté* and *Tristram of Blent*; but his vogue is almost entirely associated with *The Prisoner of Zenda* (1894) and its less effective sequel, *Rupert of Hentzau*. The Zenda romance is a tissue of adventures and complications in the imaginary kingdom of Ruritania. An enduring character was created by Sir Arthur Conan Doyle (1859-   ) in his long series of Sherlock Holmes stories. Of no great literary worth, they are fascinating and ingenious, and Doyle's Baker Street sleuth joins company with the fictional detectives of Poe and Émile Gaboriau.

Maurice Hewlett (1861-1923). A much bigger man and a much finer artist was Maurice Hewlett, whose literary work extended into the early twentieth century. He was devoted to the Middle Ages and the Renaissance and to Italian life and character. His *Little Novels of Italy* (1889) and *The Fool Errant* (1905) are rich and mellow stories, disfigured in places by misconception and unknowing prejudice, but conceived in an eminently Romantic mood and shot through with the fine fruitage of reflection and study. Hewlett's power and charm were intimated on the appearance of *The Forest Lovers* in 1898 and were widely recognized two years later when his historical novel, *The Life and Death of Richard Yea-and-Nay*, glowingly commemorated the deeds and the character of King Richard the Lion-hearted. In *Open Country: a Comedy with a Sting* Hewlett attacked the Realistic attitude in art and in life and made an artistic plea for the application of medieval ideas in modern society. Some of his characterization is accomplished in single strokes; for instance, "Mother gets herself into a hole and then looks like an early Christian." Some of Hewlett's notions are impracticable and in the narrow sense even immoral, and he missed a full appreciation of the Catholic spirit in medieval life; but he had a definite and (in essentials) a sane philosophy of living, a more than superficial knowledge of the past, and a high and original literary art. He was the last of the great Romanticists.

Realistic Novelists. A legitimate successor of George Eliot — not in life but in fiction — was Mrs. Humphry Ward (1851–1920), a niece of Matthew Arnold and the daughter of that Thomas Arnold who probably holds the record for changes in religious convictions. Like her father she was absorbed in religious problems, and her novels are almost entirely concerned with the Realistic treatment of the psychology of belief. Her *Robert Elsmere* created a sensation when it appeared in 1888; it is the drab and stodgy story of an Anglican minister who loses his faith in historic Christianity. Among her other books are *Helbeck of Bannisdale*, *Lady Rose's Daughter*, and *The Marriage of William Ashe*. She had more than George Eliot's fondness for preaching and less than George Eliot's literary skill. Mrs. Ward's opposite in almost every respect was Mrs. Craigie, who used the pseudonym of John Oliver Hobbes (1867–1906), and whose *School for Saints* and *Robert Orange* present religious problems with penetrating wit, abounding brilliancy, and rare technical skill. She was a convert to Catholicism, and her best work — and her best is very good indeed — was the outcome of her religious convictions and experiences.

George Meredith (1828–1909). A genuine poet, a novelist of exceptional ability, a philosopher of sorts, and an eminently likable man, George Meredith wrote in a style that, as has so often been said, was like chaos illuminated by flashes of lightning. He had an abundance of ideas, but when it came to expressing them he simply could not make his words behave. His style — the style of a genius given every gift save the gift of expression — is unlike anything in all literature. It sometimes recalls Lyly and sometimes Burton, sometimes Thackeray and sometimes Carlyle; but there is only one adjective to describe it — Meredithan. It is a style of clogging cleverness and dazzling obscurity. He writes, as W. E. Henley said, "with the pen of a great artist in his left hand and the razor of a spiritual suicide in his right." To Meredith may be applied the dictum of a student who heard a French writer lecturing at Oxford: "I understood every word, but not a single sentence." When reading Meredith we get the impression that we are trying to smell a rose sealed up in a glass jar or to eat a dish of ice cream through a plate-glass window.

He thinks in flashes, and writes in shorthand. He has an intellectual passion for words, but he has never been able to accustom his mind to the slowness of their service; he tosses them about the page in his anger, tearing them open and gutting them with a savage pleasure. . . . His books are like picture galleries, in which every inch of wall is covered, and picture screams at picture across its narrow division of frame. Almost every picture is good, but each suffers from its context.[1]

[1] Arthur Symons, *Figures of Several Centuries*, pp. 141–142.

His novels are sprinkled with what are most literally wild and whirling words. One character "flings a lightning" at another. Adrian "opens his mouth to shake out a coil of laughter." We read with amazement of "feeling a rotifer astir in the curative compartment of a homeopathic glob-ule" and of "a fantastical planguncula enlivened by the wanton tempers of a nursery chit." A girl's heart is "her inward flutterer." We are "amazed by the flowering up of that hard rough jaw from the tender blooming promise of a petticoat." We are not less dumfounded at the plight of one of his ladies: "The word 'Impostor' had smacked her on both cheeks from her own mouth." We are horrified by another who "called on bell-motion of the head to toll forth the utter night-cap negative." And so on, and on.

© Emery Walker Limited

GEORGE MEREDITH

From a painting by G. F. Watts in the National Portrait Gallery, London

"There is genius," wrote Henley, "but there is not felicity."

Because of such peculiarities of style and because his stories deal in a mature and sophisticated way with psychological problems of adult life, young readers will hardly find Meredith's novels congenial reading; for them he is less an author to enjoy now than an author to look forward to enjoying. His theory of fiction, the philosophy of his craft, is contained in a searching essay on *Comedy and the Uses of the Comic Spirit*, originally a lecture delivered in London in 1877. His conception of comedy is not the popular conception; to Meredith the comic spirit is a view of life that induces genial thought rather than smiles and laughter, and the comic writer is one who in a thoroughly Realistic mood "marches over sentimentalism with a birch rod" and probes to the source of human motives and character. Such is the theory that animates all Meredith's novels and many of his poems.

The first of Meredith's representative books was *The Shaving of Shagpat*, a collection of stories with an Oriental setting and characterized by fantastic humor. He really struck his stride in *The Ordeal of Richard Feverel*, partly a love story, partly a problem novel, partly a sheaf of philosophic comments on life. *Beauchamp's Career* concerns itself with love and politics; it is one of the great political novels in English. *The Egoist*, generally conceded to be Meredith's best novel, is a subtle study of a self-centered young man, Sir Willoughby Patterne; it shows us the author at his most extreme devotion to the exploitation of the comic spirit. *Diana of the Crossways*, presumably a transcript from real life, is a keen analysis of the character development of a brilliant woman of the world.

Meredith's life was far less complicated than Meredith's style. He was half Welsh and half Irish in racial descent and was born in Hampshire. He studied in Germany and lived for a time in Italy. Having married the daughter of Thomas Love Peacock, he settled down at Box Hill, a beautiful estate in Surrey, and there he led a quiet, scholarly life. Until the infirmities of old age came upon him he was fond of taking long walks in the country in all sorts of weather and of observing nature with a poet's eye. His home was often a gathering place for literary men, with many of whom Meredith was on intimate terms. In his youth unperturbed by hostile criticism and in his maturity unspoiled by praise, Meredith, with his abundant white hair and his trim, pointed beard, was the literary patriarch of the end of the Victorian Age.

CHAPTER XIV

VICTORIAN POETRY

A PERIOD OF ACHIEVEMENT

The custom of naming a period in art or literature or architecture after the sovereign then reigning comes from pre-Reformation days, when kings and popes were often patrons of the arts, extending lavish hospitality to poets and painters, supplying them with themes and materials, and organizing clubs and academies for the discussion of art problems. Hence the strict justice of our speaking of the Augustan Age in Roman Literature, the Age of Leo X in painting, the Age of Louis XIV in the history of the drama. But when we speak of the Elizabethan Age, the Queen Anne period, or the Georgian era in English Literature we do so merely as a convenient time reference and without intending to imply that the sovereigns caused or influenced the literature produced. Queen Elizabeth's ability was devoted to statecraft and to the Tudor policy of nationalism rather than to sonnet-making and the development of criticism and the encouragement of the drama; Queen Anne had as little effect on the writers of her day as a tombstone has on the song birds in a cemetery, and the German Georges had enough to do to speak the English language without bothering about English Literature.

Hence, when we speak of the Victorian Age we are not paying a tribute to Queen Victoria as a patron of the arts but are merely adopting a conventional method of indicating a period in the History of English Literature — a period extending from 1837 or thereabouts to the end of the nineteenth century. And it was a very great period in English Literature — just how great we are perhaps too near to estimate. The people living in one era are prone to belittle the spirit and the achievements of the era immediately preceding, somewhat as college freshmen, while respecting juniors and reverencing seniors, regard sophomores with suspicion and perhaps contempt. That is why in the England and the America of today the adjective Victorian is in popular vogue as an epithet connoting smugness, dullness, stupidity, even hypocrisy; it is a crushing blow to a modern "young intellectual" to dismiss his ideas as mid-Victorian. There was plenty of dullness and hypocrisy in the nineteenth century even as there is in the twentieth, but, considered in all its aspects, the Victorian Age commands respect. In history it was a period of imperial expansion, England annexing the vast territory of India and other regions. In society it was a period of notable reforms in industrial conditions and of unparalleled advance in popular education. In religion it was marked by a series of events typified by the Oxford Movement. In science it was a period of active theorizing and much practical progress. It at least held its own in the realm of art, and in literature it shone with more brilliance than any other period save possibly the Elizabethan Age. Professor Grandgent is not extreme when he expresses the belief that future generations will regard the Victorian Age "as rather a hard one to match in the annals of letters and science"; that it "bids fair to take rank with the ages of Pericles, Augustus, Elizabeth, and Louis XIV." [1]

We have already seen that in the age of Victoria fiction waxed strong and flourished; that, with the exception of Defoe, Fielding, and Scott, all the great English novelists were Victorians. It was in truth the golden age of the English novel. And yet the novel was but one literary form that flourished in the nineteenth century. That period gave us nearly all our prominent essayists; and though it produced neither a Shakespeare nor a Milton, a Chaucer nor a Dryden,

[1] *Old and New*, pp. 6, 7.

it brought forth a veritable host of poets who command a respectful hearing and several singers who have achieved a place in the literature of Europe and whose work and influence are important and enduring.

MANY VOICES

Barham and Hood. While the Victorian novelists often emphasized humor in plot and characterization, and the Victorian

THOMAS HOOD

From an original painting in the collection of George A. Plimpton

essayists were not alien to the comic spirit, most of the Victorian poets were serious souls who seldom smiled and never laughed. But there were exceptions. Though Richard Harris Barham (1788–1845) was a canon of St. Paul's Cathedral and a busy man of letters, he found time for work in lighter vein, and the result was his clever and lively *Ingoldsby Legends*, a series of poems in galloping jingles. Unfortunately Barham's strong anti-Catholic animus entered largely into his work, and the modern reader soon wearies of "the gluttonous, bibulous, amorous crew of burlesque monks, and churchmen, and saints, and devils, and frail fair ladies."[1] Barham was adroit in his use of the pun; but the past master of the punster's art was Thomas Hood (1799–1845), whose life was an incessant

[1] Walter Whyte, *The Poets and Poetry of the Century*, p. 199.

struggle with poverty and sickness but whose vast output was mostly humorous. Hood literally wrote jokes and nonsense verses to keep himself alive. It was Hood who gave us the pathetic account of the lover's death in "Faithless Sally Brown":

> His death, which happened in his berth,
>   At forty-odd befell;
> They went and told the sexton, and
>   The sexton tolled the bell.

Hood wrote a number of beautiful poems, including an "Ode to Autumn"; but he is most closely identified with a piece of popular pathos, "The Song of the Shirt," which was long a favorite in England and was translated into several European languages.

William Edmondstoune Aytoun (1813-1865). A Scot of the Scots, who rarely departed from his native land in body and never in mind, Aytoun wrote a series of stirring ballads in the spirit of Sir Walter and in the technique of Macaulay's *Lays of Ancient Rome*. Aytoun's *Lays of the Scottish Cavaliers* deserved their popularity: they embodied much of the fire of earlier singers in Scotland and much of the strength and directness of the Scottish chroniclers whom Aytoun quotes; and their appeal is universal, for readers who are not Scottish in blood or in sentiment can respond to the martial ring of the ballad of Montrose and the sad but glorious tale of Flodden Field. Aytoun deserves further remembrance for *Firmilian*, one of the best dramatic travesties in the language. There existed a group of self-important poets — one of them was Sydney Dobell — who called themselves the Spasmodists; Aytoun solemnly exaggerated their methods, and "Spasmodism" in spasms passed away.

Leigh Hunt (1784-1859). An editor, a critic, a political agitator, a helpful friend to some writers and a dependent friend of others, Leigh Hunt is now remembered — but remembered widely and well — because of two short poems, "Abou Ben

Adhem" and "Jenny Kissed Me." One of them has survived the concentrated attacks of a century of youthful elocutionists, and its last line is quoted as often as the most familiar epigrams of Pope. Here is the other poem:

> Jenny kissed me when we met,
>   Jumping from the chair she sat in.
> Time, you thief, who love to get
>   Sweets into your list, put that in.
> Say I'm weary, say I'm sad,
>   Say that health and wealth have missed me;
> Say I'm growing old, but add,
>   Jenny kissed me!

The Jenny of the poem was Jane Welsh Carlyle, wife of Thomas Carlyle and a neighbor of Hunt in Chelsea; and somebody has been unkind enough to suggest that she was moved to that sudden display of affection because the poet brought back some household utensils which Mrs. Hunt had borrowed. For there was a Mrs. Hunt and a houseful of little Hunts, and they were always borrowing things.

The Procters. It often happens that the minor poets of an epoch more adequately than the greater singers record the sentiments and reflect the fashions of the times. Much of mid-Victorianism is suggested in the poems of Bryan Waller Procter (1787–1874), who wrote over the name "Barry Cornwall," and of his daughter, Adelaide Anne Procter (1825–1864). Both exuded a sugary sentimentalism that today would be in decidedly bad form but was then expected and esteemed. But both were true poets though not great ones, and the father found in his family spirit and the daughter in her devotion to the Catholic faith (she entered the Church in 1850) inspiration for poems smooth-flowing and superficial. Adelaide Procter's verses — many of them contributed originally to Dickens's magazine, *Household Words* — are contained in *Legends and Lyrics* and *A Book of Verse*. She was especially facile as a song-writer, supplying words for nearly fifty pieces of popular music.

The poems of Barry Cornwall most in harmony with the tastes of modern readers are "The Sea" and "The Blood Horse," the latter a finely wrought description of an Arabian steed.

Mrs. Hemans (1793-1835). Popular in her generation because her lavish sentimentalism and limited range of thought eminently suited many readers, Felicia Dorothea Hemans has today become an embodiment of all in the Victorian Age which the twentieth century professes to despise. The unenviable prominence hardly does her justice. Admittedly Mrs. Hemans was a third-class poet, endowed more copiously with assiduity than with taste, with good intentions rather than with superior talents. Admittedly she wrote down to her large and undiscriminating audience; but popular poets in every age do this, the only difference being that the ignorant masses in one generation do not relish the mental pabulum which satisfied their predecessors. Mrs. Hemans at least led her admirers to perceive that England was not the entire world, for she drew most of her inspiration, such as it was, from the stream of the European Tradition. She made numerous translations from the German and from the Italian and wrote original verses on themes suggested by

> The isles of Greece, the hills of Spain,
> The purple heavens of Rome.

Two Oxford Poets. John Keble (1792-1866), a student of Balliol College, and Arthur Hugh Clough (1819-1861), a fellow of Oriel, were both identified with the beginnings of the Oxford Movement but reacted to it in opposing ways. Keble declined to follow Newman into the Catholic Church and remained in the Anglican communion, dying as vicar of Hursley after a life of zeal and study. Clough turned entirely from belief in Christianity, taught for a while at Harvard University, and died in Florence. Though less appealing than the poems of George Herbert, Keble's lyrical verses in *The Christian Year* and *Lyra Innocentium* are characterized by the spirit of devotion, considerable imaginative power, and grace of form. Clough had finer and richer poetic gifts, but his religious uncertainties affected his work and paralyzed his talents. "Say not the Struggle Naught Availeth" and "It Fortifies my Soul to Know" reveal a fine command of verse technique and express the dauntless spirit of a disillusioned mind. Reading Clough, we feel that we are watching the sun faintly shining through a mass of serried, storm-racked clouds.

Walter Savage Landor (1775–1864).

> I strove with none, for none was worth my strife;
> Nature I loved, and next to Nature, Art;
> I warmed both hands before the fire of life,
> It sinks, and I am ready to depart.

Such was the epitaph Landor wrote on himself when he had attained the age of seventy-five, and save for the first line it is characteristically true. He was always quarreling with somebody or something, a veritable Victorian war horse; but his Romantic devotion to nature and his Classical devotion to art were the two leading traits of his life and his writings. Landor's tragedy lies in the fact that the two tendencies were never wholly fused.

His life was mostly a long record of alarms and excursions. Born at Warwick, he was a trouble maker at Oxford and was suspended in 1794; he never came back. He quarreled with his neighbors when he settled in Wales; he quarreled with his wife in Italy; he quarreled indiscriminately at Bath and was obliged to leave that city as the result of a suit brought against him for libel. Perhaps his happiest years were spent in his villa at Fiesole near Florence, where he enjoyed the friendship of the Brownings and accelerated the tempo of Tuscany by throwing his cook out of the window. Despite his ungoverned temper Landor was a man of brains and character. He had high ideals of the literary art, and his scholarship, though scrappy, was vast and vital. But he never quite succeeded in achieving the greatness of performance which his friends looked for from him and which he expected of himself.

Landor's best poetry is found in brief occasional pieces like "Rose Aylmer," the little poem he wrote in memory of the girl he had loved in his youth. His more ambitious poems are *Gebir*, a romance in blank verse, and the *Hellenics*. In dramatic form — though his temperament was too individualistic for him to achieve success in the drama — he wrote *Count Julian, Fra Rupert*, and *The Siege of Ancona*; and in colorful poetic prose he composed six volumes of *Imaginary Conversations* between historic personages such as Petrarca and Boccaccio, Diogenes and Plato, Virgil and Horace, Dante and Beatrice, Henry VIII and Anne Boleyn, Steele and Addison. All his characters speak in the same style. "His *Imaginary Conversations* are not in the least dramatic. How many people have been excited by the names, and disappointed by the talk! . . . His work is as immortal as a graveyard."[1] The defect of his work, according to his most sympathetic critic, is its lack of spiritual confidence.[2] His fame also suffers from the fact that his anti-Catholic bigotry found frequent and most inartistic outlet.

John Clare (1793-1864). For a long time ignored, the poetry of John Clare, a peasant poet of Northamptonshire, has recently come into its own. Present-day students find in it a beauty, an originality, and an intensity of feeling which give it high rank, and they find too a keenness of vision which Wordsworth sought always but rarely found. Wordsworth might well have envied the man who could write of the primrose,

> With its little brimming eye
> And its yellow rims so pale
> And its crimp and curdled leaf,
> Who can pass its beauties by?

[1] Sir Walter Raleigh, *On Writing and Writers*, pp. 139–144.
[2] Lilian Whiting, *The Florence of Landor*, p. 313.

That "crimp and curdled leaf" is distinctive; and so is the unifying image in

> Yes, night is happy night,
>   The sky is full of stars,
>   Like worlds in peace they lie
> Enjoying one delight.

Clare's limitation was impatience of any poetic writing that leads to intellectual effort, that gets away from nature as nature; this is where he and Wordsworth radically differed. Perhaps Wordsworth meditated too much. Clare meditated too little — and died in a lunatic asylum. His collected poems appeared under the titles of *Poems descriptive of Rural Life and Scenery*, *The Village Minstrel and Other Poems*, *Village Stories*, and *The Rural Muse*. Edmund Blunden has gathered some recently found poems by Clare in *Madrigals and Chronicles* (1924). His own account of himself is one of the finest autobiographic poems in English:

> I lost the love of Heaven above,
>   I spurned the lust of Earth below,
> I felt the sweets of fancied love
>   And Hell itself my only foe.
>
> I lost Earth's joys, but felt the glow
>   Of Heaven's flame abound in me
> Till loveliness and I did grow
>   The bard of Immortality.
>
> I loved, but woman fell away;
>   I hid me from her faded flame.
> I snatched the sun's eternal ray
>   And wrote till Earth was but a name.
>
> In every language upon earth,
>   On every shore, o'er every sea,
> I gave my name immortal birth
>   And kept my spirit with the free.

Mrs. Browning (1806–1861). Elizabeth Barrett Browning was a true poet and an eminently womanly woman, a little spoiled and spotted by the less wholesome traits of Victorianism. For years she had been a sick-a-bed lady, a picturesque and self-conscious invalid, bullied by her father and enslaved by petty conventionalities. But she eloped with Robert Browning, six years her junior, in 1846, and thereafter enjoyed improved health and complete happiness. They lived mostly in Italy, a land they both loved, and Italian scenes and Italian national aspirations are reflected in many of her poems. Her numerous letters reveal her as gentle, but no weakling, as a loving yet shrewd and tactful wife, as a wide reader and something of a thinker as well.

© Emery Walker Limited

MRS. BROWNING

From a drawing by F. Talfourd in the
National Portrait Gallery, London

The best poems of Mrs. Browning were written after her marriage. They include *Casa Guidi Windows* and *Aurora Leigh*. Casa Guidi was the name of the house the Brownings occupied in Florence; the opening words of the poem are now engraved in marble on the façade of the dwelling:

> I heard last night a little child go singing
> 'Neath Casa Guidi windows, by the church,
> "*O bella libertà, O bella!*"

Her best-known work is *Sonnets from the Portuguese* — not translations (though Mrs. Browning did some serviceable translations from the Greek), but love poems written to her husband, who used to call her "the little Portuguese" because of her enthusiasm for the poet Camoens. Several of these sonnets are among the masterpieces of love poetry in English.

Edward Fitzgerald (1809–1883). It is possible to learn something about literature while doing our Christmas shopping early. Gift books are piled high on shelves and on counters, — books often exquisitely bound and artistically illustrated. They are books which, in the language of the trade, are "sure-fire sellers"; books which possess prestige with purchasers and recipients of presents. Stevenson's *Child's Garden of Verses* is there, and R. W. Service's narrative poems of the Klondike, and Emerson's *Essays*; and there too is *The Rubáiyát of Omar Khayyám*, "rendered into English verse" by Edward Fitzgerald.

Yet that book might not be known at all were it not for still another poet, Dante Gabriel Rossetti. Fitzgerald had produced his version of the Persian poet, submitted it to the *Fortnightly Review*, and had it returned with thanks. He published it at his own expense; but the book had no sale, so the temperamental author presented the entire edition to a bookseller. Still nobody bought *The Rubáiyát*. Then one day Rossetti was strolling in Piccadilly and paused at a bookstall to browse among some volumes marked down to a penny apiece. Among them was Fitzgerald's work. Rossetti read a little standing there in the street, bought the volume and carried it home, read it and reread it, and waxed enthusiastic. He told his friends about it, and soon the entire supply was exhausted. Fitzgerald brought out five more editions, and ever since the book has been a favorite and has assumed the proportions of an English classic.

The word *rubáiyát* means "stanzas" or "quatrains," and Fitzgerald's poem is a free translation of about one eighth of the stanzas of the Persian poet Omar Khayyám, who lived in the eleventh and twelfth centuries. Strictly speaking, it is not a translation at all, but what R. G. Moulton has called a "mediating interpretation,"[1] a theme from Omar with variations by Fitzgerald. The Persian poet's quatrains are made up of three widely different views of life: a thinker, a man of the world,

LITTLE GRANGE, WOODBRIDGE
Where Fitzgerald lived from 1874 to 1883

and a saint hold discourse and explain their several philosophies, and in Omar's work the saint seems to have the best of the argument. In the hundred and one quatrains of the standard edition of Fitzgerald's Omar we can detect the voice of the thinker and especially the utterances of the sensual man of the world; but the saint is not represented at all. Fitzgerald's *Rubáiyát* gives us a blending of the thinker in a skeptical mood and of the sensualist praising wine and extolling its delights.

In substance, therefore, Fitzgerald's *Rubáiyát* does not amount to much; writers who profess admiration of its philosophy might just as fittingly grow ecstatic over the drinking

[1] See his *World Literature*, p. 311.

song in *The Prince of Pilsen*. The secret of its charm is the beauty of its language and the freshness and richness of its imagery. It is not great poetry, because it gives us no profoundly beautiful interpretation of life; but it is real poetry, because it appeals like music to the ear, because it fills the imagination with gorgeous pictures, and because it captivates the fancy with such lines as these:

> I sometimes think that never blows so red
> The Rose as where some buried Cæsar bled;
> That every Hyacinth the Garden wears
> Dropt in her Lap from some once lovely Head.

Edward Fitzgerald was a brilliant man with a passion for reading and a disinclination to write. Most of his life he spent in Suffolk with his garden and his books; but his retreat was often invaded by the literary men of the day, and under their stimulus Fitzgerald "translated" a little of Æschylus and six of Calderón's dramas. A friend induced him to study Persian; and so one day in May, 1857, Fitzgerald read Omar in a Bedfordshire pasture "covered with butterflies and brushed by a delicious breeze." *The Rubáiyát* so impressed him that he was moved to render some of it into English. There are several more accurate and scholarly translations of the Persian poet, but none can compare with his in poetic charm.

James Thomson (" B. V.") (1834-1882). The pen name of Bysshe Vanolis was used by James Thomson as a tribute to two authors whom he held in high regard, Shelley and Novalis. He was a man in some respects like Edgar Allan Poe, a man who had suffered much, who periodically drank to excess, whose view of life was somber in the extreme, but a man, nevertheless, of unusual ability and a poet gifted with imagination and technical skill. He is remembered for one long poem, *The City of Dreadful Night*, published in 1874, "the most hopelessly sad poem in literature."[1]

---

[1] William Sharp, *Sonnets of this Century*, p. 325, note.

Gerard Manley Hopkins (1844–1889). A student at Balliol College, Oxford, becomes a Catholic; he finds himself called to the priesthood and enters the Society of Jesus; he lives the life of a saint and dies in Dublin. That is the summation of the externals of the life of Gerard Manley Hopkins, undeniably a poet deeply appreciated by a chosen few but destined never to enjoy a wide popularity. On entering the Jesuit novitiate he made a burnt offering of the poems he had written in his youth; such of his poems that we possess were written at intervals during his priestly career and are characterized by a strong devotional tone. His gifts were akin to those of Browning and Meredith, and he is open to the same charge of excessive obscurity due to compact thinking and the omission of necessary words. It requires some study, for instance, to get at the meaning of such a line as

> Squander the hell-rook ranks sally to molest him.

Aubrey de Vere (1814–1902). The Irish Wordsworth is the title that might well be bestowed upon Aubrey de Vere. In a very real and intimate sense he was Wordsworth's disciple, wholly devoted to him as man and as poet. After Wordsworth's death De Vere made an annual pilgrimage to his master's grave at Grasmere. His poetry is curiously like to Wordsworth's in several important respects; it is utterly devoid of gaiety and humor; it is filled with passages where the poetry is strangled by excessive reflection; it is charged with the belief that the poet is a "dedicated spirit," the possessor of a lofty vocation; and it is in places splendid in its pictures of nature. But the disciple was a lesser poet than his master. His tone is more even, his structure more balanced; and if De Vere never wrote ridiculously, as Wordsworth sometimes did, neither did he ever attain to the grandeur of those "purple patches" which show Wordsworth at his best.

To a great extent Aubrey de Vere was a solitary figure. His conversion to Catholicism in 1851 alienated him from most of the friends of his youth; those were days when to enter the Catholic Church was tantamount to social suicide. And he was almost equally apart from his Irish coreligionists; for though he was a true patriot and looked forward ardently to the freeing of Ireland from foreign rule, he was unalterably opposed to the methods employed by Irish nationalists. These circumstances undoubtedly affected his prestige as a poet. Indeed, it is only within our own times that De Vere's work has been accorded anything like the recognition it deserves. It remained for a twentieth-century poet, Sir William Watson, to pay noble tribute to the earlier bard:

> Poet, whose grave and strenuous lyre is still
> For Truth and Duty strung; whose art eschews
> The lighter graces of the softer muse,
> Disdainful of mere craftsman's idle skill;
> Yours is a soul from visionary hill
> Watching and hearkening for ethereal news,
> Looking beyond life's storms and death's cold dews
> To habitations of the eternal will.
>
> Not mine your mystic creed; not mine, in prayer
> And worship, at the ensanguined Cross to kneel;
> But when I mark your faith how pure and fair,
> How based on love, on passion for man's weal,
> My mind, half envying what it cannot share,
> Reveres the reverence which it cannot feel.

The octet of that ably constructed sonnet is an admirable summary of the traits of De Vere's poetry. His finest work is contained in *May Carols*, a long series of lyrics celebrating Mary Queen of May. Their theme is the mystery of the Incarnation; many of them are exquisite utterances of religious emotion and embodiments of religious thought. More popular and worthy of their vogue are his *Legends of St. Patrick*, garnerings from fifteen early lives of Ireland's patron saint. He sang too of ancient Greece, and he wrote two poetic plays, *Alexander the Great* and *St. Thomas of Canterbury* — interesting and readable closet dramas, but too permeated with Wordsworthian coolness and reserve to be effective on the stage.

Coventry Patmore (1823–1896). Human nature is so constituted that we find it hard to praise one thing without at least implying dispraise of something else. So often and so rapturously have poets — especially Catholic poets — sung the praises of virginity, and so often has literature generally enshrined the love that precedes marriage, that a reader might not unnaturally get the impression that the divinely instituted Sacrament of Matrimony has been silently disparaged. The great books of the world are filled with endless commentaries on the theme of love; but almost always they celebrate impersonal love or sinful love, frustrated love or anticipatory love — rarely nuptial love. The great lovers of literature have never been married — at least never to each other. Romeo and Juliet, Paolo and Francesca, Dante and Beatrice, represent three widely varied species of human affection, but not the affection existing between husband and wife.

COVENTRY PATMORE

The outstanding distinction of Coventry Patmore is suggested in the title bestowed upon him by his friend and biographer, Sir Edmund Gosse, "The Laureate of Wedded Love." As St. Aldhelm sang the praises of virginity, so Patmore sang the glories of matrimony. He did in a large way what Habington had done in a small way, for Patmore was the more gifted poet and the bigger man.

Patmore's poetic rendering of his philosophy of love is contained in two cycles of poems, *The Angel in the House* and *The Unknown Eros*. A third series, *Sponsa Dei*, he burned; possibly he feared that what Newman called "mixing up amorousness with religion" would create a false impression and scandalize the weak. The poems of his youth he did not destroy, because he could not; but he came to view them with scant favor. It was characteristic of Patmore that he was his own best and sternest critic.

The Angel in the House, written in simple eight-syllable iambics, consists of four parts: The Betrothal, The Espousals, Faithful Forever, and Victories of Love. *The Unknown Eros* is a series of odes distinguished for their "suave and supple loveliness." [1] His theme, introduced in *The Angel*, developed in *The Unknown Eros*, and probably completed in the lost *Sponsa Dei*, is nuptial love considered as a symbol of divine love: as man and woman are united in marriage, so God and the soul are united in religion. Human love, instead of being an obstacle to divine love, becomes in Patmore's view of it a beautiful and wholesomely natural avenue of approach to supernatural experience and eternal happiness. In the language of modern psychology, the key idea of Patmore's theory is "sublimation." His thought is intricate, his emotion is copious and fervent but artistically restrained, his word music is splendid and varied.

Patmore's love poems are as a whole too exalted and perhaps too pure ever to secure a popular audience, but even the casual reader finds inspiration and a vision of beauty in two pieces extensively quoted. "The Departure" ("It was not like your great and gracious ways!") is a touching memorial to his first wife; "The Toys," evolved from a commonplace incident in the motherless family, rises on the wings of superb art from the naughty boy sent off to bed to the sublime conception of the mercy of God, sorry for human childishness.

[1] William Sharp, *Literary Geography*. p. 18.

Sometimes writers who know little about poetry and less about matrimony give us a false impression of Coventry Patmore. They paint him as a good pious soul living in this world as though he were already in the next, intent mainly on making converts to the Holy Catholic Church and on saying his prayers in the form of superspiritualized odes. The real Patmore would have protested vigorously against that caricature. There was little conventional about him either as man or as poet. Temperamentally he was an aristocrat, inclined to snub people he did not like, to quarrel sometimes with his friends; he had a sharp tongue and never learned to suffer fools gladly. He was identified with the Pre-Raphaelite movement in literature, contributed to *The Germ*, and induced Ruskin to come to the defense of Rossetti and the other Pre-Raphaelites. He was a great talker in congenial company, was much given to picturesque exaggeration, and, like Monsignor Benson, was an assiduous smoker of cigarettes. He was thrice married, and, in the best sense of the word, was a thoroughgoing man of the world, who numbered Browning, Tennyson, De Vere, Leigh Hunt, Ruskin, and Mrs. Meynell among his friends.

Patmore's father was an amiable atheist, and the boy was brought up without any religious instruction but with every other incentive to cultural education. In his teens he became interested in religious problems and entered the Anglican communion. His first wife, so beautifully commemorated in *The Angel in the House*, was the daughter of a clergyman. Patmore was employed as assistant librarian in the British Museum until his second marriage, with a lady of wealth, enabled him to cultivate a life of scholarly leisure. He entered the Catholic Church in 1863 and was ever after enthusiastic in the practice of his faith. In Hastings, where he lived for several years among the hillside elm trees at Melward Mansion, he built the Church of Mary, Star of the Sea, far up the long and rambling high street of the old town. He died at Lymington after several years of lingering illness.

THE PRE-RAPHAELITES

The Nature of the Movement. The word *progress*, so often used and overused, and our modest insistence that we human beings are a forward-looking race, might indicate that the arts, which are expressions of the spirit of man, would always seek new worlds to conquer and let the dead past bury its dead. The facts do not justify the inference. The history of literature and painting, of sculpture and music, reveals numerous occasions when artists cried, with Wordsworth, "The world is too much with us" and sought their inspiration and the principles of their technique in the art of earlier centuries. Romanticism and Classicism in English Literature were both a looking backward, but to different times and different models. And in all the arts this periodical return to the ideas and ideals of the remote past is invariably a protest against the ideas and ideals of the proximate past; it is as though a man mistrusts his father but reverences and imitates his great-grandfather.

One such movement occurred in the middle of the last century. At exactly the time when prospectors discovered gold in California, certain artists and poets in England discovered truth and beauty in the Middle Ages. They organized themselves into a society known as the Pre-Raphaelite Brotherhood and published a magazine, *The Germ*, to expound their principles and illustrate their methods. The Brotherhood did not long endure; but the Pre-Raphaelite movement affected men who were not members of the society and left its impress on English art and literature. The name Pre-Raphaelite was no more chosen to honor Raphael than the name Anti-Saloon League was chosen to honor the saloon. The brethren condemned Raphael as artificial and conventional and harked back to his predecessors in Italian painting. In painting, in sculpture, and in poetry the Pre-Raphaelites aimed at unconventionality, at the expression of intense feeling, at great accuracy of detail, and at decorative effects. The movement was mainly a revolt against Classicism and Realism and a revival of Romanticism; but, in its insistence on detailed fidelity in portraiture, it was at the same time a reaction against some Romantic tendencies, and in its devotion to rules and precedents it developed a newer Classicism of its own.

The Rossettis. Among the persons identified with the Pre-Raphaelite movement were the artists John Millais and Holman Hunt, the sculptor Thomas Woolner, the poet William Morris, and three members of the English-Italian Rossetti family — Dante Gabriel, William Michael, and Christina. William Michael Rossetti was a writer whose work is now forgotten and whose importance, such as it is, is entirely historical. Christina Rossetti (1830–1894) was a poet of delicate fancy and of religious intensity who wrote with the childlike faith and the white-souled fervor of a medieval nun; she had none of the materialism and smugness that characterized so much of the mid-Victorian life and thought. If poetry at its best is "simple, sensuous, passionate," then Christina Rossetti is a great poet. Her representative poems include *Goblin Market*; *Annus Domini*, a sequence of prayers for every day of the year; and *Monna Innominata*, a series of beautiful love sonnets. Her singing quality is revealed in this little song:

> When I am dead, my dearest,
>   Sing no sad songs for me;
> Plant thou no roses at my head,
>   Nor shady cypress tree:
> Be the green grass above me
>   With showers and dewdrops wet;
> And if thou wilt, remember,
>   And if thou wilt, forget.
>
> I shall not see the shadows,
>   I shall not feel the rain;
> I shall not hear the nightingale
>   Sing on, as if in pain:

And dreaming through the twilight
That doth not rise nor set,
Haply I may remember, .
And haply may forget.

Both as painter and as poet Dante Gabriel Rossetti (1828–1882) was the most prominent and influential member of the Pre-Raphaelite group.

ROSSETTI'S HOME IN CHELSEA

He had little or nothing of his sister's devotional spirit, but he excelled her in variety, in force, and in decorative imagery. What was sensuous in her sometimes became sensual in him, and some of his work merited the vigorous condemnation launched against it by Robert Buchanan, the novelist, in his essay "The Fleshly School of Poetry." Rossetti's poetry, like his painting, is too sweet to be entirely wholesome; both are characterized by an affectation, a cloying colorfulness, that suggests artifice and unreality. This stricture applies more to his lyrics like "The Blessed Damozel" and to his sonnet sequence, *The House of Life,* than to his ballads like "Sister Helen" and "The King's Tragedy," which yield a sturdy echo of Coleridge.

Rossetti's fame as a poet is justified in part by his ability to coin expressions at once original and suggestive. *The House of Life* is spangled with such gems as these:

... the desultory feet of Death.

The ground-whirl of the perished leaves of Hope.

And the woods wail like echoes from the sea.

Yet if you die, cannot I follow you,
Forcing the straits of change?

He brought out some excellent translations from early Italian poets in the volume *Dante and his Circle*, and in *Sentences and Notes* he formulated some of the Pre-Raphaelite principles. For instance:

Poetry is the apparent image of unapparent realities.

Poetry should seem to the hearer to have been always present to his thought, but never before heard.

The true artist will first perceive in another's work the beauties, and in his own the defects.

The critic of the new school sits down before a picture, and saturates it with silence.

In Rossetti's poems and pictures there frequently appears a tall, slender, copper-haired lady, whose languid, unearthly beauty became characteristic of Pre-Raphaelite art. This was Elizabeth Siddall, an artists' model, whom Rossetti married after a ten years' courtship. When his young wife died in 1862, a prey to tuberculosis, Rossetti buried the manuscript of his poems in her grave, and eight years later had them unearthed and published. He was not a Catholic; though some of his works, like his picture "The Girlhood of Mary Virgin" and his exquisite sonnet on the same theme, are entirely Catholic in conception. When he lay dying on Easter Saturday at Birchington he asked for a priest. "I can make nothing of Christianity," he said, "but I only want a confessor to give me absolution for my sins!" His unbelieving friend, William Bell Scott, refused to grant the request.[1] Above his grave on

---

[1] The fact is recorded in *Autobiographical Notes of the Life of William Bell Scott*. See also Canon William Barry's *Memories and Opinions*, p. 166.

the Kentish coast is a runic cross designed by Ford Madox Brown, one of his colleagues in the Pre-Raphaelite Brotherhood, and on it this epitaph is inscribed:

Here lies Gabriel Charles Dante Rossetti, among painters as a painter, and among poets as a poet. Born in London of parentage mainly Italian, 12th May, 1828. Died at Birchington, 9th April, 1882.

HAMLET AND OPHELIA, BY ROSSETTI

Courtesy of the British Museum

William Morris (1834-1896). It is deeply symbolic of the life and work of William Morris that he was a poet who invented a chair, and that he thought more highly of his chair than he did of his poetry. He was incapable, says his latest biographer, "of looking upon writing, even writing of genius, as an adequate whole-time occupation for a healthy man."[1]

Though he wrote much, in prose and in verse, Morris preferred to be known as a "decorative artist," and regarded his wall paper and his furniture and his social experiments and theories as his greatest achievements. But his wall paper is no longer the vogue, his morris chair has already gone out of fashion, and we still have competition and class struggle in industry. Morris is remembered because he was a writer of poetry and a printer of artistic books.

[1] Holbrook Jackson, *William Morris*. The 1926 edition of this little book is a seasoned survey of Morris's personality and influence.

Right well, said Christo-   Chris-
pher; and, to say sooth, I   topher
would almost that it were   will look
night, or my bones do else,   on
that I might lie naked in a
bed.

NAY, lad, said Gilbert,
make it night now, &
we will do all that needs
must be done, while thou
liest lazy, as all kings use
to do. Nay, said Christo-
pher, I will be more a king
than so, for I will do neither
this nor that; I will not work
and I will not go to bed, but
will look on, till it is time for
me to take to the crooked
stick & the grey-goose wing
and seek venison. That is

135

William Morris studied the Middle Ages at Oxford and discovered that they produced great art because the workingman was encouraged to be an artist. He read Ruskin on the cathedral builders and Carlyle on the gospel of work, shared the Pre-Raphaelite enthusiasms of Burne-Jones and Rossetti, and determined to bring about a renaissance of medieval working conditions. That led him to oppose capitalism in industry and to favor Socialistic theories. His belief was that a man does not enjoy life until he creates something, until he becomes an artist, and he sought to make the joys of artistry not the prerogative of the few but the opportunity of the many. Even things of utility, like tapestries and chairs, were objects of art in the Middle Ages. Why could they not be such in the nineteenth century as well? And if the man who writes a book is an artist, why should not the man who prints it be an artist too? That was the idea behind Morris's varied experiments in craftsmanship, including the Kelmscott Press, which he established in 1891. He did some of the things which his fellow Pre-Raphaelites were wishing for and which Carlyle and Ruskin were writing about.

Much that Morris wrote was propaganda in favor of his industrial ideals; and some of his stories, written in half-poetic prose, are visions, like *News from Nowhere*, of the happy earth when poverty shall no longer exist and coöperation shall replace competition and every man shall find congenial occupation and abundant leisure. The relations of Pre-Raphaelitism to the Romantic Movement are clearly observable in Morris's best-known poems. *The Defence of Guenevere*, written while Morris was in the early twenties, is more authentically medieval in spirit than Tennyson's more famous work, though less pictorial and harmonious. Morris is at his best in *Sigurd the Volsung*, a vigorous and massive creation inspired by the German epic of the Nibelungs. Most characteristic of Morris, however, are *The Life and Death of Jason* and *The Earthly Paradise*, the latter a series of tales retold from Norse and

Classical sources in the spirit of Boccaccio and Chaucer. The prologue to *The Earthly Paradise,* with its refrain of "the idle singer of an empty day," reveals the essential pettiness of much of Pre-Raphaelitism and Romanticism run to seed. Morris, like so many other admirers of the Middle Ages, failed to see that Catholicism was the glowing heart of that era and its leaping inspiration. "I know no poem," wrote Sir Walter Raleigh, "that expresses better than this the weaker side of the Romantic Movement in all its phases. Decadent Romantic art can live only in the twilight of an artificial Paradise."[1]

Arthur O'Shaughnessy (1844–1881). Pre-Raphaelitism produced numerous writings that found momentary favor and then melted "like snow upon the desert's dusty face"; many writers in this kind were indeed idle singers of an empty day. Oblivion has already overtaken most of the poems of Arthur O'Shaughnessy, a Londoner, far more akin to Rossetti and Swinburne than to Mangan and Moore. His *Epic of Women* and his *Songs of a Worker* are today forgotten; but he lives, and lives vibrantly, in several short lyrics, especially that glowing and stirring defense of poetry and the poet beginning

> We are the music makers,
> And we are the dreamers of dreams.

O'Shaughnessy had an extraordinary command of metrical resources, and was declared by Francis Palgrave, compiler of *The Golden Treasury,* to be second only to Tennyson for sweetness and smoothness of versification.

Algernon Charles Swinburne (1837–1909). For sheer virtuosity of expression, for variety and skill in the singing process, most critics would award the palm to Algernon Charles Swinburne, the last of the Pre-Raphaelites and a conspicuous instance of the movement's decadence. A certain public man was once described by a candid friend as having an oratorical

[1] *On Writing and Writers,* p. 206.

vocabulary but lacking both intellect and judgment. Swinburne labored under somewhat similar limitations. He was no thinker, no moralist, no seer; he invented no morris chair, formulated no poetic principles, organized no school; he learned nothing even from experience, and never had an idea after

© Emery Walker Limited

SWINBURNE

From a painting by G. F. Watts in the National Portrait Gallery, London

he was twenty-one; as a critic he was unbalanced and as a prose writer a nightmare. But he wrote real poetry. He had nothing deep or original to sing about, but he could sing with seductive charm and with a momentarily convincing assumption of genuine passion. Swinburne was a poet.

A poet, yes, a great poet, with a perfervid fancy rather than an imagination, a poet with puny passions, a poet with no more than the momentary and impulsive sincerity of an infirm soul, a poet with small intellect — and thrice a poet. . . . I believe that Swinburne's thoughts have their source, their home, their origin, their authority and mission in those two places — his own vocabulary and the passions of other men.[1]

Born in a good Northumberland family, Swinburne attended Eton and went to Oxford, but secured no degree. He read much and dabbled in out-of-the-way reaches of Greek Literature, but never attained to the poise and restraint of the pure Attic spirit. He had an excessive admiration for some of the

[1] Alice C. Meynell, "Swinburne's Lyrical Poetry," *Dublin Review*, July, 1909.

Elizabethan poets and for Victor Hugo, took a theatrical interest in the Italian struggles for independence, and began but never completed a collection of Old English Ballads. A very small man, with sloping shoulders and a huge head surmounted by a shock of reddish hair, Swinburne was for several years a conspicuous figure in London literary circles. Ill health and indiscretions made him prematurely old; and in 1879 he was almost forced by another poet, Theodore Watts-Dunton, to live at The Pines in Putney, a London suburb on the Thames. There he continued to write until his death; but his poetic powers seemed exhausted, and he failed to fulfill the promise of his earlier poems.

Swinburne's most representative productions include *Atalanta in Calydon*, and other poetic dramas based on classical models but lacking in both dramatic sense and the authentic Greek spirit. Their choruses are the best part of them. He achieved celebrity, or rather notoriety, with his *Poems and Ballads*, many of them disfigured by witless blasphemies and a glorification of the lust of the flesh. He is less offensive in *Songs before Sunrise*, with his magnificent lyric effects and his astonishing varieties of meter. *Tristram of Lyonesse* and *The Tale of Balin* recapture something of the splendor of the Arthurian legends, but are mainly interesting for their manner rather than for their matter.

Swinburne was the possessor of high poetic gifts and sometimes, as in his tribute to St. Catherine of Siena, achieved dignity and power:

> Then in her sacred saving hands
> She took the sorrows of the lands,
> With maiden palms she lifted up
> The sick time's blood-embittered cup,
> And in her virgin garment furled
> The faint limbs of a wounded world.
> Clothed with calm love and clear desire,
> She went forth in her soul's attire,
> A missive fire.

But that note is exceptional in his verses; more prevailingly he sings in disparise of "the lilies and languors of virtue" and in eulogy of "the roses and raptures of vice." He never learned the impressive truth that man's animal passions are not the stuff of which literature is made, that atheism never has inspired great poetry and never can. Many of his poems are like music, but music that is unreal and unmeaning, for it proceeded from a mind that knew nothing of either the profundities of thought or the glow of genuine emotion. And so the last of the Pre-Raphaelites declined into senility and impotence in his semi-captivity at Putney.

BROWNING

The Dramatic Monologue. The outstanding achievement of Robert Browning (1812–1889) is a kind of poem wherein a single character does all the talking and all the thinking, but in which at the same time the alert reader is able to visualize other characters and to appreciate numerous phases of life and social conditions. This is the monodrama, or dramatic monologue. It is not to be confused with either the oration or the lyric poem, though it resembles those forms in several important respects. It is not, like the oration, addressed to a crowd, nor has it for purpose the stimulation or persuasion of an audience. And, unlike the lyric, it is not necessarily emotional; it has a wide range, and in mood it is definitely dramatic. The remarkable thing about Browning is that though he several times attempted the complete drama, as in *Strafford*, and never achieved distinction in that form, he is absolutely unapproachable in his monodramas.

Thoroughly representative of the dramatic monologue as perfected by Browning is "My Last Duchess." There is but one speaker, the Duke of Ferrara. He makes a singularly complete revelation of himself as a dry, avaricious, calculating old nobleman, just now intent on securing money through a favorable marriage, inordinately proud of his "nine-hundred-years-old name" and of his collection of paintings and curios. He is talking to an emissary of his prospective father-in-law; and in showing his guest the picture of the late duchess he unconsciously depicts the beautiful character of that unappreciated lady. We who read the short poem — it contains but fifty-six lines — get a sufficient impression of the visitor, a graphic delineation of the cold-blooded egotist who speaks, an understanding of the sweet duchess painted by Fra Pandolf, and several constructive hints of the ancestral castle and its artistic furnishings. We find characters, plot, and setting — all through the speech of one man.

That is the method employed by Browning in his construction of the dramatic monologue, the form in which he cast so many of his poems. Dramatic monologues are "A Woman's Last Word," "The Patriot," "Abt Vogler," "Andrea del Sarto," "The Bishop orders his Tomb," "Caliban upon Setebos," and the somewhat longer poem "Saul," where the monologue is rendered by David, the future King of Israel. Browning's masterpiece, *The Ring and the Book*, is a collection of monologues. The poet picked up an old yellow book one day at a bookstall in front of the Church of San Lorenzo in Florence. It contained an account of a seventeenth-century murder trial. In the poem which resulted the principal characters tell the story of the events, each from his own point of view: the town gossips, the prisoner, the young priest who was involved, the prisoner's young wife, the lawyers for the prosecution and the defense, and the pope, upon whose decision rests the culprit's fate. It is like a play in twelve acts with but one speaker in each act.

Browning's Obscurity. Browning wrote several delightfully simple poems, such as the children's classic "The Pied Piper of Hamelin," and "'How they Brought the Good News from Ghent to Aix,'" but for the most part his work makes difficult reading for anyone not initiated into the intricacies of the poet's thought and style. Browning admired Donne, and certainly imitated his "verses gnarl'd and knotted." The dramatic monologue always demands a good deal from the reader's alertness and ingenuity, and in Browning's hands it often becomes something of an intellectual puzzle. The poet once met the Chinese minister. "His Excellency," explained the polite interpreter,

A POET'S PORTRAIT OF A POET

Browning in the 40's, as painted by D. G. Rossetti. (Courtesy of the Fitzwilliam Museum, Cambridge, England)

"is a distinguished poet in his country as you are here in England." "Indeed," said Browning. "And what sort of poetry does His Excellency write?" "Chiefly poetical enigmas." Browning promptly grasped His Excellency's hand and cried, "I salute you as a brother."

The obscurity of Browning—something real enough, no matter how strenuously his admirers seek to explain it away — is due to several causes. He was fond of picking out for his themes little-known personages and historical events, and he assumed in his readers a knowledge equal to his own. Then very often he but half expresses his thoughts; like Emerson he leaps from peak to peak and leaves his less agile reader floundering in the valleys. Again, he often employs a sentence structure long and involved, drops out words necessary to complete the sense, chooses words that are odd and grotesque, and even forces familiar expressions to convey unfamiliar meanings. As he himself said, he had no desire to have his poems take the place of a cigar or a game of dominoes.

Browning the Man. Browning's obscurity is also in part explained by his life and education. Born in Camberwell, a London suburb, he attended no regular schools, but had private teachers and an oddly assorted library; thus, though he gained much, he missed the intellectual discipline and organization that come from regular courses of study and the contact of mind with mind. He was never obliged to work for a living, and spent much of his life abroad, especially in Italy, a country he deeply loved.

> Open my heart, and you will see
> Graved inside of it "Italy."

In Italy, especially at Pisa and at Florence, he spent fifteen years of perfect married happiness with Elizabeth Barrett Browning; and in Italy, at Venice, he died.

Browning was a man vigorous and robust, fond alike of the out-of-doors and of the shadowy churches and chill picture galleries of Italian cities; an active thinker, a keen observer, an assiduous reader, an energetic worker — for poetry he regarded as his essential work in life. Though he avoided public life he took an active interest in the world events of his time and maintained cordial relations with prominent men all over Europe. His life was free from unworthy conduct and his character was clean and noble. In religion his views were vague and not always consistent; he could never entirely free himself from some of the Nonconformist prejudices in which he had been brought up, but he maintained a sincere respect for Christianity and an admiration for many manifestations of the Catholic spirit in art and in life.

His long residence in Italy made him familiar with much of the history of the land and with the art and literature of earlier ages, but to the last he remained a stranger. His acquaintances were mostly English and American, and he never probed far beneath the surface of Italian life. Among churchmen he had no intimate friends; and he admitted that "as to Italian society, one may as well take to longing for the evening star, it is so inaccessible." These facts it is well to remember when reading his numerous poems on Italian subjects; they will do much to explain his occasional misreadings of history, his false judgments concerning illustrious personages, and his unconscious irreverence when describing Catholic devotional practices.

A SON'S PORTRAIT OF A POET

Browning in the 60's, as painted by R. Barrett Browning. (By permission of the Master and Fellows of Balliol College, Oxford)

Browning's Poems. *Pauline,* *Paracelsus,* and *Sordello* represent Browning's earlier experiments in poetry and constitute a truly remarkable performance for a man still young. *Sordello* possesses the further and dubious distinction of being as involved in thought and confusing in language as anything that Browning ever wrote. The finest of Browning's dramatic monologues are scattered through several collections of his poems, *Dramatic Lyrics, Dramatic Romances, Men and Women, Dramatis Personæ.* His interest in Greek Literature is shown in *Aristophanes' Apology,* really a tribute to Euripides, and in *Balaustion's Adventure,* the story of the girl of Athens who gave a dramatic reading in Syracuse. *The Ring and the Book* we have already noted.

Of individual poems it is difficult to make a selection, for nearly every one of them has interest and vitality. Besides the monologues already mentioned, the student might well consider the following: "How it Strikes a Contemporary," a revealing portrayal of a man with the gift of artistic expression; "A Grammarian's Funeral," in which Browning recaptures something of the intellectual interest and artistic enthusiasm of the Renaissance; "Rabbi Ben Ezra," voicing Browning's cheerful and constructive attitude toward life; "Prospice," an unusual and inspiring meditation on death; and the last thing he wrote, the Epilogue to *Asolando* — characteristically concluding with a battle cry and an exclamation mark.

Some Characteristics. Browning had a fondness for concentrating attention on what might be called the "high places" in emotional experience, those moments of intense feeling in which life and the world are revealed as in sudden flashes of lightning. Nearly every poem of his, and every one of his great poems, is an embodiment and interpretation of such an experience. An instance is "Fra Lippo Lippi." Lippo was an Italian painter who during a part of his life had been a monk. Browning shows him in conversation with a watchman, recalling his personal history and explaining his art and his prospects. The entire poem is conceived in a mood of vivid and almost exaggerated emotional fervor. Much the same thing might be said of "Andrea del Sarto." Here he has another painter discussing art and life, the artist known in history as the "perfect painter." Browning brings out the significant truth that the man who succeeds in technical perfection, whose work is fair and faultless, may nevertheless fail to achieve true greatness or to convey an impression of abounding life.

A favorite notion of Browning's was that "we fall to rise, are baffled to fight better, sleep to wake"; that adversity and disappointment and unrealized ambition may bring forth salutary fruits. This optimistic attitude is given its most extreme form in "Apparent Failure." The poet visits the Paris morgue, gazes upon the bodies of three men who had drowned

themselves in the Seine, and from that contemplation draws
the hopeful conclusion :

> It's wiser being good than bad;
> 　It's safer being meek than fierce:
> It's fitter being sane than mad.
> 　My own hope is, a sun will pierce
> The thickest cloud earth ever stretched;
> 　That, after Last, returns the First,
> Though a wide compass round be fetched;
> 　That what began best, can't end worst,
> Nor what God blessed once, prove accurst.

Another favorite theory of Browning's, one that if carried to
its logical conclusions would reduce civilization to barbarism,
is that it is better to follow the impulse of passion than to take
counsel of prudence and propriety. In "The Statue and the
Bust" he recounts the historical episode of Ferdinand I, Grand
Duke of Tuscany, who fell in love with a married lady and
determined to run away with her but never carried out the
determination. The poet laments the indecision of "each
frustrate ghost" and implies that they would have done better
to follow their desires. This lack of ethical sense where the
passion of love is concerned moved one of Browning's most
astute critics to call him a barbarian. The poem gets its name
from the fact that in the Piazza della Santissima Annunziata
in Florence there still stands an equestrian statue of the duke
on the spot where he first saw the lady looking from her window, and in the window is a bust of the lady herself.

The reading of Browning will result in rich cultural benefits.
He is the most "psychological" of the Victorian poets, bent
usually on giving "no more of body than shows soul." He is
adroit and subtle in analyzing character and determining motives of conduct. He is robust and manly and does much to
convince even prejudiced readers that a poet need not be a
sighful simperer. He covers a wide range of human experience
and human history. He reveals numerous points where litera-

ture links itself with art, with politics, with religion, with philosophy, with science. He has to his credit a large number of poems that are at once intellectual and emotional and that are, moreover, beautiful and moving expressions of essential truth. And his prevailing note of vibrant optimism is still potent in literature as in life.

TENNYSON

Browning and Tennyson. We can secure some notion of the contrast existing between Browning and Tennyson by comparing two poems written within the shadow of death, the Epilogue to *Asolando* and "Crossing the Bar." Here are two men, two successful and famous men, looking upon a basic fact of earthly life — the fact that it must cease; and upon a belief and a reasoned conviction — the belief and the conviction of life beyond life. They agree on fundamentals, they are willing to look death squarely in the eyes, their hearts beat expectant of life in the world to come. Yet how widely different their conceptions, how contrasted their moods, how diverse their anticipations, how antithetical their expression!

As poets and as thinkers Browning and Tennyson have little in common. As a stylist Browning is often obscure, gnarled, perverse and even freakish, difficult to make out; Tennyson writes poetry that flows as clearly and as melodiously as his own chattering brook. Browning's poems are rugged, bristling, staccato speeches; Tennyson's are tuneful, graceful, delicately fashioned songs. Browning is a cosmopolitan in time and space, choosing his material from all corners of history and from periods both near and remote; Tennyson, though occasionally he fares abroad, is the most English of poets and the most Victorian. Browning delves deep beneath the surface of life and unearths hidden motives and unsuspected strands of character; Tennyson rarely gets beyond the show of things and paints life as it seems more frequently than as it is. In Browning we catch vivid glimpses of the sounding ocean and the sky-cleaving mountains, of the storm and strife and glory of the world; in Tennyson we comfortably toast our toes before the fire or gaze serenely out across the English countryside. At times they both offend: Browning, because he is brusque and uncouth; Tennyson, because he is the perfect Victorian gentleman. Browning has been called a barbarian; Tennyson has been called "Miss Alfred."

Tennyson the Man. Alfred Tennyson (1809–1892) lived a singularly uneventful life. Born in Lincolnshire, he received a conventional education at Louth Grammar School and at Cambridge. While still a young man he began to write poetry and took a long time to perfect himself in the art. He married in due course, and in the same year (1850) became poet laureate of England; and in England, save for brief visits abroad, he lived all his life: at Cheltenham, at Pope's Twickenham, in the Isle of Wight, at Haslemere in Surrey, — "green Sussex fading into blue, with one gray glimpse of sea," — and at neighboring Aldworth, where he died. He enjoyed vast popularity during his lifetime, though his fame has since considerably declined, and he was on terms of intimacy with the leading men of letters of his day. He gave himself wholly to the writing and polishing of his poems and experimented with all kinds of poetic form.

Tennyson's Poems. Tennyson made his bardic bow at the age of eighteen with *Poems by Two Brothers* in collaboration with Charles Tennyson; three years later he won a medal at Cambridge with "Timbuctoo," and concluded his early period with two more collections of poems, including "The Lady of Shallott," "The Lotos-Eaters," "A Dream of Fair Women," and "The Palace of Art." By this time he knew enough about writing to know that he had much to learn; so for ten years he zealously read and studied world poets and practiced his art; and then in 1842 he began his mature period with a flow of poetry which kept up uninterruptedly to the year of his death. Several of his poems, like "Œnone" and "Ulysses," are on classical themes and are fine examples of the influence of the ancient writers on English Literature; others are tales in verse, like *Enoch Arden*, "Dora," and "The Northern Farmer." He attempted the poetic drama, too, as in *Becket*, a play based on the career of St. Thomas of Canterbury, but in this field he won no distinction. He is at his best in his lyrics, including the delightful songs in *The Princess* and *Maud*. The inspiration of the justly admired Bugle Song in *The Princess* he derived from a visit to Ross Castle at Killarney.

© Emery Walker Limited

TENNYSON

From a painting by G. F. Watts in the National Portrait Gallery, London

In Memoriam. As a young man Tennyson had a friend, Arthur Henry Hallam, who died in Vienna in 1833 at the age of twenty-two. Tennyson's grief over Hallam's death, and the reflections to which the event gave rise, are recorded in *In Memoriam*, first published in 1850 and amplified in succeeding editions. It is a collection of separate poems, a hundred and thirty-one in all, running in length from twelve to a hundred and twenty lines. They are mostly sonnets in substance, though not in form, each embodying a unified emotional thought. They are written in what has come to be known as the *In Memoriam* stanza, consisting of four iambic lines of four feet, in which the first line rimes with the fourth, and the second with the third:

> Nor dare she trust a larger lay,
>   But rather loosens from the lip
>   Short swallow-flights of song, that dip
> Their wings in tears and skim away.

The stanza was not invented by Tennyson. It came from the French and was used by Sidney, Jonson, and other English poets, notably by Lord Herbert of Cherbury (1583–1648).

This celebrated collection of elegiac poetry has been highly praised and roundly condemned. It has been called the English Book of Job and the "great English classic on the love of immortality and the immortality of love,"[1] "the noblest English Christian poem which several centuries have seen."[2] On the other hand, Fitzgerald declared it monotonous; Taine complained that it is "too prettily arranged"; and Arthur Christopher Benson says that it is a poor poem and adds, "Probably no modern work has done so much to undermine popular religion as *In Memoriam*."[3] Yet it is possible to select from *In Memoriam* numerous passages which defend and justify religious belief. The truth is that *In Memoriam* is a record of varying moods and of diverse lines of thought; that it is in places exquisite and inspiring and in other places flat and dull; that it is here luminous and there clotted and befogged; that the poet's grief takes a form sometimes noble and manly and sometimes almost simpering and affected. It contains some stanzas and some happy phrases which are both quotable and quoted and which justify Tennyson's admission into the company of the lords of language.

Idylls of the King. The volume of poems published by Tennyson in 1842 after his ten years of disciplinary silence contained his "Morte d'Arthur," inspired by the great prose romance of Sir Thomas Malory. This was the first of a group of poems (most of them included in the *Idylls of the King*) which seek to recapture the faith and prowess of the medieval world and to retell the tales of King Arthur and the Knights

---

[1] Henry van Dyke.   [2] Charles Kingsley.   [3] *Tennyson*, p. 151.

of the Table Round; and at times, and with limited success, the Victorian poet did reproduce something of the passion and splendor of that vanished world. "Merlin and the Gleam" is the nearest thing to a literary autobiography Tennyson ever wrote, a poem which helps us to understand the universality of literature and the qualities which in every age the makers of poetry must possess. Dramatic, ornate, rich in its suggestive atmosphere, is his version of the quest of the Holy Grail; fine and delicate and great with the simplicity of true art is his "Passing of Arthur"; sharp and convincing is his characterization of such figures as Sir Lancelot, Lynette, Merlin, Sir Modred, and King Arthur and his mobled Queen.

The modern tendency to discredit the *Idylls of the King* is less a reflection on Tennyson than on the cynicism and flippancy which just now finds fleeting favor. His King Arthur is called a prig because he makes an austere vindication of the sacredness of the marriage tie and holds in horror things which present-day paganism condones as pleasant vices. Tennyson is in this matter very close to the medieval spirit, which he was striving to interpret. The Middle Ages, like all ages, had their full quota of splendid sinners, but they did not fall into the modern looseness of thought which slurs over the sin because the sinner happens to be beautiful and charming. In the Middle Ages people were imbued with the sound Catholic principle which urged them to hate sin while loving the sinner. That is King Arthur's attitude to Queen Guinevere, and Tennyson's portrayal of it is not the least of his artistic triumphs.

The Status of Tennyson. The twentieth century depreciates Tennyson because, among other reasons, the nineteenth century exaggerated his importance; people who hold the Victorian Age in especial contempt are not likely to regard the most representative poet of that age with especial favor. And, again, in a period when excellence of style is frowned upon as something affected and artificial, when vulgarity and uncouthness are even saluted as evidences of power and originality, it is inevitable that so conscientious and painstaking a writer as Tennyson, with "his dainty felicity of phrase, his faultless chiselling, and his imperturbable refinement,"[1] should be looked upon as an impractical visionary, as a mere sower of words. Other times other manners, and it may well be that Tennyson eventually will come into his own as a linguistic goldsmith who fashioned "jewels five words long" destined to sparkle forever. But readers who are not lovers of language can hardly be lovers of Tennyson.

Perhaps Tennyson, despite his fondness for the classics and his sympathy with certain medieval ideals, was too immersed in his own country and his own time. Problems real and urgent in the nineteenth century have ceased to be problems, and since he wrote all civilized countries including his own have dropped something of their old insularity and narrowness and have taken a world view of civilization. But his age, such as it was, he reflected in almost every phase of its interest and activity. Religion, science, politics, labor, women's rights, commerce, and invention — these he studied and wrote upon ; and for the most part his views were judicial, impartial, moderate. And at times he was able, as great poets always are, to rise above the horizon of his age and assume the mantle of the poetic seer :

For I dipt into the future, far as human eye could see,
Saw the Vision of the world, and all the wonder that would be ;

Saw the heavens fill with commerce, argosies of magic sails,
Pilots of the purple twilight, dropping down with costly bales ;

Heard the heavens fill with shouting, and there rain'd a ghastly dew
From the nations' airy navies grappling in the central blue ;

Far along the world-wide whisper of the south-wind rushing warm,
With the standards of the peoples plunging thro' the thunder-storm ;

Till the war-drum throbb'd no longer, and the battle-flags were furl'd
In the Parliament of man, the Federation of the world.

[1] Frederic Harrison, *Tennyson, Ruskin, Mill*, p. 41.

Those lines occur in "Locksley Hall," and he who wrote them was a man who knew both the prophet's exaltation and the glory of words.

THE END OF THE CENTURY

Decadents and Others. A school-teacher in India and a traveler in many lands, Sir Edwin Arnold (1832–1904) wrote copiously in prose and verse on foreign themes and set forth the religious conceptions of Buddhism in his poem *The Light of Asia*. Sir W. S. Gilbert (1836–1911) collaborated with Sir Arthur Sullivan in *The Mikado*, *Pinafore*, and other comic operas, showing himself a skilled metrist and a pungent satirist in his "patter" songs and his *Bab Ballads*: "His foe was folly and his weapon wit." William Sharp (1856–1905) did much of his writing under the pen name of "Fiona Macleod" and succeeded in hiding his dual personal-

THE "GILIVAN"

A composite portrait of Gilbert and Sullivan.
(Courtesy of J. M. Dent & Sons, London)

ity from the mass of readers. His poems are in the tradition of Romanticism and recapture something of the Gaelic mystery and magic and vague picturesqueness. William Ernest Henley (1849–1903) was a poet and essayist who revealed strong convictions and wrote in a style at once forceful and fastidious.

He edited several magazines and acted as literary father confessor for a group of writers often spoken of a little contemptuously as "Henley's young men." Henley was a lifelong invalid, and his justly popular "Invictus" discloses his sturdy spirit:

> I am the master of my fate:
> I am the captain of my soul.

The Decadents were a group of writers, mostly poets, who were absorbed with unwholesome aspects of life, who devoted themselves to exotic systems of thought, and who voiced the promptings of puny passions. Some of them deliberately aimed at startling and shocking a staid and self-righteous generation and made the *Savoy* and the *Yellow Book* the organs of their campaign. Most of them lived a short life, and, like Oscar Wilde and Aubrey Beardsley, entered the Catholic Church shortly before death. One such was Ernest Dowson (1867–1900), who wrecked his life and too often degraded his considerable poetic talents, though toward the end he composed "Extreme Unction" and other religious verses which exhale a curious odor of incense and sulphur. A few of the Decadents managed to survive the mood and the movement. One of them, Francis W. Grey, is now a Catholic priest, and others, like Arthur Symons, have developed into writers fairly sedate and inconspicuous. The English Decadence of the "naughty nineties" was a pale-pink reflection of a condition that affected literature on the Continent, particularly in France.

Lionel Johnson (1867–1902). A Decadent who proved to be more than a Decadent and who, dying at the age of thirty-five, secured for himself a distinguished rank in both poetry and the less exacting sort of criticism, was Lionel Johnson. Because of one virtue he saved his soul (possibly in a spiritual sense, certainly in a literary one), and that virtue was loyalty. He was loyal to his friends, and the dedications of his individual poems show us that his friends were many. He was loyal to his mixed-race heritage — English, Irish, Welsh, and Cornish — and loved to commemorate in verse the glories of his peoples. He was loyal to the Catholic Church, to which he was an unswerving convert; and several of his poems, including that triumphant "Te Martyrum Candidatus," are among the most distinctively Catholic poetry in the English language.

He was loyal to Winchester School and to Oxford and loyal to the fine classical training he received, a loyalty he revealed in his perfection of form and his artistic discipline and abstention, — qualities which characterized his writings rather than his life.

"**Michael Field.**" A similar note of finely tempered scholarship and conscious restraint appears in certain poems of strength and distinction which won wide favor in the 80's and were attributed to one "Michael Field." Michael Field was en-

A POET AT SCHOOL

From a photograph of Lionel Johnson when he was a pupil at Winchester School. (Courtesy of The Macmillan Company and of Elkin Mathews, Ltd.)

visaged by readers as a learned and chivalrous knight in shining armor and astride a white horse, until the news came out that the poems were the work of two unmarried ladies, an aunt and a niece, Miss Katherine Bradley and Miss Edith Cooper. Then Michael Field's vogue suffered a temporary decline, and the poems which had won the enthusiastic admiration of Browning proved distasteful to readers who did not care to know that the authors were invalids, victims of cancer, who had found spiritual peace in Catholicism. Today there is a mild revival of interest in the poetic dramas of Michael Field and in such shorter poems as "The Descent from the Cross," a moving and luminous appeal to the human soul to remain on the cross of suffering with Christ. The lyrics of Michael Field appeared in collections named *Long Ago, Underneath the Bough, Sight and Song, Wild Honey*, and *Poems of Adoration*.

THOMPSON

A Master of the Lyric. There is no higher, more varied, more capable, more inspired English lyric poet than Francis Thompson (1859–1907). And Thompson is exclusively lyric; he wrote no verse narratives like *The Lady of the Lake*, no poetic dramas like Michael Field's *Tragic Mary*. Whenever he wrote in verse he wrote in lyric verse, the verse that catches an emotional mood as a mountain lake catches a star, that is rippled by the wind of circumstance but is unbroken by the shoals of controversy and unflecked by the clouds of unknowing. Yet it is rare to find two of his poems alike in other respects. Within the lyric form he exercised himself in a wide variety of meters and an even wider variety of moods. He is not merely one of the two or three masters of the lyric: he is the one master who has demonstrated how many kinds of music the lyric can evoke and how far and how high its melody can soar.

Thompson has been called the Catholic Shelley and the poetic heir of Coventry Patmore. Both titles are complimentary — to all concerned — but misleading. They imply that the man who wrote "The Hound of Heaven" is a stained-glass window reflecting the man who wrote *Alastor*, and a carbon copy of the man who wrote *The Angel in the House*. For both Shelley and Patmore he had a deep regard. His essay on Shelley is a tribute of understanding affection as well as a golden triumph of English prose, and his dedication of a group of his poems to Patmore in 1897 voices the respect of a disciple for a master. But Thompson had a range of thought, a sweep of emotion, and a fullness of life unknown to the fastidious author of *The Unknown Eros*, and he added to a technical gift the equal of Shelley's a buoyant faith and a sound philosophy of life. He was a straight thinker as well as a glorious dreamer. He is a Catholic Shelley in the sense that he wrote the sort of poetry Shelley might have written were Shelley impregnated with the rich and fruitful Catholic spirit, and he is the heir of Patmore in the sense that he mastered his master and increased and enriched their common heritage of poetry and religion. He has all Shelley's power and passion and magnificence of imagery, and more than Patmore's word artistry and religious spirit.

The Journey of his Life. Francis Thompson was born at Preston in Lancashire. His father was a Catholic and a doctor, and the boy was sent first to Ushaw College and then to Queen's College, London, to study medicine. But the dissecting room appealed to Thompson as little as it had to Keats, and he gave up his professional studies and became a homeless wanderer in the London streets. We can envisage him, gaunt and pale and ragged, a copy of Blake in one pocket, a copy of Æschylus in the other, a hapless victim of consumption and the opium habit, earning a few pence selling matches and calling cabs, haunting libraries until driven away because of his unkempt appearance, and finding his only friend in a nameless outcast. Then some things that he wrote and submitted to *Merrie England* attracted the attention of the editor, Wilfrid Meynell, who after considerable difficulty located the poet and brought him to his home. Thereafter he was the friend and honored guest of Meynell and Mrs. Meynell, making numerous acquaintances among men of letters and writing his most memorable works of poetry and prose.

Like Shelley, Thompson never quite grew up. He was always at heart a child; and his spontaneous manners, his ill-fitting, snuff-colored clothes, and his rankly odorous pipe made him an anomalous figure in the Meynell drawing room. He wrote his poems in school exercise books, often beginning on the last page and continuing wherever he chanced to come upon a blank space. He was sometimes seen in Fleet Street like a reincarnation of Izaak Walton, a fish basket hung by a strap over his shoulder; but it contained only the books which he was taking home to review from the offices of the *Academy* and the *Athenæum.* Though he lived into the twentieth century, practically all his work, and certainly his best work, had been done by 1897.

His Prose. As a prose writer Thompson, like most poets, was capable and distinguished. His essays, mostly on literary themes, are very uneven, some of them merely hack work, others keen in thought, moving in emotion, and superb in style. He wrote two lives of saints — a very good one of St. Ignatius and a very poor one of St. de la Salle — and a diverting dissertation on *Health and Holiness*, "a study of the relations between Brother Ass, the body, and his rider, the soul." His study of *Paganism Old and New*, one of the manuscripts which first won the interest of Wilfrid Meynell, is an exposition of the essential dullness and sadness of both the paganism of ignorance and the paganism of unbelief.

His Poetry. Thompson's poems, now collected in an excellent two-volume edition, originally appeared in groups : *Poems, Sister Songs*, and *New Poems*. Many of them are expressions of his regard for the members of the Meynell household : "Love in Dian's Lap" is dedicated to Mrs. Meynell, and "The Making of Viola" commemorates the birth of her youngest daughter. Some notion of Thompson's almost infinite variety may be gained by a reading of "Little Jesus," "Buona Notte," "The Passion of Mary," "An Anthem of Earth," and "To the Dead Cardinal of Westminster."

But Thompson's name and fame are most closely identified with "The Hound of Heaven," in substance and in form one of the most notable odes in universal literature. Its vision of life is clear and penetrating, its lyric sweep resembles the rise and fall of dramatic action, and its poetic imagery is rich and varied and original. Its theme is a soul-stirring application of St. Augustine's immortal saying, "Thou hast made us for Thyself, O God, and our hearts are restless ever till they rest in Thee." It shows the weak and erring soul of man fleeing timorously from the pursuing love of God, seeking comfort in human love, in the fellowship of little children, in the beauties of nature and the intricacies of art; but it finds all hollow, all aloof, all unresponsive as ever the unhurrying chase proceeds. Then of a sudden it hears the voice of Eternal Love:

> Whom wilt thou find to love ignoble thee,
> > Save Me, save only Me?
> All which I took from thee I did but take,
> > Not for thy harms,
> But just that thou might'st seek it in My arms.
> > All which thy child's mistake
> Fancies as lost, I have stored for thee at home:
> > Rise, clasp My hand, and come!

A truly great poet, Francis Thompson has the defects of his qualities. Though at times he wrote with simple grace, he is often over-elaborate and tortuously involved. His glorious flights of fancy occasionally lead him into extravagance of diction and imagery, and often we miss the spirit of the song because of the very fervor and glowing ecstasy of the singer. But, like Browning, Thompson repays careful study, and, like Keats, he shows us what poetry really is. And unlike Browning, unlike Keats, and in a far larger way than Crashaw or Patmore, he manifests religion as a source of poetic splendor. Catholicism — the Catholicism which built the great cathedrals of Europe and tempered the chisel of Michelangelo and animated the prophetic soul of Dante — is the sacred fire which burned in the heart of Francis Thompson and, at the very close of an age of unbelief and doubt and materialism, touched English poetry with aspiring flame.

CHAPTER XV

A CENTURY OF ESSAYISTS

ESSAYS AND ESSAYISTS

Besides its rich development in the field of fiction and its numerous and important contributions to English poetry, the nineteenth century is distinguished for the number and excellence of its writers of essays. In earlier periods of English Literature there were memorable essayists — More and Bacon, Dryden and Johnson, Addison and Steele; but it was not until after the year 1800 that there came a revelation of the full scope and infinite variety of the essay form. One factor in the growth of the essay was the popularity of magazines; another was the renewed interest in intellectual subjects manifested by large groups of the reading public. Then, too, the advance in poetry and fiction called for criticism and commentary, both of which necessarily took shape in essays; and the newer developments in public life — religious and social problems, the discoveries and hypotheses of scientists, the theories of educators and philosophers, the complexities of national politics and of international relations — all called for explanation and discussion. And then, as always, there were a few gifted men who, like Montaigne in sixteenth-century France, were pleased to comment gracefully and informally on life and human nature and who discovered in the prose essay the medium most congenial. The result is a collection of essays, many of them genuine literature, revealing numerous phases of experience and a diversity of points of view.

What is an essay? Meaning literally an attempt, the word has been applied to so vast a variety of prose writings that it is impossible to define it save by negation. It is not poetry and it is not fiction. It may occupy only a page or it may fill a stout volume. Its subjects range from the immortality of the soul and the meaning of *Paradise Lost* to roast pig and the man in the moon. Its method is as unstandardized as the mood in which it is written. Nothing matters very much in the literary essay except that it be literary; that is, that it possess the vitality and the art and the other essential qualities of true literature.

Perhaps the most convenient classification of essayists is that based upon their general point of view. There are third-person essayists, men like Dryden and Macaulay and Andrew Lang, who are less concerned with themselves and with their audience than with the ideas which they are seeking to convey. There are second-person essayists, who write directly at their readers and seem to keep the needs and capacity of their audience acutely in mind; such are Bacon, Steele, and Stevenson. And there are first-person essayists, who simply talk about themselves. That is what Montaigne did, and Browne, and Charles Lamb. In their case the reader rarely has occasion to think directly of himself, and he may find many of their ideas unusual, wrong-headed, or even absurd, but he is pleased and fascinated by the revelations they make of their thoughts and fancies, their theories and interpretations, their personal reactions to books and to life. All three classes of essayists are liberally represented in the literature of the nineteenth century.

LAMB

Genius on a Stool. The little man who was dismissed by Carlyle as "that stammering tomfool," who was described by Hood as running about on a pair of "immaterial legs," and who was characterized by Hazlitt as "the most delightful, the most provoking, the most witty of men" is the leading exemplar of the first-person essay in English Literature. Charles

Lamb (1775–1834) was born in London and spent some thirty-five years with those "immaterial legs" of his coiled about the rungs of a clerk's high stool in an office, first with the South Sea House and then with the East India Company. The last nine years of his life were free from drudgery, thanks to the pension he received from his employers; but most of his captivating essays were written in the odds and ends of time he secured after his day's monotonous work was done.

LAMB'S COTTAGE, EDMONTON

Lamb preserved his serenity and good nature and whole-hearted friendliness in the face of circumstances which might well have soured a sweet disposition. He was making his way in his clerical work and looked forward to a happy marriage, when his sister Mary in a moment of insanity wounded her father and killed her mother. The tragedy changed the whole course of Lamb's life. He renounced his prospect of happiness in the married state and devoted himself completely to the care of his unfortunate sister. And so they lived together in the big city and latterly at Edmonton, content with simple pleasures and the company of their friends, reading the same books and sometimes of an evening climbing up to the least expensive seats at the theater. Once in a while, too, Mary's sad malady returned, and Charles, all togged out sprucely in his shabby best clothes, would report at the office and ask for a holiday. His employers knew what that meant — that the little clerk had to take his sister to the asylum until the season of madness had passed.

The Talker. Men who knew Charles Lamb intimately were unanimous in maintaining that he was at his best in the give-and-take of familiar conversation. There are talkers and talkers, and Coleridge and Lamb, who sometimes talked at each other, represent the two extremes of the art of conversation. They were the Goliath and the David of the spoken word. Coleridge was heavy, erudite, elaborate, often truly magnificent in his discourse; his idea of a good talk was a monologue. Lamb stammered and chuckled, was often flippant and even ridiculous, yet managed to say a large number of shrewd and memorable things. Sometimes, like Oliver Goldsmith, he assumed stupidity for humorous effect. Once Coleridge — like most men in poor health, intent on giving good advice concerning diet and exercise — pompously announced that an excellent practice is to take a walk on an empty stomach. The irrepressible Lamb at once blurted out, "Whose stomach?" But though Lamb frequently donned the cap and bells, he was more than a jester; even his jokes had kernels of wisdom.

The Letter-Writer. Lamb was so delightful a conversationalist mainly because his spirits rose in congenial company, and as a letter-writer he was scarcely less delightful because to him writing a letter meant talking, pen in hand, to an understanding friend. And thus he talked, by means of the written word, to Coleridge, to Wordsworth, to numerous other friends, especially to Thomas Manning, whose prolonged absence in China occasioned the finest and most amusing of Lamb's informal epistles. He wrote mostly in the intervals of his work on the high stool "with a quill which seems more ready to glide into arithmetical figures . . . than into kindly responses and friendly recollections." Yet his letters rarely smell of aloes, ginger, and tea. They discuss, freely and frankly, the peculiarities of men and women he knew; they record his impressions of books and events; they present unstudied pictures of his mind and his heart; and sometimes, as in a letter he wrote from Coleridge's home in the Lake region, they convey lively descriptions of natural scenery, though Lamb professed to admire the busy Strand more than the mists and mountains:

We entered Coleridge's comfortable study just in the dusk, when the mountains were all dark with clouds upon their heads. Such an impression I never received from objects of sight before, nor do I suppose I can ever again. Glorious creatures, fine old fellows, Skiddaw, &c. I never shall forget ye, how ye lay about that night, like an intrenchment; gone to bed, as it seemed for the night, but promising that ye were to be seen in the morning. Coleridge had got a blazing fire in his study; which is a large, antique, ill-shaped room, with an old-fashioned organ, never played upon, big enough for a church, shelves of scattered folios, Æolian harp, and an old sofa, half-bed, &c. And all looking out upon the last fading view of Skiddaw and his broad-breasted brethren: what a night!

The Essayist. Lamb's letters read like essays in the formative stage, and his essays like letters toned down for publication. This genial informality makes him the master of the familiar essay in English. He assumes that his audience is interested in him, and he proceeds to tell what he thinks and feels and wishes and remembers. He is now humorous, now pathetic, now whimsical and illogical; at one moment he will describe an event in his daily life, at another he will dilate on the joy he derived from an unfamiliar book; here he dwells upon some bit of the London he knew so intimately and so ardently loved, there he records some winsome recollection of the good old days and the old familiar faces.

Lamb's *Essays of Elia*, fifty in all, were contributed during the thirteen years ending in 1833 to the *London Magazine* and two other publications. More than two thirds of them are frankly autobiographical (just plain Lamb), like "My Relations," "Dream-Children," and "Oxford in the Vacation." A few, like "The Child Angel" and "The New Year's Coming of Age," are half-humorous fairy tales rich in playful fancy.

Some are made up of observation and comment: "A Quakers' Meeting," "The Praise of Chimney-Sweepers," and "A Complaint of the Decay of Beggars in the Metropolis." Several of the essays, like "My First Play" and "On the Acting of Munden," disclose Lamb's deep interest in the theater, an interest which led him to bring out an annotated edition of *Specimens of English Dramatic Poets*. They are all different and all good; in *Elia* there is something to fit every day and every mood. Hard, indeed, to please must the reader be who fails to respond to the diverse appeal of such essays as "A Chapter on Ears," "Grace before Meat," and "A Dissertation upon Roast Pig."

Lamb did some other writing but never attained the high level of his essays. Of his few poems the best is "The Old Familiar Faces," really an *Elia* essay in irregular verse. *Rosamund Gray*, a novel, and *John Woodvil*,

CHARLES LAMB

Lamb and his sister Mary are buried in the quiet Edmonton churchyard. The inscription on the tall, flat stone was composed by the Reverend Henry Cary, a translator of Dante

a tragedy, are of interest to us only because Lamb wrote them. A much finer production is *Tales from Shakespeare*, written in collaboration with Mary Lamb. This book makes suitable reading for children too immature to appreciate Shakespeare at first hand and for children of a larger growth who want an easy approach to the master dramatist. Lamb's *Tales* is a classic of "mediating interpretation."

Within his limitations Lamb was a sound and judicious critic, though his enthusiasm for the Elizabethan dramatists was misproportioned; his comments on such topics as "Stage Illusion," "The Genteel Style in Writing," and "Detached Thoughts on Books and Reading" are sane and stimulating. But always it is his spirit, his style, his personality, that mainly matters. Devotees of formal rhetoric will be frequently shocked at his sentence structure and his figures of speech, and earnest students intent on learning how to write will imitate him to their undoing; for Lamb laughs at rules and baffles disciples. His is the supreme gift of being superbly alive and of conveying to his readers much of his abundant life. And, as Arthur Symons points out, Charles Lamb is good for the soul:

To read Lamb makes a man more humane, more tolerant, more dainty; incites to every natural piety, strengthens reverence; while it clears his brain of whatever dull fumes may have lodged there, stirs up all his senses to wary alertness, and actually quickens his vitality, like high pure air. . . . His jests add a new reverence to lovely and noble things, or light up an unsuspected "soul of goodness in things evil."[1]

HAZLITT

Three Critics. The mention of William Hazlitt (1778–1830) recalls a remarkable instance of the influence of mind on mind irrespective of time and place and circumstance. Hazlitt is the connecting link between two eminent literary critics, — Dr. Johnson the Englishman and Sainte-Beuve the Frenchman. Though Hazlitt is in himself and of himself important both as writer and as critic, he learned much from the Classical Dictator, and the spirit of Hazlitt's method of commenting on literature he unknowingly handed across the English Channel to the man who is esteemed one of the ornaments of French scholarship and letters. For Hazlitt this association with Johnson and Sainte-Beuve is at once a distinction and a handicap; yet he stands high, even in the company of giants.

[1] *Figures of Several Centuries*, pp. 29–30.

In his *Lives of the Poets* and other comments on literature Johnson had practically invented what has since come to be known as the biographical method of studying books. His principle was that to know the book we must know the writer, to evaluate the poem or the drama we must appreciate the man. Earlier critics, notably Longinus, had recognized the truth that literature is, among other things, an expression of the personality of the author, but Johnson reduced the theory to practice and proceeded to interpret literature in the light of the character and attainments of the men who had produced it. This method he did not follow exclusively, partly because he was devoted to the Classical ideals of literature, partly because he had the good sense to perceive that other factors besides personality enter into literary production; but to him belongs the credit of utilizing what is known about an author to throw light upon what the author has written.

This personal method of literary criticism William Hazlitt carried to lengths undreamed of by the burly dictator. Many of Hazlitt's essays, particularly his *Contemporary Portraits,* his *Lectures on the English Comic Writers,* and his *Plain Speaker,* are examples (frequently extreme) of the delineation of writers' personal characteristics for the purpose of throwing light upon the meaning of their writings. Hazlitt was read by Sainte-Beuve, and the reading led to imitation — an imitation which extended even to the titles of books. One of Sainte-Beuve's most typical productions is called *Portraits Contemporains,* and a queer and not altogether wholesome work of Hazlitt's, *Liber Amoris* (The Book of Love), was emulated by Sainte-Beuve, in matter and in manner, in his *Livre d'Amour.* As men and as writers Hazlitt and Sainte-Beuve resembled each other, though the Englishman had more force and strength, the Frenchman more sensitiveness and delicacy.

A Solitary Spirit. Born in Maidstone, William Hazlitt first purposed to follow his father into the ministry, but he became dissatisfied with Unitarianism and instead gave himself to the study of art. He early fell under the spell of Coleridge's personality and was for a time an enthusiastic admirer of Romantic ideals in literature and revolutionary ideas in life; but wide reading and his sound common sense prevented him from running to extremes, and he preserved an intellectual balance between Classicism and Romanticism. He was twice married, neither time happily. Though he had friends in London, where he engaged in a variety of literary work for the magazines, he was always much by himself and achieved the reputation of being a difficult and quarrelsome character. He spent some of his time at Winterslow, in the south of England, where he took long walks, gave many hours to silent musing before the fire, and wrote most of his memorable essays. It is difficult to include Hazlitt among the persons we should like to have met, for as a man he possessed slight appeal. He has been pictured as "of the middle size, with a handsome and eager countenance, worn by sickness and thought, and with dark hair which curled stiffly over the temples. His gait was slouching and awkward and his dress neglected."

An Enduring Essayist. However little we may find ourselves disposed to like the man, the writer Hazlitt is a prince of critics and a thoroughly delightful essayist. He was one of the truly great interpreters of great literature. His *Characters of Shakespeare's Plays* is a collection of sound and helpful comments, lacking much of the erudition which has since become associated with Shakespearean criticism, but revealing a singular skill in getting to the core of each drama and in studying the principal characters with sense and discrimination. The case is much the same with his *Lectures on the English Comic Writers*, on the Elizabethan dramatists, and on the poets of his own day. Most of his opinions have been justified by time, and his critiques of such men as Wordsworth, Cobbett, Byron, and Moore are still timely and suggestive.

Many of Hazlitt's writings are third-person essays, but he was not less adept in writing about himself and his intellectual adventures; and the highest tribute that can be paid to his style is that he succeeds in making himself interesting. Whatever the man may have been whom Lamb gently admonished and Gifford quarreled with and Patmore accused of "ingrained selfishness," there can be no doubt that the man revealed in the autobiographical essays of Hazlitt is a person of charm and urbanity. He is at his most delightful best in such essays as "On Going a Journey" and "On Living to One's-Self." In a recently discovered paper of his on "Traveling Abroad" we find a concluding paragraph which in form and substance reveals much of his power and attractiveness:

It is well to be a citizen of the world, to fall in, as nearly as one can, with the ways and feelings of others, and make one's self at home wherever one comes: or it is better still to live in an *ideal* world, superior to the ordinary one, to carry in one's breast "that peace which passeth understanding," that no accident of time or place, irritation or disappointment, can assail, except for the moment; that neither debts nor duns annoy, that reconciles itself to all situations and smooths all difficulties; not to be calm in solitude and agitated in the assemblies of men, but in the midst of a great city to retain possession of one's faculties as in perfect solitude, and in a wilderness to be surrounded with the gorgeousness of art; to owe no allegiance to the elements, nor to be the creature of circumstances, dependent on a gust of wind, a bad smell, a dinner, or a waiter at an inn, the good or bad state of the roads, but to make the best of our goings and comings, and of all circumstances, as only passages of that longer yet brief journey, that by fitful stages and various ups and downs conducts us to "our native dust and final home"!

THE PERIODICAL REVIEWERS

Literary Magazines. The beginning of the nineteenth century was marked by the appearance of several quarterly and monthly reviews mainly devoted to the discussion of books and authors. Their comments on new volumes and their statements of critical principles attracted wide attention, in some instances influenced individual writers, and served to focus attention on literary criticism as an art. The magazines or periodical reviews grew with the century and toward the end of the Victorian Age were the accepted means of expression employed by writers of essays on literature, art, history, and economics. Every one of the English essayists of the nineteenth century wrote for reviews, and some of them (for example, De Quincey) did practically nothing else.

Francis Jeffrey (1773-1850). A veritable high priest among the periodical reviewers was Francis Jeffrey, who, in the pages of the *Edinburgh Review*, vigorously championed conservative ideas in literature and unsparingly attacked the Romantic poets. He edited the *Edinburgh* from its foundation in 1802 till 1829, and he continued to contribute to it for twenty years more. A small, swarthy Scotsman with considerable learning, a wide range of interests, and strong convictions and prejudices, Jeffrey had a gift for controversy and a competent power of expression. Time has proved him a false prophet in several instances—he gravely discussed the immortality of Mrs. Hemans, Rogers, and Campbell, declared Goethe's *Wilhelm Meister* to be "so much trash," and systematically depreciated Keats, Shelley, and Wordsworth ; but he was not always making mistakes, and he had a genuine appreciation of good writing. He did more than any other man of his day to raise literary criticism to the dignity of an art.

"This will never do!" were the words with which Jeffrey began his review of Wordsworth's *Excursion* in the *Edinburgh* for November, 1814 ; and then and ever after he voiced his disapproval of the Lake Poets, whom he characterized as a "puling and self-admiring race." Preëminently a city man, he regarded descriptions of natural scenery as affected and hypocritical, suspected Coleridge's devotion to wonder and mystery, and exposed Southey's artificiality and fondness for irregular meters. Yet it is unjust to assume that Jeffrey, despite his horror of "the natural drawl of the Lakers," was mainly destructive in his criticism. Generally he was more ready to praise than to condemn, and his frequent statements of critical principles are still essentially keen and discerning. In his reception of Keats's *Endymion* he was more restrained and temperate than the other critics of the time, and cheerfully admitted that the poem is "as full of genius as of absurdity." And he was prompt to recognize the enduring merits of Hazlitt's essays on Shakespeare.

Sydney Smith (1771-1845). Associated with Jeffrey on the *Edinburgh Review* was a brilliant Yorkshire parson whom Macaulay described as "a book in breeches." Sydney Smith was more of a journalist than a critic, with the result that most of his writings have lost their interest; but he brought both wit and humor to his discussion of current literary and political topics. His peculiarly racy style may be savored in his *Letters of Peter Plymley*, a series of brilliant papers advocating the removal from Catholics of political disabilities.

William Gifford (1756-1826). The most prominent practitioner of that slashing criticism which we find in many of the literary articles appearing in the first half of the nineteenth century was William Gifford, who edited the *Quarterly Review* from its foundation in 1809 till 1824. It was he who so savagely attacked John Keats as to furnish the legend that the young poet was "snuff'd out" by the *Quarterly* article. The magazine was started to offset the prestige of the *Edinburgh*, and enlisted among its contributors certain authors, including Southey, whom Jeffrey had castigated. Gifford engaged in a fierce literary quarrel with Hazlitt and was soundly trounced in *The Spirit of the Age*. One of Gifford's contributors was Sir Walter Scott, who came over from the *Edinburgh* and wrote numerous critical articles, including an appreciation of one of his own books.

John Gibson Lockhart (1794-1854). Scott's son-in-law, John Gibson Lockhart, succeeded Gifford as editor of the *Quarterly* and was also a frequent contributor to *Blackwood's Magazine*. He was more conservative than Jeffrey, and emulated the venomous Gifford to such good purpose that he came to be known as "the scorpion." But he was more than a fighting editor. He was widely read in European Literature and made some good translations of Spanish poetry. He wrote a *Life of Burns* and achieved his masterpiece in his *Life of Scott*, a book which is almost a classic.

John Wilson (1785-1854). Using the pen name of "Christopher North," John Wilson was the mainstay of *Blackwood's Magazine* with his articles on various subjects written in a breezy, allusive style. He is mainly responsible for *Noctes Ambrosianæ*, a collection of literary dialogues on life and books originated by William Maginn (1793-1842), editor of *Fraser's Magazine*. The *Noctes* are still read and Wilson deserves his vogue. At his best he recalls the extravagant wit of Father Prout, the mellow wisdom of *My Unknown Chum*, and the acuteness and eloquence sometimes manifested by Southey in *The Doctor*.

Thomas de Quincey (1785-1859). When he was a little boy in the industrial city of Manchester, Thomas de Quincey used to play an odd game with his brother. The lads pretended they were rulers of kingdoms. Thomas's kingdom was called Gombroon, and his brother insisted that the Gombroonians had tails and suggested that their ruler make them keep sitting down to wear their tails off. Thomas thought that was a desperate remedy, whereupon his brother remarked, "If you don't like it you may abdicate."

De Quincey the writer was ever a King of Gombroon, living amid his imaginings and dangling the tails of his dreams. No amount of sitting could wear those literary tails away. He was intended by nature to be a poet, but he decided that a poet he would never be. He abdicated. He wrote prose, contributing to the *London Magazine*, to *Blackwood's*, and to other periodicals. His collected essays fill seventeen volumes, and the set might well be called The Chronicles of Gombroon. For they deal with a life as far removed from actuality as the fancied kingdom of his childhood, and though they are written in prose, it is a prose that more closely resembles poetry than anything else in the English language. Often we find prose writers — Sir Thomas Browne, Jeremy Taylor, Newman, Francis Thompson — who occasionally rise from the ground of prose and soar for a while in the pure serene of poetry; but De Quincey is the only man who, professing to tread the solid earth, is prevailingly and con- genially in the clouds.

DE QUINCEY

De Quincey is in the clouds in more ways than one. He could say something sound and practical when he was so minded, — it is De Quincey who draws the significant distinc- tion between the litera- ture of knowledge and the literature of power, — but mostly he re- duces both life and art to a rhapsody of words. With words he can do wonderful things. He makes them sing and dance, makes them paint pictures of gorgeous coloring and fantastic design, makes them bring forth a new heaven and a new earth. He had all the poet's gifts save the conviction that he could write poetry.

Like most poets, De Quincey was at his best when discussing himself, his life, his memories, his desires, and his dreams. So to know him as he thought himself to be we read his *Confessions of an English Opium Eater* — like the vastly different *Confessions* of St. Augustine in no wise a sensational book, but a series of poetical imaginings caught in the meshes of that exuberant prose style of his. And we read his *Revolt of the Tartars*, his *Joan of Arc*, his *Suspiria de Profundis*, his elaborate piece of imaginative irony called *On Murder considered as One of the Fine Arts*, not to discover anything new or profound about human history or human manners, but just to enter into his rococo visions and enjoy the flavor of his riotous rhetoric. It might be inconvenient for us to develop into literary Gombroonians, but it is broadening and refreshing to make an occasional excursion into the Kingdom of Gombroon.

Thomas Babington Macaulay (1800–1859). Though often classified as a historian because of his brilliant *History of England*, Macaulay is really a superlative periodical reviewer: in him, more than in Jeffrey, more than in De Quincey, magazine writing became literature. He brought to it vast scholarship, varied interests, an exceptional memory exceptionally well stored, and a style of writing at once dignified and interesting, vigorous and eloquent. And while Jeffrey and De Quincey continue to appeal to groups of readers interested in technical literary criticism and in prose with the lilt and splendor of poetry, Macaulay enjoys a wider if less discriminating audience. Nobody today accepts him seriously as a historian, for his distortion of facts and his political bias and his lordly indifference to original sources conspire to affect his reputation. Few readers give him much heed as a literary critic, for his prejudices were patent, his standards arbitrary, and his eye for literary beauty affected with partial myopia. His studies of men like Bacon, Walpole, and Boswell are generally discredited as biographical material, his sociological and political comments are antiquated, and his discussions of education and religion cocksure and absurd. It is possible to make out a very strong case against him. But he is still read. He is read because he is sprightly and entertaining and provocative of thought; because, whatever may be his failings as historian and critic and biographer and philosopher, he has the literary touch and the literary imagination and the literary gift of being alive.

Macaulay is often thought of as a journalist, but it is hardly fair to dismiss his representative essays as mere "journalese." If they have endured, they have endured as literature. He had the journalist's tendency to rush at conclusions, to overlook verifying his data, to make black things very black and white things very white, to sacrifice sense for sound and truth for effect. Above all, he had the journalist's consciousness of being hurried in his work and of writing for an audience neither very learned nor very exacting. But he wrote well. We may shake our heads over his frequent balanced sentences and a certain metallic quality in his style, but we must admit that it is a sort of English higher and firmer and more richly allusive and more sparklingly real than is known to journalism then or now. He may be an unsafe model for young writers, as he is certainly

MACAULAY

an injudicious exemplar for young thinkers; but he is a delight and an inspiration to any man who would know something of the resources of the written word. He was clever, perhaps, rather than truly great; but his was a clear and capable cleverness.

Macaulay's essay on Milton, which appeared in the *Edinburgh Review* when the author was only twenty-five years old, was the first of a long line of reviews which flowed rapidly and easily from his active pen. He was more than a writer. As a member of the legal profession and as a Parliamentary orator he was distinguished for his ability to amass material and present conclusions in attractive speeches, and as a conversationalist his power and energy challenged the active-minded and terrified the brainless. He tried his hand at verse-writing too, and in "Horatius," "Ivry," and "The Battle of Naseby" achieved spirited metrical narrations and descriptions.

The best thing in Macaulay's *History of England* is his third chapter, with its graphic portrayal of London life and manners in the days of James II. Of his essays the ablest is his account of Warren Hastings and the trial in Westminster Hall; Macaulay was an authority on conditions in India and brought his vast learning to bear upon his study of the impeached viceroy. As a literary critic he can be seen, for good and for ill, in such essays as those on Dante, on Milton, on Leigh Hunt, and in his review of Moore's *Life of Byron*. Every essential quality of his style may be discerned in the oft-quoted tribute to the Catholic Church contained in his not otherwise notable review of Von Ranke's *History of the Popes*. There we find his directness, his allusiveness, his extraordinary command of words, his enthusiasm, his vigor, and his fondness for concrete images and startling effects.

CARLYLE

Dumfries and Chelsea. A stretch of pleasant countryside in southern Scotland and a quiet and stately portion of the giant city of London are the two main landmarks in the life history of Thomas Carlyle (1795–1881). In Dumfriesshire, at Ecclefechan, Carlyle was born, and thither, after his funeral in Westminster Abbey, his weary old body was brought to repose; in Dumfriesshire he attended school in the town of Annan and did some teaching too; and in the same border region, at Craigenputtock, he settled with Jane Welsh, his bride, and lived six richly productive years. Then for nearly half a century he dwelt at 5 Cheyne Row,[1] Chelsea, in a narrow three-storied house with a bit of garden behind it, which he equipped with a

---

[1] Pronounced "Chainy."

sound-proof study. Here he read and dreamed and suffered from indigestion and wrote his *French Revolution* and other works; here in his dour fashion he was neighborly with Leigh Hunt and entertained Ruskin, Tennyson, Emerson, and other friends; here, after Mrs. Carlyle's sudden death in 1866, he dragged out his chill and solitary and strangely sad old age; and hither (for the house is now a Carlyle museum) come visitors from every land to the spot where Carlyle lived and labored.

CARLYLE'S HOUSE, CHELSEA

Near the Church of the Holy Redeemer, Cheyne Row

To visit Dumfriesshire and Chelsea is to draw very close to the strong and gruff and noble personality of Thomas Carlyle. At Craigenputtock we can envisage the bleak moorland farm where the essay on Burns and *Sartor Resartus* were written; at the house in Cheyne Row we can inspect his books and his souvenirs and his array of walking sticks and long clay pipes, and in the garden the grave of Nero, his favorite dog. In both places we can reconstruct the busy, toilsome, somber life he led and then go back to his essays with deepened insight and renewed appreciation.

Carlyle's Books. Few men have put so much of their essential selves into their writings. A recent biographer says:

His books are intensely, supremely personal. They review his own struggles, his slowly-won mastery over himself and his circumstances, his entire theory of human life and conduct. With a vividness almost if not quite unrivaled in the whole history of literature, they describe his ancestry and early environment, his unsystematic education, his painful quest of a career, and the spiritual conflicts by which he came to an ultimate command of himself.[1]

Much has been written about Carlyle, but nothing nearly so good as what he wrote of himself. Let us briefly consider his most representative works.

Part novel, part autobiography, and part philosophical treatise is *Sartor Resartus* (1833). The title means "The Tailor Patched," and gets its point from the fact that Carlyle pretended to comment on or patch the discourses on clothes of an imaginary German "Professor of Things in General," one Herr Teufelsdröckh of the "University of Weissnichtwo" ("I Know not Where"). The Professor is a thinly veiled and slightly caricatured portrait of Carlyle himself, and the substance of his "clothes philosophy" is thus expressed:

> The beginning of all Wisdom is to look fixedly on Clothes . . . till they become *transparent*. . . . Happy he who can look through the Clothes of a Man (the woollen, and fleshly, and official Bank-paper, and State-paper Clothes) into the Man himself; and discern, it may be, in this or the other Dread Potentate, a more or less incompetent Digestive-apparatus; yet also an inscrutable venerable Mystery, in the meanest Tinker that sees with eyes!

And so Carlyle proceeds to analyze clothing as a succession of symbols and conventions — social, professional, political, religious — and to consider the nature of man and human history from that unique point of view. The book has humor of a sort, and high seriousness, and numerous passages of fitful power and rough, glowing eloquence. Justly celebrated are the great chapters on "The Everlasting No" and "The Everlasting Yea," the one vividly picturing the barrenness of unbelief, the other concluding with Carlyle's Gospel of Work:

> I too could now say to myself: Be no longer a Chaos, but a World, or even Worldkin. Produce! Produce! Were it but the pitifullest infinites-

---

[1] Bliss Perry, *Thomas Carlyle*, "Preliminary."

imal fraction of a Product, produce it, in God's name! 'Tis the utmost thou hast in thee: out with it, then. Up, up! Whatsoever thy hand findeth to do, do it with thy whole might. Work while it is called Today; for the Night cometh, wherein no man can work.

Carlyle had given the greater part of the manuscript of *The French Revolution* to John Stuart Mill to read, and Mill's servant girl stupidly burned it as waste paper. Carlyle grimly set to work to rewrite the vast work, and the book came out in 1837. As a piece of historical writing it is most unusual. Instead of an orderly procession of names and dates and events, Carlyle gives a series of vivid, sensational pictures of men and episodes. The method has since been used by historians (by Hilaire Belloc, for instance, when writing on the same subject), but it was something distinctly new a hundred years ago. In this book Carlyle anticipated our modern motion pictures; his chapters are so many scenarios. He has frequent shifting of scenes; he utilizes large crowds, as in his account of the fall of the Bastille; and he employs effectively the device known as the "close-up." In *The French Revolution* Chelsea reached out to Hollywood.

Carlyle engaged in other historical writing, including *Cromwell's Letters and Speeches* and a *History of Frederick the Great*, and in *Heroes and Hero Worship* set forth his "great man" philosophy of history. He set his head against the so-called scientific method of seeing in history merely the operation of natural laws, and instead found the key to historical events in the great men or heroes who in one way or another dominated their own age and influenced succeeding generations. A strange assortment of such heroes he here presents: the Norse god Odin, Mahomet, Martin Luther, Dante and Shakespeare, Rousseau, Johnson and Burns, Cromwell and Napoleon; and his treatment of his heroes is as varied as the heroes themselves. No other book in English Literature is capable of awakening at once so much cordial enthusiasm and so much irreconcilable antagonism. Carlyle is frequently lopsided, wrong-headed, and inconsistent, misreading facts, and making his great men in his own image and likeness; but just as often he reveals splendid ideals, deep knowledge of human nature, and a command of forceful, glowing imagery.

Carlyle wrote a *Life of Schiller*, a *Life of Sterling*, and numerous essays on literary men; he translated Goethe's *Wilhelm Meister* and labored to make German Literature and German philosophy appreciated in England. He engaged, too, in political and social studies like *Past and Present* and *Latter-Day Pamphlets*. In *Past and Present* he gives a characteristically vigorous and pictorial account of the educational and social work of an English abbot in the Middle Ages and then makes a stirring application of the implied lesson to the nineteenth century.

Ideas and Influences. Like Cardinal Newman — and this is about the only point of resemblance between these two eminent essayists — Carlyle never wrote for the sake of writing or merely to entertain and amuse: always he had a serious purpose and was actuated by a great if sometimes misguided zeal. In a day when democratic ideals were honored and such liberalizing movements as Catholic Emancipation and the correction of abuses in the factory system were making their way in England, Carlyle sternly denounced representative government and the extension of the suffrage. "Manhood suffrage!" he snorts in *Latter-Day Pamphlets*; "presently you will be demanding horsehood suffrage." Our modern dictatorships in Spain, Italy, and Belgium would have added to his complacency, but our women casting their votes would have accentuated his dyspepsia. His distrust of popular rule sprang from his hero theory, or should we say his hero theory sprang from his distrust of popular rule? His heroes, including Prussian Frederick, were men who imposed their will upon the masses, and because they were able to do what they would they were the interpreters of the will of God. There were hardly enough of his heroes to cover all history, and especially no immediate prospect of their line continuing in the days of Queen Victoria, and that conviction saddened and embittered Thomas Carlyle.

Wrong, as we conceive it, in his idea of government, he was not less mistaken in his attitude toward religion. True, he recognized the importance of religion in life and insisted with commendable earnestness on the worth of spiritual things:

CARLYLE

From an original painting in the collection of George A. Plimpton

"A man's religion is the chief fact with regard to him." He contemptuously called materialism "pig-philosophy." But his conception of religion suffered by reason of his heredity and his personal experience. Brought up in a narrow, rigid form of Protestantism, he struck off its shackles in early manhood, and with much groaning of spirit, worshiped a vague and remote God and evolved his Gospel of Work. Why, we might ask, did he not turn to Catholicism? Because he was convinced that Catholicism was as dead as paganism. He had been taught, and he believed and expressed his belief in his essay on Luther, that the Catholic Church had grown hopelessly corrupt and that its Divine mission was transferred to Protestantism. But in his own day he saw Protestantism breaking up and losing its force — in his own day and in his own life; and, a dour and disillusioned Scotch Don Quixote, he tilted at windmills and charged on flocks of sheep. He praised Luther for fighting the principle of authority in religion, and then was pained and chagrined on seeing the spiritual children of Luther fighting authority in other departments of life. He was blind to the fact that the Catholic Church continued to maintain and extend her mission in the world and that the Protestant Rebellion, like the early heresies, was but an incident in her existence.

A CARTOON OF CARLYLE

Much of Carlyle's power and much of his erroneous philosophy of life came to him as the result of his interest in German thought and literature. His devotion to Goethe, to Schiller, and to other German poets helped to perpetuate the European Tradition, and his transfusion of German philosophy did much to enrich English thought. But it was not an unmixed good; and his admiration for Frederick the Great and militarism, so pronounced and so pervading, distorted his vision of history and his conception of democracy. To Germany, too, we must look (when we do not seek the explanation in Carlyle's own ungraceful and cantankerous nature) for the cause of his crotchety, uneven, uncouth style of writing, a style so unusual, so un-English as to deserve the name of "Carlylese." German syntax is beautiful and appropriate, in German; but not even at the hands of Carlyle could it stand transplanting.

Such are Carlyle's principal limitations, and it is not because of these that he is great. His greatness in literature is due to his rare ability to express noble thoughts nobly. And he expressed many noble thoughts: "Everywhere in life the true question is, not what we *gain*, but what we *do*," is one of his immortal maxims. His essay on Dante is a masterpiece, and so is his essay on Burns. His attacks on shams and hypocrisies, on the worship of money and the glorification of material power, are still moving and practical. And the twentieth century has much to learn from his preachments on the duty of reverence. "An irreverent knowledge is no knowledge," he laconically wrote in *Chartism*; and in *Sartor Resartus*:

I mean that Thought without Reverence is barren, perhaps poisonous; at best, dies like cookery with the day that called it forth; does not live, like sowing, in successive tilths and wider-spreading harvests, bringing food and plenteous increase to all Time. . . . The man who cannot wonder, who does not habitually wonder (and worship) . . . is but a Pair of Spectacles behind which there is no Eye.

"Carlylese." Carlyle, as we have said, is his own best biographer; perhaps, too, he is his own best critic. His remarkable individual manner of writing — a manner which alternately thrills and irritates, caricatures and adorns — he described accurately when discussing the art of the imaginary Herr Teufelsdröckh:

Of his sentences perhaps not more than nine-tenths stand straight on their legs; the remainder are in quite angular attitudes, buttressed-up by props (of parentheses and dashes), and ever with this or the other tagrag hanging from them; a few even sprawl-out helplessly on all sides, quite broken-backed and dismembered. Nevertheless, in almost his very worst moods, there lies in him a singular attraction. A wild tone pervades the whole utterance of the man, like its keynote and regulator; now screwing itself aloft as into the Song of Spirits, or else the shrill mockery of Fiends; now sinking in cadences, not without melodious heartiness, though sometimes abrupt enough, into the common pitch, when we hear it only as a monotonous hum; of which hum the true character is extremely difficult to fix. Up to this hour we have never fully satisfied ourselves whether it is a tone and hum of real Humour, which we reckon among the very highest qualities of genius, or some echo of mere Insanity and Inanity, which doubtless ranks below the very lowest.

ARNOLD

Sweet Reasonableness. Carlyle was a Hebrew prophet with a Scotch accent; Arnold was a Greek sophist with the Oxford manner. The sophists in Athens were not evil men or insincere men, though our word *sophism*, meaning a deceptive manner of reasoning, might lead us to think that the sophists were simply intellectual hypocrites. They were essentially teachers, and many of them were good teachers; but there came a time when they taught more than they learned, and accordingly fell victims to shallow scholarship and erroneous principles. Matthew Arnold (1822–1888) devoted many years of his life to educational work, inspecting schools all over England and writing copiously and often excellently on study and teaching. He was an earnest student as well; but with all his teaching and writing he had little leisure for intensive scholarship and for sage meditation and reflection, and so he unconsciously imitated the sophists and fell into some of their errors.

And as Carlyle was gruff and shrill and angular of spirit, so Arnold was suave and polished, flexible and serene. He was fond of using an expression he had borrowed from Dean Swift, "sweetness and light," and he invented for himself the term "sweet reasonableness." He waged polite but effective warfare against two classes of men whom he called Philistines and Barbarians — those who had wrong notions of intellectual culture and those who were indifferent to it altogether. That word *culture* he popularized as meaning a fine product of education and thinking and living; one of its marks, he claimed, is "flexibility of spirit," and another is freedom from "habits of unintellectual routine and one-sided growth." A passage in one of his letters suggests something of his temperament and outlook :

Partly nature, partly time and study, have also by this time taught me thoroughly the precious truth that everything turns upon one's exercising the power of *persuasion*, of *charm*; that without this all energy, reasoning power, acquirement, are thrown away and only render their owner more miserable. Even in one's ridicule one must preserve a sweetness and good humor.

Arnold's father, Thomas Arnold, was a clergyman and a distinguished educator. He was long headmaster of Rugby and there brought about a complete change for the better in study and character training. Matthew Arnold, born at Laleham on the Thames, where his father was then rector, spent his boyhood at Rugby, and after completing his studies at Oxford taught for two years under his father's direction. He was inspector of schools from 1851 to 1886 and from 1857 to 1867 taught literature at Oxford. Like most educated Englishmen he did some traveling on the Continent and even invaded the United States as a lecturer. He died suddenly at Liverpool and was buried at Laleham. Though his life was busy and distracting, he yet found time to write a considerable amount of poetry and a large number of essays.

Arnold the Poet. Though less popular than Tennyson and less spectacular than Browning, Arnold ranks high among the Victorian poets. He had a genuine lyric gift, a fastidious taste, and a mood of sweet melancholy with an intellectual cast. The note of sadness in Arnold, as suggested in his "Dover Beach," was due largely to his loss of faith in the Christian belief of his youth. A fellow feeling in this respect with Arthur Hugh Clough gives vitality and conviction to his "Thyrsis," written in commemoration of that frustrate poet. In "Rugby Chapel" Arnold gave us one of the most beautiful and inspiring poems in the English language, an affectionate eulogy of his father as man and as educator. He was at his best in elegiac verses like these and like "The Scholar-Gypsy" and "Heine's Grave," and almost as fine in several of his sonnets and in his longer lyric poems, such as "The Forsaken Merman." He was less successful when he attempted narrative in *Sohrab and Rustum*, *Balder Dead*, and *Tristram and Iseult*, though those poems contain passages of rare and almost flawless beauty.

Arnold the Essayist. Of the "big four" among the Victorian essayists, Arnold is the least impressive figure. He lacked Carlyle's titanic force, Newman's depth and range and eloquence, and Ruskin's burning zeal and florid imagination. He was closer in literary spirit to Newman than to the others, for

MATTHEW ARNOLD

From a painting by G. F. Watts in the National Portrait Gallery, London

both he and Newman had the Oxford manner, a grace and a temperance of thought and expression not shared by Carlyle and Ruskin. At times Arnold wrote exquisitely, though the general level of his style falls considerably below that of the Cardinal. Besides literature and education, politics and religion occupied much of his attention. In politics he was a moderate liberal, as is seen in his advice to his fellow countrymen concerning Ireland: "to acquire a larger and sweeter temper, a larger and more lucid mind." In religion he would be called today a modernist. Though his religious interests were strong (he was an assiduous reader of *The Imitation of Christ* and other Catholic devotional literature) his philosophical and theological scholarship was scanty; and in such books as *Literature and Dogma, God and the Bible,* and *St. Paul and Protestantism* he revealed his uncertain and inadequate grasp of his subjects. Like Carlyle he was another product of rebellion against the authority of an infallible teaching Church.

© Emery Walker Limited

Arnold the Critic. Arnold's ablest prose is found in his literary essays, especially in his two series of *Essays in Criticism*, *On Translating Homer*, *The Study of Celtic Literature*, and *Discourses in America*. Here Arnold writes with intelligence, with poise, and with enthusiasm on problems such as the influence of literary academies, and on a miscellany of writers, including Marcus Aurelius, Joubert, Wordsworth, Byron, Amiel, and Tolstoi; here we find his principles of criticism stated and his favorite theories given rein. Though some of Arnold's dicta are outmoded and disproved, it is none the less true that "his critical essays will be found in the end a broader and more lasting, as they are a saner, influence than the exaggerated æstheticism of Ruskin or the shrill prophesying of Carlyle or the scientific dogmatism of Huxley."[1]

The literary essays of Arnold hold numerous important precepts for the student who would secure the richest return on his reading investment. They inculcate "the discipline of respect for a high and flawless excellence" and insist that the power of literature "resides chiefly in the refining and elevation wrought in us by the high and rare excellence of the great style." Though by preference and training a devotee of the Greek and Latin classics, Arnold was in substantial agreement with Sainte-Beuve in recognizing as classics the best books in every language, and his comments are surest and firmest when dealing with writers of established fame. He was able, too, to recognize literary excellence even when it does not conform to established canons and precedents, and thus he avoided the mistakes of the ultra-Classical critics of the eighteenth century. Criticism, which he defined as a "disinterested endeavor to learn and propagate the best that has been known and thought in the world," Arnold regarded as an instrument of culture, and culture itself as a "study of perfection" with "its origin in the love of perfection." Thus he insisted on high standards alike in literature and in life. The method of this

[1] Paul Elmer More, *Shelburne Essays* (Seventh Series), p. 222.

cultural criticism he explained as being a "free play of the mind on all subjects which it touches," and to "approach truth on one side after another, not to strive or cry, nor to persist in pressing forward, on any one side, with violence and self-will."

NEWMAN

Infinite Riches. When we consider Cardinal Newman we consider the supreme master of English prose. In his best work (and most of what he wrote is his best) we have the finest-known examples of terse, clear, vigorous, colorful, and artistic idiomatic English. In his almost miraculous facility in manipulating the delicate and flexible instrument of language he is superbly alone. Not to know Newman is not to know English.

The collected writings of Cardinal Newman fill forty volumes, and we can gain some notion of the many-sided nature of the man and of his works if we investigate the books that bear his name. Lionel Johnson has given us an excellent summary of that five-foot shelf:

There are twelve volumes of perfect oratory, not in the main theological, but ethical and psychological; there are, at most, but seven volumes of professed technical theology. The rest contain "infinite riches": satire, humor, romance, criticism, poetry, history; he has composed Ciceronian dialogues; he has parodied prize poems; he has written African witch-chants; he has satirized newspaper articles and public speeches; he has imitated the Greek tragic chorus; he has enriched criticism with faultless judgments. To him I turn for the truest estimates of Byron or of Cicero; for the best theory of portrait-painting; for the subtlest description of musical emotion. Newman was, emphatically, a man of social habit, and his books are more full than Thackeray's of worldly knowledge. And all this wealth of matter and thought is conveyed in a style of singular charm, of most strange and haunting beauty.[1]

Lack of knowledge begets false notions of a writer, and we could easily but most unjustly form the impression that Newman was merely a devout and zealous churchman who wrote

[1] *Post Liminium*, pp. 303, 304.

mostly on dry and learned theological subjects for the enlightenment and edification of his clerical brethren. We see some of his volumes labeled *Parochial and Plain Sermons*, and we are prone to assume that sermons are necessarily dull reading. Another title — *Historical Sketches*, or *An Essay in Aid of a Grammar of Assent* — hardly raises our expectations. Now Johnson's summary of Newman's writings will help us to perceive that the illustrious Cardinal had a mind attuned to varied strains of thought and an eye intent on truth and beauty in manifold forms. And if we go a little farther and look between the covers of some of those solemn-appearing books, we shall discover that they contain prose and poetry which, whatever the subject and whatever the purpose of the writing, possess the essential traits of true and noble literature, including the quality of being alive.

NEWMAN IN THE NOONDAY
OF HIS LIFE

A Religious Spirit. A key to the understanding of John Henry Newman is a perception of his intense religious spirit. To him his own soul and God were the unfailing entities. His profound scholarship, his deep, almost uncanny knowledge of the human heart, his breadth and depth of intellectual power, his persuasive influence over the minds and hearts of others, his peerless skill as a writer, were all made possible by his ever-constant and ever-increasing sense of spiritual values. His entrance into the Catholic Church was, he tells us, like "coming into port after a rough sea. . . . O long sought after, tardily found, desire of the eyes, joy of the heart, the truth after many shadows, the fullness after many foretastes, the home after many storms." Religion was the mainspring of his life, the inspiration of his labors, the source of his greatness. Religion disciplined his mind, chastened his spirit, formed his literary style.

Newman's life was all but coextensive with the life of the nineteenth century. He was born in London in 1801 and died at Birmingham in 1890. Nearly half his years were spent at Oxford as student, as teacher, as inspirer and spiritual guide. His personality won a large following, and his sermons preached in St. Mary's Church (Anglican) made religion a vital thing to the students who flocked to hear them. His first and his last sermon as a minister of the Church of England were on the same text : "Man goeth forth to his work and to his labor until evening." The twenty years that intervened between the two sermons were filled with the labors and the strivings and the perplexities of a man who, like Dante, was no timid friend to truth.

The Oxford Movement, in which Newman was a leader, was an attempt on the part of a group of earnest, educated Anglicans to get back to the spirit and the doctrine of primitive Christianity. Many of them came to perceive that primitive Christianity and Roman Catholicism were the same thing and accordingly entered the Church. This Newman did, after long years of study, reflection, and prayer, in 1845. His conversion created a profound sensation throughout England. Figuratively and literally he went to Rome, was there ordained a priest, entered a religious congregation of the Priests of the Oratory founded by St. Philip Neri, and returned to his native land to engage in clerical and scholarly work. He was invited by the Irish bishops to assume the rectorship of the new Catholic University in Dublin, and held that post from 1854 to 1858. In 1879 Pope Leo XIII raised Newman to the cardinalate.

The last years of the venerable writer and educator were spent among his brethren of the Oratory in Birmingham, and he was buried in the community cemetery at Radnall Hill.

Poems and Novels. A volume entitled *Verses on Various Occasions* proves that Newman had high poetic gifts, largely undeveloped. The contents are uneven in tone and varied in quality, but always there is fire, point, and promise. And the promise reaches fruition in two poems which the world will not willingly let die. One of these is "The Pillar of the Cloud," more generally known as "Lead, Kindly Light." It is one of the supreme lyrics of our literature. Newman's other unique contribution to English poetry is *The Dream of Gerontius*. Considered in its formal aspects it is a marvel of metrical variety and taste, regarded in its psychological content it is a faithful and convincing record of human reactions to thoughts beyond the reaches of the soul, and studied as an interpretation of the life and experience of man it is a glowing and powerful commentary on what is and what is to be. Here Newman penetrates behind the veil before which Tennyson paused with wavering hope of answer or redress; here he boldly flings open the door to which Omar Khayyám found no key. One other poet only, the Catholic Dante, has ever carried the human spirit and human speech so far.

Loss and Gain and *Callista* are Cardinal Newman's contribution to prose fiction. They are not great novels, for their author had neither the novelist's equipment nor the novelist's training; yet they possess the stylistic distinction that inheres in everything that came from Newman's pen. Skill in character drawing, delicate though not sustained, is evidenced in *Loss and Gain*; and portions of *Callista*, notably the account of the locust invasion, are delightful bits of description. We read both these books, not because of their intrinsic worth, but because of the greatness of the man who wrote them.

Representative Essays. Newman's sermons, of which there are several volumes, possess high literary value and make excellent reading even for persons who do not associate pulpit oratory with intellectual enjoyment. His essays on historical subjects, on miracles, and on the development of Christian Doctrine, as well as his *Essay in Aid of a Grammar of Assent* (an original contribution to philosophic thought), necessarily demand a good deal from the reader because of their scholarly backgrounds and reaches of allusion, but they are far from being dry, abstract, and unduly technical. Newman is best approached, however, through *The Present Position of Catholics in England*, his university discourses, and his remarkable autobiography, *Apologia pro Vita Sua*.

© Emery Walker Limited

NEWMAN IN 1890

From a painting by E. Deane in the National Portrait Gallery, London

The Present Position is the most representative of all Newman's books. Originating as a series of lectures to explain the genesis of anti-Catholic prejudice, it developed into a splendidly written volume exhibiting every resource of style and rich with every variety of literary appeal. Augustine Birrell gives an excellent idea of it in *More Obiter Dicta*:

It is apparently a light-hearted book, written in tremendous spirits, bubbling over with fun, decorated with countless fancies — yet what was the task it set itself to perform? Nothing less than this, to roll back the great Protestant tradition, of the court, the law, society, and literature; to remove whole mountains of prejudice; to cleanse the Protestant mind of all slimy traces of slander; to shiver in pieces the prejudices of centuries; and to let the old faith of Englishmen stand forth as a body of doctrine and rule of life. What a task! Protestants though we are, we can scarce forbear to cheer. The mastery displayed by Dr. Newman in grappling with it is beyond praise, and without precedent. He is all that Burke is, and genuinely playful besides. He successfully conceals the prodigious effort he is making and the enormous importance of the verdict for which he is striving. An abler book it would be impossible to name.

Newman's university studies are collected in *The Idea of a University*, a book indispensable for any man who would know something of the Catholic ideal of education, what it means and how much it means. Among the topics discussed are elementary studies, Catholic Literature in English, the Church in its relations to literature and science, mental discipline, and knowledge in its relations to learning, to professional skill, and to religious duty. Here occurs that splendid essay on literature which in thought and in style constitutes the finest exposition of first principles in the English language; here is that description of a university, with its underlying "idea" of such breadth and depth and magnificence as to revolutionize our notions of higher education; here are the finest flowerings of Oxford training, of classical culture, of the Catholic spirit; and here are some of the most luminous specimens of Newman's glowing and flexible literary style.

Less distinguished for its literary qualities, *Apologia pro Vita Sua* is a masterpiece of autobiography. Charles Kingsley had expressed doubts as to Newman's sincerity (Kingsley was one of those men who are prone to accuse of trickery and double-dealing anybody who does not share their opinions and convictions), and Newman in the *Apologia* simply overwhelmed his adversary with facts and principles and inferences. The book was at once a withering reproof of Kingsley's impertinent insinuations and a dignified and convincing justification of Newman's religious development. It moved Coventry Patmore to express admiration of an intellect "so delicately capable of adjustment that it could crush a Hume or crack a Kingsley!"

Newman's Style. In his essay on literature Newman has drawn his own portrait. He thus describes the great author:

Whatever be his subject, high or low, he treats it suitably and for its own sake. . . . He writes passionately because he feels keenly; forcibly, because he conceives vividly; he sees too clearly to be vague; he is too serious to be otiose; he can analyze his subject, and therefore he is rich; he embraces it as a whole and in its parts, and therefore he is consistent; he has a firm hold of it, and therefore he is luminous. When his imagination wells up, it overflows in ornament; when his heart is touched, it thrills along his verse. He always has the right word for the right idea, and never a word too much. . . . He expresses what all feel but cannot say; and his sayings pass into proverbs among his people, and his phrases become household words and idioms of their daily speech.

Those few words contain the best description of Newman's style — a style that resembles a flawless window through which we can observe without distraction the workings of his mind — and a revelation of the essential secrets of the writing craft. We can recall only one bit of literature comparable with this: the speech to the players in *Hamlet*, where Shakespeare sets down with a like "lucid concision" the principles of the art of the spoken word.

There is much in Newman's writings besides doctrinal discernment, fervid devotion, priestly enthusiasm. We find, besides the vision of celestial glory, the "indispensable flavor of earth." We find a humor delicate, penetrating, masculine. We find irony keen as a finely tempered sword. We find a singular energy of thought and a sparkling vivacity of utterance, a "Shakespearean force of style," as Canon Barry says. We find notions formal and abstruse made vital and concrete through pertinent and sprightly illustrations, in accordance with Newman's own theory that "what is concrete exerts a force and makes an impression on the mind which nothing abstract can rival." We find, with Sir Edmund Gosse, that "Newman's best essays display a delicate and flexible treatment of language, without emphasis, without oddity, which hardly arrests the attention at first . . . but which, in course of time, fascinates as a thing miraculous in its limpid grace and suavity." We find, in short, the English language at its best.

What Newman Did. Let us, in conclusion, briefly summarize Newman's accomplishments as a literary dictator. For a dictator he was, however he regarded writing and criticism as but incidental to his career and however repugnant to his fastidious taste the appellation might be. First, he restated and exemplified the teachings of the ablest masters of the literary art. Secondly, he defended style as an expression of the personality of the writer, and habitually wrote in a style of extraordinary clearness, eloquence, and beauty. Thirdly, he established, both in theory and in practice, the correlation of literature with religion. Fourthly, he stressed the often forgotten truth that both religion and literature possess an intellectual as well as a merely emotional element, and he pointed out the rational approach to God as the Infinite Truth and the Infinite Beauty. Fifthly, in his life and in his books he made a contribution of inestimable value to the study of English Literature by analyzing the nature of anti-Catholic prejudice, explaining its operations, and disproving its claims. Finally, he inculcated scholarly thoroughness and scholarly toleration, and he championed a comprehensive humanism in harmony with the European Tradition in literature and in education.

RUSKIN

A Teacher of a Nation. Carlyle and Ruskin had a good deal in common. Both were Scottish in descent, though Ruskin was London-born ; Ruskin was an admirer and in a sense a disciple of Carlyle ; as writers each developed a highly original style marked by bursts of eloquence and blasts of invective ; both had little use for political expedients and mechanical progress ; and both were zealous prophets, bidding their fellow men give heed to the higher and finer interests of life. In other respects they were very different. Carlyle had a Puritan suspicion of grace and beauty which he retained all his life, whereas Ruskin emerged from his youthful prejudices, became vitally interested in poetry, painting, and architecture, and indeed made "Love beautiful things" the burden of his preachments. Carlyle, for the most part, kept aloof from the main stream of the European Tradition in art and in life, whereas Ruskin drank deep of its waters, and year by year became more and more a participator in its heritage of culture. Both were consciously and deliberately teachers of their day; but while Carlyle was as a voice crying in the wilderness, Ruskin slowly but steadily impressed his ideals and convictions on English life and thought. Many of his burning opinions on such subjects as the relations of capital and labor, on model homes for the poor, on the beautifying of cities, on the regulation of wages by law, are now accepted as natural and commonplace notions. John Ruskin (1819–1900) may not be unreservedly honored even in his own country, but the English-speaking world has accepted many of his once radical ideas. In some respects he is behind our times, but chiefly because our times have acted on his advice and bettered his instructions.

Writer and Lecturer. Ruskin's father had made a fortune as a wine merchant, so the energetic and enthusiastic apostle of beauty never suffered the handicap of poverty. He did not have to write for a living or engage in hack work to make both ends meet, and verified the saying that "to him that hath shall be given" by making large sums of money from his books. He did not hoard his wealth, however, but spent it lavishly in the support of movements designed to improve social conditions and to develop popular interest in literature and art. He secured his degree at Oxford in 1842, spent much of his time abroad, especially in Italy, and wrote and lectured untiringly. Several of his books are lectures given to workingmen. He held a professorship at Oxford during ten years. Throughout his long life he was a vigorous fighter against men and institutions and ideas that failed to meet with his approval. He was also a lifelong student. He was a bookworm at the age of five and never lost his interest in worth-while literature. "I think myself very wrong," he once wrote, "if I do not read a little bit of Plato very carefully every day."

Though Ruskin did not become a member of the Catholic Church, it is evident that Catholicism was the most powerful educational influence in his life and the inspiration of his most vibrant teachings. His studies of art and architecture opened his eyes to the glories of the great Catholic paintings and cathedrals and to the happiness and beauty of daily life in the much misunderstood Middle Ages. He drew very close to the essence of the Catholic philosophy of life when he could set forth these rules of practical conduct:

RUSKIN

Not greater wealth, but simpler pleasure. . . . Waste nothing and grudge nothing. Care in no wise to make more of money, but care to make much of it; remembering always the great, palpable, inevitable fact that what one person has, another cannot have. . . . Consider whether, even supposing it guiltless, luxury could be desired by any of us, if we saw clearly at our sides the suffering which accompanies it in the world.

Ruskin's Essays. Five volumes of *Modern Painters* — the first published in 1843 and the last in 1860 — are devoted to the formulation of art principles and to the appreciation of the English painter Turner and numerous Italian artists. The series contains some of Ruskin's best writing, numerous passages of powerful description, and strong appeals for high standards in art and in life. The same general principles and the same essential qualities of style are further applied in *The Seven Lamps of Architecture* : Truth, Beauty, Power, Sacrifice, Obedience, Labor, Memory. More restrained in style is the book which many critics consider Ruskin's best, *The Stones of Venice*, wherein he considers art and architecture as a revelation of the life of a people and the embodiment of their deepest thoughts and highest aspirations. Here we have an expression of his enthusiasm for the ideals of Catholicism, and here too some evidences of his inherited anti-Catholic prejudice — an attitude which later on he regretted and explained as a manifestation of what he called the "pert little Protestant mind."

Ruskin's most direct and stimulating contribution to social science — a contribution which has not lost its vitality — is found in *Unto This Last*, the book which he liked best of all his writings. Political economy has been called the dismal science, but Ruskin animates and brightens his treatment of it by insisting on spiritual values. If, he says in substance, the worker is regarded merely as a part of a machine, then no science of political economy is possible ; but if we remember that the individual man has a soul and immortal strivings, our efforts to improve social conditions will bear fruit. That idea he developed in his Oxford lectures and in numerous later writings, including *Fors Clavigera* (nearly a hundred open letters addressed to the English public). The title means literally "Club-bearing Fortune," and was suggested to Ruskin by the story of Hercules and his club. Ruskin plays upon the Latin words *clava*, *clavis*, and *clavus* ("club," "key," and "rudder" or "nail"), and makes them symbolical of various attitudes toward life. In *Præterita* (Things Gone By) he tells the story of his own life and endeavors ; it is one of the most readable and unusual of autobiographies. Other of his titles are *The Two Paths*, *Ethics of the Dust*, *The Crown of Wild Olive*, *The Queen of the Air*, and *The Eagle's Nest*.

Two of Ruskin's books of particular interest to students are

Sesame and Lilies and *The Bible of Amiens*. Readers of the Arabian story of the Forty Thieves will recall that the treasure cave was closed against all comers who could not utter the magic words "Open Sesame!" In *Sesame and Lilies* Ruskin tells young people how to secure profit from their study of literature; how to say "Open Sesame!" to great books. The essay in this book on "Kings' Treasuries" deals with right habits of reading, and that on "Queens' Gardens" with the education of girls. If we read nothing else of Ruskin's, this book will give us some notion of his style and spirit and an array of wise thoughts to fashion into our conception of life.

The Bible of Amiens is a little book with a big idea: it shows how a historic French cathedral is truly a sermon in stone. The substance of it Ruskin first gave as a lecture to the boys of Eton. He tells in graphic style the story of the cathedral: the missionary labors and martyrdom of St. Firmin, who came to Picardy in the year 301; the conversion to Christianity of King Clovis and his coronation at Reims; the zeal and charity of St. Martin of Tours; the legend of St. Genevieve, who "did not lead armies but stayed them"; and the literary work of "the Lion Tamer," St. Jerome, whose translation into Latin of the Holy Scriptures made the Bible the "library of Europe." Then in the fourth and final chapter Ruskin describes the cathedral and explains the meaning of its decorations in the light of the religious history of France and Europe.

Ruskin Today. A few years ago there were Ruskin clubs and Ruskin study circles in the United States. Perhaps some of them still exist. But it is true that Ruskin's books are not now popular books. They share the general condemnation of things Victorian, they are many and mostly thick, they hit and hit hard at some theories of life and art particularly dear to the young twentieth century, and they are written in a style and with a wealth of imaginative imagery rather too exacting and too unsophisticated for many modern readers. It may even be conceded that much of what Ruskin wrote will cease to be read altogether. But his best work will remain ; and Ruskin commands respect (though not always implicit obedience) as a teacher, as an economist, as an art critic, as the master of a style which sometimes mastered him.

I have had what, in many respects, I boldly call the misfortune, to set my words somewhat prettily together; not without a foolish vanity in the poor knack I had in doing so, until I was heavily punished for this pride, by finding that many people thought of the words only and cared nothing for the meaning.

He failed, it is true, to perceive the benefits which science and invention have conferred upon modern life, and too often he stood, for all the world like a bull on a railroad track, snorting furiously but impotently against the advancing train ; but he did perceive that mere mechanical progress is not a sign of civilization, that man doth not live by bread alone.

Ruskin was not in complete harmony with his own time and he is not in complete harmony with ours, which in some respects is all the worse for Ruskin and in other respects all the worse for the times; but he was in fundamental and essential harmony with that tradition of learning, of art, of culture, of education, and of religion upbuilded through the Catholic centuries and still vigorous and influential among thinking men. He has much to teach us that we well may learn : much of history, much of architecture, much of beauty in daily duties and sanity in daily living. He has left us, often nobly and impressively worded, many such wise and practical sayings as these :

Great art is adoration.

Noble ornament is man's delight in God's work.

It is useless to put your heads together if you cannot put your hearts together.

The infinite folly of modern thought is centered in the notion that liberty is good for a man, irrespective of the use he is likely to make of it.

Under all sorrow, there is the force of virtue; over all ruin, the restoring charity of God. To these alone we have to look; in these alone we may understand the past and predict the future destiny of the ages.

The great cry which rises from our manufacturing cities, louder than their furnace blast, is all in very deed for this, that we manufacture there everything but men; we bleach cotton, and strengthen steel, and refine sugar, and shape pottery; but to brighten, to strengthen, to refine, or to form a single living spirit does not enter into our estimate of advantages.

OTHER ESSAYISTS

Of minor essayists in the nineteenth century many names occur, but we shall content ourselves with noting a few writers each of whom may be regarded as broadly typical of a group of essayists in manner, in interests, and in general outlook. A glance at their contribution to English prose will enable us to see something of the variety possible to the essay form and to trace the main lines of development it assumed in the nineteenth century.

Mrs. Jameson (1794–1860). An interesting figure in the history of art criticism and literature criticism in English is Anna Murphy Jameson. "A human Irish harp," as somebody described her, she was born in Dublin, lived a great deal in England, and traveled extensively and frequently on the Continent. Mentally alert and sensitive, she responded to the appeal of European art, and in several well-written books sought to convey her impressions to English readers. Her *Legends of the Madonna, Memoirs of the Early Italian Painters*, and *Sacred and Legendary Art* won many readers and served to fortify the sense of continuity in European Literature and culture. Mrs. Jameson has her fixed place in the history of Shakespearean criticism with her *Characteristics of Women*, a series of essays in which she sympathetically analyzes and interprets the heroines of Shakespeare's plays. As a critic Mrs. Jameson avoided two extremes: she was neither a cold and remote dry-as-dust dissector, nor an ultra-impressionist making art and literature an excuse to talk about herself. Modern readers may find some of her descriptions of great paintings unduly languorous and her delineations of Ophelia and Lady Macbeth somewhat idealized, but nobody can fail to be impressed with her considerable if unobtrusive learning and the unaffected grace of her spontaneous style.

Richard Jefferies (1848-1887). Often compared with Gilbert White and our American Thoreau, Richard Jefferies lived apart from the ways of men, suffered much from ill health, and observed the passing of the birds and the splendor of the summer fields in a spirit of sad and serene contemplation which often recalls the habitual mood of Wordsworth. Jefferies was neither a scientific naturalist nor a systematic philosopher, but he was a painstaking observer and a thinker of sorts who managed to write in a style that frequently attains the status of poetic prose. His interest in religion was at once vague and insistent and produced in some of his books a strain of dreamy and not unpleasing meditation. Distinctly a minor writer, Jefferies has still a small but ardent following. He is most adequately represented in *The Story of my Heart*, a diffuse and sentimental autobiography which contains numerous fine descriptive passages. Others of his works are *The Gamekeeper at Home*, *Wild Life in a Southern County*, and *Wood Magic*.

John Addington Symonds (1840-1893). "I, for my part, feel paralyzed by the confusion round poetry, painting, philosophy, music, passion, yet without a motive force. I spin hopelessly upon my poles and never stir a step forward." In those words John Addington Symonds voiced the perplexity of a subtle and scholarly writer caught in the whirlpool of a confused and complex age; he was a Theseus in the labyrinth, but without a guiding thread and with no clear notion of where his Minotaur might be, or even if it were worth while to slay him. An Oxford man and a Greek scholar, with an active mind but without vigorous convictions, this lean and nervous lover of Hellenic grace and medieval beauty devoted his life to a study of the art and literature of the Renaissance. Some phases of the subject he did not explore, and he was original rather than trustworthy in hailing Giordano Bruno as a prominent figure in the Revival of Learning; but his *Renaissance in Italy* remains one of the ablest English studies of the movement. Recent advances in scholarship have in part outmoded his book on *Shakespeare's Predecessors in the English Drama*, though nobody has written on the pre-Shakespearean drama with more abiding charm. Symonds will be found at his best in *In the Key of Blue and Other Essays*, the title suggested by the blue clothes worn by Venetians which Symonds takes as a symbol of balanced restraint and abandon in literary style. Symonds is buried near Shelley in the Protestant Cemetery in Rome.

Walter Pater (1839-1894). A schoolboy at Canterbury read Ruskin's *Modern Painters* and thenceforth became an enthusiastic apostle of beauty in art and in life. The schoolboy was Walter Pater, who spent most of his life as student and as fellow at Oxford, where he contrived to make life interesting for the undergraduates by his eccentric habits. He liked, for instance, to deliver his lectures stretched on a sofa and smoking a pipe; and once, when required to choose the best of a number of class essays, he awarded the prize to a student whose name was Sanctuary because that struck him as being the most euphonious name on the list. When some students were called to account for starting a bonfire which caused considerable destruction, Pater defended them on the ground that the conflagration lit up the spire of St. Mary's so beautifully. A shy and unworldly man, he lived obscurely with his two maiden sisters. The temper of that academic household is indicated in the comment made by one of the Miss Paters when a visitor praised the sunset: "Yes, beautiful, of course; but rather crude, don't you think?"

Pater took infinite pains with his writing. He was known to keep for a year a book sent him to review before he was satisfied with his criticism of it. To write an essay was to Pater an act that possessed something of the sacredness of a religious ceremony. The resultant style was a thing of beauty and originality wherein the matter was often obscured by the delicacy of the manner and the substance was lost in the ornateness of the phrasing. Many a reader will agree with what Symonds wrote after reading a chapter of Pater's: "I found myself wandering about among the precious sentences just as though I had lost myself in a sugar-cane plantation." Pater deliberately chose to create an original style — a style touched as with the dim colors of a venerable bit of tapestry and laden with the odor of æsthetic incense. It has been said that style is the man; in Pater's case it was more than the man.

Soothing and refreshing as a fastidious manipulator of words, Pater as a teacher and critic hardly inspired confidence. His *Imaginary Portraits* is happily named, for in his portraiture he is less intent on painting his sitters as they were than as they appeared to his selective and overdeveloped fancy. *Plato and Platonism* makes excellent reading, but as an interpretation of the Platonic spirit it is fragmentary and misleading. Much the same thing may be said of his *Studies in the History of the Renaissance*. *Marius the Epicurean* and *Gaston de Latour* are in the form of novels, though the plots are slight and almost wholly devoid of incident; the characterization and, of course, the style constitute their attractiveness. Both might be described as romances of culture. In *Marius* Pater makes a study of a refined pagan affected by the beauties of Christianity; in *Gaston de Latour*, which remains unfinished, we have the reactions of a sensitive young Frenchman to the influence of the poet Ronsard and of the essayist Montaigne.

In *Heralds of Revolt* Canon Barry discusses Symonds and Pater as modern pagans, and in the best sense of the word that is precisely what they were. Both lost faith in the Protestantism in which they had been reared; both admired, with reservations, the Catholic Church, but hesitated to accept her teachings; both drew much of their intellectual and spiritual sustenance from Catholic art and literature; and both, because they lacked high incentives and robust convictions, frittered themselves away on miscellaneous intellectual activities. Both felt the need of a vital religion, and Pater tried to satisfy that need by worshiping at the shrine of art. It is a coincidence that he died about the time Francis Thompson was writing "The Hound of Heaven."

Oscar Wilde (1856–1900). The most conspicuous figure among the Decadents of the 90's and in his life and writings the most typical representative of Decadence, was Oscar Fingal O'Flahertie Wills Wilde, poet, dramatist, essayist, and professional æsthete and poseur. A clever Irishman with a command of words and a flair for the sensational, he was for a while a literary lion on both sides of the Atlantic and made a memorable lecture tour of the United States, startlingly arrayed in dark-green velvet knee breeches, silk stockings, and a Byronic tie. Found guilty of immoral conduct in London, he was sentenced to a prison term in 1895. On his release he lived obscurely in Paris until his death. His tragedy was the tragedy of a man who thinks that cleverness is the only requisite for success in life and in literature.

As a poet Wilde is remembered for several artfully constructed lyrics characterized by a richness and refinement of diction and by a sensuous if somewhat theatrical beauty, and by "A Ballad of Reading Gaol," into which he put more sincerity and less artifice than into anything else he wrote. It is in verse what his prison autobiography — called (though not by him) *De Profundis* — is in prose. *De Profundis* is glowingly eloquent and marred only by the impression that the author is perhaps too conscious of the attitudes he is striking. The essays of Wilde are of varying merits, distinguished for rare finish of style and for original if superficial thinking. "The Critic as Artist" and "The Decay of Lying" are permanent contributions to English Literature. In the dramatic field Wilde won attention with a number of sparkling but unsubstantial comedies including *Lady Windermere's Fan* and *The Importance of Being Earnest*. Both his essays and his dramas glitter with cynical and often amusing epigrams. He was convinced that life is too important to be taken seriously.

Andrew Lang (1844-1912). One of the many stories told of Oscar Wilde will serve to establish a contrast between him and Lang. "I am extremely fatigued," Wilde confided to an acquaintance; "I have been writing industriously all day. This morning I inserted a comma, and this afternoon I deleted it." Less self-conscious and spectacular, Lang would not be heard discussing his work; but if he wished to do so he could have said that in the morning he translated a thousand lines or so of Homer's *Iliad* and wrote two or three little poems, that in the afternoon he composed a fairy tale and an essay on anthropology, and that the evening would be taken up with the planning of a book on Scottish history and the writing of a leader for the next day's newspaper. He wrote so much and so excellently and on so many subjects that even in his lifetime he was suspected of being not one man but a syndicate.

There was gypsy blood in the veins of Andrew Lang, some of whose ancestors had wandered about Scotland mending tins and telling fortunes; and perhaps, as he himself suggests in one of his poems, the Wanderlust took in him a literary bent:

> Ye wanderers that were my sires
> Who read men's fortunes in the hand,
> Who voyaged with your smithy fires
> From waste to waste across the land;
>
> Why did you leave for garth and town
> Your life by heath and river's brink?
> Why lay your Gypsy freedom down
> And doom your child to Pen and Ink?

In his Oxford days (he was a Balliol College man) Lang crossed pens with Max Müller, the most formidable scholar of the time, on the origins of language, and during the succeeding years he engaged, with uniform good spirits and unfailing courtesy, in many another academic tilt. He united the vivacity of the journalist with the profundity of the scholar and could turn from the historical method of *The Mystery of Mary Stuart* to the metrical dexterity of *Ballades in Blue China* and *Rhymes à la Mode*. His *Letters to Dead Authors* and *Essays in Little* contain sane and helpful literary criticism, and in *How to Succeed in Literature* and *Letter to a Young Journalist* he explains the craft of writing. In his *History of English Literature* he demonstrates that even a textbook can be entertaining; particles of wit sparkle there amid the heaps of names and dates.

CHAPTER XVI

CROSS CURRENTS

Thus far we have been considering the main stream of English Literature as, enriched by the European Tradition, it follows its steady and stately course through the centuries down almost to our own time. Before we observe the principal books and writers of the twentieth century and try to discern the characteristics of the literature that is now being produced, it will be well for us to make, in this and the following chapter, a rapid survey of certain cross currents of writing which have diversified the main stream of English Literature.

As was stated at the beginning of this book, history, philosophy, science, and religion are not literature, and writers on those subjects are not necessarily littérateurs; but it may happen that a man writes on the nature of conscience, on trade conditions under the Tudors, or on insects as a menace to human continuance with literary charm and effectiveness; in other words, while writing philosophy or history or science he also produces a piece of literature. A considerable number of men have so written in English. They are chiefly and essentially historians or philosophers or scientists; but they have also in some measure, and, as it were, by the way, contributed to the literary treasure of the English-speaking peoples.

WRITERS ON HISTORY

Chroniclers. We saw in the third chapter that Alfred the Great gave an impetus to the writing of history by establishing *The Old English Chronicle*. *The Chronicle* was continued until the middle of the twelfth century. The writers were many;

and while most of them were merely prosaic recorders of facts or of what they thought were facts, some of them, unknown to us by name, revealed a literary point of view and even the possession of considerable poetic gifts. Hence *The Old English Chronicle*, though mainly a collection of documents valuable to the student of history, contains passages that appeal as well to the student of literature. The early chroniclers were all priests or monks, and their model was St. Bede the Venerable. Two of them are of especial interest. William of Malmesbury, who died about the year 1140, had read the historians of Greece and Rome and caught from them a picturesque style and an interest in world events; he saw occurrences in English history against the background of general European history. The same literary flavor is found in the work of Giraldus Cambrensis, who was born about the time William of Malmesbury died. Giraldus was chaplain to King Henry II, and a busy man of affairs who traveled much and wrote of what he saw in his *Itinerary*. He helped to preach the Third Crusade to the Welsh, and recorded some of his impressions of the country in his *Description of Wales*. He accompanied the English to Ireland in 1184. His *History of the Conquest of Ireland* is an important source book for students of Irish history. He wrote in a vigorous and lively style of the country and its inhabitants. His sympathies were all with the invaders, and his brilliant narration of the conquest has been severely criticized by later investigators.

The Paston Letters. Much rich literary material, the stuff for the making of at least a dozen novels of adventure and half a dozen stirring plays, is contained in a series of letters written by three generations of the Paston family, well-to-do dwellers in Norfolk during the Wars of the Roses. The Paston Letters cover the period between 1422 and 1509. We have here both history and literature : the history of daily perils faced by men and women living in unruly times, the literature which springs from the soil of ambition and love and war. We follow the career of John Paston and his loyal wife Margaret, a career devoted mainly to the preservation of the family estates and the conduct of business under conditions which made business a genuine adventure. Here we have the old, old situation, so beloved by writers of sensational fiction, where the daughter of the house insists on marrying a servant and is accordingly driven out into the cold, cruel world. It is all life in the rough, in the raw, with some of the details grim enough to satisfy the most exacting Realist.

Raphael Holinshed. The man who supplied Shakespeare with material for much of *Macbeth*, *Lear*, *Cymbeline*, and the ten plays dealing with English history certainly deserves commemoration in any survey of English Literature. Raphael Holinshed, however, though he was lavish of details concerning kings and prelates, was excessively sparing in writing about himself. Where he was born we do not know, but he came to London early in Queen Elizabeth's reign and secured employment with a printer and publisher named Reginald Wolfe. His duties included the compilation of the *Chronicles of England, Scotland, and Ireland*, in collaboration with William Harrison, who wrote the opening description of Britain. Holinshed was in no sense a great writer, — at best he but gathered together the dry bones which Shakespeare was to clothe with flesh and quicken with undying life, — but he could tell a story in an old-fashioned way and make moral reflections which have not yet lost their point. He died in 1580.

Clarendon (1609-1674). A scholar, an orator, a politician, and during three periods of his life an exile, Edward Hyde, Earl of Clarendon, is mainly remembered because of his skill as a historian. He was a Royalist in the Civil Wars and became Lord Chancellor when Charles II came to the throne. Then, having helped to make history, he proceeded to write it, and his *History of the Great Rebellion* in eight books was in part a detailed account of the fall of Charles I and in part a vindication of his own conduct in public life. In the portion dealing with Irish affairs (first published separately as a *History of the Irish Rebellion*) Clarendon shows a bias in favor of the Duke of Ormonde and the English policy, but in his study of the conflict with the Puritans he is remarkably impartial despite his personal identification with the royal cause. His literary abilities were distinguished. He painted vivid and convincing portraits of historical personages, and he wrote in a style clear, vigorous, and at times eloquent — a style that shows the influence of the best Latin models and the effect of his residence at the French court. In the history of the development of English prose Clarendon stands midway between More and Dryden.

William Robertson (1721–1793). The eighteenth century produced several writers now rather discredited as historians but whose books remain of interest because of the style in which they were written. Such a man was William Robertson, a Scottish Presbyterian, who wrote a *History of Scotland* and a *History of the Reign of Charles V*. He did in a small way what Gibbon did in a larger way; his manner of writing is dignified, almost pompous, and has so pronounced an element of " Johnsonese " that Johnson jokingly claimed that Robertson learned how to write from him. Robertson's view of Mary Queen of Scots is extremely adverse; his misconceptions of the Middle Ages, since exposed by Maitland and others, are due to ignorance and a strong religious prejudice. Robertson was among the first to practice the now well-established method of quoting his sources (though many documents he failed to understand), and he had a knack of picking and choosing among available material.

Edward Gibbon (1737–1794). Born in Putney, near London, Edward Gibbon went to Oxford, where he read a book which, directly and indirectly, had a tremendous influence on his life and works. The book was *The History of the Variations of the Protestant Sects*, written by Bossuet, Bishop of Meaux in France, and was (and is) a strong indictment of Protestantism based on the fundamental differences and inconsistencies of its various branches. The arguments of the learned prelate and orator deeply impressed young Gibbon, who straightway entered the Catholic Church. His conversion resulted in his expulsion from Oxford and his banishment to Switzerland by his angry father, who wrote to a clergyman of Lausanne to destroy the young man's faith in Catholicism. The order was obeyed. Gibbon lost his faith in Catholicism and his faith in the Christian revelation as well: he became a thoroughgoing skeptic and impregnated all his writings with his unbelief. He developed into a fat and selfish cynic, as his *Autobiography* shows, alternating between Lausanne and London for the rest of his life and dying of dropsy at the age of fifty-seven.

Gibbon's contribution to history is a huge work in six volumes, *The Decline and Fall of the Roman Empire*. On a visit to Rome in 1764 he stood one evening overlooking the Forum while the monks in a neighboring church, once a pagan temple, were chanting vespers; and there, face to face with the pagan past and the Christian present of the historic city, he conceived the idea of setting down the story of the fall of the one and the rise of the other. On another evening, twenty-three years later, in his summer house at Lausanne, he wrote the last sentence of his book. "After laying down my pen," he tells us in an eloquent passage of the *Autobiography*, "I took several turns in a *berceau*, or covered walk of acacias, which commands a prospect of the country, the lake, and the mountains. The air was temperate, the sky was serene, the silver orb of the moon was reflected from the waters, and all nature was silent. I will not dissemble the first emotions of joy on recovery of my freedom, and, perhaps, the establishment of my fame. But my pride was soon humbled, and a sober melancholy was spread over my mind, by the idea that I had taken an everlasting leave of an old and agreeable companion, and that, whatsoever might be the future fate of my *History*, the life of the historian must be short and precarious."

As history his *Decline and Fall of the Roman Empire,* despite the honor in which it has been traditionally held, is a biased and superficial performance. Pretending to consult original documents, Gibbon in reality drew upon the German Mosheim and other virulently anti-Catholic writers for ammunition wherewith to bombard Christianity and fire salutes to vanished paganism. As literature the fame of the *Decline and Fall* is more merited. The book is big in conception, effective in arrangement, and powerful and often beautiful in style; its narrative passages are handled with skill, and its descriptions are colorful and vivid. Gibbon's is an ornate and magniloquent prose which utilizes words of Latin derivation and long and often elaborately constructed sentences.

John Lingard (1771-1851). Robertson and Gibbon represent a sort of history writing wherein the personal prejudices of the authors distort their perspective of events, affect their selection of material, and blind them to the good qualities of men and movements they dislike. It was a Catholic priest, John Lingard, who was really the founder of the modern method of writing history — a method which aims not at persuasion, not at what today is called propaganda, not at making converts to any particular theory, but which seeks to set down the facts impartially, all the facts, and all the consequences flowing from the facts. Lingard's *History of England* is a capable and eminently impartial work; so impartial, indeed, that it was highly praised by several Protestant critics and severely attacked by Bishop Milner and other Catholic authorities. The first three of the eight volumes appeared in 1819, and the work was completed in 1830.

Lingard, who had studied in France and taught in Catholic schools in England, was made pastor of a small parish at Hornby near Lancaster, and there he lived quietly for some forty years, deep in his books and his scholarly studies. He sought the truth, and the truth made him free. He learned, as he tells us, to weigh with care "the value of authorities on which I relied, and watched with jealousy the secret workings of my own personal feeling and possessions." He declined to write of the events of his own day or the day immediately preceding, because he felt that it is only from a distance that the historian can perceive the true relations of facts; accordingly his *History of England* ends with the Orange Rebellion of 1688. Every statement he painstakingly traced to its source, every conclusion he based upon original documents.

© Emery Walker Limited

LECKY

From a painting by G. F. Watts in the
National Portrait Gallery, London

The style of Lingard is the style of a well-read and well-balanced scholar. It is leisurely and moderately colorful, though lacking the heaviness of Robertson, the ornateness of Gibbon, and the journalistic dexterity of Macaulay. It enables us to get very close to the events he narrates and the persons he describes; his characterization of Richard II, for instance, is lifelike and appealing, and his account of the rise and fall of Cardinal Wolsey is a fine example of how a competent historian can make an individual stand out against the background of national events.

A Nineteenth-Century Group. Robertson's bigoted and unscholarly account of the Middle Ages was more than offset by the histories of Henry Hallam (1777–1895), William Edward Hartpole Lecky (1838–1903), and Frederic William Maitland

(1850–1906). Hallam's most notable work is *A View of the State of Europe during the Middle Ages*, Lecky's is *The Rise and Progress of Rationalism in Europe*, and Maitland's is *Roman Canon Law in the Church of England*. Sir William Napier (1785–1860) achieved a fine piece of historical writing in his somewhat partial but highly vivid *History of the Peninsular War*, George Grote (1794–1871), a scholarly banker, made himself an authority with his *History of Greece*, and Edward Augustus Free-man (1823–1892) is still in-fluential by reason of his *History of the Norman Conquest*. Most popular of all the English historians is John Richard Green (1837–1883), whose *Short History of the English People* was the first book to minimize the "drum and trumpet" element in history and to probe social conditions. The literary value of Green's history is deservedly praised.

JUSTIN MCCARTHY

James Anthony Froude (1818–1894), for a while an Oxford disciple of Newman, wrote a *History of England* (in Tudor times) and *The English in Ireland in the Eighteenth Century*, besides numerous essays on historical and literary subjects and a much-discussed *Life of Carlyle*. As a writer Froude has been praised for force and charm and abandon, but as a historian there is literally none so poor to do him reverence. He had a positive genius for inaccuracy, and the tricks he played with quotation marks when citing authorities make him an unenviable specimen of those historians whose writings are a conspiracy against the truth. The fusion of history and journalism was accomplished by Justin McCarthy (1830–1912), a politician and miscellaneous writer, in his graphic and informing *History of our Own Times*.

Lord Acton (1834–1902). Born in Naples of an English father and a German mother, Catholic by religion and cosmopolitan by training, John Emerich Dalberg, Baron Acton, was well fitted to interpret the European Tradition in history. He wrote numerous weighty magazine articles on historical subjects, held the professorship of history at Cambridge from 1895, originated the plan of the *Cambridge Modern History*, and devoted a lifetime to collecting material for a *History of Liberty* which he did not write. A profound scholar and an independent thinker, Lord Acton was much occupied in controversy; some of his writings were censured by the Church authorities, but the condemnation cast no reflection on either the genuineness of his Catholic convictions or the probity of his personal life. Something of his spirit may be discerned in the precepts he gives the student of history:

> Be not content with the best book; seek sidelights from the others; have no favorites; keep men and things apart; guard against the prestige of great names; see that your judgments are your own, and do not shrink from disagreement; no trusting without testing; be more severe to ideas than to actions; do not overlook the strength of the bad cause or the weakness of the good; never be surprised by the crumbling of an idol or the disclosure of a skeleton; judge talent at its best and character at its worst; suspect power more than vice and study problems in preference to periods.

Cardinal Gasquet (1846–   ). Francis Aidan Cardinal Gasquet is a generally recognized authority on monasticism in England before and during the Reformation. A Londoner by birth, he joined the Benedictines, and became prior at Downside Abbey, and ultimately the superior of his order in England. His elevation to the cardinalate by Pope Pius X in 1914 was a recognition of his labors in revising the Latin text of the Bible. His representative books are *Monastic Life in England, Henry*

VIII and the English Monasteries, The Last Abbot of Glaston-bury, The Eve of the Reformation, and *The Greater Abbeys of England.*

Cardinal Gasquet's work as a historian has had the effect of dispelling from educated minds the notion that before the time of Henry VIII the English monasteries had become hopelessly corrupt and that the Tudor monarch, ever interested in purity and holiness, was regretfully obliged to suppress the abbeys and confiscate their property. Most earlier historians (Hallam, for example) had adopted some such view. Cardinal Gasquet shows, in a scholarly and judicial spirit, that the monks and nuns as a whole had been leading devout lives and that the suppression of the religious houses was an act of tyranny and rapacity on the part of the king and his favorites. The beginnings of the Protestant revolt he traces as far back as the fourteenth century, when a great pestilence known as the Black Death half depopulated Europe and seriously inter-fered with Church organization and the administration of the sacraments.

The method followed by Cardinal Gasquet in writing his studies of English history is well indicated in his own words:

My sympathies are naturally engaged, where the Church is in ques-tion, but I have striven to avoid anything like presenting or pleading a case, which indeed I felt would defeat my purpose. . . . My belief is that the facts speak strongly enough for themselves, and I have endeavored to add as little as possible of my own to the story they tell. All I desire is that my readers should judge from the letters, documents, and opinions, whether bare justice has hitherto been done to the memory of pre-Reformation Catholicism in England.

Such is the spirit in which the ablest historians in the modern world present their conclusions, and we may note that no finer and more comprehensive statement of its principles and no more logical and exemplary specimens of its application can be had than is contained in the writings of two Catholic historians, Lord Acton and Cardinal Gasquet.

WRITERS ON PHILOSOPHY AND SCIENCE

The English language contains only a part, and a relatively small part, of the world's great books on philosophy and science. One obvious explanation is that many of the world's leading scientists and thinkers have not been natives of English-speaking countries; we recall Pascal, Volta, Kant, Mendel. Another reason is that for centuries Latin was the accepted medium of communication among learned men, and English thinkers and experimenters used it rather than English in writing their treatises. John of Salisbury (1115?–1180) and William of Occam (1270?–1349?) were eminent in philosophy, and Roger Bacon (1214?–1294?) was a pioneer in science; but their writings come to us not in English but in Latin. This is especially true of most of the Catholic philosophers and scientists of England until comparatively recent times: Latin was the language of learning, as it remains in our own day the language of the Church, and because of both their learning and their Catholicism they chose it as a medium of expression.

Hobbes and the Platonists. The seventeenth century produced some philosophical writings in English which possessed a slight literary tone and which had more than a slight influence on subsequent literature. Thomas Hobbes (1588–1679), an Oxford man, was strongly impressed by certain phases of Continental thought and scientific experiment, and wrote numerous essays on government, on the physical universe, and on the nature of man. His most famous book is *Leviathan* (1651), a treatise on the theory of politics. Hobbes was a materialist and an unbeliever, and he considered self-interest the basis of all human action. His style is clear — which is something that cannot be said of all philosophers — but not otherwise distinguished. His views were opposed by a group of Cambridge University scholars, chief of whom was Henry More (1614–1687), a poet as well as a thinker and the master of a pleasing manner of writing. The Cambridge Platonists, as the group was called, opposed Hobbes's materialistic tendencies and sought, like some of the early Fathers of the Church, to teach Christianity in the light of the philosophy of Plato.

John Locke (1632-1704). Greater and more influential than Hobbes was John Locke, a practicing physician and a lecturer on Greek and rhetoric at Oxford. His fundamental doctrine was that man can learn only through experience, a doctrine which because of its narrowness tended to induce skepticism, and because of its insistence on experiment stimulated scientific research. His leading book is an *Essay concerning Human Understanding*; other productions are an *Essay concerning Toleration* and *Some Thoughts of Education*. His plain and unimaginative manner of writing had an appreciable effect on some of the leading exponents of eighteenth-century Classicism in English Literature. He was the representative thinker of "an age whose poetry was without romance, whose philosophy was without insight, and whose public men were without character." [1]

Bishop Berkeley (1685-1753). Early in the eighteenth century there came over from Ireland a man who tried with great eloquence and limited success to interest the English people in founding a college in the Bermudas for "the reformation of manners among the English in our western plantations, and the propagation of the gospel among the American savages." In pursuance of his scheme he crossed the Atlantic and lived for three years in Rhode Island, waiting in vain for funds to carry out his educational work. His college never materialized; but first-hand contact with the New World inspired him to write his "Verses on the Prospect of Planting Arts and Learning in America," of which one line has become immortal,

> Westward the course of empire takes its way;

and since in the most western portion of what is now the United States a great university stands in a city named in his

[1] Mark Pattison, *Essays and Reviews*, p. 254.

honor, his benevolent designs on the "American savages" have not wholly come to naught.

George Berkeley was born in County Kilkenny, Ireland, and educated at Trinity College, Dublin. He traveled extensively, became a clergyman, was dean of Derry and afterwards Bishop of Cloyne, and died at Oxford. He was a kindly, likable, truly noble character, a man of big ideas living in days when little ideas were more esteemed, a man of generous impulses cast into an environment where all impulses were looked upon as decidedly bad form. He was a philosophic Hamlet who found the times lamentably out of joint.

Berkeley enjoys the distinction of being the most literary of the writers of philosophy in English; his cast of mind was really artistic, and he had the ability to write on even the most abstruse subjects with vivacity of feeling and with charm and variety of diction. He was an idealist in philosophy and more akin to the Cambridge Platonists than to Hobbes and Locke. His reputation was established with his *Essay towards a New Theory of Vision* and his *Principles of Human Knowledge*. *Siris* is a somewhat amusing instance of how a great man can lose his sense of proportion. Berkeley had become convinced that the drinking of tar water would cure all bodily ills and most spiritual ones, and *Siris* is as much a philosophy of tar water as Carlyle's *Sartor Resartus* is a philosophy of clothes. His *Hylas and Philonous*, a philosophical dialogue written in imitation of Plato, is one of the most beautiful and impressive things of the kind in English.

David Hume (1711-1776). Though Berkeley was a devout believer in the Christian religion, his theory of philosophy was not based on sound principles, and his teachings were taken up by an astute Scotsman, carried to their logical conclusions, and made the justification of complete skepticism. David Hume, in such works as *Treatise of Human Nature, An Enquiry concerning Human Understanding*, and *Essays Moral and Political*, denied the fact of revelation and the possibility of miracles and reduced every circumstance in human life to the operation of purely natural laws. His *History of England* was written in the light of those principles. From the literary point of view Hume's best book is his *Autobiography*, a more pleasing work than Gibbon's, wherein the skeptic discloses himself as a hard-headed, cynical, disillusioned thinker making the best of this by no means best of all possible worlds. Hume wrote well, according to the Classical standards of his generation, with an avoidance of enthusiasm and with the crackle of a dry and canny irony.

Adam Smith (1723-1790). Though Adam Smith wrote other things, including *The Theory of Moral Sentiments*, and though he lectured on literature at Edinburgh and on logic at Glasgow his name is identified with one book which he took twelve years to write and which is still cited as an authority by writers on political economy. *An Inquiry into the Nature and Causes of the Wealth of Nations* was published in 1776. Its thesis is that national progress and well-being are best secured when private citizens are given complete freedom within the limits of justice and reason. Smith's *Wealth of Nations* owes its vogue to the fact that it makes the alleged "dismal science" interesting by working back from conditions and problems to the principles underlying them. No less an expert than Edmund Burke paid a high compliment to Smith's style: "His language is easy and spirited. . . . It is rather painting than writing."[1]

Jeremy Bentham (1748-1832). One theory of life that has had considerable prominence in the history of philosophy is known as *hedonism*, from a Greek word meaning pleasure or delight; and Jeremy Bentham was the most noted exponent of it in English with his oft-quoted contention that the basis of morality in public and in private life is the "greatest happiness of the greatest number." His system is also known by the formidable name of utilitarianism, because he maintained that the value of a thing depends on its usefulness as a means

[1] *Annual Register*, 1776.

of pleasure. Such a conception of life and duty will always appeal to men who do not think much farther than their noses and to readers who dilate on the "philosophy" of Fitzgerald's *Rubáiyát*.

Bentham was a Londoner who went to Oxford and liked the university as little as Gibbon and Smith had done, who became a lawyer but was too timid and nervous to succeed in pleading cases, and who drifted into writing under the patronage of Lord Shelburne and the encouragement of a Swiss enthusiast, Stephen Dumont. Perhaps Bentham receives more credit than he deserves, for there is a strong probability that the actual writing of his books *A Fragment on Government* and *Introduction to the Principles of Morals* was performed by Dumont, who acted as Bentham's publicity man. Bentham lived up to his principles to the last. After eighty-four years of excellent health he said to a friend at his bedside: "I now feel that I am dying; our care must be to minimize pain. Do not let the servants come into my room, and keep away the youths; it will be distressing to them and they can be of no service."

John Stuart Mill (1806–1873). A philosopher and the son of a philosopher, John Stuart Mill was the most noted disciple of Bentham and the leading champion of the utilitarian school of thought. His father kept him away from the studies and the pleasures of ordinary childhood and brought him up according to a homemade system of education. The boy started to learn Greek when he was three years old, and before he was eight he had read half a dozen of Plato's *Dialogues*. He was encouraged to suppress his feelings and to submit every thought and act to rigid reason. No religious training entered into the plan, a circumstance from which Mill suffered in his writings and his life. He early conceived the ambition of becoming a "reformer of the world" and engaged in writing to attain that end. Reading Wordsworth at the age of twenty-two, he found a new world of beauty unfolding before him, though he could not help condemning what he called the bad philosophy of the poet. Besides his *Autobiography*, Mill wrote *Political Economy, On Liberty, Considerations on Representative Government*, and other philosophical studies. His *Utilitarianism* (1861) is the clearest account we have of the theory of good living based upon pleasure and usefulness, and *The Subjection of Women* (1869) has become the corner stone of the women's rights movement. Mill's style, though heavy and humorless, is lucid and logical, strong in argument, and clever in illustration.

JOHN STUART MILL

The Evolutionists. The general theory of science loosely called evolution, a theory which just now is being tested in so many departments of life and has even been applied to music, to art, and to religion, is a subject upon which the majority of readers have but imperfect and fragmentary knowledge. The word *evolution* is a key tried on so many locks that it is worn smooth from overmuch handling. The student wishing to clarify and rectify his notions of evolution would do well to read the scholarly and discerning article on it in *The Catholic Encyclopedia*, and thus learn that it means many things and is used in several distinct senses.

In England scientific writers identified with the theory of evolution were Alfred Russel Wallace (1823–1913), whose *Malay Archipelago* stimulated the study of natural selection; Sir Charles Lyell (1797–1875), who contributed the theory of uniformity in *The Principles of Geology* and *The Antiquity of Man*; John Tyndall (1820–1893), with the exception of Huxley the most literary of all the evolutionary writers, who aroused popular interest in physics with his books *The Glaciers of the Alps, Heat as a Mode of Motion, Lectures on Sound,* and *The Forms of Water*; and especially Charles Darwin (1809–1882), whose *Origin of Species* (1859) and *The Descent of Man* (1871) exercised a tremendous influence directly on biology and indirectly on every other science and, indeed, on every aspect of life. Darwinism is one thing and evolution is another, but both theories loom large in the thought and literature of the last seventy-five years.

Darwin was essentially and even narrowly a scientist, and it is possible that his theories would have attracted the attention of only a few specialists had it not been that a copy of his *Origin of Species* fell into the hands of another man of science who was just then supporting himself by reviewing books. This was Thomas Henry Huxley (1825–1895), who at once, in his writings and his lectures, proceeded to popularize and illustrate Darwin's ideas. If Darwin was the Socrates of evolution, Huxley was its Plato, though without the serene and lofty spirit of the ancient poet-philosopher. A scientist by training and profession, Huxley was more than all else a clever controversialist and a cunning manipulator of words. He had a good deal of Arnold's skill in sarcasm and irony without Arnold's "sweet reasonableness," and many of his essays now give the impression that in those hectic Victorian days science was less a matter of calm thinking and patient experiment than an excuse for the hurling of verbal brickbats and the ascribing of unworthy motives to any and all adversaries. It has been said that the French Revolution was started by Rousseau's *Social Contract*; certainly that other revolution raised in the minds of many men within the last half century was started by *Man's Place in Nature, Science and Hebrew Tradition, Evolution and Ethics,* and other books of Huxley's. In both cases it was literary ability rather than philosophic depth which brought about the far-reaching results.

Less spectacular in his methods and more ambitious in his plans, Herbert Spencer (1820–1903) elaborated an entirely new system of philosophy based on the theory of evolution — a theory which, by the way, he had announced in his *Development Hypothesis* seven years before the publication of Darwin's *Origin of Species*. In succeeding books Spencer applied his philosophy to biology, to psychology, to sociology, to ethics, to education, and even to the art of writing. His is the dubious celebrity of expounding agnosticism, a view of life which dismisses God, the immortality of the soul, and the future life as "unknowable." "Spencer," says the Italian critic Benedetto Croce, "tried to force life into a brass bottle of his own making, but the genius will not go into his bottle." [1] Spencer, for all his earnestness and all his industry, was a singularly ignorant man. He overlooked the labors and the discoveries of earlier thinkers and the experiences and opinions of other men; he judged everything by material standards, and so his scheme of philosophy, though it attracted much attention toward the close of the nineteenth century, is already recognized as outworn and limited. In 1920 the centenary of his birth drew passing notice to the fact that today Spencer's influence is negligible and Spencer's ideas are already antiquated.

WRITERS ON RELIGION

In the Days of Elizabeth. The sixteenth century with its changes and counter-changes in the religious adherence of the nation and of individuals occasioned a vast amount of writing, nearly all controversial in character and utterly removed from the realm of literature. On the Protestant side the most remarkable offering is *The Book of Martyrs*, by John Foxe (1516–1587), a minister who retired to the Continent during the reign of Queen Mary and wrote his *Book* first in Latin and

---

[1] *Philosophy of the Practical*, p. viii.

afterwards in English. The first English edition came out in
1563 and became extremely popular; up almost to our own
time Foxe's work rivaled Bunyan's *Pilgrim's Progress* as a
favorite volume among the mass of the English people. It is
a vibrant and colorful and (as is generally admitted) highly
exaggerated account of the sufferings of the Reformers at the
hands of Queen Mary's government. No book has had a
greater effect in perpetuating the anti-Catholic tradition in
England and in sowing the seeds of intolerance even on this
side of the Atlantic.

Prominent among the Catholic writers of the period were
two ecclesiastics, Father Sander and Cardinal Allen. Nicholas
Sander (1530?–1581) was a professor of canon law at Oxford,
where he assisted Cardinal Pole to raise the standards of the
university. He had to flee from England under Elizabeth and
went to Rome; there he was ordained priest, and for the rest
of his life was identified with groups of Catholic refugees on
the Continent. He taught theology at Rouen, was present at
the Council of Trent, and went on various missions to Poland,
to Spain, and to Ireland, where he died. Among his numerous
writings distinction attaches to *The Rise and Growth of the
English Schism*.

Like Sander, William Allen (1532–1594) was an Oxford man,
and even before his ordination to the priesthood he was zealous in conserving the faith of his fellow Catholics. At length
compelled to leave the country, he established at Douai, in
France, a college for the training of English priests. Here he
took the lead in bringing out an English translation of the
Bible which has ever since been the official Catholic version
of the Holy Scriptures in English; the New Testament was
translated at Reims shortly after the college had been transferred to that city. As a writer Cardinal Allen was remarkably capable. Edmund Bolton, a seventeenth-century critic,
declared his most important work, *A Defence of English Catholics*, to be "a princely, grave, and flourishing piece of exquisite

natural English." This book was written in reply to a tract entitled *The Execution of Justice in England*, published anonymously but since discovered to have been written by Lord Burghley, the Queen's principal adviser and the treasurer of the kingdom. Burghley insisted that Catholics were being condemned not because of their religious opinions but because of treasonous acts. Cardinal Allen's *Defence* was a convincing refutation of that plea and showed that men and women were put to death for living up to the faith of their fathers. Other books of Cardinal Allen are doctrinal, devotional, and controversial in character.

Three Protestant Divines. Richard Hooker (1554?–1600) was a meek and gentle soul, unhappily married and uncongenially set in the midst of fierce religious strife. He wrote one book, *The Laws of Ecclesiastical Polity*, and thereby won an assured place among the clerical writers of English. His style is lofty and dignified, sometimes tangled in construction (as was the case with most prose before Dryden), but eloquent and musical and now and then rising to impressive grandeur. His work describes the Church of England as the happy *via media* between Catholicism and Presbyterianism.

A very different sort of man was the vigorous and pugnacious Archbishop James Ussher (1581–1656), the most notable scholar and the most untiring controversialist produced by the Protestant Church in Ireland. He was Dublin-born and a graduate of Trinity College, and for a time was chancellor of St. Patrick's Cathedral. In both England and Ireland he was recognized as the leading scholar of his time, and his interest extended to all classes of literature and science. He gathered a large and valuable library, which is now the property of Trinity College; it includes the Book of Kells, a manuscript of the Latin Gospels magnificently illuminated by eighth-century Irish monks. The last sixteen years of Ussher's life were spent in London, and today he rests (if so energetic a spirit can be said to rest) in Westminster Abbey. His works, in Latin and in English, fill seventeen large volumes. Most of them are rough-and-tumble controversy with Catholics and Presbyterians, but in *Emmanuel, or the Mystery of the Incarnation* and *Principles of the Christian Religion* he is devotional and doctrinal.

Sometimes called the English Chrysostom because of his pulpit eloquence, and recognized as one of the masters of English prose by all who are familiar with his rich and picturesque style, Jeremy Taylor (1613–1667), a barber's son and a Cambridge graduate, spent most of his clerical life now here, now there, as changes in government and the whim of his superiors decreed. His last charge was in Ireland, where as Bishop of Down and Connor he found his flock (most of them stanch Presbyterians who did not want a bishop) difficult and unruly. *Holy Living* and *Holy Dying* are books of devotion which best reveal the extraordinary affluence of his prose. He has a poetic fancy, a fund of vivid imagery, and a touch of pensive melancholy, doubtless the reflection of his troubled life. "From Plato Taylor learned the secret of his involved harmonies, and on Plato, Cicero, and Chrysostom he fashioned his diffuse and splendid eloquence."[1]

The Two Butlers. Two outstanding religious books of the eighteenth century are Butler's *Analogy of Religion* and Butler's *Lives of the Saints*. The former, the work of a Protestant bishop, Joseph Butler (1692–1752), is a learned and elaborate attempt to show the similarity existing between the Christian religion and "the constitution and course of nature"; the latter, the work of a Catholic priest, Alban Butler (1710–1773), is a collection, at once devotional and scholarly, of the lives of the men and women commemorated in the calendar of the Catholic Church. Both books reveal clerical culture and erudition, both are marked in style and thought by some of the salient traits of the literature of the eighteenth century. Recent scholarship has somewhat affected the value of both

[1] J. C. Collins, *The Study of English Literature*, p. 81.

works for the seasoned student, but there is still validity in Joseph Butler's main argument and there is still a fund of information and spiritual refreshment in Alban Butler's easy-flowing narratives and solidly pious reflections. *The Lives of the Saints* was the outcome of thirty years of intensive intellectual labor. The author was a native of Staffordshire, was educated at Douai, and at the time of his death was president of the College of St. Omer in France.

Richard Challoner (1691–1781). Since until a comparatively recent date Catholics were debarred from attendance at the English universities, practically all of them who sought higher education were compelled to study on the Continent. So it was to Douai that Richard Challoner, a native of Sussex, went to prepare himself for the priesthood, and at Douai he remained, as student and as teacher, for twenty-six years. It was an excellent preparation for his subsequent apostolate as preacher and writer in England, though so long a familiarity with Latin and French acted unfavorably on the purity and idiomatic accuracy of his English style. His life of scholarship and seclusion in the French town was in striking contrast with the troubles and sufferings of his English mission. In 1740 he was consecrated bishop and in 1758 he became vicar apostolic in London. He was a prominent Catholic leader, and in every uprising of anti-Catholic prejudice he suffered the penalty of being a marked man. He nearly met his death in the Gordon Riots.

Bishop Challoner was an active and voluminous writer on devotional and controversial subjects. *Think Well On't* and *Meditations for Every Day in the Year* are books of spiritual reflection still of practical value, and *The Grounds of the Old Religion* is an explanatory work which has not lost its force. He made a translation, yet widely used, of *The Imitation of Christ*, and he revised and annotated the Douai-Reims Bible. His style is learned yet popular, elaborate yet clear. His works have passed through numberless editions and constitute an impressive contribution to religious literature in English.

Kenelm Digby (1800-1880). One characteristic of the Romantic Movement was a renewed interest in the Middle Ages. A student at Cambridge, the son of an Irish clergyman, began to read of the past and to reflect upon Catholic times; and so it was that Kenelm Digby wrote his unique books: *The Broadstone of Honour, Mores Catholici, or Ages of Faith,* and *Compitum; or the Meeting of the Ways at the Catholic Church.* His investigations had brought him into the Church, and he wrote in all the fervor and exaltation of his new-found faith. *The Broadstone of Honour* is a treatise on the medieval institution of chivalry, and Digby enriches his theme with deep learning and rare poetic fancy. *Mores Catholici* is a vast work (it appeared originally in eleven volumes) and constitutes a veritable encyclopedia of the Middle Ages, though its style is highly wrought and picturesque and very different from the sort of writing we associate with works of reference. The *Compitum* is the symbolic story of a traveler who finds himself in the forest where all paths lead to an ancient mansion, the home of a family that had retained the Catholic faith through the Protestant centuries. In the course of the book the author describes and explores the roads symbolized as leading to the Catholic Church — the Road of the Children, the Road of the Workmen, the Road of the Priest, and the rest; and on every road the reader meets numerous historic characters — St. Paul, Pliny, St. Bede the Venerable, Lope de Vega, Savonarola, Oliver Goldsmith. The Romantic quality of the style is sufficiently indicated in the opening sentence: "What antique roofs are those rising above yon solemn wood, which the setting sun gilds with its rays?" Digby's volumes had a large share with those of Scott and the later English historians in rehabilitating the Middle Ages and offsetting the impressions of them founded on ignorance and fostered by bigotry.

Cardinal Wiseman (1802-1865). Nicholas Patrick Stephen Wiseman was born at Seville in Spain, and educated in England and in Rome, where he was ordained priest in 1825. In

1850 Catholic bishops were officially installed in England for the first time since the days of Queen Elizabeth, and Wiseman was created cardinal and appointed Archbishop of Westminster. It was an event of tremendous importance in the history of the Church in England, glowingly commemorated by Cardinal Newman in his sermon "The Second Spring."

In the course of his duties as primate Cardinal Wiseman had occasion to write many volumes on religious subjects. Some of them, like *Science and Revealed Religion*, are of little present interest; others, like *Lectures on the Principal Doctrines and Practices of the Catholic Church*, are still timely and pertinent. In substance and in style his book *The Real Presence* is an admirable performance and constitutes one of the ablest explanations of the Holy Eucharist. He wrote some short plays too, the best known of which is *The Hidden Gem*, a dramatic rendering of the story of St. Alexis. His novel, *Fabiola, or the Church of the Catacombs*, is a definite contribution to historical fiction; it has been several times dramatized and is still extensively read. The character-drawing is remarkably lifelike and the narrative is invested with strong interest and enhanced by an urbane and limpid style.

Frederick William Faber (1814–1863). An admirer and imitator of Wordsworth, Frederick William Faber while still an Oxford student wrote two poems, "The Cherwell Water Lily" and "Sir Lancelot," which are interesting and capable specimens of the Romantic school. But the young poet, intent on higher things than verse-making, became a clergyman. He was rector at Elton until 1845, when, one of the converts of the Oxford Movement, he resigned his pastorate and entered the Catholic Church. As, for the last time, he walked down the village street that gray November morning the people bade him a tearful farewell: "God bless you, Mr. Faber, wherever you go!" He became a priest, like Newman joined the Oratorians, and was superior of their London foundation from 1849 until his death.

When Father Faber announced his intention of becoming a minister, Wordsworth declared that England was losing a great poet. But in Faber's conversion England lost nothing and the Church gained much. He remained a poet even to the end, and his religious poems and hymns are familiarly used by Catholics and Protestants alike. He demonstrated that a good hymn need not be poor poetry. His Romantic fervor, deepened and purified by the intensity of his Catholic devotion, he expressed in numerous prose works on religious subjects, books such as *All for Jesus, The Creator and the Creature, Growth in Holiness, Spiritual Conferences, Bethlehem*, and *The Foot of the Cross, or the Sorrows of Mary*.

Father Faber wrote much, and sometimes his Romantic luxuriance of diction and his fondness for long-drawn descriptions and illustrations have a cloying effect on the reader; but many of his pages take very high rank in English prose. He has De Quincey's sky-soaring imagination without De Quincey's vagueness and lack of earthly contact. Faber's head was often in the clouds, but his feet were firm on the earth. He did in prose what the old painters did on canvas: he presented glowing and beautiful pictures of episodes in the life of Our Lord and His Blessed Mother and enshrined the great truths of faith in highly artistic settings. Unlike many of the Romantics, he could be keen and humorous, practical and ironic. His, indeed, were all the resources of style except possibly the saving virtue of restraint. To read even a few pages of Father Faber is to realize how practical and interesting a thing religion can be and to discover much of the power and variety of the written word.

Cardinal Manning (1808–1892). Another eminent convert to the Catholic Church was Henry Edward Manning, an Oxford graduate and Anglican rector at Lavington until 1851, when he announced his change of faith. Two months later he was ordained priest by Cardinal Wiseman, whom he succeeded as Cardinal-Archbishop of Westminster. His literary labors were but incidental to a very busy and vigorous career as leader of the Church in England, but his books reveal his clear mind and forceful personality. We find in them a keen intellectual power and a style at once simple and energetic. They include *Lectures on the Four Great Evils of the Day, The Blessed Sacrament,* and *The Temporal Mission of the Holy Ghost.*

Learned Laymen. The Victorian era was a period of strenuous intellectual activity among men of culture. Whether sociologists like Mill, statesmen like Gladstone, churchmen like Wilberforce, agnostics like Huxley, poets like Browning, or Catholics like Acton, they thought intensely, debated vigorously, and wrote in a spirit of uncompromising give-and-take little realized in our more sedate and soft-spoken generation. Numerous Catholic laymen, many

CARDINAL MANNING
From a drawing by Alphonse Legros.
(Courtesy of the British Museum)

of them converts, wrote books and contributed to reviews on matters pertaining to their faith. Sometimes they wrote for their fellow Catholics, sometimes they engaged in controversies with Protestants and unbelievers, and sometimes they wrote for the enlightenment of non-Catholics generally. Our notion of the Victorian epoch as a time of lush sentimentalism and intellectual sloth will be modified when we recall that there was founded in 1869 the Metaphysical

Society, where all manner of subjects were discussed from various points of view by such men as Ruskin, John Morley, Cardinal Manning, Tyndall, Huxley, Leslie Stephen, and Frederic Harrison.

A member of the Metaphysical Society and at one time its president was William George Ward (1812–1882), an Oxford professor who had been prominent in the Oxford Movement and had preceded Cardinal Newman into the Catholic Church. He was often called "Ideal Ward" because of a book he had written in 1844 on *The Ideal of a Christian Church*. He was for many years editor of the *Dublin Review*, a quarterly which was and is the leading organ of Catholic opinion in England. He was succeeded in the editorship by his son Wilfrid Ward (1856–1916), like his father a thoroughgoing scholar and an incisive writer. Wilfrid Ward's *Life of Cardinal Newman* is a masterpiece of impartial biography. Previously he had written a life of his father, of De Vere, and of Cardinal Wiseman. *The Wish to Believe* is an important contribution to the psychology of religion. A French critic, the Abbé Dimnet, wrote of Wilfrid Ward: "It is a rare and happy circumstance for a layman to have been disciplined in theology without losing in consequence any of his activity and independence."

Less of a publicist and more of a scholarly recluse was Thomas William Allies (1813–1903), who had been an Anglican clergyman before his entrance into the Catholic Church. He was active in educational work and did much to organize and maintain Catholic training colleges in England. *The Monastic Life* and *The Formation of Christendom* reveal his profound erudition and his mastery of a clear and winning prose style, a style in which, as his daughter and secretary, Mary Allies, has beautifully said, "the poetical vein was tenderly blended with the philosopher's wisdom." *A Life's Decision* is the story of Allies's conversion to Catholicism. Another lay defender of the faith was William Samuel Lilly (1840–1919), a Cambridge man, a lawyer, and a convert. An untiring contributor to magazines, Lilly engaged in what he liked to call the apostolate of the press and presented with knowledge and power and journalistic spiciness the Catholic point of view on numerous topics. His books include *Ancient Religion and Modern Thought, Renaissance Types, Chapters in European History*, and *Christianity and Modern Civilization*. The titles are a sufficient indication of a range of scholarship which reaches from life in the time of the Apostles to the historical backgrounds of Shakespeare's plays.

Robert Hugh Benson (1871-1914). A tourist pausing at the news stand in Waterloo Station, London, will find spread out before him the books which the English traveling public want. Some very old favorites are there and, of course, the newest things in fiction ; and there too, among the books neither very new nor very old, will the traveler see several of the novels of Monsignor Benson. *Lord of the World* and *The Necromancers* and *The Dawn of All* are distinctly popular books in England ; they are much read in America and in Australia, and they have been translated into several European languages. Their vogue is unusual in this respect : they are designedly and professedly religious stories, and most people have a suspicion (sometimes not ill-founded) that religious stories are dull reading. Readers have learned from Monsignor Benson that a novel can be strongly, even aggressively, religious and Catholic and yet be an absorbingly interesting novel.

None Other Gods recounts how a modern young Englishman — further handicapped by the name of Dick Guiseley — became a saint. *The Sentimentalists* is a study of a man who was torn between religious asceticism and the solace of his silk pajamas. *The Conventionalists* describes how a man loses a vocation and his wife wins one. *By What Authority, The King's Achievement*, and *The Queen's Tragedy* are transcripts from Catholic history in the days of persecution. *A Mirror of Shalott* is a collection of clerical ghost stories. *The Necromancers* is a warning against indiscriminate dabbling in occult science. *The Dawn of All* is a picture of ideal earthly existence, and *Lord of the World* is a forecast of its end.

Such subjects in themselves would hardly make popular novels. Rule-of-thumb critics could go over these books in detail and demonstrate that they are by no means perfect examples of the novelist's art; that there are faults of construction, lack of proportion, abrupt contrasts of sermonizing and melodrama, inconsistencies of characterization. Why are they popular? Simply because they are alive. A book may have ever so many shortcomings and still be alive, just as a man may have asthma and a harelip, a bald head and a wooden leg, and still be alive. And a book may be perfectly planned and faultlessly written and still be only a beautiful corpse. The high secret of literary effectiveness is vitality, and with vitality Monsignor Benson was thrice blessed.

Benson was first, last, and always a priest, a preacher, a missionary, a convert-maker; and writing novels was only one way in which he exercised his vocation. It was because of his power to convey living interest and living understanding to his readers that he succeeded so brilliantly as a novelist. He may fail in details, but he succeeds in totality of effect. *Lord of the World*, for instance, has its blind spots: there are paragraphs chunky and drab, incidents simply incredible, characters like statues with blank eyes, and pictures with dull areas; but it is a book crammed with ideas and replete with action — a book dominated by the sinister and mysterious figure of Felsenburgh the Antichrist, a book that in depicting universal unbelief makes this unbelief itself so shudderingly close and convincing that the reader feels he has been participating in the destruction of the earth when he reads the simple concluding words, "Then this world passed, and the glory of it." It is only afterwards that there may come to him the realization that he has been sharing the meditation of a mystic endowed with a tragic imagination and a sense of humor.

Robert Hugh Benson came of a family distinguished in clerical and literary circles. His father was the Protestant Archbishop of Canterbury, and his brothers, A. C. Benson and E. F. Benson, have been prominent writers. He went to Eton and to Cambridge, thought of the career of a soldier, and then read a novel. The novel was *John Inglesant*, and it changed his desire from the barracks to the pulpit. So he followed his father into the ministry, and then became an Anglican monk. He entered the Catholic Church in 1903, was ordained priest the following year, and for the rest of his life spent himself in preaching, lecturing, and writing in England, in Rome, and in the United States. He died at Salford, where he was preaching a series of sermons, in October, 1914.

Some Writers of Today. William Barry (1849–1930), a canon and rector of St. Peter's Church at Leamington in the Shakespeare country, during a long lifetime devoted himself to writing on Catholic subjects. He produced novels, like *The New Antigone*; essays, like *Heralds of Revolt*; biographies, like his lives of Renan and Newman; and a delightful book of reminiscences in *Memories and Opinions*. Vincent McNabb, a Dominican Father with an alert, incisive style, has contributed several important and original books, including *Where Believers may Doubt*, *Infallibility*, and *Oxford Conferences on Prayer*. Herbert Thurston (1856–   ) is a Jesuit scholar who has written an astonishingly large number of books and reviews on an astonishingly wide range of subjects. He is an adept in unearthing buried evidence and furnishing original proofs. Father Thomas Edward Bridgett (1829–1899), a learned Redemptorist, wrote an exhaustive *History of the Holy Eucharist in Great Britain*, and Father Thurston has edited and annotated that important work. At present he is engaged on a revised version of Butler's *Lives of the Saints*. Dom Anscar Vonier has written several theological works which the lay reader can both understand and enjoy, particularly *The Personality of Christ*.

THE BIBLE

A Library of Literature. Though as we know it the Bible is printed in one volume, it is in reality not a book but a library. The Bible is really a collection of books, of books originally written in more than one language and at various times. It is a collection of sacred — of inspired — writings, and as such it occupies a place of prime importance in the history of religion. But the Bible, like the Church, though of Divine origin, has also its human element. The various books which compose it were written by human hands and reflect the emotions and the conditions of human life. From one point of view the Bible is the written word of God; from another point of view it is the written word of man and a treasure house of human literature.

Sometimes in our eminently proper consideration of the Bible as a depository of sacred teaching we lose sight of it as a unique collection of literature. The Old Testament contains the history of one of the most extraordinary races of men — the Hebrews, the Chosen People; and it presents us with portraits of a large number of remarkable individuals — of Noe, of Saul, of David, of Job, of Judas Machabeus; it gives us the inspired utterances of prophets like Isaias and Jeremias, who in words of burning eloquence admonished the Jews and foretold the coming and the personality of Our Lord. The New Testament recounts the history of the Man-God, describes the foundation and organization of the Christian Church, and preserves the utterances of St. Peter (the first pope), of St. Paul (the energetic preacher of the faith to Greece and Rome), and of several of the other early Christian leaders.

Every literary form is represented in the Bible. We find in the books of *Genesis* and *Kings* and in *The Acts of the Apostles* specimens of historical narrative; we find essays in *Ecclesiastes* and the Epistles of St. Paul and St. James; we find poetry both lyrical and dramatic in the *Psalms* and the *Canticle of Canticles*; we find a supreme world drama in the book of *Job*; we find models of the short story in *Genesis*, in *Esther*, and in the parables of the New Testament; we find a rich garnering of wisdom in *Proverbs* and *Wisdom*; we find in *Josue* and *Amos* and *The Acts* masterful examples of oratory. In the Bible are fixations of all the emotional moods which go to the making of literature: fervor, pathos, humor, irony, satire, prophecy, reminiscence, sublimity. It is possible to secure the fine fruits of literary training through an exclusive study of this collection of great books.

The Bible in the European Tradition. Because of the prominence given it in the Christian scheme of civilization, the Bible assumed a formative office in the perpetuation of the European Tradition in literature. Through the centuries it was read in public and in private. Poets and painters, sculptors and dramatists, turned to it for the themes of their several arts. The prayers which generations of little children learned at their mothers' knees and the stories they heard of winter evenings by the hearth were oral transcripts from the Bible. Sermons were built upon the sacred text, stained-glass windows blazed with Biblical characters and scenes, and quotations from *Genesis* and *Exodus* and the *Psalms*, from the four Gospels and the Epistles of St. Paul and St. John, became part and parcel of familiar thought and speech. When some heroic woman performed a deed of valor, she was called the Judith of her people; when a youth proved undutiful, he was condemned as the Absalom of his family; when a man distinguished himself as a brave warrior and a successful ruler, he was saluted as a David or a Machabeus, and when he betrayed his trust he was likened to Peter, who denied his Lord, or to Judas, who delivered Him to His enemies.

Affecting thus so intimately the life of the European peoples, the Bible likewise affected the literature which was the expression of that life. Much of the literature of Europe might be said to constitute a paraphrase of the Bible. Every collection of popular literature, such as the hymns of the Church and the early miracle plays, is patently influenced by the sacred text; every great writer, such as Dante or Calderón, is indebted to the Bible alike for diction and for inspiration. The Bible was a leaven which permeated all European letters, which transformed the spirit of the literature that came down from Greece and Rome, and which animated and stimulated the newer literature that sprang up in Italy and France, Germany and Spain.

AN ILLUMINATED GOSPEL

The cover of a manuscript copy of the Gospel according to St. Matthew

From the beginning of Christianity the Bible was esteemed a treasure alike in the churches and in the libraries. Long before the fifteenth century, when printing was invented, manuscript copies of the Sacred Scriptures, often, like the Book of Kells, magnificently illuminated, were made by monastic copyists. Among the first products of the printing press were editions of the Bible in Latin and in the modern languages; a New Testament in French was published at Lyon as early as 1477, and the complete Bible in French appeared at Paris ten years later. "Not only the French and the German, but the Italian and Spanish presses also issued vernacular translations of the Scriptures half a century before the English press approached this sphere of activity."[1]

[1] Sidney Lee, *The French Renaissance in England*, p. 140.

The Bible in English. The last literary work engaged in by St. Bede the Venerable was a translation of the Gospel of St. John, and his was not an isolated instance of an early English version of the Holy Scriptures. The Lindisfarne Gospels appeared late in the seventh century, and there were the Rushworth version and the West Saxon and other translations

FROM THE FIRST PRINTED BIBLE

The beginning of the First Book of Kings in the Old Testament, printed by John Gutenberg at Mayence, Germany, about 1455. John Fust aided the work financially. (Courtesy of the British Museum)

before the Norman Conquest. It naturally came to pass that some translations were inaccurate and that much of the copying was heedless, so that the Church was compelled to insure the integrity of the Bible by legislating against unauthorized versions. John Wycliffe (1320–1384), a teacher at Oxford who eventually fell away from the Church and founded the sect of the Lollards, made a translation of the New Testament in the second half of the fourteenth century; the remainder of what is loosely called the Wycliffe Bible was the work of Nicholas of Herford, and the entire version was revised by John Purvey.

Numerous translations of the Bible, in whole and in part, appeared in England after the separation of the English Church from communion with Rome. What is known as the *Authorized Version*, the English Bible used by Protestants, is the work of forty-seven scholars appointed by King James I in 1604. Its literary quality is excellent. The English Bible used by Catholics is known as the *Douai-Reims Version* because the translation was made in France at Douai and at Reims.

In several English editions of the Bible the ambitions of the translators and the lapses of printers caused amusing errors to appear and brought unlooked-for notoriety on the versions. One edition has been called "The Wicked Bible" because the little word *not* was omitted in one of the Ten Commandments; another is known as "The Breeches Bible" because it states that our first parents in the garden made for themselves breeches of fig leaves; still another is "The Vinegar Bible" on account of a misprint of the word *vineyard*. The Classical eighteenth century was prolific in translations which sought to render the Scriptures in elaborate style. One of these begins the Parable of the Prodigal Son with the statement that "a gentleman of splendid family and opulent fortune had two sons," and describes the daughter of Herodias as "a young lady who danced with inimitable grace and elegance."

The Influence of the Bible. It would be difficult to over-estimate the influence of the Bible on the writers who have contributed to English Literature from Cædmon down. Biblical characters, Biblical events, and Biblical allusions and turns of expression appear over and over again in Shakespeare, in Milton, in Dryden, in Browning, and in Tennyson. Most of the makers of English Literature were educated men who had come into their intellectual inheritance through the study of Greek and Latin at the universities and through travel in Continental countries; but all of them drew sustenance from the diction and the imagery, from the thought and the spiritual riches, of the Bible. And so it was that

Bunyan, the Bedford tinker, and Keats, the liveryman's son, that Walton ruminating with fishing-rod in hand, and Kipling writing his best poems and stories in distant India could alike share in the educational opportunities afforded them by the Bible, could learn from the sacred text how to put words together, how to develop directness and clarity of speech, how to discipline their fancy and develop their imagination, how to transfer to the written page their observations, their aspirations, and their dreams. It was Carlyle who said that a university is a collection of books. The story of English Literature amply demonstrates that the Bible is the greatest university in the world.

CHAPTER XVII

THE IRISH CONTRIBUTION

When a visitor arrives in the city of Dublin, one of the first things he notices is that the artistic green-and-white street signs are in two languages, the familiar English and the perhaps fascinatingly mysterious Irish. As he goes through the city and through the country, he discovers everywhere this bilingual condition; the children learn both languages in the schools, and many a man he meets in the street wears a little gold circle on the lapel of his coat as an indication that he is a Gaelic speaker. English and Irish, though in different degrees, are used by the Irish people, and so we may reasonably expect to find that the literature of the Irish people is a bilingual literature. There exists a very old and very rich literature in Gaelic, a literature that even in the darkest days of Ireland's history never entirely died out and to which modern Gaelic writers are consciously contributing; and there likewise exists an expression of Irish life and thought in the English language. This Irish Literature in the English language is sometimes called Anglo-Irish Literature. It is deserving of attention in this book, not only because it is written in the English language but because it sprang from conditions made possible by English rule in Ireland, because some of it drew inspiration from English writers, and because it has had a considerable effect on the main stream of English Literature.

With the Irish Literature contained in the Gaelic tongue we are not here concerned, for that is no more English Literature than are the literatures of Portugal and Holland. Nor in this chapter shall we advert to the very voluminous contributions made to English Literature by men like the essayist Steele,

the poet Goldsmith, the dramatist Sheridan, and the historian
Lecky, for such men are recognized as holding assured rank as
English authors, in their lives and their writings more identified with the country
of their adoption than
with the country of
their birth; besides,
though born in Ireland
and of Irish parents,
they were still the Irish
"of the pale," as the
English Irish are lo-
cally designated to dis-
tinguish them from the
Irish Irish. Neither are
we to study the much
though vaguely dis-
cussed Celtic element
in the English race
and consequently in
English Literature, the
subtle strain of poetic
passion which Matthew
Arnold discovered in
Shakespeare and which
modern critics have at-
tempted to isolate in
such thoroughly Eng-
lish writers as Kipling
and H. G. Wells. We
are here to consider

MUIREDACH'S CROSS, MONASTERBOICE

Scattered throughout Ireland are ruined crosses,
exquisitely sculptured, testifying to the religious
fervor and the artistic skill of earlier ages.
Monasterboice, in the valley of the Boyne, was
a monastic school founded by St. Builhe at the
end of the fifth century. Many of the students
came from overseas

rather an extraordinary phenomenon in the history of world
literature, a state of affairs in which a subject nation, forbidden
to use its own language, adopts the tongue of the conqueror
and enriches the literature of the invaders.

THE PERIOD OF SUBJECTION

It is a fact, copiously admitted by English authorities, that the conquest of Ireland by England was made and maintained with rigor, with cruelty, and often with tyrannical injustice. For many years the Irish religion was penalized and the Irish language suppressed. Persecution did not quench Irish loyalty to Catholicism, but the imposition of the English language did for a long time almost completely wipe out the native tongue of the Irish; it is only within our own time that the Gaelic Revival has succeeded, and as yet only in part, in reëstablishing the Irish language. Especially in the cities Irish children grew up knowing nothing of the tongue of their ancestors, and so what literature was produced assumed shape in English. Hence the literature of the Period of Subjection is predominantly in the English language, and it voices the resentment and the sense of outrage of a subject people.

The Poetry of the People. One phase of the English policy in Ireland was the suppression of schools and scholars, so we shall look in vain before the nineteenth century, when the policy was modified, for a literature of learning and culture. What we do find is a literature that sprang from the heart of the race, a body of simple poetry that voiced the eternal passions of love and hate, that glowed with religious and patriotic fervor, and that reflected the life of the humble cabin and the winding road, the tilled field and the country fair; that recalled the glories of the distant and splendid national past; that kept alive stories of saints and fairies, sacred groves and haunted glens; and that served to keep alive racial ideals and national aspirations. Love poems and patriotic ballads, nearly all of them anonymous, form the bulk of this unstudied literature, which passed from generation to generation by word of mouth and was for the most part not written down until men like Sir Samuel Ferguson and Sir Charles Gavan Duffy collected and printed specimens of the poetry of the people.

Thomas Moore (1779–1852). The man who more than a hundred years ago did most to bring home to both the English and the Irish people the beauty, heroism, and pathos of Ireland's past was Thomas Moore, a Dubliner by birth and a Catholic by upbringing, who ultimately drifted both from Irish associations and the practice of his faith. While he was a student at

Trinity College he was involved with Robert Emmet in the charge of sympathizing with the United Irishmen; eighteen students, including Emmet, were expelled, but Moore was only warned as being "contumacious." All that was forgotten by the time he had gone over to London, hobnobbed with royalty, consorted with Byron and the literary set, and won the reputation of a clever man of fashion. In what seemed essentials he was more an Englishman

THOMAS MOORE

than anything else: he had been educated in Trinity College, he lived mostly in England, he married an English actress, he attended the Established Church. He wrote some poetry, including *Lalla Rookh*, an Oriental tale, and brought out lives of Sheridan and Byron. And yet Tom Moore occupies a prominent place in the history of Irish Literature, and his verses are still trembling on the lips of the Irish people.

Both fame and fortune Moore secured by the publication of his *Irish Melodies* (1807–1834); and though the fortune, as is the way with material things, disappeared, the fame was both immediate and enduring. Edward Bunting and Sir John

Stevenson had collected many of the old Irish airs, setting them down in musical form as they heard them from the lips of Irish peasants; melodies were they which had descended from a remote past, from a day when the bard, at once musician and poet, claimed parity with the scholar and the saint. It was to those traditional airs that Thomas Moore attached the graceful and singularly melodious lyrics we know as "The Minstrel Boy," and "The Meeting of the Waters," and "Let Erin Remember." With much of the true poet's clairvoyance and more of the true poet's fervor Moore could boast of his achievement and indicate the dominant traits of Irish poetry:

> Dear Harp of my Country! in darkness I found thee,
>   The cold chain of silence had hung o'er thee long,
> When proudly, my own Island Harp, I unbound thee,
>   And gave all thy chords to light, freedom, and song!
> The warm lay of love and the light note of gladness
>   Have wakened thy fondest, thy liveliest thrill;
> But, so oft hast thou echoed the deep sigh of sadness,
>   That e'en in thy mirth it will steal from thee still.
>
> .   .   .   .
>
> If the pulse of the patriot, soldier, or lover,
>   Have throbbed at our lay, 'tis thy glory alone;
> I was but as the wind passing heedlessly over,
>   And all the wild sweetness I waked was thy own.

Francis Sylvester Mahony (1804–1866). Spending most of his years abroad and engaging in a variety of literary work for English periodicals, Francis Sylvester Mahony wins his place among the Irish poets with one remarkable poem which is known wherever the English language is spoken. While he was a student for the priesthood in the Irish College at Rome, there swept over him one evening a wave of homesickness for his native city of Cork beside the River Lee, and in the fading light he scribbled on the wall beside his bed the ingenious rimes of "The Bells of Shandon." He little dreamed that in thus violating the rules of the house he was insuring his immortality.

He abandoned the priesthood and wandered over Europe, sometimes appearing in the most unexpected places. His name occurs here, there, and everywhere in the informal records of the times. Once he dropped in on the Brownings in Florence, found Robert Browning suffering from a cold, and concocted a curative drink with raw eggs and wine. Much of his time he spent in London and in Paris, where he died. On the staff of *Fraser's Magazine* he was associated with Thackeray, Ainsworth, Carlyle, Lockhart, and other literary lights, and amply lived up to his reputation for wit and learning, for gentle habits and purity of life — "a loving friend, a faithful, steadfast Irishman, and a Christian gentleman."

"FATHER PROUT"

Mahony's best work in prose and verse is contained in the two series of *The Reliques of Father Prout*. A priest of that name had lived at Watergrass Hill near Blarney, and it was Mahony's whim to attribute to the good simple man the clever and learned outcroppings of his own eccentric genius. Under that pen name Mahony wrote his delightful article on "The Rogueries of Tom Moore." He translated a number of Moore's *Melodies* into French and Latin, printed Moore's work and his own in parallel columns, and then gravely charged the self-important little poet with plagiarism from obscure authors. He made a similar French version of Charles Wolfe's "The Burial of Sir John Moore," which every ten years or so is still being "discovered" as the original of that famous poem.

THE "YOUNG IRELAND" POETS

Race-Consciousness in Literature. Thomas Moore, writing in an English environment, largely in an English manner, and with an English audience immediately in view, had little in common with a group of poets whose voices rose about the time he was winning his laurels as a sweet singer of Irish lays. The newer poets were identified with the "Young Ireland" movement, and their patriotic and political interests, while giving fire and intensity to their literary work, unquestionably narrowed their range and limited their appeal. Much of their verse was frankly pro-Irish and anti-English propaganda and from the point of view of literature possessed the defects which such material almost invariably reveals; but the Young Ireland movement also produced a body of poetry which expressed a keen and intelligent interest in the literary treasures of early Ireland and an awareness of the poet's cultural heritage. These poets looked back with passionate affection to the Old Ireland which had been the island of saints and scholars and forward to the New Ireland which they sought to realize in literature and in life. *The Nation*, a newspaper founded by Duffy, Davis, and John Blake Dillon in 1842, became the organ of the Young Ireland movement.

James Clarence Mangan (1803–1849). In his personal life and in the essential characteristics of his poetry James Clarence Mangan bears a remarkable resemblance to the American poet Edgar Allan Poe.

There is in each a prevailing note of sadness and melancholy; a love of the indefinite, the vague, the mysterious; a predilection for the preternatural and the weird; a recoiling from the world of reality, and a constant effort to find more congenial surroundings in a world which the vast majority of mankind enter only with hesitation and with a deep feeling of awe.[1]

[1] John J. O'Brien, "Mangan and Poe," *The Catholic University Bulletin*, February, 1909.

Mangan was born and lived and died in Dublin. There he knew poverty and illness and dejection; there too he feasted his spirit on the old poetry of Ireland, on bits of Oriental and Continental literature, on "many a quaint and curious volume of forgotten lore." While Tom Moore, dapper and smiling, trolled his *Irish Melodies* for the delight of lords and ladies in London drawing-rooms, this other Irish poet, trudging the squalid streets leading down to the Liffey, with the mud seeping through his tattered shoes, dreamed resplendent dreams of the past and the future and framed in leaping, passionate measures the aspirations of his race. Mangan embodied those dreams in the noblest and finest poetic contribution of an Irishman to English Literature, "Dark Rosaleen."

JAMES CLARENCE MANGAN

Ostensibly a love song, the outpouring of a lover to his lass, this very free translation of an old song by Red Hugh O'Donnell became the voice of a nation's soul. All poetry is symbolic, but this poem is doubly so. The little Dark Rose is the Irish race, and the poem caught and preserves the spirit of self-devotion and inspired ardor which even then was urging many Irishmen to desperate uprisings and forlorn hopes.

> Woe and pain, pain and woe,
>   Are my lot, night and noon,
> To see your bright face clouded so,
>   Like to the mournful moon.
> But yet will I rear your throne
>   Again in golden sheen;

'Tis you shall reign, shall reign alone,
  My Dark Rosaleen!
  My own Rosaleen!
'Tis you shall have the golden throne,
'Tis you shall reign, and reign alone,
  My Dark Rosaleen!

Here is one of the few poems in English which rise to heights sublime in "adoring, flashing, flying, laughing rapture of patriotic passion . . . the chivalry of a nation's faith struck on a sudden into the immortality of music."[1]

Other poems, some of them exquisite, many of them commonplace, came from the heart of this Irish bard with the dark hair and the wistful face and the glittering, deep-blue eyes. Not all of them were on Irish subjects, but all were heightened by Irish mystery and word magic. He found kinship in the literature of the East, a picturesqueness and a gorgeous imagery which he reproduced in his own inimitable way. His misery and melancholy he transfixed in "The Nameless One," a poem which Poe might have written in his darkest hour. In another mood he achieved a triumph of poetic vision with "The Midnight Review." A ghostly reveille echoes, the dead soldiers of Napoleon stir from their sleep in many lands, form into phantom battalions, and are reviewed by the specter of the Little Corporal as the moon sinks into the shadowy clouds:

In files the troops advance,
  And then are no longer seen.
The challenging watchword given is·"France,"
  The answer is "St. Helene."

Poets of the *Nation*. Though he died while still a young man, Thomas Osborne Davis (1814–1845) was recognized as the leader of the Young Ireland party and the most popular of the national poets. Less of a word master than Moore and less of a poet than Mangan, Davis had vigor of thought, pic-

[1] Lionel Johnson, *Post Liminium*, p. 220.

turesqueness of imagery, and the journalistic knack of creating a strong and wide appeal. His "Fontenoy," a stirring commemoration of the Irish Brigade in the French army under General Saxe in 1745, is typical of his work and remains a favorite selection for recitation. The same topic was given a more restrained but more literary treatment by Bartholomew Dowling (1823–1863). Thomas D'Arcy McGee (1825–1868), a political agitator who spent most of his life in Canada and the United States and was assassinated at Ottawa, wrote a number of well-turned and tender patriotic lyrics. Among the women contributors to the *Nation* was Lady Wilde (1826–1896), the mother of Oscar Wilde, who wrote over the pen name of Speranza. Other poets

THOMAS DAVIS

of the *Nation* were Father Charles P. Meehan, Richard Dalton Williams, Mary Anne Kelly (Eva), and John Kells Ingram.

Denis Florence MacCarthy (1817–1882). The most distinguished littérateur in the *Nation* group was Denis Florence MacCarthy, whose patriotic poems, appearing under the pseudonym of Desmond, take high rank among the lyrics of Anglo-Irish Literature. Like Mangan he was born in Dublin and died there, but he had in maturity the benefits of foreign travel; and like Mangan he managed through reading and study to garner the finest fruits of the European Tradition. He developed an early interest in Spanish Literature, and his translations of the dramas of Calderón, unsurpassed in their beauty and their fidelity to the spirit of the originals, won for him the medal of the Royal Academy of Spain. For many years he taught English Literature at the Catholic University

SIR SAMUEL FERGUSON

of Dublin. He was an enthusiastic student of early Irish Literature, bringing out *The Poets and Dramatists of Ireland* and *The Book of Irish Ballads*. MacCarthy's best original work includes a long narrative poem, *The Voyage of St. Brendan*, and such graceful, restrained, melodious offerings as "The Bridal of the Year," "The Bell-Founder," and "The Pillar Towers of Ireland."

Sir Samuel Ferguson (1810–1886). A scholarly and industrious pioneer in the Irish Literary Revival was Sir Samuel Ferguson, a Belfast lawyer who turned to the history, legends, and literature of early Ireland for the inspiration of his poems. In matter and in manner he stands among the best of the Irish poets; some discerning critics would even place him above Mangan and MacCarthy. Ferguson's reputation was established with "The Forging of the Anchor," which appeared in *Blackwood's*. His distinctively Irish poems in English are to be found in his *Lays of the Western Gael*, in *Deirdre*, a one-act play which has been extensively imitated, and in *Congal*, an epic poem in five books. His ability as a writer of narrative prose is shown in his popular humorous story, *Father Tom and the Pope*, and in his mélange of prose and verse called *Hibernian Nights' Entertainments*.

William Allingham (1824–1889). At first a bank clerk, then a customs officer, later a holder of several minor government positions, and for a time editor of *Fraser's Magazine*, William Allingham gave much of his leisure to the writing of poetry. That is not an extraordinary circumstance in the history of literature; but the distinctive thing about this man is that of all the Irish poets he was the fastest friend of the fairies. The "good people," as they are called in Ireland, the wailing banshee and the leprechaun who makes shoes, and the pooka who rides an untamed fairy steed, — these and many others whispered secrets in his ear while he estimated duties on merchandise and tried to make accounts come out right. The latter half of his life Allingham spent in London, and some critics say that his fairies came to be Anglicized in the course of time; but always his poetic fancy roved to County Donegal and the beautiful Ballyshannon of his birth, and to "the winding banks of Erne," and peopled the hills and the glens with

> Wee folk, good folk,
>   Trooping all together;
> Green jacket, red cap,
>   And white owl's feather!

Of his fairies he wrote not learnedly but knowingly; not for literal-minded grown-ups but for children of all ages who understand the wind when it drones a story and the moon when it discloses hidden things among the trees. And so it is that in Ireland and out of it Allingham's *Poems, Day and Night Songs*, and *With Songs, Ballads, and Stories*, dealing as they do with the sea and the heather, with the "good people" and ruined abbeys, with birds that mock at lovers and ducks that make merry in a pond, form a unique contribution to the English Literature that has come out of Ireland.

IRISH NOVELISTS

Gerald Griffin (1803–1840). Innocent bystanders are frequently perplexed at the Irish way of disagreeing about the merits of Irish fiction. "This book," one critic will say, "is true to the life of the peasantry; it springs from intimate

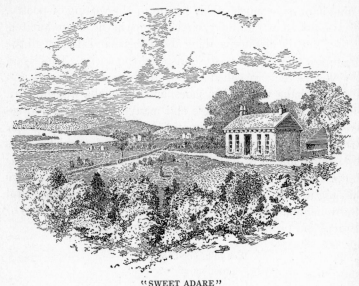

"SWEET ADARE"

Where young Gerald Griffin worked and wandered

knowledge of the land and the people, and it is written with discernment and sympathy." And against the same work another Irish critic will protest: "This book is a travesty on Irish life. It is a piece of vulgar English propaganda. It grossly misrepresents the character and habits of the race, and is the unhallowed offspring of ignorance and prejudice." One novel of Irish life, because of its sincerity, its artistry, its balance, and its charm, stands exempt from the contradictions of criticism; by all classes of Irish readers *The Collegians* is accepted as an impartial and veracious narrative.

Gerald Griffin wrote *The Collegians* when he was twenty-five; wrote it after a boyhood spent in and around his native Limerick, where he learned his art, as Stevenson was later to learn it, by transcribing and studying specimens of good English, and where he exercised his style as a contributor to the *Advertiser*. His novel is a transcript of the life he knew so intimately. The story of Hardress Cregan, a young man who met his fate because of self-indulgence and undisciplined living, is a happy fusion of Romanticism and Realism : there is sordidness in it, and vulgar villainy and a logical ending in tragic gloom; but in it too are the glamour of the Irish countryside and the idealism of men and women who seek

GERALD GRIFFIN

and find the best in life. The narrative, flowing as evenly and brilliantly as the silver Shannon, is rich in dramatic values. *The Collegians* was dramatized by Dion Boucicault under the title of *The Colleen Bawn* and enjoyed wide popularity in England and America; but the novel is immeasurably superior to the play.

Griffin wrote other stories, but never duplicated the success of *The Collegians*. *The Invasion* is a stirring Irish historical tale. He was a poet too, producing descriptive verses, tuneful lyrics, and several inimitable love songs, which, wrote Sir Charles Gavan Duffy, "smite the heart like the cry of a woman." He had studied Moore's *Irish Melodies* to good purpose and became a master of smooth and musical versification. His drama *Gisippus*, written before he was twenty, was successfully staged by Macready at Drury Lane two years after the author's death. Griffin spent several years as a journalist and miscellaneous writer in London and then, when he had won his laurels, withdrew from the world at the age of thirty-five and became a Christian Brother. Brother Joseph, as Gerald Griffin was now known, spent two happy years in prayer and teaching, and had begun a new novel, *The Holy Island*, when he died suddenly in his thirty-seventh year. He is buried in the little cemetery attached to the North Cork Monastery of the Christian Brothers.

William Carleton (1794–1869). The youngest child in a County Tyrone family of fourteen living on a farm of exactly fourteen acres, William Carleton received a good though irregular training from a hedge schoolmaster[1] named Pat Frayne. The boy thought for a while of becoming a priest, and acquired a relish for the study of Latin which never deserted him. Eventually he abandoned his clerical ambition and even drifted from the Catholic religion. He took to writing and produced a large number of stories dealing with Irish life. At first he aimed at finding an audience in England and depicted Irish life as Englishmen would like to believe it really was; later on he changed his tactics and wrote frankly for his compatriots the stories by which he is best remembered: *The Baronet's Daughter*, *The Evil Eye*, *The Irish Rapparee*, and especially *Willy Reilly*. There can be no doubt that in *Willy Reilly* Carleton has given a vivid and essentially faithful picture of life in Ireland in the days of religious persecution, that he has

[1] The policy of the English government in restricting the educational opportunities of the Catholics in Ireland resulted in the establishment of numerous informal and illegal hedge schools where learning was acquired, as it were, by stealth. Griffin had been a hedge pupil, too. The hedge schoolmasters were frequently capable and learned men, especially versed in the classics, and patriotically devoted to their work.

told a love story sufficiently conventional to win a response from all readers and sufficiently exceptional to invest it with the spice of novelty, that he has woven his tapestry of smiles and tears, of thrills and humors, with competence and a sense of design.

The Banims. Just as the first quarter of the nineteenth century was drawing to a close, a couple of young men at Kilkenny dreamed a dream. Michael and John Banim were readers, thinkers, and patriots; Michael was a man of affairs, John had already attracted distinction as dramatist and poet. The unprecedented vogue of the Waverley Novels impressed them both with the importance of a series of stories dealing with episodes in the life of a nation, and so they projected a group of novels dealing with Irish life and manners which would do for Ireland what Sir Walter Scott's stories had done for Scotland. Thus *The Tales of the O'Hara Family* came into being. The brothers engaged in genuine collaboration, freely criticizing and revising each other's work, so that it is almost impossible to apportion between them most of the novels which they turned out during the next fifteen years. John Banim (1798–1842) did most of the actual writing, and Michael Banim (1796–1874)

WILLIAM CARLETON

generously attributed to his younger brother the success of their undertaking. Among their tales are *Boyne Water*, *The Smuggler*, *Peter of the Castle*, *Crohoore of the Billhook*, *The Croppy*, *The Ghost-Hunter*, and *Father Connell*. John had planned *Father Connell*, — a story built about the personality of the parish priest of Kilkenny, — Michael had written it,

JOHN BANIM

and John was engaged in its revision at the time of his death.

Best known of the Banim novels is *Boyne Water*, a thrilling romance of Ireland in the days of King James II. The struggles of Catholics and Protestants, of Jacobites and Orangemen, reach an impressive climax in the siege of Derry, and a double love story is unfolded against the somber setting of those disastrous times. Many pages in this and other stories by the Banims are not cheerful reading, but the pictures are rarely overdrawn. John Banim especially kept free of political partisanship, but both he and his brother realized the mischief wrought on the Irish character through English rule and were unsparing in their exposure of the crushed and impoverished peasantry. "We paint from a people of a land among whom, for the last six centuries, national provocations have never ceased to keep alive the strongest and often the worst passions of our nature."

Samuel Lover (1797-1868). Samuel Lover, though usually classed among the novelists, was a man who played many parts.

Restless in a business office in his native Dublin, he turned to song-writing and painting. One of his ballads, "Rory O'Moore," he expanded into a novel which in turn he successfully dramatized for the London stage. He wrote the words for two operas of Balfe's, lived much in England, traveled in the United States and Canada, and invented a form of entertainment called Irish Evenings, consisting of poems, songs, stories, and recitations all rendered by himself. As a novelist his reputation rests on *Rory O'Moore* and *Handy Andy*. Lover had wit, broad humor, and a brisk narrative style; but he knew little of real Irish life and chose to depict what little he knew for the amusement of his English admirers. In consequence he more than anyone else is responsible for

SAMUEL LOVER

the caricature known as the stage Irishman — a care-free, rollicking, blundering ignoramus who laughs his way to fortune.

Charles Lever (1806–1872). Though often confused with Lover because of the similarity of their names and a spirit of rakish irresponsibility in their stories, Charles Lever as man and as novelist had little in common with the author of *Handy Andy*. Though born in Dublin, he was thoroughly English in blood and in sentiment, was a Trinity College man, a medical student in Germany, a diplomat at Brussels and at Spezia, a lengthy sojourner in Florence, and finally British Consul at

Trieste. There was point in Lord Derby's remark when assigning Lever to that post: "Here's six hundred a year for doing nothing, and you're just the man to do it." Lever, like the heroes in his own novels, liked action but hated work. He was extravagant and unmindful of the morrow, intent mainly on good cheer and the fascination of the gaming table. His first

CHARLES LEVER

novel, *Harry Lorrequer*, he wrote to make good his gambling debts, and his subsequent activity as a novelist was generally inspired by the same pressing need. Others of his books are *Charles O'Malley*, usually considered his best, *Tom Burke of Ours*, *The O'Donoghue*, *The Knight of Gwynne*, and *The Fortunes of Glencore*. Most of his stories are concerned with the only Irish life he knew; that is to say, the life of men and women "in the pale," the life of the English Irish. His persistent type of hero is a hot-headed scion of "the gentry" who gambles recklessly, makes love with dramatic zest, fights innumerable duels, perpetrates frequent practical jokes, and is equally free with his purse when it has anything in it and his tongue when there is occasion for back talk or self-glorification. Charles O'Malley, for instance, has a good conceit of himself and speaks as follows for the honor of Galway:

I rode boldly with foxhounds; I was about the best shot within twenty miles of us; I could swim the Shannon at Holy Island; I drove four-in-hand better than the coachman himself; and from finding a hare to hooking a salmon, my equal could not be found from Killaloe to Banagher.

Charles Joseph Kickham (1830–1882). The authentic Irish tradition in fiction was restored in the novels of Charles Joseph Kickham, which in their general features resemble the best work of Griffin, Carleton, and the Banims. *For the Old Land, Sally Cavanagh, or the Untenanted Graves*, and *Knocknagow, or the Homes of Tipperary* hold but slight appeal for readers entertained by Lover and Lever, but they are read and treasured by the Irish people at home and abroad. They are slow-moving stories, told in a style simple and unadorned, sometimes rather too filled with detail and lacking often in dramatic force, but rich in humor, accurate in observation, and in turns of dialect faithful to the speech of their author's native Tipperary. Kickham also wrote a number of simple and deservedly popular ballads. He was a journalist who became involved in the Fenian troubles and was sentenced to fourteen years of penal servitude, but was released after he had lost his eyesight in prison.

Patrick A. Sheehan (1852–1913). Doneraile (The Fort on the Cliff) is a little town a few miles beyond Mallow and close to the ruins of Kilcolman Castle, where Edmund Spenser entertained his friend Sir Walter Raleigh and wrote *The Faerie Queene*. Here Patrick A. Sheehan was parish priest — a thoughtful, studious man who had graduated from Maynooth, who had seen clerical service in both England and Ireland, and who devoted his considerable leisure to writing. In pleasant weather he would carry his paper and inkpot out to a little summerhouse in the garden behind his house and, pen in hand, reflect on life as he knew it in Ireland and beyond.

We know the results: some pleasant devotional poems, a sheaf of sage and practical essays, two collections of rich miscellaneous reflections and bits of literary criticism in *Parerga* and *Under the Cedars and the Stars*, and especially a score of novels of varying merit but all distinguished for their range of thought, spiritual insight, piquancy of dialogue, adroitness of character drawing, and a sufficiency of narrative art. Some of his pictures of Irish life rival those of John Banim in their tragic hopelessness, but others of his pages gleam with a humor nearly as strident as that of Lever and are athrill with a sense of religious reality new in English fiction. Canon Sheehan did what no Irish novelist before him had done and what very few since his time have done : while sacrificing nothing of his Irish heritage he contrived to transcend racial boundaries and to make his studies of Irish life an integral part of the European Tradition in literature. When reading his best novels we are conscious of that world view of human nature which we recognize in Cervantes, in Hugo, in Galsworthy. Tolstoy considered Sheehan the greatest novelist in the early twentieth century.

Canon Sheehan's favorite among his stories was *The Triumph of Failure*, a novel of college life which makes too heavy a demand on the reader's thinking capacity ever to win popular success; yet it remains a fine example of the psychological novel in which psychology has not forgotten the existence of the soul. He joined the best sellers with *My New Curate*, not so much a novel as a series of episodes of clerical life in Ireland. The book won readers on both sides of the Atlantic because of its bracing humor and the essential human quality of its characters. His ablest performance is *Luke Delmege*, into which he put much of his own temperament and experience. It too is a clerical story but a most unconventional one, revealing both individual and national life, and inculcating the ideal "Be a little child as well as a profound thinker." Its introductory chapter recalls Thackeray in its splendid presentation of the methods and materials of the novelist. Nearly as strong a book though less ambitious in scope is *The Blindness of Dr. Gray*, a study of a pious, rigid-minded Irish priest delightfully contrasted with his glowingly human and humane little niece from America. Other novels of

Irish life are *Glenanaar*, *Lisheen*, *The Graves at Kilmorna*, and *Miriam Lucas*, the last least successful in its American scenes, for the Canon, though he esteemed the United States and found there his first and most enthusiastic audience, had no first-hand knowledge of the country. *The Queen's Fillet*, its background the French Revolution, is an excellent historical novel.

James Owen Hannay (1865–   ). Employing the pen name of George A. Birmingham, a Protestant clergyman, the Very Reverend Canon James Owen Hannay, has made several valuable contributions to Irish fiction. He began as a serious observer of social and political conditions in Ireland with *The Seething Pot*, *Hyacinth*, and *Benedict Kavanagh*, novels that won respect and discreet praise; but he struck his true vein of fantastic and gloriously illogical comedy with *Spanish Gold*, the first of a series of fictional extravaganzas unexcelled in their delineation of the humors of Irish life. Perhaps Canon Hannay has become convinced that there is much wisdom in the words he puts into the mouth of one of his characters:

A fellow that starts off by thinking himself clever enough to know what's true and what isn't will do no good in Ireland. A simple-hearted innocent kind of man has a better chance.

At all events his later and most representative stories are simple-hearted, with the shrewdness of the Irish locution "It might" for plain "yes" or "no," and innocent, with an uncanny perception of the twists and quirps of human nature. His typical hero is one Dr. O'Grady who shines so happily in *General John Regan*, a story wherein the people of an Irish village, and ultimately the English government itself, are brought to erect a statue in honor of a native son who never existed save in the genial doctor's constructive imagination. Some present-day Irish writers take themselves and their art too solemnly; Canon Hannay tends to preserve in them a goodly sense of proportion.

THE IRISH LITERARY REVIVAL

Rise and Growth. The movement to create in Ireland a distinctive literature in the English language was but one manifestation of a spirit generated by the Young Ireland party and strengthened by a renewed race-consciousness in industrial and political life. In particular it was an outgrowth of the effort, fostered by Dr. Douglas Hyde, Father O'Growney, and others, to restore the Gaelic language. Many Irishmen, Dr. Hyde argued, would not or could not learn the tongue of their ancestors, but they might, through the English language, enter somewhat into the spirit of Irish Literature. He reduced his theory to practice and translated numerous poems from the Gaelic. And in Ireland, both north and south, were many individual writers who, like Moore, turned to the past of Ireland for the source and inspiration of their themes. Eventually groups of such authors were formed, and the revival was definitely begun.

A memorable date in the history of the revival is 1888, for in that year appeared *Poems and Ballads of Young Ireland*, containing selections from Yeats, Hyde, Katharine Tynan, and others. Four years later organizations to further the revival were formed in London and Dublin. The Irish Literary Society of London began its work with an address by the erudite Stopford Brooke (1832–1916) on " The Need and Use of Getting Irish Literature into the English Tongue." The very title of the discourse was a manifesto of the aims of the society. A similar address on " Irish Literature : Its Origin, Environment, and Influence " was delivered by George Sigerson (1839–1925), a veteran scholar of Gaelic and an industrious translator of early Irish Literature, at the inception of the National Literary Society in Dublin.

Before long similar societies sprang up in Belfast, in Cork, in Waterford, and elsewhere, and systematic efforts were made to arouse freshened interest in the poems and stories of past centuries and in training and encouraging young writers to produce for Irish readers a body of literature in the English language, mostly on Irish subjects, and always in the Irish mode. The movement made rapid progress, for it was in harmony with the national ideals of self-dependence then prevalent and with developments taking place in social and industrial life.

The Irish Drama. The revival affected poetry and fiction, but its most notable result was in the drama. Dramatic talent is a national heritage of Irishmen; numerous Irish playwrights, such as John O'Keefe (1747–1833), Charles Macklin (1690–1797), and Dion Boucicault (1822–1890), had written for the London stage, and even today many of the leading actors in London and New York are of Irish birth or ancestry. Now, however, came the deliberate attempt to create a distinctively Irish drama with the foundation in Dublin of the Irish Literary Theater in 1899. The movement spread, and within a few years there were more than a dozen similar dramatic societies in various parts of Ireland.

The drama of the revival had the advantage of possessing clear-cut and practical aims and ideals. The actors were, in the best sense, amateurs, men and women who acted for the love of acting but who submitted themselves to rigid discipline and careful rehearsal; they were schooled to be at once artistic and natural and to exemplify the Irish mode in speech and action. The theaters were small and unadorned, — the Abbey Theater in Dublin remains thoroughly unpretentious in its size and furnishings, — and the scenery was simple and suggestive. The plays chosen for presentation were based on the history and legends of Ireland and on the life of the peasants in the country and the poorer classes in the cities, and were written for the most part in the unliterary language of the Irish people.

The movement is now thirty years old and has passed beyond the experimental stage; the very fact of its continuance is an evidence of its essential success. Yet from the beginning it has been the target of violent criticism. Time and again have audiences at the Abbey Theater interrupted the players with indignant protests; and when the company attempted to enact their representative plays in New York, they met an unfavorable reception at the hands of Irish Americans. Much of the antagonism is absurd and unintelligent, but it is not without some justification. A few of the plays presented by the Abbey players have been highly offensive to the susceptibilities of Irishmen at home and abroad — especially abroad, for it is human nature to become more racially sensitive the farther we get from home — through their exclusive insistence on the vulgar and the sordid in Irish life. Synge, the greatest of the Irish dramatists, made the profound mistake of dwelling on the exceptional and abnormal and assuming it to be the usual and the representative, and younger playwrights have gone even farther in the same direction. Again, though the Catholic spirit is a conspicuous factor in Irish life and thought, it found practically no expression in the drama of the revival; nearly all the plays of the Abbey Theater have directly or by implication intimated that Ireland is dominated by ideals of gross materialism on the one hand and of a vague paganism on the other. Most of the men who have written for the Irish Literary Theater are non-Catholics: Yeats, Moore, Hyde, Synge, St. John Ervine, and more recently Sean O'Casey and Liam O'Flaherty. The only Catholic playwright prominently associated with the movement was Edward Martyn (1859–1923), who, in dramas like *The Heather Field*, *The Enchanted Sea*, and *Romulus and Remus*, opposed and even ridiculed the excessively realistic trend of the Irish drama, and who broke away from the Abbey organization and founded a theater of his own.

Despite its limitations the drama of the Irish revival has several achievements to its credit. It has emphasized the artistic treatment of familiar and ordinary life, it has encouraged its audiences to discover beauty in commonplace things, and so has accomplished one of the aims of all true art. In minimizing scenic display and refusing to exploit the personality of actors it has centered attention on what really matters in the theater; that is, on the drama itself. It has definitely discredited the Handy Andy type of stage Irishman; and though in doing so it has at times invented a different but hardly less odious caricature, on the whole it has brought possible and conceivable human beings upon the stage. It has revealed something of the possibilities of simple, homely speech as opposed to the stilted and artificial language long associated with the theater and to the use of which Irish dramatic writers have been especially prone. Aiming at naturalness of action and delivery, it has developed a fresh and sane tradition in the art of acting, a tradition which has influenced players in the commercial theater throughout the English-speaking world. Finally, in encouraging numerous playwrights and giving them opportunities of stage production it has enriched the dramatic literature of the world with several undoubted masterpieces.

John Millington Synge (1871-1909). Often we find men who write well, who write with scholarship and insight and even literary charm, but who put into their writings no breath of life. John Millington Synge thus wrote for several years after his graduation from Trinity College, Dublin; though he read much and traveled on the Continent, his essays were merely correct, conventional, respectable. Then Yeats, whom he met in Paris, gave him this advice: "Go to the Aran Islands. Live there as if you were one of the people themselves; express a life that has never found expression." And so to that practically unknown region off the west coast of Ireland Synge went; and his dead style came to life. The dramas which he wrote as a result of his stay in the Aran Islands are vivid and human and often beautiful in language and mood.

His first plays, *In the Shadow of the Glen* and *Riders to the Sea*, are true tragedies, amply realizing Aristotle's theory that the tragic poet purges the minds of his audience through pity and fear. His last play, *Deirdre of the Sorrows*, is a tragedy too, unfinished at the author's death. *The Tinker's Wedding*, a farce, is from all points of view the least satisfactory of Synge's works. His remaining plays mingle tragedy and comedy in varying proportions. *The Well of the Saints* tells the story of an old blind couple who miraculously are made to see, and then are so unhappy in the gift that when blindness comes back to them they refuse to have their sight restored. *The Playboy of the Western World*, describing honors heaped by Irish villagers on a young man who, it was supposed, had killed his father, aroused strong opposition as a misrepresentation of the Irish character; it has passages of rich and glowing beauty and deft characterizations which make it interesting as prose poetry but which do not atone for the fact that in its central conception it is a travesty less on the Irish race in particular than on humanity in general. Here Synge's mordant irony passed the bounds of truth and common sense.

The most distinctive element in the plays of Synge is his employment of English prose in the Irish mode to produce the effect of rare and delicate poetry. His diction, a slightly exaggerated reproduction of the speech of Western Ireland, leavens the strength and sturdiness of the English language with the imaginative allusiveness of the Gaelic. A heightened example of the Irish mode he puts into the mouth of Martin, the blind beggar in *The Well of the Saints*:

Ah, it's ourselves had finer sights than the like of them, I'm telling you, when we were sitting a while back hearing the birds and bees humming in every weed of the ditch, or when we'd be smelling the sweet, beautiful smell does be rising in the warm nights, when you do hear the swift flying things racing in the air, till we'd be looking up in our own minds into a grand sky, and seeing lakes, and big rivers, and fine hills for taking the plough.

Riders to the Sea shows Synge at his best. In structure and characterization the drama has the superb simplicity of true

greatness. Firm in conception, marvelous in atmosphere, direct
in unity of impression, is the picture of old Maurya, at peace
because she can suffer no more, now that all her sons have been
snatched from her by the insatiate sea:

They're all gone now, and there isn't anything more the sea can do to
me. . . . I'll have no call now to be up crying and praying when the wind
backs from the south, and
you can hear the surf in the
east, and the surf in the west,
making a great stir with the
two noises, and they hitting
one on the other. I'll have
no call now to be going down
and getting Holy Water after
Samhain, and I won't care
what way the sea is when
the other women will be
keening.

WILLIAM BUTLER YEATS

**William Butler Yeats
(1865–   ).** Though a
persistent writer of prose
essays and a reteller of
ancient stories, a founder
of the Irish National
Theater and the author
of *The Shadowy Waters*,
The Hour-Glass, and other
plays, William Butler Yeats is mainly a poet. His plays are
poetic dramas mostly, depending for their success less on their
dramatic value than on their rhythmic diction and their free
play of fancy; his prose, whether he discusses himself and his
friends in *Autobiographies* or Blake and Shelley in *Ideas of
Good and Evil*, has the lilt of rime and the lure of rhapsody.
Indeed, many of his poems are less poetical than some of his
writings which profess to be prose. *The Wanderings of Oisin*
is most characteristic of his longer pieces of verse, but his true

poetic stature may be taken from a number of his shorter poems in the collections entitled *The Secret Rose, The Wind among the Reeds*, and *In the Seven Woods*, poems written for the most part before the present century began.

Yeats was born in Dublin and received his schooling partly there and partly in London; but his education came mainly

"Æ"

From a drawing by W. R. Dublin

from reading translations of Old Irish poetry and legends. He outgrew his youthful association with Wilde, Beardsley, Dowson, and the other Decadents, and set himself to fostering and extending the literature of his native country. He imitated popular street ballads, he described bits of rural scenery, he noted the ways of thinking and speaking of people on remote farms and in hidden glens. He has dabbled in occult science, and is conveniently labeled "mystic" by numerous critics who do not altogether get his drift. He harks back in his often beautiful poetic dreams to pre-Christian Ireland and revels in tales of heroes and fairies and pagan gods. Much of what he has written is of no permanent worth, and more is incomprehensible to the generality of his countrymen, but in his writings, his lectures, and his personal influence he has had a pronounced effect on the development of literature in Ireland during the past thirty-five years.

George Russell (1867–   ). Another pagan poet of modern Ireland is George Russell, who favors the unusual pseudonym Æ; and his paganism, truly beautiful in many of its manifestations, is compounded of elements derived from ancient Ireland, — as he thinks ancient Ireland was, — from Theosophy, from the religious and philosophical concepts of India and Persia. As a philosopher Æ has little appeal, but as a poet he is remarkable for the intensity of his spirit, the richness of his emotional tone, and the profuseness of his imagery, which recalls the higher reaches in the poetry of Francis Thompson. He has gathered most of his verses in *Collected Poems* and *Gods of War*. In his simpler moods he is often convincingly devotional; the following verses might have been written by a pensive nun in studious cloister pale :

> And one thing after another
>   Was whispered out of the air,
> How God was a big, kind Brother
>   Whose home is in everywhere.
>
> His light like a smile comes glancing
>   Through the cool, cool winds as they pass,
> From the flowers in heaven dancing
>   To the stars that shine in the grass.
>
> From the clouds in deep blue wreathing
>   And most from the mountains tall,
> But God like a wind goes breathing
>   A dream of Himself in all.

The Poets of Easter Week. Three capable Irish poets perished in the Dublin rebellion of Easter week, 1916. Padraic Pearse, born in 1879, was a man who lived poetry as well as wrote it. In his plays and stories and poems and in his educational work at St. Enda's School he was animated by one idea, to revive an Ireland wherein were honored "the hero who had the most childlike heart, the king who had the largest pity, and the poet who visioned the truest image of beauty." In 1911 he gave the patrons of the Abbey Theater a grateful taste of variety by producing there an original passion play.

His poems he wrote in Gaelic, translating many of them into English in *Sleep Songs and Sorrow Songs*. Thomas Mac-

PADRAIC PEARSE

Donagh (1877–1916), educator and man of letters, published several highly important studies in *Literature in Ireland*; a play for the Abbey Theater, *When the Dawn Came*; and four collections of poems. The third of the Easter-week poets was Joseph Plunkett, whose verses in *The Circle and the Sword* are ringing expressions of patriotism and religion. Each of these men might be fittingly commemorated in a bit of Irish verse written by Pearse and translated by MacDonagh:

> I have not gathered gold;
> The fame that I won perished;
> In love I found but sorrow,
> That withered my life.
>
> Of wealth or of glory
> I shall leave nothing behind me
> (I think it, O God, enough!)
> But my name in the heart of a child.

Francis Ledwidge (1881–1917). In County Meath there roamed a young man — grocery clerk, miner, and farmer by turns — who cared little about the strife of men and the ways of the wide world and found peace and inspiration in the odors of the fields and the warblings of the birds and the rustling of the wind in the autumn leaves. He was no mystic like Yeats, no pantheist like Russell, no deliberate student of the seamy side of life like most of the Abbey Theater playwrights. He merely set down his impressions and memories, and after a while a brother poet, Lord Dunsany, encouraged him to publish *Songs of the Fields*. Less than a year later Francis Ledwidge, a soldier in the British army, met his death in the Balkans. Then came his fame, and perhaps, because of the circumstances of his death, his importance as a poet has been overestimated. He had not fully learned his craft, his gifts were not of the highest order, sometimes his singing voice was choked; but his poems serve at least to remind a time and a country which need the lesson that poetry is not poetry unless it sees and enjoys beautiful things.

Mrs. Hinkson (1861–1931). Born in Dublin and educated at the Dominican Convent at Drogheda, Katharine Tynan Hinkson, after her marriage in 1893, resided mostly in London but assumed an active part in the literary and artistic life of Ireland. She became a prolific writer of prose and verse. Among her collections of poetry are *Cuckoo Songs*, *The Wind in the Trees*, *Irish Love Songs*, and *St. Francis and the Wolf*. Her verses are symmetrical and often eloquent, convincing in their depiction of Irish scenes and in their unobtrusive devotional tone. Her long line of novels, from *The Way of a Maid* to *The Moated Grange*, are singularly even in merit and for the most part give expression to the genteel tradition in Irish life. She also brought out four volumes of personal reminiscences which afford interesting side lights on men and movements in Irish and English politics and literature during the last half century.

Lord Dunsany (1878–   ). Next to Synge, Lord Dunsany has made the most unique and original contribution to the recent Irish drama. His farces, *The Glittering Gate* and *The Lost Silk Hat*, are like no other farces in any language; his poetic plays, like *The Tents of the Arabs*, have an exotic quality which refreshes the mind and enlarges the fancy; his symbolic dramas, like *King Argimenes and the Unknown Warrior* and *The Laughter of the Gods*, reveal new possibilities of the dramatic art; his melodramatic tragedies, *The Queen's Enemies* and *A Night at an Inn*, stir the most jaded spectators to unwonted thrills. In his prose tales, such as *The Gods of Pegana*, *A Dreamer's Tales*, and *The Book of Wonder*, Lord Dunsany has

LORD DUNSANY

created a new heaven and a new earth; he has invented a paganism of his own in which there is a large infiltration of the Christian spirit. His prose style is highly individual, orotund in its cadences, massive in its simplicity, fascinating in its poetic quality. To read him is to realize what artfully arranged words can do to fill the imagination and renew the face of the earth.

Edward John Moreton Drax Plunkett, Baron Dunsany, disproves the belief entertained by many people that the littérateur is a dainty and effeminate man, out of touch with his fellows and out of harmony with the realities of daily life. There is a rugged, virile quality in his symbolic prose; and his dramas and stories appeal to us as the overflow of a singularly active mind and an abounding vitality. A soldier, a sportsman, a traveler, captain of the local cricket team, the best pistol shot in Ireland, and the master of a landed estate in County Meath near the historic Hill of Tara, Lord Dunsany's interest in literature is that of the man of the world rather than that of the scholarly recluse. Chesterton in *Manalive* has drawn his friend Dunsany to the life.

William Kirkpatrick Magee. The *enfant terrible* of the Irish Literary Revival is William Kirkpatrick Magee, better known by his pen name, John Eglington. He is an Ulster man, bred in the Protestant tradition, and a literary free lance whose principal joy in life is to attack the ideas and ideals of Yeats, Lady Gregory, Russell, and the other proponents of the new age in Irish Literature. George Moore has aptly called him "a sort of lonely thorn-tree." Magee has repeatedly assailed the dearest convictions of the Irish race, but in a prose style so terse and chaste and beautiful as to win admiration even from his enemies. Among his favorite contentions are that the Island of Saints and Scholars never produced a saint, that the Irish Irishman is the "Mere Irishman" in contradistinction to the Irishman of English stock, that Wolfe Tone was a timeserver and opportunist rather than a patriot, that the present-day revival of "the grand old tongue" is an indication of national insanity. Though he early wrote some distinguished verse, he has recently confined himself to the prose offerings contained in *Some Essays and Passages*, *Bards and Saints*, *Anglo-Irish Essays*, and other provocative and exquisitely written books.

St. John Ervine (1883–). Another Northern Ireland man is St. John Ervine, who in his plays and stories has given some vivid pictures of life among his own people. The strife of Catholic and Orangeman is the subject of two dramas, *Mixed Marriages* and *The Orangeman*. *The Magnanimous Lover*, because of its reflections on Irish morality, caused as much discussion and protest as Synge's *Playboy*. His masterpiece is *John Ferguson*, a powerful and well-constructed drama of domestic life in County Down. *Jane Clegg* is another well-knit play, with an English setting. Ervine's novels include *Mrs. Martin's Man* and *Changing Winds*. A book of reminiscences out of the ordinary is *Some Impressions of my Elders*, in which he engages in diverting criticism, mostly destructive.

Padraic Colum (1881–   ). As poet and dramatist Padraic Colum is a laureate of the soil. In *The Land*, produced at the Abbey Theater in 1905, he points an effective contrast between a father who venerates the little farm upon which he has toiled all his life and a son who looks longingly out upon the world and refuses to be tied down to "a bit of land and a house." Better yet is *The Fiddler's House*, based on a similar contrast

© Pirie MacDonald

PADRAIC COLUM

of Wanderlust versus devotion to the soil; the old fiddler leaves his little house to his younger daughter, a practical-minded person, and with his elder girl, who shares his love of the great outdoors, sets forth with his fiddle to make music and taste "the lasting kindness of the road." Colum has something of that fiddler in his own blood, for recently he sailed across the Pacific to find literary material in distant islands.

Daniel Corkery (1878–   ). A goodly measure of skill in portraiture and in the artistic suggestion of emotional backgrounds is found in the stories and short plays of Daniel Corkery, like so many of the Irish writers a student and a teacher. *The Yellow Bittern and Other Plays* show his capabilities as a dramatist, *The Hounds of Banda* contains some strong stories of the Irish struggle for national freedom, and *The Threshold of Quiet*, one of the best half-dozen novels written in English in the twentieth century, includes substantially every element in Irish life and character. He is in the forefront of the younger Irish writers.

James Stephens (1882–   ). Humble life in Dublin town has never been more sympathetically embodied in a novel than by James Stephens in his delightful descriptive and psychological story, *Mary, Mary*. Here Mary Makebelieve and Mary's mother and the big policeman and the policeman's aunt and all the other characters take their places among the unforgettable pictures in memory; and the author's confidential and limpid manner of writing is as a quavering song that floats at nightfall across the bridges of the Liffey. *Mary, Mary* shows that realistic fiction need not be sordid and offensive and that romance gladdens even the heart of a charwoman. Not less fascinating, though in another way, is *The Crock of Gold*, wherein with a constant play of humor and a rich sprinkling of homely proverbs Stephens records the words of wisdom that fall from the lips of an Irish Socrates dwelling with his Xantippe among the pines. Of his other stories the most distinguished is *The Adventures of Seumas Beg*. He has to his credit several books of pleasing verse, including *The Hill of Vision*, *Songs from the Clay*, and *The Rocky Road to Dublin*.

Other Writers. An early worker in the revival was Anna Johnston (1866–1902), somber-souled Romantic, who over the name of Ethna Carbery wrote numerous fine poems of patriotic passion and typically Irish imagery now contained in *The Four Winds of Eirinn*. Her husband, Seumas MacManus (1870–   ), has written well in verse and better in prose, his stories and sketches of Donegal in *A Lad of the O'Freels*, *Yourself and the Neighbors*, and other books bringing him a large following, especially in the United States, where he now resides. "The Little Waves of Breffny," the most perfect specimen of pure poetry which the Irish Literary Revival has produced, was written by Eva Gore-Booth (died 1926). Another woman who caught in verse the spiritual delicacy and unworldly grace of the Celtic spirit was Dora Sigerson Shorter (1872–1918), the daughter of one literary man and the wife of another, whose representative lyrics and ballads may be seen in *The Troubadour and Other Poems*. For many years identified with the Abbey Theater and a friend and adviser of Yeats, Lady Gregory

(1859–1932) brought out several plays which still enjoy favor. Among them are *The Rising of the Moon, Spreading the News,* and *The Workhouse Ward*. She recast in modern English of the Irish mode many of the old tales and legends taken down in dictation from Gaelic speakers in remote districts: *Poets and Dreamers, Gods and Fighting Men, A Book of Saints and Wonders*. Lennox Robinson (1886–   ) is one of several sad young men who specialize in plays and novels revealing the seamy side of Irish life; *The Cross Roads, The Dreamers,* and *Patriots* are dramas which convey his gloomy views of human nature and his biting criticisms of social conditions.

THE IRISH MODE

In a significant passage of his *Autobiographies* Yeats describes the holidays he used to take with his young companions when he was attending school in England. The boys would go off for the day to various spots in the vicinity of London and enjoy themselves in care-free fashion. And yet, though he played the same games with them and sat on the same grass and strolled beneath the same trees, the Irish lad was conscious of a difference between him and his classmates; they saw things that he did not see. They were English in an English country; he was Irish and in an alien land, and the finer spirit of the beautiful landscape was hidden from the eyes of his soul.

Something similar happens when a man of Irish blood writes in the English language. He may appreciate the externals of English Literature as well as an Oxford graduate, he may know English grammar almost as thoroughly as a German professor, he may have in a high degree the gift of literary expression; yet always there is a subtle difference. The language he writes in is indeed English, but behind the words which represent his thoughts and feelings are long generations of ancestors who phrased those thoughts and feelings in the Gaelic tongue, and that Irish heritage unconsciously modifies his employment of the speech of Chaucer and Shakespeare, Dryden and Newman. The modern Irishman has much in common with the modern Englishman; but his traditions are different, his outlook on life is different. All this expresses itself in his way of writing and produces what Thomas MacDonagh called the Irish mode in letters.

The Irish mode constitutes an important contribution to English Literature. When we read Sheehan's *Luke Delmege* and Benson's *Lord of the World*, we discover in the one a religious background of thought which we do not find in the other. Both books were written by priests, both are animated by earnest purpose; *Lord of the World* is even more frankly missionary in spirit than *Luke Delmege*; yet the Irish writer unconsciously reveals a depth and breadth of spiritual experience to which the English writer is a stranger. When we take up a nature poem by Shakespeare, by Wordsworth, by Tennyson, we find faithful delineation, wise reflection, fitting words, and consonant melody; but when we read in Eva Gore-Booth

The great waves of the Atlantic sweep storming on their way,
   Shining green and silver with the hidden herring shoal,
But the little Waves of Breffny have drenched my heart in spray,
And the little Waves of Breffny go stumbling through my soul,

we are aware — unless we are singularly dull of ear and mind and heart — of a turn of speech and a tint of emotion found only in the English Literature of Irish origin. "There is an Anglo-Irish language," wrote Sir Charles Gavan Duffy in his *Ballad Poetry of Ireland*, "as easily discriminated from London English as the dialect of Saxon spoken in the Lowlands of Scotland. . . . It is a dialect rich with the restless imagination, and colored with the strong passions of our nation."

The Irish mode is eminently obvious in the writings of the distinctively Irish authors, Griffin, Davis, Mangan, Mac-Carthy, Yeats, Synge, Stephens; yet it appears too in the descriptive prose of Goldsmith, in the oratorical periods of Burke, in the clever dialogue of Sheridan, in the terse brilliancy of Shaw. These men have a less lengthy line of Irish racial experience behind them than the others, but enough of it to affect their thought and style.

Not in men like Carleton and George Moore, who have written for a general audience, is the Irish mode of writing English most pronounced, but in men like the writers of the Irish Literary Revival, who produced a literature "from, by, of, to, and for the Irish people." That fact is at once their strength and their weakness. In their deliberate effort to express Irish thought and aspiration in a rhythm and speech characteristically Irish English they had the advantage of a definite incentive and a clearly seen goal, but in many instances they almost as deliberately cut themselves off from the general literary tradition of Europe and so confined their influence to the people of their own race. The Irish writers who are destined to endure in the history of English Literature are the men who, while not neglecting their peculiar Irish heritage in letters and in life, availed themselves of the training and the culture offered them by the poetry and prose of other lands. The principles of Sinn Fein, — We Ourselves, — whatever their merits in politics, have no more validity in literature than in art and in religion.

CHAPTER XVIII

THE TWENTIETH CENTURY

GENERAL CONSIDERATIONS

Perspective in Study. At first thought it might seem that the easiest of all periods of literature to analyze and evaluate would be the period of the here and now. Is not this literature a part of the life we lead? Are not contemporary men in essential respects much like ourselves? Do they not wear the same clothes, eat the same food, think the same thoughts? When we study Horace, we have to reconstruct the social and political life of Rome under Augustus and devote many hours to a study of the geography and climate of the Empire; and all the while we are laboring under the added difficulty of reading in a language which is not our own. On the contrary, when we study Max Beerbohm — rather much of a prose Horace in modern England — we have no need to read supplementary books on such subjects as "What Twentieth-Century Englishmen eat for Dinner" or "The Meaning of Railway Travel in the Western World." There seems no necessity for us to make a detailed study of literary backgrounds in Beerbohm's case; for we feel already fairly familiar — thanks to newspapers and books, moving pictures and the radio — with the life he transcribes. Then, too, we do not have to read him with a dictionary open before us; for his language is English, not Latin, and the English of today, not the English of the days of Pope or of Bacon.

Undoubtedly the student who approaches current literature escapes a quantity of drudgery which he must face in studying earlier epochs; but before he proceeds far in his investigation, he discovers that the literature of the day offers a set of difficulties all its own. For one thing, it demands far more from his good sense and judgment. If he is studying the Cavalier Poets, he knows which authors to choose and what to read of all their writings; but when he approaches the poets who have written during the last ten years, he is confused by their number and baffled by the diversity of opinion concerning the value of their poems. The writers of earlier periods listed in manuals of literature remain objects of study through successive years; a student of English Literature a hundred years from now will give at least some consideration to Donne, to Herrick, to Browning, to Thompson. But the writers of today, even though their books are now widely read, give no assurance that their worth will be permanent; sometimes a current writer ceases to be important even while we are tabulating the reasons for his supposed immortality. Swans degenerate into geese overnight, and occasionally a goose turns out to be a swan. Precisely because we are in the midst of our own day and generation it is extremely difficult for us to view it in its right perspective. "Criticism of our contemporaries," wrote Jules Lemaître, "is not criticism; it is only conversation."

The Fickleness of Fashion. It might be objected that some present-day writers are very popular, that their books have large sales and are on the waiting list in public libraries, and that such writers are sure to be permanently important. Yet popularity is no criterion of literary excellence. In August, 1907, the books most in demand in the New York Public Library were the following: Davis's *The Scarlet Car*, De Morgan's *Alice for Short*, the Williamsons' *Princess Virginia*, Alcott's *Little Women*, Ibsen's plays, O'Shea's *Dynamic Factors in Education*, and Roberts's *Haunters of the Silences*. Only two of those items would today find place in a history of literature; and one of them, *Little Women*, was a fairly old book even then, and the other, Ibsen's plays, are translations from a foreign literature. It is odd but it is true that about the surest way to fall behind the times is to confine one's reading to the books that are momentarily "the rage."

Father Time is the most discerning and the most ruthless of critics. Every year thousands of books pass under his eye, and most of them, how great soever may be their passing vogue, he promptly tosses into the waste heap of oblivion. It is only once in a while that he takes a volume from the pile and places it on the shelf of the classics. How few of the poets who sang in the days of Elizabeth are now more than dim and misty names! How few of the dramatists who were in fashion at the Restoration find place on the modern stage! If even but ten years from now another edition of this book should appear, few changes would have to be made in the earlier chapters, but it is safe to say that this chapter, dealing with very recent writers, would have to be completely rewritten.

Literature versus Journalism. Perhaps the best way of discriminating between current books that possess permanent interest and those which enjoy but a passing vogue is to keep clearly in mind the difference between books that are literature and books that are journalism. A novel dealing with the circling of the world by an aviator would today stand an excellent chance of popularity; twenty years hence, unless it should possess the characteristics of true literature, that novel would be completely forgotten, because by that time the progress of aviation will probably have made such advances that circling the globe will be as commonplace a proceeding as traveling by rail from Boston to Chicago. Journalistic books capture the mood of the moment; books that are literature embody a vision of what is permanent in human life and experience. Books that are journalism "have their day and cease to be"; but of books that are books we may say what Ben Jonson said of Shakespeare, that they are not of an age but for all time.

POETRY

Alice Meynell (1850-1922). Like most recent writers, Mrs. Meynell wrote in both prose and verse, but she is rightly placed among the poets because her verse has the authentic poetic quality and because most of her prose has poetry for its subject and is richly emotional in its coloring. In yet another way she is typical of the modern spirit in literature, for she was comprehensively catholic in her view of life and art and garnered some of the finest fruits of the European Tradition. Born in England and to a great extent educated in Italy, Mrs. Meynell was in the best sense of the word a cosmopolitan in her outlook. For many years her London home was a center of literary inspiration; there she and her husband, Wilfrid Meynell, entertained the leading writers of the late nineteenth and early twentieth centuries; there Coventry Patmore met with understanding encouragement, and there the brilliant and erratic Francis Thompson found a home.

Mrs. Meynell wrote relatively little, but that little is of uniformly high quality. Her first book of poems, *Preludes* (1875), moved Ruskin to remark that it contained some of the finest things he had seen in modern verse. In succeeding years she published other collections of poems, the edition of 1913 including only those verses which her exacting taste deemed worthy of preservation. Her best essays are to be found in *The Rhythm of Life* and *The Colour of Life*.

Mrs. Meynell might be called the Lady Poverty of English Literature. In such characteristic poems as "After a Parting" and "I Must not Think of Thee" she advocates renunciation in life and practices it in her delicate and ascetic technique. She gives us less of body than of soul. She was a convert to Catholicism, and her religious faith, though never obtrusive, lends a tone and a perfume to her poetry. Sorrow she knows and the problem of evil in the world; but she knows, too, "little solitudes of delight," and from the bitter in experience presents the sweet and the beautiful in what Thompson called "her own carved perfect way." We find Mrs. Meynell at her highest and best in "The Shepherdess":

> She walks — the lady of my delight —
>   A shepherdess of sheep.
> Her flocks are thoughts. She keeps them white;
>   She guards them from the steep;
> She feeds them on the fragrant height,
>   And folds them in for sleep.
>
> She roams maternal hills and bright,
>   Dark valleys safe and deep.
> Into that tender breast at night
>   The chastest stars may peep.
> She walks — the lady of my delight —
>   A shepherdess of sheep.
>
> She holds her little thoughts in sight,
>   Though gay they run and leap.
> She is so circumspect and right;
>   She has her soul to keep.
> She walks — the lady of my delight —
>   A shepherdess of sheep.

Austin Dobson (1840–1921). In the poetry of Mrs. Meynell we find almost flawless art and little concern with the storm and stress of world problems. A similar devotion to delicacy and a distaste of the strident and the striking we find in the poetry of Dobson, who had nothing in common with the verve and heartiness of Noyes and the aggressiveness and vulgarity of Kipling. Dobson liked to experiment with French verse forms in English, to paint poetical miniatures of men and scenes of the eighteenth century, to make little poems, slight in substance, that sing themselves sweetly and a little plaintively. In prose he did much the same thing in his *Eighteenth Century Vignettes* and in his excellent life of Horace Walpole, which reproduces the character and daily doings of the sage of Strawberry Hill. In the following lines he paints a picture of

stage conditions when Richard Burbage, Shakespeare's leading
man, first enacted Hamlet:

> When Burbage played, the stage was bare
> Of fount and temple, tower and stair;
> Two backswords eked a battle out,
> Two supers made a rabble-rout,
> The Throne of Denmark was a chair!
>
> And yet, no less, the audience there
> Thrilled through all changes of Despair,
> Hope, Anger, Fear, Delight, and Doubt,
>   When Burbage played!
>
> This is the Actor's gift, — to share
> All moods, all passions, nor to care
> One whit for scene, so he without
> Can lead men's minds the roundabout
> Stirred as of old these hearers were,
>   When Burbage played!

Sir William Watson (1858–   ). If Dobson was Classical
by preference, Sir William Watson is Classical both by temperament and reasoned conviction. In an age which has
canonized Whitman's "barbaric yawp" and has encouraged
experiments, often injudicious, in free verse and "polyphonic
prose," he has stood apart from the throng, an austere aristocrat of letters, preaching in prose and practicing in verse the
doctrine of traditional dignity and disciplined workmanship.
Of recent years his powers have given evidence of decline, but
he remains an impressive figure in twentieth-century poetry.
He early devoted himself to the expression of emotion in concise, chiseled verse, — *Epigrams of Art, Life and Nature*, —
and he continues to be the leading exponent of "the nobler
sort of epigram." He is fond, too, of writing elegiac odes and
commemorates earlier poets in such poems as "In Laleham
Churchyard," "The Tomb of Burns," "Wordsworth's Grave,"
and "Lachrymæ Musarum," the last a splendid tribute to
Tennyson.

John Masefield (1875–   ). More typical of present-day tendencies in poetry is the work of John Masefield, whose first poems appeared in 1902 after their author had taken a graduate course in the university of hard knocks. A Shropshire lad, Masefield went to sea when he was fourteen and for several years sailed before the mast. Then he landed in New York and worked in a saloon washing glasses, sweeping the floor, and occasionally ejecting undesirable patrons. It was an unusual training for a poet; but late at night, the long working day at an end, he would read himself to sleep over the one book he possessed, Malory's *Morte d'Arthur*. When he returned to England, Masefield became a husband and a father and a sedate and dignified citizen, and at the suggestion of Jack B. Yeats — William Butler Yeats's artist father — he set about describing in verse the seafaring life he had known and seen.

Masefield's first poems outdid Kipling in vulgarity and shocked the genteel tradition in letters; we can imagine Sir William Watson raising his eyebrows over that crude maritime narrative, *The Story of a Round-House*. But they were real poems. *Dauber* was an unusual study of the artistic temperament; *The Widow in the Bye-Street* was as appealing in its pathos as startling in its realism; *The Everlasting Mercy*, despite its melodramatic quality, reached unsuspected depths in its psychological portraiture of phases of religious conversion. Masefield was saved from ephemeral popularity by reason of the depth and seriousness of his view of life and his conscientious efforts to perfect himself in his art.

Least important of all his poems, *The Daffodil Fields* marks a definite transition in the work of Masefield. He here tells the tragic story of one Michael Gray, a young man who, in the words of his dying father, is "one to curb, one to be curbed"; but nobody curbs him, and accordingly he ruins his life and the lives of others through following impulse and never denying his desires. Thereafter Masefield sought and found the bulk of his material in the European Tradition and produced several dramatic poems rich in their suggestion of atmosphere, strong in their basic conceptions, distinguished in their style. In one of them, *The Tragedy of Pompey the Great*, he successfully invades the field of Shakespeare's Roman plays and presents an idealized but absorbing study of Cæsar's rival, who, loving freedom and greatly desiring it for Rome, turns against his own patrician supporters and faces certain defeat in the effort to be true to his highest conception of duty. Masefield has evoked a dreamy word music in *Philip the King*, a drama of Spain in Armada days. He abandons formal verse in *The Faithful*, a grim drama of wrong and revenge in Japan of two hundred years ago, but the meditative songs scattered through the play and the highly rhythmic quality of the prose used in the drama proper convey the effect of true poetry. His *Good Friday*, a drama of Our Lord's Passion, is dignified, reverent, and simple ; its concluding song of the blind madman strikes a chord that reverberates in much of Masefield's maturer writing :

> I cannot see what others see ;
> Wisdom alone is kind to me,
> Wisdom that comes from Agony.
>
> Wisdom that lives in the pure skies,
> The untouched star, the spirit's eyes ;
> O Beauty, touch me, make me wise.

Different in his life and in his work from John Keats, Masefield has as ardently, if perhaps neither so consistently nor so successfully, engaged in the quest of the beautiful. That quest is the burden of many of his shorter poems, including several of his finest sonnets. Ever he finds it alluring, sometimes he fears it is vain ; but he realizes that his dimly discerned vision of loveliness, whether it be a shining city splendid or a cruelly mocking mirage, has been his pillar of fire and of cloud.

Masefield has not confined himself to poetry and the drama. His little book on Shakespeare is among the most illuminating guides to the great plays; the boy who ran away to sea has bested the learned university dons in their own province. He has won a considerable following as a novelist, especially with *Sard Harker* and *Odtaa*, though the latter at least he wrote with his tongue in his cheek. They are adventure stories laid in the imaginary land of Santa Barbara in South America.

Walter de la Mare (1873–   ). A singularly capable artist, an adept in versification and word melody, Walter de la Mare holds his high place among present-day poets, first, because he excels them all in his insistence on the quest of beauty and on the inevitableness of its decline; and, secondly, because he has written much and surpassingly in the mood of fresh-eyed and illogical childhood. Beauty and childhood mold the dominant burden of his songs. In some poems he is older than his years, intent on the pursuit of loveliness even while he is disillusioned and knows how unavailing is the chase; in other poems he is a child writing for children — though in fact the children who appreciate him most are generally grown up — and heartily believing in gnomes and elves and goblins and enchanted dishes and all the other things that in childhood's imagination are gloriously and aboundingly real. If we are merely old, we accept him in "The Listeners" and "Motley"; if we are merely young, we accept him in *Songs of Childhood* and *Peacock Pie*; if we are ageless and wise, we accept him in both strains, and are grateful to him as well for his prose stories in *The Connoisseur* and *The Memoirs of a Midget*.

Alfred Noyes (1880–   ). As there are two De la Mares, the seeker after beauty and the poet of childhood fancies, so there are two Alfred Noyeses. The second and less successful Alfred Noyes has appeared but recently, a very earnest, consciously learned, and philosophical singer who in his lengthy trilogy, *The Torch-Bearers*, seeks to invent a vast blank-verse epic of human progress. What our descendants may think of *The Torch-Bearers*, or that they will think of it at all; whether they will exalt it as we have exalted *Paradise Lost* and

The Ring and the Book, or dismiss it as we have dismissed Bailey's *Festus* and Southey's *Curse of Kehama*, is an alternative beyond our powers of prophecy and prayer. But we who have known that other and younger Alfred Noyes are inclined to resent *The Torch-Bearers*, the writing of which seems to have prematurely aged an irrepressible youngster and inflicted a sin-

ALFRED NOYES

gularly tuneful singer with what threatens to be a permanent sore throat. The Noyes who vastly delighted poetry lovers and considerably enlarged their numbers with his spirited poems is the Noyes who wrote *The Barrel Organ*, *Drake*, *The Forest of Wild Thyme*, *Forty Singing Seamen*, and *Tales of the Mermaid Tavern*.

He is no philosopher, that younger Noyes, but an observer and a dreamer with a rare zest in his singing, employing a great variety of meters and succeeding surprisingly with all. He wrote much on English themes and promised to become the uncrowned laureate of England; but he went afield for many of his subjects, too, and often brought his native country into friendly contact with the wide world. In one poem he tells of a little boy in a coast town who watched the ships from his window and dreamed of "shipping as a seacook and sailing to the Golden Gate," but whom fate compelled to grow old and gray, "perched upon a high stool in London." In another, "The Realms of Gold," "written after hearing a line of Keats repeated by a passing stranger under the palms of Southern California," he imagines to what heights the

genius of Keats might have soared had his soul been enriched
by the Spanish traditions of the New World:

> He would walk at dawn by the lemon orchards,
>   And breathe at ease in that dry bright air;
> And the Spanish bells in their crumbling cloisters
>   Of brown adobe would sing to him there;
> And the old Franciscans would bring him their baskets
>   Of apple and olive and pear.

Born in Staffordshire, Alfred Noyes studied at Oxford and
then turned to poetry, intent on proving that in the modern
world a man may, if he choose, win his way with his songs.
His poems appeared quickly — some critics said too quickly —
in various English and American magazines, and several of
them, including "The Highwayman," began to be extensively
quoted. He was for several years a lecturer on modern Literature at Princeton University and conducted classes in verse-
writing. Then the World War came, and he who had hitherto
been a convinced pacifist devoted his talents to the writing of
propaganda poetry, most of which was poor as propaganda and
worse as poetry. His early joy in sonorous phrases, gorgeous
descriptions, and contagiously light-hearted songs seems to
have left him. His future development will be watched with
interest.

Helen Parry Eden (1885–   ). A voice distinguished among
the younger English poets for its clearness, its music, its range,
and its wholesomeness rises from Oxford town, where Mrs.
Helen Parry Eden lives her busy family life and writes for
publications as diverse as the English *Punch* and the American
Catholic World. Her poems have sprung from the soil of her
experiences. Some of them are clever satiric verse, the reactions of a thinking woman who observes the petty pomposities
of the dull in high places, the social aspirations of worldlings,
the sinuous insincerities of politicians. Others are happy specimens of child poetry, the flowering of play and conversation
with her daughter Betsy Jane. And yet others are movingly

devotional transcripts of religious emotion; Mrs. Eden is a convert to the Catholic faith, and the beauty of religious practices and the stability of Catholic teaching have contributed to her verse both a finish of form and a solidity of substance.

Mrs. Eden's poetry may be studied in three little volumes: *Bread and Circuses*, *Coal and Candlelight*, and *A String of Sapphires*, the last being a life of Our Lord written in rimed verse "for the young and simple." The prologue explains the spirit of the book:

> Blackberries on the highest boughs,
> Books on the highest shelves,
> Somebody else must reach you down,
> Things which, although they are your own,
> You cannot reach yourselves.
> So, like a mother, Holy Church
> Gives out of her high hoard
> To us, Her Children, all and each
> What giants on tip-toe cannot reach —
> The Truth about Our Lord.

Siegfried Sassoon (1886–   ). Lacking the consummate artistry of Walter de la Mare, the verbal riotousness of Alfred Noyes, and especially the emotional balance of Mrs. Eden, Siegfried Sassoon is nevertheless recognized as the possessor of high poetic gifts, not least the ability to convey a mood in unhackneyed words of strength and clarity. He has tried in *Satirical Poems* (1926) to lash with cynical scorn some foibles of present-day life; but thus far his most significant contributions to English poetry are the verses in *Counter Attack* and *Collected Poems*, based on his experiences in the World War. They are the vigorous and imaginative reactions of a man who fights while recognizing the baseness and futility of warfare. In places Sassoon reminds us of an actor who feels his rôle so deeply that his emotions choke his voice and partially paralyze his movements.

Other Poets. A lifelong student of poetry in English and in other languages, an untiring producer of verse, and a capable and stimulating scholar, Robert Bridges (1844-1930), late poet laureate of England, lacks the strength and the intensity of imagination requisite for making and keeping verses — even carefully composed and melodious verses — alive. The professional tragedy of Stephen Phillips (1868-1915) lies in his persisting in an attempt to write poetic dramas like *Paolo and Francesca* with an equipment almost wholly lyrical; he had been an actor, he aspired to write actable plays, but he attained only to the status of a poet whose industry and earnestness of purpose bulk larger than the intrinsic quality of his poems. A large measure of Hardy's pessimism, with appreciably less of Hardy's artistic skill, is to be found in the poems of A. E. Housman (1859-   ) collected in the volume *A Shropshire Lad*. His brother, Laurence Housman (1867-   ), was an artist for the *Yellow Book* and an associate of the Decadents; like most of them he came, in spiritual outlook though not in profession of faith, under the Catholic influence, and in *Green Arras, Rue, Spikenard, Mendicant Rhymes*, and other poems presents a pageant of tangled spirituality. Laurence Binyon (1869-   ) takes high rank as an academic poet; like Bridges, he writes much and well, but without vital inspiration. William H. Davies (1870-   ) and Rupert Brooke (1887-1915), though both authentic minor poets, enjoy an undiscriminating fame dependent upon external circumstances. Davies led the life of a tramp in the United States, returned to England, and wrote his poems in the light of his rough experiences; Brooke died in the World War, and was promptly singled out for popular canonization.

THE DRAMA

The drama in twentieth-century England is dominated by three men whose literary abilities have brought literature and play-writing closer together: Shaw, Barrie, and Galsworthy. Because of recent developments in his work, Galsworthy is more appropriately considered with the novelists. We have had numerous plays by a multitude of minor writers, most of whom are of little or no importance from the point of view of literature; the art of the theater, though it may utilize a literary product, strictly speaking does not need it, and many a play, from the practical point of view a good play, as literature is unthinkable. Like the novel, the drama toward the close of the nineteenth century manifested a decided trend toward Realism, which tendency, having reached its peak about 1925, now shows evidence of decline.

Jones and Pinero. Henry Arthur Jones (1851–   ) and Sir Arthur Wing Pinero (1855–   ), though dramatists of but moderate powers, have had a long popularity on the stage and are important as representing, with Oscar Wilde, the beginnings of the modern ascendancy of the drama of manners. Pinero is the better artist, Jones the more conscious preacher. Jones began with *The Silver King* (1882), frankly and blusteringly a melodrama; but he has since taken himself more seriously, and in *Saints and Sinners*, *The Case of Rebellious Susan*, *Mrs. Dane's Defence*, *The Liars*, and *Michael and his Lost Angel* has sought to posit and even to solve moral problems in social life. Pinero, though he has often suggested such problems, has never attempted to solve them, and he is manifestly less concerned with ethical values than with the entertaining qualities of his productions; indeed, he is at his best in such a play as *Trelawny of the Wells* (1899), in which he points with much humor and too much sugary sentiment the contrasts between life in the English peerage and in the theatrical profession. He is best known through his *The Second Mrs. Tanqueray*, which in substance and in technique shows the influence of Ibsen. Jones and Pinero have both avoided the formlessness favored by many modern dramatists.

George Bernard Shaw (1856–   ). A minor dramatist, J. Hartley Manners, has put a trenchant piece of conversation into his little play *Happiness*:

SCOWCROFT. Ah! Shaw! Bernard Shaw! What about him?

MRS. CHRYSTAL-POLE. He suggests nothing so much as an imitation diamond.

SCOWCROFT. Diamond?

MRS. CHRYSTAL-POLE. *Imitation!* He glitters, but doesn't stand analysis. He makes one so sorry for the dead and the living he is borrowing from. They put things so much better.

That criticism is undeniably clever, and clever in Shaw's own way; but like most clever writing it tells only half the truth. Shaw glitters, yes; but Shaw does stand analysis; and if he makes one sorry for the writers he has borrowed from, it is because he has put things so much better than they. Bernard Shaw can think, and he can write; but too often he thinks perversely and writes with the deliberate purpose of making his readers feel ridiculous. His method, as explained by himself, "is to take the utmost trouble to find the right thing to say, and then say it with the utmost levity." He is a consciously clever man making faces at a solemnly stupid world.

Shaw has his blind and undiscriminating admirers, and his equally blind and undiscriminating adversaries. Both usually make the mistake of taking him seriously when he is flippant, and of assuming that he is joking when he is in deadly earnest. He plays with undiminished gusto to both audiences. This highly original Irishman — he is Dublin born — is a playboy-philosopher who uses the dramatic form to confound amusement seekers with thought and to scandalize thinkers with clownish antics. That is why some people wonder if he should not spell his name with a "P" and why other people are convinced that his art and thought are summarized in the title of one of his plays, *You Never Can Tell*.

He came as a young man to London, wrote several novels, and engaged in dramatic criticism. The plays he had to review, he tells us, were so unspeakably bad that he was forced in self-defense to write plays of his own. Then, as always, his motto was: "He who can, does; he who cannot, teaches." And he has been doing and teaching ever since. He is a Socialist — of sorts — and a vegetarian; his chief form of exercise is public speaking; his means of recreation is "anything except sport."

The dramas of Shaw vary in theme and treatment. *Arms and the Man*, afterward made into a light opera, *The Chocolate Soldier*, is an adroit satire on militarism. *The Man of Destiny* is an unusual study of Napoleon with a number of characteristically Shavian twists of thought. *Cæsar and Cleopatra* possesses real fun and real dramatic power; its prologue scolds the audience for their stupidity, and the drama itself presents Cæsar, not as a great man, but only as less a fool than those about him. *The Devil's Disciple*, remarkably keen in its characterization, is set in America during the Revolutionary War. *Man and Superman* is a mass of conversation, some of it brilliant and some of it unspeakably dull. *Major Barbara* and *The Doctor's Dilemma* are satires, one on scientific charity, the other on the medical profession. In some respects the best of all Shaw's plays is *Saint Joan*, in which the French heroine is admired and her persecutors made to manifest that well-meaning stupidity which Shaw finds the dominant trait of the human spirit in all ages of the world.

GEORGE BERNARD SHAW

Shaw's activity in the drama is inspired by an aversion and an admiration; an aversion to the art of Shakespeare and an admiration for the art of Ibsen. He gave reasons for his dramatic faith. He claimed that Shakespeare lacked inventiveness, was no philosopher, had no high moral enthusiasm; that Ibsen, who could think and had moral ideals, "comes out with a double first class, whereas Shakespeare comes out hardly anywhere." But those reasons were mainly pretexts. Shaw castigated Shakespeare and eulogized Ibsen mainly because Shakespeare was lauded and Ibsen ignored. Already Shaw has lived to see that while the fame of Shakespeare endures, Ibsen is today little more than a memory; and he must enjoy the reflection that he himself has enhanced Shakespeare's reputation by denying its validity and that he has killed Ibsen by praising him to the skies.

From one point of view Shaw is more an essayist than a dramatist. As a rule — exceptions are *Arms and the Man* and *Saint Joan* — his plays read better than they act; it is the talk in them that mainly matters. And Shaw published them in book form and wrote prefaces, often more lengthy than the plays themselves, explaining his dramatic procedure and discoursing of things in general. In those prefaces are found his keenest wit, his most cutting satire, his most provocative thought.

Rightly to understand Shaw and his influence we must face the fact that in the modern world there are two essential philosophies of life, the Catholic and the pagan; the former has many adherents among people who are not members of the Catholic Church but who are none the less in varying degrees loyal to the teachings of Christ and the ideals of Christianity. Shaw is a clear-minded and consistent pagan. He does not believe in Catholic dogmas, even as those dogmas are watered down in some of the sects, and he does not accept Catholic morality as a guide to right living. He is no vulgar bigot, he is no cynical scoffer at Catholic belief; but he is definitely on the side of that philosophy which refuses to recognize any supernatural element in human life. If he is more vehemently attacked than other writers, it is because he has expressed himself more lucidly and more uncompromisingly than his fellow pagans, and especially because he has lashed with humor and ridicule the inconsistency of many men who profess Christianity but who do not live up to its implications.

Bernard Shaw has brains and industry, exceptional ability to express himself in language, an active gift of observation, and an imaginative power not to be despised. His delight in fun-making and cavorting to irritate the many and amuse the few does not minimize, though it sometimes obscures, his importance. What makes him, and keeps him, aloof from the Catholic, the Christian, theory of life is his utter lack of the bump of veneration. He is totally devoid of reverence: reverence for other thinkers, reverence for the past, reverence for ideas and ideals which in all ages noble men have held sacred. And though his eyes are eager and luminous, they are held from the vision of the ultimate truth; though his mind is clear and capacious, there is in it no space for the supreme wisdom. He is a pagan because he cannot become as a little child.

Sir James Matthew Barrie (1860-   ). An Adelphi Terrace neighbor of Shaw's has written in *Sentimental Tommy*: "The gates of Heaven are so easily found when we are little, and they are always standing open to let children wander in."

In spirit and technique Barrie is the opposite of Shaw. Where Shaw writes to unfold his destructive criticism and to vex and tickle the world, Barrie tells stories, in themselves either very simple or superbly impossible, as a boy to his mates. He is grown up, of course, but he does not want to be; and the only listeners who do not respond are children too young to enjoy his gentle satire and adults too old ever to have been children. Shaw and Barrie are both so capable as dramatists that they do not need to study the details of dramatic technique; the problem of "building" a play they leave to the lesser breed of playwright, including Pinero and Jones. Shaw and Barrie can, and sometimes do, violate all the rules of the drama so precisely set forth by professors who cannot write

plays: Shaw because his talk is usually clever and even eloquent, Barrie because he reveals the heart of a child. To know
Barrie is to love him.

Some of his plots are simplicity itself. *The Professor's Love
Story*, his first play, is on the old, old theme of the elderly lover
who loses his heart to a lass. *The Little Minister* accepts the
not less venerable stage con-
vention that in the course
of true love opposites at-
tract each other. In *Quality
Street* an old maid imper-
sonates a young one with
blissful results. In *What
Every Woman Knows* Mag-
gie cures her husband of
his foolishness by letting
him get an overdose of the
company he has found fas-
cinating. *Dear Brutus* is
a stage game in which we
pretend we are other than
ourselves and find out that
we are not. Several of the

SIR JAMES MATTHEW BARRIE

plays, notably the shorter ones, have really no plot at all:
Alice-Sit-by-the-Fire, *The Twelve-Pound Look*, *The Old Lady
shows her Medals*. But slight plot, old plot, or no plot, the
plays win us because of their genial human quality, their pleasing whimsicality, their shrewd but guileless boyishness.

When not simple, Barrie's plots are far-fetched, extravagant,
preposterous — and irresistible. Consider *The Admirable Crichton*. Bill Crichton, butler in the household of Lord Loam, is a
model servant who drops his *h's* and keeps his place. Lord
Loam and his family, together with Bill and some other servants, are wrecked on a desert island, whereupon his lordship
gravitates to the level of scullery boy and Crichton becomes

governor of the little colony. The castaways are rescued, and back in England they resume their original social positions and their pristine class consciousness. The hopelessly sophisticated reader instantly objects, "Such a yarn isn't true to life"; but the real child — of whatever age — retorts, "Of course not; it's truer than life." And so it is with *Peter Pan*, Barrie's fairy story with a difference, wherein a child's fancy is given unbridled scope. In life and in books we cease to be children, because somebody is always reminding us that what we do is not done, that what we want to do is not proper, that what we think is not thinkable. Such censors have their uses, as the wise man said of mosquitoes; but Barrie has his uses, too, when in *Peter Pan* he lets us see that the realest things are the things we can think into reality, no matter how impossible they may seem, as when the Boy Who Never Grew Up rushes down to the footlights and compels all the adult skeptics in the audience to clap their hands and thus make public profession of their belief in fairies.

Barrie was born in the little town of Kirriemuir in Scotland, a town he has immortalized in his early stories, *Auld Licht Idylls* and *A Window in Thrums*. There is much basic autobiography in *Sentimental Tommy* and its sequel, *Tommy and Grizel*; and in *Margaret Ogilvy* Barrie has paid loving tribute to his mother. After completing his studies at the University of Edinburgh he wrote for newspapers in Nottingham and in London, and from journalism gradually drifted into literature. *My Lady Nicotine*, as somebody has well said, glorified smoking as Walton's *Complete Angler* glorified fishing. Unlike Shaw, Barrie does not write lengthy prefaces for his plays, but sometimes in a few explanatory words he suggests the spirit of an entire scene. An instance occurs in *Quality Street*. Valentine is speaking:

There you wrong me, for I have discovered for myself that the school mistress in her old maid's cap is the noblest Miss Phœbe of them all. (*If he would only go away and let Miss Phœbe cry.*) When I enlisted I remember I compared her to a garden. I have often thought of that.

The italicized words suggest volumes to the actress imperson- ating Miss Phœbe. It is characteristic of Barrie thus to take the performers into his confidence and to teach them their parts from the inside. Only competent actors, however, can appreciate the subtlety of his hints, with the result that his plays suffer much at the hands of mechanically trained players.

John Drinkwater (1882–). The history of liter- ature, even of the literature of the day, offers some in- teresting transformations. Here is a poet who changed into a dramatist and who now seems likely to un- dergo a further metamor- phosis into a biographer. His poetry, which has been published at intervals since 1906, is dignified and re- strained in style and narrow in range; religious difficul- ties, the importance of do- ing things, and the power of love are the dominant

JOHN DRINKWATER

themes in successive volumes : *The Death of Leander* (1906), *Poems of Love and Earth* (1912), and *Preludes* (1923). His present interest in the writing of biography has borne fruit in several excellent and scholarly books, including *The Pilgrim of Eternity* (on Lord Byron), *Mr. Charles King of England* (on Charles II), and a life of Oliver Cromwell.

Drinkwater, already recognized as a poet, became interested in a little theater in Birmingham and wrote several short poetic plays. *The Storm* and *The God of Quiet* are more poetical than dramatic, but he completed the transition to play-writing in a third little drama, *X-O*, its scene the Trojan War and its theme the futility of warfare. Since then he has written a number of full-length dramas on famous characters in history: Mary Stuart, Cromwell, Lincoln, and Lee. Critics are sharply divided regarding the permanent worth of these plays; it has even been said that the stage success of *Abraham Lincoln* was due less to Drinkwater's skill as a dramatist than to the intrinsic interest of the subject. *Mary Stuart* has been assailed — not always judiciously — on moral grounds, but as a play it remains the finest of Drinkwater's dramas.

PROSE FICTION

The Short Story. The habits of the reading public have encouraged numerous low-priced magazines containing stories, and sometimes nothing but stories, and have made it profitable for publishers to bring out volumes of short fiction. Countless writers have necessarily engaged in story-writing, most of them possessing no claim to recognition on literary grounds. Several names stand out prominently, however. Besides Kipling, whose greatest work has been in the short story, distinction attaches to a man and a woman, a veteran and a novice, in this difficult and popular form. The man is William Wymark Jacobs (1863–   ), long a post-office employee, who has amused himself and incidentally the world with stories of seafaring men on shore leave, in *Many Cargoes*. Since that triumph he has lost nothing of his fertility in inventing plots, of his keen dialogue art, and especially of his power of comical yet human characterization. *Light Freights* and *The Lady of the Barge* are collections of the short stories of this inexhaustible humorist. The woman is Katherine Mansfield (1890–1923), whose untimely death cut short a literary career of rare achievement and rarer promise. Her short stories, some of them the merest sketches, are distinguished for keen insight into human nature, a vividness of presentation, strong character contrasts, and a unique mingling of irony and pathos.

Arthur Machen (1863–). Arthur Machen, a Welshman, is akin in his literary work to Chesterton and Belloc; he is averse to modern industrialism with its architectural horrors and seeks peace and imaginative recreation in the social and religious ideals of the Middle Ages. In religion he is a High Churchman, "with no particular respect for the Archbishop of Canterbury"; in temperament he is robustly anti-Puritan, and some of his finest essays — for he is an essayist as well as a teller of tales — are protests against Puritanism in art and in life. He has formulated this remarkable definition of literature: "Literature is the expression, through the æsthetic medium of words, of the dogmas of the Catholic Church, and that which in any way is out of harmony with these dogmas is not literature." Representative collections of his stories, some of them merging into essays, are *The Bowmen, The Great Return, Dr. Stiggins, Far Off Things*, and *Dreads and Drolls*.

Rudyard Kipling (1865–). Early distinguished as a writer of breezy, unconventional poetry and stories of army life in his native India, Kipling did his most vital and effective work in the last decade of the nineteenth century. He was the outspoken and unofficial press agent of British imperialism until the Boer War of 1899 shook his faith in the policy of "benevolent assimilation" of small nations. Since then his writings, in prose and in verse, have lacked the fire of youth and the glamour of romance. As a man, he is happily alive; as a writer, for more than a quarter of a century he has been dead.

The poems of Kipling which most matter and which best express his glorification of physical prowess are found in early volumes: *Barrack-Room Ballads, Departmental Ditties, The Seven Seas, The Five Nations*. Many of them are short stories in verse; others, such as "Mandalay," the English classic of homesickness, and "Recessional," occasioned by the jubilee of Queen Victoria, are genuine poems of careful workmanship and sustained power. In a sense different from Wordsworth's he wrote poetry in the language of simple people — the soldier in Simla, the sailor "rolling down to Rio," the veteran service man recounting, as in "Gunga Din," his experiences on some distant far-flung battle line.

Though he has written several novels, *The Light that Failed*, *The Naulahka*, *Captains Courageous*, and *Kim* — this his ablest full-length tale — Kipling has been most successful in the short story proper. English Literature has no brief prose fiction finer and more artistic than *The Man who would be King* and *Without Benefit of Clergy*. His Mulvaney stories in *Soldiers Three* and other early volumes struck a new note in fiction with their humorous and realistic portrayal of army life in India. *The Jungle Book*, *The Second Jungle Book*, and *Puck of Pook's Hill* are children's books destined to endure.

RUDYARD KIPLING

Kipling's unusual power in prose and in verse lies mainly in the vividness of his perceptions and the freshness and directness of his language. From time immemorial the camel has appeared in literature, but never so realistically as pictured in "Oonts,"

> With 'is silly neck a-bobbin' like a basket full of snakes.

The capture of hostile cities has been the subject of ever so much description in history and romance, but the reader nowhere lives through the experience so intimately and so exquisitely as in "The Taking of Lungtungpen"; allegory has been a familiar device of writers intent on making their readers see and think, but not often has it been employed so artistically as by Kipling in *The Jungle Book* description of the monkeys dwelling in a deserted man-made palace. Those Bandar-logs "never knew what the buildings were made for nor how to use them"; they would merely "scratch for fleas and pretend to be men."

Are we reading into Kipling more than he had in mind when we see in those ignorant and self-satisfied monkeys a caricature of certain "advanced" thinkers of today? Our modern Bandar-logs know but little of the history, the literature, the religion of their European ancestors, they are indifferent to the intellectual influences playing upon them from earlier epochs, and about the only use to which they put their fair cultural heritage is "to shake the rose trees and the oranges in sport to see the fruit and flowers fall." Kipling wins us to wonder if, after all, new Dark Ages may not menace our proud material civilization.

Even in our day when the proprieties are less respected than they were in the Victorian era, Kipling has been reproached for the vulgarity of many of his illustrations and comparisons; it is claimed that his crudeness is alien to the spirit of true poetry and that his offensive realism detracts from the artistic excellence of his tales. The condemnation is not without grounds. Undoubtedly Kipling has been needlessly common at times and set an example in this respect which sundry imitators have followed to their undoing. On the other hand, it must not be forgotten that touches of a realism distasteful to the sensitive appear in admittedly great literature, in Shakespeare, in Dante, in the Bible; that Kipling was depicting a manner of life scanty in the refinements and urbanities of society and was all but compelled to suit his manner to his subject; that, finally, though morality is not a matter of geography, vulgarity certainly is, and that "after all the deepest of all vulgarities is the studied avoidance of what may be thought to be vulgar."[1]

[1] A. C. Benson, *Alfred Tennyson*, p. 157.

Joseph Conrad (1857–1924). A youth in Poland, who had read Shakespeare and Cervantes and Victor Hugo in translations, responded to the lure of the sea and shipped before the mast on a French vessel that brought him to the Gulf of Mexico. Until he was forty years old Jozef Konrad Korzeniowski lived

© Underwood & Underwood

JOSEPH CONRAD

the sailor's life, rising in time to be captain in the merchant marine and sailing all over the world. He continued to read, learned English, and in 1895 had his first novel published. It was *Almayer's Folly*, a book of high simplicity with an epic sweep and that atmosphere of brooding mystery which lends a subtle charm to all Conrad's stories. The next year he abandoned the sea and settled down in England to think and write. His books slowly won recognition and at the time of his death Conrad was considered one of the two or three leading novelists of the twentieth century.

The Nigger of the Narcissus, Chance, Nostromo, and *The Arrow of Gold* are among the best-known of Conrad's novels, but his masterpiece is *Lord Jim,* the story of a man who spends his life trying to repair an early mistake. The leading character is one of a few white men on a ship carrying a crowd of Moslems across the Indian Ocean. The vessel is in danger of sinking; and while the passengers sleep on the hot decks, the German captain and three companions slip away in a small boat, and Jim joins them. Too late he is convinced that he has done a gravely dishonorable thing, and through the succeeding years as he wanders from place to place the story of his cowardice pursues him, the audible voice of his own stricken conscience. In the end, in an Eastern island among savage Malays he secures confidence and peace.

Conrad's novels are unexcelled in their depiction of the magic, the terror, the fascination of the sea; man seems but slight and trivial amid the swirling of the waters and beneath the aloof, implacable stars. These stories do more than entertain; though there is no preaching in them, no direct controversial purpose behind them, they induce reflection and probe the secret places of the heart. They are written in a style idiomatic, tense, picturesque; and though the author's narrative construction is often tangled and confusing, the characters are distinct and alive. Conrad wrote short stories also, most of them in theme and conception similar to his longer works; they are contained in several volumes, including *Youth*, *Typhoon*, and *'Twixt Land and Sea*.

Robert Hichens (1864–). The novels of Robert Hichens fall into three classes: first, stories of social satire, such as *The Green Carnation*, a clever and scathing lampoon on the Decadents of the 1890's; secondly, stories dealing with abnormal psychology, for instance, *The Dweller on the Threshold*, a study of the transference of personality; and thirdly, stories unfolding a vision of sin and repentance against an exotic background. The most impressive of this last class is Hichens's admitted masterpiece, *The Garden of Allah*, which recounts the story of a monk who broke his vows and was then induced by his wife, who had not known of his sin, to return to his monastery and make reparation. The book shows Hichens as a vigorous if somewhat verbose stylist, especially capable in his descriptions of the desert and the East. In some of his novels he shows a not altogether wholesome interest in human weakness and depravity, but he has little in common with naturalistic writers like Zola in France and the Realistic school in England and America. Hichens recognizes the importance of religion, and specifically of Catholicism, in human life, and in his treatment of the fact of sin does not fall into the facile mistake of condoning its evil nature and disintegrating consequences.

Arnold Bennett (1867–1931). Editing a ladies' magazine was but one of the journalistic offices performed by Arnold Bennett prior to his prolific career as a writer of novels; he learned the writing craft by performing all kinds of literary jobs. Even after he had gained celebrity with his stories of the Five Towns, he occasionally varied his output with plays and essays, the latter being chiefly advice on life and literature in a popular and practical form. His own story is given in *The Truth about an Author*. Some of Bennett's novels are farcical in character, like *Buried Alive*, the story of a bashful artistic genius who manages to attend his own funeral in Westminster Abbey and enjoy posthumous fame. However, Bennett's reputation rests on his seriously conceived realistic novels of dull people leading drab lives in a dreary section of England — the pottery district of Staffordshire where he spent his boyhood. His representative stories are *The Old Wives' Tale, Clayhanger,* and *Hilda Lessways.* Occasionally he relieves his pictures of dismal life with a glimmer of romance, as in another Five Towns tale, *Helen of the High Hand*; but in *Riceyman Steps* he presents us with another batch of unpleasant people. His skill in portraiture is remarkable, though clearly a matter of talent rather than of genius; he demonstrates that a moderate amount of brains, of industry, and of knowledge of "what the people want" will establish a temporary reputation in fiction.

John Galsworthy (1867–1933). Possessed of a feeling for art and a faculty of expression in verse and in prose, John Galsworthy is considered the most versatile author of our generation. Beginning as a dramatist and gradually shifting his interest to the novel, he has produced a body of prose fiction which is a distinct extension of the work of the nineteenth-century masters. In some of his poems he speaks on his own account, as is the privilege of the lyric poet; but in his plays and in his novels he rarely champions a cause or voices a preference. His is the impartiality of the artist who paints so well that he has no need to give his pictures names. Galsworthy's attitude toward life is a blending of irony and sympathy, his art a fusion of Realism and Romanticism. Like Conrad he is impressed with the mystery of the universe; like Shaw,

though in milder mood, he is grieved at the stupidity of man; with Browning he recognizes the disastrous sweep of disordered passions. Life to him is at once a pageant and a problem; in the pageant he takes a reverent delight, and to the problem he attempts to bring no solution.

Social conditions contribute substance to Galsworthy's plays. In *The Silver Box* he depicts the effects of prison life on a sensitive character, in *Strife* the futility of labor disputes, in *Jus-*

© Underwood & Underwood

JOHN GALSWORTHY

tice the irony of criminal-court procedure; in *The Eldest Son* he reveals the absurdities and inconsistencies of class distinctions; *The Pigeon* and *A Bit of Love* reveal the widespread need for sympathy, understanding, charity that is not scientific but warmly and intimately human. Some episodes and characters in these plays startle the complacent and shock the timid, but no open-minded student of them can conclude that Galsworthy tries to be sensationally suggestive. From each of them a preacher — the dramatist has no vocation to the pulpit — could point a moral as old as Mount Sinai and inculcate an exhortation as eminent as the Sermon on the Mount.

Galsworthy's ablest contribution to prose fiction is a series of stories which he calls *The Forsyte Saga*, the chronicles of a well-to-do English family through several generations. There are two strands among the Forsytes and their numerous connections through marriage — the hard-headed, tight-fisted, practical men of affairs and the dreamers and lovers and worshipers

CHEAPSIDE

This busy section of modern London, merging into the street called the Poultry, supplies the setting for several memorable scenes in Galsworthy's Forsyte stories

of beauty. The inevitable conflicts growing out of the clashing of the two strains constitute the substance of the novels, which are singularly moving in their pictures of the successes and the frustrations of the older and the younger Forsytes. The entire series — concluding with *Swan Song* — is an extended allegory suggesting the softening and enriching function of art in modern life. Other of his novels are *The Island Pharisees*, — with a short preface finer and more stimulating than the story itself, — *The Dark Flower*, and *The Patrician*. In *Caravan* Galsworthy has collected his numerous short stories.

William J. Locke (1863–1930). Frankly an entertainer rather than a teacher, William J. Locke produced numerous novels which make no great demand on brains and leave no bad taste in the mouth; some of them even stir a song in the heart. He is most himself when he introduces an amiably eccentric character, by preference a Frenchman, with little practical sense but much fundamental wisdom, and sends him careening joyously through the world, upsetting the pretentious and cheering the humble of heart. That is the basic formula of *The Beloved Vagabond*, *The Mountebank*, and *The Joyous Adventures of Aristide Pujol*, and of *The Morals of Marcus Ordeyne*, save that here the genially disturbing person is a Turkish girl who breaks into a sedate English scholar's garden. *Perella* is a delightful novel with its scene laid chiefly in Florence; the famous Ponte Vecchio, or Old Bridge, is made a happy symbol of a climax in life. Locke always has a story, and he knows how to tell it more than passing well.

Herbert George Wells (1866–   ). The Athenian painter Apelles is said to have placed one of his portraits on exhibition and then hidden himself behind a curtain to listen to the criticism of the passers-by. A cobbler scrutinized the painting and remarked upon a fault in the shoe. Apelles corrected the defect; but next day when the cobbler ventured to criticize the drawing of the leg, the painter warned him not to talk of what he did not know. *Sutor ne supra crepidam*, the reproof has come down to us in Latin; that is, "The shoemaker should not look above the shoe," or as it is more commonly and more liberally translated, "The cobbler should stick to his last."

Much of the praise and nearly all the condemnation bestowed upon H. G. Wells is due to the fact that here is a writer who has not stuck to his fountain pen, a novelist who has looked above his novels. The Athenian cobbler was doubtless a good cobbler, and Wells is a good novelist; but the cobbler and Wells have both climbed with self-constituted authority beyond the tools of their trades. When the cobbler picked flaws in the leg of Apelles's painting there were surely some in the crowd who applauded him for doing a clever thing; but the more discerning Athenians must have commented unfavorably on his presumption and reflected that a cobbler hardly knows as

© Underwood & Underwood

H. G. WELLS

much about painting as a painter does. So when H. G. Wells writes on philosophy in *First and Last Things*, when he assumes universal knowledge in his *Outline of History*, when in sundry volumes of essays he attacks beliefs which men revere and ridicules ideas which are the salt of the earth, some of his readers hail him as king, priest, and prophet, but thinking men smile or frown, according to their state of grace, and quote the Latin proverb about the shoemaker and the shoe.

Here we are to consider H. G. Wells as a novelist; as cobblers we shall stick to our last. And we must recognize that for quantity, and often for quality, he is a giant in these days. He knows how to write, not with the artistic nuances of Galsworthy nor with the crackling wit of Shaw, but with clearness and force and the ease that comes from an alert mind and long practice of the art. He has written nearly half a hundred novels, and has written most of them very well.

The novels may be conveniently classified into the Seven Ages of Wells. At first the scientific romance, like *The Time Machine*, *The War of the Worlds*, and *The First Men in the*

Moon. Then the love story, though usually not of conventional design, as *The Passionate Friends* and *Love and Mr. Lewisham.* Then stories such as *Joan and Peter*, which are reflections of educational theories and conditions. In *The New Machiavelli* and *The Research Magnificent* we have the fourth age of the Wellsian novel in stories occupied with historical retrospect and social problems. At length the novelist becomes a lay theologian and in *The Soul of a Bishop* and *The Undying Fire* gives us novels voicing and seeking to satisfy the craving of the soul for God. Sixthly, there are those stories, not negligible, like *Bealby* and *The History of Mr. Polly*, in which Wells takes a mental holiday and proceeds to enjoy himself with hilarious farce. And finally he turns his eye once more to the world of the future and of the present in *Men Like Gods* and *William Clissold* and seeks to discover what things esteemed today will be important in the eyes of the morrow.

Numerous passages in these and in other of his books are marked by flawless language, clear thinking, and rich imagination. Imagination, indeed, is the choicest gift the fairies left in Wells's cradle. The uncle in *Tono-Bungay* and Mr. Britling who did *not* see it through deserve to rank with the great creations of Dickens; Dick Remmington in *The New Machiavelli* and the dyspeptic Mr. Polly are each in his own way triumphs of creative portraiture. Scenes in *When the Sleeper Wakes* and *The First Men in the Moon* remain vivid in memory after the lapse of thirty years. Some novelists merely entertain, others are clergymen who have missed their vocation; Wells always entertains and often preaches, and no matter what he has to say we are captivated by his way of saying it. He has in his time played many parts, but always and fundamentally he is a romancer; and though he has written no formal poetry, he has a poet's heart.

In *The Undying Fire* Wells has written an excellent criticism of Wells. Mr. Huss, the schoolmaster, receives a letter from one of his former pupils which reads in part as follows:

One of the lovable things about you to us is that you have always been so jolly human to us. You've always been unequal. I've seen you give lessons that were among the best lessons in the world, and I've seen you give some jolly bad lessons.

John Ayscough (1858-1928). It is now an open secret that the novelist who signed himself John Ayscough was the Right Reverend Monsignor Francis Bickerstaffe-Drew, who became a Catholic while still an undergraduate at Oxford and who spent most of his years as a chaplain in the British army. He was fifty years of age before he began to write fiction, but in his seasoned maturity he has produced more stories than many novelists turn out in a lifetime. Yet there is in his books no heedless writing; his style is finished and pleasing, he has much humor and more irony, his characters are sharply drawn, and his sketches of backgrounds in Italy, France, and England — for his stories are laid in many lands and times — are unhackneyed and impressionistic. His most original novel, the one which may be destined in after years to identify him as a man of one book, is *San Celestino*; its hero is that St. Peter Celestine V who resigned the office of Pope of Rome and retired to a life of prayer and solitude. This is a great story, a great Catholic story, told with an economy of words which enhances its value, a story sharp in its analysis of character, bristling in its contrasts, illuminating in its presentation of thirteenth-century Italy. Other novels of John Ayscough's are *Faustula*, a tale of the vestal virgins in ancient Rome; *Monksbridge*, an exposition of snobbery in English upper-class life; *Marotz*, a tale of modern Italy; and *Dromina*, with its scene in Spain and in Ireland.

W. B. Maxwell (1866-   ). A century or so hence, were a student seeking to discover just how people lived in our age, what affections warmed their hearts and what ideas spurred them to action, he would find a generous amount of helpful material in the novels of W. B. Maxwell. Here is a man who knows modern life — both before and after the World War

— and who conveys his knowledge with artistry and power. Furthermore, were the student human enough to enjoy a surprise, Maxwell would be again accommodating, for midway in *The Devil's Garden, Mrs. Thompson, The Ragged Messenger*, and most of his other books he contrives to bring about an unexpected but natural episode or to make an amazing but logical revelation. His study of character is especially thorough and lifelike in *Glamour* and in *In Cotton Wool*, both stories of the downward development of the hero, — in the one because of emotional weakness, in the other because of selfishness and love of ease and security. Maxwell shows that to avoid "living dangerously" is sometimes dangerous.

© Underwood & Underwood

W. B. MAXWELL

Hugh Walpole (1884–). They tried to make this boy, born in New Zealand, a minister like his father, the Bishop of Edinburgh, but in his Cambridge days his soul "bumped from Rugby football to poetry and back again," never in the direction of the church. Yet few modern novelists have so immanent a sense of the reality and pervasiveness of religion as Hugh Walpole, who in *The Captives*, his best work thus far, has taken as his subject the mass of mankind "all captives in a strange country, trying to find their escape, each in his or her own fashion, back to the land of their birth." There is a strong religious motive in *The Cathedral* too, a story based upon the author's first-hand experience of Anglican clerical circles in an English town. Bigger in conception though weaker in execution is *The Dark Forest*, a war story with its setting in Russia; it brings out the great truth that unselfish love ennobles and purifies, and in its prevailing mood carries conviction of the reality of spiritual things and the relative littleness of earthly life. Walpole has also written *The Green Mirror*, *The Young Enchanted*, and *The Old Ladies*,

HUGH WALPOLE

and has rivaled De Quincey and Poe in a tale of macabre horrors in *Portrait of a Man with Red Hair*.

Moore, Phillpotts, and Others. An Irishman for a brief while identified with the Literary Revival in Dublin, George Moore (1853–1933) spent most of his life in France and England. In art and thought he is definitely separated from Irish interests. He has written *The Lake*, *Esther Waters*, and other novels and a trilogy of reminiscences, partly fantastic and partly realistic, entitled *Hail and Farewell*. He is formless and uneven in style, and owes his vogue less to real literary ability than to a carefully cultivated talent for retailing salacious gossip. Eden Phillpotts (1862–   ) is the author of a long line of novels, most of them much alike and all of them of considerable merit, pertaining to life among the rural classes in his native Dartmoor. *Widecombe Fair* and *The Whirlwind* are typical of his dignified effort to avoid the excesses of both Realism and sentimentality. Sir Hall Caine (1853–1931) won extended popularity with *The Christian* in 1897; previously he had written thrilling tales of the "blood and thunder" species and more restrained stories of life on the Isle of Man,

The Deemster and *The Manxman*. He again exploited his gift for melodrama in *The Eternal City*, and in succeeding novels has busied himself with sensational aspects of family life. Leonard Merrick (1864–   ), in *The Actor Manager, Conrad in Quest of His Youth*, and other novels, has written graceful, sentimental stories of theatrical life; in his short tales he has, like Locke, gone to France for his best inspiration. Compton Mackenzie (1883–   ), a voluminous and versatile writer of novels, poems, and plays, began with unpleasantly Realistic stories like *Sinister Street* and *Carnival*, which suggest a surface view of human nature. Latterly he has shown a more wholesome strain in *Fairy Gold* and a stronger hand in *Rogues and Vagabonds*, a tale of theatrical life. From what he has written of the novelist's art and of his professional ideals it would seem that he knows better than he builds.

Some Women Novelists. Mrs. Mary St. Leger Harrison, the daughter of Charles Kingsley, was a veteran novelist who perpetuated the dignity and reticence of an older day in *The Wages of Sin, The Far Horizon, The Golden Galleon*, and other stories. Her pen name was Lucas Malet. Trying her hand at several kinds of story and distinguishing herself in all, May Sinclair has expressed modern paganism from the point of view of a well-read and observant woman. *The Divine Fire* is acclaimed her masterpiece, but many readers prefer the quiet, sympathetic, well-balanced character analysis she supplies in *Arnold Waterlow*. Miss Sinclair is a student of philosophy, and her novels reflect her thoughtful habits. Isabel C. Clarke, since her reception into the Catholic Church in 1901, has produced a steady flow of novels of wide range and uneven quality but all permeated with a religious spirit. Her varied gifts may be estimated by a reading of *Prisoners' Years, The Secret Citadel, Their Name is Legion*, and *The Elstones*. Rose Macaulay writes glitteringly cynical novels of modern life. In *Dangerous Ages, Potterism, Told by an Idiot*, and *Crewe Train* she takes a high place among the prose satirists in English.

Disillusioned, hopeless, a little sad, but ever vivaciously aware of the humors and absurdities of the people around her, Miss Macaulay writes stories which as literature, and despite the limitations inherent in her cynical view of life, appeal strongly to readers who like brains mixed with their entertainment. Sheila Kaye-Smith (Mrs. Theodore Penrose Fry) has written several attractive novels of country life; and Susan Ertz, in *Madame Claire*, *After Noon*, and *Now East, Now West*, has struck a new and promising note in English fiction.

THE ESSAY

Frederic Harrison (1831-1923). This venerable and alert man of letters, who but a few years ago might have been seen walking his half-dozen miles on a fine afternoon along the roads of Kent, was literally the last of the eminent Victorians. Tennyson used to be a neighbor of his, he was George Eliot's legal adviser, and in amity or literary warfare or both he was associated with Arnold, Carlyle, Ruskin, Gladstone, Morley, Huxley, and Spencer. Few men knew the nineteenth century so well; no man more completely disproves the belief that it was an age of mental stagnation. Harrison shuffled out of his Protestant faith and became an admirer and follower of Auguste Comte, the founder of a now all but forgotten system of religion and culture known as Positivism; the last of the Victorians was also the last of the Positivists. Harrison's essays on life and literature form an interesting commentary on the times; several of them are searching and stimulating pieces of literary criticism.

W. H. Hudson (1841-1922). As Harrison was a wanderer among books and ideas, so Hudson was a rambler through England's meadows and cathedral towns. He loved not man the less but nature more. Even as a little boy in the Argentine he was enraptured by the blue of the skies and the sweep of the pampas and the plumage of the birds. Though a reader of books, he was primarily a student of those moments in life when "nature draws near to it, and, taking up her neglected instrument, plays a fragment of some ancient melody, long unheard on the earth." The titles of his books suggest their spirit and contents: *Idle Days in Patagonia, Birds in London, Green Mansions, Afoot in England, A Hind in Richmond Park.* He created a modern utopia in *A Crystal Age,* and told the story of his youth in *Far Away and Long Ago.* Hudson's writings serve to open the eyes and minds of modern men to the beauties and sublimities of the natural world. His style is remarkable for its prose cadences, its wealth of allusions, its skill in reproducing on the printed page the scent of the fields, the changing face of the skies, the whirring of the rooks about ancient cathedral towers.

Emily Hickey (1845–1924). When J. F. Furnivall founded the Browning Society in 1881, his co-worker and organizer was Emily Hickey, an Irishwoman resident in London. From the first she was a student and interpreter of Browning; her lectures on the poet and her essays preserved in the papers of the society had much influence in establishing and maintaining the Browning cult. She was a poet on her own account, and after her conversion to Catholicism in 1900 brought out several volumes of devotional verses. She was a frequent contributor to magazines on both sides of the Atlantic; everywhere her learning and her critical acumen and her vigorous prose style were recognized as a vital force in modern letters. Most of her essays have not been reprinted in book form.

Sir Edmund Gosse (1849–1928). England has produced several men who, devoting all their lives to study and reading, have written copiously and learnedly on literature ancient and modern. Foremost among these scholars is Sir Edmund Gosse, whose numerous essays collected in *Critical Kit-Kats, Books on the Table, Silhouettes, Leaves and Fruit,* and other volumes demonstrate that scholarship and vivacity of style are not necessarily alien to each other. He is also the author of biographies and appreciations of Donne, Browne, Taylor, Swinburne, Patmore, and Ibsen, and of a *History of Modern English Literature*.

Montgomery Carmichael (1857–). Some of the richest and most delightful prose writing in present-day English has been done by Carmichael in his meditative travel essays in *On the Old Road through France to Florence, In Tuscany*, and

other books. Completing his education in Germany, he became an authority on the history and legends of St. Francis of Assisi. *The Major-General* is a story of modern Florence, and *John William Walshe* is an autobiography in the form of a novel wherein the author describes the unusual path that led him to Catholicism.

Edward Hutton (1875–). Fond of touring on foot through his native England and especially in Italy, and deeply read in Italian Literature and his-

MAX BEERBOHM

tory, Hutton has written lives of Italian poets and artists and a vast number of books recording impressions of his travels: *England of My Heart, Studies in the Lives of the Saints, Country Walks about Florence, In Unknown Tuscany, The Val d' Arno.* A most unusual production is *The Mastiff of Rimini*, a historical novel purporting to be the memoirs of a Renaissance scholar attached to the court of a feudal lord. Hutton's style varies from the matter-of-fact manner of an encyclopedia to the ornateness, luxuriance, and emotional abandon we find in Ruskin's most glowing pages. Hutton and Carmichael have caught the essential spirit of Italian thought and culture.

Max Beerbohm (1872-   ). There have been writers who could draw and artists who could write, but Max Beerbohm impartially uses both pen and pencil to express his urbane and rather impish personality. His cartoons and his essays suggest

BEERBOHM'S CARTOON OF BYRON

From *Pilgrim of Eternity* by John Drinkwater. Published by George H. Doran Company

a man who passes through life fastidious and smiling, acutely noting the oddities about him and thoroughly enjoying the show. As a writer he is at once finished and energetic — a man's man always attired in perfectly fitting evening clothes. "He will flit through eternity," says Robert Lynd, "not as an archangel, perhaps, but as a mischievous cherub in a silk hat." He is an Oxford man, did his first writing for the *Yellow Book*, married a lady from Memphis, Tennessee, and now resides at Rapallo, Italy.

Beerbohm's liking for satire and burlesque found vent in *Zuleika Dobson*, a story of Oxford, and in *A Christmas Garland*, a series of parodies on Bennett, Henry James, George Moore, Galsworthy, and Chesterton. His best essays are contained in *More, Yet Again*, and *And Even Now*. They are unconnected papers on topics as varied as "Whistler's Writing," "The House of Commons Manner," "Servants," "On Speaking French," and "Going Out for a Walk."

Hilaire Belloc (1870–). If a prize were awarded for quantity and diversity of authorship, there would be no competition for it in modern England. Even Shaw and Wells, who have written so much and so variously and who have more than once expressed their disapproval of the man who wrote

G. B. SHAW, HILAIRE BELLOC, AND G. K. CHESTERTON
Courtesy of the *London Illustrated News*

The Path to Rome, would unhesitatingly concede that the guerdon should fall to Hilaire Belloc. For this Oxford graduate and militant Catholic, this French-Englishman who has been soldier, traveler, journalist, legislator, historian, satirist, novelist, artist, poet, and critic, has during his not overlong lifetime written nonsense rimes for children, discussions of politics and military strategy, works of philosophy, biography, and apologetics, drinking songs and nature poetry, monographs on the French Revolution, topographical studies of Roman roads, and an analysis of the Protestant Reformation. Nobody has ever compiled a complete Belloc bibliography; he probably could not do so himself. He has even run out of titles for his essays, calling one collection *On Everything*, another *On Anything*, a third *On Nothing*, and a fourth simply *On*.

Quantity is one thing and quality is another; but in Belloc's case, though the quantity is astounding, the quality, if uneven, is remarkably high; he belies the adapted adage that he who takes the pen shall perish by the pen. To his work he brings accurate scholarship, wide reading, abounding — at times disconcerting — energy, and a feeling for style. Always he suits his diction to his theme. He can be trivial and grotesque in writing verses for *The Modern Traveller* and *The Bad Child's Book of Beasts*, flippant and sardonic in *Caliban's Guide to Letters* and *The Mercy of Allah*, whimsical and lightly philosophical in *The Path to Rome* and *The Cruise of the Nona*, pictorial and graphic in his lives of Danton and Marie Antoinette, nervous and metallic in *The Servile State* and *Europe and the Faith*. His style — and this is the ultimate evidence of mastery — is as elastic as his choice of subjects and his range of moods.

His own exposition of what the art of writing means deserves consideration from students of literature:

Men are influenced by the word. Spoken or written, the word is the organ of persuasion and, therefore, of moral government.

Now, degraded as that term has become in our time, there is no proper term to express the exact use of words save the term "style."

What words we use, and in what order we put them, is the whole matter of style; and a man desiring to influence his fellow men has therefore not one, but two co-related instruments at his disposal. He cannot use one without the other. These two instruments are his idea and his style.

However powerful, native, sympathetic to his hearer's mood or cogently provable by reference to new things, may be a man's idea, he cannot persuade his fellow men to it if he have not words to express it.

And he will persuade them more and more in proportion as his words are well chosen and in the right order, such order being determined by the genius of the language whence they are drawn.[1]

Two leading traits characterize all the more serious writings of Hilaire Belloc: his energetic enthusiasm and his stalwart, even pugnacious, Catholicism. Both tend to make him more effective as a controversialist than as a distinguished scholar and exponent of Arnold's "sweet reasonableness" through the medium of the printed word. He has much of Shaw's impatience with the stupidity of mankind. The truth of certain favorite theories — the superiority of Latin to "Nordic" civilization, the continuity of the Roman race and culture in Great Britain, the evils of the present wage system, the inability of anybody not a Catholic to think philosophically — is so obvious to him that he lays down his opinions and inferences with an air of take-it-or-leave-it finality immensely heartening to men who agree with his views, but confusing and repellent to his opponents. But Belloc is at his best when he is not too serious, and few readers can resist the colorful and wide circling appeal of his *Towns of Destiny* and *Miniatures of French History*.

√ **Gilbert K. Chesterton (1874–   ).** If Belloc supplies the vinegar for the salad of modern thought, Chesterton supplies the oil — and a dash of paprika. Friends, fellow Catholics, at one in their fundamental ideas, and sometimes collaborators in literary work, they have been conceived of by Theodore Maynard as the "Chesterbelloc" in contemporary letters. Yet it is always possible to differentiate the two heads of that highly entertaining animal. If from Belloc comes a clear, resonant roar of protest and righteous wrath, from Chesterton there proceeds a gale of side-shaking and disarming laughter.

But it is not the loud laugh that speaks the vacant mind. Every man suffers from the excess of his virtues, and in some quarters Chesterton's intellectual powers are underestimated

[1] *The French Revolution*, p. 21.

because he seems to have such an uproariously good time in exercising them. Puritanism, which the "Chesterbelloc" detests, dies hard, and to its last gasp insists that in learning, as in sanctity, joviality is a suspicious circumstance. Belloc is zealous and clever, Chesterton is cheerful and clever, and in consequence both are sometimes considered superficial — so slow are certain good folk to understand that zeal is not fanaticism, that cheerfulness is not a crime, that cleverness in word and in work is evidence of brains, not of the lack thereof.

GILBERT K. CHESTERTON

The cleverness of Chesterton reveals itself in his literary style, a style — until recently at least — eminently bright and entertaining; and the most conspicuous feature of that style is its plentiful sprinkling of paradoxes. The rhetorics tell us that a paradox is a seeming contradiction in meaning or the expression of a thought running counter to generally received opinion. Some paradoxes, those of Oscar Wilde, for example, stress the words; others, like Chesterton's, stress the ideas. Chesterton's method is to take some belief that everybody accepts as true, turn it upside down or inside out, and then prove that his manipulation of it accords with reality. Thus in his essay on Lord Byron he starts with the popular assumption of the poet's skepticism and melancholy and proceeds as follows:

Surely it is ridiculous to maintain seriously that Byron's love of the desolate and inhuman in nature was the mark of vital scepticism and depression. When a young man can elect deliberately to walk alone in winter by the side of the shattering sea, when he takes pleasure in storms and stricken peaks, and the lawless melancholy of the older earth, we may deduce with the certainty of logic that he is very young and very happy. There is a certain darkness which we see in wine when seen in shadow; we see it again in the night which has just buried a gorgeous sunset. The wine seems black, and yet at the same time powerfully and almost impossibly red; the sky seems black, and yet at the same time to be only too dense a blend of purple and green. Such was the darkness which lay around the Byronic school. Darkness with them was only too dense a purple. They would prefer the sullen hostility of the earth because amid all the cold and darkness their own hearts were flaming like their own firesides.

This form of reasoning — which textbooks of logic have not yet discovered — is not merely playing with words, and still less is it playing with ideas. It is a practical protest against herd thinking. It is a manifestation of the ability to detect something untrue or even absurd in a generally accepted statement of belief. In like manner a man sufficiently ingenious might dispose of the proverb "Honesty is the best policy" by demonstrating that honesty is in fact no policy at all. Chesterton answers the question "What's wrong with the world?" by pointing out that people do not ask "What's right with the world?" He was converted to a belief in the Christian religion, he tells us in *Orthodoxy*, by reflecting on the stock arguments against Christianity. The method does not consist in "taking the opposite," but in proving the truth of the opposite; and this Chesterton generally does with a wealth of illustration and in a mood of immense self-satisfaction and contagious good humor.

The best examples of Chesterton's writing are to be found in the books he wrote before 1920; of late years — as in his profound and capable but undeniably heavy defense of religion, *The Everlasting Man* — his style has become cumbrous and opaque. All his literary essays are worth while for matter as for manner, and so are the papers contained in *All Things Considered, Tremendous Trifles, Alarms and Discursions*, and

The Uses of Diversity. In *Heretics* he engages in destructive criticism of certain modern notions promulgated by Moore, Yeats, and others; and in *Orthodoxy,* his best book, he makes a constructive study of the ground for Christian belief.

Though primarily an essayist, Chesterton has frolicked in other forms of literary expression. His short stories, recounting the extraordinary detective exploits of a Father Brown, and his novels, like *Manalive, The Napoleon of Notting Hill,* and *The Return of Don Quixote,* are unique contributions to English prose fiction; and he has written some admirable poems.

To get the most from our reading of Chesterton we should have listened to him talking, and in lieu of that we can profit from the impressions of one who has heard him. A few years ago Chesterton lectured at the Oxford Union, and one of the students in the audience thus describes the performance:

> To hear Chesterton speak is in itself an explanation of his writing. He pours out his words, suddenly says something which pleases him by its touch of fantasy, pauses, and then with a face that grows more and more smiling, and eyes that grow more and more bright, proceeds to develop that idea, to chase it, to leap ponderously after it, to hurl paradoxes in its wake, to circumvent it with every ingenious conceit.[1]

John Middleton Murry (1889–   ). Among the younger writers of literary criticism the soundest, most capable, and most promising work is being done by Middleton Murry, an Oxford graduate and miscellaneous writer, at present editor of the *Adelphi Magazine.* He steers a middle course between nineteenth-century conservatism and present-day impressionism; that is to say, he avoids both the excessive deference for established reputations shown by most of the periodical reviewers a hundred years ago and the contempt of all standards and the glorification of flippancy and ignorance characteristic

---

[1] Beverley Nichols, *25.* The unusual title is given to an autobiography written when its author was twenty-five years old. He neglected to place on the title-page an appropriate quotation from Shakespeare:

> So wise, so young, they say, do never live long.

of many contemporary commentators on literature. Here is one article of his critical credo which may well serve as a guide to students of books and authors:

What, I think, we may reasonably ask, is that criticism should be less timid; that it should openly accept the fact that its deepest judgments are moral. A critic should be conscious of his moral assumptions and take pains to put into them the highest morality of which he is capable. That is only another way of saying that the critic should be conscious of himself as an artist. He should be aware of the responsibilities imposed by his art; he should respect the technique of his craft. He should not be cheap, he should not be shallow, he should not be insincere, either in praise or in blame, but above all in these modern times, he should not be insincere in praise.[1]

Murry's essays include *Aspects of Literature, The Problem of Style, Countries of the Mind*, and *Pencillings*.

[1] *Countries of the Mind*, p. 246.

CONCLUSION

We have now reviewed the progress of English Literature from its beginnings to the present day. We have followed the stream from its small and mist-shrouded source to its happy conflux with the mighty river of the European Tradition, to its widening and deepening through the years; we have noted tributaries which have increased its volume, rocks which have temporarily divided its waters, cross currents which have diversified its flow; and if we have been observant voyagers, we have glimpsed something of the goodly country it has traversed and mayhap have caught upon its surface the splendor of starlight and the mystery of the moon.

Our journey, like all journeys, should minister to our profit and our pleasure. This has been mainly a spiritual journey and should bring forth spiritual fruits. We have learned essential facts — names of writers and of books, traits of literary movements in English Literature and in other literatures, judgments passed upon important poems and essays by critics of repute. It is well to know such things, but yet more important to think about them, to correlate them, to discuss them; and for that end it is most important of all to read as copiously as we can of the best that has been written in the English tongue. Doing thus we shall rise from facts to truth, we shall apply to our own lives and our own problems the human examples which literature supplies and the human wisdom which literature distills.

Facts are good, but principles are better. Let us hope that from our study of books we shall garner certain general ideas, certain broad and firm and basic opinions about art and about life, which will contribute to the upbuilding of our character and react upon our habits of living. Such principles are standards whereby we can distinguish between the petty and the sublime, the vulgar and the humorous, the sordid and the tragic, the flashy and the substantial, the ephemeral and the enduring. What our opinions are means much, but why we hold our opinions means more; in literature as in religion it is seemly to have reasons for the faith that is in us.

Before closing this book — with a pardonable sigh of relief — it may be well for us to turn back to that distant first chapter and in the light of our added knowledge to re-read the paragraphs which tell us what literature is and why literature is studied. There we have suggestions for an examination of conscience — perhaps even for that humble confession which is good for the soul.

SUGGESTIONS FOR READING

CHAPTER I

THE STUDY OF LITERATURE

We have many books on the study of literature which themselves are literature, and others which, though less pretentious tools, have lost none of their freshness and practical value. Again, we have recent works which deal with the old problems in a new way. The following list includes representative volumes of all three types.

G. G. LOANE. *A Short Handbook of Literary Terms.* Explains the technical language of literary study; what every student should know.

BROTHER AZARIAS. *Books and Reading.* Abounding in stimulating hints.

GEORGE SAINTSBURY. *Collected Essays and Papers,* Vol. III: "The Permanent and the Temporary in Literature."

HIRAM CORSON. *The Aims of Literary Study.*

CARDINAL NEWMAN. The essay on literature in his *Idea of a University.* Also published separately in several annotated editions.

JOHN MORLEY. *On the Study of Literature.* Sage suggestions from an eminent Victorian.

R. W. EMERSON. *The American Scholar.* Ever a timely and pertinent preachment on study.

JOHN RUSKIN. *Sesame and Lilies.* A classic on the subject of literature study.

ARLO BATES. *Talks on the Study of Literature.*

H. W. MABIE. *Short Studies in Literature; Under the Trees and Elsewhere; Books and Culture.* Invaluable as indicating the right approach to literature.

FREDERIC HARRISON. *The Choice of Books.*

C. D. WARNER. *Literature and Life.*

WOODROW WILSON. *Mere Literature.* An eloquent plea for literature as an art.

SIR ARTHUR QUILLER-COUCH. *On the Art of Reading.*

J. B. KERFOOT. *How to Read.* Novel in approach, sound in substance.

W. P. TRENT. *Greatness in Literature and Other Papers.*

C. A. SMITH. *What can Literature do for Me?*

BROTHER LEO. *Teaching the Drama and the Essay.*

W. H. CRASHAW. *The Interpretation of Literature.*

WILFRED WHITTEN (John o' London). *Unposted Letters concerning Life and Literature.* Random remarks on style, books, and authors, likely to illuminate and inspire.

Marguerite Wilkinson. *The Way of the Makers*. Poets discuss their art.

Max Eastman. *The Enjoyment of Poetry*.

E. A. G. Lamborn. *The Rudiments of Criticism*. A practical teacher of young children describes his methods of correlating the study of poetry with the practice of writing.

CHAPTER II

AN AIRPLANE SURVEY

The books here listed, because of their emphasis on the interdependence of national literatures, are of especial value in developing appreciation of the European Tradition. For the influence of individual writers on English Literature consult the bibliographies in standard encyclopedias.

R. G. Moulton. *The Modern Study of Literature*. A scholarly and highly important work.

Barrett Wendell. *The Traditions of European Literature*. A Harvard savant uncovers the roots of modern books.

R. G. Moulton. *World Literature*.

Richardson and Owen. *Literature of the World*.

C. B. Pallen. *Epochs of Literature*.

Georgina P. Curtis. *The Interdependence of Literature*. This and the three books immediately preceding amplify and enforce the airplane view of literature.

T. G. Tucker. *The Foreign Debt of English Literature*. A sure prophylactic against the isolation theory of literature.

Hadzsits and Robinson (editors). Longmans, Green & Co.'s series of volumes on *Our Debt to Greece and Rome*. Individual writers are discussed in separate books, with special attention to their influence on English writers.

Gilbert Norwood. *The Writers of Greece*. Brief and compact.

J. W. Mackail. *The Springs of Helicon*. A study of Greek and Italian influences on English poetry from Chaucer to Milton.

Gilbert Murray. *The Classical Tradition in Poetry*. Mature and stimulating lectures on the Greek and Roman influence on later literature.

Elizabeth Nitchie. *Vergil and the English Poets*.

A. H. Upham. *French Influence on English Literature*.

J. J. Walsh. *The World's Debt to the Irish*. A capable exposition of a little-appreciated literary influence.

P. J. Lennox. "The Influence of Spain on English Literature," in *The Catholic University Bulletin*, May, 1913.

Matthew Brett. *Hymns of the Breviary and the Missal*.

J. S. Phillimore. *The Hundred Best Latin Hymns*. Father Brett's book gives English translations. Phillimore's does not, but contains a brief and admirable preface.

Thomas Walsh (editor). *The Catholic Anthology*. Includes many poems translated from Continental languages.

CHAPTER III

THE HAMMER AND THE CROSS

The following are usable translations from Old English Literature:

F. KLAEBER (editor). *Beowulf and the Fight at Finnsburg.* Other, though less recent translations, are those of C. B. Tinker, F. B. Gummere, and J. D. Spaeth. Spaeth's includes a condensed version of *The Phoenix, The Wanderer,* and other poems.

MORRIS and SKEAT. *Specimens of Early English.*

GEORGE SAMPSON. *The Cambridge Book of Prose and Verse.* An anthology of English Literature from the beginnings to Chaucer. The translation has an archaic flavor and the notes are dependable.

COOK and TINKER. *Translations from Old English Prose* and *Translations from Old English Poetry.* Old and reliable texts.

Among books consisting of studies of Old English Literature the following are recommended:

R. W. CHAMBERS. *Beowulf.* A consideration of the poem in its relation to the principles of epic poetry.

R. W. CHAMBERS. *Widsith.* A study of Old English legend.

W. MACNEILE DIXON. *English Epic and Heroic Poetry.* Sound and scholarly essays.

W. P. KER. *Epic and Romance.* Essays on the literature of northern Europe.

BROTHER AZARIAS. *Development of Old English Thought.* Though some of its conclusions are untenable in the light of recent scholarship, this attractive little book remains one of the best semipopular treatises on the subject.

PETER GUILDAY (editor). *Church Historians.* Contains a notable paper on St. Bede the Venerable by F. S. Betten.

CHARLES PLUMMER. *Life and Times of Alfred the Great.* Indispensable.

BEATRICE LEES. *Alfred the Great.* Recent, pleasing in style, not too exacting in scholarship.

CHAPTER IV

MONK AND MINSTREL

General studies

GEORGE SAINTSBURY. *The Flourishing of Romance and the Rise of Allegory.*
W. H. SCHOFIELD. *English Literature from the Norman Conquest to Chaucer.*

On the Arthurian Romances

W. W. COMFORT. *The Quest of the Holy Grail.* A translation from Old French.
ERNEST RHYS. *Studies in the Arthurian Legend.*
M. W. MACCALLUM. *Tennyson's Idylls and Arthurian Story.*

J. L. WESTON. *King Arthur and his Knights.*

J. D. BRUCE. *The Evolution of Arthurian Romance from the Beginnings down to the Year 1300.* The most recent, most authoritative, and most scholarly general study of the subject. In two volumes.

Books on the life of the period

MARJORIE and C. H. B. QUENNELL. *Everyday Life in Anglo-Saxon, Viking, and Norman Times.* Simply written, copiously illustrated; based on Early English and Middle English Literature.

CRUMP and JACOB. *The Legacy of the Middle Ages.* A general and scholarly survey of religion, art, literature, philosophy, law, education, and social life.

On the religious life of the times

NEVILLE WATTS (editor). *Love Songs of Sion.* An important collection of Middle English devotional verse in modernized language.

R. A. CRAM. *The Ruined Abbeys of England.*

CARDINAL GASQUET. *The Greater Abbeys of England.* Both this book and the preceding one are of charm and value.

On the language

GREENOUGH and KITTREDGE. *Words and their Ways in English Speech.*

G. H. MCKNIGHT. *English Words and their Background.*

OWEN BARFIELD. *History in English Words.*

R. C. TRENCH. *English Past and Present.* Old, but unapproached as a fascinating study of the growth of the language.

CHAPTER V

THE AGE OF CHAUCER

General studies

T. L. CONNOLLY. *Introduction to Chaucer and Langland.* The work of a Jesuit scholar.

J. M. MANLY. *Some New Lights on Chaucer.* Not a popular book, but an excellent example of an expert's exposition of literary background.

G. G. COULTON. *Chaucer and his England.* Good for general reading.

SIDNEY DARK. *St. Thomas of Canterbury.*

FRANCIS WATT. *Canterbury Pilgrims and their Ways.* Popular and informing.

KATHERINE BRÉGY. *Poets and Pilgrims.* An interpretative study of the inclusiveness of Chaucer.

First aids to the reading of Chaucer

W. W. SKEAT. *The Student's Chaucer.*

A. W. POLLARD. *The Chaucer Primer.*

R. K. ROOT. *The Poetry of Chaucer.*

G. L. KITTREDGE. *Chaucer and his Poetry.*

Collections of Old English Ballads

ROBERT GRAVES. *The English Ballad*. A short critical survey, with thirty-four representative Ballads.

SARGENT and KITTREDGE. *English and Scottish Popular Ballads*.

W. D. ARMES. *Old English Ballads*.

J. P. KINARD. *Old English Ballads*.

KATHARINE L. BATES. *A Ballad Book*.

J. S. ROBERTS. *The Legendary Ballads of England and Scotland*.

F. B. GUMMERE. *Old English Ballads*. A thoroughgoing study and representative collection, with a formulation of the author's communal theory of Ballad origins.

HELEN L. COHEN. *The Ballade*. A study of the French verse-form.

CHAPTER VI

THE REVIVAL OF LEARNING

SIDNEY DARK. *The Story of the Renaissance*. A general view, reliable though slightly adverse.

THOMAS O'HAGAN. "The Catholic Church and the Italian Renaissance," in *The Catholic World*, February, 1919.

SELWIN BRINTON. *The Golden Age of the Medici*.

J. F. SALZMAN. *England in Tudor Times*. "The best short account of Tudor England that has appeared in many years." — *The New World*, Chicago

NELLIE S. AURNER. *Caxton — Mirror of Fifteenth Century Letters*.

H. R. PLOMER. *William Caxton*. Recent and excellent.

On More

RANDALL DAVIES. *The Greatest House at Chelsea*.

J. S. PHILLIMORE. "Blessed Thomas More and the Arrest of Humanism in England," in *The Dublin Review*, July, 1913.

J. J. DALY. "Saint and Humorist," in *The Catholic World*, July, 1920.

THEODORE MAYNARD. "Roman and Utopian," in *The Catholic World*, January, 1919.

W. P. H. KITCHIN. "Blessed Thomas More," in *The Magnificat*, February, 1926.

RICHARD LE GALLIENNE. "Some Famous Utopias," in *Munsey's Magazine*, June, 1919.

On Spenser

F. B. GUMMERE. *Selections from Spenser*.

W. L. RENWICK. *Edmund Spenser — An Essay on Renaissance Poetry*.

H. E. CORY. *Edmund Spenser — A Critical Study*. Very full and very ingenious in its development of the author's thesis.

ÉMILE LEGOUIS. *Edmund Spenser*. French in method and point of view.

J. R. LOWELL. *Essay on Spenser*. A classic.

EDWARD DOWDEN. *Transcripts and Studies*. The chapters on Spenser are still valuable.

EMILY HICKEY. "Catholicity in Spenser," in *The American Catholic Quarterly Review*, July, 1907.

On Elizabethan poets

MAUD F. JERROLD. *Francesco Petrarca*. For a sketch of the strong Italian influence on Wyatt and Surrey.

J. A. SYMONDS. *Sir Philip Sidney*.

ROBERT BELL. *Songs from the Dramatists*. A collection of the lyrics in the Elizabethan drama.

SIR EDMUND GOSSE. *More Books on the Table*. Drayton considered in the chapter entitled "The Court of Faery."

CHRISTOBEL M. HOOD. *The Book of Robert Southwell*. A recent study.

KATHERINE BRÉGY. *The Poets' Chantry*. Has an excellent chapter on Southwell.

H. J. C. GRIERSON (editor). *Donne's Poetical Works*, in two volumes. Includes an excellent commentary.

SIR EDMUND GOSSE. *Life and Letters of John Donne*. The leading modern authority.

ARTHUR SYMONS. *Figures of Several Centuries*. Contains an essay on Donne.

H. J. C. GRIERSON. *The Background of English Literature*. The chapter on the "Metaphysical Poets" is an excellent study of Donne and his imitators.

On Elizabethan prose writers

JACOB ZEITLIN (editor). *Seventeenth Century Essays*. Extracts from Bacon, Jonson, Burton, Browne, Clarendon, and others.

MEAD and CLIFT (editors). *Burton the Anatomist — Being Extracts from The Anatomy of Melancholy chosen to interest the Psychologist in Every Man*.

F. E. SCHELLING (editor). *Ben Jonson's Timber*.

STOCKTON AXSON and OTHERS. *Lectures on Francis Bacon*. Rice Institute pamphlet, January, 1926.

C. D. BROAD. *The Philosophy of Francis Bacon*.

CHAPTER VII

THE AGE OF SHAKESPEARE

On the study of the drama

ASHLEY DUKES. *Drama*. This recent addition to the Home University Library is a good popular presentation of the subject.

NELLIE B. MILLER. *The Living Drama*. A review of the historical development and a survey of modern conditions.

BRANDER MATTHEWS. *A Study of the Drama*.

RICHARD BURTON. *How to see a Play*.

A. H. THORNDIKE. *Tragedy*. A historical view, with special attention to the Elizabethans.

On the religious plays

E. K. CHAMBERS. *The Mediæval Stage.*

JOAN EVANS. *St. Joan of Orleans.* A condensed version, in English, of the fifteenth-century French pageant commemorating the delivery of the city of Orleans.

C. M. GAYLEY. *Plays of our Forefathers.* Everything essential.

H. C. SCHWEIKERT (editor). *Early English Plays.* Twenty-one plays illustrating the development of the drama in English from the liturgical *Quem Quæritis* to Dekker's *Shoemaker's Holiday* and Jonson's *Every Man in his Humour.*

On the plays of Shakespeare

W. J. LAWRENCE. *The Elizabethan Playhouse.*

G. F. BRADLEY. *About Shakespeare and his Plays.*

G. P. BAKER. *The Development of Shakespeare as a Dramatist.*

Various authors; articles in *The Catholic World*, April, 1916.

J. C. COLLINS. *Studies in Shakespeare.* Thorough and informing.

R. M. ALDEN. *A Shakespeare Handbook.*

TUCKER BROOKE. *Shakespeare of Stratford.* Much definite information in small compass.

CLARA LONGWORTH DE CHAMBRUN. *Shakespeare — Actor-Poet.* An illuminating presentation of facts and conjectures regarding the life and personality of Shakespeare.

H. S. BOWDEN. *The Religion of Shakespeare.* A mass of evidence in support of the thesis that Shakespeare was a Catholic.

SISTER MAURA. *Shakespeare's Catholicism.* A more recent study than Father Bowden's.

GERARD BRIDGE. *Shakespeare's Catholicity in Hamlet.* From the clerical point of view.

F. J. KELLY. "Shakespeare and the Art of Music," in *The Catholic World*, January, 1920.

SADAKICHI HARTMANN. *Shakespeare in Art.* An account of the paintings and statues inspired by Shakespeare's plays.

On other playwrights

ARTHUR SYMONS. *Studies in the Elizabethan Drama.*

F. E. SCHELLING. *Typical Elizabethan Plays.* Well edited.

J. L. HOTSON. *The Death of Christopher Marlowe.* The outcome of recent researches.

U. M. ELLIS-FERMOR. *Christopher Marlowe.* Some good literary criticism.

C. H. HERFORD. *Ben Jonson — The Man and his Work.* A series of ten volumes, two of which have now been published.

H. W. CARTER. *Ben Jonson's Every Man in his Humour.* A capable modern edition.

C. L. STAINER. *Jonson and Drummond.* A brilliant attempt to prove that the famous *Conversations* are an eighteenth-century forgery.

A. H. NASON. *James Shirley, Dramatist.* A recent and standard biography.

CHAPTER VIII

THE AGE OF MILTON

On the Cavalier Poets

ROBERT BROWNING. *Cavalier Tunes*. A literary rendering of the spirit of the Cavaliers.

C. M. LINDSAY. *Cavalier Poets*. A little book made up of selections and brief biographies.

C. H. HARTMANN. *The Cavalier Spirit and its Influence on the Life and Work of Richard Lovelace*. A satisfactory account of the poet's life and a good study of his poems.

F. A. STOKES (editor). *The Poems of Sir John Suckling*. The brief notes are helpful, and the introduction is more than ordinarily informing.

ZACHARY GREY (editor). *Hudibras*, by Samuel Butler.

Herrick's poems have been edited by HAZLITT (1869), by GROSART (1876), and by POLLARD (1891), with an essay by SWINBURNE.

On Milton

J. H. HANFORD. *A Milton Handbook*. A compact summary.

R. D. HAVENS. *The Influence of Milton on English Poetry*.

P. E. MORE. *Shelburne Essays* (Fourth Series). A thoughtful paper on "The Theme of Paradise Lost."

J. E. C. WELDON. "The Theology of Milton," in *The Nineteenth Century and After*, May, 1912.

C. L. VAN NOPPEN. *Vondel's Lucifer*. Includes parallelisms between Milton and the Dutch poet.

A. S. COOK (editor). *Addison's Criticism of Paradise Lost*.

On other poets

W. H. BAGGULEY (editor). *Andrew Marvell — Tercentenary Tributes*. Includes papers by Augustine Birrell, T. S. Eliot, and Sir Edmund Gosse.

BURTON CONFREY. "Crashaw's Religious Background," in *Thought*, December, 1927.

KATHERINE BRÉGY. *The Poets' Chantry*. Contains chapters on Crashaw and Habington.

JOHN MONAGHAN. "Two Poets went over to Bethlehem," in *The Catholic World*, December, 1923. A comparison of the Christmas poems of Milton and Crashaw.

L. C. MARTIN (editor). *The Poems, English, Latin, and Greek, of Richard Crashaw*. The accepted Crashaw canon, well documented and enriched with a commentary.

L. I. GUINEY. "William Habington," in *America*, January 8, 1916.

P. E. MORE. *Shelburne Essays* (Fourth Series). Has an excellent paper on Herbert.

JOHN SPARROW (editor). *The Mistress, with other Select Poems of Abraham Cowley*. A recent edition, with a helpful introduction.

L. C. MARTIN (editor). *The Works of Henry Vaughan*, in two volumes. The best modern edition. The notes trace Vaughan's indebtedness to the Bible and to early Christian writers.

EDMUND BLUNDEN. *On the Poems of Henry Vaughan — Characteristics and Intimations*. The Latin poems are translated into English verse.

GORDON CROSS (editor). *Every Man's Book of Sacred Verse*. Contains selections from Crashaw, Herbert, and other of the Religious Poets.

CHAPTER IX

THE AGE OF DRYDEN

The pros and cons of the case anent Bunyan's masterpiece are given by J. Brierley in *From Philistia* and by Francis Thompson in *A Renegade Poet and Other Essays*. Brierley's essay on " Bunyan as a Classic " presents the traditional laudatory estimate ; Thompson's essay on " Bunyan in the Light of Modern Criticism " finds Bunyan deficient in imagination and narrative skill.

LYTTON STRACHEY. *Books and Characters*. Contains a reasonable study of Browne as a stylist.

O. F. MORSHEAD (editor). *Everybody's Pepys*. A judiciously condensed version of the *Diary*, with an excellent introduction, illustrations that really illustrate, and a map of London in Pepys's days.

J. R. TANNER. *Mr. Pepys — An Introduction to the Diary together with a Sketch of his Later Life*.

H. B. WHEATLEY. *Samuel Pepys and the World he Lived In*.

KATHLEEN M. LYNCH. *The Social Mode of the Restoration Comedy*. Traces the genesis of the Restoration Comedy from the earlier English drama.

HUGH WALKER. *English Satire and Satirists*. A general review.

On Dryden

W. H. HUDSON (editor). *Dryden's Dramatic Essays*. This Everyman edition has a discerning introduction, but lacks notes.

J. C. COLLINS (editor). *The Satires of Dryden*.

RICHARD GARNETT. *The Age of Dryden*.

HALL FRYE. *Dryden and the Critical Canons of the Eighteenth Century*. Traces the influence of Dryden on the writers of the Augustan Age.

W. E. BOHN. *The Development of John Dryden's Literary Criticism*. Finds five periods.

BROTHER LEO. *Religion and the Study of Literature*. The final chapter is on "How Dryden became a Catholic."

CHAPTER X

THE CLASSICAL INFLUENCE

LANE COOPER. *Two Views of Education.* The essay on "Patterns" makes an application of the Classical spirit in the educational field.

D. N. NICHOL (editor). *The Oxford Book of Eighteenth Century Verse.*

A. S. TURBERVILLE. *English Men and Manners in the Eighteenth Century.*

AUSTIN DOBSON. *Eighteenth Century Vignettes.*

AUSTIN DOBSON. *A Dialogue to the Memory of Mr. Alexander Pope.* A sparkling piece of criticism done in riming couplets.

JOHN SARGEAUNT (editor). *Pope's Essay on Criticism.* An excellent modern edition with practical notes.

MISS E. M. SYMONDS (George Paston). *Pope, his Life and Times.* This work, in two volumes, is simple yet scholarly, and embodies the best features of previous studies by Whitwell Elwin, Mark Pattison, and Sir Leslie Stephen.

D. L. KAY. *The Glamour of Dublin.* Impressionistic thumb-nail sketches of Swift, Steele, and others.

G. A. AITKEN. *Life of Richard Steele.* Dependable.

J. J. REILLY. "'Dear Prue's' Husband," in *America*, April 16, 1921.

TEMPLE SCOTT. *The Prose Works of Jonathan Swift.* The introduction is especially worth while.

J. C. COLLINS. *Jonathan Swift.*

WALTER SICHEL. *Bolingbroke and his Times.* Two volumes of interesting lights and side lights.

F. S. MAHONY. *The Reliques of Father Prout.* Contains an impressive paper on the last days of Swift.

KATHERINE BRÉGY. "The Enigma of Dean Swift," in *The Catholic World*, October, 1920.

H. V. ABBOTT. *Boswell's Life of Johnson.* A condensed edition, with an informing introduction and adequate notes, well suited for the use of students.

ROBERT LYND. *Dr. Johnson and Company.* A sane, succinct, and stimulating survey of the life and times of Johnson.

HESTER L. PIOZZI. *Anecdotes of the Late Samuel Johnson LL.D.* A collection of Mrs. Thrale's impressions of her burly friend, recently edited by S. C. Roberts.

J. E. BROWN. *The Critical Opinions of Samuel Johnson.*

P. H. HOUSTON. *Dr. Johnson — A Study in Eighteenth Century Humanism.* A reassuring evidence of American scholarship; traces Johnson's indebtedness to the French critics, especially Boileau.

C. G. HARPER. *A Literary Man's London.* Chapter v is devoted to the haunts of Johnson. A book that makes the best possible substitute for a stroll through London town.

F. F. MOORE. *Goldsmith.* Does much to dissipate the false impression of Goldsmith invented by Boswell and accepted by most later writers.

BERTRAM NEWMAN. *Edmund Burke*. A recent and well-balanced study.

WOODROW WILSON. *Mere Literature*. Some wise remarks on Burke in the chapter on "The Interpreter of English Liberty."

WILLIAM O'BRIEN. *Edmund Burke as an Irishman*. A treasure of learning and a triumph of style in the Irish mode.

A. G. BRICKEL. "Burke and Newman," in *The Catholic World*, August, 1919. A comparison of styles.

WALTER SICHEL. *Sheridan*. A twentieth-century study, in two volumes, including all the strong points of earlier biographies and adding graces of its own.

JAMES SMITH. *Junius Unveiled*. A clever attempt to prove that Edward Gibbon was the author of *The Letters of Junius*.

ROGER COXON. *Chesterfield and his Critics*. A review of critical opinion and a reprinting of eleven essays.

CHAPTER XI

THE ROMANTIC MOVEMENT

On Romanticism

IRVING BABBITT. *The New Laokoön*. Reviews the history of Classicism and Romanticism with a few eminently human biases.

LASCELLES ABERCROMBIE. *Romanticism*. A consideration of Romanticism less in its opposition to Classicism than in its relation to Realism.

H. A. BEERS. *A History of English Romanticism in the Eighteenth Century*. Still a standard estimate, especially valuable for its first chapter on the nature of Romanticism and for its classification of eighteenth-century writers.

F. W. STOKOE. *German Influence in the English Romantic Period*. Distinguished for common sense.

On individual writers

DOROTHY M. STUART. *Horace Walpole*. A recent and valuable contribution to the English Men of Letters series.

WILLIAM HADLEY (editor). *Selected Letters of Horace Walpole*. A reflection of the life and literature of the age. The arrangement is especially helpful.

AUSTIN DOBSON. *Horace Walpole — A Memoir*. A book for profit and for delight.

J. R. LOWELL. *Essay on Gray*. The finest work of an American critic just now being depreciated by men lacking both his insight and his learning.

J. CROFTS (editor). *Gray — Poetry and Prose*. Selections from Gray and essays on him by Johnson, Goldsmith, and others.

G. C. FABER (editor). *The Poetical Works of John Gay*.

H. C. SHELLEY. *Literary By-Paths in Old England*. Background studies of Gray, Gilbert White, Goldsmith, Burns, and other writers.

WILLIAM HADLEY (editor). *The Selected Letters of William Cowper*. Includes Cowper's overestimated comments on the literature of the day.

GAMALIEL BRADFORD. "Diversions of a Lost Soul," in *Atlantic Monthly*, September, 1924. A "psychographical" investigation of Cowper's religious obsessions.

RENÉ HUCHON. *George Crabbe and his Times*. An admirable French work translated by Frederick Clarke.

GEOFFREY KEYNES (editor). *Poetry and Prose of William Blake*. Complete and scholarly.

OSBERT BURDETT. *William Blake*. A recent judicious biography and critique in less than two hundred pages.

MAX PLOWMAN. *An Introduction to the Study of Blake*. Recent.

E. H. SHORT. *Blake*. An estimate of the poet as artist and illustrator, in the British Artists series.

W. B. YEATS. *Ideas of Good and Evil*. Two interesting chapters on Blake.

PHILIP SNOWDEN (editor). *William Cobbett's Advice to Young Men*.

G. K. CHESTERTON (editor). *William Cobbett's Cottage Economy*.

G. K. CHESTERTON. *Cobbett*. A scintillating study by a man who in several respects resembles the subject of his biography.

J. J. DALY. "Charles Waterton," in *Thought*, June, 1926. Not to be missed for worlds.

LENNOX ROBINSON (editor). *Poems by Thomas Parnell*. Fifty precious pages.

WILLIAM POWER. *Robert Burns and Other Essays and Sketches*. A Scot discourses of Scottish Literature and its place in the European Tradition.

J. C. SHAIRP. *Aspects of Poetry*. An old book, but in essentials not outmoded; there is solid food in the chapter on "Scottish Song and Burns."

WILLIAM WORDSWORTH. *At the Grave of Burns*. One Romantic poet on another.

CHAPTER XII

FIVE ROMANTIC POETS

On Wordsworth

SIR WALTER RALEIGH. *Wordsworth*. One of several biographies and critical estimates, worthy of comparison with the essays by Arnold, Pater, Symonds, and Legouis.

JAMES ROWLEY. *Wordsworth and Other Essays*.

SIR EDMUND GOSSE. *Gossip in a Library*. Some vagaries of early Wordsworth criticism revived in the chapter on "Peter Bell and his Tormentors."

THOMAS O'HAGAN. "In the Footsteps of Wordsworth," in *The Catholic World*, December, 1903.

On Coleridge

J. L. LOWES. *The Road to Xanadu*. An inspiring exposition of Coleridge's artistic development.

HUGH FAUSSET. *Samuel Taylor Coleridge*. A recent estimate of the man and his work, sound in substance and judicious in temper.

AUGUSTINE BIRRELL. *More Obiter Dicta.* Contains some appealing comments on Coleridge.

L. J. CARRICO. "Pre-Raphaelitism in *The Ancient Mariner*," in *The Champlain Educator*, January, 1906. A suggestive paper which deserves to be rescued from the files of a deceased periodical.

On Keats

SIR SIDNEY COLVIN. *John Keats — His Life and Poetry, his Friends, Critics, and After-Fame.* In its latest edition the standard authority on Keats.

A. E. HANCOCK. *John Keats — A Literary Biography.* Timely and pertinent.

H. W. GARROD. *Keats.* Unexcelled in its treatment of the Odes.

On Shelley

ROGER INGPEN. *Shelley in England.* A two-volume complement of Dowden's *Life of Shelley.*

ROGER INGPEN (editor). *The Letters of Percy Bysshe Shelley.*

FRANCIS THOMPSON. *A Renegade Poet.* The essay entitled "Stray Thoughts on Shelley," though less known than the immortal *Essay on Shelley*, is a more helpful if less impassioned piece of appreciation.

HELEN R. ANGELI. *Shelley and his Friends in Italy.* Interesting and informing despite the lady's tendency to Shelley worship and her positive views on things in general.

On Byron

ETHEL C. MAYNE. *Byron.* Modern, compact, judicious.

JOHN DRINKWATER. *The Pilgrim of Eternity.* Though there is too much muckraking in the first chapter, this is the best and most authoritative book on Byron, superseding all previous studies.

AGNES REPPLIER. *Compromises.* The essay on Byron's little daughter Allegra reveals the temperamental father in a not wholly unfavorable light.

CHAPTER XIII

THE NOVEL

On prose fiction

In *The Bookman* for February, 1916, twenty-seven novelists discuss Professor Phelps's definition of the novel.

HAROLD WILLIAMS. *Two Centuries of the English Novel.*

CORNELIUS WEYGANDT. *A Century of the English Novel.*

W. L. PHELPS. *The Advance of the English Novel.* These three books are good historical summaries.

BLISS PERRY. *A Study of Prose Fiction.*

CLAYTON HAMILTON. *Materials and Methods of Fiction.*

GEORGE SAINTSBURY. *Collected Essays and Papers*, Vol. III. Contains three studies of "The Historical Novel" and a paper on "The Present State of the English Novel."

On individual novelists

W. P. TRENT. *Defoe — How to know Him.*

F. T. BLANCHARD. *Fielding the Novelist.* Recent.

WILBUR CROSS. *The History of Henry Fielding.* This three-volume study seems destined to be the authoritative work on Fielding for a long time to come.

LEWIS MELVILLE. *The Life and Letters of Tobias Smollett.*

H. S. BUCK. *A Study in Smollett.*

WILBUR CROSS. *The Life and Times of Laurence Sterne.* Two volumes.

WILFRID WARD. "The Centenary of Waverley," in *The Dublin Review,* October, 1914.

J. C. SHAIRP. *Aspects of Poetry,* chap. vii: "The Homeric Spirit in Walter Scott."

W. MACINTOSH. *Scott and Goethe.* An investigation of the considerable German influence on the writings of Scott.

J. E. GRAHAM. "Scott's Catholic Tendencies," in *The Catholic University Bulletin,* January, 1914.

ERNEST DIMNET. *The Brontë Sisters.* An estimate by a French critic.

ALICE MEYNELL. In *The Dublin Review* for April, 1911, the poet has a valuable paper on the Brontës; she indicates the stylistic superiority of Emily.

A. I. DU PONT COLEMAN. "John Inglesant," in *The Commonweal,* March 2, 1927.

M. E. SPEARE. *The Political Novel.* Disraeli's work is discussed in five chapters.

J. W. ROGERS (editor). *Learning to Write.* A collection of Stevenson's utterances on the art of writing.

CLAYTON HAMILTON. *On the Trail of Stevenson.* Interesting pilgrimages to places where Stevenson lived, and comments on his personality, his books, and his friends.

J. E. GRAHAM. "Stevenson's Treatment of Catholics," in *The Catholic University Bulletin,* October, 1912. The author discovers a growth in understanding and sympathy.

O. W. FIRKINS. *Jane Austen.* Among the latest books and one of the best.

WALTER MOBERLY. "Jane Austen," in *The Dublin Review,* July, 1914.

MARJORY A. BALD. *Women Writers of the Nineteenth Century.* Competent chapters on Jane Austen, the Brontës, George Eliot, and Mrs. Browning.

JOHN AYSCOUGH. *Levia-Pondera.* An appreciation of John Galt and *The Entail* in this book of essays.

MICHAEL SADLIER. *Trollope — A Commentary.* A favorable twentieth-century estimate.

ELIZABETH S. HALDANE. *George Eliot and her Times.*

WILLIAM BARRY. *Heralds of Revolt.* The article on "The Genius of George Eliot" is a noteworthy contribution to criticism.

MARY H. DEAKIN. *The Early Life of George Eliot.*

KONRAD BERCOVICI. "George Borrow's Gypsies," in *New York Literary Review,* August 27, 1921. Points to Borrow's ignorance and heedlessness.

C. G. Harper. *A Literary Man's London.* Contains an excellent summary of Besant's work as a novelist and descriptions of the London that figures in his books.

Lionel Johnson. *The Art of Thomas Hardy.*

Lascelles Abercrombie. *Thomas Hardy — A Critical Study.*

Charles Phillips. "The Hardy Optimist," in *The Catholic World*, March, 1919. An American Catholic man of letters offers some constructive suggestions.

G. N. Shuster. "Thomas Hardy," in *The Catholic World*, March, 1928.

J. G. Fletcher. "The Spirit of Thomas Hardy," in *The Yale Review*, January, 1924.

Lewis Melville. *William Makepeace Thackeray.* A standard life.

Mrs. Warre Cornish. "An Impression of Thackeray in his Last Years," in *The Dublin Review*, January, 1912.

P. J. Gannon. "The Religion of Thackeray," in *The Dublin Review*, January, 1912.

W. H. Rideing. *Stray Moments with Thackeray.*

E. B. Chancellor. *The London of Thackeray.* A backgrounds study.

A. C. Benson. "Master of Laughter," in *The North American Review*, March, 1912. A fine and stimulating appreciation of Dickens.

G. K. Chesterton. *Appreciations and Criticisms of the Works of Charles Dickens.* The lengthiest piece of literary criticism by G. K. C., and obviously written *con amore.*

Edwin Charles. *Some Dickens Women.* Copious and well-chosen excerpts from the novels, and appreciative comments by a confirmed Dickensian.

J. W. T. Ley. *The Dickens Circle.* Filled with otherwise inaccessible information concerning the literary men of the times.

E. B. Chancellor. *The London of Charles Dickens.* Where his characters lived and wandered.

J. W. Beach. *The Comic Spirit in George Meredith.*

J. H. E. Crees. *George Meredith — A Study of his Works and Personality.*

Robert Sencourt. "George Meredith," in *The Catholic World*, June, 1927.

CHAPTER XIV

VICTORIAN POETRY

General studies

S. T. Williams. *Studies in Victorian Literature.*

G. K. Chesterton. *The Victorian Age in Literature.*

Andrews and Percival. *Poetry of the Nineties.*

Holbrook Jackson. *The Eighteen Nineties.* Four books differing widely in outlook and treatment, but each worthy of attention.

Katherine Brégy. *The Poets' Chantry.* Chapters on De Vere, Hopkins, Patmore, Lionel Johnson, Thompson, and Mrs. Meynell.

On the Pre-Raphaelites

WALTER DE LA MARE. "Christina Rossetti." This thoughtful and comprehensive essay occurs in *Essays by Divers Hands*, being Volume VI of the Transactions of the Royal Society of Literature of the United Kingdom.

W. B. YEATS. *Ideas of Good and Evil.* Considers Morris as "The Happiest of Poets."

JOHN DRINKWATER. *William Morris — A Critical Study.* A work with all the virtues and a few of the defects of necessary youth.

ARTHUR COMPTON-RICKETT. *William Morris — A Study in Personality.*

SIR EDMUND GOSSE. *The Life of Algernon Charles Swinburne.*

MAX BEERBOHM. *And Even Now.* The dapper Max gives us a masterly description of Swinburne as Watts-Dunton's guest at Putney. The sketch should be read for the sake of Swinburne, for the sake of Beerbohm, and for the sake of the reader's own soul.

On Browning

FRANCES T. RUSSELL. *One Word More on Browning.* A classified bibliography enhances the value of this recent and original contribution to Browning study.

LILIAN WHITING. *The Brownings — Their Life and Art.* In the eyes of solemn savants this author may be found lacking; but she writes with enthusiasm and knowledge of her subject.

HIRAM CORSON. *An Introduction to the Study of Robert Browning's Poetry.* Of the vintage of 1900, and the better the more it matures. Corson was a teacher.

EMILY HICKEY. "A Study of Browning's *Saul*," in *The Catholic World*, December, 1911. A Browning expert unfolds the meaning of one of the great religious poems of the century.

W. F. P. STOCKLEY. "Browning on Faith and Morals," in *Thought*, December, 1926.

On Tennyson

T. R. LOUNSBURY. *The Life and Times of Tennyson.*

HAROLD NICOLSON. *Tennyson — Aspects of his Life and Poetry.*

C. B. PALLEN. *The Meaning of the Idylls of the King.* A commentary and interpretation untouched of time.

WILFRID WARD. "The Tennyson Centenary," in *The Dublin Review*, October, 1909.

W. F. P. STOCKLEY. "The 'Faith' of *In Memoriam*," in *The Catholic World*, March, 1925.

On Thompson

EVERARD MEYNELL. *The Life of Francis Thompson.*

SISTER MADELEVA. *Chaucer's Nuns.* One of the essays in this collection is a study of Thompson as a prose writer.

FLORENCE MOYNIHAN. "The Symbolism of Francis Thompson," in *The Catholic University Bulletin*, January, 1913.

G. N. SHUSTER. *The Catholic Spirit in Modern English Literature*, chap. viii.

On other poets

LILIAN WHITING. *The Florence of Landor.* A description of the city and a commentary on Landor's personality and writings.

J. C. REVILLE. "Walter Savage Landor," in *America,* July 10, 1920.

ROBERT BRIDGES (editor). *The Poems of Gerard Manley Hopkins.*

FRANCIS THOMPSON. *A Renegade Poet.* Contains a chapter on De Vere.

M. F. EGAN. *Lectures on Literature.* A comparison of De Vere's *St. Thomas of Canterbury* with Tennyson's *Becket.*

OSBERT BURDETT. *The Idea of Coventry Patmore.* The best existing commentary on Patmore.

LOUISE WHEATON. "Psyche and the Prophet," in *The Catholic World,* December, 1923. More light on Patmore.

KATHARINE TYNAN. "Lionel Johnson," in *America,* April 29, 1916.

MARY STURGEON. *Michael Field.*

T. STURGE MOORE. *A Selection from the Poems of Michael Field.*

A. H. GODWIN. *Gilbert and Sullivan — A Critical Appreciation of the Savoy Operas.*

CHAPTER XV

A CENTURY OF ESSAYISTS

On the Essay

SISTER ELEANORE. *The Literary Essay in English.* A modern summary, containing brief, helpful comments on representative essayists.

HUGH WALKER. *The English Essay and Essayists.*

W. C. BROWNELL. *Victorian Prose Masters.*

C. T. WINCHESTER. *A Group of English Essayists of the Early Nineteenth Century.* The group includes Jeffrey, Hazlitt, Lamb, De Quincey, Wilson, and Hunt.

On Lamb

E. V. LUCAS (editor). *The Charles Lamb Day Book.* A taste of Lamb for every day in the year.

G. T. CLAPTON (editor). *Selected Letters of Charles Lamb.*

BRANDER MATTHEWS (editor). *Lamb's Dramatic Essays.*

On Hazlitt

P. P. HOWE (editor). *New Writings by William Hazlitt.* A group of unsigned articles from the files of *The Atlas.*

P. P. HOWE. *The Life of William Hazlitt.* All in all, an excellent portrait, though perhaps unduly softened and retouched.

W. D. HOWE (editor). *Selections from William Hazlitt.* Contains a good critical introduction and a basic bibliography.

M. J. RYAN. "Hazlitt as a Critic," in *The Catholic University Bulletin,* April, 1908.

On Carlyle

BLISS PERRY. *Carlyle — How to know Him.*

WILLIAM BARRY. *Heralds of Revolt.* Contains a searching essay on Carlyle.

On Arnold

D. C. SOMERVELL (editor). *Selections from Matthew Arnold's Prose.*

S. P. SHERMAN. *Matthew Arnold — How to know Him.*

F. MOYNIHAN and BROTHER LEO. Articles on Arnold in *The Catholic World,* December, 1922.

W. H. DAWSON. *Matthew Arnold and his Relation to the Thought of our Time.*

LEONARD HUXLEY. *Thoughts on Education chosen from the Writings of Matthew Arnold.*

On Newman

J. J. REILLY. *Cardinal Newman as a Man of Letters.* A masterly book.

BERTRAM NEWMAN. *Cardinal Newman.* An excellent general study.

WILLIAM BARRY. *Cardinal Newman.*

L. E. GATES. *Three Studies in Literature.* Has a study of Newman as a prose writer.

G. J. GARRAGHAN (editor). *Prose Types in Newman.*

BROTHER AZARIAS. *Phases of Thought and Criticism.* Contains a comparison of Newman and Emerson.

On other essayists

FRANCIS JEFFREY. *Essays on English Poets and Poetry,* from *The Edinburgh Review.*

F. P. DONNELLY. *The Art of Interesting.* Contains an eminently journalistic study of Macaulay's "journalese."

J. G. WHITEHOUSE (editor). *Ruskin the Prophet.* Utterances evoked by the Ruskin centenary, from Dean Inge, John Masefield, Laurence Binyon, and others.

A. C. BENSON. *A Study in Personality — John Ruskin.*

CHAPTER XVI

CROSS CURRENTS

J. GAIRDNER (editor). *The Paston Letters.* Four volumes.

HILAIRE BELLOC. A series of papers exposing Gibbon's shortcomings as a historian, in *Studies,* December, 1917; June and September, 1918; and December, 1919.

PETER GUILDAY (editor). *Church Historians.* An article on Lingard by E. J. Ryan.

CARDINAL GASQUET. *Lord Acton and his Circle.*

A. M. GRANGE. "Dom Gasquet as an Historian," in *The American Catholic Quarterly Review,* July, 1894.

MICHAEL MAHONEY. "George Berkeley, Irish Idealist," in *Thought*, June, 1926.

WILLIAM BARRY. An article on Bishop Challoner in *The Dublin Review*, January, 1910.

WILLIAM BARRY. "Forgotten Passages in the Life of Cardinal Wiseman," in *The Dublin Review*, October, 1918.

NICHOLAS DILLON (editor). *Maxims of Christianity*. A book of selections from the writings of Kenelm Digby.

G. N. SHUSTER. *The Catholic Spirit in Modern English Literature*, chap. ii: "Kenelm Digby and the Discovery of the Past."

ALICE AYLWARD. "Father Benson as Novelist," in *The Magnificat*, November, 1911.

G. K. CHESTERTON and OTHERS. Papers on Wilfrid Ward, in *The Dublin Review*, July, 1916.

B. C. A. WINDLE. *Who's Who of the Oxford Movement*. A book crammed with interesting facts and written with manifest enjoyment.

MARY H. ALLIES. *Thomas William Allies*.

HUGH POPE. *Catholic Student's Aid to the Bible*.

A. J. BEVERIDGE. *The Bible as Good Reading*.

R. G. MOULTON. *The Literary Study of the Bible*.

J. M. LENHART. "Pre-Reformation Bibles in American Libraries," in *The Catholic World*, November, 1923.

CHAPTER XVII

THE IRISH CONTRIBUTION

Collections of Irish Literature

JUSTIN MCCARTHY (editor). *Irish Literature*. Ten volumes. Selections from Irish writers and biographical and critical comments uneven in merit but frequently pointed and judicious.

DUNN and LENNOX (editors). *The Glories of Ireland*. A survey of Irish achievements in literature and in other fields. Most of the articles are written by experts.

D. J. O'DONOGHUE (editor). *The Poets of Ireland*. A biographical and bibliographical dictionary.

A. P. GRAVES (editor). *The Book of Irish Poetry*.

PADRAIC COLUM (editor). *Anthology of Irish Verse*.

L. D. WALTERS (editor). *Irish Poets of Today*.

LENNOX ROBINSON (editor). *Treasury of Irish Verse*. The emphasis is on recent writers.

On the earlier writers

A. H. ATTERIDGE. "Thomas Moore," in *America*, March 13, 1920.

JOHN DRINKWATER. *The Pilgrim of Eternity*. An excellent estimate of Moore, pp. 172–175.

L. I. GUINEY. *James Clarence Mangan — Poems and a Study.*

C. G. DUFFY. "Personal Memoirs of Mangan," in *Dublin Review*, April, 1908.

D. J. O'DONOGHUE. *The Life and Writings of James Clarence Mangan.*

D. J. O'DONOGHUE (editor). *Poems of James Clarence Mangan.* Centenary edition.

S. J. BROWN. *Ireland in Fiction.* Biographical sketches and critical estimates by an Irish Jesuit.

H. J. HEUSER. *Canon Sheehan of Doneraile.*

On the writers of today

C. G. DUFFY, GEORGE SIGERSON, DOUGLAS HYDE. *The Revival of Irish Literature.* Addresses at the beginning of the movement.

E. A. BOYD. *Ireland's Literary Renaissance.*

E. A. BOYD. *The Contemporary Drama in Ireland.*

CORNELIUS WEYGANDT. *Irish Plays and Playwrights.*

LADY GREGORY. *Our Irish Theater.*

W. P. RYAN. *The Irish Revival — Its History, Pioneers, and Possibilities.*

LLOYD MORRIS. *The Celtic Dawn.* Comments on the writers of the revival.

W. B. YEATS. "A People's Theater," in *The Dial*, April, 1920. An open letter to Lady Gregory, explaining the objects of the literary theater.

J. J. DALY. A sound consideration of the paganism of Yeats, in *The Catholic World*, August, 1922.

PADRAIC COLUM. "An Irish Poet-Scholar," in *The Commonweal*, July 13, 1927. A tribute to George Sigerson.

PADRAIC COLUM. "An Appreciation of Francis Ledwidge," in *The New Republic*, April 7, 1920.

KATHARINE TYNAN. "Francis Ledwidge," in *The Catholic World*, November, 1917.

KATHERINE BRÉGY. *Poets and Pilgrims.* A chapter on the poetry of Katharine Tynan.

E. H. BIERSTADT. *Dunsany the Dramatist.* A capable estimate of the man and his work by an admirer who tries desperately to write like an Irishman.

THOMAS MACDONAGH. *Literature in Ireland.* Eight illuminating studies of the Irish mode of writing English, with examples drawn from Irish poetry.

CHAPTER XVIII

THE TWENTIETH CENTURY

Numerous books have been written about the leading writers of today, and literary magazines contain an abundance of comment. The following list is merely indicative of the material in existence.

General works

F. E. SCHELLING. *Appraisements and Asperities.* A veteran American university don on writers of today.

SIR EDMUND GOSSE. *Silhouettes*. Papers on Dobson and others.

J. B. PRIESTLEY. *Figures in Modern Literature*. On De la Mare, Housman, Bennett, Jacobs.

EDWARD GARNETT. *Friday Nights*. Three papers on Conrad, and studies of contemporary writers.

MARY C. STURGEON. *Studies of Contemporary Poets*.

HAROLD WILLIAMS. *Modern English Writers*. A full treatment of books published between 1890 and 1914.

S. P. B. MAIS. *Some Modern Authors*. Papers on Middleton Murry, Hugh Walpole, Arthur Machen, A. E. Housman, and others.

ROBERT LYND. *Books and Authors*. Distinctly above the average of book reviewing.

C. C. and MARK VAN DOREN. *American and British Literature since 1890*.

J. W. CUNLIFFE. *Modern English Playwrights*.

LLEWELLYN JONES. *First Impressions*. Fifteen papers on recent English and American poets.

ALFRED NOYES. *Some Aspects of Modern Poetry*. A defense of traditional ways.

JAMES GILLIS. *False Prophets*. Destructive criticism of Shaw, Wells, and others.

JOHN GALSWORTHY. *Castles in Spain*. Thoughtful and informal essays on writers and literary tendencies of the day.

GRANT OVERTON. *Authors of the Day*. Breezy papers on English and American novelists. Bennett, Walpole, Galsworthy, and Conrad are among those commemorated.

W. M. and D. B. TANNER (editors). *Modern Familiar Essays*. Specimens from both sides of the Atlantic.

HUMPHREY MILFORD (editor). *Selected Modern Essays*. Among the essayists represented are Hewlett, Belloc, Chesterton, Cunninghame Graham, and Middleton Murry.

On individual writers

ANNE K. TUELL. *Mrs. Meynell and her Literary Generation*. An appreciation based on Mrs. Meynell's complete literary product.

AGNES REPPLIER. "Alice Meynell," in *The Catholic World*, March, 1923.

ALBAN DOBSON (editor). *Austin Dobson — An Anthology of Prose and Verse*.

LOUISE NICHOLL. "John Masefield in Yonkers," in *The Bookman* (New York), January, 1919.

O. W. FIRKINS. "Mr. Masefield's Poetry," in *The Nation*, March 15, 1919.

G. K. CHESTERTON. *George Bernard Shaw*. A book that exposes much of Shaw and discloses more of Chesterton.

D. A. LORD. "Shaw's 'Apologetics,'" in *The Catholic Mind*, December 8, 1916. Reflections on *Androcles and the Lion*, salutary for readers who take Shaw seriously as a prophet of the soul.

VINCENT STARRETT. *Buried Cæsars*. Constitutes a good introduction to Arthur Machen.

RICHARD CURLE. "Conrad in the East," in *The Yale Review*, April, 1923.

JAMES HUNEKER. *Ivory, Apes, and Peacocks*. Has an excellent study of Conrad.

JESSIE CONRAD. *Joseph Conrad as I knew Him*. The novelist's widow tells intimate details of her husband's personality. Her book reënforces the conviction that to have a genius in the family is not all roses and sunshine.

FRANK PEASE. "Joseph Conrad," in *The Nation*, November 2, 1918. Helpful criticism.

W. M. HART. *Kipling the Story-Writer*.

SIDNEY DARK. *The Outline of H. G. Wells*.

H. A. HARRISON. *Frederic Harrison — Thoughts and Memories*. The essayist's son writes informally about his father.

ENID DINNIS. *Emily Hickey — Poet, Essayist, Pilgrim*.

BOHUN LYNCH. *Max Beerbohm in Perspective*. Gives an appropriate notion of "the incomparable Max." The prefatory letter, written by Beerbohm, easily the best thing in the volume.

WILBUR CROSS. "The Humor of Max Beerbohm," in *The Yale Review*, January, 1924. Includes a valuable bibliography.

THEODORE MAYNARD. "The Chesterbelloc," in *The Catholic World*, November, 1919, and following issues.

INDEX

Page numbers in italics refer to the principal or more detailed treatment of subjects. As in the body of the book, the titles of relatively short pieces of writing are printed within quotation marks, while titles of books and of lengthy pieces of writing are printed in italics. Pronunciation indications are in the nature of first-aid appliances only, and are intended neither to preclude the use of the dictionary nor to convey the sounds of words, especially non-English words, with complete accuracy.

ā as in "fate"; ă as in "fan"; ä as in "far"; ē as in "scene"; ĕ as in "let"; ī as in "nice"; ĭ as in "sit"; ō as in "old"; ū as in "rule"; ü approximately as in German "grün"; N (nasal) as in French "bon."

713